Franchise Relationship Laws
A Practical Guide

Julianne Lusthaus and Elliot Ginsburg
EDITORS

Cover design by Amanda Fry/ABA Design

The materials contained herein represent the opinions of the authors and/or the editors and should not be construed to be the views or opinions of the law firms or companies that such persons are in partnership with, associated with, or employed by, nor of the American Bar Association or the Forum on Franchising, unless adopted pursuant to the bylaws of the Association.

Nothing contained in this book is to be considered as the rendering of legal advice for specific cases, and readers are responsible for obtaining such advice from their own legal counsel. This book is intended for educational and informational purposes only.

© 2025 American Bar Association. All rights reserved.

No part of this publication may be reproduced, stored in a retrieval system, or transmitted in any form or by any means, electronic, mechanical, photocopying, recording, or otherwise, without the prior written permission of the publisher. For permission, complete the request form at www.americanbar.org/reprint or email ABA Publishing at copyright@americanbar.org.

Printed in the United States of America.

29 28 27 26 25   5 4 3 2 1

A catalog record for this book is available from the Library of Congress.

Discounts are available for books ordered in bulk. Special consideration is given to state bars, CLE programs, and other bar-related organizations. Inquire at Book Publishing, ABA Publishing, American Bar Association, 321 N. Clark Street, Chicago, Illinois 60654-7598.

www.shopABA.org

Contents

Introduction	*v*
Arkansas	1
California	39
Connecticut	93
Delaware	127
Hawaii	143
Illinois	169
Indiana	203
Iowa	219
Michigan	239
Minnesota	273
Mississippi	329
Missouri	347
Nebraska	369
New Jersey	389
Puerto Rico	421
Rhode Island	457
U.S. Virgin Islands	475
Virginia	485
Washington	499
Wisconsin	521
About the Editors	*551*
Index	*553*

Introduction

Representing franchisees and franchisors is no easy feat. In addition to federal regulations and lengthy contracts, many states have their own statutory regime when it comes to franchising. This book addresses those statutes that govern the franchise relationship once established. These laws frequently include limitations on a franchisor's right to terminate or not renew a franchise as well as other regulation of an existing franchise relationship.

We have organized the book by state. Each chapter delves into the legislative landscape of the franchise relationship law in that state as well as case law interpreting the statute. We have attempted to organize the chapters consistently to assist practitioners when comparing different state laws. The chapters each start by exploring the state's definition of a franchise and continue with regulation of the franchise relationship. Finally, there is a review of remedies for statutory violations as well as limitations on dispute resolution provisions. We hope the book will serve as a useful starting point for practitioners when facing issues related to the franchise relationship.

We thank the authors for their hard work and effort on their chapters. We also thank Ben Reed and Daniel Oates, publications officers of the Forum, as well as Teri Koller who served as the Publications Committee liaison for this book, all of whom provided advice and assistance to keep this project moving forward. We would also like to thank the ABA publications staff for helping to get this volume from our desks to yours.

Arkansas

Dawn M. Johnson

I. Introduction to Statute

Practitioners and courts refer to the Arkansas Franchise Practices Act as the AFPA.[1] Although franchise relationship statutes typically only apply to actions by franchisors, certain provisions of the AFPA apply to franchisees. In 2023, the Arkansas General Assembly amended the AFPA to clarify its applicability and to make a number of other changes that expand the scope of the statute.[2] The new law was effective on August 1, 2023.[3] Some provisions are retroactive, while others are not.

In general, the AFPA applies to franchises entered into, renewed, or transferred after March 4, 1977, the performance of which contemplates or requires the franchise to establish or maintain a place of business within the state of Arkansas, unless otherwise expressly excluded.[4]

Arkansas also has statutes that deal specifically with motor vehicle franchises, petroleum franchises, farm equipment dealers, restaurant franchises (invalidating non-Arkansas choice of venue and choice of law provisions), and beer wholesalers.[5] Although those statutes may also apply to franchises covered by the AFPA[6] (and expressly do for beer and wine wholesalers as a result of the 2023 amendments to the AFPA), these industry-specific statutes are outside the scope of this book.

---

1. Ark. Code Ann. §§ 4-72-201 to 4-72-212.
2. 2023 Ark. Acts 847 (H.B. 1783) [hereinafter "2023 Act" or "Act"], signed into law on Apr. 13, 2023. *See* https://www.arkleg.state.ar.us; 2023 LEGIS 847 (2023).
3. Ark. Code Ann. § 4-72-202.
4. *Id.* § 4-72-203(a)(1); 2023 Act § 1(6)(A).
5. *See, e.g.*, Ark. Code Ann. §§ 23-112-101 to 23-112-107 (Arkansas Motor Vehicle Commission Act); *id.* §§ 4-72-401 to 4-72-403, 4-72-501 to 4-72-503 (petroleum products, suppliers, and distributors); *id.* §§ 4-72-310 to 4-72-311 (Farm Equipment Retailer Franchise Protection Act); *id.* §§ 4-72-601 to 4-72-603 (Arkansas Procedural Fairness for Restaurant Franchisees Act); *id.* §§ 3-5-1101 to 3-5-1111 (beer wholesalers and suppliers).
6. *See, e.g.*, Ark. Op. Att'y Gen. No. 94-037, 1994 WL 118388 (Mar. 31, 1994) (considering notice of a transfer or sale under the Arkansas Motor Vehicle Commission Act and stating, "A question may remain regarding a franchisee's obligation to comply, as a separate matter, with the notice requirement in § 4-72-205 in order to avoid violation of the Arkansas Franchise Practices Act.").

The legislative findings in the 2023 Act, which are not codified, state that it was necessary to clarify the applicability of the AFPA, specifically as it relates to the 1991 amendments to the AFPA. At that time, the statute stated that it did not apply to "business relations, actions, transactions and franchises subject to the Federal Trade Commission regulations, 'Disclosure Requirements and Prohibitions Concerning Franchising and Business Opportunity Ventures,' 16 C.F.R. 436.1 et seq."[7] Two judges in the same Arkansas federal district court had reached opposite conclusions on whether the AFPA applied to franchises that are subject to the Federal Trade Commission (FTC) Franchise Rule.[8]

The legislative findings in the 2023 Act stated that the General Assembly's intent in passing the 1991 amendments was not to eviscerate post-agreement protections for franchisors and franchisees in the AFPA.[9] Rather, the legislature found that the FTC Franchise Rule involves mandatory pre-agreement disclosure requirements that apply to virtually all franchise agreements, while the subject matter of the AFPA involves post-agreement protections for both parties.[10] The 1991 amendments to the AFPA were "simply intended to reaffirm" that the FTC Franchise Rule set forth the pre-agreement disclosure requirements for franchises otherwise covered by the AFPA.[11] The 2023 amendments removed any ambiguity relating to applicability of the statute to franchises subject to the FTC rules by deleting those exceptions.[12]

Although the new law has an exemption for franchises with an initial fee of $20,000 or less and an initial term of one year or less,[13] the AFPA also now applies to the franchise relationship between wholesalers and suppliers of alcoholic and non-alcoholic beverages, regardless of the franchise fee, if any, or the initial term of the franchise.[14] These new provisions apply to franchises in existence both before and after August 1, 2023.[15]

The new law amended three sections of the AFPA: section 4-72-202 (definitions), section 4-72-203 (applicability), and section 4-72-205 (expanding provisions on transfer, assignment, and sale), which have different effective dates.[16]

---

7. 2023 Act § 3 (noting previous version of Ark. Code Ann. § 4-72-203).

8. *Compare* Lodging Dev. & Mgmt. Inc. v. Days Inns Worldwide, Inc., No. 3:00CV218 HW, 2001 WL 35756572, at *2 (E.D. Ark. Oct 18, 2001) (stating in dicta that although the AFPA stated that it was inapplicable to agreements subject to the Federal Trade Commission (FTC) Rule, "that conclusion runs counter to common sense" because it would leave nothing left for the AFPA to regulate) *with* J.K.P. Foods, Inc. v. McDonald's Corp., 420 F. Supp. 2d 966, 970–73 (E.D. Ark. 2006) (determining that the "provisions of the franchise agreements leave no doubt that the franchises are subject to the federal regulations" and thus were excluded from the coverage of the AFPA).

9. 2023 Act § 1(5).

10. *Id.* § 1(4). The legislative findings do not address the fact that the AFPA also prohibits certain pre-agreement acts in the offer or sale of a franchise. *See* Ark. Code Ann. § 4-72-207.

11. 2023 Act § 1(6)(B).

12. *Id.* § 1 (noting that the amendments in 1991 "included language that might be interpreted to exempt franchises subject to" the FTC franchise and business opportunity rules); Ark. Code Ann. § 4-72-203.

13. Ark. Code Ann. § 4-72-203(b).

14. *Id.* § 4-72-203(c).

15. *Id.* §§ 4-72-203(a)(2)(A) & (B), 4-72-203(b), 4-72-203(c); 2023 Act § 7.

16. Ark. Code Ann. §§ 4-72-202, 4-72-203, 4-72-205; 2023 Act § 7(a), (b).

It also added two new sections: section 4-72-211 (voiding choice of venue other than Arkansas) and section 4-72-212 (imposing duties of good faith and fair dealing, permitting termination only for material cause as determined under objective standards, and protecting rights of survivors), both of which apply to franchise agreements entered into or renewed on or after August 1, 2023.[17]

The original policy rationale behind the statute was to protect the public and franchisees conducting business in the state of Arkansas.[18] When the legislature enacted the AFPA in the late 1970s, it included an emergency clause that declared that some franchisors had cancelled existing franchise agreements without good cause.[19] The legislative findings in the 2023 Act stated the need for changes to the AFPA in order to further protect franchisees from unreasonable termination due to economic imbalance between the parties, the absence of free bargaining, and some franchisors' commercially unreasonable practices.[20] The 2023 Act also referred to the vital economic role of franchising.[21]

The 2023 Act provided in an uncodified section that if any provision of the act or application to any person or circumstance is held invalid, that invalidity will not affect other provisions or applications of the act that can be given effect without the invalid provisions or applications.[22] Thus, provisions of the 2023 Act are severable.

Another uncodified section of the 2023 Act clarifies the effective date of certain provisions. First, it states that section 1 (legislative findings) and section 3 (amendments to section 4-72-203) (applicability of subchapter) of the act apply retroactively to the effective dates of Act 1991, No. 411. The legislative findings, which are in the historical and statutory notes to section 4-72-203 (applicability of subchapter), clarify that the AFPA applies to franchises subject to the FTC rules.[23] Thus, the act's removal of the exception for franchises that are subject to the FTC rules is retroactive and the AFPA applies to franchises entered into, renewed, or transferred after March 4, 1977.[24]

Section 2 (amendments to section 4-72-202) (definitions), section 4 (section 4-72-205) (transfer, assignment, or sale of franchise), and section 5 (sections 4-72-211 and 4-72-212) (venue restriction and the duties of good faith and fair dealing, termination and rights of survivors) apply to franchise agreements or contracts entered into or renewed on or after the effective date of the 2023 Act on August 1, 2023.[25]

---

17. Ark. Code Ann. §§ 4-72-211, 4-72-212; 2023 Act § 7(b).
18. Capital Equip., Inc. v. CNH Am., LLC, 471 F. Supp. 2d 951, 957 (E.D. Ark. 2006) (finding the AFPA represents a fundamental public policy of the state of Arkansas).
19. *Id.* (citing Emergency Clause to Act 355 of 1977); Gunn v. Farmers Ins. Exch., 372 S.W.3d 346, 354 (Ark. 2011) (citing Act of Mar. 4, 1977, No. 355, § 13, 1977 Ark. Acts 592), *reh'g denied* (2011)).
20. 2023 Act § 1(8), (9).
21. *Id.* § 1(7) & (8)(B), (C).
22. *Id.* § 6.
23. *Id.* § 7; *see also* Ark. Code Ann. § 4-72-203, Historical and Statutory Notes.
24. 2023 Act § 7.
25. *Id.*

The fact that the 2023 Act's legislative findings and severability and retroactivity clauses are not published in the official statutory code "does not indicate that [an] act is invalid," nor does it deprive the act of the force of law.[26] The Arkansas Code Revision Commission is not required to codify certain language or sections in acts passed by the General Assembly such as legislative intent, emergency clauses, and other provisions.[27]

Courts have not yet addressed the interpretation and scope of these new provisions in the AFPA as of the writing of this chapter. However, practitioners should be aware of these recent changes when examining whether they impact the franchisor–franchisee relationship at issue.

Although the AFPA is not a disclosure statute, it prohibits certain acts, such as the making of misrepresentations in the offer or sale of a franchise and during certain other parts of the relationship.[28]

II. Commentary and Annotations

The law is known as and practitioners may cite it as the "Arkansas Franchise Practices Act."[29] The AFPA is very broad and does not include common elements that are found in other state relationship laws. The AFPA includes a definitions section.[30]

A. Definition of Franchise

1. General

a. Commentary

The AFPA defines a franchise as "a written or oral agreement for a definite or indefinite period in which a person grants to another person a license to use a trade name, trademark, service mark, or related characteristic within an exclusive or nonexclusive territory or to sell or distribute goods or services within an exclusive or nonexclusive territory at wholesale or retail, by lease agreement, or otherwise."[31] A "person" can be a natural person, corporation, partnership, trust, or other entity. In the case of an entity, a "person" includes any other entity that has a majority interest in such entity or effectively controls the other entity as well as the individual officers, directors, and other persons in active control of the activities of the entity.[32] The AFPA does not require a written contract.[33]

---

26. Hinchey v. Thomasson, 727 S.W.2d 836, 838 (Ark. 1987); Carter v. Green, 1 S.W.3d 449, 451–52 (Ark. Ct. App. 1999).
27. ARK. CODE ANN. § 1-2-303(e)(2).
28. Id. § 4-72-207.
29. Id. § 4-72-201.
30. Id. § 4-72-202.
31. Id. § 4-72-202(1)(A).
32. Id. § 4-72-202(2).
33. Id. § 4-72-202(1)(A) (franchise means "a written or oral agreement...").

The AFPA applies to a franchise entered into, renewed, or transferred after March 4, 1977.[34] However, as already noted, certain of the 2023 amendments only apply to franchise agreements entered into or renewed on and after the effective date of the 2023 Act, which was August 1, 2023.[35]

The AFPA only applies to a relationship if the agreement's performance contemplates or requires the franchise to establish or maintain a "place of business" within the state of Arkansas.[36] The AFPA defines a "place of business" as a "fixed geographical location at which the franchisee displays for sale and sells the franchisor's goods or offers for sale and sells the franchisor's services."[37] A franchise agreement can either explicitly or implicitly require performance from a fixed location.[38] If the parties enter into the agreement in Arkansas, but the agreement contemplates locations only in another state, the AFPA will not apply.[39] In addition, if the franchisee is to perform the agreement in Arkansas, but the agreement does not contemplate or require a fixed geographical location for selling products or services, the AFPA will not apply.[40]

Before the legislature amended the AFPA in 1991, the AFPA's definition of a franchise was limited to a license to sell or distribute goods or services within an exclusive territory.

Therefore, there are cases before the 1991 amendments where courts concluded that a franchisee that had only a nonexclusive territory could not assert claims under the AFPA.[41] The legislature amended the AFPA in 1991 to include nonexclusive territorial relationships within its coverage. As of the date of this writing, there does not appear to be any published case law where a court found there was no territory at all and thus no franchise under the AFPA.

The AFPA has several exclusions. It excludes from the definition of a franchise (1) a lease, license, or concession granted by a retailer to sell goods or furnish services on or from premises occupied by the retailer-grantor primarily for its own merchandising activities and (2) door-to-door sales complying with Arkansas Code section 4-89-101-110, which governs home solicitation sales.[42] The AFPA also excludes business relations, actions, transactions, and franchises

---

34. *Id.* § 4-72-203(a)(1).
35. 2023 Act §§ 2, 4, 5 (applicable to Ark. Code Ann. §§ 4-72-202, 4-72-205, 4-72-211, 4-72-212).
36. Ark. Code Ann. § 4-72-203(a)(1).
37. *Id.* § 4-72-202(6).
38. Dr. Pepper Bottling Co. v. Frantz, 842 S.W.2d 37, 40–41 (Ark. 1992); S&S Sales, Inc. v. Pancho's Mexican Foods, Inc., No. 2:08CV00220-WRW, 2010 WL 749562, at *3 (E.D. Ark., Mar. 3, 2010).
39. *See* JRT Inc. v. TCBY Sys., 52 F.3d 734, 736 (8th Cir. 1995) (finding franchise agreement only contemplated the opening of yogurt stores in Michigan, so the AFPA did not apply).
40. *See* Bridgman v. Cornwell Quality Tools Co., 831 F.2d 174, 175 (8th Cir. 1987); Mary Kay, Inc. v. Isbell, 999 S.W.2d 669, 671–73 (Ark. 1999).
41. Consol. Naturals, Inc. v. Wm. T. Thompson Co., 623 F. Supp. 458, 461–62 (W.D. Ark. 1985) (finding that the AFPA did not apply to one of the contracts at issue because the agreement explicitly stated that the parties' arrangement was a nonexclusive distributor); Chrysler Motors Corp. v. Thomas Auto Co., Inc., 939 F.2d 538, 544 (8th Cir. 1991) (finding AFPA did not apply because dealer only had a nonexclusive territory).
42. Ark. Code Ann. § 4-72-202(1)(B).

subject to Arkansas Code section 4-72-401-403 and Arkansas Code section 4-72-501-503 (petroleum products suppliers, dealers and distributors).[43]

The AFPA does not apply to sales representatives or brokers who merely solicit orders or promote products, but who do not have the right to consummate the sale.[44]

The 2023 amendment to the AFPA also excludes franchises where the initial franchise fee is $20,000 or less and the initial term of the franchise is one year or less. However, the AFPA applies to relationships between wholesalers and suppliers of wine, spirits, beer, nonalcoholic beverages, or any other alcoholic beverages regardless of the initial franchisee fee, if any, or the initial term of the franchise.[45]

b. Annotations

(i) Written, Oral, or Other Agreement

Courts have determined that the Arkansas statute of frauds does not apply to the AFPA. The AFPA defines a franchise as "a written or oral agreement" for a definite or indefinite period, in which a person grants to another person a license . . . to sell or distribute goods or services. . . ."[46] Thus, the court denied the manufacturer's motion to dismiss on the grounds that a verbal agreement could constitute a franchise despite the statute of frauds. *Thomas Bridgers, d/b/a Bridgers Superior Coach Sales & Leasing v. StarLine Enter.*, Case No. LRC81208, 1981 WL 764051, at *1 (E.D. Ark. Sept. 30, 1981).[47]

Disputed material issues of fact precluded summary judgment regarding whether there was an oral franchise agreement under the AFPA between a dental products manufacturer and its dealer to sell the manufacturer's products or whether the arrangement was simply to allow the dealer to purchase the products and resell them however it wanted. *Otto Dental Supply, Inc. v. Kerr Corp.*, No. 4:06CV01610-WRW, 2008 WL 410630, at *3 (E.D. Ark. Feb. 13, 2008).

Although the distributor did not have any rights to acquire additional brands or territories and thus was not a "franchise" for these brands, the distributor could still assert a claim under the AFPA with respect to its ownership of other brands and territories for the manufacturer's failure to deal with it in a commercially reasonable manner and in good faith. The manufacturer adopted and executed a plan to eliminate the distributor, applied pressure to other distributors in furtherance of that plan, and prevented the distributor

---

43. *Id.* § 4-72-203.
44. Consol. Naturals, Inc. v. Wm. T. Thompson Co., 623 F. Supp. 458, 462 (W.D. Ark. 1985) (finding that agreement did not give broker the right to sell or distribute goods or services because the supplier could accept or reject orders); Kent Jenkins Sales, Inc. v. Angelo Bros. Co., 804 F.2d 482, 487 (8th Cir. 1986) (finding manufacturer's representative had authority to negotiate price, but he did not have unqualified authorization to transfer the product at the point of an agreement to sell, so he was merely a promoter rather than a seller of goods).
45. ARK. CODE ANN. § 4-72-203(b), (c).
46. *Id.* § 4-72-202(1)(A).
47. This decision was before the AFPA amendment that added "nonexclusive" territory to the definition of a franchise. *Id.* However, that change would not impact the outcome in this case.

from acquiring other brands that would help it grow its business and increase revenues, which was critical to its ability to remain competitive. *Miller Brewing Co. v. Ed Roleson, Jr., Inc.*, 223 S.W.3d 806, 811–12 (Ark. 2006).

A boilerplate disclaimer in the agreement that stated that the parties' agreement "does not create any franchise . . ." between the parties was not sufficient to resolve the issue of whether the plaintiff was a franchise within the meaning of the AFPA. The court held that the issue must be determined based on an examination of the parties' relationship rather than the label that defendant placed on it in the agreement. *Britelink, Inc. v. Telecorp PCS, Inc.*, No. 3:03-CV-00207 GTE, 2004 WL 5509416, at *8 (E.D. Ark. May 6, 2004).

The parties created a franchise relationship, even though there was no signed contract. *South Beach Bev. Co. v. Harris Brands, Inc.*, 138 S.W.3d 102, 103 (Ark. 2003).

(ii) Location Requirement

A previous course of business with a predecessor company whose rights a distributor bought may have resulted in the parties implicitly contemplating that the distributor would maintain a distributorship operation in the state of Arkansas. The distributor's warehouse had no signage, no posted hours of operation, and allegedly did not display the manufacturer's products at the warehouse. However, the manufacturer admitted that the distributor sold some of its products from the warehouse and the distributor offered evidence that it did display products at its warehouse. The court held that disputed issues of material fact on whether the warehouse operations constituted a "place of business" under the AFPA required denial of the manufacturer's motion for summary judgment. *S&S Sales, Inc. v. Pancho's Mexican Foods, Inc.*, No. 2:08CV00220-WRW, 2010 WL 749562, at *3 (E.D. Ark. Mar. 3, 2010).

The AFPA did not apply to a distributorship agreement between an exclusive distributor of a supplier's products within a specific geographic territory in Arkansas and Tennessee. The agreement did not contemplate or require the distributor to establish or maintain a place of business in the state of Arkansas, as the AFPA requires. The court distinguished the *South Beach Beverage Co. v. Harris Brands, Inc.* and *Dr. Pepper Bottling Co. v. Frantz* cases because plaintiff did not allege that the supplier suggested it set up a place of business in Arkansas or that plaintiff actually did set up a place of business in Arkansas, nor did plaintiff allege that it had a place of business in Arkansas. *Jack Tyler Engineering Co., Inc. v. TLV Corp.*, No. 07-2580 STA-dkv, 2008 WL 2998840, at *3 (W.D. Tenn. July 31, 2008).

An Oklahoma-based distributor and a manufacturer contemplated a place of business in Arkansas when the manufacturer acknowledged that the distributor might need to open a satellite warehouse in Arkansas if the business developed as anticipated. The distributor anticipated that the warehouse would have a telephone, forklift, products for distribution, personnel, a message center, and sales displays. Therefore, substantial evidence existed to meet the definition of "place of business" under the distributor's claim for wrongful termination under the AFPA. In addition, the distributor already had an Arkansas outlet for the manufacturer's products with a sub-distributor with the manufacturer's permission. *South Beach Beverage Co. v. Harris Brands, Inc.*, 138 S.W.3d 102, 106 (Ark. 2003).

Occasional sales from a consultant's home or a customer's home do not satisfy the AFPA's requirement of a fixed location. A Mary Kay beauty consultant agreed to promote and sell Mary Kay products to customers at home demonstration parties. The agreement prohibited her from selling or displaying the products in retail sales or service establishments, so sales occurred either at the consultant's home or at the customer's home. After the consultant began leasing space and conducting activities prohibited by her agreement, Mary Kay terminated her on 30 days' notice. The court held that the agreement did not contemplate or require a fixed location for selling products or services. The court distinguished *Dr. Pepper Bottling Co. of Paragould v. Frantz*, 842 S.W.2d 37, 39–41 (Ark. 1992), where the franchisee maintained regular business hours at his warehouse where he displayed and sold products. Mary Kay would not allow its consultant to use retail space for displays and product sales. Therefore, the relationship was not a franchise under the AFPA. *Mary Kay, Inc. v. Isbell*, 999 S.W.2d 669, 671–73 (Ark. 1999).

In *JRT, Inc. v. TCBY Systems, Inc.*, 52 F.3d 734, 736, 739 (8th Cir. 1995), the court of appeals affirmed dismissal of the franchisee's AFPA claims because it agreed that the AFPA only applies if the franchisee is required to do business in Arkansas (citing the AFPA that contemplates or requires the franchise to establish or maintain a place of business in Arkansas). Because the franchise agreements contemplated yogurt stores in Michigan only, the court found that the district court had correctly dismissed claims alleging violations of the AFPA.

A distribution agreement between a soft drink company and a distributor was a franchise under the AFPA even though the agreement did not require the distributor to display and sell products from a fixed location or to maintain a particular place of business. The distributor operated vehicles and a warehouse, and displayed and sold some product from the warehouse that the distributor built with the manufacturer's knowledge. Because the AFPA applies to agreements "the performance of which contemplates the franchise to establish or maintain a place of business within the State of Arkansas,"[48] the court focused on the "more encompassing" word "contemplates." The court found nothing in the agreement prohibited the distributor from selling at a fixed location, the distributor testified that he operated from both a mobile and a fixed location, and there was no evidence that the manufacturer ever challenged what the distributor contemplated in performing the agreement. The distributor had a warehouse, which one would expect in order for the distributor to handle the number of products the agreement required him to handle. In affirming judgment for the distributor, the court also considered the fact that the legislature designed the AFPA for the public's protection. *Dr. Pepper Bottling Co. v. Frantz*, 842 S.W.2d 37, 37–38, 40–41 (Ark. 1992).

Franchisee's use of his home for administrative matters and occasional demonstrations did not afford him the protections of the AFPA. The AFPA only applies when the agreement "contemplates or . . . requires the franchise to

---

48. ARK. CODE ANN. § 4-72-203(a)(1); 2023 Act § 1(6)(A).

establish or maintain a place of business within the State of Arkansas,"[49] which is defined as a fixed geographical location. Even if plaintiff had operated on a regular basis from his home, the crucial question under the AFPA was whether the parties' agreement contemplated a home office.[50] The franchisee admitted that it was his intent to operate all of his business from his van and nothing in the agreement required him to maintain any kind of permanent place of business, other than the van. A multi-county area served from a van was not a "fixed geographical location" under the AFPA's "place of business" requirement. Thus, the AFPA did not apply. *Bridgman v. Cornwell Quality Tools Co.*, 831 F.2d 174, 175–76 (8th Cir. 1987).

(iii) Territory Requirement

A farm equipment dealer had a "franchise" as defined by the AFPA because the parties' agreement contemplated that the dealer would serve an area and achieve a satisfactory market share within that area, even though the agreement did not define the boundaries of the territory.

The AFPA does not require that the agreement specify territory boundaries, only that it contemplate a territory. *Larry Hobbs Farm Equipment, Inc. v. CNH America, LLC*, No. 2:08CV00049 JLH, 2008 WL 3931323, at *7 (E.D. Ark. Aug. 22, 2008).

An authorized dental products dealer satisfied the AFPA's territory requirement. Its nonexclusive territory was the United States because the manufacturer prohibited it from selling its products to foreign countries. The manufacturer had argued that there was no territory and thus no franchise because there was no geographical limitation on the distributor or its sales. *Otto Dental Supply, Inc. v. Kerr Corp.*, No. 4:06CV01610-WRW, 2008 WL 410630, at *4 (E.D. Ark. Feb. 13, 2008).

(iv) Right to Sell, Offer, or Distribute

Insurance agent could not change the terms of any insurance policy and did not have the "unqualified authorization" to transfer a product at the time of sale or to permanently bind the insurer to a contract. The authority to enter into a temporary binder of insurance, which by definition an insurer could cancel at any time at its discretion, does not equate to the ability to sell. The agent was most fairly characterized as a promotor or solicitor for the insurance procured. An essential element of a franchise agreement is the ability to transfer the franchisor's goods or services or commit the franchisor to a transaction at the moment of the agreement to sell. Thus, the agent was not a franchisee under the AFPA. *Gunn v. Farmers Insurance Exchange*, 372 S.W.3d 346, 355–57 (Ark. 2010).

In *Otto Dental Supply, Inc. v. Kerr Corp.*, the court denied summary judgment as to whether or not a franchise relationship existed. There were material issues of fact as to whether the manufacturer of dental products and its distributor

---

49. Ark. Code Ann. § 4-72-203(a)(1); 2023 Act § 1(6)(A).

50. As of the writing of this chapter, there was no case law addressing whether a franchise that provides virtual services where a franchisee is permitted to work from home but can work anywhere would qualify as a "fixed geographical location" under the AFPA.

entered into an oral agreement that the distributor would market and sell the manufacturer's products using its name and trademarks for an indefinite time. The manufacturer did not sell products directly to customers but relied on dealers to distribute products to customers. Plaintiff argued that the parties entered into an oral agreement to sell and market the manufacturer's products. The manufacturer argued that there was no contract or agreement between the parties to sell the manufacturer's products and that plaintiff "was merely a purchaser of catalogued items which Plaintiff resold however it wanted." *Otto Dental Supply, Inc. v. Kerr Corp.*, No. 4:06CV01610-WRW, 2008 WL 410630, at *3 (Feb. 13, 2008).

A sales representative who maintained no inventory, had no authority to set prices, and could not enter into a binding contract of insurance did not establish a franchise relationship under the AFPA because the representative only had authority to solicit and procure applications for insurance rather than sell insurance. *Stockton v. Sentry Ins.*, 989 S.W.2d 914, 916–17 (Ark. 1999).

A sales representative did not take title or possession of any of the manufacturer's products, and, although he had some authority to negotiate price, he did not have an unqualified authorization to transfer the product at the point and moment of the agreement to sell. Therefore, he was a promoter or solicitor of sales rather than an actual seller of goods. Thus, he was not a franchisee under the AFPA. The court relied on reasoning of courts construing similar provisions of the Wisconsin Fair Dealership Act. *Kent Jenkins Sales, Inc. v. Angelo Bros. Co.*, 804 F.2d 482, 486–87 (8th Cir. 1986).

2. Trademark Element

a. Commentary

The AFPA has a broad definition that includes granting to another person a license to use a trade name, trademark, service mark, or related characteristic.[51] There is no definition in the law or clarification in cases regarding the meaning of "related characteristic." As of the date of this writing, no cases address what acts would constitute the grant of a license under the AFPA.

The AFPA's definition of a franchise, as written, is not limited to the use of a trademark. Section 4-72-202(1)(A) provides that a franchise is an agreement to use a trademark *or* "to sell or distribute goods or services within an exclusive or nonexclusive territory at wholesale or retail" (emphasis added). Given the use of the word "or" in the definition of a franchise, one Arkansas federal court held that the AFPA is not limited to the use of a trademark because it also defines a franchise as a written agreement "to sell or distribute goods or services within an exclusive or nonexclusive territory at wholesale or retail."[52] However, the Arkansas Supreme Court has found the application of the AFPA is clear and the legislature plainly intended for it to apply where a person grants another

---

51. Ark. Code Ann. § 4-72-202(1)(A).
52. Larry Hobbs Farm Equip., Inc. v. CNH Am., LLC, No. 2:08CV00049 JLH, 2008 WL 3931323, at *11 (E.D. Ark. Aug. 22, 2008).

person a license to sell or distribute goods or services within an exclusive or nonexclusive territory.[53]

b. Annotations

A contract did not contemplate the exclusive use of a trade name, trademark, service mark, or related characteristic where it merely appointed an entity with the exclusive right to act as its broker within a prescribed territory by soliciting and promoting the sale of defendant's products. *Consolidated Naturals, Inc. v. Wm. T. Thompson Co.*, 623 F. Supp. 458, 461–62 (W.D. Ark. 1985).

The AFPA's definition of a franchise is not limited to the use of a trademark. Section 4-72-202(1)(A) defines a franchise in the disjunctive: as a written agreement in which a person grants a license to use a trade name, trademark, service mark, or related characteristic *or* "to sell or distribute goods or services within an exclusive or nonexclusive territory at wholesale or retail." Thus, the fact that a dealer agreement gave a dealer the right to sell or distribute products within a nonexclusive territory at retail was sufficient to find a franchise under the AFPA, even if there was no mention of the right to use the original manufacturer's trademark and trade name. *Larry Hobbs Farm Equipment, Inc. v. CNH America, LLC*, No. 2:08CV00049 JLH, 2008 WL 3931323, at *11 (E.D. Ark. Aug. 22, 2008).

3. Franchise Fee Element

a. Commentary

The AFPA does not include a franchise fee element.[54]

b. Annotations

Not applicable.

4. Community of Interest; Significant Degree of Control; Joint Marketing Plan

a. Commentary

Not applicable.

b. Annotations

Not applicable.

---

53. Stockton v. Sentry Ins., 989 S.W.2d 914, 917 (Ark. 1999) (citing Dr. Pepper Bottling Co. v. Frantz, 842 S.W.2d 37, 39 (Ark. 1992)).

54. However, the 2023 amendments to the AFPA exclude from its coverage any franchise for which the initial franchise fee paid by the franchisee or franchise owner does not exceed $20,000 and the initial term of the franchise does not exceed one year. ARK. CODE ANN. § 4-72-203(b).

B. Scope and Jurisdiction

1. Commentary

The AFPA applies to franchises entered into, renewed, or transferred after March 4, 1977.[55] The AFPA is primarily a relationship statute that addresses termination, nonrenewal, transfers, and other aspects of the relationship, including releases and waivers, choice of law and venue, the right to free association, and inventory repurchase rights, among others. The AFPA is not a registration or disclosure statute, but it does contain provisions prohibiting fraud or fraudulent omissions in connection with the "offer, sale, purchase, transfer, or assignment of any franchise in this state."[56]

The Arkansas legislature initially enacted the AFPA for the protection of franchisees conducting business within the state of Arkansas. When enacted, the statute included an emergency clause that declared that the distribution and sale of franchise agreements in Arkansas "vitally affects" the general economy, public interest, and public welfare.[57] The legislature found that some franchisors were cancelling or threatening to cancel existing franchise agreements without cause, which prejudiced citizens, and the only way to remedy the situation was to enact the AFPA immediately in order to preserve public peace, health, and safety.[58] Amendments to the AFPA in 2023 recited many of these same factors as reasons to further define the franchise relationship and responsibilities of franchisors and franchisees.[59]

Courts should liberally construe the AFPA in order to bring about its remedial purposes and legislative goals.[60] The Arkansas General Assembly's statutory enactment of protections for franchisees in the AFPA reflects fundamental public policy decisions, which a franchisor cannot displace by obtaining contractual agreements to avoid or limit the franchisor's liability under the AFPA.[61]

2. Annotations

The AFPA represents the fundamental public policy of the state, particularly with respect to the termination only for cause and notice provisions. That is based on the specific language of the emergency clause and the statutory language, "which departs significantly from customary contract principles permitting the parties to define the terms of their terminations, and the fact that the statute was enacted to protect a weaker economic party from the oppressive use of superior bargaining power." *Britelink, Inc. v. Telecorp PCS, Inc.*, No. 3:03-CV-00207 GTE, 2004 WL 5509416, at *8 (E.D. Ark. May 6, 2004).

---

55. Ark. Code Ann. § 4-72-203.
56. *Id.* § 4-72-207.
57. An emergency clause allows legislation in Arkansas to become law immediately when the governor signs it, rather than taking effect 90 days after the General Assembly adjourns.
58. Capital Equip., Inc. v. CNH Am., LLC, 471 F. Supp. 2d 951, 957 (E.D. Ark. 2006) (quoting Emergency Clause to Act 355 of 1977).
59. 2023 Act §§ 1(2), (7), (8), (9).
60. Stockton v. Sentry Ins., 989 S.W.2d 914, 917 (Ark. 1999); Dr. Pepper Bottling Co. v. Frantz, 842 S.W.2d 37, 41 (Ark. 1992).
61. Capital Equip., Inc. v. CNH Am., LLC, 471 F. Supp. 2d 951, 958 (E.D. Ark. 2006).

A dealer agreement stating that "the laws of the State of Texas shall govern its interpretation" did not displace the AFPA but merely meant that Texas rules of contract interpretation apply. That contract language did not give the dealer sufficient warning that it would forfeit its rights under the AFPA. Because the agreement did not have a choice of law provision except with respect to the "interpretation" of the contract, the court applied the "most significant contacts" test and found that Arkansas had the most significant contacts with the contracts at issue. Thus, the AFPA applied to the relationship and the dealer could assert claims under the AFPA. *Heating & Air Specialists, Inc. v. Jones*, 180 F.3d 923, 930–31 (8th Cir. 1999).

There was substantial evidence from which the jury could have found that changes a franchisor made to its policies and procedures manual after March 4, 1977, the effective date of the AFPA, constituted a new agreement governed by the AFPA such that the franchisor terminated the agreement without proper notice and an opportunity to cure. *The Trane Co. v. Miller Engineering, Inc.*, No. CA 87-58, 1987 WL 19735, at *2 (Ark. Ct. App. Nov. 11, 1987).

Courts should liberally construe the AFPA to carry out the legislative goal of protecting the public. *Gunn v. Farmers Insurance Exchange*, 372 S.W.3d 346, 354 (2010), *reh'g denied* (2011).

C. Termination

1. What Constitutes Termination or Cancellation

a. Commentary

The AFPA does not define termination or cancellation of a franchise, nor are there any cases that discuss what constitutes termination or cancellation. Until the 2023 amendments to the AFPA, the statute prohibited a franchisor from terminating or cancelling a franchise without good cause.[62] The AFPA defines eight reasons that constitute "good cause."[63] The 2023 amendments added the requirement, in a different section of the statute, that agreements entered into or renewed after the effective date of the act on August 1, 2023, can only be terminated for "material cause as determined under objective standards."[64] The AFPA does not define what is meant by "material cause" or "objective standards," or whether the AFPA's eight grounds that constitute "good cause" will also constitute "material cause."

b. Annotations

In *Capital Equipment, Inc. v. CNH America, LLC*, 471 F. Supp. 2d 951, 959–61 (E.D. Ark. 2006), the court declined to rule on whether a franchisee can assert a claim for constructive termination under the AFPA, noting that no Arkansas case had addressed the issue of whether a franchisee may pursue an action for termination when the termination is constructive rather than actual. The franchisor had

---

62. Ark. Code Ann. §§ 4-72-204(a)(1), 4-72-202(7)(A)–(H).
63. *Id.* § 4-72-202(7)(A)–(H).
64. *Id.* § 4-72-212(b).

argued that the franchisee could not prevail on its theory that the franchisor terminated it without good cause under the AFPA because it voluntarily resigned its dealership. The franchisee argued that Arkansas courts would reject the franchisor's position and would recognize de facto or constructive terminations violated the AFPA's good cause requirement for terminating a franchisee. In a subsequent ruling, the court said it preferred to address these novel legal issues on a fully developed record at trial. *Capital Equipment, Inc. v. CNH America, LLC*, No. 4:04-CV-00381 GTE, 2006 WL 2788667, at *2 (E.D. Ark. Sept. 28, 2006). The parties ultimately dismissed the case with prejudice before trial. There are no Arkansas cases addressing whether there is a cause of action for constructive termination under the AFPA.

2. Restrictions on Termination or Cancellation

a. Commentary

As already discussed, the AFPA requires a franchisor to have good cause to terminate or cancel a franchise.[65] The AFPA lists eight grounds for termination that constitute good cause. Good cause is defined as: (A) the franchisee's failure to substantially comply with the franchisor's requirements imposed on the franchisee or similarly situated franchisees; (B) the franchisee's failure to act in good faith and in a commercially reasonable manner; (C) the franchisee's abandonment of the franchise; (D) the franchisee's conviction of an offense punishable by a prison term in excess of one year that is substantially related to the franchise business; (E) a franchisee's act that substantially impairs the franchisor's trademark or trade name; (F) a franchisee's insolvency or bankruptcy or assignment of assets for a creditor's benefit; (G) the franchisee's loss of the right to occupy the franchise business premises; and (H) the franchisee's failure to pay amounts owed to the franchisor within ten days' receipt of notice of past due sums.[66] If none of these grounds exists, then a franchisor cannot terminate the franchise.

However, a 2023 amendment to the AFPA created a new section that states a franchisor can terminate a franchise agreement "only for material cause as determined under objective standards" to terminate a franchise agreement.[67] The amendment did not define "material cause" or reference the existing termination provisions of the AFPA. This particular amendment applies to franchise agreements or contracts entered into or renewed on or after the effective date of the 2023 Act on August 1, 2023. Thus, it is unclear whether the existing "good cause" requirements and definition in the AFPA will apply to those agreements.

b. Annotations

The plain language of the AFPA, along with the canon of statutory construction *expression unius est exclusion alterisus*, prohibits an interpretation of the AFPA's list of circumstances constituting "good cause" for termination that includes

---

65. *Id*. § 4-72-204(a)(1).
66. *Id*. § 4-72-202(7)(A)–(H).
67. *Id*. § 4-72-211.

circumstances not specifically listed in section 4-72-202. *Larry Hobbs Farm Equipment, Inc. v. CNH America, LLC*, 291 S.W.3d 190, 196 (Ark. 2009).

The market withdrawal of a product or of a trademark and trade name for the product is not "good cause" to terminate a franchisee under the AFPA. The AFPA clearly defines what constitutes good cause, and market withdrawal is not included. *Larry Hobbs Farm Equipment, Inc. v. CNH America, LLC*, 291 S.W.3d 190, 193–96 (Ark. 2009).

A dental products manufacturer could terminate a distributor for "good cause" if the distributor did not meet the purchasing requirements or if the distributor sold products in the gray market, which refers to goods sold outside the normal distribution channels. However, if those were the grounds for termination, the manufacturer must give the distributor proper notice and time to correct the deficiency under the AFPA. *Otto Dental Supply, Inc. v. Kerr Corp.*, No. 4:06CV01610, 2008 WL 410630, at *5 (E.D. Ark. Feb. 13, 2008).

A franchisor of heating and air conditioning products had good cause to terminate the franchisee for defaulting on its payment obligations. The franchisor had informed the franchisee that it would terminate the franchisee in 90 days if the franchisee failed to cure the defaults within ten days. Although the parties disputed the precise amount owed, the uncontroverted evidence at trial showed that the franchisee's account was past due on the date of the default notice, that franchisee had ten days to cure to prevent the termination, and that franchisee failed to repay any amount owed within those ten days. Therefore, the franchisee's claim for unlawful termination under the AFPA failed. *Heating & Air Specialists, Inc. v. Jones*, 180 F.3d 923, 931 (8th Cir. 1999).

3. Notice Requirement

a. Commentary

Before terminating, cancelling, or failing to renew a franchise, the franchisor must (1) give notice to the franchisee at least 90 days in advance of the action; (2) set forth the reasons for the termination, cancellation, or failure to renew the franchise; and (3) in the case of termination, provide the franchisee with 30 days to rectify any claimed deficiency.[68] However, the AFPA does not require a franchisor to give notice where the reason for termination or cancellation is for good cause as defined in section 4-72-202(7)(C)–(H): (C) voluntary abandonment of the franchise; (D) conviction of the franchisee of an offense, punishable by a term of imprisonment in excess of one year, substantially related to the business conducted pursuant to the franchise; (E) any act by the franchisee which substantially impairs the franchisor's trademark or trade name; (F) insolvency or bankruptcy proceedings by or against a franchisee, or any assignment or attempted assignment by a franchisee of the franchise or the assets of the franchise for the benefit of the creditors; (G) loss of the franchisor's or franchisee's right to occupy the premises from which the franchise business is operated; or (H) the franchisee's failure to pay to the franchisor within ten days after receipt of notice of any sums past due the franchisor and relating to the

---

68. *Id*. § 4-72-204(b).

franchise. Thus, the only notice and opportunity to cure that a franchisor would be required to give in those circumstances is notice, if any, required by the franchise agreement.

The AFPA protects a franchisor and its officers, agents, and employees from liability for any "cause of action of any nature (other than as provided by this subchapter)" relating to the franchisor's furnishing of information about the reasons for termination, cancellation, or an intent not to renew, or for submitting evidence at a hearing or trial in connection with termination, cancellation, or an intent not to renew.[69] Although the language of this protection appears broad, there are no cases interpreting it.

b. Annotations

A dental products manufacturer could terminate a distributor for "good cause" if the distributor did not meet the purchasing requirements or if the distributor sold products in the gray market outside normal distribution channels. However, if those were the grounds for termination, the manufacturer must give the distributor proper notice and time to correct the deficiency under the AFPA. *Otto Dental Supply, Inc. v. Kerr Corp.*, No. 4:06CV01610, 2008 WL 410630, at *5 (E.D. Ark. Feb. 13, 2008).

A dealer's allegation that the manufacturer gave it insufficient notice of termination under the AFPA could state a claim where the manufacturer (1) said the dealer could not order new products as of a date that was only 17 days after the date on which the manufacturer gave notice of termination, (2) failed to set forth the reasons for termination, and (3) failed to provide the dealer with the requisite time to rectify any claimed deficiency. However, the dealer failed to allege that the deficient notice itself was the proximate cause of any specific damages, so the court dismissed its claim without prejudice. *Larry Hobbs Farm Equipment, Inc. v. CNH America, LLC*, No. 2:08CV00049 JLH, 2008 WL 3931323, at *9 (E.D. Ark. Aug. 22, 2008).

There was substantial evidence from which the jury could have found that changes a franchisor made to its policies and procedures manual after March 4, 1977, the effective date of the AFPA, constituted a new agreement governed by the AFPA. The old agreement gave the parties the right to terminate with 30 days' notice. Under the AFPA, the franchisor is required to give 90 days' notice and 30 days to cure any deficiencies, which franchisor failed to do. *The Trane Co. v. Miller Engineering, Inc.*, No. CA 87-58, 1987 WL 19735, at *2 (Ark. Ct. App. Nov. 11, 1987).

4. Grounds for Termination

a. Commentary

As already noted, good cause for termination is limited to eight scenarios listed in the statute.[70] However, as also discussed earlier, the 2023 amendments to the AFPA created a new section that states that a franchisor can terminate a

---

69. *Id.* § 4-72-210.
70. *Id.* § 4-72-202 (7)(A)–(H).

franchise agreement "only for material cause as determined under objective standards."[71] The amendment did not define "material cause" or reference the existing termination provisions of the AFPA. This particular amendment applies to franchise agreements or contracts entered into or renewed on or after the effective date of the 2023 Act on August 1, 2023. Thus, it is unclear whether the existing "good cause" requirements and definition in the AFPA will also apply to agreements entered into after August 1, 2023.

b. Annotations

A dental products manufacturer could terminate a distributor for "good cause," including failure to comply substantially with the requirements imposed upon the franchisee by the franchisor, or sought to be imposed by the franchisor, if the distributor did not meet the purchasing requirements or if the distributor sold products in the gray market. Because it was unclear whether the manufacturer terminated the distributor for those reasons or whether it treated the distributor in a commercially reasonable manner and in good faith, the court denied the manufacturer's motion for summary judgment. *Otto Dental Supply, Inc. v. Kerr Corp.*, No. 4:06CV01610, 2008 WL 410630, at *6 (E.D. Ark. Feb. 13, 2008).

The eight grounds enumerated in the AFPA are the exclusive means for a franchisor to terminate a franchisee for good cause, except for those entered into on or after August 1, 2023. The appellate court affirmed the district court's grant of summary judgment to the dealer finding that the manufacturer had terminated their agreement without good cause under the AFPA. The manufacturer admitted that it did not terminate the dealer agreement for any of the specific reasons listed in the AFPA, but it contended that those eight grounds were not an exclusive list. It argued that it had good cause to terminate based on its desire to rebrand acquired businesses under a single trademark and to use dealers who were willing to carry the entire product line. The court disagreed, based on principles of statutory construction. *Volvo Trademark Holding Aktiebolaget v. Clark Machinery Co.*, 510 F.3d 474, 481–84 (4th Cir. 2007); *Volvo Trademark Holding Aktiebolaget v. AIS Construction Equipment Corp.*, 416 F. Supp. 404, 410–12 & nn.2–3 (W.D.N.C. 2006).

The court found an issue of fact as to whether a manufacturer terminated a distributorship for good cause under the AFPA. The manufacturer informed the distributor that it did not meet minimum distribution requirements and gave the distributor 90 days to correct the deficiency.

Manufacturer then gave distributor written notice that it was terminating the distributor on 30 days' notice because it had acquired another company. Whether the manufacturer terminated the distributor for good cause for failure to comply substantially with the agreement's requirements was one for the jury, considering that there was evidence from which the jury could readily find that termination was attributable to the manufacturer acquiring another company rather than the distributor's failures to meet sales goals. *Dr. Pepper Bottling Co. v. Frantz*, 842 S.W.2d 37, 42 (Ark. 1992).

---

71. *Id.* § 4-72-212.

The AFPA invalidated a provision in a dealer agreement that permitted either party to terminate without good cause. Nevertheless, the court found that the franchisor had good cause to terminate the agreement under the AFPA because the dealer failed to pay amounts due to the franchisor within the statutorily required ten-day cure period. This was regardless of the dealer's allegations that it could not pay amounts due because the franchisor breached the agreement by failing to provide start-up costs, co-op payments, and special financing terms. The amounts due to the franchisor far exceeded the amount of any payments that the dealer claimed it was entitled to receive, so the debt could not have resulted from the franchisor's alleged breaches. *Heating & Air Specialists, Inc. v. Jones*, 180 F.3d 923, 931 (8th Cir. 1999).

The market withdrawal of a product or of a trademark and trade name for the product is not "good cause" to terminate a franchise under the AFPA. The AFPA clearly defines what constitutes good cause and market withdrawal is not included. *Larry Hobbs Farm Equipment, Inc. v. CNH America, LLC*, 291 S.W.3d 190, 193–96 (Ark. 2009).

5. Required Cure Period

a. Commentary

Pursuant to the AFPA, the franchisee has 30 days to rectify any claimed deficiency before termination.[72] However, this cure period is shortened to ten days when the reason for termination is (1) repeated deficiencies within a 12-month period that gives rise to good cause under section 4-72-202(A) (franchisee's failure to substantially comply with the franchisor's requirements); (2) section 4-72-202(B) (franchisee's failure to act in good faith and in a commercially reasonable manner); or (3) failure to pay the franchisee within ten days after receipt of notice of any sums past due the franchisor and relating to the franchise under section 4-72-202(7)(H). Timely curing the defaults voids the termination notice.[73]

b. Annotations

There was substantial evidence from which the jury could have found that changes a franchisor made to its policies and procedures manual after March 4, 1977, the effective date of the AFPA, constituted a new agreement governed by the AFPA. The old agreement gave the parties the right to terminate with 30 days' notice. Under the AFPA, the franchisor is required to give 90 days' notice and 30 days to cure any deficiencies, which franchisor failed to do. *The Trane Co. v. Miller Engineering, Inc.*, No. CA 87-58, 1987 WL 19735, at *2 (Ark. Ct. App. Nov. 11, 1987).

6. Repurchase Obligations

a. Commentary

The franchisor does not have any repurchase obligation where the termination is proper under the AFPA. However, if a franchisor terminates a franchise

---

72. *Id.* § 4-72-204(b).
73. *Id.* § 4-72-204(d).

without good cause, the franchisee may choose to require the franchisor to repurchase the franchisee's inventory, supplies, equipment, and furnishings that the franchisee bought from the franchisor or its approved sources. The repurchase price will be at the franchisee's net cost less a reasonable allowance for depreciation or obsolescence. The franchisor does not have to repurchase personalized items that have no value to the franchisor.[74] If a franchisee files a lawsuit and seeks damages against a franchisor for termination without good cause, the franchisee must include a claim for inventory repurchase in the same lawsuit or the claim will be barred by res judicata in a later lawsuit.[75]

b. Annotations

A franchisee's second lawsuit seeking a mandatory injunction to force a franchisor to repurchase its inventory was rejected on the grounds of res judicata because the franchisee failed to assert the claim in a prior lawsuit for unlawful termination. The court rejected the franchisee's argument that it could not have asserted its claim for inventory repurchase until after the first case was completed. It is the act of termination without good cause that triggers the auxiliary remedy of repurchase, not the entry of judgment of termination without good cause. The AFPA does not require a franchisee to pursue another remedy prior to seeking repurchase of its inventory. The jury could have considered the value of the inventory in calculating damages in the first lawsuit, so res judicata barred the second lawsuit for repurchase of the inventory. *American Standard, Inc. v. Miller Engineering, Inc.*, 772 S.W.2d 344, 346–47 (Ark. 1989).

D. Restrictions on Nonrenewal

1. What Constitutes Nonrenewal

a. Commentary

Franchisors are precluded from failing to renew a franchise except for (1) good cause or (2) in accordance with the current policies, practices, and standards established by the franchisor that in their establishment, operation, or application are not arbitrary or capricious. The AFPA does not state what constitutes nonrenewal.[76]

b. Annotations

There is no case law addressing a failure to renew under the AFPA.

2. Restrictions on Nonrenewal

a. Commentary

As already indicated, franchisors can only refuse to renew where there is good cause or where the refusal is in accordance with the current policies, practices,

---

74. *Id.* § 4-72-209.
75. Am. Standard, Inc. v. Miller Eng'g, Inc., 772 S.W.2d 344, 347 (Ark. 1989).
76. Ark. Code Ann. § 4-72-204(a)(2).

and standards established by the franchisor that in their establishment, operation, or application are not arbitrary or capricious.[77]

b. Annotations

There is no case law addressing a failure to renew under the AFPA.

3. Notice Requirement

a. Commentary

A franchisor must give a franchisee written notice of its intent not to renew the franchise at least 90 days "in advance of such action" and the franchisor must set forth the reasons for its intention not to renew the franchise.[78]

The AFPA, section 4-72-204(2)(c), states that notice is not required for a "termination or cancellation" that is based on one of the grounds for good cause in section 4-72-202(7)(C)–(H) of the AFPA, without mentioning a failure to renew.[79] Because the preceding section of the AFPA, section 4-72-204(2)(b), requires notice for nonrenewal, a court would likely conclude that a franchisor must give notice of nonrenewal even if the nonrenewal was based on one of the grounds for good cause listed in section 4-72-202(7)(C)–(H). Thus, although a franchisor can terminate a franchise without notice for abandonment, for example, a franchisor must provide notice of its intent to not renew the franchise for abandonment.

To protect a franchisor from liability for stating its reasons for nonrenewal, the AFPA prohibits any causes of action against the franchisor (such as defamation), other than as provided by the AFPA.[80]

b. Annotations

There is no case law addressing the notice requirements for nonrenewal.

4. Grounds for Nonrenewal

a. Commentary

As already discussed, the franchisor can only refuse to renew a franchise where (1) the franchisor has good cause based on one of the eight grounds enumerated in the statute, or (2) the failure to renew is in accordance with the current policies, practices, and standards established by the franchisor that in their establishment, operation, or application are not arbitrary or capricious.[81] The 2023 amendments to the AFPA do not address nonrenewal.

b. Annotations

There is no case law addressing grounds for nonrenewal.

---

77. *Id.*
78. *Id.* § 4-72-204(b).
79. *Id.* § 4-72-204(c).
80. *Id.* § 4-72-210.
81. *Id.* § 4-72-204(a)(2).

5. Required Cure Period

a. Commentary

The AFPA requires franchisors to permit franchisees to cure certain defaults that would otherwise constitute good cause for nonrenewal if the franchisor's reasons for failing to renew the franchise are (1) the franchisee's repeated deficiencies within a 12-month period giving rise to good cause under section 4-72-202(7)(A) (defined as the franchisee's failure to comply substantially with the requirements imposed by the franchisor), or (2) the franchisee's failure to act in good faith and in a commercially reasonable manner in carrying out the terms of the franchise.[82] In those cases, the franchisee has ten days to rectify the repeated deficiencies and void the notice.[83] It is unclear how a franchisee would cure those defaults but if it does, the franchisor would have to renew the franchise.

Where the refusal to renew is based on any other "good cause" scenario, the franchisee is not entitled to a cure period.

b. Annotations

There is no case law addressing the cure period for nonrenewal.

6. Limitations on Franchisors' Right to Impose Conditions for Renewal

a. Commentary

Other than the restrictions on nonrenewal discussed earlier, the AFPA does not expressly limit the franchisors' right to impose conditions for renewal. Thus, presumably a franchisor could require a franchisee to, for example, sign a new franchise agreement or pay a renewal fee.

b. Annotations

Not applicable.

7. Repurchase Obligations

a. Commentary

Although the AFPA contains a repurchase requirement (at franchisee's option) for franchisors who terminate a franchise without good cause, the statutory repurchase obligation addresses only "termination" without good cause and does not expressly state that it applies to a failure to renew a franchise.[84]

b. Annotations

Not applicable.

---

82. *Id.* § 4-72-204(d).
83. *Id.*
84. *Id.* § 209 ("Upon termination of any franchise by a franchisor without good cause . . .").

E. Transfers and Succession

1. Commentary

For franchise agreements entered into, renewed, or transferred after March 4, 1977, but before August 1, 2023, the AFPA requires a franchisee to provide prior written notice to a franchisor of its intent to transfer, assign, or sell a franchise or interest in a franchise to another person. The franchisee must set forth the prospective franchisee's name, address, statement of financial qualification, and business experience during the previous five years.[85] The franchisor has 60 days after receiving the notice to inform the franchisee in writing that it either (1) approves the transfer, assignment, or sale to the proposed transferee or (2) rejects the proposed transferee and provides a material reason relating to the character, financial ability, or business experience of the proposed transferee.[86] If the franchisor fails to respond to the franchisee's request within 60 days, the request is deemed granted.[87] However, the transfer, assignment, or sale is not valid unless the transferee agrees in writing to comply with all of the requirements of the franchise then in effect.[88]

The legislature amended the AFPA's transfer and succession provisions in 2023 to broaden protections for franchisees. For franchise agreements entered into or renewed on and after August 1, 2023,[89] a franchisee or franchise owner (defined in the amendments as a person who owns a financial interest in a franchise or is a guarantor under a franchise agreement)[90] is not required to obtain the franchisor's approval for a transfer of a franchise by a franchisee or franchise owner to the spouse, child, or heir of a franchisee or franchise owner who is operationally and financially qualified.[91] The amendments do not define "operationally and financially qualified," although this provision would appear to imply that a franchisor would need to determine if the transferee is qualified to own the franchise which, in and of itself, would constitute approval. The 2023 amendments also prohibit a franchisor or its related entities from exercising a right of first refusal for a transfer, sale, or assignment to the spouse, child, or heir of a franchisee or franchise owner.[92] Otherwise, franchisors are permitted to exercise a contractual right of first refusal to purchase a franchise or all or substantially all of the assets of a franchise business on the same terms and conditions as a bona fide offer from a proposed purchaser.[93]

---

85. Act of Mar. 4, 1977, No. 355 § 6 (previous version of Ark. Code Ann. § 4-72-205(a)).
86. *Id.*
87. *Id.*
88. *Id.*
89. The uncodified retroactivity provision of the act states that the new transfer provisions in this § 4-72-205 (section 4 in the act) only apply to franchise agreements or contracts entered into or renewed on and after the effective date of the act. The provision does not mention whether it applies to agreements that were transferred. 2023 Act § 7(b). *See supra* note 16.
90. Ark. Code Ann. § 4-72-202(4), (9).
91. *Id.* § 4-72-205(d).
92. *Id.* § 4-72-205(e).
93. *Id.* § 4-72-205(f).

In addition, the time period for the franchisor to approve or disapprove the transfer, assignment, or sale was shortened from 60 to 30 days. Within 30 days after receiving the notice of franchisee's intent to transfer, sell, or assign its interest, the franchisor must provide written notice (1) to either the franchisee or the franchise owner approving the sale, transfer, or assignment to the proposed transferee or (2) to the franchisee and franchise owner of the unacceptability of the proposed transferee.[94] The notice of unacceptability must state a "material deficiency relating to the character, financial ability, or business experience of the proposed transferee based on the application of the franchisor's then-existing standards consistently and uniformly applied to similarly situated franchisees operating within the franchise brand."[95] If the franchisor does not reply within the 30 days, the franchisor's approval is deemed granted.[96] The 2023 amendments changed the requirement that the transferee must agree in writing to comply with the requirements of the franchise then in effect to those "reasonable and legal" requirements of the franchise then in effect.[97]

The 2023 amendments to the AFPA also created a new section, separate from the transfer provisions, requiring the franchisor to treat a survivor of a franchisee in good faith and to provide the survivor a "sufficient opportunity" to become an owner of the franchise.[98] A "survivor" as used in that provision means "an immediate family member or designated heir of the franchisee or franchise owner."[99]

Franchisees are prohibited from transferring, assigning, or selling their franchise or an interest in the franchise without first providing the franchisor with written notice of its intent and that notice must include the prospective transferee's name, address, financial qualifications, and previous five years' business experience to the franchisor.[100]

Although the AFPA states that a franchisee violates the statute if it does not provide the proper notice to the franchisor of a transfer, assignment, or sale, a franchisor does not have an independent cause of action or remedy against the franchisee for a violation under the AFPA. If a franchisor has no right under the franchise agreement to receive notice from the franchisee of a proposed transfer, assignment, or sale or to terminate a franchisee due to the unacceptability of a proposed transferee, a franchisor cannot terminate a franchisee for "good cause" under the AFPA because the AFPA defines good cause as a failure by a franchisee to comply substantially with the requirements imposed by the franchisor.[101]

The AFPA protects a franchisor and its officers, agents, and employees from liability for any "cause of action of any nature (other than as provided by this

---

94. *Id.* § 4-72-205(b)(1)(B).
95. *Id.*
96. *Id.* § 4-72-205(b)(2).
97. *Id.* § 4-72-205(c).
98. *Id.* § 4-72-212(c)(1).
99. *Id.* § 4-72-212(c)(2).
100. *Id.* § 205(a).
101. Ark. Op. Att'y Gen. No. 89-113, 1989 WL 298185 (May 15, 1989).

subchapter)" for furnishing information about, making statements about, or submitting evidence at a hearing or trial in connection with the unacceptability of a proposed transferee, or relating to the character, financial ability, or business experience of a proposed transferee.[102] There are no cases interpreting this section of the AFPA.

2. Annotations

A former automobile franchisee who had sold his dealership but was attempting to buy it back was not a franchisee under the AFPA after he sold his business. Therefore, the court found that the lower court properly dismissed franchisee's claim that it would be fundamentally unfair for the franchisor to refuse to renew, reassign, or transfer a franchise back to him. *J.D. Fisher v. Jones*, 816 S.W.2d 865, 867–68 (Ark. 1991).

A wholesale beer distributor claimed that its supplier violated the AFPA by refusing to approve a buyer other than the supplier's preferred buyer, which caused it to sell the distributorship at a price less than fair market value. The distributor claimed that the supplier refused to deal with it in a commercially reasonable manner and in good faith as required by section 4-72-206 of the AFPA. The supplier argued that the claim failed because the distributor did not meet the statutory requirements to trigger the supplier's obligations to review or approve any potential buyers other than the supplier's choice of buyer, so it could not have acted in a commercially unreasonable and bad faith manner. The court found there was a genuine issue of material fact that precluded summary judgment, entitling the distributor to submit its claim to a jury. *Southeastern Distributing Co. v. Miller Brewing Co.*, 237 S.W.3d 63, 70–71 (Ark. 2006). There is no subsequent published decision on this case.

F. Other Regulation of the Franchise Relationship

1. Commentary

The AFPA has a number of provisions that generally regulate the franchisor–franchisee relationship. These include prohibitions on certain contractual releases, free association of franchisees, changes in franchisee management, restrictions on certain kinds of franchisee sales, advertising fee regulations, requiring franchisors to deal with franchisees in a commercially reasonable and good faith manner, and imposing a general duty of good faith and fair dealing on the relationship. Another requirement limits franchisors' discriminatory treatment of franchisees.

a. Standards of Conduct

The AFPA prohibits franchisors, through an officer, agent, or employee, from engaging, directly or indirectly, in any of the following practices:

(1) Requiring a franchisee to assent to a release, assignment, novation, waiver, or estoppel that would relieve any person from liability imposed by the AFPA;

---

102. ARK. CODE ANN. § 210.

(2) Prohibiting directly or indirectly the right of free association among franchisees for a lawful purpose;
(3) Requiring or prohibiting a change in management of any franchisee unless the requirement or prohibition of change is for reasonable cause, which cause must be stated in writing by the franchisor;
(4) Restricting the sale of any equity or debenture issue or the transfer of any security of a franchisee or in any way preventing or attempting to prevent the transfer, sale, or issuance of shares of stock or debentures to employees, personnel of franchisee, or heirs of the principal owners as long as basic financial requirements of the franchisor are complied with, if the sale, transfer, or issuance does not have the effect of accomplishing a sale of the franchise;
(5) Providing any term or condition in any lease or other agreement ancillary or collateral to a franchise, which term or condition directly or indirectly violates the AFPA;
(6) Refusing to deal with a franchise in a commercially reasonable manner and in good faith; or
(7) Collecting a percentage of the franchisee's sales as an advertising fee and not using the funds for the purpose of advertising the business conducted by the franchisee.[103]

The act does not define "commercially reasonable manner and in good faith." The Arkansas Supreme Court has not defined that phrase either, but it has held it is a question for the jury.[104] The Arkansas Supreme Court Committee on Jury Instructions-Civil has noted that the concept of "commercial reasonableness" in the context of the Uniform Commercial Code "is a flexible concept."[105]

In addition to the requirement that franchisors deal with franchisees in a commercially reasonable manner and in good faith, the 2023 amendments to the AFPA imposed "governing principles and the obligations of good faith and fair dealing" on a "transaction" under the AFPA.[106] A "transaction" is not defined. Under Arkansas law, the governing principles and the obligations of good faith and fair dealing are those imposed on every party to a contract—to act in good faith in the performance and enforcement of a contract and not to do anything

---

103. *Id.* § 4-72-206(a)(1)–(7).
104. *See* Distrib. Co. v. Miller Brewing Co., 237 S.W.3d 63, 71 (Ark. 2006) (holding that distributor had presented proof demonstrating a material issue of fact on whether supplier's actions constituted a refusal to deal with a franchise in a commercially reasonable manner and in good faith by allegedly preventing distributor from obtaining offers from potential purchasers by forcing a sale to supplier's preferred purchaser); Miller Brewing Co. v. Ed Roleson, Jr., Inc., 223 S.W.2d 806, 811–12 (Ark. 2006) (finding substantial evidence to support the jury's finding that franchisor refused to deal with its franchisee in a commercially reasonable manner and in good faith).
105. Ark. Model Jury Instr., comment to Civil AMI 2805 (quoting Marks v. Powell, 162 B.R. 820, 829 (E.D. Ark. 1993)).
106. ARK. CODE ANN. § 4-72-212(a).

that would prevent, hinder, or delay performance.[107] There is no separate cause of action for breach of the implied covenant of good faith and fair dealing.[108]

b. Liability Relating to Franchisor's Provision of Information

The AFPA states that a franchisor is not liable, except as provided under the AFPA, for furnishing information about the reasons for termination, cancellation, intent not to renew, failure to renew, refusal to do business, or substantial change in competitive circumstances, unacceptability of a proposed transferee or relating to the character, financial ability, or business experience of a proposed transferee, or for statements made or evidence submitted at a hearing or trial conducted therewith.[109] No cases interpret this provision.

c. Right of Free Association

The AFPA makes it unlawful for a franchisor to prohibit directly or indirectly the right of free association among franchisees for a lawful purpose.[110] No cases interpret this provision.

d. Franchisee Management and Ownership

The AFPA makes it unlawful for a franchisor to require or prohibit a change in management of a franchisee unless the requirement or prohibition of change is for a reasonable cause, which cause the franchisor must state in writing.[111] No cases interpret this provision.

e. Ancillary Documents

The AFPA makes it unlawful for a franchisor to provide any term or condition in a lease or other agreement ancillary or collateral to a franchise if the term or condition directly or indirectly violates the AFPA.[112] No cases interpret this provision.

f. Advertising Fees

The AFPA makes it unlawful for a franchisor to collect a percentage of the franchisee's sales as an advertising fee and not use the funds to advertise the business conducted by the franchisee.[113] No cases interpret this provision.

g. Discrimination

The AFPA does not directly prohibit a franchisor from discriminating against franchisees. However, if a franchisor is terminating or failing to renew a franchise for good cause due to the franchisee's failure to comply substantially

---

107. Cmty. Bank of N. Ark. v. Tri-State Propane, 203 S.W.3d 124, 128 (Ark. Ct App. 2005).
108. Wilkins v. Simmons Bank, 2023 WL 1868142, No. 3:20-cv-116-DPM, at *2 (E.D. Ark. Feb. 9, 2023) (citing Ark. Rsch. Med. Testing, LLC v. Osborne, 2011 WL 1423993, at *2 (Ark. Apr. 14, 2011)).
109. ARK. CODE ANN. § 4-72-210.
110. *Id.* § 4-72-206(a)(2).
111. *Id.* § 4-72-206(a)(3).
112. *Id.* § 4-72-206(a)(5).
113. *Id.* § 4-72-206(a)(7).

with the franchisor's requirements, the requirements cannot be discriminatory as compared to requirements imposed on other similarly situated franchisees, either by their terms or how they are enforced.[114] No cases interpret this provision.

The 2023 amendments to the AFPA also indirectly address discrimination in the transfer, assignment, or sale of a franchise. If a franchisor rejects a proposed transferee, the franchisor's reasons must be based on the application of the franchisor's then-existing standards consistently and uniformly applied to similarly situated franchises operating within the franchise brand.[115]

2. Annotations

A wholesale beer distributor alleged that its supplier committed fraud under the AFPA because the supplier falsely stated that its preferred buyer for the distributorship would be the only approved buyer for the distributorship. The court affirmed summary judgment to the supplier, finding that any statements regarding its intention to approve a prospective buyer were projections of a future event, not statements of fact, and therefore were not actionable. *Southeastern Distributing Co. v. Miller Brewing Co.*, 237 S.W.3d 63, 73–75 (Ark. 2006).

A franchisor's attempt to force a franchisee out of business may constitute a failure to deal with a franchisee in a commercially reasonable manner and in good faith under the AFPA, which is a question of fact for the jury. Substantial evidence supported the jury's verdict that a brewing company refused to deal with its distributor in a commercially reasonable manner and in good faith, in violation of the AFPA by attempting to force it out of business as part of its plan to consolidate its distributor network. Evidence showed that the brewing company had developed an internal consolidation plan, without the distributor's knowledge, to reduce the number of wholesale distributors in Arkansas. In order to effectuate its plan, the brewer thwarted the plaintiff distributor's efforts to buy another distributor by interfering in the sale. The brewer instructed another one of its distributors, which it planned to keep in its network, to buy the distributor that plaintiff was negotiating with, and that plaintiff needed in order to grow its market share and remain commercially viable as the brewer required. The court also found that the AFPA claim was not preempted by the Arkansas Beer Wholesaler's Act. The distributor's claim under the AFPA was not a claim against the manufacturer by a proposed purchaser of a wholesaler's business, but by its own franchisee. The distributor's claim was that Miller refused to deal with it in a commercially reasonable manner by attempting to put the distributor out of business. Miller's alleged interference with the potential purchase of another distributor was merely evidence used to support the distributor's claim. *Miller Brewing Co. v. Ed Roleson, Jr., Inc.*, 223 S.W.3d 806, 811–14 (Ark. 2006).

Whether a party treats another party in a commercially reasonable manner and in good faith under the AFPA is a fact question for the jury. *Otto Dental*

---

114. *Id.* § 4-72-202(7)(A).
115. *Id.* § 4-72-205(b)(1)(B).

Supply, Inc. v. Kerr Corp., No. 4:06-CV-01610-WRW, 2008 WL 410630, at *6 (E.D. Ark. Feb. 13, 2008); *Miller Brewing Co. v. Ed Roleson, Jr., Inc.*, 223 S.W.3d 806, 811 (Ark. 2006).

Selling the same products as its dealer but with different colors and different brand names in the dealer's territory did not provide the dealer with a claim under the AFPA for dealing with a franchise in a commercially unreasonable manner or in bad faith. The AFPA recognizes the reasonableness of a franchisor's dual distribution to multiple franchisees in the same area by defining a franchise as the use of a trademark or sale of a particular product "within an exclusive or nonexclusive" territory. The dealer agreement stated that the dealer would be a nonexclusive dealer, so even if the franchisor engaged in dual distribution, this dual distribution was not commercially unreasonable. *Larry Hobbs Farm Equipment, Inc. v. CNH America, LLC*, No. 2:08CV00049 JLH, 2008 WL 3931323, at *7 (E.D. Ark. Aug. 22, 2008).

A dealer agreement allowed a dealer to operate facilities outside its area of responsibility only with the manufacturer's permission. When the plaintiff dealer complained about another dealer operating an unauthorized facility in its area of responsibility, the manufacturer did not stop the other dealer from doing so. A jury could reasonably conclude that the manufacturer had an obligation to investigate and prevent another dealer from operating a facility in plaintiff's territory and that it acted in bad faith by failing to do so when it became aware of it. Therefore, summary judgment was improper on the dealer's claims for breach of the implied covenant of good faith and fair dealing and violation of the AFPA for failing to act in a commercially reasonable manner and in good faith. *Southern Implement Co., Inc. v. Deere & Co.*, 122 F.3d 503, 507–08 (8th Cir. 1997).

G. Remedies and Administrative Action

1. Restrictive Covenants

a. Commentary

The AFPA does not address restrictive covenants. However, Arkansas enacted a statute, effective July 15, 2015, that governs and greatly expanded the enforceability of covenants not to compete in the context of an employment relationship "or part of an otherwise enforceable employment agreement or contract."[116] Contrary to Arkansas common law, the statute allows courts to "blue pencil" or reform an agreement to make it enforceable.[117] The legislature may have intended to exclude franchise agreements from its applicability as it expressly states that "[t]his subsection does not apply to a covenant not to compete agreement that is ancillary to other contractual relationships, including any type of agreement for the sale and purchase of a business, franchise agreement, and any other agreement not ancillary to an employment relationship or employment

---

116. *Id.* § 4-75-101.
117. *Id.* § 4-75-101(f).

contract."[118] That provision appears to have created confusion by incorrectly referring to "this subsection" rather than "this section" because a legislator introduced a bill in January 2023 to strike the word "subsection" in that provision and replace it with "section."[119] That bill died before adjournment, so it is not clear whether franchise agreements are excluded. However, even without the proposed clarification to the statute, commentators have interpreted the statute to exclude franchise agreements from its coverage.

A provision within that same subsection that excludes franchise agreements states that existing common law principles governing a covenant not to compete outside the employment background remain in effect.[120] Arkansas common law precludes courts from rewriting or reducing an overly broad covenant not to compete.[121] Thus, assuming that franchise agreements are excluded from the noncompete statute, common law principles will continue to apply to noncompetition covenants in franchise agreements, meaning that courts are not likely to blue pencil noncompetes in the franchise context.

Under Arkansas common law, courts generally disfavor covenants not to compete, although the "general rule is that a contract in restraint of trade ancillary to a sale or a business transaction, which is reasonably limited as to time and place, is not against public policy and is not invalid."[122] Such covenants need to meet three requirements: (1) there must be a valid interest to protect, (2) the time limit in the covenant must be reasonable, and (3) the scope of the covenant must not be overly broad.[123] One Arkansas court has applied the generally applicable common law in a case that addressed a covenant against competition in the context of a franchise relationship and the sale of a franchised business.[124]

b. Annotations

The court found a covenant not to compete was unreasonable, even though it was ancillary to the sale of the business, because it prohibited the franchisee from engaging in the business of catfish preparation within 100 miles of the location of his restaurant for one year after termination of the franchise agreement. The franchisor had operated a catfish restaurant and then sold it to a buyer, who signed a franchise agreement in which he agreed to refrain from operating a catfish restaurant within 100 miles of the restaurant for one year after termination of the franchise agreement. The franchisor sued the franchisee

---

118. *Id.* § 4-75-101(h)(1).
119. Ark. House Bill No. 1130, introduced Jan. 12, 2023 (L. Johnson); died in the Arkansas House of Representatives on May 1, 2023.
120. ARK. CODE ANN. § 4-75-101(h)(2).
121. Federated Mut. Ins. Co. v. Bennett, 818 S.W.2d 596, 599 (Ark. Ct. App. 1991) (noting that it has long been the rule that Arkansas courts will not rewrite an overly broad covenant not to compete).
122. Hobbs v. Pool, No. CA 86-145, 1987 WL 8004, at *2 (Ark. Ct. App. Mar. 18, 1987).
123. Optical Partners, Inc. v. Dang, No. 10-629, 2011 Ark. 156, at *12 (Ark. 2011) (finding covenant not to compete in lease agreement with Pearle Vision franchisee was unreasonable because parties were not in direct competition and their businesses served different functions and provided different services).
124. Hobbs v. Pool, No. CA 86-145, 1987 WL 8004, at *2 (Ark. Ct. App. Mar. 18, 1987).

for continuing to operate a similar business with a different name at the same location. The appellate court found that the 100-mile radius was unnecessarily large, particularly because the franchisor had introduced other catfish operations within that radius in competition with franchisee's restaurant and it precluded the franchisee from not only operating another catfish restaurant, but from engaging in any phase of "catfish preparation." That could include raising, processing, or distributing catfish. Therefore, the covenant was invalid. *Hobbs v. Pool*, No. CA 86-145, 1987 WL 8004, at *3 (Ark. Ct. App. Mar. 18, 1987).

2. Damages

a. Commentary

A franchisee harmed by a violation of the anti-fraud provisions of the AFPA is entitled to recover treble damages, injunctive relief, reasonable attorneys' fees, and costs of litigation.[125] A franchisee harmed by other sections of the AFPA, including those governing terminations, transfers, and other unlawful practices, can recover actual damages, injunctive relief, reasonable attorneys' fees, and costs of litigation.[126] Arkansas also has model jury instructions for damage claims based on unlawful practices of franchisors.[127]

b. Annotations

A manufacturer was not entitled to summary judgment on a distributor's claim for treble and punitive damages where the distributor alleged violations of the AFPA. The distributor contended that, in connection with the unlawful termination of its oral agreement, the manufacturer knowingly made untrue statements and omitted material facts about the basis for the termination and thus violated the AFPA by failing to give proper notice and an opportunity to cure. The distributor's claim did not relate solely to future events, as the manufacturer contended, because the timing of the events was "in connection with the termination, transfer and assignment of" the distributor's rights. The distributor also contended that the manufacturer "knowingly" made the alleged misrepresentations and did not treat it in a commercially reasonable manner and in good faith under the AFPA. Therefore, the distributor adequately pled its claims for treble and punitive damages under Arkansas law because there were issues of fact as

---

125. ARK. CODE ANN. § 4-72-208(a) (referring to violations of § 4-72-207 for fraud in connection with the offer, sale, purchase, transfer, or assignment of any franchise in the state, which in addition to civil actions, allows criminal prosecutions as Class B felonies).

126. ARK. CODE ANN. § 4-72-208(b).

127. Ark. Model Jury Instr., Civil AMI 2805, which are based on violations under ARK. CODE ANN. § 4-72-206, with the exception of § 4-72-206(1), which makes it an unlawful practice to require a franchisee at the time of entering into a franchise arrangement to agree to a release, assignment, novation, waiver, or estoppel that would relieve any person from liability under the act. Although the Arkansas Supreme Court Committee on Jury Instructions-Civil believes that provision could be a basis for a damages claim, the committee believes it would ordinarily operate to negate a defense by a franchisor. A court has nullified a damages limitation in a franchise agreement based on this provision. *See* Capital Equip., Inc. v. CNH Am., LLC, 471 F. Supp. 2d 951, 958 (E.D. Ark. 2006).

to whether the manufacturer made fraudulent misrepresentations regarding the basis of the termination and whether the manufacturer knew such statements were false when made. *Otto Dental Supply, Inc. v. Kerr Corp.*, No. 4:06CV01610-WRW, 2008 WL 410630, at *3 (E.D. Ark. Feb. 13, 2008); *Otto Dental Supply, Inc. v. Kerr Corp.*, No. 4:06-CV-01610-WRW, 2008 WL 4974910, at *1 (E.D. Ark. Nov. 13, 2008) (clarifying Feb. 13, 2008, order).

A dealer sufficiently alleged that the manufacturer's violations of the AFPA proximately caused lost profit damages. The dealer had alleged that terminating its right to buy certain branded products preceded its actual withdrawal of those products from the market, the dealer agreement conferred the right to sell those products without conditioning the right on how the products were branded, and the manufacturer's decision to withdraw branded products from the market could constitute a termination or cancellation of the franchise without good cause. Whether market withdrawal constitutes good cause under the AFPA was an issue for the Arkansas Supreme Court. *Larry Hobbs Farm Equipment, Inc. v. CNH America, LLC*, No. 2:08CV00049 JLH, 2008 WL 3931323, at *10–12 (E.D. Ark. Aug. 22, 2008).

Substantial evidence supported the jury's verdict of $1,600,000 in damages on a wholesale beer distributor's claim under the AFPA that the brewing company refused to deal with it in a commercially reasonable manner and in good faith when it interfered with the distributor's efforts to increase its market share by purchasing another distributor, which was critical to remaining competitive. As part of its secret plan to consolidate distributors and eliminate the plaintiff as a distributor and force it out of business, the brewer applied pressure to other distributors in furtherance of its plan. The court found it irrelevant that the distribution agreement did not specifically address the distributor's acquisition of other brands and territories and that the brewer may not have caused the distributor to lose the brands and territories listed in the existing distribution agreement. The brewer's actions effectively forced the distributor out of business in violation of the AFPA. *Miller Brewing Co. v. Ed Roleson, Jr., Inc.*, 223 S.W.3d 806, 811–14 (Ark. 2006).

The parties' service agent agreement that included an arbitration clause limiting liability for punitive damages; lost profits for more than six months; or any other indirect, special, exemplary, incidental, or consequential damages did not necessarily make the agreement unenforceable due to an alleged conflict with the AFPA's broader damages provisions. The parties agreed to arbitrate the dispute, including the AFPA claim, and it was for the arbitrator to decide any question concerning the extent of remedies available. *Arkcom Digital Corp. v. Xerox Corp.*, 289 F.3d 536, 538–40 (8th Cir. 2002).

The correct measure of damages for a claim of wrongful termination under the AFPA is loss of the profits the franchisee was reasonably certain to have made had the contract not been terminated. Substantial evidence supported the jury's verdict based on the accountant's testimony regarding proof of loss based on a valuation of the company immediately prior to the termination date and immediately after. *The Trane Co. v. Miller Engineering, Inc.*, No. CA 87-58, 1987 WL 19735, at *3 (Ark. Ct. App. Nov. 11, 1987).

3. Rescission

a. Commentary

The AFPA does not explicitly refer to a right to rescission and there is no case law in Arkansas addressing rescission under the AFPA.

b. Annotations

Not applicable.

4. Injunctive Relief

a. Commentary

A franchisee harmed by relationship sections of the AFPA, including those governing terminations, transfers, and other unlawful practices, can recover actual damages, injunctive relief, reasonable attorneys' fees, and costs of litigation.[128]

b. Annotations

Distributor's claims for injunctive relief to prohibit the alleged continued violations of the AFPA were moot, warranting dismissal of the claim. During a lawsuit between the distributor and manufacturer, the manufacturer terminated the parties' distribution agreement on the basis that the distributor failed to satisfy the agreement's minimum purchase quantity provision. The distributor amended its lawsuit and sought monetary damages and injunctive relief to prohibit the manufacturer from continuing to violate the AFPA and the parties' distribution agreement. The manufacturer then rescinded its termination letter and reinstated the parties' distribution agreement effective immediately and filed a motion to dismiss the injunctive relief claims and to compel arbitration of the remaining claims. The manufacturer argued that the injunctive relief claims were moot because the distributor had terminated the agreement and the manufacturer had rescinded the termination and reinstated the distribution agreement. The court agreed that the injunctive relief claims were moot, and the court referred the remaining claims to arbitration. *Ground Connections, LLC v. Krinner Schraubfundamente GMBH*, Case No. 5:18CV00181-JM, 2019 WL 3504235, at *3–4 (E.D. Ark. Aug. 1, 2019).

5. Control Person Liability

a. Commentary

The AFPA defines a franchisor and a franchisee to include a "person," which includes individual officers, directors and other persons in active control of the entity.[129] The AFPA's anti-fraud provisions are applicable to any "person" who directly or indirectly, in connection with the offer, sale, purchase, transfer, or assignment of any franchise in Arkansas.[130] The AFPA makes it a Class B felony

---

128. ARK. CODE ANN. § 4-72-208(b).
129. *Id.* § 4-72-202(2)–(4).
130. *Id.* § 4-72-207(a).

to violate the anti-fraud provisions.[131] The AFPA also gives the attorney general the authority to file a petition seeking injunctive relief against any person violating any provision of the AFPA (including the relationship laws), as well as the state securities commissioner from taking appropriation action if a franchise constitutes a security under the Arkansas Securities Act.[132]

b. Annotations

There are no cases addressing director, officer, or other employee liability under the AFPA.

6. Attorneys' Fees

a. Commentary

The AFPA states that any franchisee harmed by a violation of the AFPA shall be entitled to recover, where appropriate, reasonable attorneys' fees and costs of litigation.[133] Courts have interpreted this to mean it is within the court's discretion whether to award fees. *Volvo Trademark Holding Aktiebolaget v. Clark Machinery Co.*, 510 F.3d 474, 485 (4th Cir. 2007).

The AFPA allows recovery of reasonable attorneys' fees and costs of litigation, the amount of which is within the sound discretion of the trial court. *The Trane Co. v. Miller Engineering, Inc.*, No. CA 87-58, 1987 WL 19735, at *4 (Ark. Ct. App. Nov. 11, 1987).

b. Annotations

Even though a manufacturer violated the AFPA when it terminated a distributor without good cause, the district court did not abuse its discretion when it found that the distributor was not entitled to recover an attorneys' fee award under the AFPA after a jury concluded that the distributor incurred no damage by the violation. *Volvo Trademark Holding Aktiebolaget v. Clark Machinery Co.*, 510 F.3d 474, 485 (4th Cir. 2007).

The AFPA does not expressly limit a "harmed" franchisee to one that recovers actual damages, nor does the AFPA require an attorneys' fee award upon proving a mere violation of the AFPA. However, a party seeking attorneys' fees under the AFPA must demonstrate the harm suffered as a result of the violation. The AFPA's attorneys' fee provision plainly reserves the issue of whether to award attorneys' fees to the court's discretion. *Volvo Trademark Holding Aktiebolaget v. CLM Equipment Co., Inc.*, Civil Nos. 1:00CV238, 1:00CV232, 2006 WL 2828768, at *2–4 (W.D.N.C. Oct. 2, 2006).

To determine the reasonableness of an attorneys' fee award under the AFPA, courts consider (1) the experience and ability of counsel; (2) the time and labor required to perform the legal service properly; (3) the amount involved in the case and the results obtained; (4) the novelty and difficulty of the issues involved; (5) the fee customarily charged in the locality for similar services;

---

131. *Id.* § 4-72-207(b).
132. *Id.* § 4-72-208(c).
133. *Id.* § 4-72-208.

(6) whether the fee is fixed or contingent; (7) the time limitations imposed upon the client or by the circumstances; and (8) the likelihood, if apparent to the client, that the acceptance of the particular employment will preclude other employment by the lawyer. *South Beach Beverage Co., Inc. v. Harris Brands, Inc.*, 138 S.W.3d 102, 108 (Ark. 2003).

7. Limitations on Damage Waivers

a. Commentary

The AFPA does not contain a specific prohibition on damage waivers. However, it prohibits a franchisor from requiring a franchisee at the time of entering into the franchise to agree to a waiver that would relieve a person from liability under the AFPA.[134]

b. Annotations

A contractual limitation of damages provision in a franchise agreement was inapplicable and therefore unenforceable to the extent that it limited the statutory protections available under the AFPA. The court's conclusion was bolstered by the AFPA's anti-waiver provision in section 4-72-206. Thus, to the extent that lost profits are available to the franchisee under the AFPA, franchisee may recover such damages notwithstanding a contractual limitation of damages. *Capital Equipment, Inc. v. CNH America, LLC*, 471 F. Supp. 2d 951, 957–58 (E.D. Ark. 2006).

A company could enforce an agreement to arbitrate, even though it precluded the arbitrator from awarding damages specifically authorized by the AFPA. Whether the agreement validly limited the arbitrator's remedies for an AFPA violation went to the merits of the dispute and was an issue for the arbitrator to decide, as well as what state law applied and whether the agreement created a franchise. *Arkcom Digital Corp. v. Xerox Corp.*, 289 F.3d 536, 539 (8th Cir. 2002).

8. Administrative Action

a. Commentary

In addition to the other remedies provided to franchisees, the AFPA grants the attorney general the authority to file a petition seeking an injunction prohibiting any person, firm, corporation, partnership, or other entity from engaging in any of the AFPA's prohibited practices.[135]

The AFPA also gives the state's securities commissioner the authority to take "appropriate action" when a franchise constitutes a security under the Arkansas Securities Act.[136] Under that act, the securities commissioner can take various types of action, including administrative action.[137]

---

134. *Id.* § 4-72-206(b).
135. *Id.* § 4-72-208(c).
136. *Id.*
137. *Id.* §§ 23-42-101 to 23-42-509.

b. Annotations

There are no cases addressing administrative action under the AFPA.

H. Dispute Resolution

1. Limitations on Franchisors' Ability to Restrict Venue

a. Commentary

For franchise agreements entered into or renewed before August 1, 2023, the AFPA does not contain a limitation on a franchisor's ability to restrict venue. Thus, courts may grant motions to transfer venue if the parties agreed to a venue outside Arkansas.

For franchise agreements entered into or renewed on and after August 1, 2023, the 2023 amendments to the AFPA state that any provision in a franchise agreement that restricts venue to a forum outside Arkansas is void with respect to any claims arising under or relating to the franchise agreement involving a franchise operating or conducting business in Arkansas.[138] Thus, an Arkansas court considering claims under the AFPA is likely to deny a motion to transfer venue outside the state.

The AFPA states that a condition, stipulation, or provision requiring the application of the law of another state in lieu of the AFPA is void.[139] This provision was added to the 2023 Act in 2019. At that time, the AFPA applied to franchises entered into, renewed, or transferred after March 4, 1977.[140]

b. Annotations

Court granted franchisor's motion to transfer venue from Arkansas federal court to Texas federal court following removal based on the parties' forum-selection clause. The court found the clause ("You and the Owners must file any suit against us . . .") was broad enough to encompass franchisee's claims brought under the AFPA alleging misrepresentations and omissions before the parties executed the agreements, rejecting franchisee's argument that the clause was not intended to encompass all claims of any sort that may have arisen between the parties. The court rejected franchisee's claim that enforcement of the clause violated Arkansas public policy because doing so would displace the protection afforded to it by the AFPA's enactment. The court found this was not an unusual case where the forum selection clause should not apply. *Ajax Holdings, LLC v. Comet Cleaners Franchise Group, LLC*, No. 4:15CV00494 SWW, 2015 WL 5898310, at *4 (E.D. Ark. Oct. 9, 2015).

The court granted the franchisor's motion to transfer venue from Arkansas to a New York federal court based on the parties' forum selection clause. The court rejected the franchisee's argument that the forum selection clause did not govern its AFPA claims. The court found the clause was broad and unambiguous because it applied to "all suits for causes of action relating to or arising

---

138. *Id.* § 4-72-211.
139. *Id.* § 4-72-206(b).
140. *Id.* § 4-72-203(a)(1).

directly or indirectly from this Agreement." The court found that the parties' unequal bargaining power, their lack of negotiation, or the fact it was a form contract did not make the forum selection clause invalid. *Applied Energy of AR-LA-MS, Inc. v. Pall Corp.*, No. 5:14CV00180 JLH, 2014 WL 7011093, at *1–2 (E.D. Ark. Dec. 10, 2014).

The court examined a choice of law clause that stated that the "validity, interpretation and construction of this Agreement shall be governed by and construed in accordance with the laws of the United States of America and the Commonwealth of Virginia." The court first concluded that the provision applied to plaintiffs' termination and implied good faith claims. However, it did not apply to plaintiffs' AFPA fraud-related claim because the fraud claim included allegations of fraud in the inducement of the agreement itself, which was beyond the scope of the choice of law provision that applied to the "validity, interpretation, and construction of the Agreement." Second, the court applied Arkansas conflicts of law principles and determined that applying Virginia law, rather than Arkansas law, would result in "a substantial loss of protection provided by the AFPA for Arkansas franchisees." Even though Virginia has its own franchisee protection law, the contract was negotiated and performed in Arkansas so the franchisee could not take advantage of Virginia law. The court found that Arkansas had a materially greater interest in ensuring that the AFPA protects franchisees operating within its borders and that on the facts of this case, such protection would be lost altogether if Virginia law applied. Thus, the court concluded that the AFPA represents a fundamental public policy of the state and found it unnecessary to address plaintiff's argument that application of Virginia law would violate the AFPA's anti-waiver provision. Virginia law could not displace the AFPA. *Britelink, Inc. v. Telecorp PCS, Inc.*, No. 3:03-CV-00207 GTE, 2004 WL 5509416, at *7–8 (E.D. Ark. May 6, 2004).

If the AFPA applied, an arbitration provision in a distribution agreement that required the parties to submit claims and disputes under the agreement to arbitration did not limit or waive any substantive rights that the distributor had under the AFPA. AFPA claims and other claims that the distributor may have must be resolved in the arbitral forum. *Gruma Corp. v. Morrison*, 362 S.W.3d 898, 904–05 (Ark. 2010).

The AFPA does not override an arbitration provision in a distribution agreement. By submitting to arbitration, the franchisee did not waive the substantive rights granted under the AFPA, but it was merely submitting the resolution of those rights in an arbitral forum. *Platinum Distrib., Inc. v. Cytosport, Inc.*, Case No. 09-2036, 2009 WL 1873502, at *2 (W.D. Ark. 2009).

A choice of law provision in a dealer agreement, which stated that "the laws of the State of Texas shall govern its interpretation," does not effectively displace the entire body of Arkansas protective legislation but merely provides that Texas rules of contract construction apply. The choice of law language did not provide the dealer with fair warning that it would forfeit its right to protection under the AFPA. Under the "principal contacts analysis," Arkansas had the most significant contacts with the contracts at issue. Thus, the substantive laws of Arkansas govern the parties' rights and responsibilities under the agreements. Thus, the AFPA applied. *Heating & Air Specialists, Inc. v. Jones*, 180 F. 3d 923, 930–31 (8th Cir. 1999).

2. Limitations Period

a. Commentary

The AFPA does not contain a statute of limitations for civil actions. In one case, the Arkansas Supreme Court held that the three-year statute of limitations for liability imposed by statute applies.[141] In a case ten years later, it held that the five-year, catch-all statute of limitations under Arkansas law applies to AFPA claims, rejecting its earlier holding based on the facts in the first case.[142] Therefore, it appears that courts will apply the Arkansas five-year, catch-all statute of limitations to AFPA claims.

Parties to a contract may agree upon "a limitation period which is shorter than that prescribed by the applicable statute of limitation, so long as the stipulated time is not unreasonably short and the agreement does not contravene some statutory requirement or rule based upon public policy." Conversely, the parties may agree to lengthen the limitation period for a reasonable time.[143]

b. Annotations

The five-year, catch-all statute of limitations applied to AFPA claims rather than the three-year breach of oral contract or five-year breach of written contract statutes of limitation where a wholesale beer distributor claimed that the brewing company interfered with its attempt to expand its business by buying other distributors. The Arkansas Supreme Court noted that the AFPA does not have a statute of limitations for civil actions, the parties had a written franchise agreement, and other statutes of limitation did not specifically apply. The court rejected its seemingly conflicting decision in *Chalmers*, which applied a three-year statute of limitations, distinguishing that case because it involved a fraud claim and whether the claim was tolled by fraudulent concealment and the continuing tort doctrine. The court said the five-year, catch-all statute of limitations applied because none of the other statutes specifically applied and to hold otherwise would negate the purpose of the AFPA. In doing so, it cited a federal court's decision that the five-year, catch-all statute applied to the Arkansas Unfair Practice Act because that act did not contain a statute of limitations. *Miller Brewing Co. v. Ed Roleson, Jr., Inc.*, 223 S.W.3d 806, 815–16 (Ark. 2006).

The Arkansas Supreme Court affirmed summary judgment on grounds that an automobile dealer's contract, fraud, and AFPA claims against an importer and two regional distributors were barred by the statute of limitations, including the three-year statute of limitations for liability imposed by statute.[144]

---

141. Chalmers v. Toyota Motor Sales, USA, Inc., 935 S.W.2d 258, 260–61 (Ark. 1996).
142. Miller Brewing Co. v. Ed Roleson, Jr., Inc., 223 S.W.3d 806, 815–16 (Ark. 2006).
143. 2 Ark. Civ. Prac. & Proc. § 5:4 (5th ed.) (citations omitted).
144. "As early as 1890 the Arkansas Supreme Court ruled that a statutorily created liability had a three year limitations period unless that liability was part of a written agreement which would then have a five year limitations period under what is today § 16-56-111." Med. Liab. Mut. Ins. Co.

Although the case does not identify the AFPA claims, the dealer's theory was that Toyota allowed regional distributors to force dealers in the region to accept vehicles loaded with options and accessory packages not required of other nearby dealers, which resulted in pricing disparity that destroyed their ability to compete in their economic market. The court would not toll the statute of limitations based on a theory of continuous tort because Arkansas did not recognize the continuing tort theory. *Chalmers v. Toyota Motor Sales, USA, Inc.*, 935 S.W.2d 258, 260–61 (Ark. 1996).

Arkansas's five-year statute of limitations barred franchisee's lawsuit filed in 1985. Distributor claimed that the 1980 termination of its exclusive distributorship violated the AFPA. Arkansas's savings statute, which allows the refiling of a suit within one year of its dismissal, did not apply to an earlier lawsuit claiming unlawful termination in 1981 of a 1980 nonexclusive distributorship because it did not relate back to the earlier case. The two complaints stated facts involving different breaches, different contracts, and occurring in different years, and they would have required different evidence to prove. *Morgan Distributing Co., Inc. v. Unidynamic Corp.*, 868 F.2d 992, 994–96 (8th Cir. 1989).

---

v. Alan Curtis LLC, 519 F.3d 466, 472 (8th Cir. 2008). "We have found no Arkansas case questioning the general proposition that where a statute creates a liability but does not include a limitations provision and no other statute of limitations applies, a claim to enforce the statutory liability is an action 'founded on . . . liability, expressed or implied' under § 16-56-105 and is subject to a three year limitations period." *Id.* at 473.

California

Barry Kurtz and Filemon Carrillo[1]

I. Introduction to Statutes

A. Introduction to Statute

California's franchise relationship law, the California Franchise Relations Act (CFRA),[2] governs the ongoing relationship between franchisors and franchisees and regulates defaults, terminations, renewals, and transfers of franchises. The CFRA was made effective on January 1, 1981, and applies to franchise agreements entered into or last renewed between January 1, 1981, and December 31, 2015.[3] The CFRA was amended in October 2015; however, the amended provisions only apply to franchise agreements entered into or renewed on or after January 1, 2016, and to any franchise agreement of an indefinite duration that may be terminated by the franchisor or the franchisee without cause.[4] As a result, the date a franchise agreement was entered into or renewed will determine whether the CFRA adopted in 1981 (1981 CFRA) or the CFRA as amended in 2016 (2016 CFRA) will apply to the franchise agreement. While many of the provisions of the 1981 CFRA and the 2016 CFRA are identical, the 2016 CFRA imposes additional restrictions on franchisors' termination of or refusal to renew franchise agreements, increases franchisors' post-termination obligations, and bolsters franchisees' rights to sell their franchised businesses.

On September 29, 2022, sections 20015, 20022, and 20041 of the 2016 CFRA were amended, and section 20044 was added. The amended CFRA (2022 CFRA) only applies to franchise agreements entered into or renewed on or after January 1, 2023, and to franchises of an indefinite duration that may be terminated by the franchisee and franchisor without cause.[5] However, amendments to franchise agreements entered into or renewed on or after January 1, 2023, that are initiated by a franchisee and do not substantially and adversely impact the

---

1. The authors wish to thank Sandra Gibbs, a colleague and friend of Mr. Carrillo, and Caitlyn Dillon, an associate at Lewitt Hackman, for their contributions to this chapter.
2. CAL. BUS. & PROF. CODE §§ 20000–20044.
3. *Id.* § 20041 (effective 1/1/81).
4. *Id.* § 20041(b) (effective 1/1/16).
5. *Id.* § 20041(c) (effective 1/1/23).

franchisee's rights, benefits, privileges, duties, obligations, or responsibilities under the franchise agreement are exempted from coverage.[6]

The amendments adopted in 2022 impose additional restrictions on franchisors' rights of termination and nonrenewal of franchise agreements. New section 20015(b) provides that any provision of a franchise agreement requiring the franchisee to waive any provisions of the CFRA are contrary to public policy, void, and unenforceable.[7] Amended section 20022(h) limits the franchisor's right to offset against the amounts owed by a franchisee to those amounts that the franchisee agrees to or those amounts established by a final adjudication.[8] New section 20044 provides that a franchisor is prohibited from modifying a franchise agreement or requiring a general release, in exchange for any assistance related to a declared state or federal emergency.[9]

The CFRA overrides and supersedes inconsistent terms of franchise agreements on the subjects it covers.

B. Policy Rationale

The CFRA does not contain a statement of policy; however, California courts have relied on the broad statement of policy in the California Franchise Investment Law (CFIL) to give both the CFRA and the CFIL wide-ranging application to protect franchisees. The CFIL was intended to "provide each prospective franchisee with the information necessary to make an intelligent decision regarding franchises being offered" and to "prohibit the sale of franchises where the sale would lead to fraud or a likelihood that the franchisor's promises would not be fulfilled and to protect the franchisor and the franchisee by providing a better understanding of the relationship between the franchisor and the franchisee with regard to their business relationship."[10]

II. Commentary and Annotations

A. Definition of Franchise

A "franchise" under the CFRA is a contract or agreement, express or implied, whether oral or written, by two or more persons in which (1) a franchisee is granted the right to engage in the business of offering, selling, or distributing goods or services under a marketing plan or system prescribed in substantial part by the franchisor; and (2) the operation of the business pursuant to that plan or system is substantially associated with the franchisor's trademark, service mark, trade name, logotype, or advertising or other commercial symbol designating the franchisor or its affiliate; and (3) the franchisee is required to

---

6. *Id.*
7. *Id.* § 20015(b).
8. *Id.* § 20022(h).
9. *Id.* § 20044.
10. Cal. Corp. Code § 31001.

pay, directly or indirectly, a franchise fee for the right to enter into the business.[11] The term "franchise" also includes an area franchise.[12]

The CFRA does not apply to motor vehicle franchises;[13] to franchises governed by the Petroleum Marketing Practices Act;[14] to lease departments, licensees, or concessions at a general merchandise retail store that are incidental or ancillary to the operation of the store;[15] or to nonprofit organizations operated on a cooperative basis by and for independent retailers which wholesale goods and services primarily to its member retailers who meet other statutory requirements, including providing members with a franchise disclosure document.[16]

1. *Trademark Element*

a. Commentary

To constitute a franchise under the CFRA, the operation of the franchisee's business must be substantially associated with the franchisor's commercial symbol, such as a trademark, service mark, trade name, or logotype.[17] Any trademark license agreement with a trademark licensed by one party to another could satisfy this requirement. However, merely selling products with the licensor's trademark affixed is not substantially associating with the licensor's trademark.[18]

The substantial association requirement can only be satisfied if use of the commercial symbol is communicated to the franchisee's customers so that the customers regard the franchisee's business as one in a chain identified with the franchisor. If use of the commercial symbol is not evident to the franchisee's customers, the business is not substantially associated with the franchisor's commercial symbol.[19]

The substantial association requirement can be satisfied even if the franchisee is not obligated to display a franchisor's commercial symbol[20] and even if a franchisee is prohibited from using the franchisor's name.[21]

b. Annotations

Notwithstanding the distributor's argument that it conducted business under the manufacturer's name, a court ruled that there was no evidence of a franchise relationship presented to the trial court where a distributor operated under its own name and was not known to its customers under the manufacturer's

---

11. CAL. BUS. & PROF. CODE § 20001 (effective 1/1/81).
12. *Id.* § 20006.
13. *Id.* § 20042.
14. *Id.* § 20001(d)(1).
15. *Id.* § 20001(d)(2).
16. *Id.* § 20001(d)(3).
17. Cal. Dep't of Corps., Comm'r Op. No. 3-F: When Does an Agreement Constitute a "Franchise" (June 22, 1994) [hereinafter Release 3-F].
18. Gabana Gulf Distrib. v. Gap Int'l Sales, Inc., 2008 U.S. Dist. LEXIS 1658 (N.D. Cal. Jan. 9, 2006).
19. Cal. Dep't of Corps., Comm'r Op. No. 73/5F (Feb. 2, 1973); Cal. Dep't of Corps., Comm'r Op. No. 78/1F (May 9, 1978).
20. Cal. Dep't of Corps., Comm'r Op. No. 73/20F (May 21, 1973) [hereinafter Opinion 73/20F].
21. Kim v. Servosnax, Inc., 10 Cal. App. 4th 1346, 13 Cal. Rptr. 2d 422 (1992).

trademark, logo, advertising, or other commercial symbol designating the manufacturer or its product lines. *Bestest International Inc. v. Futrex Inc.*, No. SA CV 00-119 AHS (ANx), 2000 U.S. Dist. LEXIS 23825 (C.D. Cal. Aug. 14, 2000).

The contract between a clothing distributor and a manufacturer of Gap clothing products was not a "franchise" under the CFRA because the distributor's business was not substantially associated with the Gap trademark, logo, or commercial symbol. The parties' agreement expressly forbade the distributor from "adopt[ing] any trademark, service mark, trade name, trade dress or any element thereof," and prohibited the distributor from using the Gap trademark. The court rejected the distributor's argument that the distributor met the substantial association requirement because the distributor traded exclusively in Gap products, finding that the distributor "must establish something more., i.e., that its customers associated [the distributor] with the Gap trademark." The court also rejected the distributor's argument that the manufacturer granted it the right to use the Gap trademark simply because the trademark appeared on Gap clothing sold by the distributor. *Gabana Gulf Distribution v. Gap International Sales, Inc.*, No. C 06-02584 CRB, 2008 U.S. Dist. LEXIS 1658 (N.D. Cal. Jan. 9, 2006).

Where a food service licensee was contractually prohibited from using its licensor's name in the operation of a food service business, a court found that the licensee was substantially associated with the licensor's trademark because the licensee relied on the communication of the licensor's name to the host company, which was considered the licensee's customer. The court held that the licensee's key association with the name and goodwill of the licensor when a host company selects the licensor from among other competitors fulfilled the substantial association element of the definition of a franchise. The licensor's trade name was communicated through billings for catering services provided by the licensee, in the licensor's contract with the host company, and in correspondence about cafeteria items and prices. The licensee was intimately associated with the licensor in the mind of the host company. *Kim v. Servosnax, Inc.*, 10 Cal. App. 4th 1346, 13 Cal. Rptr. 2d 422 (1992).

A genuine dispute of material fact as to substantial association with a trademark was found where a distributor provided evidence of its permitted use of its supplier's trademarks even though the distribution agreement did not allow the distributor to conduct its business under its supplier's name or use the supplier's trademarks in any way except upon receiving the supplier's written consent. Evidence that customers communicated with the supplier about the distributor created a dispute as to whether the distributor's customers substantially associated the supplier's trademarks with the distributor's operations. *Macedonia Distribution v. S-L Distribution Co.*, LLC, 2018 U.S. Dist. LEXIS 227914 (C.D. Cal. Aug. 7, 2018).

An opinion letter issued by the commissioner looked into the relationship between various manufacturing plants with which the franchisor entered into service contracts which were later assigned to the franchisees. The commissioner found that the manufacturing plants were considered "customers" of the franchisees. Since the franchisor communicated its name to these customers as a result of negotiating the service contracts and by being a named party to the service contracts, the commissioner concluded that the franchisees' businesses were substantially associated with the commercial symbol of the franchisor. California Department of Financial Protection and Innovation, Comm. Op. No. 74/7F (1974).

While substantial association with the franchisor's commercial symbol must be communicated to the customers of the franchisee, an opinion letter issued by the commissioner stated that it is not necessary to require the franchisee to use the franchisor's symbol; rather the granting of the right to use the franchisor's commercial symbol on material, in such a way as to communicate the symbol to its customers, is sufficient to conclude that the operation of the franchisee's business is substantially associated with the franchisor's commercial symbol. California Department of Corporations, Comm. Op. No. 73/20F (1973).

2. Franchise Fee Element

a. Commentary

A "franchisee fee" is broadly defined in the CFRA as any fee or charge that a franchisee must pay or agrees to pay for the right to enter into a business under a franchise agreement, including the franchisee's payment for goods and services, regardless of the designation given to, or the form of the payment.[22]

A payment made for the right to enter into a business distinguishes the payment from a payment for goods or services made entirely for the goods or services. A voluntary payment is not a franchise fee. Payments a licensee must make to its licensor, or affiliates of the licensor, under its license agreement are franchise fees. Payments a licensee must make to third parties unaffiliated with the licensor under its license agreement are not franchise fees.[23] Payments for ordinary business expenses incurred during the course of business are not a franchise fee.[24] Payments for the purchase of promotional materials can be a franchise fee if the materials are required or suggested by the franchisor as essential for the success of the business.[25]

Express exclusions from the definition of a franchise fee include (1) the purchase or agreement to purchase goods "at a bona fide wholesale price," unless the franchisee is obligated to purchase quantities in excess of what a reasonable businessperson normally would purchase for a starting inventory or supply or to maintain an ongoing inventory or supply; (2) credit card service charges; (3) payments to trading stamp companies; (4) franchise fees that do not exceed $100 annually; and (5) payments that do not exceed $1,000 to purchase or rent fixtures, equipment, or other tangible property to be used in the franchised business, if the purchase price or rental charge does not exceed the cost incurred by the franchisee acquiring the item at the fair market purchase price or rental charge.

---

22. H.C. Duke & Son, LLC v. Prism Mktg. Corp., 2013 U.S. Dist. LEXIS 140254 (C.D. Ill. Sept. 30, 2013).
23. Bestest Int'l, Inc. v. Futrex, Inc., 2000 U.S. Dist. LEXIS 23825 (C.D. Cal. Aug. 14, 2000).
24. Thueson v. U-Haul Int'l, Inc., 144 Cal. App. 4th 664, 50 Cal. Rptr. 3d 669 (2006).
25. Release 3-F, *supra* note 17; Boat & Motor Mart v. Sea Ray Boats, Inc. 825 F.2d 1285 (9th Cir. 1987).

Under CFRA section 20007(a), payments made for the purchase of goods in an amount not exceeding the "bona fide wholesale price" of such goods are not a franchise fee, because no substantial prejudice will come to a person buying a business and paying only the bona fide wholesale price for merchandise which that person proposes to sell in the business.[26] Under these circumstances, the payment is not made for the right to enter into the franchised business.[27]

"Bona fide wholesale price" means the price at which goods are purchased and sold by a manufacturer or wholesaler to a wholesaler or dealer where there is ultimately an open and public market in which sales of the goods are effected to consumers of the goods.[28] "Bona fide wholesale price" does not include the price of goods for which there is no open and public market, or for goods sold primarily to a person engaged in their redistribution.[29]

The bona fide wholesale price exception is applicable only to the purchase of tangible goods that the franchisee is authorized to distribute by the franchise agreement, not to payments that the franchisee must make to the franchisor under the franchise agreement for services or items other than goods.[30] Furthermore, payments for fixtures, equipment, or other items to be used by the franchisee in the operation of the franchised business, such as display cases, tools, equipment, and, in the case of a restaurant franchise, table linen, napkins, flatware, and other service utensils are franchise fees.[31] However, the payment of a sum of not exceeding $1,000 annually for the purchase or rental of fixtures, equipment, or other tangible property to be utilized in, and necessary for, the operation of the franchised business is not a franchise fee if the price or rental fee charged does not exceed the cost the franchisee would pay to acquire the items from other sellers in the open market.[32]

The bona fide wholesale price exception is not available if the quantity of goods required to be purchased exceeds the amount a reasonable businessperson normally would purchase for its starting inventory or its ongoing inventory.[33] Further, if the price of goods is negotiable, use of the bona fide wholesale price exception would not be available, because the seller cannot contend that sales are made at the bona fide wholesale price when the sales price will vary according to the ability of the purchaser to negotiate beneficial terms.[34] In addition, a purchase of goods above the bona fide wholesale price is an indirect franchise fee even if

---

26. Release 3-F, *supra* note 17.
27. Opinion 73/20F, *supra* note 20.
28. Release 3-F, *supra* note 17.
29. Cal. Dep't of Corps., Comm'r Op. No. PL/20F (Apr. 15, 1971); Cal. Dep't of Corps., Comm'r Op. No. 71/52F (Aug. 26, 1971); Cal. Dep't of Corps., Comm'r Op. No. 73/1F (Jan. 22, 1973); Cal. Dep't of Corps., Comm'r Op. No. 74/2F (Jan. 24, 1974).
30. Release 3-F, *supra* note 17.
31. *Id.*
32. CAL. CODE REGS. tit. 10, § 310.011.1; Cal. Dep't of Corps., Comm'r Op. No. 74/6F (Oct. 25, 1973).
33. Sunflora, Inc. v. Nat. Sols., LLC, 2021 U.S. Dist. LEXIS 257677 (C.D. Cal. Dec. 16, 2021).
34. Release 3-F, *supra* note 17.

there is no obligation to purchase or pay for a quantity of goods in excess of what a reasonable businessperson would normally purchase.[35]

b. Annotations

Payments for promotional materials can qualify as a franchise fee if they are required or suggested as essential. The court noted that the Guidelines for Determining Whether an Agreement Constitutes a "Franchise," California Department of Corporations Release 3-F (1974) specified that "a payment by a franchisee, though nominally optional, may in reality be a required one, if the article for which the payment is made is essential, or if the franchisor intimates or suggests that it is essential, for the operation of the business." When a dealer purchased video cassettes, films, floats, banners, posters, and brochures as required by the manufacturer and all were suggested by the manufacturer as essential, there was a question of fact as to whether these purchases constituted "goods" bought at a bona fide wholesale price or a franchise fee. If the products were "goods" purchased at the bona fide wholesale price in order to start or maintain an inventory, they would not constitute franchise fees under the CFRA. If "goods" meant only the product that the franchisee distributes, then the purchases may still be excluded as franchise fees, if the purchase price did not exceed $1,000 annually. "In view of this uncertainty and in the absence of California precedent on the meaning of 'goods,' we abstain from deciding whether a franchise fee was paid." *Boat & Motor Mart v. Sea Ray Boats, Inc.*, 825 F.2d 1285 (9th Cir. 1987).

The wages a distributor pays its employees are not franchise fees even if the distributor hired more employees than it would otherwise have hired because of the distributorship agreement. The court relied on the Guidelines for Determining Whether an Agreement Constitutes a "Franchise," California Department of Corporations Release 3-F (1974), which defines a franchise fee to include any fee or charge the franchisee is required to pay to the franchisor or franchisor's affiliate for the right to engage in business. The court held that while wages and other payments made to the distributor's employees were related to the conduct of business, the payments were not made for the right to engage in business. "[A]s a matter of law, such personal expenses . . . do not constitute a 'franchise fee' within the meaning of" the CFRA. *Premier Wine & Spirits of South Dakota, Inc. v. E. & J. Gallo Winery*, 644 F. Supp. 1431 (E.D. Cal. 1986).

A distribution agreement with no required payment, but whose predecessor made past due payments to the manufacturer for goods previously purchased by a third party, was not a franchise relationship. A payment to or for the account of third parties not affiliated with the franchisor is not a franchise fee within the meaning of the statute. *Bestest Int'l, Inc. v. Futrex, Inc.*, No. SA CV 00-119 AHS (ANx), 2000 U.S. Dist. LEXIS 23825 (C.D. Cal. Aug. 14, 2000).

California statutes define a franchise fee as a fee paid for the right to do business, not ordinary business expenses paid during the course of business. An indirect franchise fee was not found in a dealership agreement requiring the payment of monthly fees for a local telephone line, a local computer terminal,

---

35. *Sunflora, Inc.*, 2021 U.S. Dist. LEXIS 257677.

and other business expenses. *Thueson v. U-Haul International, Inc.*, 144 Cal. App. 4th 664, 50 Cal. Rptr. 3d 669 (2006).

An insurance agent's relationship with an insurance company was not a "franchise" under the CFRA because the agent did not pay the insurance company a "franchise fee" for the right to conduct its business. The agent made voluntary payments to the insurance company for advertising, promotional materials, signage expenses, and computer expenses, all of which were not required by the contract. Such payments, the court held, did not qualify as payments required for the right to conduct the business. *Vice v. State Farm Mutual Automobile Insurance Co.*, Bus. Franchise Guide (CCH) ¶ 13,897 (Cal. Super. Apr. 14, 2008). [This is an unpublished opinion.]

The payment of an initial $62,040 fee by a distributor was found to be an initial franchise fee because the distributor placed its own funds at risk in exchange for entering into its business relationship with the supplier. By paying for the exclusive right to distribute authorized products to authorized retailers within its territory, the distributor was required to make a considerable investment in the supplier at the commencement of their relationship. If the venture had been unsuccessful early on in the business relationship, the distributor would not have been able to recoup its investment. That the distributor could sell its exclusive territory was insufficient to show there was not a payment of a franchise fee. *Macedonia Distributing Inc. v. S L Distribution Co., LLC*, 2018 U.S. Dist. LEXIS 227914 (C.D. Cal. Aug. 7, 2018).

Under the CFRA, a "franchise fee" is "any fee or charge that a franchisee or subfranchisor is required to pay or agrees to pay for the right to enter into a business under a franchise agreement including, but not limited to, any payment for goods or services." The payment must exceed $100 on an annual basis, or it is not a "franchise fee." A distributor agreement requiring the distributor to assume the debt of a prior distributor, taken together with multiple payments for enough goods to have "ample stock of service and repair parts," and advertising and marketing materials is sufficient to plead the existence of a franchise fee. A payment may be a franchise fee "regardless of the designation given to, or the form of, such payment." *H.C. Duke & Son, LLC v. Prism Marketing Corp.*, No. 4:11-cv-04006- SLD-JAG, 2013 U.S. Dist. LEXIS 140254 (C.D. Ill. Sept. 30, 2013).

An individual who entered into an agreement to be an independent agent operator for a car rental company was not treated as a franchisee for purposes of determining whether she was an employee or independent contractor in her labor dispute with the rental company. The car rental company contended that the agent was functionally indistinguishable from a franchisee and should be treated as such, and that the presumption of employment should not apply. It was undisputed that the agent did not pay the rental car company a franchise fee for the right to enter into the business. The court found that, but for the requirement that a franchise fee be paid, the relationship would be categorized as a franchise under California law. The court determined that without the fee element, the agent should not be treated as a franchisee, since she did not have the rights and remedies of a franchisee. *Ambrose v. Avis Rent a Car System*, No. 2:11-cv-09992-CAS(AGRx), 2014 U.S. Dist. LEXIS 170406 (C.D. Cal. Dec. 8, 2014).

Payment of an annual franchise fee of $100 or less under the CFRA is not considered a franchise fee. *Gingiss International v. L&H Tuxes*, Case No. 01 C 7272, 2002 U.S. Dist. LEXIS 12792 (N.D. Ill. July 11, 2002).

A payment to, or for the account of third parties not affiliated with the franchisor is not a "franchise fee." *Premier Wine & Spirits of South Dakota, Inc. v. E. & J. Gallo Winery*, 644 F. Supp. 1431 (E.D. Cal. 1986).

An opinion letter issued by the commissioner stated that fees a distributor was required to prepay a third party for newspaper advertising when the contract in question was executed and quarterly thereafter were paid "for the account and benefit of the franchisor" to "enhance the business of the franchisor" and could be considered a franchise fee. California Department of Corporations, Comm. Op. No. 73/17F (1973). There are no cases adopting or rejecting this opinion, although the opinion was cited in California Department of Corporations, Comm. Op. No. 73/29F (1973).

3. Third Element (Community of Interest; Significant Degree of Control; Joint Marketing Plan)

a. Commentary

A business is a franchise under the CFRA if it is operated under a marketing plan or system prescribed in substantial part by the franchisor. A marketing plan may be express or implied, written or oral, and is one of the important means by which the appearance of centralized management and uniform standards is achieved.[36]

According to the commissioner, a franchise exists if the franchised business is one of many business arrangements presented to the public as a unit or marketing concept, and for all units the franchisor has "ostensibly" assumed responsibility for the outlets by causing them to be operated "with the appearance of some centralized management and uniform standards regarding the quality and price of the goods sold, services rendered and other material incidents of the operation."[37] A marketing plan will likely exist when a licensee must comply with the licensor's directions or obtain the licensor's approval on significant elements of the licensee's business, such as the selection of locations and the use of trade names, advertising, signs, sources of supply, fixtures and equipment, employee uniforms, hours of operation, and similar requirements at the licensee's business premises. Limitations on a distributor's territory, use of the licensor's trade name and sales of competitive products, an obligation to use the licensor's price list, and get the licensor's prior consent to advertising constitute a marketing plan or system "prescribed" in substantial part by the licensor.[38]

A marketing plan or system may be "prescribed" if the franchisor provides specific sales programs, training materials, courses, or seminars. An optional program may be "prescribed" if there are negative covenants against the use of alternatives. A marketing plan or system may not be prescribed if the

---

36. Cal. Dep't of Corps., Comm'r Op. No. 73/39F (Oct. 25, 1973).
37. Release 3-F, *supra* note 17.
38. Cal. Dep't of Corps., Comm'r Op. No. 73/30F (July 18, 1973).

performance requirements are customarily observed in business relationships in the particular trade or industry, even though, to some extent, they may restrict the freedom of action or the discretion of the operator.[39]

The determination of when directions given to the franchisee are "substantial" requires "an evaluation of all of the provisions in an agreement and the effect which these provisions have as a whole on the ability of the person engaged in the business to make decisions substantially without being subject to restrictions or having to obtain the consent or approval of other persons . . . and may be made in the light of applicable principles of general law and of customs prevailing in the particular trade or industry."[40]

b. Annotations

A dealership agreement that only required the dealer to "aggressively" market its boats was too vague to constitute a marketing plan under the CFRA. However, the manufacturer also provided the dealer with a marketing program and a computer printout of prospective customers; would not allow the dealer to advertise outside of its assigned territory; and provided the dealer with press kits, promotional tools, and marketing advice. The manufacturer "provided detailed instructions on what [the dealer's] salesmen should do, especially at boat shows. It provided instructions on how to lay out the booth, including the instruction that all boats should be wiped down each day. It said that a telephone was 'a must,' as was a carpet. It gave detailed instructions as to other booth accessories. It insisted on a dress code for salesmen. It told [the dealer] what to supply the salesmen with." The court concluded the dealer followed a system prescribed in substantial part by the manufacturer. *Boat & Motor Mart v. Sea Ray Boats, Inc.*, 825 F.2d 1285 (9th Cir. 1987).

No marketing plan or system should be deemed to be prescribed when the franchisee is left entirely free to operate the business according to its own marketing plan or system, even if the franchisee paid a fee in exchange for the right to distribute a manufacturer's goods. Where evidence made it clear that a manufacturer did not prescribe any marketing plan and the agreement stated only that the distributor was required to use its best efforts to sell the products and each distributor had absolute discretion regarding sales, marking, merchandising, and personnel, there was no marketing plan prescribed by the franchisor. *Bestest International, Inc. v. Futrex, Inc.*, No. SA CV 00-119 AHS (ANx), 2000 U.S. Dist. LEXIS 23825 (C.D. Cal. Aug. 14, 2000).

Evidence that a distributor was granted the right to distribute authorized products only within its territory, that the supplier established uniform pricing and a centralized billing system, provided its distributor with marketing materials and held sales meetings to discuss new marketing and promotion was sufficient to create a genuine dispute of material fact as to whether the distributor operated pursuant to a marking plan or system prescribed in part by the supplier. *Macedonia Distributing v. S-L Distribution Co.*, LLC, 2018 U.S. Dist. LEXIS 227914 (C.D. Cal. Aug. 7, 2018).

---

39. Cal. Dep't of Corps., Comm'r Op. No. 71/42F (July 27, 1971).
40. Release 3-F, *supra* note 17.

A distributor's alleged development of a market for a product at the outset of its relationship with its supplier was insufficient to give rise to a reasonable inference that the supplier substantially prescribed a marketing plan or system for the distribution of its beers. *Boon Rawd Trading International Co., Ltd. v. Paleewong Trading Co.*, 688 F. Supp. 2d 940 (N.D. Cal. 2010).

A lubricant distributor seeking protection under the CFRA adequately alleged the existence of a marketing plan by alleging that the supplier modified the agreement to include the grant of an exclusive territory, a prohibition on sales of competing products, the provision of specialized training, advice on ways to sublicense the supplier's trademark, and supplier approval of the distributor's advertising and sales brochures. *US Mac Corp. v. Amoco Oil Co.*, Business Franchise Guide (CCH) ¶ 11,963 (Cal. Ct. App. Aug. 16, 2000). [This opinion is not published.]

The court found that the existence of a prescribed marketing plan was sufficiently alleged where an affiliate agreement limited resale prices, prescribed what products were allowed to be carried, placed restrictions on the use of advertising, provided detailed directions and advice about store operations, assigned an exclusive territory, and prohibited the sale of similar products within 100 miles of the affiliate's store. *Sunflora, Inc. v. Natural Solutions, LLC*, No. CV 20-01141-CJC (MRWx), 2021 U.S. Dist. LEXIS 257677 (C.D. Cal. Dec. 16, 2021).

A relationship was not a franchise when the required fee and marketing plan elements were absent and the dealer agreed in the Dealer Agreement that "nothing stated in this agreement shall be construed as creating the relationship of . . . franchisor and franchisee." *Absolute USA, Inc. v. Harman Professional, Inc.*, CV 2:21-cv-06410-MEMF (MAAx), 2023 U.S. Dist. LEXIS 26835 (C.D. Cal. Feb. 14, 2023).

B. Scope and Jurisdiction

1. Commentary

Both the 1981 CFRA and the 2016 CFRA applied to any franchise where either the franchisee was domiciled in California or the franchised business was or had been operated in California.[41] Consequently, an out-of-state franchised location was still subject to the CFRA if the franchisee was domiciled in California. The 2022 CFRA provides that the CFRA will apply to any franchise where either the franchisee or its owners are domiciled in California, or the franchised business is or will be in California.[42]

2. Annotations

The CFRA did not apply to a Pennsylvania dealer despite a California choice-of-law provision in the franchise agreement. The CFRA applies only to franchises where the franchisee is domiciled in California, or the franchise is or was operated in California. *Bunch v. Artech International Corp.*, 559 F. Supp. 961 (S.D.N.Y. 1983).

---

41. CAL. BUS. & PROF. CODE § 20015 (effective 1/1/81); *id.* § 20015 (effective 1/1/16).
42. *Id.* § 20015(b) (effective 1/1/23).

The CFRA did not apply to a South Dakota wine distributor who was not domiciled in California and who did not operate a franchise in California. The CFRA only applies to franchisees domiciled or franchised locations operated in California. *Premier Wine & Spirits of South Dakota, Inc. v. E. & J. Gallo Winery*, 644 F. Supp. 1431 (E.D. Cal. 1986). The fact that a putative franchisor is located in California is not—in and of itself—sufficient to result in application of the CFRA.

Multiple franchise agreements provided for California choice of law even though the franchisee and the restaurants were located outside of California. The court noted the CFRA was neither designed nor intended to regulate claims of nonresidents arising from conduct occurring entirely outside California. The franchisor entered into franchise agreements for multiple Texas restaurant locations with two individuals, who, on the same day, assigned the franchise agreements to an entity. Although the original individual franchisee was domiciled in California, there was no allegation that the individual had an ownership interest in the franchisee entity and therefore no basis to apply the protections of the CFRA to the franchisee entity and none of the relevant restaurants had ever operated in California. The court found the franchisee entity could not meet the CFRA's jurisdictional requirement and dismissed the CFRA claim. *Jack in the Box Inc. v. San Tex Restaurants, Inc.*, 2021 U.S. Dist. LEXIS 7924 (W.D. Tex. 2021).

A distribution agreement provided for the application of California law, although the dealer was not domiciled in California and the business was operated outside California. A choice-of-law provision stipulating that California law applies cannot override the CFRA's domicile requirement. The territorial limitation was an integral part of the CFRA and helped establish its boundaries. *Fred Briggs Distributing Co. v. California Cooler, Inc.*, No. 92-35016, 1993 U.S. App. LEXIS 20732 (9th Cir. Aug. 11, 1993).

A distributor not domiciled in California argued that the CFRA applied because his distribution agreement provided for the application of California law. When a law contains geographical limitations as to its application, courts will not apply it to parties falling outside those limitations even if the parties stipulate that the law should apply. *Peugeot Motors of America, Inc. v. Eastern Auto Distributors, Inc.*, 892 F.2d 355, 358 (4th Cir. 1989), *cert. denied*, 497 U.S. 1005 (1990).

A court ruled that the CFRA did not apply to a distribution agreement when the distributor was not domiciled in California despite the distribution agreement's California choice-of-law provision. The definitional limitation of the CFRA was an integral part of the CFRA and helped establish its boundaries. *Fred Briggs Distributing Co. v. California Cooler, Inc.*, No. 92-35016, 1993 U.S. App. LEXIS 20732 (9th Cir. Aug. 11, 1993).

C. Termination

1. What Constitutes Termination or Cancellation

a. Commentary

Termination of a franchise agreement occurs when a franchisee ceases operation of its franchised business upon demand by the franchisor before the expiration of its term for "good cause." No franchisor may terminate a California franchise prior to the expiration of its term, except for good cause.[43]

b. Annotations

The franchisor violated the implied covenant of good faith and fair dealing owed to its franchisee by failing to exercise its option to renew the lease for the premises used by the franchisee for its franchised business. A franchisor wrongfully terminates a franchise in violation of the CFRA if the franchisor's failure to exercise its option to renew its lease for the franchised premises results in a termination of the franchise before the end of its term. The court noted that the CFRA prohibits franchisors from terminating franchisees without good cause. *Magna Cum Latte, Inc. v. Diedrich Coffee, Inc. (In re Magna Cum Latte, Inc.)*, Nos. 07-31814, 07-03304, 2007 Bankr. LEXIS 4265 (Bankr. S.D. Tex. Dec. 13, 2007).

2. Restrictions on Termination or Cancellation

a. Commentary

Under the 1981 CFRA, California franchisors cannot terminate a franchise before the expiration of its term except for "good cause," which includes, but is not limited to, the franchisee's failure to comply with any lawful requirement of the franchise agreement following notice and a reasonable opportunity to cure the default, which need not exceed 30 days.[44]

The 2016 CFRA modified the definition of "good cause" and substantially extended the notice and cure periods for franchisee defaults. Under the 2016 CFRA, "good cause" is limited to a franchisee's failure to "substantially" comply with the lawful requirements of the franchise agreement and the failure by the franchisee to cure the identified noncompliance within the cure period. Exceptions are defaults relevant to the franchise that allow a franchisor to immediately terminate a franchise agreement following notice without affording the franchisee an opportunity to cure as discussed later in subsection C.4.a.[45]

b. Annotations

The trial court did not err in applying New Jersey law to a contract containing a New Jersey choice-of-law provision because the franchise agreement contained a "good cause" provision for termination that is the same as the requirement under the CFRA. The court held that, under the circumstances, the application of New Jersey law was not contrary to a fundamental policy of California because the contract provided the franchisee with the same relevant protections as the CFRA. *Century 21 Real Estate LLC v. All Profional Realty, Inc.*, 600 F. App'x 502 (9th Cir. 2015).

A real estate franchisor terminated its franchisee for failure to make the required payments under its franchise agreement. If a franchisor has good cause

---

43. *Id.* § 20020 (effective 1/1/16).
44. CAL. BUS. & PROF. CODE § 20020.
45. *Id.* § 20021.

to terminate a franchise agreement, its motive for doing so is irrelevant. There is no requirement of good faith (or the absence of bad faith) in the CFRA. *Century 21 Real Estate, LLC v. All Professional Realty, Inc.*, 889 F. Supp. 2d 1198 (E.D. Cal. 2012).

A franchisor that made a sale of an unregistered master franchise agreement that contained a provision allowing for the agreement's termination without cause must refrain from interfering with the franchisee's normal and usual business arrangements under the master franchise agreement, unless and until the franchisor has good cause to terminate the agreement under the CFRA. *In re Commissioner of Business Oversight v. Royal Tea Taiwan Co., Ltd.*, Fil. Org. ID. 352363 (May 26, 2020).

The choice-of-law provision in the franchise agreement of a California-based franchisee called for application of Washington law. The franchise agreement was terminated by the franchisor for not reporting revenue, which constituted reasonable cause under California law, but not under Washington law. Washington choice of law was upheld, notwithstanding CFRA's nonwaiver provision, because Washington law was more protective of the rights of the franchisee. *1-800-Got Junk? LLC v. Superior Court*, 189 Cal. App. 4th 500, 116 Cal. Rptr. 3d 923 (2010).

3. Notice Requirement

a. Commentary

Both the 1981 CFRA and the 2016 CFRA provide specific requirements for the contents and delivery of a notice of termination of a franchise agreement. A notice of termination must (1) be in writing; (2) be sent by registered, certified, or other receipted mail, by telegram, or personally delivered to the franchisee; (3) contain a statement of the franchisor's intent to terminate the franchise agreement; (4) state the reasons for termination; and (5) state the effective date of termination.[46]

b. Annotations

A hotel franchisor did not violate the CFRA when it terminated a franchise agreement without providing further notice and an opportunity to cure, because the franchisee had repeatedly failed to comply with the payments provisions in the franchise agreement. The notice requirement of the CFRA to terminate a franchise is satisfied where the franchisee is given two notices of default within one year, whether or not the franchisee cured the default. The good cause requirement of the CFRA to terminate a franchise based on repeated defaults is satisfied by two distinct defaults. *Ramada Franchise Systems, Inc. v. Kouza*, Business Franchise Guide (CCH) ¶ 13,282 (S.D. Cal. 2005). [This opinion is not published.]

A franchisor's failure to provide written notice of immediate termination when the franchisee allegedly abandoned the franchise location violated the CFRA. While the CFRA provides certain exceptions to the good cause requirement for termination, allowing for immediate termination without a cure period, the CFRA still requires a franchisor to provide written notice of termination regardless of whether a cure period is required under the CFRA or whether

---

46. *Id.* § 20030 (effective 10/1/81).

the franchise can be immediately terminated under the CFRA. *Tikiz Franchising, LLC v. Piddington*, No. 17-cv-60552 -BLOOM/Valle, 2017 U.S. Dist. LEXIS 221704 (S.D. Fla. July 31, 2017) (denying motion to dismiss by franchisor finding that franchisee properly alleged a violation of the CFRA based on franchisor's failure to send notice of termination). Since franchisor's failure to provide the notice of termination entitled the franchisee to receive the fair market value of the franchised business and franchise assets plus any other damages caused by the franchisor's violation of the CFRA under section 20035 of the 2016 CFRA, the franchisor could have likely avoided that burden thereafter by issuing the notice of termination following the court's ruling.

A franchisor's use of a form termination letter did not meet the requirements of the CFRA. The franchisor sent the termination letter to the franchisee by express mail and, in accordance with the franchisor's custom and practice, stated that the termination was "effective immediately." With respect to the reasons for the termination, the letter stated only that "[a]fter full and complete consideration of the information provided, it was the decision [of the Board] to cancel all aspects of the property's membership effective immediately." The court concluded that this "form" letter did not satisfy the requirements of the CFRA. *Mahroom v. Best Western International*, 2010 U.S. Dist. LEXIS 160279 (N.D. Cal. Mar. 29, 2010).

4. Grounds for Termination

a. Commentary

No franchisor may terminate a franchise prior to the expiration of its term, except for good cause.[47]

Under the 1981 CFRA, "good cause" included the franchisee's failure to comply with any lawful requirement of the franchise agreement following notice and a reasonable opportunity to cure the default, which need not exceed 30 days.[48] Under the 2016 CFRA, a franchisor cannot terminate a franchise unless the franchisee fails to "substantially comply" with the lawful requirements imposed upon the franchisee by the franchise agreement. A franchisee must be given at least 60 days' prior notice of the potential termination of its franchise. However, the period to exercise the right to cure need not exceed 75 days unless there is a separate agreement between the franchisor and franchisee to extend the time.[49]

Both the 1981 CFRA and the 2016 CFRA provide for exceptions to these notice and cure period requirements for certain defaults by the franchisee when immediate notice of termination without an opportunity to cure is permitted, which include (1) the bankruptcy or insolvency of the franchisee; (2) the abandonment of the franchise for five consecutive days, except for events of force majeure; (3) the written agreement of the franchisor and franchisee to terminate the franchise; (4) material misrepresentations in the purchase of the franchise,

---

47. *Id.* § 20020 (effective 1/1/16).
48. *Id.* § 20020 (effective 10/1/81).
49. *Id.* § 20020 (effective 1/1/16).

conduct that reflects materially and unfavorably upon the operation and reputation of the franchise business or system; (5) the franchisee's failure, for a period of ten days after notification of noncompliance, to comply with any federal, state, or local law or regulation, including, but not limited to, all health, safety, building, and labor laws or regulations; (6) seizure or foreclosure by the government or a creditor; (7) the franchisee's conviction of a felony; (8) failure to pay any franchise fees or other amounts due within five days after receiving written notice that such fees are overdue; (9) when the continued operation of the franchise by the franchisee will result in an imminent danger to public health or safety; and (10) upon the termination or nonrenewal of a motor fuel franchise operated by the franchisee at the same business premises of an additional franchised business granted by the same franchisor or an affiliate.[50]

b. Annotations

The CFRA was not violated where a franchisor terminated its franchisee without notice or opportunity to cure as a result of the material misrepresentations the franchisee made in its franchise application, pursuant to a provision in the franchise agreement allowing for such termination. An opportunity to cure was not required because the misrepresentation could not be cured. *El Pollo Loco, Inc. v. Hashim*, 316 F.3d 1032 (9th Cir. 2003).

A dealer agreement granting the manufacturer the right to terminate the agreement without cause with 90 days' notice is invalid under the CFRA. Where a franchisor terminates a dealer agreement consistent with the contract but in violation of the CFRA, the franchisee can pursue damages. *JRS Products, Inc. v. Matsushita Electric Corp. of America*, 115 Cal. App. 4th 168, 8 Cal. Rptr. 3d 840 (2004). Notably, a franchisee can seek damages provided under the CFRA and breach of contract damages under the common law. *Id.*

A leak detection franchisee's continued failure to pay royalties when due under the franchise agreement justified terminating the franchise without an opportunity to cure. The franchisee was given two written notices related to the breach of the franchise agreement and was terminated without an opportunity to cure on the third notice. *Hiromoto v. Evans*, Business Franchise Guide (CCH) ¶ 10,943 (Cal. App. 1996). [This is an unpublished opinion.]

5. Required Cure Period

a. Commentary

Under the 1981 CFRA, the franchisee's reasonable opportunity to cure its default is limited to 30 days after a default notice is given.[51] Under the 2016 CFRA, a franchisee must cure its defaults within at least 60 days, but no more than 75 days, after a default notice is given, unless there is a separate agreement between the franchisor and franchisee to extend the cure period beyond 75 days.[52]

---

50. *Id.* § 20021 (effective 10/1/81); *id.* § 20021 (effective 1/1/16).
51. *Id.* § 20020 (effective 10/1/81).
52. *Id.* § 20020 (effective 1/1/16).

b. Annotations

Providing a cure period was not required under the CFRA where a franchisee was selling unauthorized yogurt products to its customers while operating an ice cream franchise. The CFRA allows immediate termination without a cure period if the "franchisee engages in conduct which reflects materially and unfavorably upon the operation and reputation of the franchise business or system," such as selling unauthorized products. *Franchising v. Mihranian*, No. CV 08-07022-RGK (PJWx), 2009 U.S. Dist. LEXIS 135725 (C.D. Cal. Jan. 22, 2009).

A franchisor argued that it properly terminated a franchise agreement based on its interpretation of a provision in the franchise agreement stating that the agreement automatically terminated when the franchisee missed two consecutive payments, and that the franchisee missed two consecutive payments. The court rejected this argument, noting that California law prohibits a franchise agreement from automatically terminating without notice to the franchisee and an opportunity to cure. The court found the franchisor's argument was contrary to California law. *Fantastic Sams Salons Corp. v. Moassesfar*, 2015 U.S. Dist. LEXIS 6934 (C.D. Cal. Jan. 21, 2015).

6. Repurchase Obligations

a. Commentary

Under the 2016 CFRA, the franchisor must, even where there is lawful termination, repurchase all inventory, supplies, equipment, fixtures, and furnishings purchased or paid for under the franchise agreement or any ancillary or collateral agreement by the franchisee to the franchisor or its approved suppliers and sources that are at the time of the notice of termination in the possession of the franchisee or used by the franchisee in the franchised business at the value of price paid minus depreciation. The franchisor will have the right to receive clear title to and possession of all items purchased from the franchisee.[53] This repurchase obligation does not apply to personalized items, items not reasonably required to operate the franchised business, to items for which the franchisee cannot convey good title and possession, the franchisee declines a bona fide renewal offer, the franchisee is allowed to retain control of the principal place of the franchised business, or the franchisor completely withdraws from franchising in the geographic market.[54] The franchisor's repurchase obligation does not apply to inventory, supplies, equipment, fixtures, or furnishings that the franchisee sold between the date of notice of termination and the cessation of the franchise's operation pursuant to termination.[55] The franchisor is permitted to offset the purchase price of the assets against any money owed to the franchisor or its subsidiaries by the franchisee under the franchise agreement or any ancillary agreement. The 2022 update to section 20022(h) of the 2016 CFRA

---

53. *Id.* § 20022 (effective 1/1/16).
54. *Id.* § 20035 (effective 1/1/16).
55. *Id.* § 20022.

authorizes setoff rights only if the franchisee agrees to the amount of the proposed offset or the franchisor has received a final adjudication of the amount of the offset.[56]

Where the franchisor terminates a franchise agreement in violation of the 2016 CFRA, the franchisor must pay the franchisee "the fair market value of the franchised business and franchise assets," as well as any other damages caused by the franchisor's violation of the CFRA.[57] The franchisor is permitted to offset the purchase price of the assets against any money owed to the franchisor or its subsidiaries by the franchisee under the franchise agreement or any ancillary agreement.[58]

b. Annotations

A franchisor terminated a franchise agreement on 90 days' notice, without setting forth a cause for the termination or giving the franchisee an opportunity to cure. On appeal, the franchisor did not assert that it had good cause or that it gave adequate notice and conceded that the termination was wrongful under the CFRA. However, the franchisor claimed that the repurchase of the franchisee's inventory was the sole remedy for its violation of the CFRA. The court disagreed, explaining that if that was the case, franchisors would have no incentive to refrain from wrongfully terminating franchisees' businesses and taking over such businesses with the very inventory they would need to continue operating it. Instead, because the franchisor breached the franchise agreement, the franchisee could pursue damages under a breach of contract claim in addition to the repurchase of inventory. *JRS Products, Inc. v. Matsushita Electric Corp. of America*, 115 Cal. App. 4th 168, 8 Cal. Rptr. 3d 840 (2004).

D. Restrictions on Nonrenewal

1. What Constitutes Nonrenewal

a. Commentary

Nonrenewal of a franchise agreement occurs when a franchisor or franchisee elects not to extend the duration of a franchise agreement for a successive term when its prior term expires.

b. Annotations

An ice cream franchisor was purchased by another corporation and altered the manner and method in which its ice cream was distributed, resulting in a lawsuit brought by its franchisees. The court dismissed the franchisees' claim for wrongful termination and/or nonrenewal of the franchise under the CFRA, finding that the franchisees did not allege actual termination or nonrenewal. The court held that the CFRA contemplates an actual stripping of franchise rights from affected franchisees and does not discuss detrimental activities

---

56. *Id.* § 20022(h) (effective 1/1/23).
57. *Id.* § 20035 (effective 1/1/16).
58. *Id.* § 20036.

short of complete franchise destruction. The statutes are only meant to address actual termination or nonrenewal. *Carlock v. Pillsbury Co.*, CIVIL 4-87-517, CIVIL 4-87-586, 1988 U.S. Dist. LEXIS 18666 (D. Minn. Oct. 13, 1988).

2. Restrictions on Nonrenewal
a. Commentary
A franchisor can refuse to renew a franchise only if the franchisor gives the franchisee at least 180 days prior written notice of its intent not to renew and if the franchisor complies with one of the following: (1) the franchisor permits the franchisee to sell his business to a qualified purchaser during the 180-day period; or (2) the franchisor's refusal to renew is not for the purpose of converting the franchised business to a company-owned business for the franchisor's own account, except under a right of first refusal provision in the franchise agreement, and the franchisor agrees not to enforce any covenant not to compete against the nonrenewed franchisee; or (3) termination of the franchise agreement for good cause would be permitted under sections 20020 or 20021 of the CFRA; or (4) the franchisee and the franchisor mutually agree not to renew the franchise; or (5) the franchisor withdraws from distributing its products or services through franchises in the geographic market served by the franchisee, provided that (a) the franchisor does not seek to enforce any covenant not to compete against the nonrenewed franchisee; (b) the refusal to renew is not for the purpose of converting the franchised business to a company-owned business for the franchisor's own account; (c) the franchisor offers the franchisee a 30-day right of first refusal to match any offer to purchase the premises of any company-owned business; and (d) on a sale of the franchisor's interest to another franchisor, the other franchisor offers the franchisee the right to purchase one of its franchises on substantially the same terms and conditions currently being offered to other franchisees; or (6) the franchisor and the franchisee fail to agree to changes or additions to the terms and conditions of the franchise agreement, if the changes or additions would result in renewal of the franchise agreement on substantially the same terms and conditions on which the franchisor is then customarily granting renewal franchises, or on the terms and conditions on which the franchisor is then customarily granting original franchises.[59]

b. Annotations
The CFRA requires that the franchisor provide a franchisee with 180-days' notice of the franchisor's intent not to renew the franchise. The statute also requires that at least one additional circumstance out of the CFRA's enumerated circumstances be met before a franchisor may decline to renew a franchise. *Amcobeauty Corp. v. Armstrong*, No. D054249, 2009 Cal. App. Unpub. LEXIS 9279 (Nov. 23, 2009). [This opinion is not published.]

Nonrenewal under sections 20025(a) and (b) of the CFRA is permissible without cause. Subsection (a) requires the franchisor to provide the franchisee

---
59. *Id*. § 20025 (effective 10/1/81).

180 days prior to the expiration of the franchise to sell its business to a purchaser meeting the franchisor's then current requirements for granting renewal franchise and subsection (b) allows the franchisor to refuse to renew but not for the purpose of converting the franchisee's business to a company-owned operation and if the franchisor agrees not to enforce any post-term noncompete. Nonrenewal pursuant to section 20025(c) is permissible only in circumstances in which termination prior to the end of the franchise term would be permitted by sections 20020 and 20021, which typically require good cause and that the franchisee be given the opportunity to cure. *Dale Carnegie & Associates v. King*, 31 F. Supp. 2d 359 (S.D.N.Y. 1998).

No restriction on nonrenewal shall prohibit a franchisor from exercising a right of first refusal to purchase the franchisee's business. The expectation is that California courts will ordinarily enforce a franchisor's right of first refusal to purchase an interest in a franchisee. *Prudential Real Estate Affiliates, Inc. v. PPR Realty, Inc.*, 204 F.3d 867 (9th Cir. 2000).

A franchisor that agreed to extend the term of the franchise for approximately seven months complied with the CFRA's mandate of providing 180 days prior written notice of any intent to not renew. "Nothing in Section 20025 shall prohibit a franchisor from offering or agreeing before expiration of the current franchise term to extend the term of the franchise for a limited period in order to satisfy the time of notice of nonrenewal requirement of that section." *West L.A. Pizza, Inc. v. Domino's Pizza, Inc.*, 2008 U.S. Dist. LEXIS 45977 (C.D. Cal. 2008).

3. Notice Requirement

a. Commentary

The CFRA provides specific requirements for the contents and delivery of a notice of nonrenewal of a franchise agreement. A notice of nonrenewal must (1) be in writing; (2) be sent by registered, certified, or other receipted mail, by telegram, or personally delivered to the franchisee; (3) contain a statement of intent to not renew the franchise; (4) state the reasons for the nonrenewal; and (5) state the effective date of the nonrenewal or expiration. The CFRA prohibits nonrenewal of a franchise unless the franchisor gives the franchisee at least 180 days prior written notice of the franchisor's intention not to renew the franchise.[60]

b. Annotations

Section 20030 of the CFRA, which requires that a franchisor give notice of termination or nonrenewal and include a statement of the reasons, does not require a specific statement of reasons for nonrenewal when the nonrenewal is made pursuant to section 20025(a) or (b) because these provisions do not require good cause for termination. The only constraint under section 20025(a) is that the franchisor is required to afford the franchisee an appropriate opportunity to sell its franchised business. Further, the only constraints under section 20025(b) are that the nonrenewal not be for the purpose of the franchisor's conversion of the franchised business to operation by employees or agents of the franchisor and

---

60. *Id.* § 20030.

that the franchisor not enforce a post-term noncompete. *Dale Carnegie & Associates v. King*, 31 F. Supp. 2d 359 (S.D.N.Y. 1998).

4. Grounds for Nonrenewal
a. Commentary
Under the 2016 CFRA, a franchisor can refuse to renew a franchise only if the franchisor gives the franchisee at least 180 days prior written notice of its intent not to renew and only if the franchisor is in compliance with the following: (1) the franchisor must permit the franchisee to sell his business to a qualified purchaser during the 180-day period; or (2) the franchisor's refusal to renew is not for the purpose of converting the franchised business to a company-owned business for the franchisor's own account, except under a right of first refusal provision in the franchise agreement, and the franchisor agrees not to enforce any covenant not to compete against the nonrenewed franchisee; or (3) termination of the franchise agreement for good cause would be permitted under sections 20020 or 20021 of the CFRA; or (4) the franchisee and the franchisor mutually agree not to renew the franchise; or (5) the franchisor withdraws from distributing its products or services through franchises in the geographic market served by the franchisee, provided that (a) the franchisor does not seek to enforce any covenant not to compete against the nonrenewed franchisee; (b) the refusal to renew is not for the purpose of converting the franchised business to a company-owned business for the franchisor's own account; (c) the franchisor offers the franchisee a 30-day right of first refusal to match any offer to purchase the premises of any company-owned business; and (d) on a sale of the franchisor's interest to another franchisor, the other franchisor offers the franchisee the right to purchase one of its franchises on substantially the same terms and conditions currently being offered to other franchisees; or (6) the franchisor and the franchisee fail to agree to changes or additions to the terms and conditions of the franchise agreement, if the changes or additions would result in renewal of the franchise agreement on substantially the same terms and conditions on which the franchisor is then customarily granting renewal franchises, or on the terms and conditions on which the franchisor is then customarily granting original franchises.[61]

b. Annotations
In evaluating the remedies available under the CFRA where a manufacturer failed to provide 180 days' notice of nonrenewal to a dealer but still permitted the dealer to sell its business to a purchaser, the court held that repurchase of inventory was the exclusive remedy under the CFRA for failure to provide the required notice for nonrenewal. *Boat & Motor Mart v. Sea Ray Boats, Inc.*, 825 F.2d 1285 (9th Cir. 1987). However, a franchisee can pursue damages available under common law claims. *See JRS Products, Inc. v. Matsushita Electric Corp. of America*, 115 Cal. App. 4th 168, 175 *as modified on denial of reh'g* (Feb. 25, 2004);

---

61. *Id.* § 20025 (effective 1/1/16).

Mahroom v. Best Western International, Inc., No. C 07-2351 JF (HRL), 2010 WL 11575097, at *9 (N.D. Cal. Mar. 29, 2010).

A general release executed by a franchisee in consideration of a renewal was not unconscionable or in violation of California public policy because the release did not purport to absolve the franchisor of future liability for fraud or other intentional wrongs. *Lee v. GNC Franchising, Inc.*, 73 Fed. Appx. 202 (9th Cir. 2003).

A franchisee's current franchise agreement specifically gave the franchisor authority to impose materially different terms upon renewal, including terms more onerous to franchisees, provided those terms constituted the "then current form" of the franchisor's standard franchise agreement. Such practice was expressly permitted under the CFRA. *West L.A. Pizza, Inc. v. Domino's Pizza, Inc.* (C.D. Cal. Feb. 26, 2008).[62]

5. Required Cure Period
Not applicable.

6. Limitations on Franchisor's Right to Impose Conditions for Renewal
Not applicable.

7. Repurchase Obligations

a. Commentary
A franchisor's repurchase obligations will vary depending on whether it complies or fails to comply with the requirements of the CFRA.

If a franchisor fails to comply with the 2016 CFRA on a nonrenewal, the franchisor must offer to repurchase the franchisee's resalable current inventory that meets the franchisor's standards and is required to be sold under the franchise agreement or commercial practice.[63] The purchase price will be the lower of the fair wholesale market value or the price paid by the franchisee.[64] The franchisor need not purchase personalized items which have no value to the franchisor or the business it franchises.[65] The franchisor is permitted to offset against any repurchase offer any sums owed by the franchisee to the franchisor or its subsidiaries.[66]

If the franchisor complies with the 2016 CFRA on a nonrenewal, the franchisor must purchase from the franchisee "at the value of price paid, minus depreciation, all inventory, supplies, equipment, fixtures, and furnishings purchased or paid for" by the franchisee, from the franchisor or its approved suppliers and sources.[67] The franchisee must be in possession of the assets when it ceases operating the business as a franchise, and must be able to grant the franchisor

---

62. The authors did not find more recent cases.
63. CAL. BUS. & PROF. CODE § 20035 (effective 1/1/16).
64. *Id.*
65. *Id.*
66. *Id.* § 20036.
67. *Id.* § 20022.

clear title to the assets.[68] The franchisor is permitted to offset the purchase price of the assets against the money that the franchisee owes to the franchisor or its subsidiaries.[69]

This repurchase requirement will not apply, however, if (1) the assets to be purchased are personalized items, inventory, supplies, equipment, fixtures, or furnishings not reasonably required to conduct the operation of the franchise business in accordance with the franchise agreement or any ancillary or collateral agreement; or (2) the franchisee is unable to give the franchisor clear title to, and possession of, the assets; or (3) the franchisee declined a bona fide offer from the franchisor to renew the agreement; or (4) the franchisor does not prevent the franchisee from retaining control of the franchise business location after the termination or nonrenewal; or (5) the franchisor's termination or nonrenewal is based on a publicly announced, nondiscriminatory decision to completely withdraw its franchise activity from the geographic market area where the franchisee is located; or (6) the parties mutually agree in writing to terminate or to not renew the franchise.[70]

b. Annotations

Until January 1, 2016, under the CFRA, a franchisee's only remedy for wrongful nonrenewal is the franchisor's repurchase of the franchisee's inventory—there is no right to damages. *Boat & Motor Mart v. Sea Ray Boats, Inc.*, 825 F.2d 1285 (9th Cir. 1987). For franchise agreements entered into or renewed on or after January 1, 2016, the CFRA provides that a "franchisee shall be entitled to receive from the franchisor the fair market value of the franchised business and franchise assets and any other damages caused by the violation of this chapter." California Business and Professions Code §§ 20035, 20041(b).

E. Transfers and Succession

1. Commentary

Sections 20028 and 20029, which were added to the CFRA in 2015, regulate the rights and responsibilities of franchisors and franchisees in transferring or selling the assets of a franchised business. A franchisee is permitted to sell or transfer a franchise, all or substantially all of the assets of the business, or an interest in the business to another person so long as the transferee (1) is qualified under the franchisor's standards for the approval of new or renewing franchises; and (2) complies with the transfer conditions in the franchise agreement.[71] The franchisor must make available to the franchisee its then-existing standards for new or renewing franchisees. These standards must be consistently applied to similarly situated franchisees.

The CFRA does not give the franchisee the right to sell, transfer, or assign the franchise, its assets, or an interest in the franchise business without the

---

68. *Id.*
69. *Id.* § 20036.
70. *Id.* § 20022.
71. *Id.* § 20028(a).

written consent of the franchisor.[72] However, the franchisor's consent cannot be withheld unless the buyer, transferee, or assignee does not meet the standards for new or renewing franchisees or does not comply with the transfer conditions specified in the franchise agreement.

The franchisee must notify the franchisor of the franchisee's intent to sell, transfer, or assign the franchise, its assets, or an interest in the franchise business prior to the sale, transfer, or assignment.[73] This notice must be delivered to the franchisor by business courier or receipted mail and must include the transferee's name and address; a copy of all agreements related to the sale, assignment, or transfer; and the transferee's franchise application. The franchisor is required to provide forms and notify the franchisee and the proposed transferee of any additional information needed.

The franchisor must notify the franchisee of the approval or disapproval of the proposed sale, assignment, or transfer within 60 days after the receipt of all the necessary information and documentation, or as otherwise agreed to by the parties in writing.[74] If the franchisor does not take action pursuant to the requirements of the CFRA, the proposed sale, assignment, or transfer shall be deemed approved. If disapproved, the franchisor must provide notice and set forth the reasons for disapproval. The reasonableness of a disapproval is a question of fact requiring consideration of all existing circumstances.

A franchisor is not required to exercise a right of first refusal but is not prohibited from exercising such a right as long as it pays an amount at least equal to the value of the bona fide offer.[75]

Sections 20028 and 20029 of the CFRA do not explicitly confer any rights on prospective buyers, although the language in these statutes is arguably broad enough to protect prospective buyers, as well as franchisees.[76] In 2022, the state legislature added a new provision to the CFIL specifying what information a prospective franchisee must provide to the franchisor and requiring the franchisor to notify the prospective franchisee in writing of its approval or disapproval.[77] If the proposed sale is not approved, the franchisor is required to state its reasons.[78] The new law provides that a franchisor's failure to comply with these obligations is a violation of the CFIL.[79]

The CFRA requires a franchisor to permit the surviving spouse, heirs, or estate of either a deceased franchisee or the majority shareholder of the franchisee to participate in the operation of a franchise for a reasonable time after the death of the franchisee or the majority shareholder of the franchisee.[80] During

---

72. *Id.* § 20028(b).
73. *Id.* § 20029(a).
74. *Id.* § 20029(b).
75. *Id.* § 20028(b)(3), (c).
76. *See id.* § 20029(b)(2) ("In any action in which the franchisor's disapproval of a sale, assignment, or transfer pursuant to this subdivision is an issue, the reasonableness of the franchisor's decision shall be a question of fact requiring consideration of all existing circumstances.").
77. CAL. CORP. CODE § 31126.
78. *Id.* § 31126(d)(1).
79. *Id.* § 31221.
80. CAL. BUS. & PROF. CODE § 20027(a).

that time, the surviving spouse, heirs, or estate must either satisfy the requirements to become a franchisee or sell the franchise to a person who can satisfy those requirements. This provision does not prohibit the franchisor from exercising a right of first refusal if the surviving spouse, heirs, or estate receive a bona fide offer to purchase the franchise.[81] The surviving spouse, heirs, or estate must maintain the standards and obligations of the franchise during the time they are allowed to operate the franchise.[82]

2. Annotations

Franchisor's withholding of consent for franchisee's transfer of franchise to buyers based on their failure to pass English language proficiency assessment did not constitute breach of franchise agreement, as it was reasonable to require compliance with the company-wide policy of passing the English language proficiency assessment. *De Walshe v. Togo's Eateries, Inc.*, 567 F. Supp. 2d 1198, 1202 (C.D. Cal. 2008).

Franchisor was entitled to withhold its consent to a sale of franchisee's restaurant to any prospective purchaser who has not completed the applicant training program. *Perez v. McDonald's Corp.*, 60 F. Supp. 2d 1030, 1034 (E.D. Cal. 1998).

Provision restricting franchisor from denying the right of a surviving spouse, heir, or estate of a deceased franchisee or a majority stockholder to participate in the ownership of the franchise for a reasonable time does not prohibit a franchisor from exercising a right of first refusal to purchase a franchise. *Prudential Real Estate Affiliates, Inc. v. PPR Realty, Inc.*, 204 F.3d 867, 875 (9th Cir. 2000).

Franchisor was entitled to exercise its right of first refusal to purchase business based on stipulated appraisal value in arbitration of partnership dispute. *Bhullar v. Midland Oil Group, LLC*, No. E072486, 2022 WL 2207837 (Cal. App. June 21, 2022) [unpublished/not citable].

Where franchise agreement requires a bona fide offer to be in a "dollar amount," offer that was based in part on the buyer's future performance was not a bona fide offer and did not trigger franchisor's right of first refusal. The court remanded the case for a determination of whether, by attempting to exercise a right of first refusal, the franchisor had waived its right to disapprove the transfer. *IJLSF, LLC v. It's Just Lunch International, LLC*, E071940, 2021 WL 3012850 (Cal. App. July 16, 2021) [unpublished/not citable].

F. Other Regulation of the Franchise Relationship

California relies on its statutory codes (such as the Civil Code and the Code of Civil Procedure), in addition to the CFRA and CFIL, to provide the answers to various franchise-related legal questions. As a result, it is not sufficient to look solely to the CFRA and the CFIL to find the law applicable to California franchises. Rather, one must examine the entirety of California's statutory and case law to ascertain how a franchise agreement governed by California law will be construed.

---

81. *Id.* § 20027(b).
82. *Id.* § 20027(a).

For example, California statutes *other than* the CFRA and CFIL govern issues such as enforcement of post-term noncompetes,[83] the reciprocity of attorneys' fees provisions,[84] the enforceability of a general release as to unknown claims,[85] advance waivers of the right to a jury trial,[86] accrual of a cause of action for purposes of starting the statute of limitations,[87] and the calculation of damages and restitution.[88]

In addition, certain provisions of the CFRA and CFIL regulate the franchise relationship in ways that are, if not unique, at least uncommon in the franchise-related laws of most states. Most notably, as discussed later, a material modification of an existing franchise agreement is deemed to be a "sale" of a franchise and is subject to certain disclosure and notice requirements.

1. Associational Rights

a. Commentary

The CFIL prohibits a franchisor from restricting or inhibiting the right of franchisees to join a trade association or associate with other franchisees for any lawful purposes.[89] A separate enforcement provision authorizes an action for temporary and permanent injunctive relief and for damages, if any, as well as the costs of suit including reasonable attorneys' fees.[90] No damages need be proven to obtain injunctive relief, but the statute contains a two-year statute of repose.[91]

b. Annotations

Prohibiting certain franchisees from attending franchise meetings and events does not necessarily violate this provision because franchisees are not barred from otherwise communicating with other franchisees outside of the meetings or events. *United Studios of Self Defense, Inc. v. Rinehart*, No. 8:18-CV-01048, 2019 WL 1109682 (C.D. Cal. Feb. 22, 2019).

A franchisor's request that franchisees refrain from making disparaging comments does not violate this section. *Overturf v. Rocky Mountain Chocolate Factory, Inc.*, No. SACV08-00365, 2009 WL 10675269 (C.D. Cal. Feb. 13, 2009).

After a franchisee has received a notice of termination, the terminated franchisee has no rights under this section. *Devore v. H&R Block Tax Services LLC*, No. CV 16-946, 2018 WL 1942384 (C.D. Cal. Mar. 29, 2018).

---

83. *Id.* § 16600; *see* the chapter on California law in COVENANTS AGAINST COMPETITION IN FRANCHISE AGREEMENTS (4th ed. 2022).
84. CAL. CIV. CODE § 1717.
85. *Id.* § 1542.
86. CAL. CIV. PROC. CODE § 631.
87. *Id.* § 312.
88. CAL. CIV. CODE §§ 3274–3424; *see also* the commentary at subsection II.G.2 in this chapter.
89. CAL. CORP. CODE § 31220.
90. *Id.* § 31302.5(A).
91. *Id.* § 31302.5(A), (B).

2. Encroachment

a. Commentary

There is no provision in the CFRA specifically relating to encroachment. Instead, franchisees aggrieved by a franchisor's approval of a nearby competitor generally assert a breach of the implied covenant of good faith and fair dealing.

b. Annotations

Franchisor breached the covenant of good faith and fair dealing by constructing a competing restaurant within a mile and a half from franchisee's restaurant where franchise agreement was silent as to whether territory was exclusive. *In re Vylene Enterprises, Inc.*, 90 F.3d 1472, 1477 (9th Cir. 1996).

Franchisor did not breach the implied covenant of good faith and fair dealing when it allowed a large franchisee to place two franchises in close proximity to the plaintiff's office. The franchise agreement expressly provided that franchisor could place additional franchises in franchisee's market territory. *Hobin v. Coldwell Banker Residential Affiliates, Inc.*, 144 N.H. 626, 744 A.2d 1134 (N.H. 2000) (applying California law). However, where a court finds a provision expressly providing a franchisor the right to place additional franchises in the franchisee's market to be unconscionable, the franchisee can successfully seek damages for encroachment. *Bryman v. El Pollo Loco, Inc.*, Case No. MC026045 (Cal. Super. Ct. Mar. 30, 2017) (order granting summary judgment finding provision unconscionable); *Bryman v. El Pollo Loco, Inc.*, Case No. MC026045 (Cal. Super. Ct. Aug. 1, 2018).[92] Summary judgment is inappropriate where the franchisor reserved itself the right under the automobile franchise agreement to approve competing dealerships "near" the franchisee, but the term "near" was undefined. *Ri-Joyce, Inc. v. New Motor Vehicle Board*, 2 Cal. App. 4th 445, 3 Cal. Rptr. 2d 546 (1992).

3. Material Modifications

a. Commentary

Unlike most state franchise disclosure statutes, the CFIL does not stop applying when the franchise agreement is signed. The definition of "sale" and "offer" in the CFIL provides that "a material modification of an existing franchise, whether upon renewal or otherwise, is a 'sale' within the meaning of this section."[93]

Under California Corporations Code section 31125, it is unlawful even to solicit the agreement of a franchisee to a proposed material modification of an existing franchise contract without first providing the franchisee a copy of the proposed modification in a form approved by the Department at least five days before the modification is signed, unless the modification is exempt.[94]

A material modification is exempt from the registration requirement if:

---

92. Both authors were involved in this case.
93. CAL. CORP. CODE § 31018(c).
94. *Id.* § 31125(b).

- It is offered on a voluntary basis and does not "substantially and adversely impact the franchisee's rights, benefits, privileges, duties, obligations, or responsibilities under the franchise agreement."[95]

OR

- It is not within 12 months of the day the franchise agreement was executed, and does not waive any of the franchisee's rights under the CFRA; and
- The franchisee receives the complete modification at least five days prior to signing it, or is given a right to rescind it within five days of signing; and
- It is either:
    - Made in connection with the resolution of a bona fide dispute between the parties, and is not offered on a system-wide basis; or
    - Offered on a voluntary basis to fewer than 25 percent of the franchisees in the system within any 12-month period.[96]

If the material modification is not exempt under either of these tests, then a franchisor must submit an application for registration of the material modification to the Department.[97] Due to this unusual law, it is important for a franchisor to assess both the law and the available statutory exemptions any time it seeks to amend an existing franchise agreement with a California-based franchisee.

b. Annotations

Where the changes are made as a result of discretionary power reserved to the franchisor under the franchise agreement, the changes are not "material" for the purposes of this section. *R.N.R. Oils v. BP West Coast Products LLC*, No. B219126, 2011 WL 37962 (Cal. App. Jan. 6, 2011) [unpublished/not citable].

Where there was a material modification of an "interim agreement" and the material modification was within the statute of limitations, the franchisee's claim was not time barred. *MZ Ventures LLC v. Mitsubishi Motor Sales of America, Inc.*, No. CV9902395, 1999 WL 33597219, Business Franchise Guide (CCH) ¶ 11,692 (C.D. Cal. Aug. 31, 1999).

A modification of a "rental policy" that increased the rent for the franchisees was not a material modification within the meaning of the CFIL, where the franchisees agreed to a possible rent modification at the time the franchisees entered into their dealer station leases. *In re ConocoPhillips Co. Service Station Rent Contract Litigation*, No. M:09-cv-02040, 2011 1399783 (N.D. Cal. Apr. 13, 2011).

CFIL section 31101 states that a franchisor's material modification of an existing franchise is exempt from the registration and disclosure provisions of the CFIL so long as the franchisor "discloses in writing to each franchisee [getting the modification] information concerning the specific sections of the franchise agreement proposed to be modified and such additional information as

---

95. *Id.* § 31125(d).
96. *Id.* § 31125(c).
97. *Id.* § 31125(a); CAL. CODE REGS. tit. 10, § 310.125.

may be required by rule or order of the commissioner." *DT Woodard, Inc. v. Mail Boxes Etc., Inc.*, No. B194599, 2007 WL 3018861, Business Franchise Guide (CCH) ¶ 13,746 (Cal. App. Oct. 17, 2007) [unpublished/not citable].

Where franchisor's new marketing program allegedly imposes costs not previously disclosed, franchisee's claim for violation of this section survives motion to dismiss. *BP Products North America, Inc. v. Grand Petroleum, Inc.*, No. 20-cv-901, 2020 WL 1987605 (N.D. Cal. Apr. 27, 2020).

4. No Waiver Clauses

a. Commentary

The CFRA contains three separate "no waiver" provisions: the first prohibits "any condition, stipulation or provision purporting to bind any person to waive compliance with any provision" of the CFRA;[98] the second, effective January 1, 2023, declares void any provision of a franchise agreement requiring a franchisee to waive the provisions of the CFRA;[99] the third specifically voids any agreement to restrict venue to a forum outside of California.[100] The first two provisions are discussed in this section; the venue-specific provision is discussed in the dispute resolution section that follows. In addition, as some provisions of the CFIL affect the relationship between franchisors and franchisees, it should be noted that the CFIL has its own anti-waiver provision.[101]

The anti-waiver provision may void a choice-of-law provision where it requires a franchisee to waive compliance with the CFRA.[102] Section 20010 may apply even where an agreement specifically stated that no franchise relationship was created.[103] A party must be a resident or domiciled in California or have agreed to be treated as such for the CFRA's anti-waiver provision to be applicable.[104]

Section 20015(b), added in 2022, is by its terms nearly identical to—but arguably narrower than—section 20010, which has been part of the CFRA since 1980. Whereas section 20015(b) is limited to provisions in the franchise agreement, section 20010 arguably applies to any "condition, stipulation or provision" between the parties. Available legislative history is silent as to the legislature's perceived need for this additional provision.

In addition, California law provides that contracts intended "to exempt anyone from responsibility for his own fraud, or willful injury or property of another, or violation of law, whether willful or negligent, are against the policy

---

98. CAL. BUS. & PROF. CODE § 20010.
99. *Id.* § 20015(b), added by Cal. Assembly Bill 676, effective Sept. 29, 2022.
100. CAL. BUS. & PROF. CODE § 20040.5.
101. CAL. CORP. CODE § 31512.
102. 1-800 Got Junk? LLC v. Super. Ct., 189 Cal. App. 5th 500, 116 Cal. Rptr. 3d 923 (2010).
103. Gabana Gulf Distrib., Ltd. v. Gap Int'l Sales, Inc., 2006 WL 2355092 (N.D. Cal. Aug. 14, 2006).
104. *Gabana Gulf Distrib., Ltd.*, 2006 WL 2355092.

of the law" and unenforceable.[105] And a law established for a "public reason" may not be contravened by private agreement.[106]

b. Annotations

Franchise agreement provision that stated that contract claims cannot be waived by any action or inaction of the parties defeated affirmative defenses of waiver and ratification. *Stillwell v. RadioShack Corp.*, 676 F. Supp. 2d 962, 980 (S.D. Cal. 2009).

Contractual no-waiver clauses can themselves be waived. *Auntie Anne's, Inc. v. Wang*, No. CV 14-01049, 2014 WL 11728722 (C.D. Cal. July 16, 2014).

5. Unfair Competition Law

a. Commentary

California's broad Unfair Competition Law (UCL) prohibits, among other things, "any unlawful, unfair or fraudulent business act or practice."[107] The UCL has been described as "sweeping, embracing anything that can properly be called a business practice and at the same time is forbidden by law."[108] This provision is frequently used as the basis for claims by franchisees against their franchisor. Available remedies for violation of the UCL are restitution and injunctive relief; damages are not available.[109] To establish standing to sue under the UCL, a party must show injury in fact, and the loss of money or property, as a result of unfair competition.[110]

A business practice is "unlawful" and independently actionable under the UCL if it would offend another law, "be it civil or criminal, federal, state, or municipal, statutory, regulatory, or court-made."[111] If a defendant can demonstrate that there is no violation of the "predicate" law, however, the UCL claim may fail.[112]

Courts have devised at least three different tests to determine whether an "unfair" business practice violates the UCL: First, that (1) the consumer injury is substantial; (2) the injury is not outweighed by any countervailing benefits to consumers or competition; and (3) the injury could not reasonably have been avoided by consumers themselves. Second, that the practice offends an established public policy, as reflected in specific constitutional, statutory, or

---

105. CAL. CIV. CODE § 1668.
106. *Id.* § 3513.
107. CAL. BUS. & PROF. CODE § 17200.
108. Cel-Tech Commc'ns, Inc. v. L.A. Cellular Tel. Co., 20 Cal. 4th 163, 180 (1999).
109. SDMS, Inc. v. Rocky Mountain Chocolate Factory, Inc., 2008 WL 4838557 (S.D. Cal. Nov. 6, 2008); Fresno Motors, LLC v. Mercedes Benz USA, LLC, 771 F.3d 1119 (9th Cir. 2014).
110. Blue Mako Inc. v. Minidis, 2008 WL 11334205 (C.D. Cal. June 23, 2008); United Studios of Self Defense, Inc. v. Rinehart, 2019 WL 6973520 (C.D. Cal. Sept. 9, 2019) (potential loss of money is insufficient).
111. Saunders v. Super. Ct., 27 Cal. App. 4th 832, 838–39, 33 Cal. Rptr. 2d 438 (1994).
112. Acedo v. DMAX, Ltd., 2015 WL 12696176 (C.D. Cal. Nov. 13, 2015); Flexpand, LLC v. CREAM, Inc., 2020 WL 13504973 (N.D. Cal. June 16, 2020); *but see* Ronald Cohn, Inc. v. Sprouts Farmers Mkt., Inc., 2021 WL 120896 (S.D. Cal. Jan. 13, 2021).

regulatory provisions. And third, that it is immoral, unethical, oppressive, unscrupulous, or substantially injurious to consumers.[113]

A "fraudulent" business practice is prohibited by the UCL where the practice is likely to deceive reasonable members of the public, even if the deception is not intended.[114]

b. Annotations

Franchisees' employees' claim that franchisor engaged in an "unfair" business practice by requiring franchisee to use software that undercounted hours worked fails because franchisor is not the employees' employer. *Aleksick v. 7-Eleven, Inc.*, 205 Cal. App. 4th 1176, 140 Cal. Rptr. 3d 796 (2012).

Injunction under UCL is appropriate to prevent franchisor from seeking to enforce unlawful noncompetition provision. *Robinson v. U-Haul Co. of California*, 4 Cal. App. 5th, 209 Cal. Rptr. 3d 81 (2016).

UCL claims that are based on contractual disputes between two private parties that otherwise have no connection to competition or the general public must be dismissed. *Macedonia Distributing, Inc. v. S-L Distribution Co., LLC*, No. SACV 17-1692, 2018 WL 6190592 (C.D. Cal. Aug. 7, 2018).

Although claims based on an alleged breach of contract do not generally fall within the "unlawful" theory of the UCL, allegations as to tortious conduct related to contractual relationship may be within its scope. *Nestle USA, Inc. v. Crest Foods, Inc.*, No. LA CV16-07519, 2018 WL 7506166 (C.D. Cal. June 6, 2018); *Gabana Gulf Distribution, Ltd. v. Gap International Sales, Inc.*, No. C 06-02584, 208 WL 111223 (N.D. Cal. Jan. 9, 2008). *But see R. N. Beach, Inc. v. Country Visions, Inc.*, No. 2:15-cv-02014, 2016 WL 1682046 (E.D. Cal. Apr. 27, 2016).

A private plaintiff may bring a UCL action even when there is no private right of action under the predicate law. *Ronald Cohn, Inc. v. Sprouts Farmers Market, Inc.*, No. 19-cv-848, 2021 WL 120896 (S.D. Cal. Jan. 13, 2021).

6. Discrimination/Protected Classification

a. Commentary

The California Constitution prohibits a person from being disqualified from entering into or pursuing a business because of sex, race, creed, color, or national or ethnic origin.[115] The Cartwright Act, California's antitrust statute, prohibits the exclusion of any person from a business transaction on the basis of a written policy requiring discrimination on the basis of any protected characteristic[116] or "on the basis that the person conducts or has conducted business in a particular location."[117] This provision has been interpreted to require a showing of antitrust injury.[118]

---

113. Dallas & Lashmi, Inc. v. 7-Eleven, Inc., 112 F. Supp. 3d 1048 (C.D. Cal. 2015); Power Quality & Elec. Sys., Inc. v. BP W. Coast Prods. LLC, 2016 WL 6524408 (N.D. Cal. Nov. 3, 2016).
114. Yi v. Circle K Stores, Inc., 258 F. Supp. 3d 1075 (C.D. Cal. 2017); Samica Enters. LLC v. Mail Boxes Etc., Inc., 460 F. App'x 664 (9th Cir. 2011).
115. CAL. CONST. art. I, § 8.
116. The statute references the state's Unruh Civil Rights Act, CAL. CIV. CODE § 51(b), (e).
117. CAL. BUS & PROF. CODE § 16721.
118. Wilson v. Avemco Ins. Co., 59 Fed. App'x 928 (9th Cir. 2003).

Section 51.8 of the California Civil Code prohibits a franchisor from discriminating in the granting of franchises solely on account of any protected characteristic of the franchisee or of the composition of a neighborhood or geographic area where the franchise is located.[119] This prohibition is not intended to prohibit a program "to make franchises available to persons lacking the capital, training, business experience, or other qualifications ordinarily required of franchisees, or any other affirmative action program adopted by the franchisor."[120] Like section 16721 of the Cartwright Act, this section adopts by reference the characteristics protected by the Unruh Civil Rights Act.[121]

In 2022, the legislature amended the CFIL to add a provision virtually identical to section 51.8 of the California Civil Code, except that in addition to prohibiting the discriminatory refusal to grant a franchise, the new provision also prohibits a franchisor from discriminatorily refusing to provide financial assistance "that has been granted or provided to other similarly situated franchisees or prospective franchisees."[122]

As of 2023, the characteristics protected under the Unruh Civil Rights Act are sex, race, color, religion, ancestry, national origin, disability, medical condition, genetic information, marital status, sexual orientation, primary language, and immigration status.[123]

b. Annotations

Neither automobile franchisor's minority recruitment policy, coupled with its policy of recommending franchise candidates on a one-at-a-time basis, nor its statements concerning selection of franchisor's recruited candidates gave rise to inference of required racial exclusion necessary to violation of section 16721 of the Cartwright Act, where existence and race of franchisee's candidate for franchise were not contemplated by franchisor's policy, and submitted documents did not show that franchisor was excluding franchisee's candidates or that their race was considered. *Burke v. Superior Court (General Motors Corp.)*, 128 Cal. App. 3d 661, 180 Cal. Rptr. 537 (1982).

Where notices of default were justified and not pretextual, franchisor's alleged demand that franchisee terminate Filipino employees does not support a claim for discrimination under the Unruh Civil Rights Act. *Reyes v. Atlantic Richfield Co.*, 12 F.3d 1464 (9th Cir. 1993).

7. Sources of Supply

a. Commentary

The CFRA and CFIL contain no provisions prohibiting franchisors from specifying where or from whom franchisees must purchase certain products or services. Some California franchisees have asserted claims under the Sherman Act,

---

119. CAL. CIV. CODE § 51.8(a).
120. *Id.*
121. *Id.*
122. CAL. CORP. CODE § 31212.
123. CAL. CIV. CODE § 51(b), (e).

the Clayton Act, and/or the Cartwright Act on various theories, including tying, price fixing, and market allocation; these claims have generally been unsuccessful.

b. Annotations

Franchisor could impose a requirement that franchisees buy all of their ice cream from Baskin-Robbins as it was necessary to assure uniform product quality and maintain goodwill and value of the trademark. The product (ice cream) and the trademark were so interrelated in the minds of the consumers that they were not separate items for antitrust tie-in purposes. *Krehl v. Baskin-Robbins Ice Cream Co.*, 664 F.2d 1348, 1354 (9th Cir. 1982).

Franchisor's ability to "coerce" its franchisees into buying certain products does not show market power and does not invoke antitrust concerns. A tying arrangement disclosed in advance through a franchise agreement is a part of a negotiated business relationship and not a restraint on trade. *Exxon Corp. v. Superior Court (Koutney)*, 51 Cal. App. 4th 1672, 60 Cal. Rptr. 2d 195 (1997).

Franchises, almost by definition, necessarily consist of "bundled" and related products or services—not separate products. Where the challenged aggregation is an essential ingredient of the franchised system's formula for success, there is but a single product and no tie-in exists as a matter of law. *Rick-Mik Enterprises, Inc. v. Equilon Enterprises LLC*, 532 F.3d 963, 974 (9th Cir. 2008).

Franchisor's receipt of kickbacks or commissions from banks for processing its franchisees' transactions did not violate antitrust laws. *Rick-Mik Enterprises, Inc. v. Equilon Enterprises LLC*, 532 F.3d 963 (9th Cir. 2008).

A franchisor's failure to disclose payments or kickbacks received from suppliers, which omission is relied on by the franchisee in deciding to enter into the franchise agreement, could constitute a misrepresentation in violation of section 31200 of the CFIL. *California Bagel Co. v. American Bagel Co.*, No. CV 97-8863, 2000 WL 35798199 (C.D. Cal. June 7, 2000).

A manufacturer's requirement that its distributor purchase a certain amount of nonbranded equipment can constitute an unlawful tying arrangement, because the allegedly tied products are not identified by the manufacturer's trademark. The court dismissed the claim with leave to amend, however, where the distributor failed to allege that it was coerced to purchase the nonbranded equipment. *Strawflower Electronics, Inc. v. Radioshack Corp.*, No. C-05-0747, 2005 WL 2290314 (N.D. Cal. Sept. 20, 2005).

Franchisee's tying claim fails because required inventory is not a distinct product from the offering of franchises. *Flip Flop Shops Franchise Co., LLC v. Amy Neb*, No. CV 16-7259, 2017 WL 2903183 (C.D. Cal. Mar. 14, 2017).

Observing, outside of the franchise context, that no poach agreements among competitors are per se violations of the Sherman Act but distinguishing certain "no poach" agreements in the franchise context, which are vertical. *Markson v. CRST International, Inc.*, No. 2022 WL 790960 (C.D. Cal. Feb. 24, 2022).

8. Price Control

a. Commentary

The CFRA and CFIL do not expressly prohibit or otherwise restrict the franchisor's ability to control the pricing of products and services that franchisees offer.

However, the California Supreme Court in 1978 held, in *Mailand v. Burckle*, that a minimum resale price agreement between a franchisor and a franchisee was per se unlawful under the Cartwright Act, California's antitrust statute.[124] The *Mailand* ruling may have survived the Supreme Court's ruling in *Leegin Creative Leather Products v. PSKS, Inc.*, which overruled long-standing judicial precedent and held that vertical minimum resale price restraints are to be judged according to the rule of reason.[125] Since *Leegin* involved interpretation of a federal statute (the Sherman Act), not the Cartwright Act, courts have ruled that *Mailand* is good authority and that minimum resale price maintenance clauses are still per se illegal in California.[126] The California Supreme Court had not yet revisited the issue post-*Leegin*. As recently as 2022, California's attorney general has taken the position that "[a]ny agreement between a seller and a buyer regarding the price at which the buyer resells a product is illegal."[127]

A party's control of the pricing of products and services has been held to be a factor supporting the existence of a franchise relationship.[128]

b. Annotations

An arrangement under which franchisees are required to purchase products from the franchisor is not a device to evade price control, so there is no claim for price discrimination under the Robinson Patman Act, 15 U.S.C. § 13. *Casey v. Diet Center, Inc.*, 590 F. Supp. 1561 (N.D. Cal. 1984).

G. Remedies and Administrative Action

1. Restrictive Covenants

a. Commentary

California Business and Professions Code section 16600 prohibits "every contract by which anyone is restrained from engaging in a lawful profession, trade, or business of any kind" except as provided elsewhere in the statute.[129] Among the explicit exceptions are covenants not to compete following the sale of a business in order to protect the purchased goodwill.[130]

Despite the facially absolute nature of section 16600's prohibition, courts applying the law have often found circumstances justifying certain restraints

---

124. Mailand v. Burckle, 20 Cal. 3d 367 (1978).

125. Leegin Creative Leather Prods. v. PSKS, Inc., 551 U.S. 877 (2007).

126. Bodine v. First Co., 2019 WL 5684399 (S.D. Cal. Nov. 1, 2019); Alan Darush MD APC v. Revision LP, 2013 WL 1749539 (C.D. Cal. Apr. 10, 2013); Alsheikh v. Super. Ct., 2013 WL 5530508 (Cal. Ct. App. Oct. 7, 2013) [unpublished/non-citable].

127. Off. of the Att'y Gen. of Cal., Antitrust Enforcement in California: How You Can Help, https://oag.ca.gov/sites/all/files/agweb/pdfs/antitrust/antitrust.pdf (last visited Mar. 18, 2025).

128. Kim v. Servosnax, Inc., 10 Cal. App. 4th 1346, 13 Cal. Rptr. 2d 422 (1992); Gentis v. Safeguard Bus. Sys., Inc., 60 Cal. App. 4th 1294 (1998); Boat & Motor Mart v. Sea Ray Boats, Inc., 825 F.2d 1285, 1289 (9th Cir. 1987).

129. Cal. Bus & Prof. Code § 16600.

130. *Id.* § 16601 (sale of business entity); § 16602 (dissolution of a partnership); § 16602.5 (sale of an LLC).

that would appear to be prohibited by the statute.[131] In general, trial and intermediate appellate courts upheld covenants that applied during the term of a contract ("in-term" covenants) and generally invalidated contracts that restricted trade after a contract had terminated ("post-term" covenants).[132] Some courts also found that "partial" restraints—those that permitted the restrained party to engage in some, but not all, activities—could be upheld.

In *Edwards v. Anderson LLP*, the California Supreme Court held that ***all*** covenants not to compete are invalid in California "even if narrowly drawn, ***unless*** they fall within the applicable statutory exceptions of section 16601, 16602, or 16602.5."[133] *Edwards* concerned an employee who was induced to sign a post-termination noncompete in order to retain his job at his employer's successor company. Following *Edwards*, several courts held that post-term noncompetes and other contractual restraints are unenforceable regardless of the reasonableness of the restraint.[134]

In *Ixchel Pharma, LLC v. Biogen, Inc.*,[135] the California Supreme Court narrowed *Edwards* to the employment context and held that restrictive covenants between businesses must be judged by the rule of reason. The court pointed to a long history of courts applying a reasonableness standard to section 16600 and to the need to consider section 16600 consistently with its statutory neighbor, the Cartwright Act, California's antitrust law. As long as a commercial restraint does not "harm[] competition more than it helps" and there is no intent to establish or exploit a monopoly, it may be enforced. *Ixchel* concerned a collaboration agreement that contained an in-term, "exclusive dealing" provision under which the companies were prohibited from dealing with a third-party competitor.

After *Ixchel*, intermediate appellate courts in California have applied the rule of reason to uphold post-term covenants as well as in-term covenants.[136]

---

131. *See, e.g.*, Great Western Distillery Prods., Inc. v. John A. Wathen Distillery Co., 74 P.2d 745, 10 Cal. 2d 442 (1937); Comedy Club, Inc. v. Improv West Assocs., 553 F.3d 1277 (9th Cir. 2009) (in-term covenant enforceable); Webb v. West Side Dist. Hosp., 144 Cal. App. 3d 946 (1983), *disapproved on other grounds in* Moncharsh v. Heily & Blasé, 3 Cal. 4th 1 (1992) (reasonable covenant is enforceable).

132. *Comedy Club, Inc.*, 553 F.3d 1277; Schwartz v. Rent A Wreck of Am., Inc., 468 Fed. App'x 238 (4th Cir. 2012); Dayton Time Lock Serv., Inc. v. Silent Watchman Corp., 52 Cal. App. 3d 1, 124 Cal. Rptr. 678 (1975); Kelton v. Stravinski, 138 Cal. App. 4th 941, 41 Cal. Rptr. 3d 877 (2006); Gatsinaris v. ART Corp. Sols., Inc., 2015 WL 4208595 (C.D. Cal. July 10, 2015); Great Harvest Franchising v. Artim, Bus. Franchise Guide (CCH) ¶ 11,259 (E.D. Cal. June 23, 1997) (upholding a post-term covenant that prohibited an ex-franchisee from operating a business that baked bread or rolls containing 25 percent or more whole wheat, on the basis that the restraint did not keep the franchisee from pursuing an entire trade or business).

133. Edwards v. Anderson LLP, 44 Cal. 4th 937, 946 (2008) (emphasis added).

134. SriCom, Inc. v. EbisLogic, Inc., 2012 WL 4051222 (N.D. Cal. Sept. 13, 2012); Silguero v. Creteguard, Inc., 187 Cal. App. 4th 60 (2010); Golden v. Cal. Emergency Physicians Med. Grp., 782 F.3d 1083 (9th Cir. 2015).

135. 9 Cal. 5th 1130, 470 P.3d 571 (2020).

136. Quidel Corp. v. Super. Ct., 57 Cal. App. 5th 155, 271 Cal. Rptr. 3d 237 (2020) (holding that in-term exclusive dealing provision must be judged under rule of reason); GreenLink Fin., LLC v. Freedom Debt Relief, LLC, 2022 WL 780655 (Cal. Ct. App. Mar. 15, 2022) [unpublished/non-citable] (applying rule of reason to uphold post-term covenant not to compete); Howroyd-Wright

And in an even further departure from the notion that restrictive covenants are per se invalid, some courts, both inside and outside California, have placed the burden on the party challenging the restraint to demonstrate that it is unreasonable under section 16600.[137]

b. Annotations

Determination of whether a noncompete provision is enforceable under the rule of reason is a heavily fact-based inquiry into the "circumstances, details, and logic" of the arrangement, and may require expert testimony on the definition of the relevant market and the extent of the defendant's market power. *Sandler Partners, LLC v. Masergy Communications, Inc.*, 848 F. App'x 798 (9th Cir. 2021).

In a commercial contract, "as long as a noncompetition provision does not negatively affect the public interests, is designed to protect the parties in their dealings, and does not attempt to establish a monopoly, it may be reasonable and valid." *Quidel Corp. v. Superior Court (Beckman Coulter, Inc.)*, 57 Cal. App. 5th 155, 166–68, 271 Cal. Rptr. 3d 237 (2020).

California Business and Professions Code section 16600 generally prohibits a post-termination covenant not to compete that restrains someone from engaging in a lawful profession, trade, or business. But that prohibition does not apply to a covenant that restricts someone from a small or limited part of the business or profession. Therefore, it would not likely prohibit a covenant not to compete in a franchise agreement that restricts a franchisee from operating a retail ice cream store in the same storefront or building as the former franchised store. *Baskin-Robbins, Inc. v. Patel*, 264 F. Supp. 2d 607 (N.D. Ill. 2003).

California law differentiates between "post-contract" noncompete covenants, which are generally unenforceable, and "in-term" covenants, which courts have found enforceable. As a result, the court upheld an "in-term" covenant not to compete in areas where the franchisor has franchisees. *Comedy Club, Inc. v. Improv West Associates*, 554 F.3d 1277 (9th Cir. 2009).

Exclusive dealing clause that restricted distributor from selling or leasing any similar product did not violate California Business and Professions Code section 16600. The "in-term" noncompete was effective during the life of the franchise. *Dayton Time Lock Services, Inc. v. Silent Watchman Corp.*, 52 Cal. App. 3d 1, 124 Cal. Rptr. 678 (1975).

Franchisor may employ an exclusive dealing contract to promote and protect the franchise. *Kelton v. Stravinski*, 138 Cal. App. 4th 941, 41 Cal. Rptr. 3d 877 (2006).

Interpreting California Business and Professions Code section 16600 in light of the case law yields the conclusion that an in-term exclusive dealing agreement in the context of a franchise agreement does not run afoul of section 16600,

---

Emp't Agency, Inc. v. Springboard Sols. LLC, 2021 WL 4145092 (Cal. Ct. App. Sept. 13, 2021) [unpublished/non-citable] (upholding placement fee under rule of reason standard).

137. Ho v. Marathon Patent Grp., Inc., 2022 WL 1600048 (C.D. Cal. Feb. 11, 2022); Cota v. Art Brand Studios, LLC, 2021 WL 4864588 (S.D.N.Y. Oct. 15, 2021) (claim is dismissed where plaintiff failed to plead facts demonstrating that restraint was unreasonable).

provided that it does not foreclose competition in a substantial share of the market. *Schwartz v. Rent A Wreck of America, Inc.*, 468 F. App'x 238 (4th Cir. 2012).

A provision requiring assignment of any invention disclosed within one year after termination of employment, based on a presumption that the invention was conceived during the period of employment, is void under section 16600. *Applied Materials, Inc. v. Advanced Micro-Fabrication Equip. (Shanghai) Co.*, 630 F. Supp. 2d 1084 (N.D. Cal. 2009).

2. Damages

a. Commentary

(i) Termination or Nonrenewal

The original version of the CFRA (effective as to franchises entered and last amended on or before December 31, 2015) did not expressly provide for damages. The only statutory remedy for a termination or nonrenewal of a franchise in violation of the CFRA was a requirement that the franchisor repurchase the franchisee's "resalable current inventory meeting the franchisor's present standards" at the lesser of either the current fair wholesale market value or the price paid by the franchisee.[138] The franchisor was given the right to offset any amount owed under the franchise agreement or any ancillary agreement against the purchase price.[139]

The CFRA does provide that nothing contained in the law "shall abrogate the right of a franchise to sue under any other law."[140] Some courts opined that repurchase of inventory was the exclusive remedy for a wrongful nonrenewal under the original version of the CFRA.[141] Others disagreed, reasoning that such an interpretation would render section 20037 a nullity.[142]

Revisions to the CFRA in 2015 (effective for franchises entered and last amended on or after January 1, 2016, and to franchises of indefinite duration terminable without cause) added more serious consequences for both lawful and unlawful terminations or failures to renew.

First, for a *lawful* termination or nonrenewal of a franchise agreement, the franchisor must purchase from the franchisee (at the price paid less depreciation) substantially all inventory, supplies, equipment, fixtures, and furnishings purchased or paid for under the terms of the franchise agreement or related agreements.[143] However, this provision does not apply

---

138. CAL. BUS. & PROF. CODE § 20035 (superseded).
139. CAL. BUS. & PROF. CODE § 20036.
140. *Id.* § 20037.
141. Boat & Motor Mart v. Sea Ray Boats, Inc., 825 F.2d 1285 (9th Cir. 1987); Mahroom v. Best W. Int'l, Inc., 2009 WL 2216578 (N.D. Cal. July 22, 2009); Andersen v. Griswold Int'l, LLC, 2014 WL 12694138 (N.D. Cal. Dec. 16, 2014); Dale Carnegie & Assocs. v. King, 31 F. Supp. 2d 358 (S.D.N.Y. 1999).
142. JRS Prods., Inc. v. Matsushita Elec. Corp. of Am., 115 Cal. App. 4th 168, 8 Cal. Rptr. 3d 840 (2004) (CFRA § 20037 allows franchisee to seek any common law or statutory remedy for wrongful termination of the franchise, including a breach of contract action).
143. CAL. BUS. & PROF. CODE § 20022(a).

- To personalized items, items not reasonably required to operate the franchised business, or to items for which the franchisee cannot convey good title;
- If the franchisee declines a bona fide renewal offer;
- If the franchisee is allowed to retain control of the principal place of the franchised business;
- To a termination or nonrenewal due to a publicly announced and non-discriminatory decision by the franchisor to completely withdraw from all franchise activity in the market; or
- If the parties mutually agree to terminate.[144]

Revised section 20022 also gave the franchisor the right to offset amounts owed to it against any amounts due under this provision.[145]

For a termination or nonrenewal that is *unlawful* under the CFRA, the franchisee is entitled to receive the fair market value of the franchised business and any other damages caused by the franchisor's CFRA violation.[146] The franchisor is allowed to offset against this payment any amounts previously paid to the franchisee pursuant to CFRA section 20022 as well as any amounts that the franchisee owes to the franchisor.[147] The revised section 20035 also authorizes a court to grant preliminary and permanent injunctions for a violation or threatened violation of the CFRA.[148]

In 2022, section 20022 was revised to specify that the offset is conditioned on either the franchisee's agreement as to the amount owed or on a final adjudication of the amount owed.[149]

(ii) CFRA Violations Other than Termination or Nonrenewal

The remedies available for violations of CFRA provisions other than termination and nonrenewal are found in the California Civil Code (sections 3274 through 3424), which contains comprehensive remedies available in California. Section 3274 of that Code provides:

As a general rule, compensation is the relief or remedy provided by the law of this State for the violation of private rights, and the means of securing their observance; and specific and preventive relief may be given in no other cases than those specified in this Part of the Civil Code.[150]

In *Spreckels v. Hawaiian Commercial & Sugar Co.*,[151] the California Supreme Court held that this part of the Civil Code (that is, sections 3274 through 3424) is "intended as a comprehensive statement of the entire law upon the subject [of remedies]."

---

144. *Id.* § 20022(b)–(f).
145. *Id.* § 20022(h).
146. *Id.* § 20035(a).
147. *Id.* § 20036.
148. *Id.* § 20035(b).
149. *Id.* § 20022(h).
150. Cal. Civ. Code § 3274.
151. 117 Cal. 377 (1897).

The Civil Code distinguishes two broad types of injuries giving rise to damages: breach of contract[152] and everything else.[153] The "everything else" category includes tort claims and damages arising out of statutory violations. The main difference is that damages for breach of contract are limited to the damages that could have been anticipated at the time of contracting. There is no such limitation on damages from noncontractual causes.

Damages are the basic civil remedy prescribed for violation of the CFIL. Although the CFIL does not define damages, the California Civil Code defines damages as follows: "Every person who suffers detriment from the unlawful act or omission of another, may recover from the person in fault a compensation therefor in money, which is called damages."[154]

For a franchise entered into before January 1, 2023, a claim for damages for breach of the CFRA is governed by Civil Code section 3333, which contemplates an award of an amount necessary to "compensate for all the detriment proximately caused [by the violation], whether it could have been anticipated or not."

(iii) Lost Future Royalties

In the seminal case of *Postal Instant Press, Inc. v Sealy*,[155] a franchisor terminated a franchisee for failing to pay royalties and then sued for past-due royalties and—under a provision entitling the franchisor to the "benefit of its bargain"—for anticipated royalties (less expenses) for the remainder of the franchise term. Reversing the trial court, the California Court of Appeal held that a franchisor is not entitled to recover lost future royalties where the proximate cause of the loss was the franchisor's own decision to terminate the franchisee. The *Sealy* court acknowledged that the nature and extent of the breach was critical; a franchisee's "total" breach—such as thorough abandonment—could justify the award of lost future royalties.[156] As a "second independent and sufficient rationale" for its decision, the *Sealy* court also ruled that, under the facts of the case, award of lost future royalties would result in "unreasonable, unconscionable, or grossly oppressive" in violation of California Civil Code section 3359.[157]

The reasoning in *Sealy* has been rejected by most (but not all[158]) courts outside of California, and even California-based courts have distinguished it on various grounds, including

- *Sealy* does not prohibit parties from agreeing to a specific, reasonable liquidated damages provision.[159]

---

152. Addressed in CAL. CIV. CODE §§ 3300–3322.
153. *Id.* §§ 3333–3343.7.
154. *Id.* § 3281.
155. 43 Cal. App. 4th 1704, 51 Cal. Rptr. 2d 365 (1996).
156. *Id.* at 1711–13.
157. *Id.* at 1713–18 (discussing the "gross bargaining disparity" between franchisors and franchisees).
158. *See* I Can't Believe It's Yogurt v. Gunn, 1997 WL 599391 (D. Colo Apr. 15, 1997); Burger King Corp. v. Hinton, Inc., 203 F. Supp. 2d 1357 (S.D. Fla. 2002); Kissinger, Inc. v. Singh, 204 F. Supp. 2d 944 (W.D. Mich. 2003).
159. Radisson Hotels Int'l, Inc. v. Majestic Towers, Inc., 488 F. Supp. 2d 953 (C.D. Cal. 2007).

- *Sealy* does not prevent a franchisor from recovering lost future royalties where the franchisee's breach constituted a total failure to perform.
- *Sealy* may not bar lost future royalties where the franchisee terminated contract.[160]
- Summary judgment is inappropriate where a reasonable jury could find that plaintiff's lost profits and reputational harm were a "natural and direct" consequence of defendants' manufacture and sale of contaminated pet food.[161]

(iv) Liquidated Damages

Liquidated damages in California are governed by California Civil Code section 1671. Under that provision, liquidated damages in a commercial contract are presumed to be reasonable, and the burden is on the party seeking to avoid enforcement of the liquidated damages provision to prove that the amount was unreasonable at the time the contract was made or that the provision is both procedurally and substantively unconscionable.[162] A liquidated damages provision may be invalidated as a penalty "if it bears no reasonable relationship to the range of actual damages that the parties could have anticipated would flow from the breach."[163]

An agreement to waive a challenge to the validity of a liquidated damages provision is unenforceable as against public policy.[164] In addition, parties may not circumvent the public policy reflected in the statute by characterizing a liquidated damages provision as something else.[165]

b. Annotations

The measure of damages for breach of a statute (such as the CFRA) is broader than the measure of damages for breach of contract. In particular, damages for breach of contract are limited to those reasonably anticipated by the parties at

---

160. It's Just Lunch Franchise, LLC v. BLFA Enters., LLC, 2003 WL 21735005 (S.D. Cal. July 21, 2003).

161. Party Animal Inc. v. Evanger's Dog & Cat Food Co., Inc., 2020 WL 2477688 (C.D. Cal. Mar. 11, 2020).

162. *See* H.S. Perlin Co. v. Morse Signal Devices, 209 Cal. App. 3d 1289, 258 Cal. Rptr. 1 (1989) (liquidated damages provision in commercial contract that limits alarm company's liability to $250 is not objectively unreasonable or unconscionable); Mahroom v. Best W. Int'l, Inc., 2010 WL 11575097 (N.D. Cal. Mar. 29, 2010) (finding liquidated damages provision unconscionable and therefore unenforceable in a contract of adhesion that lacked an analogous provision protecting the franchisee in the event of wrongful termination). *See also* CAL. CIV. CODE § 1670.5 (specifying procedures upon finding that a contractual provision is unconscionable).

163. 911 Restoration Franchise, Inc. v. Blakeney, 2015 WL 12698290 (C.D. Cal. Sept. 22, 2015) (declining to enforce liquidated damages provision, citing gross disparity between liquidated damages amount and actual damages incurred); Tesoro Ref. & Mktg. Co. LLC v. S&S Fuel, Inc., 2020 WL 3203057 (C.D. Cal. Mar. 30, 2020) (enforcing liquidated damages provision based on an agreed-upon price multiplied by the contractual minimum gallons of fuel for the remainder of the term).

164. Cook v. King Manor & Convalescent Hosp., 40 Cal. App. 3d 782 (1974).

165. 911 Restoration Franchise, Inc., 2015 WL 12698290.

the time of contracting, but there is no such limit on damages for violations of a statute. *Overgaard v. Johnson*, 68 Cal. App. 3d 821, 137 Cal. Rptr. 412 (1977).

The term "damages" in Civil Code section 3281 "is intended to represent the plain and ordinary meaning of the word 'damages.'" *AIU Insurance Co. v. Superior Court (FMC Corp.)*, 51 Cal. 3d 807, 825, 799 P.2d 1253 (1990).

In a case involving wrongful termination of a master franchise (subfranchisor) agreement, the court held that the proper measure of damages consisted of anticipated (net) royalties from the existing location plus reimbursement of excess expenses from attempts to develop additional sites. It was not proper to award damages measured by initial franchise fees and anticipated royalties for proposed locations that had not yet opened. *Parlour Enterprises, Inc. v. The Kirin Group, Inc.*, 152 Cal. App. 4th 281, 61 Cal. Rptr. 3d 243 (2007).

A franchisor was entitled to both liquidated damages for breach of franchise agreement as well as damages for violation of the Lanham Act where franchisee continued to use trademarks after termination of franchise agreement. *Villager Franchise Systems, Inc. v. Dhami, Dhami & Virk*, No. CV-F- 04-6393, 2006 WL 224425 (E.D. Cal. Jan. 26, 2006).

A franchisor that wrongfully terminates a franchise may be liable to the franchisee for breach of contract, not for the tort of intentional interference with prospective business advantage. *JRS Products, Inc. v. Matsushita Electric Corp. of America*, 115 Cal. App. 4th 168, 8 Cal. Rptr. 3d 840 (2004).

Plaintiff must provide some factual allegations to support an inference that it is a franchise within the meaning of the CFRA to bring a claim for wrongful termination under CFRA. Simply alleging that a plaintiff is a franchise within the meaning of the CFRA does not suffice. *Boon Rawd Trading International Co. v. Paleewong Trading Co.*, 688 F. Supp. 2d 940 (N.D. Cal. 2010).

3. Rescission

a. Commentary

The CFRA contains no provision regarding rescission of a franchise agreement. Because the CFRA expressly acknowledges the right of a franchisee to sue under any other law,[166] however, a franchisee may seek rescission under general equitable principles. The statute of limitations for such an action is four years.[167]

The CFIL does authorize rescission as a remedy for willful violation of certain provisions of the statute, including those relating to registration and misrepresentation.[168]

b. Annotations

Under section 31300 of the CFIL, the term "willful" refers to an act that is committed knowingly and intentionally; a plaintiff need not prove that the defendant knew that the act was unlawful or was reckless as to the possibility. *Dollar Systems, Inc. v. Avcar Leasing Systems, Inc.*, 890 F.2d 165 (9th Cir. 1989).

---

166. Cal. Bus. & Prof. Code § 20037.
167. Cal. Civ. Proc. Code § 337(c).
168. Cal. Corp. Code § 31300.

4. Injunctive Relief

a. Commentary

For franchises entered into after January 1, 2016, the CFRA explicitly provides for preliminary and permanent injunctive relief to remedy a violation or threatened violation of the CFRA.[169] For franchises entered into before 2016, equitable relief is available in accordance with Civil Code sections 3420–3424 and general equitable principles.

The federal court, in *Prudence Corp. v Shred-It America, Inc.*,[170] addressed the availability of equitable relief for violation of (the original version of) the CFRA. In that case, the franchisee tried to renew its franchise agreement, and the franchisor delayed (for more than a year) any attempt to renew without any legitimate excuse. Finding that the franchisor had breached the contract by failing to follow renewal procedures, the trial court ordered (and the Ninth Circuit affirmed) that the franchisor was deemed to have offered renewal on the terms of the original agreement, and that the franchisee was deemed to have accepted that offer of renewal.

b. Annotations

A violation of CFRA, which prohibits termination of franchise agreements without good cause, may permit injunctive relief as a remedy. *Mahroom v. Best Western International, Inc.*, No. C 07-2351, 2009 WL 248262 (N.D. Cal. Feb. 2, 2009).

5. Control Person Liability

a. Commentary

The CFRA contains no provision extending liability to individual directors or officers of a franchisor. The CFIL, however, does extend liability for certain CFIL violations to "[e]very person who directly or indirectly controls" the franchisor, as well as "every person occupying a similar status or performing similar functions, [and] every employee of a person so liable who materially aids in the act or transaction constituting the violation" unless the person "had no knowledge of or reasonable grounds to believe in the existence of the facts by reason of which the liability is alleged to exist."[171]

In an enforcement proceeding brought in superior court under section 31400 of the CFIL, "the court may prohibit, conditionally or unconditionally, and permanently or for such period of time as it shall determine, any person who violated Section 31200, 31201, or 31202"—all relating to "fraudulent practices"—"from acting as an officer or director of any franchisor if the person's conduct demonstrates unfitness to serve as an officer or director of the franchisor."[172]

---

169. CAL. BUS. & PROF. CODE § 20035(b).
170. Bus. Franchise Guide (CCH) ¶ 14,334 (C.D. Cal. Sept. 30, 2008), *aff'd*, 365 Fed. App'x 859 (9th Cir. 2010).
171. CAL. CORP. CODE § 31302.
172. *Id.* § 31400.1.

b. Annotations

Officers and directors who ratified an employee's unlawful sale of franchises are individually liable under this section. *Spahn v. Guild Industries Corp.*, 94 Cal. App. 3d 143, 156 Cal. Rptr. 375 (1979).

Ignorance of the law is no defense to liability under section 31302. *Dollar Systems, Inc. v. Avcar Leasing Systems, Inc.*, 890 F.2d 165 (9th Cir. 1989).

Liability under section 31302 is joint and several. *Dollar Systems, Inc. v. Avcar Leasing Systems, Inc.*, 890 F.2d 165 (9th Cir. 1989).

6. Attorneys' Fees

a. Commentary

California follows the "American Rule," which provides each party involved in litigation is responsible for paying his own attorneys' fees and costs unless provided otherwise by statute or contract.[173] However, California's Civil Code section 1717 transforms any unilateral attorneys' fee provision into a reciprocal one. When the contract provides for attorney fees to either a particular party or the prevailing party, the prevailing party "on the contract" is entitled to recover reasonable attorney fees regardless of whether that party was the party specified in the contract.

The CFRA does not grant a party a statutory right to attorneys' fees for prevailing on a claim. The CFIL provides a narrow statutory ground for obtaining attorneys' fees where a claim for violation of section 31220 (right of free association) is brought.[174] Where an administrative action is brought against a franchisor, the administrative law judge may also grant the commissioner reasonable attorneys' fees.[175]

California also authorizes the award of attorneys' fees, under the "private attorney general doctrine," to a successful party in an action that results in the "enforcement of an important right affecting the public interest if: (a) a significant benefit . . . has been conferred on the general public or a large class of persons, (b) the necessity and financial burden of private enforcement, or of enforcement by one public entity against another public entity, are such as to make the award appropriate, and (c) such fees should not in the interest of justice be paid out of the recovery, if any."[176]

b. Annotations

Where franchisor attempted to fabricate the disclosure date, the district court did not abuse its discretion by assessing attorneys' fees on the ground that the party acted in bad faith, vexatiously, wantonly, or for oppressive reasons. *Dollar Systems, Inc. v. Avcar Leasing Systems, Inc.*, 890 F.2d 165 (9th Cir. 1989).

A court's ruling that a service station franchisor's transfer policy violated the California Vehicle Code resulted in a significant benefit to a large class of

---

173. Cal. Civ. Proc. Code § 1033.5(a)(10).
174. Cal. Corp. Code § 31302.5.
175. *Id.* § 31408.
176. Cal. Civ. Proc. Code § 1021.5.

current and future franchisees; accordingly, the trial court should have awarded attorneys' fees to the plaintiff under the private attorneys general doctrine. *California Service Station & Automotive Repair Association v. Union Oil Co. of California*, 286 Cal. Rptr. 723 (Cal. App. 1991) [unpublished/not citable].

Trial court award of attorneys' fees under the private attorneys general doctrine is subject to review for abuse of discretion. *Robinson v. U-Haul Co. of California*, 4 Cal. App. 5th 304, 209 Cal. Rptr. 3d 81 (2016).

7. Limitations on Damage Waivers

a. Commentary

Neither the CFRA nor the CFIL specifically prohibit franchisees from waiving certain types of damages. California Civil Code section 1668, however, prohibits a person from contracting away liability for fraud or deceit based on intentional misrepresentation.[177]

Franchisees seeking to avoid a contractual damages waiver typically assert that the provision is unconscionable. Limitations on a party's statutory rights or a lack of mutuality are typically cited as grounds for substantive unconscionability.[178] Waivers of certain damages such as punitive damages have been held not to be substantively unconscionable.[179]

b. Annotations

Punitive damages waiver is substantively unconscionable as it lacks mutuality; a franchisor is more likely to be defending against punitive damages than seeking them. *IJL Dominicana S.A. v. It's Just Lunch International, LLC*, No. CV 08-5417, 2009 WL 305187 (C.D. Cal. Feb. 6, 2009).

8. State or Federal Emergency

a. Commentary

In 2022, the legislature added a provision to the CFRA prohibiting a franchisor from modifying a franchise agreement, or requiring a general release, in exchange for any assistance related to a declared state or federal emergency.[180]

b. Annotations

There is no case law addressing this issue.

---

177. CAL. CIV. CODE § 1668; Negrel v. Drive N Style Franchisor SPV LLC, 2018 WL 6136151 (C.D. Cal. Aug. 27, 2018) (finding exculpatory provision unenforceable under section 1668 as to claims sounding in fraud).

178. Bencharsky v. Cottman Transmission Sys., LLC, 625 F. Supp. 2d 872 (N.D. Cal. 2008); Johnston v. Fairway Divorce Franchising, Inc., 2012 WL 12891392 (C.D. Cal. July 27, 2012).

179. Chin v. Advanced Fresh Concepts Franchise Corp., 194 Cal. App. 4th 704, 712, 123 Cal. Rptr. 3d 547, 555 (2011); Monster Energy Co. v. Olympic Eagle Dist. & King Beverage, Inc., 2015 WL 12781213 (C.D. Cal. Sept. 29, 2015).

180. CAL. BUS. & PROF. CODE § 20044.

9. Administrative Action

a. Commentary

There is no provision for administrative enforcement of the CFRA. The CFIL, by contrast, contains extensive enforcement provisions in favor of the Department of Financial Protection and Innovation.[181]

b. Annotations

There is no case law addressing this issue.

H. Dispute Resolution

1. Limitations on Franchisors' Ability to Restrict Venue

a. Commentary

Section 20040.5 of the CFRA renders void any provision that purports to restrict venue to a forum outside of California for "any claim arising under or relating to a franchise agreement" involving a California franchisee. This provision "expresses a strong public policy of the State of California to protect California franchisees from the expense, inconvenience, and possible prejudice of litigating in a non-California venue."[182]

This provision is preempted by the Federal Arbitration Act for franchise agreements that require arbitration of such claims.[183] Accordingly, franchisors that wish to ensure a non-California venue for a franchise agreement governed by the CFRA should include an enforceable arbitration provision in their franchise agreements.

Mandatory out-of-state mediation has been deemed outside the scope of this provision because it does not constitute a "claim." In *Delamater v. Anytime Fitness, Inc.*,[184] the court concluded that a forum selection clause that required mediation outside of California as a condition precedent to filing a lawsuit was not void under CFRA section 20040.5.[185] The court concluded that section 20040.5 was limited to forum selection clauses applicable to claims for relief or demands for a legal remedy, and a mediation clause did not contemplate submission of a "claim."[186]

(i) Effect of Atlantic Marine

In 2013, the U.S. Supreme Court ruled that "a valid forum-selection clause [should be] given controlling weight in all but the most exceptional cases."[187]

---

181. *See* CAL. CORP. CODE §§ 31400–31408.
182. Jones v. GNC Franchising, Inc., 211 F.3d 495, 498 (9th Cir. 2000).
183. Bradley v. Harris Rsch., Inc., 275 F.3d 884 (9th Cir. 2001). *See* subsection II.H.3, in this chapter, relating to arbitration.
184. 722 F. Supp. 2d 1168 (E.D. Cal. 2010).
185. *Id.*
186. *Id.* at 1178.
187. Atlantic Marine Constr. Co., Inc. v. U.S. Dist. Ct., 571 U.S. 49, 63 (2014).

Most (but not all) courts have held that section 20040.5 renders a forum-selection clause not "valid," making it unenforceable despite *Atlantic Marine*.[188]

Other courts have treated *Atlantic Marine* as binding regardless of whether the forum-selection clause is "valid" as a matter of substantive state law;[189] or requiring that the party seeking to enforce section 20040.5 demonstrate that state public policy protecting franchisees outweighs the federal policy favoring enforcement of forum-selection provisions.[190]

(ii) "Meeting of the Minds" Angle

Some litigants have successfully argued that an out-of-state forum selection clause should not be enforced because there was no "meeting of the minds" on the subject. This argument is typically based on California regulations mandating that franchisors disclose, in their Franchise Disclosure Documents, that prospective franchisees should consult an attorney to determine "the applicability of California and federal law . . . to any provisions of a franchise agreement restricting venue to a forum outside of the State of California."[191] In *Laxmi Investments v. Golf USA*,[192] the court held that the disclosure created sufficient doubt in the mind of the franchisee that an out-of-state forum would apply that there was no meeting of the minds.

In *Roberts v. Synergistic International, LLC*, an addendum to the franchise agreement stated that if the parties could not agree on a location for the arbitration, it would take place in Texas, but then stated, "This provision may not be enforceable under California law."[193] Applying California law, the district court agreed there was no meeting of the minds as to the venue provision, but the remainder of the arbitration provision was enforceable, and compelled arbitration, subject to the parties' meet and confer about the proper location for the arbitration.

b. Annotations

Section 20040.5 "expresses a strong public policy of the State of California to protect California franchisees from the expense, inconvenience, and possible prejudice of litigating in a non-California venue." *Jones v. GNC Franchising, Inc.*, 211 F.3d 495, 498 (9th Cir. 2000).

Where franchise agreement includes a forum selection provision, franchisor bears a heavy burden of showing that enforcement of the provision will not deprive a California franchisee of its rights under the CFRA. *Wimsatt v. Beverly Hills Weight Loss Clinics International, Inc.*, 32 Cal. App. 4th 1511, 38 Cal. Rptr. 2d 612 (Cal. App. 1995).

Even though the dispute was related to a financing agreement, rather than a franchise agreement, the state policy of protecting franchisees that is embodied

---

188. Weber v. Saladworks, LLC, 2014 WL 12581768 (C.D. Cal. Jan. 27, 2014); Frango Grille USA, Inc. v. Pepe's Franchising Ltd., 2014 WL 7892164 (C.D. Cal. July 21, 2014).
189. Postnet Int'l Franchise Corp. v. Wu, 521 F. Supp. 3d 1087 (D. Colo. 2021).
190. Pinnacle Foods of Cal., LLC v. Popeyes Louisiana Kitchen, Inc., 2021 WL 3557744 (C.D. Cal. Apr. 21, 2021). Mr. Carrillo was involved in this matter.
191. CAL. CODE REGS. tit. 10, § 310.114.1(c)(5)(B)(iv).
192. 193 F.3d 1095 (9th Cir. 1999).
193. 676 F. Supp. 2d 934, 948 (E.D. Cal. 2009).

by section 20040.5 is broad enough to be applicable to agreements that are attendant to the franchise agreement, such as addenda or other documents that amend the terms of the franchise agreement. *T-Bird Nevada LLC v. Outback Steakhouse, Inc.*, No. B219861, 2010 WL 1951145 (Cal. App. May 17, 2010) [unpublished/not citable].

Section 20040.5 only applies to claims made under an existing franchise agreement. *Pinnacle Foods of California, LLC v. Popeyes Louisiana Kitchen, Inc.*, No. 2:21-cv-02050, 2021 WL 3557744 (C.D. Cal. Apr. 21, 2021).[194]

Where an arbitration provision is deemed to be invalid and unenforceable because it contains an unlawful pre-dispute waiver of claims under the Private Attorneys General Act (PAGA),[195] section 20040.5 is not preempted by the Federal Arbitration Act. *Fleming v. Matco Tools Corp.*, 384 F. Supp. 3d 1124 (N.D. Cal. 2019).

2. Limitations Period

a. Commentary

The CFRA does not contain its own statute of limitations. The general limitations period for an action on a statute is three years.[196]

For alleged violations of the CFIL, sections 31303 and 31304 contain statutes of repose requiring private actions to enforce liability under certain provisions of the CFIL—including those requiring registration and disclosure and prohibiting certain misrepresentations—to be brought within four years or two years, at the latest, depending on the statutory violation.[197] Both statutes shorten this period to the lesser of one year from the discovery of facts constituting the violation or 90 days from delivery of a written notice, approved by the Department, disclosing the violation.

In addition, section 31302.5 requires that any claims to enforce liability created under section 31220 (relating to associational rights) must be brought before the expiration of two years after the violation or the expiration of one year after the discovery of the facts constituting the violation, whichever occurs first.[198]

b. Annotations

Sections 31303 and 31304 are statutes of repose; there is no equitable tolling due to delayed discovery of the facts constituting the violation. *People ex rel. Department of Corporations v. SpeeDee Oil Change Systems, Inc.*, 95 Cal. App. 4th 709, 116 Cal. Rptr. 2d 497 (2002).

At the time a franchisee signs the franchise agreement, it is "almost invariably" aware of the facts constituting a violation of CFIL section 31119, which requires a franchisor to provide a franchise disclosure document. *JB Brothers,*

---

194. Mr. Carrillo was involved in this matter.
195. CAL. LAB. CODE §§ 2698, *et seq.*
196. CAL. CIV. PROC. CODE § 338.
197. CAL. CORP. CODE §§ 31303, 31304.
198. *Id.* § 31302.5.

Inc. v. Poke Bar GA Johns Creek I, LLC, No. 2:21-cv-1405, 2022 WL 3012822 (C.D. Cal. June 6, 2022).

3. Arbitration

a. Commentary

The CFRA expressly recognizes that a franchisor and a franchisee may agree to submit claims arising under the CFRA to binding arbitration, as long as the standards applied to the arbitration are "not less than" the CFRA's requirements and the arbitrator is "chosen from a list of impartial arbitrators supplied by the American Arbitration Association or other impartial person."[199]

Arbitration clauses may be challenged under generally applicable contract defenses, such as fraud, duress, or unconscionability. California courts have long recognized that franchise agreements have characteristics of contracts of adhesion and thus may be procedurally unconscionable.[200] Courts have pointed to the "vastly superior bargaining strength" of the franchisor in finding procedural unconscionability.[201] On the other hand, at least one court has noted that since franchising requires detailed disclosures and a waiting period there is no procedural unconscionability.[202]

A finding of unconscionability requires both procedural and substantive unconscionability. Limitations on a party's statutory rights or a lack of mutuality are typically cited as grounds for substantive unconscionability.[203] California Civil Code section 1670.5(a) gives "a trial court some discretion as to whether to sever or to restrict the unconscionable provision or whether to refuse to enforce the entire agreement."[204] Where the major part of the arbitration provision was substantively unconscionable and imposed on the franchisee without any opportunity to negotiate the provision, the unconscionability "permeated" the arbitration provision and warranted voiding the entire provision rather than merely severing the offending unconscionable provisions.[205]

The Ninth Circuit has held that the Federal Arbitration Act preempts section 20040.5 of the CFRA, to the extent that the CFRA voids the venue selection clause of a franchise agreement which requires a California franchisee to arbitrate disputes with the franchisor in a venue outside of California.[206] However, if the arbitration provision contains a pre-dispute waiver of claims under the California Private Attorneys General Act (PAGA),[207] it is unlawful under

---

199. CAL. BUS. & PROF. CODE § 20040.

200. Bridge Fund Cap. Corp. v. Fastbucks Franchise Corp., 622 F.3d 996, 1004 (9th Cir. 2010); Roberts v. Synergistic Int'l, LLC, 676 F. Supp. 2d 934, 952–53 (E.D. Cal. 2009).

201. Nagrampa v. MailCoups, Inc., 469 F.3d 1257, 1281 (9th Cir. 2006).

202. Kairy v. Supershuttle Int'l, Inc., 2012 WL 4343220, at *7 (N.D. Cal. Sept. 20, 2012).

203. Bencharsky v. Cottman Transmission Sys., LLC, 625 F. Supp. 2d 872 (N.D. Cal. 2008); Johnston v. Fairway Divorce Franchising, Inc., 2012 WL 12891392 (C.D. Cal. July 27, 2012).

204. Armendariz v. Found. Health Psychcare Servs., Inc., 24 Cal. 4th 83 (2000).

205. Bridge Fund Cap. Corp. v. Fastbucks Franchise Corp., 622 F.3d 996 (9th Cir. 2010).

206. Bradley v. Harris Rsch., Inc., 275 F.3d 884 (9th Cir. 2001), *abrogated in part on other grounds by* Sakkab v. Luxottica Retail N. Am., Inc., 803 F.3d 425 (9th Cir. 2015).

207. CAL. LAB. CODE §§ 2698, *et seq.*

California law and may render the entire arbitration provision unenforceable, depending on the severability provision. The PAGA authorizes an "aggrieved employee" to sue under the state's labor laws on their own behalf and on behalf of other current or former employees.[208] In *Fleming v. Matco Tools Corp.*, 384 F. Supp. 3d 1124 (N.D. Cal. 2019), the plaintiff franchisee asserted that it was an employee but had been improperly classified as an independent contractor. Because of an unlawful pre-dispute PAGA waiver and unusual severability language in the distribution agreement, the entire arbitration provision (including the Ohio forum selection provision) was deemed invalid, enabling the franchisee to avoid both arbitration and transfer.

b. Annotations

California Corporations Code section 31512, which requires judicial consideration of claims brought under the CFIL and precluding enforceability of arbitration agreement, conflicts with section 2 of Federal Arbitration Act, violates the supremacy clause, and is therefore invalid. *Southland Corp. v. Keating*, 465 U.S. 1 (1984).

Where an offering circular stated that a forum selection provision "may not be enforceable under California law" a contractual provision for arbitration in Oklahoma was not enforced because there was no clear meeting of the minds between the parties. *Laxmi Investments, LLC v. Golf U.S.A.*, 193 F.3d 1095, Business Franchise Guide (CCH) ¶ 11,706 (9th Cir. 1999).

"To defeat an arbitration clause, the litigant must show both procedural and substantive unconscionability, although 'the more substantively oppressive the contract term, the less evidence of procedural unconscionability is required to conclude that the term is unenforceable, and vice versa.'" *Bridge Fund Capital Corp. v. Fastbucks Franchise Corp.*, 622 F.3d 996, 1004 (9th Cir. 2010).

A mandatory waiver of nonwaivable statutory rights granted under the CFIL "are the sort of one-sided and overly-harsh terms that render an arbitration provision substantively unconscionable." *Bridge Fund Capital Corp. v. Fastbucks Franchise Corp.*, 622 F.3d 996, 1004–05 (9th Cir. 2010) (citation omitted). Class action waivers are usually considered substantively unconscionable. Terms granting the franchisor, but not the franchisee, the right to seek injunctive relief are substantively unconscionable. If the place and manner restriction of the forum selection provision is unduly oppressive or has the effect of shielding the stronger party from liability, the forum selection clause is unconscionable.[209]

In *Bencharsky v. Cottman Transmission Systems, LLC*, 625 F. Supp. 2d 872, 881 (N.D. Cal. 2008), the court found that the arbitration provision in a franchise agreement was procedurally unconscionable as a contract of adhesion. The court also found the agreement substantively unconscionable because it (1) lacked mutuality (the franchisee was forced to arbitrate, but the franchisor reserved for itself the ability to seek judicial or arbitral remedies), (2) limited the franchisee's statutory rights (barred punitive damages and imposed a one-year

---

208. *Id.* § 2699(a).
209. *Id.*

statute of limitations), and (3) limited the arbitrator's power to alter or modify any provision. *Id.* at 882.

Unlike the Ninth Circuit in *Bridge Fund Capital*, the district court in *Bencharsky* refused to invalidate the entire arbitration provision because the unconscionable provisions could be severed. The "central purpose" of the franchise agreement in *Bencharsky* was to allow the plaintiff to open franchises, which was not illegal. The illegal and unconscionable provisions can be severed without harming the central purpose of the franchise.

In *Roberts v. Synergistic International, LLC*, 676 F. Supp. 2d 934 (E.D. Cal. 2009), the court came to the opposite conclusion regarding enforcement of the arbitration clause. The franchisee sued the franchisor for breach of contract but refused to arbitrate his claim pursuant to the arbitration provision in the franchise agreement because, it argued, that provision was unconscionable. The district court agreed that the arbitration provision was procedurally unconscionable because it is a contract of adhesion. But the district court concluded the franchisee did not establish that the arbitration provision was substantially unconscionable. Although the franchisee stated that many provisions of the franchise agreement are "unconscionably one-sided," no authority was cited to support the broad assertion. *Id.* at 952–53.

Arbitration provision in a franchise agreement is procedurally unconscionable where the agreement, a standardized contract, was given on a "take-it-or-leave-it" basis and was not the product of any real negotiation. The court also noted that franchise agreements have some characteristics of contracts of adhesion because of the "vastly superior bargaining strength" of the franchisor. Franchisor's forum selection clause and arbitration carve-out for provisional remedies and injunctive relief were substantively unconscionable. *Nagrampa v. MailCoups, Inc.*, 469 F.3d 1257 (9th Cir. 2006).

A provision in an adhesive franchise agreement limiting recovery to actual compensatory damages while barring noneconomic and punitive damages was not unconscionable where the damages limitation was facially mutual and no damages were available under the statutes cited in franchisee's complaint against franchisor. *Chin v. Advanced Fresh Concepts Franchise Corp.*, 194 Cal. App. 4th 704, 123 Cal. Rptr. 3d 547 (2011).

Arbitration provision which waived either party's right to exemplary or punitive damages did not shock the conscience and thus was not substantively unconscionable. *Monster Energy Co. v. Olympic Eagle Distribution & King Beverage, Inc.*, No. EDCV1500819, 2015 WL 12781213 (C.D. Cal. Sept. 29, 2015).

Arbitration clause in a franchise agreement was procedurally unconscionable where there was no meaningful negotiation or discussion of terms and clause appeared on pages 44–47 of a 66-page agreement. Clause was substantively unconscionable as it allowed franchisor to bring almost any claim it wanted in court but prohibited franchisee from litigating any claim in court. *Johnston v. Fairway Divorce Franchising, Inc.*, No. EDCV1200952, 2012 WL 12891392 (C.D. Cal. July 27, 2012).

The court found that there was not a significant amount of procedural unconscionability, as franchise agreements are subject to a considerable amount of regulation including requiring detailed disclosures to prospective franchisees and providing a waiting period between provision of the disclosure document and the sale of the franchise. *Kairy v. Supershuttle International, Inc.*, No. C 08-02993, 2012 WL 4343220 (N.D. Cal. Sept. 20, 2012).

A franchise agreement is not unconscionable merely because the franchisor has superior bargaining power. Further, a franchisor has no obligation to highlight the arbitration clause of its contract or to specifically call that clause to the franchisee's attention. *Han v. Synergy Homecare Franchising, LLC*, No. 16-CV-03759, 2017 WL 446881 (N.D. Cal. Feb. 2, 2017).

The incorporation of AAA rules constitutes clear and unmistakable evidence that the contracting parties agreed to arbitrate. *Capelli Enterprises, Inc. v. Fantastic Sams Salons Corp.*, No. 5:16-CV-03401, 2016 WL 4492588 (N.D. Cal. Aug. 26, 2016).

State court exceeded its jurisdiction by lifting a stay of litigation pending arbitration merely because franchisees maintained that they could not afford the costs associated with the arbitration ordered by a court in a sister state. *MKJA, Inc. v. 123 Fit Franchising, LLC*, 191 Cal. App. 4th 643, 660, 119 Cal. Rptr. 3d 634 (2011).

Where a claimant lacked the resources to pay for arbitration and the respondent was unwilling to front the fees, claimant could pursue case in court regardless of arbitration clause. *Tillman v. Tillman*, 825 F.3d 1069 (9th Cir. 2016).

Although trademark issues were carved out of arbitration clause, the parties could choose to arbitrate those issues, and arbitrator did not exceed his authority by deciding them. *Jay Bharat Developers, Inc. v. Minidis*, No. B219498, 2011 WL 3918977 (Cal. App. Sept. 7, 2011) [unpublished/not citable].

Class arbitration waiver is neither unconscionable nor against public policy under California law. *Gold v. Melt, Inc.*, No. B210452, 2010 WL 1509795 (Cal. App. Apr. 16, 2010) [unpublished/not citable].

4. Jury Trial Waiver

a. Commentary

California has a strong public policy favoring trial by jury, and since the California Supreme Court's 2005 decision in *Grafton Partners, L.P. v. Superior Court (PriceWaterhouseCoopers L.L.P.)*, contractual pre-dispute jury trial waivers have been held invalid in cases in California state courts unless otherwise expressly authorized by statute.[210] *In re County of Orange*, in 2015, extended the prohibition to federal courts sitting in diversity, where the state law is more protective of the right to a jury trial than federal law.[211]

b. Annotations

Conducting a choice-of-law analysis, the court rejected defendant's argument that it must apply California law because its policy with respect to jury trials is more protective than that in New York. *U.S. Securities Holdings, Inc. v. Andrews*, No. CV 21-2263, 2021 WL 6104394 (C.D. Cal. Sept. 15, 2021).

---

210. Grafton Partners, LP v. Super. Ct., 36 Cal. 4th 944, 955, 116 P.3d 479 (2005).
211. *In re* Cnty. of Orange, 784 F.3d 520 (9th Cir. 2015).

5. Choice of Law

a. Commentary

Although contracting out of application of the CFRA is not easy, the converse is not necessarily true. There has been at least one case in which a choice-of-law clause served to make the CFRA applicable despite failure to satisfy the jurisdictional requirements of the law.[212] As a result, care must be taken in drafting choice-of-law provisions not to subject a franchise to the CFRA inadvertently when the franchise does not otherwise meet the jurisdictional requirements of the law.

b. Annotations

In a case of first impression, the district court determined the CFRA applied to a distribution agreement between a California supplier and a distributor organized in the United Kingdom with principal offices in Switzerland and operating in the Middle East. The distribution agreement designated application of California law. But a simple choice-of-law clause is not sufficient to mandate application of the CFRA. A court must determine if the statutory requirements of the CFRA permit application. However, in at least one case, a court determined that because the agreement stated that California law applies "as applied to agreements entered into and to be performed entirely within California between California residents," the jurisdictional limits of the CFRA were satisfied and applied the CFRA to their franchise agreement. *Gabana Gulf Distribution, Ltd. v. Gap International Sales, Inc.*, No. C 06-02584, 2006 WL 2355092 (N.D. Cal. Aug. 14, 2006).

The CFRA does not invalidate a Florida choice-of-law provision in a franchise agreement between a Florida franchisor and a California franchise for a fast-food franchise operated in California.

The CFRA prohibition against restricting venue to an out-of-state forum does not invalidate an unambiguous choice-of-law provision. The franchisee did not claim the franchisor's actions breached the CFRA except to the extent the franchise agreement required application of Florida law. A "California Addendum" to the franchise agreement stated that, to the extent required by law, the Florida choice-of-law clause shall not abrogate the franchisee's rights under the CFRA. That provision did not amend the franchise agreement to eliminate Florida as the designated forum or the designated law. *Burger King Corp. v. Midland Management, L.L.C.*, Business Franchise Guide (CCH) ¶ 12,332 (S.D. Fla. 2002).

The Ninth Circuit applied California law to invalidate an arbitration provision in a franchise agreement even though the agreement had a Texas choice-of-law provision. Texas had a substantial relationship to the parties and the transaction because it was the franchisor's principal place of business and the place where the franchise agreement was formed. But application of Texas law would be contrary to a fundamental public policy of California. *Id.* California

---

212. *See* Gabana Gulf Distrib. v. Gap Int'l Sales, Inc., 2006 WL 2355092 (N.D. Cal. Aug. 14, 2006) (applying CFRA to franchisee not located in California and not operating in California, on basis of choice of law provision choosing California law "as applied to agreements entered into and to be performed entirely within California between California residents").

has a materially greater interest in applying its law than Texas has in applying Texas law. Although Texas has a significant interest in enforcing contracts executed by its citizens in Texas, "California has a substantial, case-specific interest in protecting its resident franchisees from losing statutory protections against fraud and unfair business practices." *Bridge Fund Capital Corp. v. Fastbucks Franchise Corp.*, 622 F.3d 996, 1003 (9th Cir. 2010).

The court refused to apply the Nevada choice-of-law provision of the franchise agreement to a franchisee's claim against the franchisor for violation of the CFIL. The franchisor is a Nevada corporation that resides in California and the franchisee resides in New York. Although Nevada has an interest in applying its laws, California's franchise law embodies a fundamental policy, and California has a materially greater interest than Nevada in enforcing its laws with respect to claims for violation of the CFIL. *It's Just Lunch International LLC v. Island Park Enterprise Group, Inc.*, No. EDCV 08-367, 2008 WL 4683637 (C.D. Cal. Oct. 21, 2008).

Absent a public policy exception, choice-of-law provisions are generally enforceable. A contractual choice-of-law provision designating Washington in a contract between a Vancouver, B.C.-based franchisor and a California-based franchisee was upheld because the parties had a reasonable basis for selecting Washington law because franchisors have an interest in uniformity across operations. The Washington choice-of-law provision, which gave the franchisee enhanced protection (as compared to the CFRA), was not barred by California's stated public policy in the CFRA. *1-800-Got Junk? v. Superior Court (Millennium Asset Recovery, Inc.)*, 189 Cal. App. 4th 500, 116 Cal. Rptr. 3d 923 (2010).

In a dispute between a Texas-based franchisor and California franchisees, the franchise disclosure document stated that "[t]he franchise agreement requires application of the laws of Texas. This provision may not be enforceable under California law." The franchise disclosure document also included other provisions that made it clear the franchisor would insist on application of Texas law. In finding that the franchisees failed to identify an actual conflict between Texas law and California public policy, the court applied Texas law. *Meadows v. Dickey's Barbecue Restaurants, Inc.*, 144 F. Supp. 3d 1069 (N.D. Cal. 2015).

Under a California choice-of-law analysis, application of New Jersey law to a dispute involving a California real estate brokerage franchisee and a New Jersey franchisor would not diminish the franchisee's rights because any claims that the franchisee could have under the California Franchise Relations Act (CFRA) could be pursued as breach of contract claims under the parties' franchise agreements. Thus, the choice of New Jersey law provision in the parties' agreements would not effectuate a waiver of the franchisee's protections under the CFRA and was enforceable. *Century 21 Real Estate v. All Professional Realty*, 889 F. Supp. 2d 1198 (E.D. Cal. 2012).

A choice-of-law clause applying Washington's franchise relations law to a franchisee domiciled and operating in California was not precluded by the CFRA where Washington's law provided greater protection. *1-800-Got Junk? v. Superior Court (Millennium Asset Recovery, Inc.)*, 189 Cal. App. 4th 500, 116 Cal. Rptr. 3d 923 (2010).

The court rejected a franchisee's argument that California law—and specifically section 16600's prohibition on enforcing post-termination noncompetes—was incorporated into the franchise agreement through the California Addendum to the franchisor's Franchise Disclosure Addendum.

Finding that the Addendum, which warned that post-termination noncompetes may not be enforceable under California law, was intended merely to put the franchisee on notice that California law was different than Tennessee law, the court enforced the post-term noncompete. *Servpro Industries, Inc. v. Woloski*, No. 3:17-cv-01433, 2020 WL 5629452 (Sept. 21, 2020 M.D. Tenn. 2020).

Connecticut

Kristin Corcoran

I. Introduction to Statute

Connecticut has a robust franchise relationship law in the Connecticut Franchise Act (Connecticut Act),[1] which is considered remedial in nature and liberally construed to protect franchisees.[2]

Connecticut does not have any registration or disclosure laws, but the Connecticut Business Opportunity Investment Act[3] may apply to franchise systems without a federally registered trademark. Franchise systems with federally registered trademarks qualify for an exemption from that statute's requirements.[4] Additionally, Connecticut General Statutes section 42-133j–n addresses franchise agreements involving gasoline dealers.[5] These statutes are beyond the scope of this chapter, but practitioners should be aware of their potential application.

II. Commentary and Annotations

A. Definition of Franchise

1. Commentary

The Connecticut Act defines a "Franchise" as

> an oral or written agreement or arrangement in which (1) a franchisee is granted the right to engage in the business of offering, selling or distributing goods or services under a marketing plan or system prescribed in substantial part by a franchisor, provided nothing contained herein shall be deemed to create a franchisor-franchisee relationship between the grantor and grantee of a lease, license or concession to sell goods or services upon or appurtenant to the premises of the grantor, which

---

1. CONN. GEN. STAT. §§ 42-133e, *et seq.*
2. Hartford Elec. Supply Co. v. Allen-Bradley Co., Inc., 250 Conn. 334, 345, 736 A.2d 824, 831 (Conn. 1999); Muha v. United Oil Co., Inc., 180 Conn. 720, 433 A.2d 1009, 1013 (Conn. 1980).
3. CONN. GEN. STAT. §§ 36b-60, *et seq.*
4. *Id.* § 36b-61(2)(D).
5. *Id.* §§ 42-133j, *et seq.*

premises are occupied by the grantor primarily for its own independent merchandising activities; and (2) the operation of the franchisee's business pursuant to such plan or system is substantially associated with the franchisor's trademark, service mark, tradename, logotype, advertising or other commercial symbol designating the franchisor or its affiliate, and includes any agreement between a manufacturer, refiner or producer and a distributor, wholesaler or jobber, between a manufacturer, refiner or producer and a retailer, or between a distributor, wholesaler or jobber and a retailer[.][6]

As described in this excerpt, the elements in the definition of franchise include (1) the right granted to the franchisee to engage in the business of offering, selling, or distributing goods or services; (2) the business to be operated will be pursuant to the franchisor's marketing plan or system; and (3) the business to be operated is substantially associated with the franchisor's trademark or other commercial symbol.[7] Courts similarly have held that the parties' use of, or disavowal of the term "franchise," is relevant, but not dispositive, when deciding whether the act applies.[8] A written agreement is not required for a franchise to exist.[9] The use of the term "franchise" in a written agreement is not conclusive evidence that a franchise exists under the act.[10]

In two recent cases, putative franchisees seeking protection under the Connecticut Act were found to not be franchisees within the meaning of the statute. In *Trade Links, LLC v. BI-QEM SA de CV*, a sales representative was not a franchisee for purposes of the Connecticut Act because the representative did not buy and sell goods and was simply an order-taker acting as defendant's agent.[11] The court in *Purugganan v. AFC Franchising*, in deciding franchisor's

---

6. *Id.* § 42-133e(b).

7. Hartford Elec. Supply Co. v. Allen-Bradley Co., Inc., 250 Conn. 334, 736 A.2d 824, 831 (Conn. 1999); Jenkins v. Haworth, Inc. 572 F. Supp. 591, 599–600 (W.D. Mich. 1983).

8. Sorisio v. Lenox, Inc., 701 F. Supp. 950, 961 (D. Conn. 1988), *aff'd*, 863 F.2d 195 (2d Cir. 1988); Kinsley Grp., Inc. v. MWM Energy Sys., No. 3:12cv1286 (JBA), 2014 WL 4740577, at *5 (D. Conn. Sept. 23, 2014) (disavowal of a franchise relationship is a relevant consideration that weighs against a finding of a franchise relationship); B & E Juices, Inc. v. Energy Brands, Inc., No. 3:07CV1321, 2007 WL 3124903 (D. Conn. Oct. 25, 2007) (Noting that the label given to the relationship by the parties, while relevant, is not determinative of the existence of a franchise relationship. Nor is the relationship of the parties governed solely by the parties' written agreement. Rather, the statutory test is "whether the parties' conduct, in addition to their words, constitutes an agreement or arrangement" under the act.).

9. *See, e.g., Jenkins*, 572 F. Supp. at 600 ("[A] franchise agreement is an unnecessary addition to the legal relationship.").

10. *See id.* (absence of term "franchise" in written agreements between parties was not determinative but lent support to the court's conclusion that a franchise did not exist); McKeown Distribs., Inc. v. Gyp-Crete Corp., 618 F. Supp. 632, 642 (D. Conn. 1985) (failure of agreement to refer to the relationship between the parties as a "franchise" was a factor in court's determination that a franchise did not exist); *Sorisio*, 701 F. Supp. at 961 ("use of the word 'franchise' in an agreement between the manufacturer and a dealer may be a probative factor" in determining whether a franchise relationship exists).

11. Trade Links, LLC v. BI-QEM SA de CV, Docket No. 3:19-CV-00308 (KAD), 2020 U.S. Dist. LEXIS 49536 (D. Conn. Mar. 23, 2020).

motion to dismiss several claims, found that even though the master developer had an agreement with the franchisor, he was not a franchisee for purposes of the Connecticut Act because the developer was limited to soliciting, evaluating, and screening individuals for the franchisor approval and "[franchisee] does not 'have the right to offer, sell or distribute goods or services' of the kind offered under [the franchisor's] mark."[12] However, those two cases can be compared to *Kollar v. Allstate Insurance Co.*, where the allegations that an exclusive insurance agent was a franchisee for purposes of the Connecticut Franchise Act was deemed sufficient to withstand a motion to dismiss, because a Connecticut Act inquiry "is fact-based, customized, and includes an analysis of the control asserted by a purported franchisor."[13] And most interesting, in the matter of *Mujo v. Jani-King International*, where cleaning franchisees claimed to be "misclassified" and were employees rather than independent contractors under Connecticut law, the U.S. Court of Appeals for the Second Circuit found that the Connecticut Act applied holding that, "[i]f an individual qualifies as both a franchisee and an employee, she would be entitled to the protections of both the Connecticut Franchise Act and the employment-related provisions of Connecticut law."[14]

2. Annotations

In granting partial summary judgment, the court found no support for the proposition that the Connecticut Act was intended to apply to prospective franchisees who had been granted a conditional right to develop a location but had not yet completed the franchise sales process. *Stetzer v. Dunkin' Donuts, Inc.*, 87 F. Supp. 2d 104 (D. Conn. 2000).

A plaintiff claiming to be a franchisee under the Connecticut Act must show "(1) there was an oral or written franchise agreement"; (2) plaintiff was "substantially associated" with franchisor; and (3) franchisor "substantially subscribed" the plaintiff's business. Although the operative agreement "on its own is not dispositive, the parties' express disavowal of a franchise relationship is a relevant consideration that weighs against a finding of a franchise relationship." *Kinsley Group, Inc. v. MWM Energy Systems*, No. 3:12cv1286 (JBA), 2014 WL 4740577 (D. Conn. Sept. 23, 2014).

The statutory test to determine whether there is a franchise relationship is based on reality: on the parties' conduct and words and not solely by their written agreement. *Edmands v. CUNO, Inc.*, 277 Conn. 425, 892 A.2d 938 (Conn. 2006)

The statutory test is "whether the parties' conduct, in addition to their words, constitutes an agreement or arrangement" under the Connecticut

---

12. Purugganan v. AFC Franchising, LLC, No. 3:20-cv-00360 (KAD), 2021 U.S. Dist. LEXIS 34284 (D. Conn. Feb. 24, 2021), quoting Getty Petroleum Mktg., Inc. v. Ahmad, 253 Conn. 806, 813, 757 A.2d 494 (2000) (quoting Chem-Tek, Inc. v. General Motors Corp., 816 F. Supp. 123, 127 (D. Conn. 1993)).

13. Kollar v. Allstate Ins. Co., Docket No. 3:16-cv-1927 (VAB), 2018 U.S. Dist. LEXIS 167569 (D. Conn. Sept. 28, 2018).

14. Mujo v. Jani-King Int'l, 13 F.4th 204 (2d Cir. 2021).

Franchise Act. *B & E Juices, Inc. v. Energy Brands, Inc.*, No. 3:07CV1321, 2007 WL 3124903 (D. Conn. Oct. 25, 2007).

Plaintiff insurance agent's assertion that the parties had a contractual relationship, and it had the right to offer, sell, or distribute defendant insurance company's goods and services was enough to plausibly plead that the relationship established under the contract could state a claim for relief under the act. *Garbinski v. Nationwide Mutual Insurance Co.*, No. 3:10cv1191(VLB), 2011 WL 3164057 (D. Conn. July 26, 2011), *but see further ruling at Garbinski v. Nationwide Mut. Ins. Co.*, 3:10cv1191(VLB), 2012 WL 3027918 (D. Conn. July 24, 2012), *aff'd, Garbinski v. Nationwide Prop. & Cas. Ins. Co.*, 523 F. App'x 24 (2d Cir. 2013) (granting summary judgment and holding that the Connecticut Act did not apply to insurer–agent relationship).

The court found that an insurance agent had satisfied the first element of the Connecticut Act by presenting substantial evidence from which a jury could conclude that the agent not only had the right to sell, offer, or distribute the insurance company's product but could bind policies. *Charts v. Nationwide Mutual Insurance Co.*, 397 F. Supp. 2d 357 (D. Conn. 2005).

Kitchen appliance retailer failed to show it was "substantially associated" with its distributor. It did not present evidence to dispute that distributor's products accounted for less than half of retailer's sales and it did not show that customers considered doing business with the seller as one and the same as doing business with the distributor. Therefore, the forum selection clause in the parties' agreement was not invalidated by the Connecticut Act. *Contractors Home Appliance, Inc. v. Clarke Distribution Corp.*, 196 F. Supp. 2d 174 (D. Conn. 2002).

In granting the manufacturer's motion for summary judgment, the court found that the substantial association prong was not satisfied, and the parties' contractual relationship was not governed by the Connecticut Act's remedial provisions where the sales representative only provided conclusory statements regarding the impact of contract termination, noting most or all of the sales representative's business must be derived from association with the manufacturer. *Rudel Machinery Co., Inc. v. Giddings & Lewis, Inc.*, 68 F. Supp. 2d 118, 128–29 (D. Conn. 1999).

Gas station lessee/operator was not a franchisee under the Connecticut Act because the lessee/operator did not have the right to sell or offer the product but rather was deemed the "temporary custodian of the gasoline, the caretaker of the property, the cashier" responsible for selling the gasoline, and collecting payments to be forwarded to petroleum company. *Getty Petroleum Marketing, Inc. v. Ahmad*, 253 Conn. 806, 757 A.2d 494 (Conn. 2000), quoting *Automatic Comfort Corp. v. D & R Services, Inc.*, 627 F. Supp. 783 (D. Conn. 1986).

Granting a franchisee authority to convey title to goods under the franchisor's trademark is sufficient to constitute a "right to engage in the business of offering, selling or distributing products or services." *Chem-Tek, Inc. v. General Motors Corp.*, 816 F. Supp. 123 (D. Conn. 1993).

When his employment was terminated, Jenkins, president of a subsidiary of defendant, Haworth, Inc., claimed the subsidiary was a franchise. Because the subsidiary never purchased goods, maintained an inventory, resold goods, or took actual title to goods and merely sold goods as an agent for the parent corporation, the subsidiary was not "offering, selling or distributing" the parent's goods. *Jenkins v. Haworth, Inc.*, 572 F. Supp. 591 (W.D. Mich. 1983).

An independent contractor that did not have authority to enter into contracts of sale with customers and was limited to soliciting orders for products did not "offer" or "sell" within the meaning of the Connecticut Act. *George R. Darche Associates, Inc. v. Beatrice Foods Co.*, 538 F. Supp. 429, 434 (D.N.J. 1981), *aff'd*, 676 F.2d 685 (3d Cir. 1982).

B. Trademark Element

1. Commentary

Under the Connecticut Act's trademark element, a franchisee's business must be "substantially associated with the franchisor's trademark, service mark, tradename, logotype, advertising or other commercial symbol designating the franchisor or its affiliate."[15] This requirement of substantial association can be satisfied when the franchisee extensively uses the manufacturer's name and logo so that it appears to be a franchisee.[16] The "substantial association" requirement does not mean that the franchisee must be completely associated with the franchisor's marks, have no separate identity, or be exclusively dependent on the franchisor,[17] but rather that the franchised business is "substantially associated with the franchisor's trademark, service mark, tradename, logotype, advertising or other commercial symbol."[18]

In *Hartford Electric*, this element was satisfied under the circumstances where a distributor was substantially associated with the franchisor's trademark, because of a variety of factors, including that the distributor provided the manufacturer's catalogs and promotional materials containing the manufacturer's logo and used signage prominently containing the manufacturer's name at distributor's premises for 50 years.[19] The two were so closely linked that customers considered the parties as one and the same. Additionally, the agreement's termination would result in the distributor losing half of its gross annual sales of $20 million and the opportunity to distribute other products that were associated with the manufacturer.[20]

In *Grand Light*, a Connecticut federal district court held that because a small portion of the franchisee's business was conducted in accordance with the franchisor's marketing plan, it was "substantially associated" with the franchisor's

---

15. CONN. GEN. STAT. § 42-133e(b).
16. Dittman & Greer, Inc. v. Chromalox, Inc., No. 3:09-cv-1147, 2009 WL 3254481, at *5 (D. Conn. Oct. 6, 2009).
17. Hartford Elec. Supply Co. v. Allen-Bradley Co., Inc., 250 Conn. 334, 736 A.2d 824, 838 (Conn. 1999); *see also* Grand Light & Supply Co. Inc. v. Honeywell, Inc., 771 F.2d 672, 678 (2d Cir. 1985). Muha v. United Oil Co., Inc., 180 Conn. 720, 433 A.2d 1009 (Conn. 1980) (indicating that, while exclusivity is not required, the absence of exclusivity would be significant); *accord* Chem-Tek, Inc. v. Gen. Motors Corp., 816 F. Supp. 123, 129 (D. Conn. 1993).
18. CONN. GEN. STAT. § 42-133e(b).
19. *Hartford*, 736 A.2d at 838–39.
20. *Id.*

trademark, and a franchise existed.[21] The Second Circuit Court of Appeals held that such a literal reading of the Connecticut Act was not required and rejected the lower court's conclusion that "damages may be awarded for a violation of Connecticut's Franchise Act."[22] While there is no clear test for the required "substantial" association, the Second Circuit held that the Connecticut Act's purpose is to protect the franchisee that would face "economic disaster" if the franchisor severed the parties' relationship without good cause or sufficient notice.[23] The court highlighted that "[w]here the franchisee is completely dependent on the public's confidence in the franchised product *for most or all of his business*, abrupt severance of the franchise tie, without good cause and without sufficient notice, could spell ruination."[24] Because only a minor portion (3 percent) of plaintiff's business was derived from defendant's products, plaintiff was not dependent on defendant.[25] However, the Connecticut federal district court later held in *Spear-Newman, Inc. v. E.I. du Pont de Nemours & Co.* that 23 and 27 percent of the franchisee's business was enough for the franchisee to be "sufficiently dependent on [the franchisor's products] that it is likely to face 'ruination' if the [product] line was abruptly terminated" and therefore found this percentage to be enough to be substantially associated with a franchisor's trademark, trade name, advertising, and other commercial symbols.[26]

Although, generally, courts have found a level of association higher than 25 percent of the business to be substantial, the district court in *Dittman & Greer, Inc. v. Chromalox, Inc.*, held that a distributor's business was not substantially associated with the manufacturer's trademark where the manufacturer's products accounted for 42 percent of the distributor's total sales and 33 percent to 34 percent of its gross profits.[27] Although the percentage seemed significant on its face, the court distinguished *Dittman & Greer, Inc. v. Chromalox, Inc.*, from other cases such as *Hartford Electric*, and found that the distributor could withstand the loss of the manufacturer's business and therefore fell short of meeting the requirements of substantial association.[28] Similarly, in *Walker Industrial Products, Inc. v. Intelligent Motion Systems, Inc.*, a superior court held that losing its agreement with a manufacturer would not fatally injure a distributor's business

---

21. Grand Light & Supply Co. Inc. v. Honeywell, Inc., 771 F.2d 672 (2d Cir. 1985).
22. *Id.* at 674.
23. *Id.* at 677.
24. *Id.* (emphasis added); *see also* Chem-Tek, Inc. v. Gen. Motors Corp., 816 F. Supp. 123, 129 (D. Conn. 1993) ("The franchisee must be sufficiently dependent on the franchisor that termination would be not only harmful, but disastrous.").
25. *Grand Light*, 771 F.2d at 677; *see also* Sorisio v. Lenox, Inc., 701 F. Supp. 950, 961–62 (D. Conn. 1988), *aff'd*, 863 F.2d 195 (2d Cir. 1988) (no substantial association when, among other things, line constituted less than 10 percent of luggage dealer's purchases); Advanced Mach. Co., Inc. v. Trumpf, Inc., No. CV940538577S, 1996 WL 457211, at *3 (Conn. Sup. Ct. July 18, 1996) (no franchise found where less than 1 percent of plaintiff's revenues were attributable to the sale of defendant's products).
26. Spear-Newman, Inc. v. E. I. du Pont de Nemours & Co., No. 3:91CV00652WWE, 1991 WL 318725, at *10 (D. Conn. Jan. 17, 1991) (quoting *Grand Light*, 771 F.2d at 677).
27. Dittman & Greer, Inc. v. Chromalox, Inc., No. 3:09-cv-1147, 2009 WL 3254481, at *6 (D. Conn. Oct. 6, 2009).
28. *Id.* at *20.

and refused to find substantial association when 35 percent of the distributor's business was attributable to the manufacturer.[29] The Seventh Circuit Court of Appeals has suggested that a showing of 50 percent of lost sales is required.[30]

Besides looking at the percentage of a putative franchisee's business that depends on the franchisor's products, various courts have considered additional factors that may show the requisite association. The court in *Spear-Newman, Inc. v. E.I. du Pont de Nemours & Co.*, considered factors such as the franchisee's substantial advertising link with the franchisor's product names and symbols, use of the franchisor's trade names on its business cards and delivery trucks, and references to the franchisor's trade names on its telephone answering system.[31] In another case, the court considered that the franchisee was licensed to use the franchisor's trademark and made extensive use of the trademark, the franchisee's office telephone was answered by announcing the franchisor's product name and trademark, and that the franchisee's business stationery and business entrance prominently featured the franchisor's product name and trademark.[32] However, in *Garbinski v. Nationwide Mutual Insurance Co.*, the district court found no substantial association between an insurance company and its insurance agent, where the agent was allowed to sell other companies' insurance products and could not show a level of dependence whereby Nationwide's termination would result in economic disaster for the agent's business.[33]

Although the Connecticut Act does not contain an explicit "significant degree of control" or "significant assistance" element, factors relating to control and assistance are often relevant in courts' analyses of the "marketing plan" or system element.

2. Annotations

The Connecticut Act did not apply to a distribution agreement, where (1) the putative franchisor did not control various factors of putative franchisee's marketing (e.g., hours and days of operation, lighting, employee uniforms, pricing, sales quotas, or trading stamps); and (2) putative franchisee failed the "most if not all" substantial association test since its sales of franchisor's products varied by year and accounted for only a fraction of its annual revenue. *Bryka, LLC v. Holt Integrated Circuits, Inc. et al.*, 2024 WL 4264390 (D. Conn. 2024).

---

29. Walker Indus. Prods., Inc. v. Intelligent Motion Sys., Inc., No. DBDCV094010861, 2009 WL 3417438 (Conn. Super. Ct. Oct. 1, 2009).

30. Echo, Inc. v. Timberland Machs. & Irrigation, Inc., 661 F.3d 959 (7th Cir. 2011) (where range of sales associated with franchisor over time was 29.95 percent to 34.97 percent, court emphasized failure was to show more than 50 percent of its business resulted from its relationship with plaintiff supplier); B & E Juices, Inc. v. Energy Brands, Inc., No. 3:07CV1321, 2007 WL 3124903, at *16 (D. Conn. Oct. 25, 2007) (losing 40 percent of sales insufficient).

31. Spear-Newman, Inc. v. E. I. du Pont de Nemours & Co., No. 3:91CV00652WWE, 1991 WL 318725, at *10 (D. Conn. Jan. 17, 1991).

32. Carlos v. Philips Bus. Sys., Inc., 556 F. Supp. 769, 776 (E.D.N.Y.), *aff'd*, 742 F.2d 1432 (2d Cir. 1983).

33. Garbinski v. Nationwide Mut. Ins. Co., 3:10cv1191(VLB), 2012 WL 3027918, at *8–*9 (D. Conn. July 24, 2012), *aff'd*, Garbinski v. Nationwide Prop. & Cas. Ins. Co., 523 F. App'x 24 (2d Cir. 2013).

Master developer with an agreement with a franchisor to recruit prospective franchisees and to support franchisees was not a franchisee for purposes of the Connecticut Act because he did not assume the financial risk of opening and operating a franchise and did not "have the right to offer, sell or distribute goods or services of the kind offered under [the franchisor's] mark." *Purugganan v. AFC Franchising, LLC*, Docket No. 3:20-cv-00360 (KAD), 2021 U.S. Dist. LEXIS 205591 (D. Conn. Aug. 31, 2021).

Allegations that an exclusive insurance agent was a franchisee for purposes of the Connecticut Act were sufficient to withstand a motion to dismiss. "Connecticut Franchise Act inquiry is fact-based, customized, and includes an analysis of the control asserted by a purported franchisor." *Kollar v. Allstate Insurance Co.*, Docket No. 3:16-cv-1927 (VAB), 2018 U.S. Dist. LEXIS 167569, at *24 (D. Conn. Sept. 28, 2018).

The Connecticut Act is "more specific" than the FTC Rule and requires a combination of a "marketing plan or system subscribed by the franchisor" and "a substantial association with the franchisor's marks," while the FTC Rule requires "a significant degree of control over the franchisee's method of operation or significant assistance with the franchise's method of operation." *Safe Step Walk in Tub Co. v. CKH Industries, Inc.*, 242 F. Supp. 3d 245, 257–58 (S.D.N.Y. 2017).

Cabinet manufacturer granted distributor exclusive rights to distribute its trademarked cabinets. Upon termination by cabinet manufacturer, distributor claimed he was a franchisee of the manufacturer. However, because (1) the exclusive distribution agreement granted distributor a nonexclusive right to use the cabinet manufacturer's marks for its *product*, not for the sale of franchises, and (2) the distributor's franchise agreements granted his franchisees' rights under a different trademark and logo, the court concluded that the substantial association test could not be met, even if distributor could demonstrate that distributor's business and its franchisees were harmed by cabinet manufacturer's termination of the agreement. *Rogovsky Enterprises, Inc. v. Masterbrand Cabinets, Inc.*, No. 3:15-cv-00022- RLY-WGH, 2015 WL 7721223 (D. Conn. Nov. 30, 2015). Putative franchisee deriving less than 10 percent of revenue from the franchise was insufficient evidence to demonstrate a substantial association with franchisor. *Kinsley Group, Inc. v. MWM Energy Systems*, No. 3:12cv1286 (JBA), 2014 WL 4740577 (D. Conn. Sept. 23, 2014).

No substantial association between an insurance company and its insurance agent, where agent did not have an exclusive or near-exclusive agency relationship. *Garbinski v. Nationwide Mutual Insurance Co.*, 3:10cv1191(VLB), 2012 WL 3027918, at *8–*9 (D. Conn. July 24, 2012), *aff'd, Garbinski v. Nationwide Prop. & Cas. Ins. Co.*, 523 F. App'x 24 (2d Cir. 2013).

Distributor failed to demonstrate substantial association with supplier's trademark, trade name, or other commercial name or symbol when it failed to show that more than 50 percent of its business resulted from its relationship with the plaintiff supplier (range over time was 29.95 percent to 34.97 percent). *Echo, Inc. v. Timberland Machines & Irrigation, Inc.*, 661 F.3d 959 (7th Cir. 2011).

Distributor's business was not "substantially associated" with manufacturer's trademark where distributor sold products of 19 other manufacturers, depicted several manufacturers' trademarks and logos on its website, and manufacturer's products accounted for 42 percent of distributor's total sales, and 33 percent to 34 percent of distributor's gross profits. *Dittman & Greer, Inc. v. Chromalox, Inc.*, No. 3:09-cv-1147, 2009 WL 3254481 (D. Conn. Oct. 6, 2009).

"Substantial association" was not satisfied where distributor only attributed 35 percent of its business to manufacturer. *Walker Industrial Products, Inc. v. Intelligent Motion Systems, Inc.*, No. DBDCV094010861, 2009 WL 3417438 (Conn. Super. Ct. Oct. 1, 2009).

Beverage distributor was not substantially associated with beverage manufacturer for purposes of the Connecticut Act where 40 percent of its sales would be lost as a result of termination. *B & E Juices, Inc. v. Energy Brands, Inc.*, No. 3:07CV1321, 2007 WL 3124903 (D. Conn. Oct. 25, 2007).

Distributor's business was not exclusively or nearly exclusively associated with the manufacturer's trademark and therefore was not "substantially associated." Association with the manufacturer accounted for only 14.68 percent of the distributor's total net income for the year, which the court found insufficient to satisfy the "nearly exclusive" requirement. *Terex Corp. v. Cubex Ltd.*, No. 3:06-CV-1639-G, 2006 WL 3542706 (N.D. Tex. Dec. 7, 2006).

Retailer did not meet the substantial association test where it failed to present evidence that its business involved the use of distributor's trademark or symbol, sold any products marketed with distributor's name, used the distributor's name as part of its own trade name, or featured distributor's name on its letterhead or business cards. *Contractors Home Appliance, Inc. v. Clarke Distribution Corp.*, 196 F. Supp. 2d 174 (D. Conn. 2002).

Where franchisee distributed franchisor's catalogs and promotional materials with both companies' names, displayed franchisor's sign on franchisee's premises, franchisee's fliers contained franchisor's logo, franchisee was widely recognized as the leading distributor of the franchisor's products, and customers believed the franchisee and franchisor were the same enterprise, franchisee's business was "substantially associated" with franchisor's trademark. *Hartford Electric Supply Co. v. Allen-Bradley Co., Inc.*, 250 Conn. 334, 736 A.2d 824 (Conn. 1999).

Business not "substantially associated" with trademark where the portion of revenues attributable to the sale of putative franchisor's products was minor (less than 1 percent). *Advanced Machinery Co., Inc. v. Trumpf, Inc.*, No. CV9405385775, 1996 WL 457211 (Conn. Sup. Ct. July 18, 1996).

The substantial association requirement does not require exclusivity but does require franchisee to be sufficiently dependent on the franchisor that termination of the franchise would not only be harmful but also disastrous. Additionally, authority to convey title by a franchisee to goods under the franchisor's trademark is sufficient to constitute a "right to engage in the business of offering, selling or distributing products or services." *Chem-Tek, Inc. v. General Motors Corp.*, 816 F. Supp. 123 (D. Conn. 1993).

Although exclusivity is not required, franchisee must provide evidence that some portion of its business operated pursuant to a marketing plan to be substantially associated with the franchisor's trademark. *M & S Audio, Inc. v. Bogen Communications, Inc.*, No. CV91-0239171S, 1992 WL 231459 (Conn. Sup. Ct. Sept. 14, 1992).

The court concluded that franchisee's business was substantially associated with franchisor's trademark where between 23 percent and 27 percent of its business was derived from the sale of franchisor's products. *Spear-Newman, Inc. v. E.I. Du Pont de Nemours & Co.*, No. 3:91CV00652WWE, 1991 WL 318725 (D. Conn. Jan. 17, 1991).

Business was not "substantially associated" with putative franchisor's trademark where less than 10 percent of total product purchases by putative franchisee were of putative franchisor's merchandise. *Sorisio v. Lenox, Inc.*, 701 F. Supp. 950 (D. Conn.), *aff'd*, 863 F.2d 195 (2d Cir. 1988).

C. Franchise Fee Element

1. Commentary
Not applicable.

2. Annotations
Not applicable.

D. Community of Interest; Significant Degree of Control; Joint Marketing Plan

1. Commentary

In reviewing whether "a marketing plan or system prescribed in substantial part by a franchisor meets this element,"[34] courts focus on the amount of control exercised by the franchisor in the conduct of the franchisee's business.[35] In determining the amount and the type of control exercised by a franchisor, in addition to determining whether a written marketing plan exists, courts may consider factors such as the franchisor's ability to establish prices; examine and audit the franchisee's books; inspect the franchisee's premises; hire and fire the franchisee's employees; regulate the conduct of the franchisee's employees; establish sales quotas; require training of the franchisee's employees; provide management training and financial support; set hours of operation; and approve marketing or advertising.[36]

However, "[t]here is no precise formula as to how many of such factors must exist, in the aggregate, before the control exercised by a manufacturer rises to a marketing plan or system prescribed in substantial part by a franchisor."[37]

---

34. *Id.*
35. Hartford Elec. Supply Co. v. Allen-Bradley Co., Inc., 250 Conn. 334, 736 A.2d 824 (Conn. 1999).
36. Consumers Petroleum of Conn., Inc. v. Duhan, 38 Conn. Supp. 495, 452 A.2d 123, 125 (Conn. Sup. Ct. 1982); *accord* Petereit v. S.B. Thomas, Inc., 63 F.3d 1169, 1180 (2d Cir. 1995) (listing additional factors); Chem-Tek, Inc. v. Gen. Motors Corp., 816 F. Supp. 123, 129 (D. Conn. 1993); Sorisio v. Lenox, Inc., 701 F. Supp. 950, 960 (D. Conn. 1988), *aff'd*, 863 F.2d 195 (2d Cir. 1988); McKeown Distribs., Inc. v. Gyp-Crete Corp., 618 F. Supp. 632 (D. Conn. 1985); Hydro Air of Conn., Inc. v. Versa Techs., Inc., 599 F. Supp. 1119 (D. Conn. 1984); *Hartford*, 736 A.2d at 834.
37. *Sorisio*, 701 F. Supp. at 960.

The specifics of each case will differ and may impact the court's ultimate determination of whether the putative franchisee has met its burden.[38]

In *Hartford Electric*,[39] a frequently cited case finding the existence of a sufficient marketing plan, plaintiff, Hartford Electric Supply Company (HESCO), distributed electrical supplies and equipment manufactured by defendant, Allen-Bradley Co., Inc. (A-B). HESCO and A-B had a written distributorship agreement that, among other things, required HESCO to prepare a business plan for selling A-B products, which it approved and constantly monitored for compliance.[40] This business plan helped establish that HESCO operated under a marketing plan or system prescribed by A-B. A-B also constantly monitored business plan compliance and, when HESCO did not adequately adhere to it, intervened in HESCO's operations. The court held that HESCO's business plan, "once it was approved by A-B, became A-B's marketing plan to enforce upon HESCO."[41]

However, the mere existence of a written marketing plan is not dispositive, and an annual plan created by both parties to formulate a strategy for identifying new customers or emphasizing certain product lines is not necessarily a "substantially prescribed" marketing plan but is rather a normal sales planning activity between manufacturers and sales representatives.[42]

Courts also consider putative franchisors' control over pricing as potential evidence of the requisite marketing plan or system.[43]

Similarly, a Connecticut superior court found this element satisfied where a manufacturer required the distributor to keep a technical employee, trained by the manufacturer, on staff to support both salespeople and customers in the application of the manufacturer's products. The court considered the required training an important factor in determining whether the manufacturer substantially prescribed the distributor's marketing plan or system.[44]

2. Annotations

Where an insurance agent was specifically prohibited from selling other insurance companies' policies, the exclusive agent's assertions that he was a franchisee for purposes of the Connecticut Franchise Act were sufficient to withstand a motion to dismiss. The court noted, "Connecticut Franchise Act inquiry is fact-based, customized, and includes an analysis of the control asserted by a

---

38. B & E Juices, Inc. v. Energy Brands, Inc., No. 3:07CV1321, 2007 WL 3124903, at *13 (D. Conn. Oct. 25, 2007).
39. *Hartford*, 736 A.2d 824.
40. *Id.* at 834.
41. *Id.*
42. Dittman & Greer, Inc. v. Chromalox, Inc., No. 3:09-cv-1147, 2009 WL 3254481, at *3 (D. Conn. Oct. 6, 2009).
43. *See Hartford*, 736 A.2d 834; Petereit v. S.B. Thomas, Inc., 63 F.3d 1169, 1181 (2d Cir. 1995) ("[p]rice is perhaps the most fundamental aspect of a marketing plan"); *Dittman*, 2009 WL 3254481, at *3 (reaffirming the importance of control over pricing but holding that while direct pricing is not necessary to find a marketing plan, merely offering a discount for resale and suggesting retail prices is insufficient to satisfy the price-setting factor).
44. Walker Indus. Prods., Inc. v. Intelligent Motion Sys., Inc., No. DBDCV094010861, 2009 WL 3417438, at *7–8 (Conn. Super. Ct. Oct. 1, 2009).

purported franchisor." *Kollar v. Allstate Insurance Co.*, Docket No. 3:16-cv-1927 (VAB), 2018 U.S. Dist. LEXIS 167569, at * 24 (D. Conn. Sept. 28, 2018).

Plaintiff failed to show that the marketing plan or system were substantially prescribed by franchisor where franchisor could not, per the agreement, dictate or control plaintiff's prices or hiring decisions so as to deprive the franchisee of the "right to exercise independent judgment in conducting its business." *Kinsley Group, Inc. v. MWM Energy Systems*, No. 3:12cv1286 (JBA), 2014 WL 4740577 (D. Conn. Sept. 23, 2014).

The relationship between an insurance company and its insurance agent was not a franchise where the factors reviewed showed that the agent offered various insurance products for numerous insurers and the agent did not purchase the products from the insurer before reselling them and was not required to meet any minimum sales quotas. Additionally, the court found that the agent did not have an exclusive or near-exclusive agency relationship, and the insurance company did not prescribe the manner the insurance agent was to conduct its business. *Garbinski v. Nationwide Mutual Insurance Co.*, 3:10cv1191(VLB), 2012 WL 3027918 (D. Conn. July 24, 2012), *aff'd, Garbinski v. Nationwide Property & Casualty Insurance Co.*, 523 F. App'x 24 (2d Cir. 2013).

Merely suggesting retail prices without specifically fixing prices and offers of discounts for resale did not support a finding that a franchise relationship exists. The court found that requiring a supplier to keep a certain level of inventory on hand and to participate in ongoing promotions or requiring minimum purchase volumes on a short-term basis, was insufficient to show the existence of a marketing plan controlled by a franchisor. An annual plan between two parties to formulate a strategy for identifying new customers or emphasizing certain product lines does not necessarily indicate a marketing plan that is substantially prescribed by a franchisor to a franchisee and in fact such plans are commonplace between manufacturers and sales representatives. *Dittman & Greer, Inc. v. Chromalox, Inc.*, No. 3:09-cv-1147, 2009 WL 3254481 (D. Conn. Oct. 6, 2009).

Manufacturer exercised sufficient control by, among other factors, (1) reviewing and participating in the various plans, including annual, territory, and mutual action plans; (2) requiring distributor to maintain a manufacturer-trained technical employee; (3) controlling product promotion; and (4) setting and recommending certain pricing. *Walker Industrial Products, Inc. v. Intelligent Motion Systems, Inc.*, No. DBDCV094010861, 2009 WL 3417438 (Conn. Super. Ct. Oct. 1, 2009).

There is no precise set of factors, nor does any one factor control if there is a substantially prescribed marketing plan for the offering, selling, or distribution of goods or services by distributor. The factors, instead, largely depend on the type of business that is involved and must be reviewed in detail and include matters such as hours of operation, uniforms, hiring and employee training, stock levels, pricing, sales quotas, advertising, and other issues. *B & E Juices, Inc. v. Energy Brands, Inc.*, No. 3:07CV1321, 2007 WL 3124903 (D. Conn. Oct. 25, 2007).

Based on the contract and the parties' actions, the court found that manufacturer exercised sufficient control over its distributor because, among other factors, manufacturer had sole control over billing to retailers, had sole discretion in changing its product lines and packaging, and trained distributor and his employees, who were encouraged by manufacturer to wear manufacturer's logoed clothing. *Hillegas v. V.B.C., Inc.*, No. CV074007774S, 2007 WL 3173462 (Conn. Super. Ct. Oct. 15, 2007).

Despite manufacturer monitoring monthly sales and sending distributor reports that compared actual sales to projections, when all factors were reviewed, including that manufacturer did not force distributor to take specific corrective measures or impose punitive measures, nor dictate how distributor was to achieve its sales objectives, it was reasonable for the court to conclude that the manufacturer did not exercise sufficient control over distributor's marketing plan for the offering, selling, or distributing of goods or services, and, therefore, distributor failed to meet the elements of a franchise. In addition, even though manufacturer dictated some terms, it did not require, among other things, distributor to maintain particular stock levels or to carry specific products. *Edmands v. CUNO, Inc.*, 277 Conn. 425, 892 A.2d 938 (Conn. 2006).

A jury verdict finding a franchise was upheld where testimony was presented showing that insurance agents had to follow a marketing plan and the company's standards. *Charts v. Nationwide Mutual Insurance Co.*, 397 F. Supp. 2d 357 (D. Conn. 2005).

Factors for review by the court in determining whether franchisee's business is operated pursuant to a marketing plan or system substantially prescribed by franchisor are whether franchisor (1) requires a marketing plan, (2) has power over pricing, (3) has power over hiring and firing franchisee's personnel, (4) has power to require training of franchisee's personnel, and (5) has power to examine franchisee's financial records and require an audit. Factors demonstrating control over franchisee's business included franchisor's use of a special program to remedy franchisee's underperformance, franchisor's demands for improvement, and franchisor's rigorous enforcement of franchisee's business plan. *Hartford Electric Supply Co. v. Allen-Bradley Co., Inc.*, 250 Conn. 334, 736 A.2d 824 (Conn. 1999).

Manufacturer's control over prices effectively deprives distributors of independent judgment in conducting their business and is a significant indication of a franchisor's control. *Petereit v. S.B. Thomas, Inc.*, 63 F.3d 1169 (2d Cir. 1995).

In determining whether the definition of a franchise is satisfied, the amount of control the franchisor exercises in the conduct of the franchisee's business, including control over hours and days of operation, advertising, financial support, auditing of books, inspection of premises, control over lighting, employee uniforms, prices, trading stamps, hiring, sales quotas, and management training are significant factors. *Chem-Tek, Inc. v. General Motors Corp.*, 816 F. Supp. 123 (D. Conn. 1993).

A distributor showed the existence of a marketing plan where manufacturer exerted significant operational control over the distributor's marketing efforts, controlled advertising, indirectly restricted distributors to certain geographical territories, exerted control over pricing, required distributor to employ a specialist, required regular reporting of financial and sales information, and offered training seminars. *Spear-Newman, Inc. v. E.I. Du Pont de Nemours & Co.*, No. 3:91CV00652WWE, 1991 WL 318725 (D. Conn. Jan. 17, 1991).

The word "franchise" in an agreement between a manufacturer and a dealer may be probative but is not enough to establish the existence of a franchise relationship. The evidence failed to show that manufacturer prescribed operations, required uniforms, controlled hiring, set sales quotas, audited books, provided financing, conducted periodic or repetitive inspections, or set prices and therefore no franchise was found. While there is no precise formula, the dealer was not able to establish enough factors to meet the definition of franchise. *Sorisio v. Lenox, Inc.*, 701 F. Supp. 950 (D. Conn.), *aff'd*, 863 F.2d 195 (2d Cir. 1988).

Whether the franchisor set the hours of operation, controlled the number of employees, determined the placement of advertising, hired employees, provided management training, or offered financial support are factors relevant to determining whether a franchisee was granted the right to do business under a marketing plan or system prescribed by a franchisor. Because the putative franchisor failed to dispute the putative franchisee's facts, the court denied putative franchisor's motion for summary judgment, concluding that this was an issue for the trier of facts. *Hydro Air of Connecticut, Inc. v. Versa Technologies, Inc.*, 599 F. Supp. 1119 (D. Conn. 1984).

Motion for preliminary injunction was granted where a franchisee rejected the franchisor's offer to enter into a new dealership agreement that would result in loss of exclusive territory rights. Franchisee had been granted a license to use the franchisor's trademark, encouraged to associate its business with franchisor's trademark, made extensive use of the trademark, including answering its business phone with franchisor's trade name and trademark, and prominently featured franchisor's trade name and trademark on franchisee's business stationery and store front. *Carlos v. Philips Business Systems, Inc.*, 556 F. Supp. 769 (E.D.N.Y.), *aff'd*, 742 F.2d 1432 (2d Cir. 1983).

Lessor's control over lessee's business was not sufficient to show the existence of a marketing plan or system, despite lessor's control over lessee's hours of operation, number of employees, advertising, and lending lessee equipment to use in the business. *Consumers Petroleum of Connecticut, Inc. v. Duhan*, 38 Conn. Supp. 495, 452 A.2d 123 (Conn. Sup. Ct. 1982).

E. Scope and Jurisdiction

1. Commentary

The Connecticut Act is remedial in nature and is to be liberally construed in favor of those whom the legislature intends to benefit.[45] Its purpose was to protect franchisees and correct abuses in franchise relationships, particularly in the petroleum industry.[46] The Connecticut Act's "genesis was recognition of the disparity between the franchisor's superior economic strength of the franchisor and that of the franchisee and an attempt to remedy historic abuses within the

---

45. *Hartford*, 736 A.2d 824.
46. *Muha v. United Oil Co., Inc.*, 180 Conn. 720, 433 A.2d 1009 (Conn. 1980).

franchise field,"[47] and it was designed to prevent franchisors from taking unfair advantage of the relative economic weakness of the franchisee.[48]

The Connecticut Act, on its face, does not apply to franchises located outside the state and applies only to franchise agreements "the performance of which contemplates or requires the franchisee to establish or maintain a place of business in this state."[49] A franchisee, however, can qualify for protection of its Connecticut operations, even if it is not headquartered in Connecticut.[50] As seen in the following two cases, franchisees arguing that the Connecticut Act applies in circumstances where a Connecticut choice-of-law clause is found in the franchise agreement have had mixed results. In one matter, a federal district court rejected of an out-of-state franchisee's argument that the Connecticut Act applied due to a contractual Connecticut choice-of-law clause because "only franchisees who have established or maintained a place of business in Connecticut are covered by the act."[51] Conversely, a Connecticut superior court allowed an out-of-state franchisee to pursue a claim for violation of the Connecticut Act based upon the parties' inclusion of a Connecticut choice-of-law provision in their agreement.[52]

According to the Connecticut Act, any franchise agreement entered into or amended on or after June 12, 1975, that seeks to waive the franchisee's termination, cancellation, and nonrenewal rights under sections 42-133f or 42-133g is void.[53] Courts generally apply the Connecticut Act in cases involving a purported franchisee located in Connecticut, even if a choice-of-law provision applies the law of another state or contains a forum selection clause placing jurisdiction in another forum.[54] In *B & E Juices*, for example, the court applied the Connecticut Act despite a choice-of-law provision stating that New York law should apply.[55] In *R & R Associates of Connecticut, Inc. v. Deltona Corp.*, where a Florida franchisor and Connecticut franchisee entered into an agreement governed by the laws of Florida, a Connecticut federal district court relied on section 42-133f(f) in refusing to give effect to the parties' contractual choice

---

47. *Hartford*, No. CV965620615, 1997 WL 297256, at *3 (Conn. Sup. Ct. May 28, 1997), *aff'd*, 250 Conn. 334, 736 A.2d 824 (Conn. 1999).

48. *Id.*; *see also* Chem-Tek, Inc. v. Gen. Motors Corp., 816 F. Supp. 123, 129 (D. Conn. 1993); M & S Audio, Inc. v. Bogen Comm'ns, Inc., No. CV91-02391715, 1992 WL 231459, at *3 (Conn. Sup. Ct. Sept. 14, 1992); Grand Light & Supply Co., Inc. v. Honeywell, Inc., 771 F.2d 672, 677 (2d Cir. 1985).

49. CONN. GEN. STAT. § 42-133h.

50. New England Surfaces v. E. I. du Pont de Nemours & Co., 546 F.3d 1, 8 (1st Cir.), *decision clarified on denial of reh'g*, 546 F.3d 11 (1st Cir. 2008).

51. Forbes v. Joint Med. Prods. Corp., 976 F. Supp. 124, 126 (D. Conn. 1997) (a choice-of-law clause in a franchise agreement is not sufficient to override the jurisdictional prerequisites of the Act); *see also* H.J., Inc. v. ITT Corp., 867 F.2d 1531, 1546 (8th Cir. 1989) ("it is doubtful that the Connecticut franchise law applies extraterritorially").

52. Diesel Injection Serv. v. Jacobs Vehicle Equip., No. CV980582400S, 1998 WL 95086 (Conn. Sup. Ct. Dec. 4, 1998).

53. CONN. GEN. STAT. § 42-133f(f).

54. B & E Juices, Inc. v. Energy Brands, Inc., No. 3:07CV1321, 2007 WL 3124903 (D. Conn. Oct. 25, 2007).

55. *Id.* at *11.

of Florida law to govern their relationship.[56] The court concluded "[u]nder . . . section [42-133f(f)] of the Act, the choice of Florida law provision of the parties' agreement, to the extent that it would operate to deprive the plaintiff of his rights under the Act, must be considered void."[57]

2. Annotations

Cleaning franchisees claimed to be "misclassified" and that they were employees rather than independent contractors under Connecticut law. The U.S. Court of Appeals for the Second Circuit held that, "[i]f an individual qualifies as both a franchisee and an employee, she would be entitled to the protections of both the Connecticut Franchise Act and the employment-related provisions of Connecticut law" but affirmed dismissal of franchisees' Connecticut Minimum Wage Act and unjust enrichment claims, concluding that the payment of franchise fees was not unlawful, even if cleaning franchisees could be considered "employees" under Connecticut law. *Mujo v. Jani-King International*, 13 F.4th 204 (2d Cir. 2021).

The court determined nothing in the Connecticut Act explicitly bars franchisors and franchisees from agreeing to forum-selection clauses to adjudicate their disputes outside of Connecticut. *Columbia Aircraft Sales, Inc. v. Piper Aircraft, Inc.*, 2020 WL 7353912 (D. Conn. 2020).

Without determining whether a franchise relationship exists under the Connecticut Act, the trial court, in hearing an appeal of an administrative award of unemployment compensation benefits, determined that the statutory test for determining the existence of an employment relationship under the unemployment compensation statutory scheme contains no express exemption for franchises, and therefore no exception applies. *Jason Robert's, Inc. v. Administrator, Unemployment Compensation Act, et al.*, 127 Conn. App. 780, 15 A.3d 1145 (Conn. App. 2011).

Anti-waiver provisions of the Connecticut Act protect franchisees from franchisors that may require franchisees to agree to certain terms that are against their interest, including forum selection. In light of the clear anti-forum selection clause provision of the Connecticut Act, the Texas forum selection clause in the parties' franchise agreement was unreasonable and therefore unenforceable. *Phoenix Surgicals, LLC v. Blackstone Medical, Inc.*, No. 3:10-cv-1643 (WWE), 2011 WL 63992 (D. Conn. Jan. 3, 2011).

Enforcement of the forum selection of the federal court located nearest franchisor's "National Office" (then, in Norfolk, Virginia) was invalid because Connecticut has a strong public policy preventing a franchisor from unfairly exerting its economic leverage to take advantage of a franchisee. *Sherman Street Associates, LLC v. JTH Tax, Inc.*, No. 3:03-cv-1875, 2009 WL 426469 (D. Conn. Feb. 20, 2009).

Even if its headquarters are located outside of the state, a franchisee is not protected merely because the franchisor is a Connecticut company, but place-of-business provisions in the Connecticut Act allow a franchisee to qualify for

---

56. R & R Assocs. of Conn., Inc. v. Deltona Corp., Bus. Fran. Guide (CCH) ¶ 7525 (D. Conn. May 19, 1980).

57. *Id.*

protection of at least its Connecticut operations. *New England Surfaces v. E.I. du Pont de Nemours & Co.*, 546 F.3d 1 (1st Cir.), *decision clarified on denial of reh'g*, 546 F.3d 11 (1st Cir. 2008).

Despite the parties' agreement that New York law would apply, the court considered the applicability of the Connecticut Act before concluding that there was no franchise relationship between the parties, as that term is defined by the Connecticut Act. *B & E Juices, Inc. v. Energy Brands, Inc.*, No. 3:07CV1321, 2007 WL 3124903 (D. Conn. Oct. 25, 2007).

In a diversity action, the Connecticut Act does not render a forum selection clause per se unenforceable in federal court. *Sherman Street Associates, LLC v. JTH Tax, Inc.*, No. CIVA3:03CV1875(CFD), 2004 WL 2377227 (D. Conn. Sept. 30, 2004).

Although the franchise agreement called for Pennsylvania courts as the forum, franchisee filed a five-count complaint (two claims under Connecticut Act General Statutes section 42-133f and other claims alleged common law breach of contract and violations of unfair trade practice acts) in Connecticut. A forum selection clause in a franchise agreement is generally enforced, absent evidence of fraud, or overreaching. The court granted franchisor's motion to dismiss, except for the two claims under Connecticut Act General Statutes section 42-133f because, under the Connecticut Act, any franchisee's waiver of rights under the act contained in any franchise agreement is void. *Pepe v. GNC Franchising, Inc.*, 46 Conn. Supp. 296, 750 A.2d 1167 (Conn. Super. Ct. 2000).

In a matter involving a franchisee doing business outside of Connecticut, what the parties intended when they choose Connecticut law is a question to be explored during discovery or perhaps trial. *Diesel Injection Service v. Jacobs Vehicle Equipment*, No. CV980582400S, 1998 WL 950986 (Conn. Sup. Ct. Dec. 4, 1998).

The Connecticut Act applies only to a franchise agreement to be performed in Connecticut or where the franchisee is required to maintain a place of business in Connecticut. Where the franchise agreement provides that Connecticut law applies to an out-of-state franchisee, a distributor agreement's Connecticut choice-of-law provision governs only which state's laws applies to disputes, not whether the jurisdictional perquisites of the Connecticut Act have been satisfied. *Forbes v. Joint Medical Products Corp.*, 976 F. Supp. 124 (D. Conn. 1997).

A franchisee cannot waive the protections of the Connecticut Act by agreeing that another state's law applies to all disputes between the franchisor and franchisee. *R & R Associates of Connecticut, Inc. v. Deltona Corp.*, Business Franchise Guide (CCH) ¶ 7525 (D. Conn. May 19, 1980).

F. Termination

As prerequisites to termination or cancellation, Connecticut Act section 42-133f(a) requires that the franchisor (1) have "good cause," which may include circumstances such as the franchisee's refusal or failure to comply substantially with any material and reasonable obligation of the franchise agreement and (2) provide at least 60 days' advance written notice of such termination or cancellation, stating the cause for termination.[58] There are, however, two circumstances

---

58. CONN. GEN. STAT. § 42-133f(a).

where the Connecticut Act does not require good cause and 60 days' notice: (1) the franchisee's voluntary abandonment of the franchise relationship, and (2) the franchisee is convicted of an offense punishable by an imprisonment term in excess of one year and is directly related to the franchised business conducted by the franchisee.[59] In both instances, notice is still required: (1) for voluntary abandonment, 30 days' notice is required, and (2) for said conviction of an offense, notice may be given at any time following the conviction and will be effective upon delivery and the franchisee's receipt of the notice.[60]

1. What Constitutes Termination or Cancellation

a. Commentary

Beginning in 1995 in *Petereit v. S.B. Thomas, Inc.*,[61] franchisees have raised claims of "constructive termination," resulting from their franchisor taking action adverse to the franchisee without explicitly terminating the relationship. In *Petereit*, three franchisees alleged that the franchisor's realignment of their sales territories caused a substantial loss of revenue and constituted termination, albeit constructive, under the Connecticut Act. Although the Second Circuit Court of Appeals recognized that a cause of action exists for constructive termination of a franchise, it reversed the district court's finding that such a constructive termination had taken place in this instance, holding that "[w]e agree that total abrogation of a franchise is not required to trigger the Act's protections, but cannot agree that *any* negative impact on franchise income resulting from the franchisor's realignment of territories is alone sufficient to be deemed a termination."[62] Constructive termination would clearly be found in a case where a franchisor attempts to drive its franchisee out of business or refuses to continue doing business with the franchisee. Additionally, the court stated that constructive termination will be found when a franchisor's actions result in a *"substantial decline"* in the franchisee's net income.[63]

Determining whether a "substantial decline" has occurred will depend on the particular facts of each case, and that analysis should be "strictly financial, except in close cases, where non-financial factors may have some bearing."[64] Although, ultimately, the case was remanded to the district court for a factual determination of the effect the franchisor's realignment of the franchisees' sales territories had on the franchisees' business, the court provided useful guidance by stating that one franchisee's alleged annual loss of 12 percent of its income and another franchisee's alleged annual loss of $6,000 "do not in our estimation meet the test of a substantial decline in income, in either absolute terms or as a percent of income, so as to justify a finding of constructive termination."[65]

---

59. *Id.*
60. *Id.*
61. 63 F.3d 1169 (2d Cir. 1995), *cert. denied*, 517 U.S. 1119 (1996).
62. *Id.* at 1182 (emphasis in original).
63. *Id.* at 1183 (emphasis in original).
64. *Id.*
65. *Id.*

b. Annotations

Realignment of franchisee's sales territory could constitute constructive termination of franchise under Connecticut Act. To support a finding of constructive termination, the loss must be greater than de minimis but can be less than driving franchisee out of business. Negative impact on franchise income resulting from the franchisor's realignment of sales territories is not, without more, sufficient to be deemed a termination. *Petereit v. S.B. Thomas, Inc.*, 63 F.3d 1169 (2d Cir. 1995).

2. Restrictions on Termination or Cancellation

As already noted, section 42-133f(a) of the Connecticut Act requires, as prerequisites to termination or cancellation, that the franchisor (1) have "good cause," and (2) provide at least 60 days' advance written notice of such termination or cancellation, with the cause stated thereon.[66] The two circumstances where the Connecticut Act's provisions requiring good cause and 60 days' notice do not apply (1) where the franchisee voluntarily abandons the franchise relationship, and (2) where the franchisee is convicted of an offense that is punishable by a term of imprisonment in excess of one year and is directly related to the franchisee's business conducted pursuant to the franchise.[67] In both instances, notice is still required: (1) for voluntary abandonment, 30 days' notice is required and (2) for said conviction of an offense, notice may be given at any time following the conviction and will be effective upon delivery and the franchisee's receipt of the notice.[68]

a. Commentary

See discussion in Section F.1.a.

b. Annotations

See annotations in Section F.1.b.

3. Notice Requirement

a. Commentary

Except for the limited circumstances set forth in the statute, franchisors must provide at least 60 days' advance written notice of termination or cancellation of the franchise agreement, and said notice must state the reasons for termination.[69] The limited exceptions are: (1) if the franchisee voluntarily abandons the franchise, then only 30 days' notice is required; or (2) if the franchisee is convicted of an offense punishable by a term of imprisonment in excess of one year and the offense is directly related to the business conducted by the franchisee pursuant to the franchise agreement, then no notice of termination is necessary.[70]

---

66. CONN. GEN. STAT. § 42-133f(a).
67. Id.
68. Id.
69. Id. § 42-133f(a).
70. Id.

Connecticut Act section 42-133f(b) applies to franchises operating on premises leased by the franchisor to the franchisee under a lease that terminates upon the termination of the franchise. If the franchisor seeks to terminate the lease, notice must be served on the franchisee by a sheriff or other disinterested person and state that the lease shall terminate upon termination of the franchise[71] and that the franchisee may have certain rights under sections 42-133f and 42-133g (Action for Violation). Copies of those sections must be reproduced and attached to the notice.[72]

b. Annotations

Court denied franchisee's motion for temporary restraining order (TRO) seeking to restrain franchisor's activities relating to termination. Terminated franchisee claimed that statutorily required notice was defective but failed to establish irreparable harm sufficient for TRO. In addition, "[w]hen a franchisor fails to afford the required sixty-day notice . . . the appropriate remedy is generally limited to the franchisee's lost profits for the time period the termination was in effect without the proper notice." Accordingly, lack of proper notice can be remedied through money damages that the franchisee suffered during the required notice period. *A.B. Corp. v. Dunkin' Donuts Franchising, LLC*, No. 3:22-CV-1474 (SVN), 2022 U.S. Dist. LEXIS 215371 (D. Conn. Nov. 30, 2022).

Notice of default or notice to cure immediately followed by a notice of termination for failure to cure did not comply with the requirement to give 60 days' notice of termination under the Connecticut Act.

Where a franchisor fails to give adequate notice of termination under the Connecticut Act, however, damages are limited to franchisee's provable loss during the 60-day required notice period. In this case there were no damages because evidence at trial established that the franchisee was operating at a loss. *Sherman Street Associates, LLC v. JTH Tax, Inc.*, No. 3:03-CV-1875 CFD, 2011 WL 3837078, at *8–*9 (D. Conn. Aug. 30, 2011).

4. Grounds for Termination

a. Commentary

Whether or not a franchisor had "good cause" to terminate the franchise relationship is often litigated. The Connecticut Act states that good cause "shall include, but not be limited to the franchisee's refusal or failure to comply substantially with any material and reasonable obligation of the franchise agreement."[73] The Connecticut Act originally prohibited termination without 60 days' written notice but was amended in 1973 to provide that no franchise could be terminated except for "good cause." However, at that time, "good cause" was not defined nor explained. The Connecticut Act was again amended in 1974 to provide that good cause included but was not limited to the franchisee's refusal or failure to comply substantially with any material and reasonable obligation of

---

71. *Id.* § 42-133f(b).
72. *Id.*
73. *Id.* § 42-133f(a).

the franchise agreement. This last amendment was an attempt to address the vagueness of the phrase "good cause" and address the concern expressed by some franchisors that the vagueness gave franchisees an advantage in litigation.

The Second Circuit Court of Appeals in *Petereit v. S.B. Thomas, Inc.* held that "good cause is not limited to proving actual contractual breaches of the franchise agreement but may be based on a franchisor's legitimate business reasons."[74] The franchisor's legitimate business reason for termination was its determination that it could increase sales by realigning the sales territories of its franchisees. The franchisees claimed this act resulted in a constructive termination of their franchises due to a substantial reduction in revenue they experienced. According to the Second Circuit, "[a] seller of goods in the marketplace is justified in identifying untapped opportunities or unutilized potential and adjusting its distribution network to realize greater profits. When the franchisor demonstrates that its business decision is legitimate and made in good faith—even if shown by hindsight to be made in error—a court should not replace the grantor's decision with its own."[75] And further, the court stated that a franchisor need not show unprofitability to establish a legitimate business reason for terminating the franchise. The court found that the franchisor had a legitimate business need to increase sales and that this constituted "good cause" under the act.[76]

The Connecticut Supreme Court in *Hartford Electric Supply Co. v. Allen-Bradley Co., Inc.* affirmed that the trial court correctly decided that a decision to terminate based exclusively on the franchisee's alleged poor performance did not amount to a legitimate business reason under the facts of the case.[77] Instead, it held that to prove that the franchise was terminated for good cause, the franchisor must establish that the franchisee failed substantially to perform essential provisions of the parties' agreement.[78] The franchise agreement in *Hartford* required the franchisee to "vigorously and aggressively promote and develop the market" for the sale of the franchisor's goods.[79] By failing to show how the franchisee's sales performance compared to that of similar distributors or to the growth of the franchisor's sales regionally or nationally in the same period, the court concluded that the franchisor failed to establish that the franchisee substantially failed to fulfill its obligation under the agreement to promote the franchisor's products "vigorously and aggressively."

Though given ample time to make other credit arrangements, the franchisee in *Central Sports, Inc. v. Yamaha Motor Corp.* failed to maintain the line of credit required by the agreement. The court agreed that the franchisor had good cause

---

74. Petereit v. S.B. Thomas, Inc. 63 F.3d 1169, 1184 (2d Cir. 1995).
75. *Id.* at 1184.
76. *Id.* at 1185.
77. Hartford Elec. Supply Co. v. Allen-Bradley Co., Inc., 250 Conn. 334, 736 A.2d 824 (Conn. 1999).
78. *Hartford*, 736 A.2d at 840–41; *see also* Power Draulics-Nielsen, Inc. v. Libbey Owens-Ford Co., No. 82-CIV-1134 (MBM), 1988 WL 31880 (S.D.N.Y. Mar. 11, 1988) (although materiality is a concept the act applies to violations of a franchise agreement, the concept also applies in determining "good cause" for termination when no contractual term is at issue).
79. *Id.*

to terminate the franchise agreement with the franchisee, holding that the franchisee failed to comply with a reasonable material provision of the franchise agreement despite being given 180 days' notice of its violation.[80]

b. Annotations

If a franchise relationship between insurance company and insurance agent had been deemed to exist, the insurance company would have had good cause to terminate the relationship where the agent, contractually obligated to maintain a good reputation in the community, to conduct himself with integrity and to comply with the law, failed to do so and, instead, drew significant local media attention for a significant domestic disturbance requiring police intervention. *Garbinski v. Nationwide Mutual Insurance Co.*, 3:10cv1191(VLB), 2012 WL 3027918 (D. Conn. July 24, 2012), *aff'd, Garbinski v. Nationwide Property & Casualty Insurance Co.*, 523 Fed. Appx. 24 (2d Cir. 2013).

Franchisor successfully established good cause for termination because the franchisee was provided with notice of its failure to comply with a reasonable, material franchise provision and the franchisor gave franchisee more than six months to make substantial progress toward compliance. Franchisee failed to maintain the line of credit as required in the agreement, and franchisor agreed franchisee could seek another financing source or make other credit line arrangements, which franchisee was unsuccessful in obtaining. *Central Sports, Inc. v. Yamaha Motor Corp., U.S.A.*, 477 F. Supp. 2d 503 (D. Conn. 2007).

Nationwide terminated an insurance agent, claiming the agent violated the Connecticut Insurance Code. Because the court could not assess the weight of conflicting evidence, Nationwide's post-verdict motion for judgment was denied, where jury could have found that evidence submitted by Nationwide was not persuasive and jury had enough evidentiary support to find that Nationwide did not have good cause for termination. *Charts v. Nationwide Mutual Insurance Co.*, 397 F. Supp. 2d 357 (D. Conn. 2005).

Good faith, legitimate business decision of franchisor that is based on grounds independent from the actions of franchisee may constitute good cause under the act. *Hartford Electric Supply Co. v. Allen-Bradley Co. Inc.*, 250 Conn. 334, 736 A.2d 824 (Conn. 1999).

5. Required Cure Period

a. Commentary

Not applicable.[81]

b. Annotations

Not applicable.

---

80. Central Sports, Inc. v. Yamaha Motor Corp., U.S.A., 477 F. Supp. 2d 503, 510 (D. Conn. 2007).
81. CONN. GEN. STAT. § 42-133f(a).

6. Repurchase Obligations

a. Commentary

Upon termination, except for any personalized items that have no value to the franchisor, the franchisor must provide the franchisee with "fair and reasonable compensation" for the franchisee's inventory, supplies, equipment, and furnishings purchased from the franchisor.[82] Franchisors are not required to compensate a franchisee for inventory or supplies not purchased directly from the franchisor or its approved sources.[83]

b. Annotations

The author was unable to locate any decisions specifically discussing repurchase obligations under the Connecticut Act other than reciting the statutory language.

G. Restrictions on Nonrenewal

As with termination, section 42-133f(a) of the Connecticut Act requires, as a prerequisite to the failure to renew a franchise, that the franchisor (1) have "good cause" and (2) provide at least 60 days' advance written notice of intent not to renew, with the cause stated thereon.[84] Again, two circumstances where the Connecticut Act does not require 60 days' notice: (1) the franchisee's voluntary abandonment of the franchise relationship, and (2) the franchisee is convicted of an offense punishable by an imprisonment term in excess of one year and is directly related to the franchised business conducted by the franchisee.[85] In both instances, notice is still required: (1) for voluntary abandonment, 30 days' notice is required, and (2) for said conviction of an offense, notice may be given at any time following the conviction and will be effective upon delivery and the franchisee's receipt of the notice.

Except for "good cause" and its exceptions as noted later, section 42-133f states that no franchisor shall fail to renew a franchise "for the reasons stated in subsection (e) of this section."[86] That section states:

> A franchisor may elect not to renew a franchise which involves the lease by the franchisor to the franchisee of real property and improvement, in the event the franchisor (1) sells or leases such real property and improvements to other than a subsidiary or affiliate of the franchisor for any use; or (2) sells or leases such real property to a subsidiary or affiliate of the franchisor, except such subsidiary or affiliate shall not use such real property for the operation of the same business of the franchisee; or (3) converts such real property and improvements to a use not covered by the franchise agreement; or (4) has leased such real property from a person not the franchisee and such lease from such person is terminated or not renewed.[87]

---

82. *Id.* § 42-133f(c).
83. *Id.*
84. *Id.* § 42-133f(a).
85. *Id.*
86. *Id.*
87. *Id.* § 42-133f(e).

1. What Constitutes Nonrenewal

a. Commentary

The Connecticut Act does not specifically define "Nonrenewal." A claim for "constructive non-renewal," would likely be governed by the same standards as the "constructive termination" claims already discussed in the termination section.

b. Annotations

The author was unable to locate any published decisions specifically discussing what constitutes nonrenewal under the Connecticut Act.

2. Restrictions on Nonrenewal

a. Commentary

Refusal by a franchisor to renew a franchise agreement without good cause or to provide the requisite notice is a violation of the Connecticut Act.[88]

b. Annotations

The author was unable to locate any decisions specifically discussing nonrenewal restrictions under the Connecticut Act other than reciting the statutory language.

3. Notice Requirement

a. Commentary

Termination, cancellation, and failure to renew a franchise requires similar notice. For nonrenewal, a franchisor must provide at least 60 days' written notice stating the reasons for nonrenewal prior to the expiration and nonrenewal of the franchise agreement.[89] Similar to termination, if the franchisee voluntarily abandons the franchise, then the required notice period is only 30 days. If the franchisee is convicted of an offense that is punishable by a term of imprisonment in excess of one year and is directly related to the franchisee's business conducted pursuant to the franchise agreement, then no advanced notice is necessary.[90] Longer notice of nonrenewal (as compared to termination) arises when the nonrenewal is based on any of the four reasons set forth in section 42-133f(e). If the franchisor elects not to renew a franchise that involves the lease by the franchisor of real property and improvements for reasons set forth in section 42-133f(e), then the franchisor must give the franchisee written notice of such intent not to renew at least six months prior to the expiration of the franchise agreement.[91]

If the franchise that is subject to a failure to renew arises under the circumstances provided in section 42-133f(b), that is, "operated on premises leased by

---

88. *Id.* § 42-133f(a).
89. *Id.*
90. *Id.*
91. *Id.*

the franchisor to the franchisee under a lease which terminates upon termination of the franchise, and if the franchisor seeks to terminate the lease," notice must be served on the franchisee by a sheriff or other disinterested person and state that the lease shall terminate upon termination of the franchise.[92] The notice must also state that the franchisee may have certain rights under sections 42-133f and 42-133g (Action for Violation), and copies of those sections must accompany the notice.[93]

b. Annotations

The author was unable to locate any decisions that specifically discuss nonrenewal notice requirements under the Connecticut Act other than reciting the statutory language.

4. Grounds for Nonrenewal

a. Commentary

Where the franchisor leases property to the franchisee, the Connecticut Act states that the franchisor may chose not to renew when the franchise (1) sells or leases such real property and improvements to other than a subsidiary or affiliate of the franchisor for any use; (2) sells or leases such real property to a subsidiary or affiliate of the franchisor, except such subsidiary or affiliate shall not use such real property for the operation of the same business of the franchisee; (3) converts such real property and improvements to a use not covered by the franchise agreement; or (4) has leased such real property from a person not the franchisee and such lease from such person is terminated or not renewed.[94] In all other ways, the good cause analysis for nonrenewal is the same as the analysis for termination.

b. Annotations

The author was unable to locate any decisions that specifically discuss nonrenewal notice requirements under the Connecticut Act other than reciting the statutory language.

5. Required Cure Period for Nonrenewal

a. Commentary

Not applicable.[95]

b. Annotations

Not applicable.

---

92. *Id.* § 42-133f(b).
93. *Id.*
94. *Id.* § 42-133f(e).
95. *Id.* § 42-133f(a).

6. Limitations on Franchisors' Right to Impose Conditions for Renewal

a. Commentary

The Connecticut Act does not explicitly address franchisors' rights to impose conditions for renewal.

b. Annotations

Not applicable.

7. Repurchase Obligations

a. Commentary

Certain special requirements related to "termination" of the franchise are discussed earlier in the termination section, but the Connecticut Act does not explicitly state that these special requirements apply to "nonrenewal," and whether these special requirements extend to nonrenewal has not been litigated.

b. Annotations

The author was not able to locate any decisions that specifically discuss franchisors' obligations with respect to nonrenewal.

H. Transfers and Succession

1. Commentary

The Connecticut Act does not contain any restriction on a franchisor's right to object to transfer. However, some of Connecticut's industry-specific franchise laws do restrict a franchisor's right to object to transfer and some specify that consent to assignment of the franchise cannot be unreasonably withheld.[96] Similarly, some of Connecticut's industry-specific franchise laws restrict a franchisor's right to object to transfer on death of a franchisee.[97]

2. Annotations

Not applicable.

I. Other Regulation of the Franchise Relationship

1. Commentary

Not applicable.

2. Annotations

Not applicable.

---

96. *See, e.g., id.* § 42-133m(a) (concerning petroleum marketing franchises) and § 42-133cc(10) (concerning motor vehicle dealerships).

97. *See, e.g., id.* § 42-133m(b) (concerning petroleum marketing franchises) and § 42-133y (concerning motor vehicle dealerships).

J. Remedies and Administrative Action

1. Restrictive Covenants

a. Commentary

The Connecticut Act does not address restrictive covenants.

b. Annotations

Not applicable.

2. Damages

a. Commentary

Any franchisee may bring an action for violation of sections 42-133e to 42-133g, inclusive, to seek to recover damages for a violation of the Connecticut Act.[98] The amount of the franchisee's recoverable damages depends on which provisions of the Connecticut Act the franchisor allegedly violated. A franchisee's recoverable damages caused by the wrongful termination are limited to those that are "directly related" to the franchisee's termination.[99] If a franchisor failed to provide the requisite 60 days' notice, but otherwise complies with the Connecticut Act, a franchisee will only be able to recover its lost profits for the time period that it would have remained in business before the termination would have been effective if notice had been properly given under the Connecticut Act.[100] In *Charter Practices*, no damages were recoverable where the franchisor took control of the franchise's operations during the notice period because the franchisor continued to provide the revenue from the franchise's operations to the franchisee.[101]

No court has directly ruled on whether punitive damages may be recovered against a franchisor who wrongfully terminates a franchise, but in the district court in *Petereit v. S.B. Thomas, Inc.*, a claim for punitive damages was denied.[102]

Under section 42-133g, a franchisee bringing an action, "if successful," is entitled to "costs, including, but not limited to, reasonable attorneys' fees."[103] Interestingly, on its face only franchisees are entitled to costs, and "successful" franchisors cannot recover an award of attorneys' fees. "Successful" is not defined in the statute and the term in this section of the Connecticut Act has not been addressed in any reported decision by any Connecticut state or federal

---

98. CONN. GEN. STAT § 42-133g.
99. Power Draulics-Nielsen, Inc. v. Libbey Owens-Ford Co., No. 82-CIV-1134 (MBM), 1988 WL 31880, at *2 (S.D.N.Y. Mar. 11, 1988).
100. *See* Petereit v. S.B. Thomas, Inc., 63 F.3d 1169, 1186–87 (2d Cir. 1995); Keown Distrib., Inc. v. Gyp-Crete Corp., 618 F. Supp. 632, 643 (D. Conn. 1985).
101. *See* Charter Practices Int'l, LLC v. Robb, No. 3:12-cv-1768 (RNC), 2017 WL 4366717 (D. Conn. Sept. 30, 2017).
102. 853 F. Supp. 55, 63 (D. Conn. 1993), *aff'd in part, rev'd in part*, 63 F.3d 1169 (2d Cir. 1995) (finding that franchisor's acts did not reach the level of being "immoral, unethical, oppressive or unscrupulous").
103. CONN. GEN. STAT. § 42-133g(a).

court, but has been addressed by the First Circuit Court of Appeals.[104] The court in *Virzi* looked to analogous state and federal laws and a New Jersey case that determined that the franchisee had been "successful" because it obtained a temporary restraining order barring the termination of its franchise, even though the franchisee's claims were ultimately dismissed as moot.

The *Virzi* court applied the same analysis used in determining if attorney fees should be awarded for bringing a federal civil rights action.[105] That federal civil rights statute provides that a party may recover attorneys' fees, without a final favorable judgment on the merits, if (1) the lawsuit was a "necessary and important factor" in achieving the relief obtained; and (2) the lawsuit was not "frivolous, unreasonable or groundless."[106] Relying on the findings of the district court, the *Virzi* court found that the franchisee lawsuit was necessary and important to the continuation of the franchise and that the action was not frivolous, unreasonable, or groundless. The *Virzi* court found that the franchisee was a "successful" party and entitled to attorney's fees.

Also, section 42-133g of the Connecticut Act provides that any franchisee may bring an action "in the superior court" to recover damages for violations of the Connecticut Act, but this provision is not intended to exclude actions from being arbitrated if the terms of a franchise agreement provide for arbitration.[107] In *Stodolink*, the franchisee refused the franchisor's demand to arbitrate, claiming that the Connecticut Act provides the franchisee with the right to access to state courts to seek redress and that this right could not be waived.[108] However, the Federal Arbitration Act (FAA) requires enforcement of arbitration clauses voluntarily agreed to by the parties to a contract, leading the *Stodolink* court to conclude that "the state law is not controlling in the face of congressional exercise of authority over interstate commerce" and the franchisee's claims were properly heard by the arbitrators.[109]

There is no express language in the statute granting a right to a trial by jury. Because the Connecticut Act created rights that did not exist at common law, some courts have held that the statute did not give rise to the right to a jury trial. A Connecticut federal district court agreed, holding that a jury trial is not available under the Connecticut Act in the absence of a statutory provision.[110]

b. Annotations

Court did not interpret bad faith and punitive damages as harmonious, and, therefore, jury could find franchisor's actions met the "bad faith" standard, but

---

104. Virzi Subaru, Inc. v. Subaru of New England, Inc., 742 F.2d 677 (1st Cir. 1984).
105. *See* 42 U.S.C. § 1988.
106. *Id.* (quoted in *Virzi*, 742 F.2d at 681).
107. CONN. GEN. STAT. § 42-133g(a).
108. Stodolink v. Yankee Barn Homes, Inc., 574 F. Supp. 557 (D. Conn. 1983).
109. *Id.* at 558; Ironson v. Ameriprise Fin. Servs., Inc., No. 3:11-cv-899 (JBA), 2012 WL 3940141 (D. Conn. Sept. 10, 2012).
110. Sherman Street Assocs., LLC v. JTH Tax, Inc., No. 3:03-cv-1875, 2010 WL 1240748 (D. Conn. Mar. 22, 2010) (striking jury claim).

not the punitive damages standard. *Charts v. Nationwide Mutual Insurance Co.*, 397 F. Supp. 2d 357 (D. Conn. 2005).

Punitive damages were not recoverable where franchisor's acts were not immoral, unethical, oppressive, or unscrupulous in nature. *Petereit v. S.B. Thomas, Inc.*, 853 F. Supp. 55 (D. Conn. 1993), *aff'd in part, rev'd in part*, 63 F.3d 1169 (2d Cir. 1995).

Franchisee is limited to recovering damages that result directly from termination of the franchise. *Power Draulics-Nielsen, Inc. v. Libbey Owens-Ford Co.*, No. 82-CIV-1134 (MBM), 1988 WL 31880 (S.D.N.Y. Mar. 11, 1988).

Where franchisor's only arguable violation of the Connecticut Act was its failure to give 60 days' notice, franchisee was only entitled to recover lost profits associated with the proper notice period. *McKeown Distributors, Inc. v. Gyp-Crete Corp.*, 618 F. Supp. 632 (D. Conn. 1985).

Franchisee, who obtained temporary restraining order and was able to sell franchise on favorable terms prior to termination, was entitled to an award attorneys' fees because his action was deemed "successful," even though there was no final judgment on merits. *Virzi Subaru, Inc. v. Subaru of New England, Inc.*, 742 F.2d 677 (1st Cir. 1984).

The FAA preempts the Connecticut Act with respect to the contractual obligation, and therefore the franchisee's claims are properly heard by the arbitrators. *Stodolink V. Yankee Barn Homes, Inc.*, 574 F. Supp. 557 (D. Conn. 1983).

3. Rescission

a. Commentary
Not applicable.

b. Annotations
Not applicable.

4. Injunctive Relief

a. Commentary
Franchisees may obtain injunctive relief from franchisors to prevent the termination or cancellation of the franchise agreement.[111] Section 42-133g provides that such causes of action may be brought in the superior court.[112]

b. Annotations
In denying franchisee's motion for temporary restraining order (TRO) seeking to restrain franchisor's activities relating to termination, the court found the franchisee failed to establish irreparable harm or imminent "economic disaster" in that terminated franchisee had continued its operations up to the time of the TRO hearing. Terminated franchisee claimed that statutorily required notice was defective but failed to establish irreparable harm sufficient for TRO. In addition,

---

111. Hillegas v. V.B.C., Inc., No. CV074007774S, 2007 WL 3173462 (Conn. Super. Ct. Oct. 15, 2007).
112. CONN. GEN. STAT. § 42-133g(a).

"[w]hen a franchisor fails to afford the required sixty-day notice . . . the appropriate remedy is generally limited to the franchisee's lost profits for the time period the termination was in effect without the proper notice." Accordingly, lack of proper notice can be remedied through money damages. *A.B. Corp. v. Dunkin' Donuts Franchising, LLC*, No. 3:22-CV-1474 (SVN), 2022 U.S. Dist. LEXIS 215371 (D. Conn. Nov. 30, 2022).

Issuance of a temporary injunction preventing termination is appropriate where the franchisor fails to demonstrate good cause for termination. *Hillegas v. V.B.C., Inc.*, No. CV074007774S, 2007 WL 3173462 (Conn. Super. Ct. Oct. 15, 2007).

5. Control Person Liability

a. Commentary
Not applicable.

b. Annotations
Not applicable.

6. Attorneys' Fees

a. Commentary
Franchisees prevailing on a Connecticut Franchise Act claim are entitled to "costs, including, but not limited to, reasonable attorneys' fees."[113] See previous discussion.

b. Annotations
Attorneys for prevailing plaintiff were entitled to fee award under the act and Connecticut Unfair Trade Practices Act that was greater than one provided for by contingency agreement due to the novelty and difficulty of the questions presented, skill required to perform the proper legal service, the amount involved, result obtained, and the experience, reputation and ability of the attorneys. *Charts v. Nationwide Mutual Insurance Co.*, 397 F. Supp. 2d 357 (D. Conn. 2005).

To recover attorneys' fees, the franchisee must be "successful," by meeting a two-part test: obtaining a practical benefit as a result of his attorney's efforts and the lawsuit was not "frivolous, unreasonable or groundless." *Virzi Subaru, Inc. v. Subaru of New England, Inc.*, 742 F.2d 677 (1st Cir. 1984).

Even where the case is eventually dismissed for mootness, the court can find that the franchisee's attorney obtained a practical benefit for his client and is entitled to fees. *Virzi Subaru, Inc. v. Subaru of New England, Inc.*, 742 F.2d 677 (1st Cir. 1984).

7. Limitations on Damage Waivers

a. Commentary
The Connecticut Act states that any waiver of the franchisee's rights under section 42-133f or section 42-133g (which address termination, cancellation,

---

113. *Id.*

and nonrenewal) that is contained in any franchise agreement entered into or amended on or after June 12, 1975, is void.[114] This rule stems from Connecticut's strong public policy preventing a franchisor from unfairly exerting its economic leverage to take advantage of a franchisee.[115] The court reaffirmed this rule in *B & E Juices*, and applied the act despite a choice-of-law provision stating that New York law should apply.[116]

b. Annotations

Relying on section 42-133f(f), in *R & R Associates of Connecticut, Inc. v. Deltona Corp.*,[117] a Connecticut federal district court refused to give effect to the parties' contractual choice of Florida law to govern their relationship. There, a Florida franchisor and Connecticut franchisee entered into an agreement that stated that it "shall be governed by the laws of Florida."[118] Despite this provision, the court held that the franchisee was entitled to the protections of the act: "Under . . . section [42-133f(f)] of the Act, the choice of Florida law provision of the parties' agreement, to the extent that it would operate to deprive the plaintiff of his rights under the Act, must be considered void."[119]

8. Administrative Action

a. Commentary

Not applicable.

b. Annotations

Not applicable.

K. Dispute Resolution

1. Limitations on Franchisors' Ability to Restrict Venue

a. Commentary

The Connecticut Act provides that a franchisee "may" bring an action in the Connecticut superior court,[120] but it does not prohibit parties from litigating or arbitrating elsewhere and the Federal Arbitration Act (FAA) requires enforcement of arbitration clauses voluntarily agreed to by the parties to a contract.[121]

b. Annotations

In a matter involving the nonrenewal of a commercial dealership agreement, dealer asserted violations of the Connecticut Act and the Connecticut Unfair

---

114. *Id.* § 42-133f(f).
115. Sherman St. Assocs., LLC v. JTH Tax, Inc., No. 3:03-cv-1875, 2009 WL 426469, at *2 (D. Conn. Feb. 20, 2009).
116. B & E Juices, Inc. v. Energy Brands, Inc., No. 3:07CV1321, 2007 WL 3124903, at *11 (D. Conn. Oct. 25, 2007).
117. Bus. Franchise Guide (CCH) ¶ 7525 (D. Conn. May 19, 1980).
118. *Id.*
119. *Id.*
120. CONN. GEN. STAT. § 42-133g(a).
121. Stodolink v. Yankee Barn Homes, Inc., 574 F. Supp. 557 (D. Conn. 1983).

Trade Practices Act, and the U.S. District Court for the District of Connecticut granted the manufacturer's motion to transfer to the U.S. District Court for the Southern District of Florida on the basis of a forum selection clause in the parties' dealership agreement. The dealer argued that the claims asserted were outside the scope of the forum selection clause and that "enforcement of the forum-selection clause as to the Connecticut Act claim contravenes a strong public policy of the State of Connecticut in favor of allowing it to litigate a Connecticut Act claim in the courts of Connecticut," but the court disagreed, noting that the fact that the Connecticut Act "allows a plaintiff to file a lawsuit in the state courts of Connecticut does not necessarily mean that it is the strong public policy of the State of Connecticut that any rights under the [Connecticut Act] must be litigated *only* in the courts of Connecticut rather than in any other court." *Id.* at *13–15 (emphasis in original). *Columbia Aircraft Sales, Inc.* v. *Piper Aircraft, Inc.*, Docket No. 3:20-cv-00701 (JAM), 2020 U.S. Dist. LEXIS 184978 (D. Conn. Oct. 6, 2020).

A Uniform Franchise Offering Circular's statements regarding Connecticut having a state relationship statute that may supersede the Franchise Agreement did not expressly mention arbitration and therefore was not evidence that the parties meant to exempt claims under the Connecticut Act from the arbitration clause. The Connecticut Act's right of access to state court and anti-waiver provisions do not render an otherwise valid arbitration clause unenforceable. *Ironson v. Ameriprise Financial Services, Inc.*, No. 3:11-cv-899 (JBA), 2012 WL 3940141 (D. Conn. Sept. 10, 2012).

Because the Connecticut Act created rights that did not exist at common law, some courts have held that the statute did not give rise to the right to a jury trial. A Connecticut federal district court agreed, holding that a jury trial is not available under the Connecticut Act in the absence of a statutory provision. *Sherman Street Associates, LLC v. JTH Tax, Inc.*, No. 3:03-cv-1875, 2010 WL 1240748 (D. Conn. Mar. 22, 2010) (striking jury claim and collecting cases).

Even if the Connecticut Act provides a right to a trial by jury, knowing and voluntary waivers of that right would be enforceable. *Sherman Street Associates, LLC v. JTH Tax, Inc.*, No. 3:03-cv-1875, 2010 WL 1240748, at *2 (D. Conn. Mar. 22, 2010).

Although the act secures a franchisee's right of access to the Connecticut state courts for redress of any violations of the act, enforcement of an arbitration clause in the parties' franchise agreement pursuant to the Federal Arbitration Act does not constitute a waiver of the franchisee's rights under the act and the arbitration clause is not void. *Stodolink v. Yankee Barn Homes, Inc.*, 574 F. Supp. 557 (D. Conn. 1983).

2. Limitations Period

a. Commentary

The Connecticut Act does not contain a limitations period, and no cases have litigated the applicable limitations period. Under Connecticut law, if a statute includes no express statute of limitations, the court borrows the most suitable statute of limitations on the basis of the nature of the cause of action or of the right sued upon.[122] The two most likely candidates would be the Connecticut statute of limitations for contract claims and tort claims.[123] The limitations period for contract claims in Connecticut is six years after the right of action accrues, and the limitations period for tort claims in Connecticut is three years from the date of the act or omission complained of.[124]

b. Annotations
Not applicable.

---

122. *See, e.g.*, Bellemare v. Wachovia Mortg. Corp., 284 Conn. 193, 199, 931 A.2d 916 (2007).
123. CONN. GEN. STAT. § 52-576 (contract), § 52-577 (tort).
124. *Id.*

Delaware

Jaime S. Paoletti

I. Introduction to Statute

Delaware is not a franchise registration state and does not have a franchise disclosure law applicable to the sale of franchises. It does, however, have franchise relationship laws that govern certain franchises. The Delaware Franchise Security Law (DFSL) regulates any franchise that meets its definition. The DFSL was created to protect franchisees from unjust franchisor conduct, including unjust terminations, nonrenewals, and unreasonable rents.[1] The DFSL prevents franchisors from providing short-term contracts with no renewal rights and instead effectively requires such contracts, at the franchisor's peril, to extend into the indefinite future terminable only upon certain conditions.[2] As one court put it, the DFSL protects the "franchise distributor" who is economically dependent on the sale of the franchisor's products and who has used its efforts in promoting them.[3]

Delaware also has the Motor Vehicle Franchising Practices Act (MVFPA), but this industry-specific law is beyond the scope of this chapter.[4]

II. Commentary and Annotations

A. Definition of Franchise

Under the Federal Trade Commission (FTC) rule, a franchise exists where there are three elements present: (1) use of a trademark; (2) required payment or fee; and (3) significant assistance or control in the method of operation. The DFSL looks to similar elements but is drafted toward protection of "franchised

---

1. Globe Liquor Co. v. Four Roses Distillers Co., 281 A.2d 19, 21 (Del. 1971).
2. *Id.*
3. *Id.* at 19, 21.
4. The MVFPA regulates vehicle manufacturers, distributors, or wholesalers and factory or distributor representatives, and the franchises issued by same. DEL. CODE ANN. tit. 6, §§ 4901 *et seq.* Franchised distributors who operate a service station, filling station, store, garage, or other place of business for the sale of *motor fuel* for delivery into the service tank or tanks of any vehicle propelled by an internal combustion engine are governed by the DFSL. *See* DEL. CODE ANN. tit. 6, § 2551(2)(d).

distributors."[5] Therefore, the DFSL's somewhat unique definition, including the purchase or distribution of product, provides sweeping coverage of product and service distribution relationships without requiring the same level of franchisor control over day-to day operations required by the FTC rule and other franchise relationship laws. Under the DFSL, a franchise relationship may exist even when the franchisor does not exert substantial control over the franchised distributors method of doing business.[6] The DFSL's definitions, which include selling trademarked product in or through "retail outlets" and operating a services station for the sale of "motor fuel" are potentially becoming antiquated in light of e-commerce and the rise of electronic vehicle charging franchises. It will be interesting to see how the definitions change, or their interpretations evolve, as commerce advances.

1. Trademark Element

a. Commentary

The DFSL expressly contemplates that a franchised distributor will be purchasing or taking on consignment products that bear the franchisor's trademark or trade name for the primary purpose of selling such products to retail outlets.[7] Although the definition does not expressly reference use of the franchisor's trademark when the products being distributed are publications or petroleum and automotive products, in practicality, most petroleum and automotive products offered by distributors are likely to be associated with the franchisor's trade name or trademark.[8] As such, although a franchised distribution relationship may still exist where there is no trademark license, most franchised distributers will be selling product under a trademark.

Although the DFSL is drafted to toward protecting "franchised distributors," the definition of a "franchised distributor" is likely to encompass other franchise relationships as well. The DFSL's definition of franchised distributor includes an entity that through a retail outlet sells products that bear the trademark or trade name of no more than three manufacturers, producers, publishers, trademark licensors, or trade name licensors.[9] The DFSL then defines products as "any tangible items offered for sale irrespective of their nature."[10] Accordingly, most services franchises, including quick service restaurants and convenience stores, will sell tangible items from a retail outlet that bear only one franchisor's trademark. Indeed, in *Sandhu v. 7-Eleven, Inc.*, the court held that the DFSL governed the 7-Eleven franchise relationship.[11]

---

5. DEL. CODE ANN. tit. 6, § 2551.
6. Id.
7. Id. § 2551(2); id. § 2551(3).
8. Id. § 2551(3).
9. Id. § 2551(2) (b).
10. Id. § 2551(4).
11. *See, e.g.*, Sandhu v. 7-Eleven, Inc., 45 F. Supp. 3d 426, 430 (D. Del. 2014) (holding DFSL applied to 7-Eleven constructive termination case).

b. Annotations

In *Globe Liquor Co. v. Four Roses Distillers Co.*, the distributor and manufacturer entered into a franchise agreement for one year.[12] Before the end of the year, the manufacturer notified the distributor that it would not be renewing the franchise agreement.[13] Globe sued the manufacturer arguing that the language in the DFSL prevented Four Roses from not renewing the franchise agreement as a unilateral decision without just cause.[14] Four Roses argued that the DFSL was unconstitutional because it impaired the obligations of a contract and would force them to continue working with Globe past the agreed upon term between the parties, the language was vague, and the act was unreasonable in its distinction between wholesale and retail franchise distributors.[15] The Delaware Supreme Court contemplated the constitutionality of the DFSL against four separate sections of law: article 1, section 10, and the 14th Amendment of the Constitution of the United States, and article 1, sections 7 and 8 of the Constitution of the State of Delaware.[16] The court agreed with Four Roses and found that the DFSL was unconstitutional under article 1, section 10 of the U.S. Constitution for requiring substantive changes under the terms of the contract that was entered into before the DFSL was enacted.[17] The court reasoned that the DFSL was to transform the contract between Globe and Four from a one-year contract "with no right of renewal on the part of Globe to a contract to extend into the indefinite future which Four Roses may terminate only upon certain conditions and at its peril."[18] However, the court upheld application of the DFSL against the vagueness argument because "good cause" and "bad faith" have settled meaning in law. Specifically, the court found that the term "bad faith" may be defined by referring to other law, such as the Uniform Commercial Code (UCC), that contains the same term.[19] The UCC defines good faith as "honesty in fact and the observance of reasonable commercial standards of fair dealing in the trade."[20]

The court also found that the DFSL's distinction between dealers who carry "no more than 3" lines of trademark or trade name products and those who carry more than three is not unconstitutional because the State has the ability to determine the need to protect certain classes of businesses over others.[21]

2. Franchisee Fee Element

a. Commentary

The definition of a franchise under the DFSL requires a payment of $100 or more by the franchised distributor to the franchisor; however, arrangements

---

12. 281 A.2d at 19, 20.
13. *Id.*
14. *Id.*
15. *Id.* at 21–23.
16. *Id.* at 20.
17. *Id.* at 21.
18. *Id.*
19. *Id.* at 19–21.
20. U.C.C. § 2-103.
21. *Globe Liquor Co.*, 281 A.2d at 22–23.

involving the sale of petroleum products and operation of a service station need not satisfy the fee element to qualify as a franchise.[22]

b. Annotations

In *James v. Tandy Corp.*, the court determined that the DFSL applied because the plaintiff, a Radio Shack distributor, met the definition of franchised distributor and paid more than $100 to enter into the agreement with Radio Shack, even though the payment was in the form of a "security deposit."[23] In so holding the court reasoned that the security deposit was not fully refundable because, by the terms of the agreement between plaintiff and Radio Shack, a portion of the security deposit could be retained by Radio Shack to compensate for low profit's at plaintiff's store.[24] Likewise, the court found the plaintiff would never fully receive back the interest that his money has or could have earned for the past 12 years.[25] In sum, the court found, "Radio Shack received a monetary benefit from the use of plaintiff's security deposit and plaintiff gave up a corresponding value."[26]

In *Del-Way Petroleum Co. v. Phillips Petroleum Co.*, the purchaser brought a claim against the supplier for wrongful termination of certain contracts and alleged, inter alia, protection under the DFSL.[27] The court held that a fee paid for goods or services cannot be a "franchise fee" because it is not paid for the right to enter into the relationship.[28] In so holding, the court reasoned that "in view of the nominal amount established as the standard, i.e., $100, it seems unrealistic to think that any and all payments required in connection with the business arrangement, including the wholesale cost of goods for resale, were contemplated as being sufficient to turn the relationship into a protected 'franchise' which could only be terminated thereafter by the supplier for good cause."[29]

In *A.R. Dervaes Co. v. Houdaille Industries*, the plaintiff distributor brought an action for injunctive relief against defendant manufacturer, seeking to enjoin an alleged wrongful contract termination pursuant to the DFSL.[30] The court found that the distributor was not a franchisee within the meaning of the DFSL because the required minimum inventory purchase was not a "franchise fee."[31]

In *Dave Greytak Enterprises, Inc. v. Mazda Motors of America, Inc.*, a car dealer who paid a $30,000 up-front payment for signs and equipment did not pay a "franchise fee," under the DFSL because the costs were construed as an investment necessary to enable the dealer to perform and carry out the dealer agreement.[32]

---

22. DEL. CODE ANN. tit. 6, §§ 2551(1), 2551(2)(d).
23. James v. Tandy Corp., Civil Action No. 7033, 1984 Del. Ch. LEXIS 571, at *8–9 (Ch. Nov. 1, 1984).
24. *Id.* at *9.
25. *Id.*
26. *Id.*
27. No. 4802, 1977 Del. Ch. LEXIS 187, at *1 (Del. Ch. Mar. 10, 1977).
28. *Id.* at *7.
29. *Id.*
30. C.A. No. 6471, 1981 Del. Ch. LEXIS 545, at *1 (Del. Ch. Sept. 29, 1981).
31. *Id.* at *8–*9.
32. 622 A.2d 14, 19 (Del. Ch. 1992).

Although the car dealer met the definitional requirements of the MVFPA, the defendant manufacturers' actions were not prohibited by the MVFPA.[33]

In *Uniroyal Chemical Co. v. Syngenta Crop Protection, Inc.*, the court held the DFSL did not apply where corporation had not paid more than $100 to enter the agreements because money expended to develop new uses for products is not a franchise fee under DFSL.[34]

The DFSL applies to franchises that import liquor so long as they pay at least a $100 franchise fee.[35]

3. Community of Interest; Significant Degree of Control; Joint Marketing Plan

a. Commentary

Unlike the FTC rule, the definition of franchise under the DFSL does not require a marketing plan, system, or other showing of significant assistance or control over the franchisee's method of operation. This distinction is likely because the DFSL was drafted to regulate a distribution relationship even if there is no particular marketing plan or system, such as the exclusive rights to distribute a product within a certain market area, without a requirement as to standardized procedure for distribution that the franchisee is required. A distribution agreement may take an infinite number of forms and still constitute a franchise relationship.[36] The most common scenario is one in which a manufacturer, producer, assembler, importer, refiner, publisher, or any provider of services ("franchisor") wants to reach new markets by selling a third party the right to be the franchisor's distributor in a selected territory.[37] The DFSL protects any purchaser of trademarked products who resells those products to retail outlets.[38] As such, the DFSL provides broad coverage of product and/or services distribution relationships.

b. Annotations

In *Doe v. Massage Envy Franchising, LLC*, the plaintiff alleged that the franchisor who controlled the franchisee's day-to-day operations should be liable where a franchised Massage Envy employee sexually assaulted her and that prior to working at Massage Envy, the employee worked for another franchisee where he was the subject of several complaints for inappropriate touching.[39] The court denied the franchisor's motion to dismiss and held that where a franchise agreement goes beyond setting standards and the franchisor exercises the right to control daily operations, an agency relationship exists under Delaware law.[40]

---

33. *Id.* at 21.
34. 2006 WL 516749 (D. Conn. Mar. 1, 2006).
35. Del. Alcoholic Bev. Control Comm'n v. B-F Spirits, Ltd., 429 A.2d 975, 977–78 (Del. 1981).
36. H. Bret Lowell & John F. Dienelt, *Drafting Distribution Agreements: The Unwitting Sale of Franchises and Business Opportunities*, 11 DEL. J. CORP. L. 725, 728 (1986).
37. *Id.*
38. DEL. CODE ANN. tit. 6, § 2551(1).
39. 2021 Del. Super. LEXIS 18, at *4.
40. *Id.* at *6.

B. Scope and Jurisdiction

1. Commentary

The DFSL applies to anyone with a place of business within Delaware who pays a fee of $100 or more to become a wholesaler of a trademark or trade name products; a retailer of products that bears the trademark or trade name of no more than three manufacturers; a wholesaler of a publication; or an operator of gas station or similar outlet for selling petroleum products. The $100 fee requirement does not apply to gas stations or petroleum distributors that otherwise meet the statutory definition of franchise.[41]

2. Annotations

An office and/or residence located in Delaware constitutes a "place of business" within the meaning of the DFSL.[42] However, even though the distributor agreement was governed by Delaware law, a Massachusetts and New York dealer could not avail itself of the protections of the DFSL because it did not have a place of business in Delaware by virtue of having paid fees related to Dupont's Delaware "Warranty Center."[43] Similarly, a manufacturer's representative who solicited orders in Delaware, but neither accepted goods on consignment in Delaware nor operated a retail outlet in the state, could not invoke the protections of the DFSL.[44]

The DFSL may be applied to any contract entered into or renewed after July 8, 1970.[45] In *Globe Liquor Co.*, the distributor and manufacturer entered into a franchise agreement for one year.[46] Before the end of the year, the manufacturer notified the distributor that it would not be renewing the franchise agreement.[47] The court looked at the constitutionality of the DFSL and held that it would be unconstitutional to apply the DFSL to any contract entered into before, and not renewed after, July 8, 1970.[48]

C. Termination

1. What Constitutes Termination or Cancellation

a. Commentary

A franchise agreement may end through cancellation or termination when the franchisor terminates the contract or refuses or fails to renew the franchise agreement. The DFSL provides franchisees with protection from unjust

---

41. DEL. CODE ANN. tit. 6, § 2551(1), (2).
42. 33 Flavors of Greater Del. Valley, Inc. v. Bresler's 33 Flavors, Inc., 475 F. Supp. 217, 228 n.32. (D. Del. 1979).
43. KBQ, Inc. v. E.I. duPont deNemours and Co., 6 F. Supp. 2d 94, 99 (D. Mass. 1998).
44. George R. Darche Assocs., Inc. v. Beatrice Foods Co., 538 F. Supp. 429, 434 (D.N.J. 1981).
45. Paradee Oil Co., Inc. v. Phillips Petroleum Co., 320 A.2d 769 (Del. Ch. 1974), *aff'd*, 43 A.2d 610 (Del. 1975).
46. 281 A.2d at 19–20.
47. *Id.*
48. *Id.* at 21.

terminations and nonrenewals.[49] It also protects franchisees from constructive terminations, prohibiting franchisors from "unjustly refusing to deal with a franchised distributor with whom the franchisor has been dealing for at least 2 years."[50] Although the statute does not define constructive terminations, in *Sandhu v. 7-Eleven, Inc.*, the court held that the DFSL "does permit a cause of action for constructive or *de facto* termination, consistent with the law's general purpose which is to remedy the imbalance of power in the franchise relationship by adding a few statutory pounds to the franchisee's side of the scales."[51]

b. Annotations

The DFSL permits a cause of action for "constructive or de facto termination" when the franchisor's actions are so egregious to amount to a repudiation of the contract.[52]

In *Sandhu v. 7-Eleven, Inc.*, a 7-Eleven franchisee alleged constructive termination following its failure of the franchisor's announced audit.[53] In its motion for injunctive relief, franchisee argued that the DFSL standard applied instead of the usual injunctive relief standard.[54] The court agreed that the DFSL permits a cause of action for constructive termination and requires that in order to maintain the status quo pending a full hearing, a franchisee must show "some probability" that the franchisor was attempting to terminate the relationship in bad faith or without just cause, but found nonetheless that the franchisee failed to carry this burden.[55]

The court issued an injunction maintaining status quo after finding that abandoning a goods distributor with less than four months' notice, while continuing to supply nearby distributors, may be "bad faith."[56]

Terms "good cause" and "bad faith" are not unconstitutionally vague and may be defined by reference to other laws and similar terms, such as the National Labor Relations Act, the Uniform Commercial Code, the Unemployment Compensation Act, and Rule 46 of the Delaware Alcoholic Beverage Control Commission.[57]

A nonrenewal is unjust when it is found to be unfair or unconscionable "such as no man in his senses and not under delusion would make on the one hand, and as no honest or fair man would accept, on the other."[58] To show unfairness or unconscionability, the franchise must show that the contract terms bear "no reasonable relation to the business risks involved," or that they are "so

---

49. Del. Code Ann. tit. 6, § 2552.
50. *Id.* § 2552(i).
51. 45 F. Supp. 3d 426, 428–29 (D. Del. 2014) (internal quotations omitted).
52. Kirkwood Kin Corp. v. Dunkin' Donuts, Inc., No. 94C-03-189-WTQ, 1997 Del. Super. LEXIS 30, 1997 WL 529587 (Del. Super. Jan. 29, 1997).
53. 45 F. Supp. 3d 426, 428–29 (D. Del. 2014).
54. *Id.* at 429.
55. *Id.* at 430.
56. Paradee Oil Co., Inc. v. Phillips Petroleum Co., 320 A.2d 769 (Del. Ch. 1975).
57. Globe Liquor Co. v. Four Roses Distillers Co., 281 A.2d 19, 22 (Del. 1971).
58. Tulowitzki v. Atl. Richfield Co., 396 A.2d 956, 960 (Del. 1978).

one-sided as to be oppressive."[59] The Trial Court properly refused to grant an injunction against termination of a gas station franchisee that would not purchase "vapor recovery equipment" that the Environmental Protection Agency might require.[60]

2. Restrictions on Termination or Cancellation

a. Commentary

The DFSL prohibits "unjust" terminations of a franchise, meaning (1) without good cause or (2) in bad faith.[61] Any contract provision that permits such a termination is "against public policy and shall not be enforced in the courts of [Delaware]."[62] The statute, however, does not expressly define "good cause" or "bad faith."

b. Annotations

Plaintiff bears the burden to establish an unjust termination.[63]

3. Notice Requirement

a. Commentary

The DFSL requires 90 days' notice prior to any termination or nonrenewal.[64] Accordingly, notwithstanding any provision to the contrary in the franchise agreement, any termination of a franchise or election not to renew must be made on at least 90 days' notice.

b. Annotations

There are no applicable annotations.

4. Grounds for Termination

a. Commentary

The DFSL prohibits "unjust" franchise terminations, which means a franchisor cannot terminate a franchise without (1) good cause or (2) in bad faith.[65] Contracts that permit such termination are against Delaware public policy and shall not be enforced.[66] A termination is considered unjust if it is "without good cause or in bad faith."[67]

---

59. *Id.*
60. *Id.*
61. DEL. CODE ANN. tit. 6, § 2552.
62. *Id.*
63. James v. Tandy Corp., Civil Action No. 7033, 1984 Del. Ch. LEXIS 571 (Ch. Nov. 1, 1984).
64. DEL. CODE ANN. tit. 6, § 2555.
65. *Id.* § 2552.
66. *Id.*
67. *Id.*

b. Annotations

Terms "good cause" and "bad faith" are not unconstitutionally vague and may be defined by reference to other laws and similar terms, such as the National Labor Relations Act, the Uniform Commercial Code, the Unemployment Compensation Act, and Rule 46 of the Delaware Alcoholic Beverage Control Commission.[68]

5. Required Cure Period

a. Commentary

Not applicable.[69]

b. Annotations

Not applicable.

6. Repurchase Obligations

a. Commentary

Although the DFSL does not specifically require the franchisor to buy back the franchisee's inventory upon termination or nonrenewal, the statute allows the franchisee to seek an order from the Court of Chancery requiring the franchisor to deal with the franchised distributor on fair and competitive terms. Although the DFSL does not specifically require that the franchisor buy back inventory, it is possible that a franchised distributor may use the language of statute requiring the franchisor to deal with the franchised distributor on "fair and competitive terms" to seek a buyback of inventory used in the franchised business.[70]

b. Annotations

There are no applicable annotations for this section.

D. Restrictions on Nonrenewal

1. What Constitutes Nonrenewal

a. Commentary

The DFSL declares that "the failure of a franchisor to renew a franchise shall be deemed to be "unjust" or to have been made "unjustly," if such failure to renew is without good cause or in bad faith.[71]

The DFSL prohibits "unjust" franchise nonrenewals, which means a nonrenewal cannot be made without (1) good cause or (2) in bad faith.[72] Contracts that permit such termination are against Delaware public policy and shall not be enforced.[73]

---

68. Globe Liquor Co. v. Four Roses Distillers Co., 281 A.2d 19, 22 (Del. 1971).
69. *See* DEL. CODE ANN. tit. 6, § 2555.
70. DEL. CODE ANN. tit. 6, § 2553(b).
71. *Id.* § 2552(b).
72. *Id.*
73. *Id.* § 2552(f).

b. Annotations

In *Tulowitzki v. Atlantic Richfield Co.*, plaintiff lessee operated an automotive service station in Delaware pursuant to a lease.[74] Before the expiration date of the lease, defendants sent plaintiff a new lease with an addendum for rent for certain equipment that the EPA might require.[75] Plaintiff argued the terms of the new lease created a constructive nonrenewal.[76] On appeal, the Delaware Supreme Court assumed arguendo that the DFSL applied, but held that there was no unjust termination or nonrenewal.[77] In so holding, the court reasoned and held that the terms of the renewal were not unjust, because to be unjust the terms must be unconscionable and to be unconscionable "there must be an absence of meaningful choice and contract terms unreasonably favorable to one of the parties."[78]

2. Restrictions on Nonrenewal

a. Commentary

Nonrenewals must not be "without good cause or in bad faith."[79]

b. Annotations

The key to eligibility for relief under this subchapter is found at this section where the term "unjustly" is defined as being "without good cause or in bad faith."[80]

The trial court properly refused to grant an injunction against termination of a gas station that would not purchase "vapor recovery equipment" that the Environmental Protection Agency might require because there is no unjust termination or failure to renew a lease without good cause, nor any act of bad faith, where the franchisor demonstrates that the terms of an addendum to the lease constitutes a reasonable increase in rent.[81]

For a term of a proposed renewal agreement to be the basis of an "unjust" nonrenewal, it must bear no reasonable relation to the business risk involved or be so one-sided as to be oppressive.[82] For a business requirement to be reasonable, it need not necessarily be profitable for the franchisee.[83]

---

74. 396 A.2d 956, 958 (Del. 1978); *see also* discussion subsection D.4.a in this chapter.
75. *Tulowitzki*, 396 A.2d at 958.
76. *Id.* at 959.
77. *Id.* at 960.
78. *Id.*
79. DEL. CODE ANN. tit. 6, § 2552.
80. Paradee Oil Co., Inc. v. Phillips Petroleum Co., 320 A.2d 769, 775 (Del. Ch. 1975).
81. *Id.*
82. *Id.*
83. *Id.*

3. Notice Requirement

a. Commentary

The DFSL requires 90 days' notice prior to franchisor's election not to renew a franchise.[84] Accordingly, notwithstanding any provision to the contrary in the franchise agreement, any election not to renew the franchise agreement must be made on at least 90 days' notice.

b. Annotations

There are no annotations applicable to this section.

4. Grounds for Nonrenewal

a. Commentary

Under the DFSL, no franchisor may unjustly fail or refuse to renew a franchise.[85] The statute does not specifically define "just cause," but rather states, "the failure of a franchisor to renew a franchise shall be deemed to be "unjust," or to have been made "unjustly" if such failure to renew is without good cause or in bad faith."[86] Such broad definitions allow courts to apply a totality of the circumstances analysis.[87]

b. Annotations

A court refused to issue an injunction for potential constructive nonrenewal where franchisor terminated the exclusive distribution agreement but offered to continue selling its products to distributor at an increased price. *Artoss, Inc. v. Artoss GmbH*, No. 20-cv-00741, 2021 WL 7416584 (D. Del. Dec. 9, 2021). In denying the motion, the court noted that the distributor could not show irreparable harm where it could continue buying products, even at a loss, because the loss of funds could be calculated and ascertained as part of a jury award of damages.[88]

5. Required Cure Period

a. Commentary

Not applicable.[89]

b. Annotations

There are no applicable annotations.

---

84. DEL. CODE ANN. tit. 6, § 2555.
85. *Id.* § 2552(h).
86. *Id.* § 2552(b).
87. *See, e.g., Tulowitzki*, 396 A.2d at 956.
88. *Id.*
89. DEL. CODE ANN. tit. 6, § 2555.

6. Limitations on Franchisors' Right to Impose Conditions for Renewal

a. Commentary

A franchisor cannot impose conditions on renewal that would make the renewal unjust.[90] Accordingly, a franchisor should ensure that conditions for renewal are reasonable and related to legitimate business interests, as courts may consider if renewal requirements are justifiable and not excessively burdensome. The DFSL does not expressly address whether, as a condition of renewal, a franchisor may require that the franchisee pay a fee and execute the then-current franchise agreement. However, if the franchise agreement contains language spelling out that the franchisee's right to renew is conditioned on the franchisee's acceptance and agreement to new terms, and the new terms are made system-wide to reflect changes necessitated by the market or other legitimate business reasons, such a condition on renewal is likely to be upheld.

There is no unjust termination or failure to renew a lease without good cause, nor any act of bad faith, where the franchisor demonstrates that based on the totality of circumstances, the terms of an addendum to a lease constitutes a reasonable increase in rent based on an estimate of the franchisor's increase in expenditures imposed upon it by a third party.[91]

b. Annotations

There is no case law addressing this issue.

E. Transfers and Succession

1. Commentary

Not applicable.

2. Annotations

Not applicable.

F. Other Regulation of the Franchise Relationship

1. Commentary

Under the DFSL, a franchisor may not charge a franchised distributor excessive rent for real or personal property.[92] The issue of whether the rent is excessive must be considered "in light of the use to which the property has been placed by the franchisor and/or the interest of the franchisor in the real or personal property."[93] Charging excessive rent is actionable as if it were "an unjust

---

90. DEL. CODE ANN. tit. 6, § 2552(h).
91. *Tulowitzki*, 396 A.2d at 960.
92. DEL. CODE ANN. tit. 6, § 2552(j).
93. *Id.*

termination of the franchise."[94] This provision applies when the impact of the excessive rent is a de facto termination or nonrenewal of the franchise.[95]

Under the DFSL, a franchisor may not "unjustly" refuse to deal with a franchisee with whom it has been dealing for at least two years.[96]

G. Remedies and Administrative Action

1. Restrictive Covenants

a. Commentary

The DFSL does not address restrictive covenants; however, it does state that "[i]ndividuals or entities who are parties to a franchise agreement as set out by the Federal Trade Commission shall not be deemed employees for purposes of Chapter 11 of Title 19 (Wage and Payment Collection)."[97] This classification clarification may bear on restrictive covenant analysis under appliable laws.

b. Annotations

There are no applicable annotations.

2. Damages

a. Commentary

If a franchisor threatens, attempts to, or actually unjustly terminates or fails to renew, the franchised distributor may seek damages related to lost assets, goodwill, and profits. The franchised distributor may also seek injunctive relief.[98] A fractional portion of the franchised distributor's tangible assets may be awarded as damages using a formula related to a proportion of the franchisee's gross sales in the state.[99] Damages for loss of goodwill, lost profits of no less than five times profits in most recently completed fiscal year, attorneys' fees, and all other damages are also available under the law.[100] A wrongfully nonrenewed franchised distributor may sue for damages and injunctive relief plus reasonable attorneys' fees and expenses.[101]

b. Annotations

Although the statute details certain damages that any award "shall include," it is unconstitutional for a court to award the listed statutory damages without proof of actual damages.[102]

---

94. *Id.*
95. Kirkwood Kin Corp. v. Dunkin Donuts, Inc., No. 94C-03-189-WTQ, 1997 Del. Super. LEXIS 30, 1997 WL 529587 (Del. Super., Jan 29, 1997); Sandhu v. 7-Eleven, Inc., 45 F. Supp. 3d 426 (D. Del. 2014).
96. DEL. CODE ANN. tit. 6, § 2552(i).
97. *Id.* § 2554.
98. *See* Section G.4 in this chapter.
99. DEL. CODE ANN. tit. 6, § 2553(c)(1).
100. *Id.* § 2553(c)(2)–(5).
101. *Id.* § 2553.
102. Globe Liquor Co. v. Four Roses Distillers Co., 281 A.2d 19, 24 (Del. 1971).

3. Rescission

a. Commentary
Not applicable.

b. Annotations
Not applicable.

4. Injunctive Relief

a. Commentary
The DFSL allows a franchised distributor to seek injunctive relief but does not require a court to enjoin a threatened violation of the statute; that decision is within the court's discretion.[103] It is, however, easier to obtain an injunction under the DFSL than the usual common law standard because a party seeking an injunction under the DFSL need not show a "substantial likelihood of success on the merits," and instead only has to show some probability that the franchisor was terminating in bad faith or without just cause.

b. Annotations
Although the DFSL uses the word "shall" to describe the right to injunctive relief under the statute, the legislature's intent was not to grant an aggrieved franchisee the right to an "automatic" injunction.[104]

To obtain an injunction under the DFSL, a franchisee was not required to show a "substantial likelihood" of success on the merits, but instead was required to demonstrate "some probability" that the franchisor was attempting to terminate the franchise relationship in bad faith or without just case, regardless of the franchise agreement language.[105]

5. Control Person Liability

a. Commentary
Not applicable.

b. Annotations
Not applicable.

6. Attorneys' Fees

a. Commentary
The DFSL allows for recovery of "reasonable counsel fees and expenses incurred" in actions brought pursuant to the DFSL.[106] The statutory language explicitly provides for an award of counsel fees where the franchisor violates the DFSL.

---

103. Paradee Oil Co., Inc. v. Phillips Petroleum Co., 320 A.2d 769, 775 (Del. Ch. 1975).
104. *Id.*
105. Sandhu v. 7-Eleven, Inc., 45 F. Supp. 3d 426, 430 (D. Del. 2014).
106. DEL. CODE ANN. tit. 6, § 2553(c)(5).

b. Annotations
There are no applicable annotations.

7. Limitations on Damages Waivers
a. Commentary
Not applicable.

b. Annotations
Not applicable.

8. Administrative Action
a. Commentary
Not applicable.

b. Annotations
Not applicable.

H. Dispute Resolution

1. Limitations on Franchisor's Ability to Restrict Venue
a. Commentary
The DFSL does not expressly restrict venue or choice of law. Under Delaware law, a choice-of-law provision is likely to be upheld so long as the jurisdiction selected bears some material relationship to the transaction and the law of the foreign jurisdiction is not repugnant to the public policy of Delaware.[107] That said, the DFSL is likely to apply regardless of choice of law because it embodies Delaware's strong public policy to protect franchised distributors.[108]

b. Annotations
Plaintiff franchisee sued defendant in Delaware state court, seeking a declaratory judgment that an amendment to the franchise agreement was void.[109] The franchisor removed the case to federal court and moved to dismiss or transfer to the District of Connecticut.[110] The district court denied the motion to dismiss

---

107. Shadewell Grove IP, LLC v. Mrs. Fields Franchising, LLC, No. 1691-N, 2006 Del. Ch. LEXIS 85, 2006 WL 1375106 (Del. Ch., May 8, 2006); *see also* BBDova, LLC v. Automotive Techs., Inc., 358 F. Supp. 2d 387 (D. Del. 2005) (choice of forum provision not per se violation of public policy of DFSL but may be a violation where litigant would face blatant prejudice); McGurk v. Swisher Hygiene Franchise Corp., No. 02-1337-SLR, 2003 WL 252124, 2003 U.S. Dist. LEXIS 1549 (D. Del. Jan. 30, 2003) (choice of forum clause selecting North Carolina enforceable even though franchisee was located in Delaware and had medical problems causing franchisee to be immobile).

108. 33 Flavors of Greater Delaware Valley, Inc. v. Bresler's 33 Flavors, Inc., 475 F. Supp. 217, 227 n.29 (D. Del. 1979) (indicating in dicta that if the DFSL applies it may override a contrary choice-of-law provision).

109. BBDova, LLC v. Auto. Techs., Inc., 358 F. Supp. 2d 387, 388 (D. Del. 2005).

110. *Id.*

but granted the motion to transfer.[111] In support of its decision, the court held that a choice of forum provision did not violate public policy or the DFSL, but there may be a violation of federal law where a litigant can show that it would face "blatant prejudice in the foreign forum" if the forum selection provision is upheld.[112]

The DFSL embodies Delaware's public policy and might void contrary choice-of-law provisions.[113] A choice of law provision is likely enforceable so long as the jurisdiction selected bears some material relationship to the transaction and the law of the foreign jurisdiction is not repugnant to the public policy of Delaware.[114]

2. Limitations Period

a. Commentary

The Delaware Superior Court has applied a three-year statute of limitations to DFSL violations.[115]

b. Annotations

In *Kirkwood Kin Corp.*, a former Dunkin' Donuts franchisee sued the franchisor and the owners of a competing franchisee for inter alia violations of the DFSL.[116] The court applied the general three-year statute of limitations found in Delaware Code section 8106 to the case.[117]

The DFSL does not support a claim for "a continuing unjust termination."[118] By definition, once a termination has occurred, the franchise cannot continue, and the limitations period does not toll.[119]

---

111. *Id.*
112. *Id.*
113. *33 Flavors of Greater Delaware Valley, Inc.*, 475 F. Supp. at 227–28.
114. Shadewell Grove IP, LLC. v. Mrs. Fields Franchising, LLC, 2006 WL 1375106 (Del. Ch., May 8, 2006).
115. *See* Kirkwood Kin Corp. v. Dunkin' Donuts, C.A. No. 94C-03-189, 1995 Del. Super. LEXIS 297, at *23–24 (Super. Ct. June 30, 1995) (applying the general three-year statute of limitations found codified in Del. Code Ann. tit. 10, § 8106).
116. *Kirkwood Kin Corp.*, 1995 Del. Super. LEXIS 297, at *9.
117. *Id.* at *21.
118. *Id.* at *9.
119. *Id.*

Hawaii

Michael Levitz

I. Introduction to Statute

The Hawaii Franchise Investment Law (HFIL) is primarily focused on the registration, offer, and sale of franchises.[1] However, HFIL section 6 contains provisions governing the relationship between a franchisee and franchisor.[2] Among other things, it requires that both parties to the franchise relationship act in good faith, declares certain conduct by a franchisor to be "an unfair or deceptive act or practice or an unfair method of competition," and entitles a franchisee to compensation following a prohibited termination or failure to renew.[3] The provisions of section 6 also govern relationships between a sub-franchisor and sub-franchisee.

HFIL section 9 imposes civil liability on franchisors for violations of section 6, by declaring that conduct constituting an unfair or deceptive act or practice or an unfair method of competition under section 6 "shall constitute an unfair or deceptive act or practice under [Hawaii Revised Statute section] 480," Hawaii's law of general application regulating competition.[4] However, section 9 does not independently create a private right of action in favor of a franchisee harmed by a franchisor's violation of section 6, and therefore standing must be determined by looking to Hawaii Revised Statute section 480.[5] In the case of deceptive practices, Hawaii Revised Statute section 480-2(d) "limits standing to consumers, the attorney general, and the director of the office of consumer protection [of the Department of Commerce and Consumer Affairs]."[6] A corporate franchisee is not a "consumer" as defined by Hawaii Revised Statute section 480-1, and thus lacks standing to pursue a franchisor for deceptive practices.[7] Less clear is whether an individual franchisee would be a consumer within the

---

1. Haw. Rev. Stat. §§ 482E-1 to -12.
2. *Id.* § 482E-6.
3. *Id.*; *see also* Lui Ciro, Inc. v. Ciro, Inc., 895 F. Supp. 1365, 1386 (D. Haw. 1995) (covenant of good faith and fair dealing implied in a franchise agreement).
4. Haw. Rev. Stat. § 482E-9(a); *Lui Ciro*, 895 F. Supp. at 1386.
5. *Lui Ciro*, 895 F. Supp. at 1387.
6. *Id.* (citing Haw. Rev. Stat. § 480-2(d)).
7. *Lui Ciro*, 895 F. Supp. at 1388 (dismissing shareholders' claim for deceptive practices).

meaning of Hawaii Revised Statute section 480-1, which defines the term "consumer": "Consumer" means a natural person who, primarily for personal, family, or household purposes, purchases, attempts to purchase, or is solicited to purchase goods or services or who commits money, property, or services in a personal investment.

Although not considered in the franchising context, at least one case has held that when an individual makes an investment primarily for business purposes, that individual is not making a "personal investment" and is therefore not a "consumer" within the meaning of Hawaii Revised Statute section 480-1.[8] In contrast, both individuals and corporate franchisees have standing to bring claims for unfair competition by franchisors under Hawaii Revised Statute section 480-13.[9]

II. Commentary and Annotations

Only a small number of reported cases have been decided under the HFIL. As such, cases interpreting similar laws may be persuasive.[10] Final orders issued by the commissioner of the Department of Commerce and Consumer Affairs (DCCA) in enforcement actions brought under the HFIL may also aid in the interpretation of the HFIL.

A. Definition of Franchise

1. Trademark Element

a. Commentary

For a relationship to be a "franchise" within the meaning of the HFIL, the putative franchisee must be granted a license to use a "trade name, service mark, trademark, logotype or related characteristic."[11] There is no requirement that the mark have federal or state registration status. Because the HFIL does not require that a franchise agreement be written, it logically follows that the trademark license need not be express and therefore may be determined to exist based on the manner and degree to which the putative franchisee has been permitted to use the marks.

b. Annotations

In *Prim Limited Liability Co. v. Pace-O-Matic, Inc.*, the supplier of electronic amusement devices sought partial summary judgment, contending that the

---

8. Sung v. Hamilton, 710 F. Supp. 2d 1036, 1052–53 (D. Haw. 2010) (land purchased by a natural person for use in the development and operation of a water bottling business was not a "personal investment").

9. *Lui Ciro*, 895 F. Supp. at 1388–89 (franchisee stated a claim for unfair competition based on discrimination in the supply of inventory).

10. *See* JJCO, Inc. v. Isuzu Motors Am., Inc., No. 10-16597, 2009 WL 1444103 (D. Haw. May 22, 2009) (considering cases from other jurisdictions when ruling on whether a dealership was within the scope of the HFIL).

11. Haw. Rev. Stat. § 482E-2.

distribution relationship under which a distributor purchased and sold the amusement devices and game play credits was not a franchise.[12] The court ruled in favor of the supplier, concluding that the relationship was not a franchise because, among other things, the distribution agreement did not give the distributor the right to use the supplier's trademarks.[13]

In *The Gold Refinery, LLC v. Aloha Island Gold, LLC*, the plaintiff, a purchaser of gold jewelry, sued its commissioned agents who it contended had misappropriated trade secrets and began competing against it.[14] The defendant counterclaimed, including three counts for violations of the HFIL. With respect to the HFIL counts, after a thorough and thoughtful discussion as to the level of details required for adequate pleading, the court noted that the allegations essentially tracked the language of the HFIL, but failed to articulate any facts supporting the contention that a franchise existed.[15] Of particular note, the counterclaim failed to identify "what trade name, service mark, trademark, logotype or related characteristic was covered by the purported franchise," resulting in dismissal of the three HFIL counts.[16]

2. Franchise Fee Element

a. Commentary

In order for a relationship to be a "franchise" within the meaning of the HFIL, the putative franchisee must pay "directly or indirectly, a franchise fee."[17] The HFIL generally defines "franchise fee" as "any fee or charge that a franchisee or subfranchisor is required to pay or agrees to pay for the right to enter into a business or to continue a business under a franchise agreement" and then goes on to include specific payments that would be considered a "franchise fee" as well as several statutory exceptions.[18] In general, to constitute a "franchise fee" the payment must be received by the franchisor.[19] Initial investment costs paid to a third party, such as travel expenses to attend a training program, do not constitute a "franchise fee."[20] The HFIL, like a number of other franchise and dealer protection laws, excludes certain expenditures from the definition of "franchise fee," including "the purchase or agreement to purchase goods at a bona fide wholesale price."[21] This particular exclusion will preclude a traditional product distributorship from being within the ambit of the HFIL, provided that the only payment being made to the supplier is the bona fide wholesale price of the goods that the distributor will resell.

---

12. No. 10-617, 2012 WL 6553819 (D. Haw. Dec. 14, 2012).
13. *Id.*
14. No. 11-00522, 2012 WL 518396, at *1 (D. Haw. Feb. 15, 2012).
15. *Id.* at *5.
16. *Id.*
17. Haw. Rev. Stat. § 482E-2.
18. *Id.*
19. JJCO, Inc. v. Isuzu Motors Am., Inc., No. 10-16597, WL 2009 WL 1444103, at *11 (9th Cir. July 5, 2012).
20. *Id.*
21. Haw. Rev. Stat. § 482E-2.

In addition to the definition of "franchisee fee" in the HFIL, regulations under the HFIL may aid in the determination of whether a putative franchisee has paid a "franchise fee," in that the regulations define "bona fide wholesale transaction" and outline different circumstances under which a "franchise fee" may be determined to have been paid.[22] For example, the regulations contemplate consideration of whether the price paid to the supplier of goods is solely for those goods, or includes a payment for the right to continue to do business under the agreement defining the parties' relationship.[23]

b. Annotations

In *Prim Limited Liability Co. v. Pace-O-Matic, Inc.*, the supplier of electronic amusement devices sought partial summary judgment, contending that the distribution relationship under which a distributor purchased and sold the devices and game play credits was not a franchise.[24] The distributor argued that the game play credits constituted a franchise fee, because the price of the credits greatly exceeded the cost of the few keystrokes necessary to generate the credits.[25] The court disagreed, explaining that the fact that the supplier realized a profit on the sales did not transform the payments for the credits into a franchise fee, and granted summary judgment to the supplier.[26]

In *JJCO, Inc. v. Isuzu Motors America, Inc.*, prior to trial, the judge denied the supplier's motion for summary judgment on the issue of whether the relationship between an automobile supplier and its dealer was a franchise under the HFIL.[27] To decide the issue, the court analyzed each of the expenses that the dealer contended to be a franchise fee. With respect to the dealer's purchase of tools, parts, and equipment from the supplier, the court held that these types of purchases could constitute a franchise fee if they exceeded fair market value, but that the dealer had not established that the purchases satisfied that criteria.[28] In response to the dealer's argument that the HFIL's franchise fee exception for goods purchased at fair market value only applied to goods purchased from the supplier for resale by the dealer, the court observed that the HFIL "contains no such limitation."[29] With respect to the dealer's payment of a communications licensing fee for a system used to communicate sales information, submit warranty claims, and other information, the court held that "unclear from the record is whether the fee was incurred for the right to do business with Isuzu or was the kind of expense JJCO would have had to incur even without the kind of agreement it had with Isuzu."[30] With regard to direct payments made by the dealer for marketing expenses and point of sale signage, the court,

---

22. HAW. CODE R. § 16-37-1.
23. *Id.*
24. No. 10-617, 2012 WL 6553819 (D. Haw. Dec. 14, 2012).
25. *Id.* at *5.
26. *Id.* at *6.
27. No. 08-00419, 2009 WL 1444103 (D. Haw. May 22, 2009).
28. *Id.* at *7.
29. *Id.*
30. *Id.* at *8.

relying on decisions from other jurisdictions considering similar statutes, held that marketing expenses and costs of point of sale signage were not a "franchise fee" because the dealer failed to establish that the amounts charged were unreasonable.[31]

The court also considered the dealer's contention that expenses incurred to send employees to attend the supplier's training program constituted a franchise fee, characterizing this contention as "the most persuasive" of the dealer's arguments, noting that "'training fees or training school fees or charges' are expressly included in the statutory definition of 'franchise fee.'"[32] However, the court concluded that expenses paid to third parties for travel did not constitute a franchise fee, and there was insufficient evidence to conclude that the dealer's payments to the supplier for training materials were payments for the training itself.[33] Finally, the court concluded that neither a financing program, with respect to which the dealer selected the lender, or an optional service pricing program in which the dealer elected to participate were franchise fees.[34] Ultimately, the court held that whether the expenses the dealer contended to be a franchise fee was a question of fact, and the dealer had not met its burden of establishing that it paid a franchise fee.[35]

At trial, the jury found in favor of the supplier, Isuzu.[36] The dealer, JJCO, then sought an order altering or amending the judgment, or a new trial.[37] In respect to JJCO's contention that its obligations, under its dealership agreement, to pay for signs and to submit financial statements constituted a franchise fee, the court noted that JJCO never complied with those requirements, and therefore the requirements were not "for the right to do business with Isuzu."[38] With respect to JJCO's reimbursement of its employees' travel expenses to attend training seminars, the court again held that the payments to third parties were not a franchise fee.[39] The court also held that the requirement that JJCO maintain a financing relationship with a bank could not be a franchise fee, as JJCO was free to select a lender, and chose a lender that did not have a special relationship with Isuzu.[40] Revisiting the issue of the communications system, the court noted that the jury had a reasonable basis to conclude that the use of the system was not required for JJCO to continue its business.[41] Ultimately, the court declined to overturn the jury's determination that the JJCO had not paid a franchise fee.[42]

---

31. *Id.* at *10.
32. *Id.* (quoting HAW. REV. STAT. § 482E-2).
33. *JJCO*, 2009 WL 1444103, at *11.
34. *Id.*
35. *Id.* at *12.
36. No. 08-00419 2010 WL 2541794 (D. Haw. June 22, 2010).
37. *Id.*
38. *Id.* at *5.
39. *Id.*
40. *Id.*
41. *Id.*
42. *Id.* at *7, *aff'd*, 492 Fed. App'x 715, 717 (9th Cir. 2012) (court correctly decided that "jury's finding was not against the clear weight of the evidence").

In *Rogovsky Enterprise, Inc. v. Masterbrand Cabinets, Inc.*, Rogovsky, a remodeling system franchisor, signed an "Exclusive Distribution Agreement" under which it agreed that its franchisees would use the defendant's MasterBrand cabinets on an exclusive basis.[43] After Masterbrand terminated the agreement, Rogovsky sued MasterBrand in the U.S. District Court for the District of Minnesota, contending that the agreement was a franchise under the HFIL, the Minnesota Franchise Act, and several other state franchise laws.[44] MasterBrand moved to transfer to Indiana, based on the agreement's forum selection clause. To decide whether to enforce the forum selection clause, the court had to first consider whether the agreement was a franchise under the Minnesota Franchise Act, in which case the forum selection clause would have been invalidated by the act's anti-waiver provision.[45] Ultimately, the judge in Minnesota concluded that the agreement was not a franchise, and transferred the case to the U.S. District Court for the Southern District of Indiana.[46] Masterbrand then moved for dismissal for failure to state a claim for relief that can be granted. Although a motion to dismiss would normally be based on the allegations of the pleadings, under the law of the case doctrine, the court in Indiana concluded that there was no reason to revisit the well-reasoned conclusions made by the court in Minnesota.[47] With respect to the franchise fee element, Rogovsky argued that the $300,000 it spent to remodel and completely stock its showroom and training facility with the defendant's products was a "franchise fee" under the HFIL and several other state laws.[48] Based on the analysis that had already been made in Minnesota, the Indiana court concluded that the expenses were not a "franchise fee" because they fell within the HFIL's exception for fixtures and supplies necessary to start or continue the business under the parties' agreement.[49] The court granted Masterbrand's motion to dismiss, concluding that, although Masterbrand may have indirectly benefited from the expenditures, the primary benefit was to Rogovsky, which sold cabinets and other remodeling materials to consumers from its showroom.[50]

In *Cycle City, Ltd. v. Harley-Davidson Motor Co., Inc.*, the court considered a motion to dismiss filed by motorcycle manufacturer Harley-Davidson, contending that a terminated motorcycle distributorship was not a "franchise" within the meaning of the HFIL because the distributor had not paid a franchise fee.[51] Cycle City operated dealerships in Oahu and Maui. In addition to its dealerships, Cycle City had two separate agreements with Harley-Davidson; an exclusive distributorship agreement under which it purchased and sold motorcycles, parts, and accessories to other Hawaii dealers; and a separate licensing

---

43. No. 3:15-cv-00022, 2015 WL 7721223 (S.D. Ind. Nov. 30, 2015).
44. *Id.* at *2.
45. *Id.*
46. *Id.*
47. *Id.* at *4.
48. *Id.* at *5.
49. *Id.*
50. *Id.* at *7.
51. No. 14-00148, 2015 WL 3407825 (D. Haw. May 26, 2015).

agreement under which it manufactured branded merchandise, such as t-shirts. In denying Harley-Davidson's motion to dismiss, the court concluded that royalties paid under a licensing agreement for the right to manufacture and sell branded goods, even though separate from the distributorship agreement, might satisfy the franchise fee element under the HFIL.[52] The court also rejected Harley-Davidson's argument that royalties paid under the license agreement were part of the bona fide wholesale price of the motorcycles and other items purchased from Harley-Davidson under the dealership agreement, because royalties paid under the license had no relationship to the prices the dealer paid Harley-Davidson for the motorcycles and other items.[53]

3. Community Interest; Significant Degree of Control; Joint Marketing

a. Commentary

In order for a relationship to be a "franchise" within the meaning of the HFIL, there must be "a community interest in the business of offering, selling, or distributing goods or services at wholesale or retail, leasing, or otherwise."[54] The HFIL defines "community interest" as "a continuing financial interest between the franchisor and franchisee in the operation of the franchise business."[55] There is relatively little case law construing "community interest" under the HFIL, and as such practitioners and courts might look to cases decided under other states' laws in which "community of interest" is an element of a franchise or dealership, such as the New Jersey Franchise Practices Act,[56] the Wisconsin Fair Dealership Law,[57] and the Minnesota Franchise Act.[58] As illustrated by the annotations, there are also several opinions issued by the DCCA providing guidance with respect to the "community interest" element.

b. Annotations

In *Cycle City, Ltd. v. Harley-Davidson Motor Co., Inc.*, the court considered a motion to dismiss filed by motorcycle manufacturer Harley-Davidson, contending that a terminated motorcycle distributorship was not a "franchise" within the meaning of the HFIL.[59] The court considered cases decided under the Wisconsin Fair Dealership Law and New Jersey Franchise Practices Act, and it set

---

52. *Id.* at *8.
53. *Id.*
54. Haw. Rev. Stat. § 482E-2.
55. *Id.*
56. N.J. Stat. Ann. § 56:10-3 (2023) ("'Franchise' means a written arrangement for a definite or indefinite period, in which a person grants to another person a license to use a trade name, trade mark, service mark, or related characteristics, and in which there is a community of interest in the marketing of goods or services at wholesale, retail, by lease, agreement, or otherwise.").
57. Wis. Stat. § 135.02 ("'Community of interest' means a continuing financial interest between the grantor and grantee in either the operation of the dealership business or the marketing of such goods or services.").
58. Minn. Stat. § 80C.01 subdiv. 4 (a required element of a "franchise" is that the relationship be one "in which the franchisor and franchisee have a community of interest in the marketing of goods or services at wholesale, retail, by lease, agreement, or otherwise").
59. No. 14-00148, 2015 WL 3407825 (D. Haw. May 26, 2015).

out a list of nonexhaustive factors developed under the Wisconsin Fair Dealership Law: (1) the duration of the business relationship; (2) the nature and extent of the parties' contractual arrangement; (3) the proportion of time and revenue the alleged dealer devotes to the alleged grantor's products or services; (4) the percentage of gross profits that the alleged dealer derives from the alleged grantor's products or services; (5) the nature and extent of the alleged grantor's territorial grant to the alleged dealer; (6) the nature and extent of the alleged dealer's uses of the alleged grantor's proprietary marks; (7) the nature and extent of the alleged dealer's investment in facilities, inventory, and goodwill in furtherance of the alleged dealership; (8) the personnel devoted by the alleged dealer to the alleged dealership; (9) the amount spent by the alleged dealer on advertising or promotions for the alleged grantor's products and services; and (10) the nature and extent of any supplementary services provided by the alleged dealer to consumers of the alleged grantor's products and services.[60]

Ultimately, the court concluded that the dealer had adequately pled the existence of a "community interest" by alleging that it was required to purchase all new motorcycles exclusively from Harley-Davidson; had made substantial investments in inventory, advertising, and sale of licensed products; and Harley-Davidson exercised considerable control over the dealer's sale and distribution of products.[61]

In the Matter of Richard Craft, Jr., the DCCA ordered the putative franchisor to cease the sale of unregistered franchises.[62] In concluding that the respondents had engaged in the sale of franchises, the DCCA concluded that the putative franchisor and putative franchisee had a community interest where: (1) the putative franchisee was granted a protected territory; (2) the respondents received monthly "franchise payment[s]"; (3) the putative franchisee was required to pay rents under a restaurant lease that was in the putative franchisor's president's name; and (4) the putative franchisee was required to pay a monthly advertising fee.[63] With respect to a second franchise, the DCCA concluded that there was a community interest where: (1) the putative franchisee was required to pay a monthly franchise fee; (2) the putative franchisee was required to pay rents under a restaurant lease that was in the putative franchisor's president's name; (3) the putative franchisee was required to pay respondents for advertising, and had "acknowledged the 'importance of the standardization of advertising and promotion to the goodwill and public image of the . . . System'"; and (4) the putative franchisee was required to maintain accurate books in records in the form prescribed by the respondent.

In the Matter of Lovelle, the DCCA ordered the putative franchisor to cease the sale of unregistered coffee store franchises.[64] In concluding that the respondents had engaged in the sale of franchises, the DCCA concluded that there was

---

60. *Id.* at *8–9 (citing Girl Scouts of Manitou Council, Inc. v. Girl Scouts of U.S. of Am., Inc., 549 F.3d 1079, 1093 (7th Cir. 2008)).
61. *Cycle City*, 2015 WL 3407825, at *9.
62. No. SEU-2008-051, DCCA (Preliminary Order to Cease and Desist, May 2, 2012).
63. *Id.*
64. No. SEU-2011-012, DCCA (Preliminary Order to Cease and Desist, Oct. 26, 2012).

a community interest where: (1) the putative franchisee paid the respondents for advertising; (2) the putative franchisee was obligated to purchase its coffee and related supplies from the respondent; (3) the agreement specified where the putative franchisee could do business and the hours of operation; (4) there was a noncompetition covenant requiring the putative franchisee to obtain the respondents permission to sell any products not obtained from the respondent; (5) putative franchisor was granted the authority with respect to handling customer complaints, use of credit cards, advertising, and termination of the agreement; (6) the agreement required the return of all trademarked products upon termination; and (7) the putative franchisor indirectly controlled the putative franchisee's possibility of success by controlling the volume and types of products sold.[65]

In the Matter of Fuller, the commissioner concluded that a roadside assistance business satisfied the community interest requirement, where, among other things, the putative franchise was required to use the putative franchisor's dispatch, accounting, and billing services; the putative franchisor deducted a percentage from insurance reimbursements prior to remitting them to the putative franchisee on a weekly basis; and the putative franchisee paid the putative franchisor for the dispatching and billing services.[66]

B. Scope and Jurisdiction

1. Commentary

The HFIL does not specify whether its relationship law has extraterritorial application. In contrast, Hawaii Revised Statute section 482-4 expressly provides that HFIL's pre-sale disclosure laws do not apply to "[t]he offer or sale to a franchisee or prospective franchisee where the franchisee or prospective franchisee is not domiciled in this State and where the franchise business will not be operated in this State." Even assuming that there might be a constitutional basis for application of section 6 outside of Hawaii, presumably a court, in determining the applicability of section 6, would be guided with respect to legislative intent by Hawaii Revised Statute section 482-4.

2. Annotations

In *Keurig Green Mountain, Inc. v. Global Baristas US, LLC*, the court held that, by its terms, the HFIL did not apply to the formation of a contract where the franchisee operated in Washington but also had the right to operate in "every state in the United States."[67] The court held that having the right to operate in Hawaii does not result in application of the HFIL—there must be some sort of concrete connection between the franchise and Hawaii in order for the HFIL to apply.[68]

---

65. Id.
66. No. SEU-2010-011, DCCA (Preliminary Order to Cease and Desist, May 12, 2013, attached to Final Order dated Nov. 20, 2013).
67. 18-cv-0095 (LAK), 2018 WL 4926446 (S.D.N.Y. Oct. 10, 2018).
68. Id.

In *Century 21 Real Estate v. All Professional Realty*, although the court held that the franchisor had good cause to terminate the franchises operated in Hawaii, it also held that the HFIL was inapplicable to the parties' relationship because the franchise agreement contained a valid choice of law provision specifying New Jersey law.[69]

In *RM Yogurt Hawaii LLC v. Red Mango Franchising Co.*, the court enforced the parties' contractual choice of venue, concluding that the HFIL does not reflect a "'strong public policy' against forum selection clauses."[70] The court reasoned that, unlike California's franchise relationship law, which expressly prohibits a franchisor requiring litigation outside of California, the HFIL contains no such prohibition.[71]

C. Termination

1. What Constitutes Termination or Cancellation

a. Commentary

There is very little case law discussing termination under the HFIL. As such, practitioners and courts may look to other laws and the cases decided under them. If the contract at issue is a product distribution agreement, then it would likely be a contract for the sale of goods, within the scope of article 2 (Sales) of the Uniform Commercial Code.[72] Article 2 includes definitions for each "termination" and "cancellation."[73]

b. Annotations

In the bench trial of a case brought under Hawaii's Motor Vehicle Industry Licensing Act, the trial court concluded that the supplier's breaking off communications and ceasing to provide the dealer with information and resources necessary for the sale of the supplier's products, was a termination of the dealership.[74]

2. Restrictions on Termination or Cancellation

a. Commentary

The HFIL makes it an "unfair or deceptive act or practice or an unfair method of competition" for a franchisor to terminate a franchise other than for good cause, and on a nondiscriminatory basis.[75] The HFIL does not delineate all

---

69. 889 F. Supp. 2d 1198, 1241 (E.D. Cal. 2012), *aff'd*, 600 Fed. Appx. 502, 507 (9th Cir. 2015).
70. RM Yogurt Haw., LLC v. Red Mango Franchising Co. 2010 WL 11534419 (D. Haw. June 29, 2010).
71. *Id.* (distinguishing Jones v. GNC Franchising, Inc. 211 F.3d 495 (9th Cir. 2000), *cert. denied*, 531 U.S. 928 (2000)).
72. Paulson, Inc. v. Bromar, Inc., 775 F. Supp. 1329, 1333 (D. Haw. 1991) (holding that Hawaii supreme court would likely decide that the UCC is applicable to distribution agreements).
73. Haw. Rev. Stat. § 490:2-106(3), (4).
74. Soderholm Sales & Leasing, Inc. v. Byd Motors, Inc., Civ. No. 19-00160 (D. Haw. Sept. 22, 2021), *aff'd*, No. 21-16778 (9th Cir. Nov. 10, 2022).
75. Haw. Rev. Stat. § 482E-6(2)(H).

those circumstances that might constitute good cause for termination; but it does expressly provide that good cause for termination includes a failure of a franchisee to comply with any material provision of the franchise agreement, after notice and a reasonable cure opportunity.[76] A failure to satisfy the franchisor's standards and a failure to cure can be good cause for termination, if the franchisor can establish that it applies those standards in a nondiscriminatory manner, or that any distinction in treatment of franchisees is justifiable and not arbitrary.[77]

b. Annotations

In *Century 21 Real Estate v. All Professional Realty*, the court held that, although the HFIL was inapplicable to the parties' relationship in view of their contractual choice of law, the franchisor's termination of the franchises would have satisfied the HFIL because the franchisor notified the franchisee of the franchisee's financial default, and the franchisee failed to pay amounts owing.[78]

3. Notice Requirement

a. Commentary

The HFIL does not permit a franchisor to terminate a franchise without first providing the franchisee with notice and a reasonable opportunity to cure.[79] In view of the HFIL's nonwaiver provision (discussed later), a court might conclude that a franchisor must permit a cure opportunity even in the case of a breach that the franchise agreement defines as "non-curable."

b. Annotations

In *Century 21 Real Estate v. All Professional Realty*, the court held that, although the HFIL was inapplicable to the parties' relationship in view of their contractual choice of law, the franchisor's termination of the franchises satisfied the HFIL because it notified the franchisee of the franchisee's financial default, and the franchisee failed to pay amounts owing.[80]

4. Grounds for Termination

a. Commentary

As already discussed, the HFIL does not provide an exhaustive list of those things that would be good cause for termination of a franchise agreement. However, the HFIL defines good cause for termination to include, without limitation, "the failure of the franchisee to comply with any lawful, material provision of the franchise agreement after having been given written notice thereof and an opportunity to cure the failure within a reasonable period of time."[81]

---

76. Id.
77. Id.
78. 889 F. Supp. 2d 1198, 1241 (E.D. Cal. 2012), *aff'd*, 600 Fed. Appx. 502, 507 (9th Cir. 2015).
79. HAW. REV. STAT. § 482E-6(2)(H).
80. 889 F. Supp. 2d 1198, 1241 (E.D. Cal. 2012), *aff'd*, 600 Fed. Appx. 502, 507 (9th Cir. 2015).
81. HAW. REV. STAT. § 482E-6(2)(H).

b. Annotations

In *Century 21 Real Estate v. All Professional Realty*, the court held that, although the HFIL was inapplicable to the parties' relationship in view of their contractual choice of law, the franchisor's termination of the franchises satisfied the HFIL because it notified the franchisee of the franchisee's financial default, and the franchisee failed to pay amounts owing.[82]

5. Required Cure Period

a. Commentary

The HFIL requires that prior to termination a franchisee be given notice of the grounds for termination, and a "reasonable period of time" to cure."[83] The statute does not provide guidance as to the amount of time that would be reasonable. Whether a particular cure period is reasonable is fact dependent, considering the nature of the default, and the actions required to correct the circumstances constituting the default. If the parties have agreed, in the franchise agreement, to a specified cure period, a court would likely consider the agreed upon period to be reasonable.

b. Annotations

The author was unable to locate any published cases addressing this issue.

6. Repurchase Obligations

a. Commentary

The HFIL requires a franchisor, at the time of termination, to purchase the "franchisee's inventory, supplies, equipment and furnishings purchased from the franchisor, or from a supplier designated by the franchisor."[84] As written, the repurchase obligation is not tied to whether the franchisor acted improperly, and therefore might be construed as imposing a repurchase obligation irrespective of the circumstances underlying the termination. Excluded from the repurchase obligation are "personalized materials which have no value to the franchisor."[85]

b. Annotations

The author was unable to locate any published cases addressing this issue.

D. Restrictions on Nonrenewal

The HFIL limits a franchisor's right to not renew a franchise.[86] It is unclear whether the statute is intended to establish an independent right to renew a franchise agreement that makes no mention of renewal; or is simply intended to apply in those instances in which the franchise agreement contemplates

---

82. 889 F. Supp. 2d 1198, 1241 (E.D. Cal. 2012); *aff'd*, 600 Fed. Appx. 502, 507 (9th Cir. 2015).
83. Haw. Rev. Stat. § 482E-6(2)(H).
84. *Id.* § 482E-6(3).
85. *Id.*
86. *Id.* § 482E-6(2)(H).

renewal. However, the statute would likely apply in the absence of a contractual renewal right, if the franchisor did not offer to renew a franchise but routinely renewed other franchises under similar circumstances. If the franchisor refuses to renew a franchise in order to take over the franchisee's business, then the franchisor must compensate the franchisee for the loss of goodwill.[87]

1. What Constitutes Nonrenewal

a. Commentary

The HFIL does not define the meaning of "not renew." Typically, "not renew" would be understood to describe a party's decision to not continue the franchise relationship beyond the expiration of the existing franchise. The language of the HFIL infers that, as a condition of renewal, the franchisor may require the franchisee to agree to the franchisor's current terms, if those terms were being uniformly offered to its other renewing franchisees, or any variation from those the terms being offered to other renewing franchisees was for justifiable reasons.[88]

b. Annotations

In *Cycle City, Ltd. v. Harley-Davidson Motor Co., Inc.*, a dealer and distributor of Harley-Davidson's motorcycles, and licensee with respect to the manufacture of Harley-Davidson's merchandise, contended that Harley-Davidson violated the HFIL when, following a negotiating impasse, it did not renew the distributorship and license agreement upon expiration, despite having previously done so as a matter of routine.[89] Harley-Davidson sought dismissal, contending that the relationship was not a franchise under the HFIL. The court denied the motion, holding that Cycle City had adequately stated a claim for relief under the HFIL.[90]

2. Restrictions on Nonrenewal

a. Commentary

The HFIL does not establish restrictions on nonrenewal, other than to require the franchisor to have grounds for nonrenewal, as discussed further later. However, if the reason for nonrenewal is so that the franchisor may convert the franchisee's business to one operated by the franchisor, then the franchisor must compensate the franchisee for the lost goodwill.[91]

b. Annotations

The author was unable to locate any published cases addressing this issue.

---

87. *Id.* § 482E-6(3).
88. *Id.*
89. No. 14-00148, 2015 WL 3407825, *3 (D. Haw. May 26, 2015).
90. *Id.* at *10.
91. Haw. Rev. Stat. § 482E-6(3).

3. Notice Requirement

a. Commentary
Not applicable.

b. Annotations
Not applicable.[92]

4. Grounds for Nonrenewal

a. Commentary
A franchisor's decision to not renew a franchise, to be lawful, must be based on one of two justifications. The first justification is that a franchisor may decline to renew a franchise for "good cause."[93] Although section 6 defines "good cause" in the context of a termination, it does not do so with respect to nonrenewal.[94] This suggests that the legislature understood, and accepted, that a franchisor might have justifiable reasons for not remaining in a relationship, even if those same reasons would not have enabled the franchisor to lawfully terminate the same franchise. Section 6 does not provide any clear indication of whether "good cause" could include a franchisor's self-interest, such as the determination that supporting a franchised business in Hawaii might not make economic sense. However, the statute's requirement that the franchisor compensate the franchisee for a loss of goodwill in those instances in which the franchisor converts a franchisee's business to the franchisor's business seemingly allows a franchisor to justify nonrenewal based on its own business objectives.[95]

The second justification for nonrenewal is that a franchisor may decline to renew a franchisee if the franchisee does not meet the franchisor's then-current standards and requirements, applied on a nondiscriminatory basis, or which discriminate for justifiable reasons.[96] Where the franchisor makes nonrenewal decisions based on classifications, or other distinctions, it has the burden of proving that its decisions are "justifiable and proper" and "not arbitrary."[97]

b. Annotations
In *Cycle City, Ltd. v. Harley-Davidson Motor Co., Inc.*, Cycle City, which was both a dealer and distributor of Harley-Davidson motorcycles, and a licensee with respect to Harley-Davidson branded merchandise, alleged that Harley-Davidson's nonrenewal of the distributorship and merchandise license violated the HFIL.[98] Cycle City argued that the nonrenewal violated the HFIL, because Harley-Davidson was attempting to end Cycle City's role as a distributor, "to recapture for itself the significant benefits now being realized by Cycle City as

---

92. *Id.* (Notice and cure requirement is preceded by "in a termination case.").
93. Haw. Rev. Stat. § 482E-6(2)(H).
94. *Id.*
95. *Id.* § 482E-6(3).
96. *Id.*
97. *Id.*
98. No. 14-00148, 2015 WL 3407825 (D. Haw. May 26, 2015).

the Harley-Davidson Hawaii distributor for over the past 48 years."[99] The court concluded that Cycle City had adequately pleaded a claim for relief, and denied Harley-Davidson's dismissal motion.[100]

5. Required Cure Period

a. Commentary
Not applicable.[101]

b. Annotations
Not applicable.

6. Limitations on Franchisors' Right to Impose Conditions for Renewal

a. Commentary
The HFIL permits a franchisor to establish conditions for renewal, as long those conditions are applied on a nondiscriminatory basis or are based on differentiating factors that the franchisor can justify.[102] This would presumably include the franchisor's right to insist on the execution of the franchisor's most current form of franchise agreement.

b. Annotations
The author was unable to locate any published cases addressing this issue.

7. Repurchase Obligations

a. Commentary
The HFIL requires a franchisor, at the time of nonrenewal, to purchase the "franchisee's inventory, supplies, equipment and furnishings" which were purchased from the franchisor, or from a supplier designated by the franchisor."[103] As written, the repurchase obligation is not tied to whether the franchisor acted improperly, so it might be construed as imposing a repurchase obligation irrespective of the circumstances underlying the nonrenewal. Excluded from the repurchase obligation are "personalized materials which have no value to the franchisor."[104]

b. Annotations
The author was unable to locate any published cases addressing this issue.

---

99. *Id*. at *3.
100. *Id*. at *10.
101. Haw. Rev. Stat. § 482E-6(H) (Notice and cure requirement is preceded by "in a termination case.").
102. *Id*.
103. Haw. Rev. Stat. § 482E-6(3).
104. *Id*.

E. Transfers and Succession

1. Commentary

The HFIL makes it an "unfair or deceptive act or practice or an unfair method of competition" for a franchisor to decline to consent to a proposed transfer "except for good cause."[105] Good cause includes but is not limited to (1) the proposed transferee not satisfying the franchisor reasonable, standard requirements; (2) the proposed transferee being, or being affiliated with, a competitor of the franchisor; (3) the inability or unwillingness of the proposed transferee to sign the franchisor's current form of franchise agreement; and (4) the failure of the proposed transferee to cure any existing defaults at the time of the transfer.[106]

Upon receiving written notice of a proposed transfer, the franchisor has 30 days to approve or disapprove the proposed transfer; and if the franchisor fails to timely act then it will be deemed to have granted its approval.[107] In view of this automatic approval element, if a franchisor's transfer process will take more than 30 days, then the franchisor should consider articulating, in writing, the conditions that have yet to be satisfied, making clear that until those conditions are satisfied, the proposed transfer is "not approved."

2. Annotations

The author was unable to locate any published cases addressing this issue.

F. Other Regulation of the Franchise Relationship

1. Freedom of Association

a. Commentary

Laws intended to protect franchisees have in numerous instances been enacted, in part, due to the perception that franchisees do not have equal bargaining power. The right of franchisees to form an association that can be an advocate for those franchisees, and that can help the franchisor to understand the day-to-day dynamics experienced by franchisees, can be very important. The HFIL makes it an "unfair or deceptive act or practice or an unfair method of competition" for a franchisor to "[r]estrict the right of the franchisees to join an association of franchisees."[108]

b. Annotations

The author was unable to locate any published cases addressing this issue.

---

105. *Id.* § 482E-6(2)(I).
106. *Id.*
107. *Id.*
108. *Id.* § 482E-6(2)(A).

2. Restricting Sources of Supply

a. Commentary

Source restrictions are often a legitimate means of ensuring uniformity and quality within a franchising system; and can also be important to achieving critical mass necessary for negotiating favorable supply arrangements. However, limiting franchisees' choices can lead to reduced competition, and higher prices, or may be motivated more by the franchisor's self-interest that the needs of the franchisees and system. The HFIL makes it an "unfair or deceptive act or practice or an unfair method of competition" for a franchisor to require a franchisee to make purchases from or lease from the franchisor or designated source, unless there is a legitimate business purpose for the requirement.[109] The HFIL makes clear that sources suggested by the franchisor or approved by the franchisor are not to be "deemed designated sources of supply."[110] Presumably, however, the exercise of approval rights over a new supplier could be the equivalent of a source restriction.

b. Annotations

The author was unable to locate any published cases addressing this issue.

3. Discrimination Between Franchisees

a. Commentary

The HFIL requires franchisors and franchisees to deal with each other in good faith.[111] The HFIL makes it an "unfair or deceptive act or practice or an unfair method of competition" for a franchisor to "[d]iscriminate between franchisees in the charges offered or made for royalties, goods, services, equipment, rentals, advertising services, or in any other business dealing" in the absence of an applicable justifying exception.[112]

Justifiable exceptions for treating franchisees differently are that the differentiation (1) is reasonably related to the franchises having been granted at materially different times; (2) results from the franchisor's offering different terms "to persons with insufficient capital, training, business experience, education, or lacking other qualifications"; (3) relates to regional, local, or experimental variations; (4) relates to franchisees' efforts to cure operational deficiencies or contractual defaults; or (5) is based on other reasonable, nonarbitrary distinctions, taking into account the purposes of the HFIL.[113]

b. Annotations

In *West v. International House of Pancakes, LLC*, the court reversed a magistrate judge's granting of a protective order precluding a franchisee, whose franchise was terminated pre-opening, from pursuing certain lines of discovery relevant

---

109. *Id.* § 482E-6(2)(B).
110. *Id.*
111. *Id.* § 482E-6(1).
112. *Id.* § 482E-6(2)(C).
113. *Id.*

to the issue of whether the franchisor had discriminated by subsequently giving another franchisee more time to open for business at the same location.[114] The court reasoned that the discovery might establish that the other franchisee had been given more leeway to open for business, supporting the franchisee's claims of discrimination and, in turn, unlawful termination.[115]

In *Lui Ciro, Inc. v. Ciro, Inc.*, the plaintiff claimed that the franchisor had discriminated against it by providing it with inferior inventory and diverting inventory to other stores.[116] The court, considering a motion to dismiss, held that the plaintiffs had adequately stated a claim for violation of Hawaii Revised Statute section 482E-6(2)(B), and unfair competition under Hawaii Revised Statute section 480.[117]

4. Prohibition on Secret Rebates

a. Commentary

The HFIL makes it an "unfair or deceptive act or practice or an unfair method of competition" for a franchisor to receive monetary or nonmonetary consideration, based on its franchisee's purchases, without communicating its intention to do so to the franchisee prior to receiving that consideration.[118] The language is not clear as to whether "in advance" means prior to the franchisee's signing the franchise agreement. As such, by way of example, even if a franchise agreement permits a franchisor to receive rebates, based on its franchisees' purchases, section 6 might be construed as requiring the franchisor to affirmatively communicate its intent to exercise that right as to any new rebate that franchisor plans to receive.

This prohibition is consistent with commercial bribery and other laws prohibiting secret rebates and kickbacks.[119] The rationale for the prohibition is that a franchisor's motivation for establishing a supply or services relationship may be more for the franchisor's benefit than for the benefit of the franchisees and system and might result in the franchisees paying a higher price for something than would otherwise be the case.

b. Annotations

The author was unable to locate any published cases addressing this issue.

5. Prohibition on Encroachment

a. Commentary

The HFIL makes it an "unfair or deceptive act or practice or an unfair method of competition" for a franchisor to directly or indirectly establish a competing

---

114. West v. Int'l House of Pancakes, LLC, 2011 WL 2607173, at *9 (D. Haw. June 30, 2011).
115. *Id.*
116. 895 F. Supp. 1365, 1377, 1388 (D. Haw. 1995).
117. *Id.* at 1388–89.
118. HAW. REV. STAT. § 482E-6 (2)(D).
119. *See id.* § 708-880 (making commercial bribery a misdemeanor or felony, depending upon the value of the undisclosed benefit).

business within an existing franchisee's exclusive territory; other than to the extent expressly contemplated by the franchise agreement.[120] The provision makes clear that the solicitation of sales by the franchisor or another franchisee in a franchisee's exclusive territory "shall not constitute the establishment of a similar business within the exclusive territory."[121]

b. Annotations

The author was unable to locate any published cases addressing this issue.

6. Anti-Waiver Provision

a. Commentary

Like a number of other laws enacted to protect franchisees and dealers, the HFIL contains an anti-waiver provision to prevent parties from contracting around its protections. It is an "unfair or deceptive act or practice or an unfair method of competition" for a franchisor to require a franchisee, at time of entering into a franchise, to waive any rights it may have under the HFIL; and any provision that purports to deprive a franchisee of the protections of the HFIL is declared to be void.[122] The prohibition, by its terms, does not extend to settlements of disputes.[123]

Courts considering similar laws have refused to enforce contractual choice of law provisions if doing so would contravene a statutory anti-waiver provision. However, one court has held that the HFIL was inapplicable to a franchise dispute involving a franchised business in Hawaii, where the parties' franchise agreement specified New Jersey law.[124]

b. Annotations

In *Century 21 Real Estate v. All Professional Realty*, although the court held that the franchisor had good cause to terminate the franchises operated in Hawaii, it also held that the HFIL was inapplicable to the parties' relationship because the franchise agreement contained a valid choice of law provision specifying New Jersey law.[125] It is unclear whether the court was aware of the HFIL's anti-waiver provision; but the court considered a comparable provision the California Franchise Relations Act (CFRA), which franchisees also contended to have been violated.[126] The court explained that the anti-waiver provision in the CFRA did not preclude enforcing the New Jersey choice of law provision, because the franchise agreement itself contained the same protections as those that existed

---

120. Haw. Rev. Stat. § 482E-6(2)(E).
121. *Id.*
122. *Id.* § 482E-6(2)(F).
123. *Id.*
124. Century 21 Real Estate v. All Pro. Realty, 889 F. Supp. 2d 1198, 1241 (E.D. Cal. 2012); *aff'd*, 600 Fed. App'x 502, 507 (9th Cir. 2015).
125. *Id.* at 1241.
126. *Id.* at 1217 (considering Cal. Bus. & Prof. Code § 20015).

under the CFRA, being that termination be for good cause, and that the franchisee be given a reasonable cure opportunity.[127]

7. Prohibition on Unreasonable and Arbitrary Standards

a. Commentary

The HFIL makes it an "unfair or deceptive act or practice or an unfair method of competition" for a franchisor to "[i]mpose on a franchisee by contract, rule, or regulation, whether written or oral, any unreasonable and arbitrary standard of conduct."[128]

b. Annotations

In *Cycle City, Ltd. v. Harley-Davidson Motor Co., Inc.*,[129] the court denied a manufacturer's motion to dismiss, determining that the dealer had adequately pled the elements of a franchise.[130] Among the dealer's contentions was that manufacturer, Harley-Davidson, had imposed unreasonable and arbitrary standards of conduct in violation of the HFIL.[131] Although the court did not delineate the alleged unreasonable and arbitrary conduct, the complaint alleged that Harley-Davidson had "maliciously, arbitrarily and capriciously increased . . . prices, charges and terms . . . to force Cycle City to relinquish its rights under the Distributorship Agreement."[132]

G. Remedies and Administration Action

Section 9 of the HFIL imposes civil liability on franchisors for violations of section 6, by declaring violations to "constitute an unfair or deceptive act or practice under chapter 480," Hawaii's law of general application regulating competition.[133] A corporate franchisee can pursue a franchisor for unfair competition under Hawaii Revised Statute section 480-13.[134] The attorney general of the state of Hawaii and the DCCA may bring an action against franchisors that commit deceptive practices within the scope of section 6.[135] The DCCA may also seek to recover a civil penalty for any violations of the HFIL, or rule promulgated under the HFIL, up to $100,000.[136] However, the DCCA does not appear to have initiated any enforcement actions on account of a violation of section 6.

---

127. *Id.*
128. HAW. REV. STAT. § 482E-6(2)(E).
129. No. 14-00148, 2015 WL 3407825 (D. Haw. May 26, 2015).
130. *Cycle City*, 2015 WL 3407825, at *9.
131. *Id.*
132. *Cycle City*, No. 14-00148, Complaint, ¶ 53.
133. HAW. REV. STAT. § 482E-9(a); Lui Ciro, Inc. v. Ciro, Inc., 895 F. Supp. 1365, 1386 (D. Haw. 1995).
134. *Lui Ciro*, 895 F. Supp. at 1388–89 (franchisee stated a claim for unfair competition based on discrimination in the supply of inventory).
135. *Id.* at 1386.
136. HAW. REV. STAT. § 482E-10.5(a).

1. Restrictive Covenants

a. Commentary
Not applicable.

b. Annotations
Not applicable.

2. Damages

a. Commentary
As already noted, HFIL section 9 imposes civil liability on franchisors for violations of section 6, by declaring that conduct constituting an unfair or deceptive act or practice or an unfair method of competition under section 6 "constitute an unfair or deceptive act or practice under chapter 480," Hawaii's law of general application regulating competition.[137] Damages awarded for a violation of section 6 "may be based on reasonable approximations but not on speculation."[138]

b. Annotations
The author was unable to locate any published cases addressing this issue.

3. Rescission

a. Commentary
Not applicable.[139]

b. Annotations
Not applicable.

4. Injunctive Relief

a. Commentary
There is no provision contemplating injunctive relief in a civil action initiated by a franchisee harmed by a franchisor's violations of the HFIL, but a court would have the authority to order injunctive relief consistent with that present in other civil actions.[140]

b. Annotations
In *Wahaba, LLC v. USRP (DON), LLC*, a case that included counts for alleged wrongful termination of a franchise under Hawaii Revised Statute section 486H, applicable to gasoline dealerships, the Hawaii Supreme Court held that the defendants could not be held in contempt for violating an ex parte temporary restraining order issued by the circuit court, because the circuit court

---

137. *Id.* § 482E-9(a); *Lui Ciro*, 895 F. Supp. at 1386.
138. Haw. Rev. Stat. § 482E-6.
139. *Id.* § 482E-9(a)–(b).
140. *See* Haw. Rev. Stat. § 603-23 (granting circuit courts the power to enjoin violations of state laws).

exceeded its authority by affirmatively requiring the defendants to reinstall and restore equipment removed by the defendants, whereas the court's authority to issue a temporary restraining order was solely for purposes of maintaining the status quo.[141]

5. Control Person Liability

a. Commentary

Although there do not appear to be any cases expressly deciding the issue, HFIL's definitions of "franchisor" and "person" could be construed as extending liability for violations of section 6 to officers, directors, and other persons controlling the franchisor. The HFIL defines "franchisor" as "a *person* who grants a franchise to another person."[142] The HFIL defines a "person" to include, "in the case of an entity . . . any other entity which has a majority interest in such an entity or effectively controls such other entity as well as the *individual officers, directors, and other persons* [that control] the activities of each such entity."[143]

b. Annotations

In *Lui Ciro, Inc. v. Ciro, Inc.*, the plaintiff, owners of four franchised jewelry stores, claimed that the franchisor and chairman of the board had engaged in various fraudulent activities, as well as discrimination in violation of Hawaii Revised Statute section 482E-6(b).[144] The court expressly determined that the allegations of fraud and other conduct were sufficient to preclude dismissal of the complaint as against the franchisor's chairman.[145] In addressing the franchisee's unfair competition claim under Hawaii Revised Statute section 480 and Hawaii Revised Statute section 482E(9)(a), predicated on the franchisor's alleged discrimination in violation of Hawaii Revised Statute section 482E-6(b), the court did not expressly address the issue of director liability but held that the complaint adequately pled a claim against the chairman for violation of Hawaii Revised Statute section 482E-6(b).[146]

6. Attorneys' Fees

a. Commentary

As explained earlier, violations of section 6 may be pursued under Chapter 480, Hawaii's unfair competition law. An award of attorney's fees is available to a prevailing plaintiff under Chapter 480.[147]

b. Annotations

The author was unable to locate any published cases addressing this issue.

---

141. 106 P.3d 1109, 106 Haw. 466 (2005).
142. HAW. REV. STAT. § 482E-2 (emphasis added).
143. *Id.*
144. 895 F. Supp. 1365 (D. Haw. 1995).
145. *Id.* at 1385.
146. *Id.* at 1387.
147. HAW. REV. STAT. §§ 480-13(a)(1), 480-13(a)(2)(b)(1).

7. Limitations on Damage Waivers

a. Commentary

As discussed earlier, the HFIL contains a general prohibition on any waiver of its protections.[148] To the extent that the HFIL establishes a right to damages, any attempt to waive a right to the damages contemplated by the HFIL would presumably be void.[149]

b. Annotations

The author was unable to locate any published cases addressing this issue.

8. Administrative Action

a. Commentary

Although section 6, together with section 9(a), enables franchisees to pursue a private right of action under Hawaii Revised Statute section 480, the HFIL does not exclude the provisions of section 6 from the enforcement powers of the attorney general and the DCCA. It is therefore conceivable, by way of example, that an administrative action might be commenced to enforce section 6 as against a franchisor that interfered with its franchisees' free association rights.[150] Similarly, the DCCA could issue a stop order to halt sales by a franchisor that violated section 6, although such action would typically be used to prevent sales violations.[151]

Additionally, the DCCA can bring a civil action to recover a civil penalty for violations of Section 6, for an amount not exceeding $100,000.[152] However, the DCCA does not appear to have initiated any enforcement actions on account of a violation of section 6.

b. Annotations

In *Lui Ciro, Inc. v. Ciro, Inc.*, the court, discussing the interrelationship of Hawaii Revised Statute section 482E-9(a) and section 480, held that Hawaii Revised Statute section 482E-9(a) "allows the allows the attorney general and the [DCCA]" to bring an enforcement action "against those franchisors who commit deceptive practices."[153]

H. Criminal Liability

1. Commentary

Criminal liability may attach to violations of the HFIL, and in this regard the HFIL does not distinguish between franchise sales violations and prohibitions

---

148. *Id.* § 482E-6(2)(F).
149. *See id.*
150. *See* Lui Ciro, Inc. v. Ciro, Inc., 895 F. Supp. 1365, 1387–88 (D. Haw. 1995) (violations of section 6 can be enforced by the attorney general and the DCCA).
151. Haw. Rev. Stat. § 482E-8.
152. *Id.* § 482E-10.5.
153. 895 F. Supp. 1365, 1387–88 (D. Haw. 1995).

with respect to the franchise relationship.[154] In the case of violations resulting in harm to the victim of under $5,000, a violation of the HFIL is a class C felony.[155] In the case of harm exceeding $5,000, a violation is a class B felony.[156] There are also provisions for property forfeiture.[157] However, the DCCA does not appear to have initiated any enforcement actions on account of a violation of section 6.

2. Annotations
The author was unable to locate any published cases addressing this issue.

I. Dispute Resolution
1. Limitations on Franchisors' Ability to Restrict Venue
a. Commentary
Not applicable.

b. Annotations
In *Vierican, LLC v. Midas International, LLC*, the court stayed a case relating to a purported wrongful termination, pending the decision of an arbitrator as to arbitrability of a franchise dispute, where the franchise agreement contained a provision specifying arbitration in Florida, and expressly required arbitrability questions be decided by the arbitrator.[158]

In *RM Yogurt Hawaii LLC v. Red Mango Franchising Co.* the court enforced the parties' contractual choice of venue, concluding that the HFIL does not reflect a "'strong public policy' against forum selection clauses."[159] The court reasoned that, unlike California's franchise relationship law, which expressly prohibits a franchisor requiring litigation outside of California, the HFIL contains no such prohibition.[160]

2. Limitations Period
a. Commentary
It is important to recognize that actions initiated by franchisees for violations of section 6 would likely be subject to the limitation periods established in Hawaii Revised Statute section 480, and not those established by the HFIL. The limitations period for actions under Hawaii Revised Statute section 480 must be commenced within four years of the accrual of the cause of action.[161] In the case of a continuing violation, the cause of action accrues "at any time during the period

---

154. Haw. Rev. Stat. § 482E-10.6.
155. *Id.*
156. *Id.*
157. *Id.*
158. No. 19-00620, 2020 WL 4430967 (D. Haw. July 31, 2020).
159. 2010 WL 11534419 (D. Haw. June 29, 2010).
160. *Id.* (distinguishing Jones v. GNC Franchising, Inc. 211 F.3d 495 (9th Cir. 2000), *cert. denied*, 531 U.S. 928 (2000)).
161. Haw. Rev. Stat. § 480-24.

of the violation."[162] Of note however, in the unlikely event of a state enforcement action under Hawaii Revised Statute section 480 for a violation of section 6, the four-year limitations period is tolled, and a private action may be commenced within one year of the conclusion of the state action.[163]

The HFIL contains a five-year statute of limitations provision, in respect to civil actions initiated by the DCCA, under the HFIL, although a discovery rule permits a civil action to be commenced within two years after discovery, but "in no event shall any civil action be brought later than seven years subsequent to the date of the violation."[164] There is a similar limitations provision with respect to felony prosecutions for violations of the HFIL.[165]

b. Annotations

In *Flynn v. Marriott Ownership Resorts, Inc.*, the court held that the four-year statute of limitations applicable to claims under Hawaii Revised Statute section 480 time barred a claim for a violation of Hawaii's law respecting timeshare ownerships, which, like section 6 of the HFIL, declares that certain delineated conduct "shall constitute an unfair or deceptive practice" under Hawaii Revised Statute section 480.[166]

---

162. *Id.*
163. *Id.* § 480-22.
164. *Id.* § 482E-10.5(b).
165. *Id.* § 482E-10.6(f).
166. 165 F. Supp. 3d 955, 964 (D. Haw. 2016); Haw. Rev. Stat. § 514E.

Illinois

Allison Grow Ryan and Xiaoyin Cao[1]

I. Introduction to the Statute

The Illinois Franchise Disclosure Act of 1987 (the Act), which replaced a prior 1974 version, took effect in 1988. The last substantive amendment to the law became effective on October 1, 2009, and was intended to bring the Act more in line with the Federal Trade Commission's (FTC) Franchise Rule. In addition to its registration and disclosure requirements, the Act regulates certain aspects of the franchise relationship, such as termination and renewal.

The relationship provisions are contained primarily in sections 17 through 20 of the Act, and they contain a range of requirements, such as limiting franchisors from restricting franchisees' participation in trade associations, prohibiting discrimination among franchisees, requiring good cause for termination or an opportunity to cure certain types of curable defaults, and prohibiting franchisors from refusing to renew franchise agreements without either compensating franchisees or providing them with sufficient notice and the ability to continue their business under another trade name. The Act states that its intent in the relationship provisions is, in part, "to protect the franchisee and the franchisor by providing a better understanding of the business and the legal relationship between the franchisee and the franchisor."[2]

II. Commentary and Annotations

A. Definition of Franchise

Subject to specified exemptions, the Act defines a "franchise" as any oral, written, express, or implied contract or agreement between two or more individuals or entities in which:

> (a) a franchisee is granted the right to engage in the business of offering, selling, or distributing goods or services, under a marketing plan or system prescribed or suggested in substantial part by a franchisor; and

---

1. The authors extend sincere appreciation to Max DeLeon for his invaluable assistance in preparing this chapter. His expertise and diligence greatly contributed to the quality of the work.
2. 815 Ill. Comp. Stat. § 705/2(2)(b).

(b) the operation of the franchisee's business pursuant to such plan or system is substantially associated with the franchisor's trademark, service mark, trade name, logotype, advertising, or other commercial symbol designating the franchisor or its affiliate; and

(c) the person granted the right to engage in such business is required to pay to the franchisor or its affiliate, either directly or indirectly, a franchise fee of $500 or more.[3]

All three elements of the definition must be satisfied for a franchise relationship to exist.[4] Whether the parties intended to form a franchise relationship does not affect the analysis.[5] Further, the parties cannot avoid the creation of a franchise relationship merely by disclaiming its existence.[6] The "relationship" protections afforded to franchisees by the Act only attach once a franchise exists, meaning they do not protect prospective franchisees.[7]

1. Trademark Element

a. Commentary

Under the Act, for a "franchise" to exist the franchisee's business must be operated according to a plan or system "substantially associated" with the franchisor's trademark, service mark, and so on. According to the regulations, a franchised business is "substantially associated" with a franchisor's trade or service mark if the business is or is permitted to be primarily identified by the mark, or if the mark is otherwise used or permitted to convey to the public that the franchised business is one of the franchisor's outlets.[8] Substantial association may be found even in situations where a franchisor has not specifically authorized the use of its mark in the parties' contract if the franchised business or other circumstances permit or require the franchisee to identify its business primarily by the mark.[9]

b. Annotations

In *Chicago Male Medical Clinic, LLC v. Ultimate Management, Inc.*, a federal district court in California concluded that the parties had a franchise relationship under the Act despite the purported license agreement containing no authorization for the franchisee's use of the franchisor's trademarks.[10] The court rea-

---

3. *Id*. § 705/3(1); Hickory Hills Foodmart, Inc. v. Equilon Enters., LLC, 2023 WL 4273664, at *4 (N.D. Ill. June 29, 2023) (allegedly oral franchise agreement could fall within the protections of the Act, because the definition of "franchise" under the Act is defined to include both oral and implied agreements).

4. BJB Elec., LP v. N. Cont'l Enters., Inc., 2010 WL 502746, at *2 (N.D. Ill. Feb. 9, 2010) (citing Vitkauskas v. State Farm Mut. Auto. Ins. Co., 509 N.E.2d 1385, 1391 (Ill. App. Ct. 1987)).

5. Honeywell Int'l, Inc. v. Automated Bldg. Controls, LLC, 2016 WL 5349462, at *6 (N.D. Ill. Sept. 22, 2016) (citing Brenkman v. Belmont Mktg., Inc., 410 N.E.2d 500, 503 (Ill. App. Ct. 1980)).

6. *See* Peter v. Stone Park Enters., LLC, 1999 WL 543210, at *7 (N.D. Ill. July 23, 1999).

7. Smith v. Molly Maid, Inc., 415 F. Supp. 2d 905, 917 (N.D. Ill. 2006).

8. ILL. ADMIN. CODE tit. 14, § 200.103.

9. *Id.*

10. 2014 WL 7180549, at *7–8 (C.D. Cal. Dec. 16, 2014).

soned that extrinsic evidence—including that the franchisee was listed on the franchisor's website like the franchisor's affiliate-owned outlets; the franchisee was provided a logo that used the same font, styling, and caduceus symbol in the same position as the franchisor's mark; and the franchisor was contractually obligated to provide advertising support—demonstrated that the franchisee's business operations were substantially associated with the franchisor's trademark, trade name, logo, advertising, or other commercial symbols to satisfy the Act's trademark element.[11]

In *Salkeld v. V.R. Business Brokers*, a sub-licensee executed a purported sub-licensing agreement with an alcoholic beverage distributor that granted the sub-licensee a specific territory in which to sell the maker's beverage with use of certain trademarks and sales support. The sub-licensee later sued the maker and its related entities for violations of the Act. On appeal, the court held that the relationship constituted a franchise, determining that the agreement's grant of rights to use the distributor's marks satisfied the Act's trademark element, despite no actual use of the marks by the sub-licensee.[12]

In *Account Services Corp. v. DAKCS Software Services, Inc.*, the Illinois Appellate Court held that the Act's definition of a franchise is not met where optional trademark rights are offered.[13] Specifically, the court determined that application of the Act could not rest on an allegation that the "agents" could choose whether to become associated with the franchisor's name or advertising. More recently, in *McKeever v. Pepperidge Farm, Inc.*, the Illinois Appellate Court found that having permission to use the putative franchisor's trademark on trucks and equipment could "convey to the public that plaintiff was an outlet" of the putative franchisor and was thus sufficient to survive a summary judgment motion on the Act's trademark element.[14]

In *Blankenship v. Dialist International Corp.*, the court concluded that the trademark element was satisfied where a distributor instructed the plaintiff's "sales representative" to rely on the "good name" of the product, which was the same as the distributor's, in marketing the distributor's product in a designated territory.[15] This, the court reasoned, created a significant association between plaintiff's business and the distributor's mark.[16]

---

11. Id.
12. 548 N.E.2d 1151, 1156 (Ill. App. Ct. 1989) ("It is our opinion that these representations were substantially associated with [franchisee's] business such that the second statutory requirement was satisfied."); *but see* Fosdick Poultry Processors, Inc. v. Eager, 555 N.E.2d 62, 65 (Ill. App. Ct. 1990) (distinguishing *Salkeld* and finding that no franchise existed because the "benefits to be derived from the use of the logos were not specifically mentioned in the contract" as they were in *Salkeld*).
13. 567 N.E.2d 381, 385 (Ill. App. Ct. 1990).
14. 2014 WL 2968683, at *5 (Ill. App. Ct. June 27, 2014).
15. 568 N.E.2d 503, 507 (Ill. App. Ct. 1991).
16. Id.

2. Franchise Fee Element

a. Commentary

The Act defines a "franchise fee" as "any fee or charge that a franchisee is required to pay directly or indirectly for the right to enter into a business or sell, resell, or distribute goods, services or franchises under an agreement, including, but not limited to, any such payment for goods or services[.]"[17] The case law interpreting it shows that this element is fairly easy to meet.

The regulations confirm that a franchise fee is to be construed broadly and may be present regardless of the designation or form given to the fee. The requirement may be satisfied by cumulative installment payments or those that are contingent on future sales, profits, purchases, or the sale or transfer of the business (except for transfer costs that represent reasonable expenses incurred in connection with the transfer) so long as those payments ultimately meet the $500 threshold.[18] That said, a payment to the franchisor for equipment, materials, real estate, or other items is not considered a fee if the items are not required or if they may be purchased from available sources outside of the franchisor and its affiliates.[19]

Likewise, the Act itself exempts certain payments by the franchisee to the franchisor from the definition of a franchise fee, including (1) the payment of a reasonable service charge to the issuer of a credit card by an establishment that accepts or honors the credit card; (2) amounts paid to a trading stamp company by a person issuing trading stamps in connection with the retail sale of merchandise or services; (3) the purchase or agreement to purchase goods for which there is an established market at a bona fide wholesale price; (4) the payment for fixtures necessary to operate the business; (5) the payment of rent that reflects payment for the economic value of the property; and (6) the purchase or agreement to purchase goods for which there is an established market at a bona fide retail price subject to a bona fide commission or compensation plan.[20]

Under the regulations, the bona fide wholesale or retail price exceptions apply only to goods to be resold—no part of the price may be for the right to enter the franchised business in the first place.[21] As such, the exceptions generally do not apply to things like services, rental payments, and training programs (which are typically considered services, not goods).[22] The bona fide wholesale and retail price exceptions are satisfied when the price charged for the good is fair given the level of distribution at which it is purchased.[23] Whether the product has an "established market" is determined in accordance with a series of factors in Illinois or an area with similar market characteristics, including how long such products have been sold, the quantity and price of such products, the

---

17. 815 Ill. Comp. Stat. § 705/3(14).
18. *Id.*; Ill. Admin. Code tit. 14, § 200.104.
19. Ill. Admin. Code tit. 14, § 200.105.
20. 815 Ill. Comp. Stat. § 705/3(14).
21. Ill. Admin. Code tit. 14, § 200.106(a)–(b).
22. *Id.* § 200.106(c).
23. *Id.* § 200.106(a).

ability of a purchaser to resell the product around the same price, and the number of outlets of the seller or similar businesses.[24]

Despite the bona fide wholesale and retail price exceptions, an indirect franchise fee—meeting the statutory definition of "franchise fee"—may be found if the buyer is required to purchase a quantity of goods so "unreasonably large" that such goods may not be resold within a "reasonable time," as determined by the relevant price of the goods, markup, consumer demand, location of product suppliers, and seasonal demand variations.[25]

b. Annotations

The court in *Marathon Petroleum Co. v. LoBosco* agreed with a service station operator who claimed that Marathon's requirement that he purchase 100,000 gallons of gasoline per month could constitute an indirect "franchise fee" under the Act—even if he was unable to purchase that amount for all months—if the requirement itself was an unreasonable volume given consumer demand.[26]

With respect to "indirect" franchise fees, the Seventh Circuit explained in *Wright-Moore Corp. v. Ricoh Corp.* that the fee element ensures that "only those entities that have made a firm-specific investment are protected under the franchise laws; where there is no investment, there is no fear of inequality of bargaining power."[27] The cost of excessive inventory, for example, signals "inequality of bargaining power" because the franchisor could essentially "prevent [the franchisee] from being liquid" by asserting that it is no longer an authorized franchise.[28] In contrast, ordinary business operations, such as sales quotas or materials not unique to the business, are not franchise fees.[29]

The Seventh Circuit in *Digital Equipment Corp. v. Uniq Digital Technologies, Inc.* found that a distributor was not required to pay an "indirect" franchise fee for purchase of excessive inventory because the relevant contract did not require it to purchase any inventory.[30] The court rejected the distributor's argument that it was forced to stockpile an excessively large inventory due to a 12-month lag between orders from the manufacturer and delivery to the distributor, because

---

24. *Id.* § 200.107.
25. *Id.* § 200.108.
26. 623 F. Supp. 129, 134 (N.D. Ill. 1985); *but see* Kempner Mobile Elecs., Inc. v. Sw. Bell Mobile Sys., LLC, 2003 WL 22595263, at *8 (N.D. Ill. Nov. 7, 2003), *aff'd sub nom.*, Kempner Mobile Elecs., Inc. v. Sw. Bell Mobile Sys., 428 F.3d 706 (7th Cir. 2005) (holding that purchase of cellular phone equipment did not constitute franchise fee where, even if plaintiff could show that it was required to maintain an excessively large inventory, it had not proffered any evidence that its inventory "could not be resold within a reasonable time").
27. 908 F.2d 128, 135–36 (7th Cir. 1990) (applying Indiana's franchise statute but referencing the Act, "which is almost identical to Indiana's statute").
28. *Id.* at 136.
29. *Id.* ("[U]nless the expenses result in an unrecoverable investment in the franchisor, they should not normally be considered a fee.").
30. 73 F.3d 756 (7th Cir. 1996).

the record established that the distributor sold inventory an average of 16 days after receipt from the manufacturer.[31]

In *Dupage Fork Lift Services, Inc. v. Machinery Distribution, Inc.*, the court held that mere revocation of a discount or rebate cannot constitute payment of an indirect franchise fee.[32] The court also rejected the notion that a training program need only be made available to the franchisee to constitute payment of a franchise fee, and stated, "[t]he Act clearly provides that a franchisee must be 'required to pay,' either indirectly or directly, a franchise fee of $500. The argument that a franchisee may passively meet this requirement, without any sacrifice on its part, simply if a franchisor makes a training session 'available,' is preposterous."[33]

For a payment to be considered a franchise fee, it must be consideration paid for the right to operate a franchise business.[34] In *Kocjancich v. Bridges*, the court held that the plaintiff's payment to defendants of $5,000 as a settlement for hiring defendants' employees in violation of the franchise agreement, which was not paid until more than eight months after the franchisee had gone into operation, was not a franchise fee because it was not made in return for the right to enter into the business itself.[35]

In *Smith v. Molly Maid, Inc.*, the court found that a franchise did not exist where the prospective franchisee failed to pay the full franchise fee.[36] Specifically, the franchisor declined to continue with granting the franchise when the prospective franchisee only paid $6,900 toward the $43,351 franchise fee, and the franchisor returned the amount paid to the franchisee.[37] Accordingly, the court held that a franchise relationship had not existed, and thus the prospective franchisee's claim under the Act failed.[38]

In *P & W Supply Co. v. E.I. du Pont de Nemours & Co.*, the court found that an indirect franchise fee was properly alleged where the defendant manufacturer required the plaintiff supplier to maintain an inventory sufficient to satisfy any conceivable customer need.[39] The defendant argued that the bona fide wholesale price exception should apply because there was a nationwide market for the required purchases, but the court noted that under the Illinois regulations,

---

31. *Id.* at 760; *cf.* Fluid Power Eng'g Co., Inc. v. Cognex Corp., 2022 WL 16856395, at *2 (N.D. Ill. Nov. 10, 2022) (rejecting allegation that franchisee's required purchase of demonstration equipment constituted an indirect franchise fee because it amounted to an agreement to purchase goods for which there was an established market, which the Act specifies does not constitute a franchise fee—franchisee remained free to resell the equipment).

32. 1995 WL 125774, at *5 (N.D. Ill. Mar. 15, 1995).

33. *Id.* at *7.

34. *See, e.g.*, Rhine Enters. LLC v. Refresco Beverage US, Inc., 2022 WL 195109, at *3 (S.D. Ill. Jan. 22, 2022) ("On its own, the mere incurrence of unspecified expenses does not reasonably equate to an inference that Plaintiff actually *paid* a $500 franchise fee to Defendant or Defendant's affiliate. Moreover, . . . Plaintiff has not pled any factual details to infer whether the $500 expenses it incurred fit within the statutory definition for a 'franchise fee.'").

35. 417 N.E.2d 694, 698 (Ill. App. Ct. 1981).

36. 415 F. Supp. 2d 905, 917 (N.D. Ill. 2006).

37. *Id.*

38. *Id.*

39. 747 F. Supp. 1262, 1266 (N.D. Ill. 1990).

the bona fide exception was inapplicable when an "unreasonably large" quantity of goods were required to be purchased, and the plaintiff alleged inventory in excess of normal customer needs by over $500.[40] Even though the plaintiff could have returned the unsold products to the defendant for an exchange, it would have had the same number of products and thus would still be required to stock products beyond normal customer needs.[41]

In *Rhine Enterprises, LLC v. Refresco Beverage US, Inc.*, the court held that an indirect franchise fee could be found where the franchisee alleged that the franchisor charged more than a bona fide wholesale price for required products, that there was no established market for the products in the relevant area, and that the franchisor thereby required the franchisee to purchase product in excess of reasonable consumer demand, resulting in unsold inventory in excess of $500.[42]

The franchise fee must be a mandatory, rather than optional, payment or expense.[43] In *Bly & Sons, Inc. v. Ethan Allen Interiors, Inc.*, the court found an indirect franchise fee where the license agreement required a "mandatory contribution" from the licensee of 2 percent of its invoices to an advertising fund, even though the money was paid to an advertising agency rather than the franchisor itself.[44]

In *Burford v. Accounting Practice Sales, Inc.*, the court found that there was no franchise fee between a broker and an accounting practices marketer where the broker only paid a percentage commission on any sales that he made, because it was a contingent commission, not a mandatory fee.[45] The court declined to consider the commissions an indirect fee because the amount was not guaranteed to be anything at all, let alone $500.[46]

There is no time limit in which the franchisee's payments must accumulate to $500 for a "franchise fee" to be found. For example, in *To-Am Equipment Co., Inc., v. Mitsubishi Caterpillar Forklift America, Inc.*, the distributor paid for parts and service manuals over several years at a total price of more than $500, and the court found that a franchise fee had been paid.[47] In affirming this decision, the appellate court noted that "[t]hese definitions [of the elements of a franchise] are obviously sweeping in their scope. The sum of $500, all that has to be paid over the entire life of a franchise, is less than small change for most businesses of any size."[48] The "Illinois legislature and the . . . Attorney General could not have been more clear" that a "wide class of dealers, distributors, and other 'franchisees'" were intended to fall within the scope of the Act.[49] As such,

---

40. *Id.*
41. *Id.*
42. 2022 WL 2439966, at *3 (S.D. Ill. July 5, 2022).
43. *See* Account Servs. Corp. v. DAKCS Software Servs., Inc., 567 N.E. 2d 381, 385 (Ill. App. Ct. 1990).
44. 2006 WL 2547202, at *3 (S.D. Ill. Sept. 1, 2006).
45. 2014 WL 2974064, at *2 (S.D. Ill. July 1, 2014).
46. *Id.*
47. 152 F.3d 658, 662 (7th Cir. 1998).
48. *Id.*
49. *Id.*

a "franchise fee" may be found where various required small purchases were made over time on an installment or infrequent basis.[50] The court also rejected the manufacturer's arguments that payments for manuals required in the business were not fees but were ordinary business expenses since there was no evidence presented of a market for the franchisor's proprietary manuals.[51]

Notably, the specific equipment dealership in *To-Am* that was found to be a franchise was subsequently exempted from the provisions of the Act by an amendment, effective January 1, 2000, to the Illinois Equipment Fair Dealership Law, which provides that "retailers and wholesalers, manufacturers, and distributors of inventory are not subject to the provisions of the Franchise Disclosure Act of 1987."[52] A "retailer" under that statute is defined as "any person, firm or corporation engaged in the business of selling and retailing outdoor power equipment including but not limited to all-terrain vehicles or off-highway motorcycles, farm implements, farm machinery, attachments accessories or repair parts and retailers of construction or industrial equipment, attachments or accessories or repair parts, but shall not include retailers of petroleum and motor vehicles and related automotive care and replacement products normally sold by such retailers."[53]

In *Flynn Beverage Inc. v. Joseph E. Seagram & Sons, Inc.*, the court held that allegations that a manufacturer required an alcohol distributor to purchase "excess inventory" stated a claim for an indirect franchise fee.[54]

3. Community of Interest; Significant Degree of Control; Joint Marketing Plan

a. Commentary

The Act's third element for what constitutes a "franchise" is a "marketing plan or system." The Act defines a "marketing plan or system" as "a plan or system relating to some aspect of the conduct of a party to a contract in conducting business, including but not limited to (a) specification of price, or special pricing systems or discount plans, (b) use of particular sales or display equipment or merchandising devices, (c) use of specific sales techniques, or (d) use of advertising or promotional materials or cooperation in advertising efforts[.]"[55] However, under the Act, an agreement does not include a marketing plan or system solely because a manufacturer or distributor of goods reserves the right to occasionally require sales at a special reduced price which is advertised on the product's regular container or packaging material, if the reduction in price is absorbed by the manufacturer or distributor.[56] The regulations further clarify the nonexclusivity of the listed examples by providing generally that a

---

50. *Id.* at 662–63.
51. *Id.* at 663.
52. 815 Ill. Comp. Stat. § 715/10.1.
53. *Id.* § 715/2(4).
54. 815 F. Supp. 1174, 1179 (C.D. Ill. 1993).
55. 815 Ill. Comp. Stat. § 705/3(18).
56. *Id.*

marketing plan or system simply "means advice given to the purchaser on how to sell the franchisor's product or service."[57]

To satisfy this element of the definition of a "franchise," the marketing plan or system must be "prescribed or suggested in substantial part by a franchisor."[58] The regulations state that this can occur even if the franchisee is an independent contractor and notwithstanding any agreement purporting to grant the franchisee complete freedom in operating its business.[59] Rather, whether or not a plan or system is prescribed or suggested in substantial part depends on the extent to which the following assistance is provided by the franchisor: "site selection, the grant of an exclusive territory, assistance on constructing or remodeling or decorating business premises, advice on fixtures or equipment or signs, advice on dress, training programs, advice on business hours, limitations on products or services to be sold, advertising assistance, suggested prices or credit practices, customer relations advice, and warranty advice."[60] The Illinois Appellate Court has stated that this element is met when a franchisor provides a marketing plan, even if it is optional.[61] The court held that the definition of "marketing plan" does not include the requirement that the franchisee participate in the plan; instead, the "prescribed or suggested" language in the Act focuses on the existence of the plan or system.[62]

b. Annotations

In *Smith v. Molly Maid, Inc.*, the court found that a franchise did not exist where the alleged franchisee paid only a portion of the franchise fee and thus never became eligible to receive training on the purported franchisor's marketing tools or to operate a business pursuant to the franchisor's suggested marketing plan.[63]

In *Account Services Corp. v. DAKCS Software Services, Inc.*, the court was "not persuaded" that plaintiffs had pled the existence of a marketing plan or system because the defendants did not give the plaintiffs any advice as to how to sell their services. The alleged "plan," while it described a "structure" whereby the defendants would obtain bad debts from hospitals and assign them to various collections agencies, "[did] not assist plaintiffs in the affirmative act of their selling or their offering of debt collection services."[64]

In *Salkeld v. V.R. Business Brokers*, the court held that the marketing plan requirement was met with the provision of a sales manual that detailed product information and sales strategies for a sub-licensed cocktail distribution business, particularly where the sub-licensee was promised support in marketing,

---

57. ILL. ADMIN. CODE tit. 14, § 200.102(a).
58. 815 ILL. COMP. STAT. § 705/3(1)(a).
59. ILL. ADMIN. CODE tit. 14, § 200.102(c).
60. *Id.* § 200.102(b).
61. Blankenship v. Dialist Int'l Corp., 568 N.E. 2d 503, 506–07 (Ill. App. Ct. 1991).
62. *Id.*
63. 415 F. Supp. 2d 905, 917 (N.D. Ill. 2006).
64. 567 N.E.2d 381, 385 (Ill. App. Ct. 1990).

training, advertising, and promotion and where the "sub-licensee program" was described as one where the company is "with you every step of the way."[65]

Advice given by the manufacturer about how to conduct a business does not need to be comprehensive for it to be a "marketing plan," nor must it be obligatory.[66] In *Blankenship v. Dialist*, a licensee was held to have received a marketing plan when it was given a detailed explanation of the licensor's business system, instruction on how to market the product, promises that additional instruction about the system would be forthcoming, a manual containing product information, sales points, promotional material, sample advertisements, numerous letters from purported customers announcing their participation in the public relations program, and later assistance from the licensor in proving the system's credibility to third parties.[67] The court reached this conclusion even though the parties' agreement allowed the licensee to develop the territory "without interference."[68]

B. Scope and Jurisdiction

1. Commentary

While the scope of the Act's registration provisions applies when (1) the franchisee is domiciled in Illinois, or (2) the offer of the franchise is made or accepted in Illinois, and the franchise business is or will be located in Illinois,[69] each of the Act's three primary relationship sections—those prohibiting discrimination and limiting termination and nonrenewal—provide only that franchisors are subject to those sections when the franchised business is located within Illinois.[70]

The vast majority of courts that have considered the scope of the Act's termination provisions have interpreted them to only apply to franchises located in Illinois, holding that choice-of-law provisions cannot extend the jurisdictional

---

65. 548 N.E. 2d 1151, 1153–56 (Ill. App. Ct. 1989).
66. *See, e.g.*, To-Am Equip. Co., Inc. v. Mitsubishi Caterpillar Forklift Am., Inc., 953 F. Supp. 987, 994 (N.D. Ill. 1997); Peter v. Stone Park Enters, LLC, 1999 WL 543210, at *7 (N.D. Ill. July 23, 1999) (holding that "[a]lthough the license agreement disclaims that [franchisor] has any obligation to provide [franchisee] with a marketing plan, [franchisee] may be able to allege that the brochure was an offer for a franchise, and that [franchisor] therefore gave [franchisee] 'the right' to sell under the marketing plan described in the brochure"); *see also Blankenship*, 568 N.E. 2d, at 506 (the focus of the marketing plan element of the "franchise" definition is not the franchisee's required use of the marketing plan, but the existence of the right under an agreement to sell or distribute under such a marketing system).
67. 568 N.E. 2d, at 506–07.
68. *Id.* at 506 (the focus of the marketing plan element of the "franchise" definition is not the franchisee's required use of the marketing plan, but the existence of the right under an agreement to sell or distribute under such a marketing system).
69. 815 Ill. Comp. Stat. § 705/10. The anti-fraud provision of the Act is broader and covers franchise sales when (1) the offer to sell or buy the franchise is made in Illinois and accepted within or outside of Illinois; (2) the offer is made outside of Illinois and accepted in Illinois; (3) the prospective franchisee is domiciled in Illinois; or (4) the franchised business is or will be located in Illinois. *Id.* § 705/6.
70. *Id.* §§ 705/18–705/20.

scope to include out-of-state franchisees.[71] Further, in an unreported decision, a federal court held that the Act does not provide a remedy for Illinois franchisees who claim damages for lost sales outside of Illinois, and as such, any damage claims would be limited to sales occurring within the state.[72]

2. Annotations

In *Cromeens, Holloman, Sibert, Inc. v. AB Volvo*, the plaintiff franchisees were located in Texas, Maine, Montana, New York, Alberta, and Saskatchewan, but argued that section 19 of the Act nonetheless applied to their wrongful termination claims against the franchisor because the dealer agreements at issue contained an Illinois choice-of-law provision.[73] The Seventh Circuit agreed with the franchisor, however, that the plain language of the Act excludes franchisees from its protection to the extent they are not located within the state of Illinois.[74]

In *H.R.R. Zimmerman Co. v. Tecumseh Products Co.*, the plaintiff franchisee sued its former franchisor for wrongful termination and claimed damages for the loss of its territory in Illinois, Indiana, Iowa, Wisconsin, and Michigan.[75] The franchisor sought to limit the franchisee's claimed damages to bar the allowance

---

71. *See* Cromeens, Holloman, Sibert, Inc. v. AB Volvo, 349 F.3d 376, 386 (7th Cir. 2003); Auto Driveaway Franchise Sys., LLC v. Auto Driveaway Richmond, LLC, 2019 WL 3302223, at *7 (N.D. Ill. July 23, 2019); McDonald's Corp. v. C.B. Mgmt. Co., 13 F. Supp. 2d 705, 714 (N.D. Ill. 1998); H.C. Duke & Son, LLC v. Prism Mktg. Corp., 2013 WL 5460209, at *8 (C.D. Ill. Sept. 30, 2013). Notably, however, several lower courts have suggested in dicta that the Act's termination provisions could apply to out-of-state franchises when the franchise agreement designates Illinois law in its choice-of-law provision. JTH Tax LLC v. Natalie Grabowski, Supernat LLC, 2020 WL 6203355, at *2 (N.D. Ill. Oct. 22, 2020) (court was "skeptical" that the Act would not apply simply because the supposed franchisee's territory was outside of Illinois, because "[i]t would seem that the parties' express undertaking to apply Illinois law to disputes between the parties with respect to the Agreement or dealings of the parties related thereto amounts to a decision to opt into Illinois law even if it might not otherwise apply," but holding that the Act nonetheless did not apply because no franchise fee was paid) (cleaned up); *see also* Lift Truck Lease & Serv., Inc. v. Nissan Forklift Corp., N. Am., 2012 WL 3891615, at *4–5 (E.D. Mo. Sept. 7, 2012) (the court was "not persuaded" that the Act would not apply because not only did the dealer's territory include 20 Illinois counties in addition to Missouri counties but also because the dealership agreement contained an Illinois choice-of-law provision; nonetheless, the court found that all claims under the Act should be dismissed because no franchise fee was paid).

72. H.R.R. Zimmerman Co. v. Tecumseh Prods. Co., 2002 WL 31018302, at * 3–4 (N.D. Ill. Sept. 9, 2002).

73. 349 F.3d 376, 385 (7th Cir. 2003).

74. *Id.* at 386 ("The [franchisees] paradoxically argue that the application of the IFDA is required, not by the law of Illinois, but rather by the intention of the parties. This is a circle from which the[y] cannot successfully emerge. If they insist (as they must, because the contract chooses Illinois law) that Illinois law applies, then we must look to the law of Illinois to determine the scope of application. The IFDA limits its scope to franchises located within the state, and the [franchisees] may not claim its protections."). The court further noted that Wisconsin's Fair Dealership Law and New York's Franchised Motor Vehicle Act—which have similarly restrictive language—had been construed by the Seventh Circuit and Fourth Circuit, respectively, to only apply to in-state franchisees. *Id.* at 385–86 (citing Peugeot Motors of America, Inc. v. Eastern Auto Distributors, Inc., 892 F.2d 355 (4th Cir.1989) and Generac Corp. v. Caterpillar Inc., 172 F.3d 971, 973 (7th Cir. 1999)).

75. 2002 WL 31018302, at * 1 (N.D. Ill. Sept. 9, 2002).

of any lost sales that occurred outside of Illinois. The Northern District of Illinois agreed with the franchisor, noting that under Illinois Supreme Court precedent, when a statute is silent as to its extraterritorial effect, there is a presumption that it has none.[76] Further, allowing the extraterritorial reach that the franchisees sought would present constitutional issues under the Dormant Commerce Clause, a problem that was avoided by interpreting the Act—as its silence about extraterritorial effects suggested—to only apply to economic activity occurring in Illinois.[77] As such, the franchisees' damages would be restricted to their lost sales within Illinois.[78]

C. Termination

1. What Constitutes Termination or Cancellation

a. Commentary

While the Act itself does not specify what constitutes termination of a franchise, at least one court has noted that a "constructive termination" of a franchise agreement might constitute termination under the Act.[79]

b. Annotations

Analogizing to other state franchise protection statutes and the Illinois Human Rights Act, the court in *Bell v. Bimbo Foods Bakeries*, in dicta, noted that "a constructive termination should qualify as a 'termination' under the Act."[80]

2. Restrictions on Termination

a. Commentary

Termination of a franchise without "good cause" is a violation of the Act, as discussed later in the chapter in Subsection II.C.4.

b. Annotations

See annotations under the following Subsection II.C.3 and Subsection II.C.4.

3. Notice Requirement

a. Commentary

The Act does not require advanced notice of termination per se once there is "good cause," but providing up to 30 days' notice of and an opportunity to cure contractual defaults is one means by which a franchisor can establish good cause, as discussed next in Subsection II.C.4.

---

76. *Id.* at *3.
77. *Id.* at *4.
78. *Id.* at *5–6.
79. Bell v. Bimbo Foods Bakeries Distrib., 2012 WL 2565849, at *3 (N.D. Ill. July 2, 2012).
80. *Id.* (finding, nonetheless, that no constructive discharge had occurred because the franchisee never stopped operating the franchise).

b. Annotations

In *Scholl's 4 Seasons Motor Sports, Inc. v. Arctic Cat Sales, Inc.*, a ten-day notice to cure payment defaults after months of attempting to collect monies owed was reasonable to support the termination of a franchise agreement, even though the franchisor did not specifically note that the franchise would be terminated if the franchisee did not comply.[81]

Because the Act states that the cure period *"in no event"* must be more than 30 days, the court in *McDonald's Corp. v. C.B. Management Co., Inc.* found that the franchisor's provision of a 30-day period for franchisee to cure unpaid rents and fees complied with the Act even though the franchisor knew that the franchisee would take more than 30 days to cure and even though it gave the franchisee reason to believe it would not terminate after 30 days.[82]

The Act requires notice of a default and a reasonable opportunity to cure but does not require notice of the franchisor's potential intent to terminate.[83]

4. Grounds for Termination

a. Commentary

As already discussed, termination of a franchise without "good cause" is a violation of the Act. One way that a franchisor may satisfy the Act's requirement of "good cause" to terminate is to first provide notice that the franchisee has defaulted on any lawful provision of the franchise agreement and to give a reasonable opportunity to cure, which "in no event need be more than 30 days."[84] Good cause is also satisfied, even without notice or opportunity to cure, where the franchisee (1) "makes an assignment for the benefit of creditors or a similar disposition of the assets of the franchise business"; (2) "voluntarily abandons the franchise business"; (3) "is convicted of a felony or other crime which substantially impairs the good will associated with the franchisor's trademark, service mark, trade name or commercial symbol"; or (4) "repeatedly fails to comply with the lawful provisions of the franchise or other agreement."[85] Further, because the Act states that good cause includes, but is not limited to, the preceding enumerated situations, the existence of good cause is not necessarily limited to the specific situations listed in the statute.[86]

The Act's prohibition against termination of franchises without good cause applies equally to relationships without a fixed duration and those with a fixed

---

81. 2010 WL 4736495, at *2 (N.D. Ill. Nov. 16, 2010).
82. McDonald's Corp. v. C.B. Mgmt. Co., Inc., 13 F. Supp. 2d 705, 715 (N.D. Ill. 1998).
83. Honeywell Int'l, Inc. v. Automated Bldg. Controls, LLC, 2016 WL 5349462, at *7 (N.D. Ill. Sept. 22, 2016) (declining to follow as "unpersuasive" the reasoning of H.R.R. Zimmerman Co. v. Tecumseh Prod. Co., 2001 WL 1356153 (N.D. Ill. Nov. 2, 2001), in which the Magistrate Judge had recommended that a franchisor must advise both as to the existence of a default and that the franchise is at risk if the default is not cured).
84. 815 Ill. Comp. Stat. § 705/19(b).
85. *Id.* § 705/19(c).
86. Rhine Enters. LLC v. Refresco Beverage US, Inc., 2022 WL 195109, at *3 (S.D. Ill. Jan. 22, 2022).

duration.[87] A franchisor's right to terminate a franchisee exists irrespective of any claims the franchisee might have against the franchisor.[88]

b. Annotations

In *Zeidler v. A & W Restaurants, Inc.*, a franchisor sent notices threatening to terminate a franchisee for failure to follow sanitation standards and for a lapsed insurance policy that were both required under the license agreement.[89] The franchisee then stopped operations, arguing that the franchisor's threats were in bad faith and made the business impossible to run, and the franchisor subsequently terminated.[90] The Seventh Circuit held that the termination was explicitly justified under section 19 of the Act, which lists "voluntary abandonment" as good cause.[91] Noting its earlier opinion in *Interim Health Care of Northern Illinois, Inc. v. Interim Health Care, Inc.*, the Seventh Circuit acknowledged that termination might not be justified in a situation where the franchisor's bad faith actions forced the franchisee to stop operating.[92] In this case, however, the franchisor's threats of termination—even if made in bad faith—could not have made the business impossible to run, and, thus, the franchisee's abandonment was voluntary.[93]

In *7-Eleven, Inc. v. Dar*, the court opined that the termination of a franchise agreement without good cause was wrongful under the Act, even though the franchise agreement did not require good cause for termination.[94] The court noted that contracts at odds with the Act are ineffectual.[95]

In *Honeywell International, Inc. v. Automated Building Controls, LLC*, good cause for termination under section 19(b) of the Act existed where the franchisee repeatedly paid fees late, even after the franchisor had notified it on several occasions that its payments were late and requested timely payment.[96] Even if no notice had been given, good cause existed for the franchisee's "repeated" violations because the undisputed record established that every single monthly statement showed an overdue balance for well over a year.[97]

In *McDonald's Corp. v. C.B. Management Co., Inc.*, the court held that the franchisor had "good cause" under the Act to terminate the franchise agreement based on the franchisee's failure to satisfy a legal requirement under the

---

87. *See* Carl A. Haas Auto. Imports, Inc. v. Lola Cars Ltd., 933 F. Supp. 1381, 1393–94 (N.D. Ill. 1996); *see also Rhine Enters. LLC*, 2022 WL 2439966, at *4 (noting that the crux of what section 19 requires is that the franchise "still be in effect when it is terminated by the franchisor").
88. 7-Eleven, Inc. v. Spear, 2011 WL 830069, at *4 (N.D. Ill. Mar. 3, 2011) (citing McDonald's Corp. v. Robertson, 147 F.3d 1301, 1309 (11th Cir. 1998)).
89. 301 F.3d 572, 573 (7th Cir. 2002).
90. *Id.*
91. *Id.* at 574.
92. *Id.* at 574–75 (citing Interim Health Care of N. Illinois, Inc. v. Interim Health Care, Inc., 225 F.3d 876 (7th Cir. 2000)).
93. *Id.* at 575.
94. 757 N.E.2d 515, 522 (Ill. App. Ct. 2001).
95. *Id.*
96. 2016 WL 5349462, at *6–7 (N.D. Ill. Sept. 22, 2016).
97. *Id.*

agreement—timely payment of rents and fees—where the franchisor issued a written default notice and provided the franchisee with 30 days to cure the defaults.[98] The court reached this conclusion even though the franchisee argued that the franchisor had not provided it with a "reasonable opportunity" to cure since the franchisor sent the default notice knowing the default was not curable in 30 days.[99] The court relied on the statutory language that a "reasonable opportunity" to cure "in no event" need be more than 30 days to hold that "[u]nder the explicit terms of the IFDA, [the franchisor] was justified in terminating the franchises."[100]

In *Pearle Vision, Inc. v. Romm*, the court found that a franchisor had sufficient good cause to terminate four franchise agreements with a franchisee because the franchisee had violated numerous material terms of the agreement, including the obligation to report monthly revenues and make a payment to the franchisor based on a percentage of those revenues.[101] Significantly, despite the franchisor sending notices of default after nearly all of the violations, the franchisee's reporting and payment violations had not been cured, even after two default notices had been sent.[102]

In *7-Eleven, Inc. v. Shakti Chicago, Inc.*, the court held that the franchisor had good cause to terminate a franchisee that had repeatedly failed to comply with the franchise agreement, even though the franchisor allegedly terminated for other reasons, because whether the franchisor had an "improper motive" was "irrelevant" as to whether it objectively had the legal right to terminate.[103]

5. Required Cure Period

a. Commentary

As noted earlier in Subsection II.C.4, one means by which a franchisor may satisfy the Act's requirement of "good cause" is to provide the franchisee with notice and an opportunity to cure any defaults under the agreement, which "in no event need be more than 30 days," or to terminate under the four enumerated situations without notice or opportunity to cure.[104]

b. Annotations

In *H Guys LLC v. Hallal Guys Franchise, Inc.*, the court denied the franchisee's motion for a temporary restraining order enjoining the franchisor from

---

98. 13 F. Supp. 2d 705, 714–15 (N.D. Ill. 1998).
99. *Id.*
100. *Id.*
101. 2005 WL 2172393, at *5–6 (N.D. Ill. Sept. 1, 2005).
102. *Id.*
103. 2019 WL 3387001, at *2 (N.D. Ill. July 26, 2019).
104. 815 Ill. Comp. Stat. § 705/19(b)–(c) (no notice or opportunity to cure is required where the franchisee: (1) "makes an assignment for the benefit of creditors or a similar disposition of the assets of the franchise business"; (2) "voluntarily abandons the franchise business"; (3) "is convicted of a felony or other crime which substantially impairs the good will associated with the franchisor's trademark, service mark, trade name or commercial symbol"; or (4) "repeatedly fails to comply with the lawful provisions of the franchise or other agreement").

terminating the franchise agreement because the franchisor likely had good cause to immediately terminate pursuant to the Act's cure period exceptions based on the franchisee's "repeated" failures to comply with the franchise agreement's food safety standards.[105] The court credited detailed reports of at least three failed inspections, which included photographs documenting the franchisee's serious violations of sanitation and food safety standards.[106] Further, the court discounted the franchisee's argument that the failed inspections were mere pretext for the franchisor's desire to terminate due to personal animus and to resell the territory without paying the franchisee, noting that "it certainly is possible that [the franchisor] did not like [the franchisee] and its principals, yet still had good cause to terminate the Franchise Agreement due to [the franchisee's] repeated poor performance on health and safety inspections."[107]

In *Tilted Kilt Franchise Operating, LLC v. 1220, LLC*, the franchisor sought a declaratory judgment that it could lawfully terminate an area developer agreement under the Act without any cure period where the area developer allegedly provided misleading financial performance representations to prospective franchisees on several occasions.[108] On the franchisee's motion to dismiss, the court held that the franchisor stated a claim for proper termination without notice under the Act for two reasons: (1) the Act's 30-day cure period arguably does not apply to a "material" and "incurable" breach of the franchise agreement; and (2) the franchisee's alleged actions fell within the Act's enumerated exceptions to the cure requirement because they were arguably "crimes" under the Act and the FTC's Franchise Rule and constituted "repeated" failures to comply with the franchise agreement.[109]

In *In re Neely Group, Inc.*, the franchisor sent the franchisee default notices when it failed to pay past due amounts owed under two franchise agreements.[110] The franchisor demanded that the franchisee cure the defaults within 30 days to avoid termination, following which, the franchisee paid and cured the defaults.[111] Two months later, however, the franchisee again fell behind on payments and had accrued another past due balance.[112] Without offering another cure period, the franchisor sent a notice of immediate termination on the grounds that the franchisee had "repeatedly" failed to abide by the franchise agreements, thereby giving the franchisor good cause to terminate without affording an opportunity to cure under section 19 of the Act.[113] The franchisee challenged the termination in court, arguing that the franchisor should have provided another cure period because two breaches do not constitute "repeated" violations within the

---

105. 2019 WL 3337116, at *4 (N.D. Ill. July 25, 2019).
106. Id.
107. Id.
108. 2016 WL 4063172, at *6–7 (N.D. Ill. July 29, 2016).
109. Id.
110. 2024 WL 2946219, at *2 (Bankr. N.D. Ill. June 11, 2024).
111. Id.
112. Id.
113. Id.

meaning of the Act.[114] The court disagreed, finding that the structure of the Act requires notice and an opportunity to cure for one default (under section 19(b)), but does not require notice or an opportunity to cure for "repeated" defaults (under section 19(c)(4)): "So 'repeatedly' must mean more than once. Otherwise, the statute's coverage would have a gap: the possibility of two defaults."[115] The court further held that "[h]ad the General Assembly wanted section 19(c) to apply only after three or more franchisee defaults, it could have said so," but "[i]t did not say so in section 19."[116] Therefore, the franchisor had good cause under the Act to immediately terminate the franchisee after its second payment default without offering any cure period.[117]

6. Repurchase Obligations

a. Commentary
Not applicable.

b. Annotations
Not applicable.

D. Restrictions on Nonrenewal

1. What Constitutes Nonrenewal

a. Commentary
The nonrenewal provision of the Act applies when a franchise agreement expires by its terms and the franchisor refuses to renew it.[118] This provision only applies to franchise agreements with fixed expiration dates.[119]

b. Annotations
In *Jamb Optical, Inc. v. American Vision Centers, Inc.*, the franchisor leased a location that was subleased to the franchisee for operation of the franchised business.[120] When the landlord terminated the lease, the franchisor granted the franchisee the right to relocate the franchise, but then denied the franchisee's request to transfer the franchise.[121] After the transfer request was denied, the franchisee stopped operating.[122] The franchisee argued that the term "nonrenewal" should be read broadly to encompass a situation where the franchisee "causes the discontinuation of a franchise." However, the court disagreed, noting that there was no refusal to renew and section 20 did not apply because the

---

114. *Id.* at *4.
115. *Id.* at *5.
116. *Id.* at *6.
117. *Id.*
118. 815 Ill. Comp. Stat. § 705/20.
119. H.R.R. Zimmerman Co. v. Tecumseh Prod. Co., 2001 WL 1356153, at *9 (N.D. Ill. Nov. 2, 2001), *adopted as modified*, 2002 WL 31018302, at *8 (N.D. Ill. Sept. 9, 2002).
120. 1998 WL 292398, at *1 (N.D. Ill. May 19, 1998).
121. *Id.* at *1–2.
122. *Id.*

franchisee "could have continued operating the franchise in another location if they had chosen to do so."[123]

2. Restrictions on Nonrenewal

a. Commentary

It is a violation of the Act for a franchisor to refuse to renew without compensating the franchisee either by repurchase or "other means for the diminution in the value of the franchised business caused by the expiration of the franchise" unless (1) the franchisor provides at least six months' notice of nonrenewal to the franchisee; and (2) the franchisee is not barred from competing in substantially the same business in the same area under a different trademark after nonrenewal, either because the franchise agreement does not contain any post-expiration noncompetition requirements or because the franchisor waives any such requirements at least six months prior to expiration.[124]

b. Annotations

In *Auto Driveaway Franchise System, LLC v. Auto Driveaway Richmond, LLC*, the franchisor's complaint for breach of the post-termination noncompetition covenants alleged that the parties entered into a five-year franchise agreement that expired in January 2018, at which point the franchisee refused to execute a renewal agreement and the parties continued the old agreement on a month-to-month basis until the franchisor terminated the franchisee in September 2018.[125] The court held that the franchisor's alleged actions did not violate section 20 of the Act because the franchisor had not refused to renew the franchise agreement at the end of its term.[126]

3. Notice Requirements

a. Commentary

As already explained in Subsection II.D.2, to avoid the compensation provisions of the Act, a franchisor must provide both (1) at least six months' notice of nonrenewal prior to the franchise agreement's expiration date or any extension thereof; and (2) six months' notice that it will waive any noncompetition requirement that bars the franchisee from competing in substantially the same business in the same area under a different trademark after nonrenewal (if such a provision exists in the parties' franchise agreement).[127]

b. Annotations

In *Dunkin' Donuts Inc. v. Benita Corp.*, three months before the parties' franchise agreement was scheduled to expire, the franchisor offered to extend the agreement for an additional three months (for a total of six months) and notified

---

123. *Id.* at *4.
124. 815 Ill. Comp. Stat. § 705/20.
125. 2019 WL 3302223, at *1–2 (N.D. Ill. July 23, 2019).
126. *Id.* at *7.
127. 815 Ill. Comp. Stat. § 705/20.

the franchisee that it would not renew after that date.[128] The franchisee argued that the franchisor had violated section 20 of the Act because it did not give six months' notice of nonrenewal prior to the scheduled expiration date, but the court held that the franchisor had likely complied with the plain language of section 20 because the notice was given six months prior to the expiration "or any extension thereof of the franchise."[129]

4. Grounds for Nonrenewal

a. Commentary

"Good cause" is not a basis upon which franchisors may end the franchise relationship in the renewal context as it is in the termination context (see Subsection II.C.4). As such, if a franchisor refuses to renew a franchisee's agreement, the only way the franchisor may avoid compensating the franchisee is to provide the requisite notice and (if applicable) waiver of any noncompetition covenants.[130]

b. Annotations

Although no cases have thus far noted the interplay between the Act's termination provision, which does not require compensation, and the nonrenewal provision, which does require compensation, theoretically the Act incentivizes franchisors to terminate franchisees when there is good cause to do so, even if they are at the end of their term, rather than allow their franchise agreements to expire without renewal.

5. Required Cure Period

a. Commentary
Not applicable.

b. Annotations
Not applicable.

6. Limitations on Franchisors' Right to Impose Conditions for Renewal

a. Commentary
Not applicable.

b. Annotations

In *Auto Driveaway Franchise System, LLC v. Auto Driveaway Richmond, LLC*, the renewal of the relevant franchise agreement was contingent on "certain conditions" being met.[131] According to the franchisor's complaint, the franchisee refused to sign a renewal agreement, and the parties continued on a month-to-month basis until the franchisor terminated.[132] Although the issue was not

---

128. 1998 WL 67613, at *1 (N.D. Ill. Feb. 10, 1998).
129. *Id.* at *4.
130. 815 Ill. Comp. Stat. § 705/20.
131. 2019 WL 3302223, at *1 (N.D. Ill. July 23, 2019).
132. *Id.* at *2.

central to the court's decision, it held that the franchisor's allegations would satisfy the Act's requirements because it was the franchisee, not the franchisor, that refused to renew.[133]

7. Repurchase Obligations

a. Commentary

Unless the franchisor provides six months' notice and waives any noncompetition requirements barring the franchisee from competing in substantially the same business in the same area under a different trademark after nonrenewal, a franchisor that refuses to renew must compensate the franchisee either by repurchase or "other means for the diminution in the value of the franchised business caused by the expiration of the franchise."[134]

b. Annotations

There is little case law construing the Act's renewal provision regarding compensation. In dicta, the Sixth Circuit has noted that the section requires compensation for the full value of the franchise as a going concern.[135] In contrast, at least one franchisor has attempted to argue that because section 20 of the Act only requires six months' notice, damages must be limited to no more than six months.[136]

E. Transfers and Succession

1. Commentary

Not applicable.

2. Annotations

In *Jamb Optical, Inc. v. American Vision Centers, Inc.*, the court found that the nonrenewal provision of the Act does not apply to a franchisor's alleged unreasonable refusal to approve transfer of a franchise to new franchisees, "which is a very different thing" from a franchisor's refusal to renew the franchise.[137]

F. Other Regulation of the Franchise Relationship

The Act prohibits franchisors from restricting franchisees' participation in trade associations[138] and unreasonably discriminating between similarly situated franchisees.[139] Additionally, it voids any agreement that purports to waive compliance with the Act's provisions.[140] It does not, however, contain sections directly

---

133. *Id.* at *7.
134. 815 ILL. COMP. STAT. § 705/20.
135. *See* Gen. Aviation, Inc. v. Cessna Aircraft Co., 13 F.3d 178, 182 (6th Cir. 1993).
136. *See* H.R.R. Zimmerman Co. v. Tecumseh Prod. Co., 2002 WL 31018302, at *8 (N.D. Ill. Sept. 9, 2002) (the court ultimately held that the renewal provisions were inapplicable to the dispute at issue because the franchise agreement had no fixed term and thus did not concern a renewal).
137. 1998 WL 292398, at *4 (N.D. Ill. May 19, 1998).
138. 815 ILL. COMP. STAT. § 705/17.
139. *Id.* § 705/18.
140. *Id.* § 705/41.

addressing territory rights, pricing restrictions, restrictions of sources of supply, advertising funds, or standards of conduct.

1. Discrimination

a. Commentary

The Act prohibits franchisors from "unreasonably and materially" discriminating between franchisees "in the charges offered or made for franchise fees, royalties, goods, services, equipment, rentals or advertising services, if such discrimination will cause competitive harm to a franchisee who competes with a franchisee that received the benefit of the discrimination."[141] Because this language specifically targets price, the Northern District of Illinois has interpreted section 18 of the Act to only cover price discrimination.[142]

Discrimination between franchisees is not a violation of the Act when it is (1) based on franchises granted at different times; (2) related to one or more programs for making franchises available to those with insufficient capital, training, business experience or education, or lacking other qualifications; (3) related to local or regional experimentation with product or service lines or business formats or designs; (4) related to efforts by one or more franchisees to cure deficiencies in their business; or (5) based on other reasonable distinctions "considering the purposes of [the] Act and is not arbitrary."[143]

b. Annotations

In *P & W Supply Co., Inc. v. E.I. DuPont de Nemours & Co., Inc.*, the franchisee alleged that the franchisor discriminated against it in two ways: (1) terminating an agreement due to the franchisee's refusal to sign the revised agreement; and (2) refusing to sell a "specific Du Pont product" to the franchisee prior to the termination of the agreement.[144] The court rejected the franchisee's claims, holding that section 18 only prohibits price discrimination, which the plaintiff had not alleged.[145] The court provided two examples of what would constitute prohibited price discrimination under the Act: "a fast-food franchisor cannot sell hamburger meat to one franchisee at 30 cents a pound while selling the same meat to a competing franchisee for 60 cents a pound. Similarly, the franchisor cannot require one of its franchisees to sell a hamburger for $2.00 and at the same time allow a competing franchisee to sell a hamburger for only $1.00."[146] The Southern District of Illinois recently followed *P & W Supply Co., Inc.*, holding that the type of discrimination prohibited under the Act refers only to price discrimination on the part of franchisors against competing franchisees.[147]

---

141. *Id*. § 705/18.
142. P & W Supply Co., Inc. v. E.I. DuPont de Nemours & Co., Inc., 747 F. Supp. 1262, 1267 (N.D. Ill. 1990).
143. 815 Ill. Comp. Stat. § 705/18.
144. 747 F. Supp. 1262, 1266–67 (N.D. Ill. 1990).
145. *Id*. at 1267.
146. *Id*.
147. Rhine Enters. LLC v. Refresco Beverage US, Inc., 2022 WL 195109, at *3 (S.D. Ill. Jan. 22, 2022).

2. Association Rights

a. Commentary

The Act prohibits a franchisor from restricting any franchisee in any way from joining or participating in any trade association.[148] As discussed in the following case annotations, however, a franchisor's termination of a franchisee for objective good cause cannot be overcome by the fact that the franchisor may have an improper motive, such as to prevent the franchisee from joining or participating in a trade association.[149]

b. Annotations

In *7-Eleven, Inc. v. Shakti Chicago, Inc.*, 7-Eleven terminated the franchise agreements after the issuance of five default notices alleging various breaches, including failures to comply with wage and hour laws and failures to submit accurate payroll information.[150] The franchisee countersued alleging that 7-Eleven terminated the franchise agreements because of his leadership within the Franchise Owners Association of Chicagoland as well as his criticism of 7-Eleven's business practices, in violation of section 17 of the Act.[151] On 7-Eleven's Rule 12(b)(6) motion to dismiss, 7-Eleven argued that motive was irrelevant because it had good cause to terminate the franchise agreement.[152] The court found that because the franchisee did not dispute the accuracy of the five default notices, under a Rule 12(b)(6) standard it was established that 7-Eleven had good cause to terminate the franchise agreements.[153] The court found that the franchisee did "not provide, and the Court has not found, any legal support for the argument that a termination for good cause can be 'overcome by the presence of an improper motive.'"[154]

3. Restriction on Waivers

a. Commentary

The Act voids any provision that purports to waive compliance with the Act, such as statements involving unregistered financial performance representations, timely disclosure, warranty, material misrepresentations, or limitation of liability.[155] The Act does not, however, prohibit a settlement agreement or general release regarding a potential or actual lawsuit for claims under the Act, nor does it prohibit an agreement that provides for arbitration as the method of dispute resolution.[156]

---

148. 815 ILL. COMP. STAT. § 705/17.
149. 7-Eleven, Inc. v. Shakti Chicago, Inc., 2019 WL 3387001, at *2 (N.D. Ill. July 26, 2019).
150. *Id.* at *2.
151. *Id.* at *1.
152. *Id.* at *2.
153. *Id.*
154. *Id.*
155. 815 ILL. COMP. STAT. § 705/41; ILL. ADMIN. CODE tit. 14, § 200.609.
156. *See generally* 815 ILL. COMP. STAT. § 705/41.

b. Annotations

In *Sound of Music Co. v. Minnesota Mining & Manufacturing Co.*, the franchisee appealed the district court's entry of summary judgment on its claim under the Act, breach of contract claim, and Minnesota franchise act claim.[157] While the Seventh Circuit upheld the district court's ruling that the franchisee's claim under the Act was barred by the statute of limitations, it noted that it was proper to consider the claim under the Act despite the presence of a valid Minnesota choice-of-law provision.[158] Specifically, the court noted that although the "agreement provided that it would be governed by Minnesota law, Sound of Music's offices were all in Illinois. The Illinois franchise statute contains an anti-waiver provision."[159] Through this provision, "Illinois, like many other states, has made it clear that parties cannot opt out of the coverage of the act for Illinois franchisees."[160]

In *Window World of Chicagoland, LLC v. Window World, Inc.*, the franchisee was located in Illinois but the franchise agreement contained a North Carolina choice-of-law provision; when the franchisee brought claims under the Act and for common law breach of contract, the court—based on the Act's anti-waiver provision—applied Illinois law to the claims under the Act while applying North Carolina law to the common law breach of contract claims.[161]

In *Sanchez v. CleanNet USA, Inc.*, the franchisor moved to dismiss a representative franchisee's putative class action claim for misclassification based on a mandatory arbitration provision in the franchise agreement.[162] The court found that the arbitration provision was enforceable and compelled arbitration, but only after severing the franchise agreement's remedial limitations—specifically, its punitive damages and attorneys' fees and costs waivers.[163] The court explained that those waivers are unenforceable because the Act voids provisions that waive compliance with the Act and makes franchisors liable for damages and attorneys' fees in the event they violate the Act.[164]

In *7-Eleven, Inc. v. Dar*, reviewing a wrongful termination claim, the court upheld an arbitrator's determination that a franchisor could supplant the limitations period provided under the Act by entering an agreement containing a shorter limitations period.[165]

---

157. 477 F.3d 910, 915 (7th Cir. 2007).
158. *Id.* at 917–18.
159. *Id.* at 918 n.2.
160. *Id.* (quoting To-Am Equip. Co., Inc. v. Mitsubishi Caterpillar Forklift Am., Inc., 152 F.3d 658, 662 (7th Cir. 1998)).
161. 2015 WL 2193752, at *8 (N.D. Ill. May 7, 2015) (following *Sound of Music Co.*, 477 F.3d, at 917–18 n.2).
162. 78 F. Supp. 3d 747 (N.D. Ill. 2015).
163. *Id.* at 757.
164. *Id.*
165. Bus. Franchise Guide (CCH) ¶ 12,057 (Ill. App. Ct. 2001).

G. Remedies and Administrative Action

1. Restrictive Covenants

a. Commentary

As discussed earlier in Subsection II.D, the Act does not permit a franchisor to refuse to renew a franchise agreement unless the franchisor waives the franchisee's obligation to comply with any noncompetition covenants and gives notice of the nonrenewal, or provides compensation to the franchisee.

b. Annotations

See annotations in Subsection II.D.

2. Damages

a. Commentary

Section 26 of the Act states that franchisees may sue for damages when the franchisor "offers, sells, terminates, or fails to renew a franchise in violation of this Act."[166] In other words, section 26 provides franchisees a private cause of action for fraudulent misrepresentations, material omissions, wrongful termination, or failure to renew. Damages, including lost future profits, are recoverable for such violations, and the additional remedy of rescission is also available for sales violations arising out of sections 5, 6, 10, 11, or 15 of the Act.[167]

Because the only relationship provisions referred to in section 26 are termination and nonrenewal, it is unclear whether there is any private cause of action for violations of section 17's prohibition on associational restrictions or section 18's prohibition on price discrimination. On its face, section 26 appears to exclude those provisions by omission, and section 28 states that "except as explicitly provided," no civil liability shall arise "by implication from or as a result of the violation of any provision of this Act."[168] As of publication, the only published decision referring to an alleged violation of section 17's prohibition on associational restrictions was in the context of an allegedly unlawful termination (see Subsection II.F.2).[169] And while there are several published decisions analyzing franchisors' alleged violations of section 18's prohibition on discrimination (see Subsection II.F.1), the franchisors in those cases do not appear to have challenged the franchisee's statutory standing.

The history of the Act also suggests that there is no private right of action for the nonspecified relationship provisions. While the original 1974 version of the Act focused only on franchise sales, it was amended in 1979 to prohibit termination except for "good cause," and its enforcement section, entitled "Private Civil Actions," gave franchisees the right to sue for any "violation of this

---

166. 815 Ill. Comp. Stat. § 705/26.
167. *Id.*; To-Am Equip. Co. v. Mitsubishi Caterpillar Forklift Am., Inc., 953 F. Supp. 987, 995 (N.D. Ill. 1997).
168. 815 Ill. Comp. Stat. § 705/28.
169. 7-Eleven, Inc. v. Shakti Chicago, Inc., 2019 WL 3387001, at *2 (N.D. Ill. July 26, 2019).

Act."[170] When the entire statute was revised in 1987, the enforcement sections were reworded to provide a right of action against any person "who offers or sells a franchise in violation of this Act."[171] Then, in 1992, section 26 was revised yet again to include reference to termination and nonrenewal, along with an additional sentence stating that "[t]his amendatory Act of 1992 is intended to clarify the existence of a private right of action under existing law with respect to the termination or nonrenewal of a franchise in violation of this Act."[172] As such, while the 1979 version of the Act provided a private cause of action for any violation of the Act, and the 1992 version explicitly provided a cause of action for termination and nonrenewal, the 1987 version's enforcement section did not mention termination or nonrenewal and only explicitly provided a private cause of action for wrongful sales.

In several cases regarding disputes arising out of franchise terminations that had occurred between 1987 and 1992, franchisors argued that franchisees had no statutory standing to sue for wrongful termination under the plain language of the Act.[173] Courts rejected those arguments, however, holding that because the 1992 amendment stated that it was intended to "clarify" existing law, it meant that franchisees had a private cause of action to sue for wrongful termination even in disputes that arose during the 1987–1992 period when section 26 said nothing about termination or nonrenewal.[174] That said, the best justification for those decisions—particularly given that Illinois statutes are to be interpreted according to their plain language—is simply that the 1992 amendment was given retroactive effect because it explicitly stated that the Act allowed suits for wrongful termination and nonrenewal under "existing law."[175] Because the Act provides no such "clarification" for trade associations or price discrimination, there is less reason to believe that modern courts will take a similarly expansive view of section 26's application to those sections, at least outside the context of termination or nonrenewal issues.

The Act itself does not provide for punitive damages.[176] While the Act states that "[n]othing in this Act shall limit any liability which may exist by virtue of any other statute or under common law," because punitive damages are not generally recoverable for breach of contract (including the implied covenant of good faith and fair dealing), it is unlikely that Illinois franchisees would be

---

170. H.R.R. Zimmerman Co. v. Tecumseh Prod. Co., 2001 WL 1356153, at *6 (N.D. Ill. Nov. 2, 2001) *adopted as modified*, 2002 WL 31018302 (N.D. Ill. Sept. 9, 2002) (explaining history of the Act's private cause of action sections).

171. *Id.*

172. *Id.*; 815 ILL. COMP. STAT. § 705/26.

173. Dudley Enters., Inc. v. Palmer Corp., 832 F. Supp. 221, 227 (N.D. Ill. 1993); *Zimmerman*, 2001 WL 1356153, at *6.

174. *Zimmerman*, 2001 WL 1356153, at *6.

175. *Id.*

176. Bonfield v. AAMCO Transmissions, Inc., 708 F. Supp. 867, 887 (N.D. Ill. 1989) ("Punitive damages (as contrasted with 'damages' generally) are absent from the remedies listed [in the Act], raising at least the inference of their unavailability under the Act. After all, the General Assembly knows how to specify the recovery of punitive damages should it choose to do so.").

able to obtain punitive damages for wrongful termination or nonrenewal.[177] It could be possible for a franchisee to seek punitive damages for an intentional tort that occurs during the franchise relationship, such as fraudulent inducement of additional investments in a franchised business, but as of publication, no Illinois cases have examined such claims.

b. Annotations

In *To-Am Equipment Co. v. Mitsubishi Caterpillar Forklift America, Inc.*, the expert witness for a forklift dealer seeking to establish damages for wrongful termination under the Act calculated damages by predicting future sales and the resulting profits had it remained a dealer, which the expert then capitalized and then subtracted the value of pre-termination assets.[178] While the court chided the expert's calculation as "fishy," it upheld the jury's $1.525 million award, determining that the expert persuaded the jury and citing Illinois case law that permits juries to split the difference between competing expert damages calculations.[179]

3. Rescission

a. Commentary

The Act expressly states that recission is only available for violation of sections 5, 6, 10, 11, or 15 of the Act, which pertain to disclosure, registration, and the offer or sale of a franchise, not the Act's relationship provisions.[180]

b. Annotations

Not applicable.

4. Injunctive Relief

a. Commentary

While the Act does not affirmatively provide for injunctive relief as a remedy for violations, it does not prohibit it, stating that "nothing in this Act shall limit any liability which may exist by virtue of any other statute or under common law."[181] And, as discussed in the annotations, courts have explicitly recognized that injunctive relief is available in the case of threatened termination.

b. Annotations

In *Stuller, Inc. v. Steak N Shake Enterprises, Inc.*, the court granted a franchisee's motion for a preliminary injunction against its franchisor's implementation of a new policy that required all franchisees to follow a set menu (except for breakfast) and offer all of the franchisor's promotions as published.[182] Notably,

---

177. 815 Ill. Comp. Stat. § 705/28.
178. 953 F. Supp. 987, 995 (N.D. Ill. 1997), *aff'd*, 152 F.3d 658 (7th Cir. 1998).
179. *Id.* at 995–96.
180. 815 Ill. Comp. Stat. § 705/26.
181. *Id.* § 705/28.
182. 2011 WL 2473330, at *14 (C.D. Ill. July 21, 2011), *aff'd*, 695 F.3d 676 (7th Cir. 2012).

it determined that absent an injunction, the franchisee would suffer irreparable harm and there was no other adequate remedy because the franchisor had threatened to terminate the franchise agreement if the franchisee did not abide by the policy during the pendency of the lawsuit.[183]

5. Control Person Liability

a. Commentary

A franchisor's directors, partners, principal executive officers, persons directly or indirectly in control, and employees "who materially aid[] in the act or transaction constituting the violation" can be held jointly and severally liable in a private civil action for violating the Act, unless such person "had no knowledge or reasonable basis to have knowledge of the facts, acts or transactions constituting the alleged violation."[184] Because individual liability is made explicit under the Act, corporate veil-piercing is not required.[185]

b. Annotations

To date, while the issue of individual liability under the Act has been litigated in the disclosure context, no cases were located discussing it in the relationship context.[186]

6. Attorneys' Fees

a. Commentary

The Act provides that prevailing franchisees are entitled to costs, including reasonable attorneys' fees, if they are successful in bringing claims under the Act.[187] Conversely, it does not provide that franchisors who successfully defend claims brought pursuant to the Act may recover any costs or attorneys' fees. In practice, however, many franchise agreements explicitly allow the franchisor to recover attorneys' fees if it is a prevailing party in any litigation with the franchisee, including by successfully defending against a franchisee's claims.

b. Annotations

In *Bly & Sons, Inc. v. Ethan Allen Interiors, Inc.*, the franchisor sent out a termination letter and then, just 26 days later, rescinded the termination.[188] Despite the rescindment, the court found that the termination had been wrongful and

---

183. *Id.* at *11 (citing Semmes Motors, Inc. v. Ford Motor Co., 429 F.2d 1197, 1205 (2d Cir. 1970)).
184. 815 ILL. COMP. STAT. § 705/26.
185. Geri's West, Inc. v. Ferrall, 505 N.E.2d 1348, 1350–51 (Ill. App. Ct. 1987) (franchisor president was not insulated from individual liability for alleged registration and disclosure violations when the president admitted that he alone represented the franchisor during the sales process, and the Act had a "comprehensive strategy of individual liability for all those acting for a franchisor" based on the Act's individual-encompassing definitions of "franchise broker" and "salesperson," as well as the "other persons" catchall in Section 21).
186. *See, e.g.*, To-Am Equip. Co. v. Mitsubishi Caterpillar Forklift Am., 913 F. Supp. 1148 (N.D. Ill. 1995).
187. 815 ILL. COMP. STAT. § 705/26.
188. 2006 WL 2547202, at *2 (S.D. Ill. Sept. 1, 2006).

without cause and ordered the franchisor to pay the franchisee's costs and attorneys' fees related to the termination of the agreement for the 26-day period.[189]

In *To-Am Equipment Co., Inc. v. Mitsubishi Caterpillar Forklift America, Inc.*, the prevailing franchisee requested an attorneys' fees award of $500,000, even though the hours expended at the lawyers' normal rates only totaled $234,482.[190] The franchisee argued that it was entitled to the greater award either based on a risk of nonpayment multiplier or the continent-fee arrangement between the franchisee and its law firm.[191] The court rejected the franchisee's argument, noting that under the U.S. Supreme Court's holding in *Burlington v. Dague*, multipliers are never appropriate when calculating the amount of fees to be imposed on a losing litigant.[192] It also rejected the franchisee's argument that the Illinois Appellate Court condoned the consideration of fee arrangements when crafting the award in *Blankenship v. Dialist International Corp.*, explaining that *Blankenship* predated *Dauge*, does not require consideration of such arrangements, and noting that nothing in the Act suggests an intended departure from the traditional fee-shifting statutes.[193] Ultimately, the court awarded the franchisee attorneys' fees for its work in pursuing its claims under the Act, based on an adjusted lodestar method rather than a risk-adjusted method.[194] Moreover, the court refused to award the franchisee its expert-witness fees, finding that such fees are not covered by section 705/26 of the Act.[195]

7. Limitations on Damage Waivers

a. Commentary

The Act does not address punitive damages or limitations on damage waivers directly. However, the Act's anti-waiver section voids any agreement to waive compliance with the Act.[196] At least one court has interpreted the anti-waiver provision as prohibiting a punitive damages waiver.[197]

b. Annotations

See earlier discussion of *Sanchez v. CleanNet USA, Inc.* in Subsection II.F.3.[198]

8. Administrative Action

a. Commentary

The Illinois attorney general has the authority to suspend, terminate, or deny a franchisor's ability to register or sell franchises if it finds that the franchisor

---

189. *Id.*
190. 953 F. Supp. 987, 997 (N.D. Ill. 1997), *aff'd*, 152 F.3d 658 (7th Cir. 1998).
191. *Id.*
192. *Id.* at 998.
193. *Id.*
194. *Id.* at 99–1000.
195. *Id.* at 1000.
196. 815 ILL. COMP. STAT. § 705/41.
197. Sanchez v. CleanNet USA, Inc., 78 F. Supp. 3d 747, 757 (N.D. Ill. 2015).
198. *Id.*

has violated the Act.[199] The Act does not provide a statute of limitations for the state's ability to prosecute administrative actions.[200]

b. Annotations

As of publication, no case law addresses actions taken against franchisors by the Illinois attorney general for violations of the relationship provisions of the Act.

H. Dispute Resolution

1. Limitations on Franchisors' Ability to Restrict Venue

a. Commentary

The Act voids any contractual provision "that designates jurisdiction or venue in a forum outside of this State."[201] However, it does permit agreements to arbitrate outside of the state.[202] Further, the plain language of the Act only voids contractual provisions which designate venue outside of Illinois; the Act does not mandate that litigation occur in Illinois if venue is independently proper in another state.[203] As such, while some courts have given deference to an Illinois forum given the state's interest in enforcing the Act, others have declined to force venue in Illinois.[204]

b. Annotations

In *ECC Computer Centers of Illinois, Inc. v. Entre Computer Centers, Inc.*, the franchisor moved to either dismiss the plaintiff's contract, tort, and claims under the Act or, alternatively, transfer the case to Virginia based on the franchise agreement's venue provision.[205] The court denied both motions, holding that regardless of whether state or federal law controlled the analysis the case should remain in Illinois—under state law because the Act voided the venue provision and under federal law because enforcing the venue provision would contravene the strong public policy reflected in the Act.[206] Illinois venue is proper even though the franchise agreement between an Illinois franchisee and a Virginia franchisor specified Virginia as the forum, because the Act expressly renders

---

199. 815 Ill. Comp. Stat. § 705/22(a).
200. *Id.* § 705/22.
201. *Id.* § 705/4.
202. *Id.*
203. *Id.; see also* Jackson Hewitt Inc. v. O & W Taxes, Inc., 2022 WL 17466428, at *2 n.4 (D.N.J. Dec. 5, 2022).
204. *Compare* O & W Taxes, Inc., 2022 WL 17466428, at *2 n.4 (declining to grant franchisee's motion to transfer because the franchisee did not meet its burden to show that a transfer to Illinois was appropriate) *with* Hofbrauhaus of Am., LLC v. Oak Tree Mgmt. Serv., Inc., 2023 WL 24179, at *9 (D. Nev. Jan. 3, 2023) (granting franchisee's motion to transfer because Illinois has a strong interest in protecting its franchisees, due in part to the Act's language voiding forum selection clauses calling for litigation outside of Illinois).
205. 597 F. Supp. 1182, 1183 (N.D. Ill. 1984).
206. *Id.* at 1184–86.

void any provision of a franchise agreement that designates jurisdiction or venue in a forum outside of Illinois.[207]

In *Bo Foods, Inc. v. Bojangles' of America, Inc.*, the court also recognized the strong public policy reflected in the Act, which prevented enforcement of an out-of-state venue provision.[208]

In *Jacob v. C&M Video, Inc.*, the court reversed the trial court's denial of the franchisor's motion to dismiss the franchisees' tort, contract, and claims under the Act, concluding that the franchise agreement contained an enforceable agreement to arbitrate.[209] Specifically, the court observed that the franchise agreement designated arbitration as the sole venue for disputes arising out of the franchise agreement and determined that arbitration would provide the franchisees the protection afforded under the Act, as the arbitrator was capable of awarding the relief requested by the franchisees.[210]

In *DNB Fitness, LLC v. Anytime Fitness, LLC*, 14 franchisees brought breach of contract and Clayton Act claims against their Minnesota franchisor, alleging that the franchisor violated the fee provision in the franchise agreement and used its leverage as the franchisor to enhance sales in the fitness website market in violation of section 3 of the Clayton Act.[211] The franchisees filed the action in Illinois based on several franchisees' locations in Illinois.[212] However, the court granted the franchisor's motion to dismiss the Illinois franchisees' claims, holding that they effectively released their claims prior to the lawsuit.[213] The court, thereafter granted the franchisor's motion to transfer the venue to Minnesota, "as none of the remaining plaintiffs in this matter reside in Illinois, plaintiffs have not set forth any reason why the Illinois Franchise Disclosure Act should apply to their claims."[214]

In *Jackson Hewitt Inc. v. O & W Taxes, Inc.*, a franchisor filed claims for breach of contract and trade secret misappropriation against the franchisee and its guarantors in federal court in New Jersey, and the defendants moved to transfer to federal court in Illinois pursuant to 28 U.S.C. § 1404(a).[215] The parties' franchise agreements contained a provision in which the franchisee consented to venue and personal jurisdiction "in the appropriate federal or state court in Illinois to the extent required by the laws of Illinois" or "if permitted by the laws of Illinois," state or federal court in New Jersey.[216] The court concluded that this language amounted to a permissive, and not a mandatory venue provision, and thus declined to undertake the adjusted *forum non conveniens* analysis

---

207. *Id.*
208. *See* 1987 WL 5904, at *2 (N.D. Ill. Jan. 23, 1987) (denying improper venue motion and refusing to enforce Nevada forum selection clause given "Illinois policy of declaring forum clauses contained in franchise agreements void").
209. 618 N.E.2d 1267, 1275 (Ill. App. Ct. 1993).
210. *Id.* at 1272.
211. 2012 WL 1952662, at *1 (N.D. Ill. May 30, 2012).
212. *Id.* at *3–4.
213. *Id.*
214. *Id.* at *5.
215. 2022 WL 17466428, at *1 (D.N.J. Dec. 5, 2022).
216. *Id.* at *1–2.

prescribed by *Atlantic Marine Construction Company, Inc. v. United States District Court for the Western District of Texas*, proceeding instead under ordinary section 1404(a) principles.[217] In support of their motion, the defendants argued the Act mandated litigation of the claims in Illinois.[218] The court rejected this argument, explaining that "[b]y its plain language, the [Act] only voids certain contractual provisions which designate venue outside of Illinois, but it does not mandate venue in Illinois."[219] The court went on to hold that while the Act may void the franchise agreement's venue provision, the defendants failed to satisfy their burden for transfer, and thus denied the motion.[220]

In *Honest Abe Roofing Franchise, Inc. v. Lesjon Holdings, LLC*, a franchisor filed suit against the franchisee's guarantor in Indiana.[221] The parties' franchise agreement required venue to be in Illinois pursuant to the Act, whereas the contemporaneously executed guaranty called for venue to be in Indiana. The franchisor argued that the guaranty was a separate agreement whereas the franchisee argued that the two agreements were linked and that allowing an Indiana venue would eviscerate the protections of the Act. The court noted that the two venue provisions were conflicting and could not both be enforced, and it analyzed the franchise agreement and guaranty to determine which was primary and which was secondary. It found that the franchise agreement was the primary contract and therefore granted the guarantor's motion to transfer to Illinois.

In *Hofbrauhaus of America, LLC v. Oak Tree Management Services, Inc.*, a Nevada franchisor filed suit against its former Illinois franchisee in Nevada for continuing to operate its franchised business and for violating the franchisor's trademark rights after termination of the agreement.[222] The franchise agreement's venue provision called for a Nevada forum but also contained language acknowledging that it was subject to the Act. The franchisee filed a motion to transfer the dispute to the Southern District of Illinois, where the franchisee was located. The court granted the motion to transfer after applying the standard 28 U.S.C. § 1404 analysis, finding in relevant part that Illinois had a greater connection to the dispute because the franchisee was located in Illinois, and noting that Illinois had a strong interest in protecting its residents who become franchisees, in part because it voids provisions in franchise agreements that designate a forum outside of Illinois.

2. Limitations Period

a. Commentary

The statute of limitations for private causes of action under the Act is three years after the violation, one year after the franchisee becomes aware of the facts that

---

217. 571 U.S. 49, 62 (2013); *O & W Taxes, Inc.*, 2022 WL 17466428, at *3.
218. *O & W Taxes, Inc.*, 2022 WL 17466428, at *3 n.4.
219. *Id.*
220. *Id.* at *3–4.
221. 2023 WL 8452415, at *5 (S.D. Ind. Dec. 6, 2023).
222. 2023 WL 24179, at *9 (D. Nev. Jan. 3, 2023).

give rise to the claim, or 90 days after the franchisee receives notice disclosing the violation, whichever occurs first.[223]

b. Annotations

Courts have held that the three-year statute of limitations period set forth in section 27 of the Act is a statute of repose and does not incorporate the discovery rule as a basis for tolling the limitations period absent fraudulent concealment.[224]

In construing the one-year limitation period, courts have held that it runs from the time the franchisee acquires not only knowledge of the facts giving rise to the violation but also of the legal right to sue under the statute.[225]

The predominant view among courts interpreting the 90-day limitation period of section 27 is that the notice required to start the 90-day period must mention the Act, admit the franchisor's violation, and make an express reference to the 90-day time limitations imposed by the Act.[226]

In *Port City Leasing v. Loffredo*, the franchisor argued that its franchisee's disclosure claims under the Act were barred by the Act's statute of limitations and thus should be dismissed because the franchisee first raised the nondisclosure issue nearly three years after he became aware of the withheld information, nearly two years after the one-year limitations period expired.[227] The Illinois Appellate Court, however, held that the franchisee's claim was not barred by the statute of limitations, explaining that "knowledge of [Act] violations present[ ] mixed questions of law and fact on which laymen are entitled to acquire their first knowledge from an attorney."[228]

In *Sound of Music Co. v. Minnesota Mining & Manufacturing, Co.*, a dealer's claim against the defendant, a background music provider, was time-barred under the Act because it was filed more than 14 months after the defendant terminated the parties' agreement, pursuant to which the defendant provided background music to the dealer.[229] The Act requires a party to file a lawsuit within one year of becoming "aware of facts or circumstances reasonably indicating that [it] may have a claim for relief."[230] Although the dealer argued that its attorney did not become aware of the claims under the Act because the

---

223. 815 Ill. Comp. Stat. § 705/27.
224. *See* Putzier v. Ace Hardware Corp., 50 F. Supp. 3d 964, 977 (N.D. Ill. 2014); *see also* Window World of Chicagoland, LLC v. Window World, Inc., 2015 WL 2193752, at *7 (N.D. Ill. May 7, 2015); Manning & Silverman, Ltd. v. H&R Block Tax Servs. LLC, 2020 WL 6287407, at *2 (N.D. Ill., 2020).
225. Hengel Inc. v. Hot 'N Now, Inc., 825 F. Supp. 1311, 1319–20 (N.D. Ill. 1993).
226. RWJ Mgmt. Co. v. BP Prods. N. Am., 2011 WL 101727, at *2 (N.D. Ill. Jan. 12, 2011) (citing H.R.R. Zimmerman Co. v. Tecumseh Prods. Co., 2001 WL 289867, at *3 (N.D. Ill. Mar. 14, 2001) & R.N.F. Enters., Inc. v. Ecowater Systems, Inc., 2002 WL 1377860, at *2 (N.D. Ill. June 21, 2002)).
227. *See* 449 N.E.2d 907, 909–10 (Ill. App. Ct. 1983).
228. *Id.*; *see also* Proimos v. Fair Auto. Repair, Inc., 808 F.2d 1273 (7th Cir. 1987) (case remanded for a determination of when each of the four franchisees learned of the franchisor's omissions and misstatements).
229. 389 F. Supp. 2d 988, 1001 (N.D. Ill. 2005) (noting that the question of whether the parties had a franchise relationship and thus whether the dealer had actionable claims under the Act, were not necessary to reach given the expiration of the statute of limitations).
230. *Id.*

franchise fees were allegedly "hidden" and "disguised," the court found that it was not credible for the attorney to claim that he could not have discovered these fees at the time of termination.[231]

In *R.N.F. Enterprises v. Ecowater Systems, Inc.*, a franchisee filed a lawsuit for wrongful termination against its franchisor a full year after receiving a notice of termination from the franchisor.[232] The Act requires that private actions be filed within "90 days after delivery to the franchisee of a written notice disclosing the violation." The court ruled that the franchisee's claim was barred by the statute of limitations and there was no reason to toll the statute of limitations because the franchisee was fully aware of the facts and circumstances reasonably indicating a claim within 90 days of receiving a notice of termination even if the notice did not expressly state that a violation had occurred. In contrast, in *H.R.R. Zimmerman Co. v. Tecumseh Products Co.*, the court held that "the ninety-day statute of limitations requires an actual admission of liability by the franchisor under the IFDA before the statute of limitations will begin to run."[233]

Construing both *R.N.F Enterprises* and *H.R.R. Zimmerman*, the court in *RWJ Management Co. v. BP Products North America* held that, at least where a notice does not signal a "flat-out violation" of the Act such as occurred in *R.N.F Enterprises*, a notice must at least mention the legal requirements of the Act and reference the 90-day limitations period in order to trigger that limitations period under section 27 of the Act.[234]

---

231. *Id.* at 1002–03.
232. 2002 WL 1377860, at *2 (N.D. Ill. June 24, 2002).
233. 2001 WL 289867, at *3 (N.D. Ill. Mar. 15, 2001) (analogizing to the Seventh Circuit's treatment of the Act's one-year limitations period in Pyramid Controls Inc. v. Siemens Industrial Automation, Inc., 172 F.3d 516, 520 (7th Cir. 1999)).
234. 2011 WL 101727, at *6–7 (N.D. Ill. Jan. 12, 2011).

Indiana

Larry LaTarte

I. Introduction to the Statutes

The Indiana Franchise Act (IFA)[1] and the Indiana Deceptive Franchise Practices Act (IDFPA)[2] were enacted by the Indiana General Assembly in 1975 and 1976, respectively. Together, these two statutes, along with the modest body of case law that has developed over the past 50 years interpreting them, govern franchise relationships in Indiana. The IFA is the franchise disclosure statute under which the securities commissioner is empowered to ensure sufficient and reliable franchise disclosures and to investigate and prevent the commission of fraud. The IDFPA governs the relationship between franchisor and franchisee and sets forth unlawful provisions in franchise agreements and unlawful actions and practices by franchisors.

Although Indiana statutes lack legislative history to help interpret legislative intent,[3] IFA section 47, which sets out the purpose of that statute, provides that the powers it grants "shall be liberally construed to the end that the practice or commission of fraud may be prohibited and prevented," and that sufficient information should be disclosed by franchisors to "afford reasonable opportunity for the exercise of independent judgment of the persons involved[.]"[4] The IFA and IDFPA together reflect "crucial policy choices affirmatively made by the legislature in an effort to balance, in a way that makes sense in the commercial and social life of Indiana, the freedom to enter into contracts and the need to regulate the practices of the franchise industry."[5]

---

1. IND. CODE § 23-2-2.5.
2. *Id.* § 23-2-2.7.
3. Courts interpreting Indiana law do not have the benefit of legislative history. *See* Wright-Moore Corp. v. Ricoh Corp., 908 F.2d 128, 142 (7th Cir 1990) (Ripple, J., dissenting).
4. IND. CODE § 23-2-2.5-47.
5. *Wright-Moore Corp.*, 908 F.2d at 142 (Ripple, J., dissenting).

II. Commentary and Annotations

A. Definition of Franchise

The IFA defines a franchise as a "contract by which: (1) a franchisee is granted the right to engage in the business of dispensing goods or services, under a marketing plan or system prescribed in substantial part by a franchisor; (2) the operation of the franchisee's business pursuant to such a plan is substantially associated with the franchisor's trademark, service mark, trade name, logotype, advertising, or other commercial symbol designating the franchisor or its affiliate; and (3) the person granted the right to engage in this business is required to pay a franchise fee."[6] A franchise expressly "includes a contract whereby the franchisee is granted the right to sell franchises on behalf of the franchisor."[7] The IDFPA expressly incorporates this franchise definition.[8] As in many other jurisdictions, there are few Indiana cases addressing the first two elements.

The IFA specifically excludes certain preexisting businesses from the definition of a franchise. A "franchise" does not include "a contract where the franchisee, or any of its officers or directors at the time the contract is signed, has been in the type of business represented by the franchise or a similar business for at least two (2) years, and the parties to the contract anticipated, or should have anticipated, at the time the contract was entered into that the franchisee's gross sales derived from the franchised business during the first year of operations would not exceed twenty percent (20%) of the gross sales of all the franchisee's business operations."[9]

The IDFPA defines a franchise by reference to the IFA definition, with one exception. An agreement "which relates to the business of selling automobiles and/or trucks and the business of selling gasoline and/or oil primarily for use in vehicles with or without the sale of accessory items" is a franchise even if the putative franchisee is not required to pay a franchise fee.[10]

1. Trademark Element

a. Commentary

As already noted, under Indiana law, a franchise is a contract by which the franchisee's business is "substantially associated with the franchisor's trademark, service mark, trade name, logotype, advertising, or other commercial symbol designating the franchisor or its affiliate."[11] Put simply, where a franchisor licenses the use of its trademark to a franchisee and the franchisee's business is "substantially associated" with the trademark, the trademark element is almost certainly satisfied. Distribution of products or services covered by the franchisor's trademarks is sufficient to satisfy the substantial association requirement.

---

6. IND. CODE § 23-2-2.5-1(a).
7. Id.
8. IND. CODE § 23-2-2.7-5.
9. Id.
10. Id. § 23-2-2.7-5.
11. Id. § 23-2-2.5-1(a).

b. Annotations

In *Master Abrasives Corp. v. Williams*, the court found that a manufacturer's admission that products were private labeled under its trademark and sold by franchisee was sufficient to support finding that franchisee was substantially associated with franchisor's trademarks.[12]

Where a copier distribution agreement permitted a distributor to state in writing that it was an authorized distributor of certain of manufacturer's products and was provided with advertising materials bearing manufacturer's trademark, even where distribution agreement otherwise prohibited distributor from using manufacturer's name or trademark, the court in *Wright-Moore Corp. v. Ricoh Corp.* found that the "substantial association" requirement was clearly met.[13]

Where there was no dispute that a basketball team purchased the right to use a basketball league's logo at its own discretion, where the entertainment produced by games between the team and other teams "plainly constituted the distribution of services" covered by the league's trade name, and where the league owned and controlled all national advertising, the court in *Continental Basketball Association, Inc. v. Ellenstein Enterprises, Inc.* found that the franchisee basketball team was substantially associated with the league's service mark, trade name, and advertising.[14]

2. Marketing Plan or System Element

a. Commentary

The touchstone of the marketing plan or system element is that the plan or system must be "prescribed in substantial part" by a franchisor.[15] Courts considering whether there is a marketing plan or system prescribed in substantial part by a franchisor look to the "nature of the obligations that the agreement imposes upon the putative franchisee, particularly with respect to franchisor mandates regarding sales of goods or services."[16] This is inherently a fact-intensive inquiry, so while courts have identified a variety of factors that they consider to be important, no specific test has been identified.

b. Annotations

In *Master Abrasives Corp. v. Williams*, the Indiana Court of Appeals concluded that a marketing plan existed because the contract between the putative franchisor and franchisee divided the state into marketing areas, authorized the establishment of sales quotas, gave the franchisor the right to approve the hiring of sales personnel, and required sales training for sales personnel.[17] Further, testimony at trial established that the franchisor did, in fact, provide field training in sales

---

12. Master Abrasives Corp. v. Williams, 469 N.E.2d 1196, 1999 (Ind. Ct. App. 1984).
13. Wright-Moore Corp. v. Ricoh Corp., 794 F. Supp. 844, 847 (N.D. Ind. 1991).
14. Continental Basketball Ass'n, Inc. v. Ellenstein Enter., Inc., 640 N.E.2d 705, 708–09 (Ind. Ct. App. 1994).
15. IND. CODE § 23-2-2.5-1(a).
16. Horner v. Tilton, 650 N.E.2d 759, 762 (Ind. Ct. App. 1995).
17. 469 N.E.2d 1196, 1200 (Ind. Ct. App. 1984).

techniques and that franchisee employees were provided with sales materials and instructed about the types of customers to solicit and how to solicit them.[18]

The court in *Hoosier Penn Oil Co. v. Ashland Oil Co.* held that the marketing plan element was not satisfied where the parties' agreement was a nonexclusive distributorship, where, among other things, the putative franchisor had no control over the distributor's hiring of sales employees, where sales training was optional, and where—despite the existence of minimum purchase requirements—there was no sales quota.[19] The court found all of these factors distinguished this case from *Master Abrasives Corp.*[20]

Examining the court's reasoning in *Master Abrasives Corp.*, the Indiana Court of Appeals found in *Horner v. Tilton* that it is apparent that courts should examine "the nature of the obligations that the [franchise] agreement imposes upon the putative franchisee, particularly with respect to franchisor mandates regarding sales of goods or services."[21] In doing so, the court found that where the putative franchisee was not subject to sales quotas, not included in a marketing scheme, and where a specified geographical location was only used to define the limits of the trademark license, "the agreement did not subject the [putative franchisee] to the degree of control and oversite . . . which is necessary to constitute a marketing plan."[22]

The court in *Richard I. Spiece Sales Co. v. Levi Strauss North America* rejected distributor's argument that it was a franchisee where it had invested heavily in marketing manufacturer's products because those investments were not required by the manufacturer and because the manufacturer did not set pricing, did not have purchase requirements, and where any marketing plan between the parties was oral and mutually agreed.[23]

Granting a motion to dismiss in favor of manufacturer, the court in *Ervin Equipment Inc. v. Wabash National Corp.* found that the putative franchisee dealer failed to state a claim because the underlying agreement did not reference a marketing plan or system prescribed by the putative franchisor but instead specifically provided that the dealer "controls its business and decision making" including "its pricing and marketing."[24]

3. Franchise Fee Element

a. Commentary

The IFA defines a franchise fee as "any fee that a franchisee is required to pay directory or indirectly for the right to conduct a business to sell, resell, or distribute goods, services, or franchises under a contract agreement, including, but not limited to, any such payment for goods or services."[25] Specifically exempted

---

18. *Id.*
19. 934 F.2d 882, 885 (7th Cir. 1991).
20. *Id.*
21. *Horner*, 650 N.E.2d at 762.
22. *Id.*
23. 19 N.E.3d 345, 357 (Ind. Ct. App. 2014).
24. 187 F. Supp. 3d 968, 977 (N.D. Ind. 2016).
25. Ind. Code § 23-2-2.5-1(i).

from this definition are "(1) the payment of a reasonable service charge to the issuer of a credit card by an establishment accepting or honoring the credit card; (2) the amounts paid to a trading stamp company by a person issuing trading stamps in connection with the retail sale of goods or services; or (3) the purchase or agreement to purchase goods at a bona fide wholesale price."[26] Thus, several elements comprise the payment of a franchise fee. At its core, it is a fee paid for the right to participate in the franchise business. The fee may be direct or indirect; it may be part of a payment for goods or services; it may be a fee for the right to sell not just goods or services but also franchises. On the other hand, payments for goods at a bona fide wholesale price and payments for ordinary business expenses are not franchise fees. Whether a fee is or is not a franchise fee depends on the facts of the particular case.[27]

b. Annotations

The court in *Wright-Moore Corp. v. Ricoh Corp.* rejected two arguments made by a copier distributor that expenses it incurred were actually indirect franchise fees.[28] First, the required purchase of excess inventory was not a franchise fee because the distributor received a large discount on the inventory and sold almost all of the inventory for a profit before payment was due.[29] In other words, the goods purchased by the distributor were purchased at or below the bona fide wholesale price. Second, expenses incurred training dealers were not indirect franchise fees because these were ordinary business expenses that the distributor recovered because its dealers received expert training that allowed the dealers to service products sold.[30]

The court in *Communications Maintenance, Inc. v. Motorola, Inc.* held that an agreement to enter into subcontracts for the installation and maintenance of goods sold, as well as performing the work to the manufacturer's specifications, is not a franchisee fee.[31] This is because "the passing of consideration in the form of a promise to perform a future act" does not lie within "the parameters of any reasonable definition" of a franchise fee under the IFA.[32] Likewise, the court rejected the distributor's argument that its performance of maintenance work at a price lower than the manufacturer charged was a discount that amounted to an indirect franchise fee.[33] This is because the contract between the parties made it clear that the distributor's service fee was not discounted from its normal rates.[34]

The court in *Implement Service, Inc. v. Tecumseh Products Co.* rejected an argument that services provided to customers at a discount were indirect franchise

---

26. Id.
27. *See* Wright-Moore Corp. v. Ricoh Corp., 908 F.2d 128, 136 (7th Cir. 1990).
28. 980 F.2d 432, 436 (7th Cir. 1992).
29. Id.
30. Id.
31. 761 F.2d 1202, 1206 (7th Cir. 1985).
32. Id.
33. Id.
34. Id.

fees because the discount was provided to the customer and not the putative franchisor and therefore could not be construed as an indirect franchise fee.[35] For the same reason, free warranty work and free training provided to customers cannot be an indirect franchise fee.[36]

Nor is it an indirect franchise fee when a distributor is required to purchase demonstration equipment and contractually prohibited from reselling that equipment for two years. The court in *Neff Group Distributors, Inc. v. Cognex Corp.* held that while the distributor would need permission to sell the equipment, the distributor retained the right to sell the equipment, and the manufacturer could not prevent the equipment from ever being liquid.[37]

Adopting the Seventh Circuit's reasoning from *Wright-Moore Corp. v. Ricoh Corp.*, the Indiana Court of Appeals determined that a distributor must show that alleged indirect franchisee fees were "an unrecoverable firm specific investment" in the manufacturer that is required for the right to conduct business with the manufacturer.[38] Ordinary business expenses, the court also held, cannot be deemed franchise fees.[39] Applying this standard, the court found that the distributor failed to establish that it was "required" by the manufacturer to purchase certain items for displaying product because doing so was customary in the industry.[40]

B. Scope and Jurisdiction

1. Commentary

The IFA "applies to an offer or franchise if: (a) the offeree or franchisee is an Indiana resident; or (b) the franchised business contemplated by the offer or franchise will be or is operated in Indiana."[41] Likewise, the IDFPA declares it unlawful for any franchisor to engage in certain enumerated conduct "with a franchisee who is either a resident of Indiana or a nonresident operating a franchise in Indiana[.]"[42] The statute exempts offers from having been made in Indiana if the offer was either made via radio or television programming originating outside of Indiana, or if found in a "bona fide newspaper or other publication of general, regular and paid circulation" to which two-thirds of its subscribers were outside Indiana during the preceding year.[43] However, parties to a franchise agreement may elect another state's law to govern their agreement, and that choice of law will control so long as it does not conflict with the IFA.[44]

---

35. 726 F. Supp. 1171, 1178–79 (S.D. Ind. 1989).
36. *Id.*
37. 642 F. Supp. 3d 173, 179 (D. Mass. 2022) (applying Indiana law).
38. 714 N.E.2d 1196, 1201 (Ind. Ct. App. 1999).
39. *Id.*
40. *Id.* at 1202.
41. IND. CODE § 23-2-2.5-2.
42. *Id.* § 23.2.2.7-2.
43. *Id.* § 23-2-2.5-2.
44. Gre-Ter Enter., Inc. v. Mgmt. Recruiters Int'l, Inc., 329 F. Supp. 3d 667, 675–76 (S.D. Ind. 2018).

2. Annotations

Notwithstanding the applicability of the IFA and IDFA, the court in *Gre-Ter Enterprises, Inc. v. Management Recruiters International, Inc.* held that where parties to a franchise agreement chose another state's law—in this case, Ohio law—and there is no conflict between that law and Indiana franchise law, "to that extent the parties' choice of law controls."[45]

In a dispute between Indiana franchisee and out-of-state franchisor, the court in *Baskin Robbins Franchising LLC v. Blu Moo Ice Cream Inc.* applied Massachusetts law because franchise agreements contained a choice of law provision dictating that disputes be governed by Massachusetts law.[46]

C. Termination

1. What Constitutes Termination or Cancellation?

Neither the IDFPA nor cases discussing it define termination or cancellation of the franchise relationship.

2. Restrictions on Termination or Cancellation

a. Commentary

The IDFPA requires that that franchisor have good cause (and that it not act in bad faith) for a unilateral termination of a franchise.[47] Good cause is statutorily defined to include "any material violation of the franchise agreement."[48] A franchisee has a cause of action against a franchisor where the franchise agreement is terminated without good cause.[49]

b. Annotations

In *Continental Basketball Association, Inc. v. Ellenstein Enterprises, Inc.*, the Indiana Supreme Court declined to consider whether a franchise agreement was terminated without good cause because although "a determination of good cause could, in appropriate circumstances be made as a matter of law, we note that more often it seems to be a question of fact."[50] Thus, because the parties had not briefed the good cause issue and because "it could turn on a factual determination," the court remanded the issue to the trial court.[51]

In *Hacienda Mexican Restaurant of Kalamazoo Corp. v. Hacienda Franchise Group, Inc.*, the Indiana Court of Appeals rejected the franchisee's argument that the franchisor violated the IDFPA when it terminated the franchise after the franchisee missed three royalty payments in an 18-month period of time.[52] The franchise

---

45. 329 F. Supp. 667, 675 (S.D. Ind. 2018).
46. No. 1:24-cv-00293-JRS-CSW, 2024 WL 2730252, at *4 (S.D. Ind. May 7, 2024).
47. Ind. Code § 23-2-2.7-1(7).
48. *Id.* § 23-2-2.7-1(7).
49. *Id.* § 23.2.2.7-4; Continental Basketball Ass'n, Inc. v. Ellenstein Enter., Inc., 669 N.E.2d 134, 139 (Ind. 1996).
50. *Continental Basketball Ass'n, Inc.*, 669 N.E.2d at 139.
51. *Id.*
52. 569 N.E.2d 661, 667 (Ind. Ct. App. 1991).

agreement expressly allowed such a termination, did not require notice or an opportunity to cure, and the missed payments were clear defaults of the agreement such that franchisor had good cause to terminate.[53]

3. Notice of Termination or Cancellation

a. Commentary

The IDFPA requires at least 90 days' notice for termination of a franchise, unless otherwise provided for in the franchise agreement.[54] Thus, if the franchise agreement includes a termination provision that differs from the statutory requirement, courts are likely to enforce that contractual provision.

b. Annotations

Franchisor was not required to give 90 days' notice where franchise agreement expressly provided for immediate termination upon franchisee's receipt of written notice of termination.[55]

4. Grounds for Termination

a. Commentary

As noted earlier, the IDFPA requires that that franchisor have good cause (and that it not act in bad faith) for termination or nonrenewal of a franchise.[56] Good cause is statutorily defined to include "any material violation of the franchise agreement."[57]

b. Annotations

In *Continental Basketball Association, Inc. v. Ellenstein Enterprises, Inc.*, the Indiana Supreme Court declined to consider whether a franchise agreement was terminated without good cause because although "a determination of good cause could, in appropriate circumstances be made as a matter of law, we note that more often it seems to be a question of fact."[58] Thus, because the parties had not briefed the good cause issue and because "it could turn on a factual determination," the court remanded the issue to the trial court.[59]

In *Hacienda Mexican Restaurant of Kalamazoo Corp. v. Hacienda Franchise Group, Inc.*, the Indiana Court of Appeals rejected the franchisee's argument that the franchisor violated the IDFPA when it terminated the franchise after the franchisee missed three royalty payments in an 18-month period of time.[60] The franchise agreement expressly allowed such a termination, did not require

---

53. *Id.*
54. IND. CODE § 23-2-2.7-3.
55. Snihurowycz v. AAMCO Transmissions, Inc., 418 N.E.2d 1190, 1192 (Ind. Ct. App. 1981).
56. IND. CODE § 23-2-2.7-1(7), (8).
57. *Id.* § 23-2-2.7-1(7).
58. 669 N.E.2d 134, 139 (Ind. 1996).
59. *Id.*
60. 569 N.E.2d 661, 667 (Ind. Ct. App. 1991).

notice or an opportunity to cure, and the missed payments were clear defaults of the agreement such that franchisor had good cause to terminate.[61]

5. Required Cure Period

Indiana law does not require a franchisor to provide an opportunity to cure to avoid termination.

6. Repurchase Obligations

Indiana law does not impose repurchase obligations when a franchise agreement is terminated.

D. Restrictions on Nonrenewal

1. What Constitutes Nonrenewal?

Neither the IDFPA nor cases discussing it define nonrenewal of the franchise relationship.

2. Restrictions on Nonrenewal

a. Commentary

The IDFPA requires that that franchisor have good cause (and that it not act in bad faith) for nonrenewal of a franchise.[62] Good cause is statutorily defined to include "any material violation of the franchise agreement."[63] Notwithstanding these restrictions, the franchise agreement may provide for expiration of the agreement upon its term, and it may also impose contractual conditions on renewal.[64] A franchisee has a cause of action against a franchisor where the franchise agreement is terminated without good cause or not renewed without good cause.[65]

b. Annotations

The Seventh Circuit held that the internal economic reasons of the franchisor—in this case a change in marketing strategy relating to product distribution—was not a good cause reason for nonrenewal under the IDFPA because "the purpose of the franchise statute is to protect the franchisee" and the franchisor's suggested reading "is contrary to this purpose and would effectively nullify the statute."[66]

Franchisor was not required to show good cause where franchise agreement expired consistent with its nonrenewable one-year term, which agreement required a new agreement in order to continue the relationship.[67]

---

61. *Id.*
62. IND. CODE § 23-2-2.7-1(8).
63. *Id.* § 23-2-2.7-1(7).
64. *Id.* § 23-2-2.7-1(8).
65. *Id.* § 23.2.2.7-4; Continental Basketball Ass'n, Inc. v. Ellenstein Enter., Inc., 669 N.E.2d 134, 139 (Ind. 1996).
66. Wright-Moore Corp. v. Ricoh Corp., 908 F.2d 128, 139 (7th Cir 1990).
67. Wright-Moore Corp. v. Ricoh Corp., 980 F.2d 432, 437 (7th Cir. 1992).

3. Notice of Nonrenewal

a. Commentary

The IDFPA requires at least 90 days' notice for election not to renew a franchise, unless otherwise provided for in the franchise agreement.[68] Thus, if the franchise agreement includes a nonrenewal provision that differs from the statutory requirement, courts are likely to enforce that contractual provision.

b. Annotations

There are no Indiana cases discussing the 90-day notice requirement for nonrenewal of a franchise agreement.

4. Grounds for Nonrenewal

a. Commentary

As noted earlier, the IDFPA requires that that franchisor have good cause (and that it not act in bad faith) for nonrenewal of a franchise.[69] Good cause is statutorily defined to include "any material violation of the franchise agreement."[70] Notwithstanding these restrictions, the franchise agreement may provide for expiration of the agreement upon its term, and it may also impose contractual conditions on renewal.[71] A franchisee has a cause of action against a franchisor where the franchise agreement is terminated without good cause or not renewed without good cause.[72]

b. Annotations

The Seventh Circuit held that the internal economic reasons of the franchisor—in this case a change in marketing strategy relating to product distribution—was not a good cause reason for nonrenewal under the IDFPA because "the purpose of the franchise statute is to protect the franchisee" and the franchisor's suggested reading "is contrary to this purpose and would effectively nullify the statute."[73] Franchisor was not required to show good cause where the franchise agreement expired consistent with its nonrenewable one-year term, which agreement required a new agreement in order to continue the relationship.[74] Thus, the IDFPA's prohibition on nonrenewal for good cause does not create a right to renew where none otherwise exists.

5. Required Cure Period

Indiana law does not require a franchisor to provide an opportunity to cure.

---

68. IND. CODE § 23-2-2.7-3.
69. Id. § 23-2-2.7-1(8).
70. Id. § 23-2-2.7-1(7).
71. Id. § 23-2-2.7-1(8).
72. IND. CODE § 23-2-2.7-4; Continental Basketball Ass'n, Inc. v. Ellenstein Enter., Inc., 669 N.E.2d 134, 139 (Ind. 1996).
73. Wright-Moore Corp. v. Ricoh Corp., 908 F.2d 128, 139 (7th Cir 1990).
74. Wright-Moore Corp. v. Ricoh Corp., 980 F.2d 432, 437 (7th Cir. 1992).

6. Limitations on Franchisors' Right to Impose Conditions for Renewal

a. Commentary

A franchisor may impose contractual conditions on the franchisee for purposes of renewal. The only condition the IDFPA places on such renewal conditions is that failure to renew may not be without good cause or in bad faith.[75] A franchisor is not prohibited from providing that the agreement "is renewable if the franchisee meets certain conditions specified in the agreement."[76]

b. Annotations

Franchisor's change in marketing strategy relating to product distribution was not a good cause reason for nonrenewal under the IDFPA because "the purpose of the franchise statute is to protect the franchisee" and the franchisor's suggested reading "is contrary to this purpose and would effectively nullify the statute."[77]

7. Repurchase Obligations

Indiana law does not impose a repurchase obligation on a nonrenewing franchisor.

E. Transfers and Succession

1. Commentary

Indiana law does not impose restrictions on a franchisor's ability to reasonably restrict franchise transfers. However, the IDFPA prohibits a franchisor from "denying the surviving spouse, heirs, or estate of a deceased franchisee the opportunity to participate in the ownership of the franchise under a valid franchise agreement for a reasonable time after the death of a franchisee," so long as the successor heir(s) maintain "all standards and obligations of the of the franchise."[78]

2. Annotations

There are no Indiana cases discussing Indiana Code section 23-2-2.7-2(3) or successor rights.

F. Other Regulation of the Franchise Relationship

1. Discrimination

a. Commentary

The IDFA prohibits unfair discrimination by the franchisor among franchisees in relation to the franchise agreement.[79] Indiana courts, however, have not defined "unfair discrimination" or otherwise discussed what it means.[80]

---

75. IND. CODE § 23-2-2.7-1(8).
76. Id.
77. Wright-Moore Corp., 908 F.2d at 139.
78. IND. CODE § 23-2-2.7-2(3).
79. Id. § 23.2-2.7-2(5).
80. Andy Mohr Truck Ctr., Inc. v. Volvo Trucks N. Am., 869 F.3d 598, 603 (7th Cir. 2017) ("There is a dearth of precedent that might shed light on the meaning of discrimination for purposes of the

b. Annotations

Interpreting Indiana law, the Seventh Circuit Court of Appeals predicted that an Indiana court would find that "discrimination among franchisees means that as between two or more similarly situated franchisees, and under similar financial and marketing conditions, a franchisor engaged in less favorable treatment toward the discriminatee than toward other franchisees."[81] Thus, in order to prove discrimination, a franchisee was required to make a showing of "arbitrary disparate treatment among similarly situated individuals or entities."[82] Applying that standard, the court rejected a franchisee's contention that price concessions were unfair simply because a sampling of price concessions suggested that some were worse than that provided to other franchisees.[83]

The court in *Truck Country of Indiana, Inc. v. Daimler Vans USA, LLC* rejected franchisees claim of discriminatory treatment because it found that differences between comparators were "so significant as to make any comparison effectively useless."[84]

Where franchisor was "the only true national distributor," other "so-called national distributors" that operated in smaller regions of the country were not similarly situated such that there could be no comparator for unfair discrimination purposes.[85]

2. Exclusive Territory and Encroachment

a. Commentary

Subject to certain specific statutory exceptions, franchisors are prohibited from establishing "a franchisor-owned outlet engaged in a substantially identical business to that of the franchisee within the exclusive territory granted the franchisee by the franchise agreement, or if no exclusive territory is designated, competing unfairly with the franchisee within a reasonable area."[86] The statute does not address, and therefore does not expressly prohibit, encroachment by other franchisees on a franchisees' exclusive territory.

b. Annotations

There are no Indiana cases addressing statutory prohibition on franchisors competing with franchisees.

3. Restrictions on Supply

a. Commentary

The IDFPA makes it unlawful for a franchisor to require a franchisee to purchase goods, supplies, inventories, or services "exclusively from the franchisor

---

IDFPA. As best we can tell, Indiana's courts have not clarified what is meant by 'unfair discrimination' in the statute, nor what would be sufficient to make a showing.").

81. *Id.* at 604 (citing Canada Dry Corp v. Nehi Beverage Co., Inc. of Indianapolis, 723 F.2d 512, 521 (7th Cir. 1983).
82. *Id.*
83. *Id.* at 605–07.
84. No. 3:21-cv-00156-RLY-MPB, 2022 WL 16958638, at *6 (S.D. Ind. Aug. 17, 2022).
85. Wright-Moore Corp. v. Ricoh Corp., 908 F.2d 128, 139 (7th Cir. 1990).
86. IND. CODE § 23-2-2.7-2(2).

or sources designated by the franchisor" when goods of comparable quality are available from other sources.[87] This prohibition does not restrict the franchisor from providing a list of approved suppliers or from setting specifications and standards for supplies.[88] Nor does this restriction apply to "the principal goods, supplies, inventories, or services manufactured or trademarked by the franchisor."[89]

b. Annotations

There are no Indiana cases addressing statutory prohibition on franchisors placing restrictions on franchisee supplies.

4. Restrictions on Releases or Waivers

a. Commentary

The IDFPA contains a broad nonwaiver provision prohibiting a franchisor from "limiting litigation brought for breach of the agreement in any manner whatsoever."[90] Likewise, a franchisor may not "requir[e] the franchisee to prospectively assent to a release, . . . waiver, or estoppel which purports to relieve any person from liability to be imposed by this chapter."[91] This nonwaiver principle does not, however, prevent the parties from waiving the right to a jury trial via an arbitration agreement.[92]

b. Annotations

The court in *Wright-Moore Corp. v. Ricoh Corp.* discussed Indiana's strong public policy against contractual waiver of actions under its franchise laws in the context of rejecting a choice of law provision that would have negated application of the IDFPA.[93] "The public policy, articulated in the nonwaiver provisions of the statute is clear: a franchisor, through its superior bargaining power, should not be permitted to force the franchisee to waive the legislatively provided protections, whether directly through waiver provisions or indirectly through choice of law."[94] The court found that Indiana had a materially greater interest in the litigation than the contractually chosen state because the franchisee was an Indiana corporation located in Indiana with its witnesses and documents in Indiana; further, the contract negotiation occurred in Indiana and was largely performed in Indiana.[95] As such, applying the contractually chosen law would violate public policy.

Although the IDFPA allows parties to waive the right to a jury trial in favor of arbitration, a jury trial waiver on its own is a waiver of a substantive legal

---

87. *Id.* § 23-2-2.7-1(1).
88. *Id.*
89. *Id.*
90. *Id.* § 23-2-2.7-1(10).
91. *Id.* § 23-2-2.7-1(5).
92. *Id.*
93. 908 F.2d 128, 132–34 (7th Cir. 1990).
94. *Id.* at 132.
95. *Id.* at 133.

right that is governed by "the clear statutory limitations in the IDFPA which prohibits a franchise agreement from 'limiting litigation brought for breach of the agreement in any manner whatsoever.'"[96]

5. Other Standards of Conduct

In addition to the unlawful acts and practices in Indiana Code section 23-2-2.7-2 described earlier, that section makes it unlawful for franchisors to engage in a number of other types of conduct. For example, a franchisor may not engage in coercing franchisees to order or receive unnecessary goods, participate in advertising or marketing above the level required in the franchise agreement, or enter into any agreement with the franchisor under threat of termination or nonrenewal.[97] Likewise, a franchisor may not obtain improper benefits from any other person with whom the franchisee does business due to the franchisee's business with the other person other than for fair compensation provided to the franchisor; increase the price of goods without prior written notice of the price increase; or engage in deceptive advertising.[98]

G. Remedies and Administrative Action

1. Restrictive Covenants

a. Commentary

The IDFPA makes unlawful restrictive covenants requiring a franchisee "not to compete with the franchisor for a period longer than three (3) years or in an area greater than the exclusive area granted by the franchise agreement or, in the absence of such a provision in the agreement, an area of reasonable size, upon termination of or failure to renew the franchise."[99]

b. Annotations

Applying Indiana common law pertaining to the reasonableness of a restrictive covenant, the court in *South Bend Consumers Club, Inc. v. United Consumers Club, Inc.* held that a restrictive covenant was facially unreasonable because it was not limited to the area of the former franchisee's operations, but rather sought to bar competition in any area in the 15 states in which the franchisor operated.[100] While the court discussed the possibility of "blue penciling" the restrictive covenant, the court declined to do so because to do so would require it to rewrite the entire covenant, which is impermissible under Indiana law.[101]

---

96. Carrel v. George Weston Bakeries Distrib. Inc., No. 1:05-CV-1769-SEB-JPG, 2006 WL 2524124, at *2 (S.D. Ind. Aug. 29, 2006).
97. IND. CODE § 23-2-2.7-2(1).
98. *Id.* § 23-2-2.7-2(6)–(8).
99. *Id.* § 23-2-2.7-1(9).
100. 572 F. Supp. 209, 213 (N.D. Ind. 1983).
101. *Id.* at 215.

2. Damages

The IDFPA provides franchisees with a private right of action. Franchisees who are parties to franchise agreements entered into or renewed after July 1, 1976, and who are injured by an unfair practice set forth in the IDFPA or are party to a franchise agreement containing an unlawful provision may bring an action for damages.[102]

3. Rescission

The IDFPA does not address rescission.

4. Injunctive Relief

The IDFPA does not address injunctive relief.

5. Control Person Liability

The IDFPA does not address control person liability.

6. Attorneys' Fees

The IDFPA does not provide for attorneys' fees.

7. Limitation on Damages

The IDFPA does not provide for a statutory limitation on damages.

8. Administrative Action

The IDFPA does not provide for administrative action.

H. Dispute Resolutions

1. Limitation on Franchisors' Ability to Restrict Venue

a. Commentary

As already noted, the IDFPA prevents a franchisor from "[l]imiting litigation brought for breach of the agreement in any manner whatsoever."[103] Thus, the plain text of the statute appears to prevent a franchisor from requiring a franchisee to agree to restrict venue.

b. Annotations

No Indiana case specifically addresses a franchisor's ability to restrict venue in the franchise agreement.

---

102. IND. CODE § 23-2-2.7-4.
103. *Id.* § 23-3-2.7-1(10).

2. Limitations Period

a. Commentary

The IDFPA imposes a two-year statute of limitations.[104] The two-year period begins to run at contract formation for claims seeking relief for unlawful provisions in the franchise agreement under Indiana Code section 23-2-2.7-1.

b. Annotations

The two-year statute of limitations provision in the IDFPA barred franchisee from asserting a contractual violation by the franchisor as a defense to an action more than two years after signing the franchise agreement because the franchisee's use of the defense was barred by the statute of limitations.[105]

The court in *Craig & Landreth, Inc. v. Mazda Motor of America, Inc.* found that the doctrine of continuing wrong did not toll the two-year statute of limitations period where the plaintiff franchisee complained to the franchisor about alleged discriminatory practices more than two years before suit was filed.[106] That franchisor denied wrongdoing during the entire time period was insufficient because plaintiff was aware of the facts that gave rise to the discovery of the cause of action for more than two years.[107]

---

104. *Id.* § 23-2-2.7-7.
105. Volvo Trucks N. Am. v. Andy Mohr Truck Ctr., No. 1:12-cv-448-WTL-DKL, 2014 WL 4794185, at *8 (S.D. Ind. Sept. 25, 2014).
106. 744 F. Supp. 2d 818, 830–31 (S.D. Ind. 2010).
107. *Id.*

Iowa

Rush Nigut

I. Introduction to Statute

While the Iowa legislature has not codified a franchise registration or disclosure law of general applicability, it does have two versions of a franchise relationship law.[1] In 1992, the legislature enacted the Iowa Franchise Act, Iowa Code sections 523H.1 *et seq.* (1992 Act) "to provide greater protection for franchisees by leveling bargaining power between franchisees and franchisors; promoting good faith business practices and fair dealing in franchise relationships; and protecting franchisees from fraud and overreaching on the part of franchisors."[2] The 1992 Act was amended in 2000 to clarify that it governs "all actions with respect to a franchise agreement entered into prior to July 1, 2000, no matter when the occurrence giving rise to such actions occurs."[3] The 1992 Act states that "[p]rior law governs all actions based on facts occurring before July 1, 1992."[4] However, in 1993, in *McDonald's Corp. v. Nelson*[5] as well as in 1994 in *Holiday Inns Franchising, Inc. v. Brandstad*,[6] the federal courts found the 1992 Act's retroactive application unconstitutional and the 1992 Act was deemed to only apply to franchise agreements entered into between July 1, 1992, and June 30, 1999.

Following the Eighth Circuit's decision in *Holiday Inns Franchising, Inc. v. Branstad*, 29 F.3d 383 (8th Cir. 1994), the Iowa legislature created and codified a new general franchise relationship law, found in Iowa Code section 537A.10 (2000 Act) to ensure the applicability of its franchise law going forward. The 2000 Act was expressly made applicable to new or existing franchises operated in Iowa and subject to agreements entered on or after July 1, 2000.

While the 2000 Act does not repeal the 1992 Act, it does limit the application of the 1992 Act to franchise agreements entered into before July 1, 2000.

---

1. Iowa also has codified the Motor Vehicle Franchisers Act at IOWA CODE §§ 322A.1, *et seq.*
2. Holiday Inns Franchising, Inc. v. Branstad, 537 N.W.2d 724, 728–29 (Iowa 1995).
3. IOWA CODE § 523H.2A(2).
4. *Id.* § 523H.15.
5. McDonald's Corp. v. Nelson, 822 F. Supp. 597, 606 (S.D. Iowa 1993) (specifically finding sections 523H.5–523H.8 unconstitutional as applied retroactively), *aff'd*, Holiday Inns Franchising, Inc. v. Branstad, 29 F.3d 383, 385 (8th Cir. 1994), *cert. denied*, Iowa v. Holiday Inns Franchising, Inc., 513 U.S. 1032 (1994).
6. Holiday Inns Franchising, Inc. v. Branstad, 29 F.3d 383 (8th Cir. 1994).

Accordingly, the 1992 Act applies to franchise agreements from July 1, 1992, until June 30, 2000, and the 2000 Act applies to all franchise agreements from July 1, 2000, to the present. Both relationship laws are, by their own terms, to be liberally construed to effectuate their purposes. Both the 1992 Act and the 2000 Act (collectively, the Iowa Acts) provide that they do not limit liability that may exist under other statutes or common law.[7]

The purposes of both the 1992 Act and 2000 Act are to protect franchisees operating in Iowa from abuses by franchisors, level the bargaining power between franchisors and franchisees, promote good faith and fair dealing in business practices, and to protect franchisees from fraudulent actions and overreaching by franchisors.[8] However, both statutes only apply to franchises where the premises from which the franchise is operated is physically located within Iowa.[9]

The two acts, while substantially the same, do have some differences. Both statutes provide similar provisions for termination, nonrenewal, transfer, and encroachment. However, the 2000 Act includes a provision that limits a franchisor's rights to require franchisees to purchase goods or services from the franchisor if alternatives are available in the marketplace.[10]

II. Commentary

A. Definition of Franchise

The Iowa relationship laws define "franchise" as an oral or written agreement, either express or implied, which provides all of the following: (1) grants an individual or an entity the right to distribute goods or provide services under a marketing plan prescribed or suggested in substantial part by the franchisor; (2) requires payment of a franchise fee to a franchisor or its affiliate; and (3) allows the franchise business to be substantially associated with a trademark, service mark, trade name, logotype, advertisement, or other commercial symbol of or designating the franchisor or its affiliate.[11] Also covered by both statutes is a "master franchise," which is defined as "an agreement by which a person pays a franchisor for the right to sell or negotiate the sale of franchises."[12]

Pursuant to the Iowa Acts, a business operated under lease or license on the premises of a lessor or licensor (commonly referred to as a "leased department") is not considered a franchise as long as the business is incidental to the business conducted by the licensor or lessor on the premises.[13] This includes "leased departments, licensed departments, and concessions" when "the leased

---

7. IOWA CODE §§ 523H.15, 537A.10(15).
8. Holiday Inns Franchising, Inc. v. Branstad, 537 N.W.2d 724, 728–29 (Iowa 1995); Equip. Mfrs. Inst. v. Janklow, 300 F.3d 842, 861 (8th Cir. 2002).
9. IOWA CODE §§ 523H.2, 537A.10(2).
10. *Id.* § 537A.10(9)(a).
11. *Id.* §§ 523H.1(3)(a), 537A.10(1)(c)(1).
12. *Id.* §§ 523H.1(8), 537A.10(1)(h).
13. *Id.* §§ 523H.1(3)(b), 537A.10(1)(c)(2).

or licensed department operates only under the trademark, trade name, service mark, or other commercial symbol designating the lessor or licensor."[14] Additionally, a franchise governed by the acts does not include contracts governed by the Petroleum Marketing Practices Act,[15] or franchise relationships regarding the sale of construction equipment, lawn or garden equipment, or real estate under both Iowa Acts.[16]

1. Trademark

a. Commentary

Unfortunately, no Iowa cases to date have elaborated on the trademark element of the statute. However, because the language tracks the language of other, similar franchise statutes that require only "substantial association," with a "trademark, service mark, trade name, logotype, advertisement or other commercial symbol,"[17] decisions under those statutes may be persuasive.[18]

b. Annotations

There is no case law addressing this issue under the Iowa Acts.

2. Franchise Fee

a. Commentary

A franchise fee, under both the 1992 Act and the 2000 Act, consists of a payment, either direct or indirect, to purchase or operate a franchise.[19] However, franchise fees do not include (1) payment of reasonable credit card related service charges; (2) "[p]ayment to a trading stamp company by a person issuing trading stamps in connection with a retail sale"; (3) "[a]n agreement to purchase at a bona fide wholesale price a reasonable quantity of tangible goods for resale"; (4) "[t]he purchase or agreement to purchase at fair market value any fixtures, equipment, leasehold improvements, real property, supplies or other materials reasonably necessary to enter into or continue a business"; (5) "[p]ayments by a purchaser pursuant to a bona fide loan from a seller to the purchaser"; (6) "[p]ayment of rent which reflects payment for the economic value of leased real or personal property"; or (7) "[t]he purchase or agreement to purchase promotional or demonstration supplies, materials, or equipment furnished at fair market value and not intended for resale."[20]

---

14. *Id.*
15. 15 U.S.C. §§ 2801 *et seq.*
16. Iowa Code §§ 523H.1(3)(c), 537A.10(1)(c)(3).
17. *Id.* §§ 523H.1(3)(a), 537A.10(1)(c)(1).
18. *See, e.g.*, California Franchise Investment Law, Cal. Corp. Code §§ 31000 *et seq.*; Connecticut Franchise Act, Conn. Gen. Stat. § 42-133e; Indiana Franchise Law, Ind. Code § 23-2-2.5-1; Illinois Franchise Disclosure Act of 1987, 815 Ill. Comp. Stat. § 705/3; Michigan Franchise Investment Law, Mich. Comp. Laws § 445.1502.
19. Iowa Code §§ 523H.1(4), 537A.10(1)(d).
20. *Id.*

b. Annotations

As reasoned in *Jones Distributing Co. v. White Consolidated Industries, Inc.*, because a distributor of appliances failed to reference direct or indirect franchise fees and did not refute the manufacturer's claim that possible indirect franchise fees were actually normal business expenses, the court dismissed the distributor's Iowa Franchise Act claim on summary judgment finding that the franchisee failed to rebut the franchisor's argument that any possible "indirect" franchise fees were anything but a normal business expense.[21]

As of the writing of this chapter, there are no more recent Iowa cases addressing what constitutes a franchise fee.

3. Community of Interest; Significant Degree of Control; Joint Marketing Plan

a. Commentary

A "marketing plan" is defined in both Iowa Acts as "a plan or system concerning a material aspect of conducting business."[22] Signs or elements of marketing plans may include things like price specifications; special pricing systems or discount plans; sales or display equipment or merchandising devices; sales techniques; promotional or advertising materials or cooperative advertising; trading regarding the promotion, operation, or management of the business; or operational, managerial, technical, or financial guidelines or assistance.[23]

b. Annotations

There is no case law addressing this issue under the Iowa Acts.

B. Scope and Jurisdiction

1. Commentary

The Iowa Acts limit applicability to those franchises that are operated in Iowa, which is defined to mean that the premises from which the franchise is operated are physically located in Iowa.[24] Franchises that involve "marketing rights" within Iowa are deemed to be operated in the state only if the franchisee's principal business office is actually physically located in Iowa.[25] This requirement was addressed in *Holiday Inns Franchising, Inc. v. Branstad*,[26] wherein the Iowa Supreme Court determined that, under the express language of the 1992 Act, the statute would not apply to a franchisee located outside of Iowa who did not have a principal place of business within the state of Iowa, even if the Iowa laws would apply under a conflict-of-laws analysis. Because the relevant language of the 2000 Act is the same, it is likely that Iowa courts would interpret the 2000 Act in the same manner.

---

21. Jones Distrib. Co. v. White Consol. Indus., Inc., 943 F. Supp. 1445, 1458 (N.D. Iowa 1996).
22. IOWA CODE §§ 523H.1(7), 537A.10(1)(g).
23. *Id.*
24. *Id.* §§ 523H.2, 537A.10(2).
25. *Id.*
26. Holiday Inns Franchising, Inc. v. Branstad, 537 N.W.2d 724, 730 (Iowa 1995).

Pursuant to the Iowa Acts, clauses or terms in franchise agreements restricting jurisdiction to venues outside of Iowa are void with respect to claims brought under the Iowa Acts. Instead, actions may be brought wherever jurisdiction exists, notwithstanding a contractual choice-of-forum clause.[27] Under the 1992 Act, parties may agree to alternative dispute resolution, including arbitration and mediation.[28] However, no similar provision exists in the 2000 Act, and it is silent as to whether alternative dispute resolution is permitted or prohibited, although arbitration provisions are likely enforceable.

The Iowa Acts expressly state that "[a] condition, stipulation, or provision requiring a franchisee to waive compliance with or relieving a person of a duty or liability imposed by or a right provided by this [Act] . . . is void."[29] Similarly, the Iowa Acts state that "[a] condition, stipulation, or provision requiring the application of the law of another state in lieu of this [Act] is void."[30] Accordingly, parties may not contract around the Iowa Acts.

2. Annotations

In *McDonald's Corp. v. Nelson*, the court held that the retroactive application of the Iowa Franchise Act substantially impaired the franchisor's contractual rights because prior regulation in Iowa and other states at the time the agreements were executed was insufficient to put plaintiffs on notice that they would be subject to regulations such as the act.[31] Ultimately, the court determined that the retroactive application of the 1992 Act violated the contracts clauses of both the United States and Iowa constitutions.[32] Accordingly, the 1992 Act could only apply to franchise agreements entered into from and after June 1, 1992.

The Iowa Supreme Court held that the reasonable interpretation of "out-of-state franchisee" in the sentence "[t]he provisions of this chapter do not apply to any existing or future contracts between Iowa franchisors and out-of-state franchisees" in section 523H.2 of the 1992 Act means a franchisee operating a franchise outside of the borders of Iowa. *Holiday Inns Franchising, Inc. v. Branstad*.[33] Further, even if Iowa law applies under conflict-of-laws analysis, the Iowa Franchise Act "shall never apply to a franchise operated beyond the borders of the state of Iowa."[34]

The U.S. District Court, Eastern District of California, determined that failure to plead that a principal business office was physically located within the state of Iowa and failure to plead facts that make a showing of the business presence of the franchisee in Iowa resulted in dismissal without prejudice.[35]

---

27. Iowa Code §§ 523H.3, 537A.10(3).
28. *Id.* § 523H.3(3).
29. *Id.* §§ 523H.4, 537A.10(4).
30. *Id.* §§ 523H.14, 537A.10(14).
31. McDonald's Corp. v. Nelson, 822 F. Supp. 597, 606 (S.D. Iowa 1993).
32. *Id.*
33. Holiday Inns Franchising, Inc. v. Branstad, 537 N.W.2d 724, 730 (Iowa 1995).
34. *Id.*
35. G.P.P., Inc. v. Guardian Prot. Prods., Inc., Case No. 1:15-cv-00321-SKO, 2015 WL 3992878, at *10–11 (E.D. Cal. June 30, 2015).

C. Termination

1. What Constitutes Termination

a. Commentary

The Iowa Acts are relationship laws that address termination, nonrenewal, transfer, encroachment, no-waiver provisions, venue, and other aspects of the franchise relationship. Neither of the Iowa Acts expressly define "termination." The language of the Iowa Acts, when read as a whole, suggests that termination is considered the ending or cancellation of a franchise agreement during or at the end of the term of the agreement.[36] No court has answered whether constructive termination would qualify as termination under the Iowa Acts.

b. Annotations

There is no case law addressing this issue under the Iowa Acts.

2. Restrictions on Termination or Cancellation

The restrictions for termination under both Iowa Acts are contained in the following Notice Requirement and Grounds for Termination sections.

3. Notice Requirement

a. Commentary

Under the Iowa Acts, prior to terminating a franchise for default under or breach of the franchise agreement, the franchisor must provide the franchisee written notice and an opportunity to cure the default.[37] Written notice must include the basis or reason for the proposed termination and give the franchisee a reasonable period of time to cure the default.[38] Under the Iowa Acts, a "reasonable period of time" is no "less than thirty days or more than ninety days."[39] If the reason for termination is for failure to pay monetary amounts due under the franchise agreement, the period to cure provided by the franchisor need not exceed 30 days.[40]

However, notice and opportunity to cure is not required, under either Iowa Act, when

(1) The franchisee or the franchisee's business related to the franchise is declared bankrupt or judicially determined to be insolvent;
(2) All or a substantial part of the assets of the franchisee or the franchisee's business related to the franchise are assigned to or for the benefit of a creditor;
(3) The franchisee voluntarily abandons the franchise by failing to operate the business for five consecutive business days during which the franchisee is required to operate the business under the terms of the franchise, or any

---

36. IOWA CODE §§ 523H.7, 537A.10(7).
37. *Id.* §§ 523H.7(2), 537A.10(7)(b).
38. *Id.*
39. *Id.*
40. *Id.*

shorter period if it is not unreasonable, under the facts and circumstances, for the franchisor to conclude that the franchisee does not intend to continue to operate the franchise, unless the failure to operate is due to circumstances beyond the control of the franchisee;

(4) The franchisor and franchisee agree in writing to terminate the franchise;

(5) The franchisee knowingly makes any material misrepresentations or knowingly omits to state any material facts relating to the acquisition or ownership or operation of the franchise business;

(6) The franchisee repeatedly fails to comply with one or more material provisions of the franchise agreement and the enforcement of such material provisions is not arbitrary or capricious, regardless of whether or not the franchisee complies after receiving notice of the failure to comply;

(7) The franchised business or business premises of the franchisee are lawfully seized, taken over, or foreclosed by a government authority or official;

(8) The franchisee is convicted of a felony or any other criminal misconduct which materially and adversely affects the operation, maintenance, or goodwill of the franchise in the relevant market; and/or

(9) The franchisee operates the franchised business in a manner that imminently endangers the public health and safety.[41]

The 1992 Act also provides that a franchisor need not give a franchisee written notice of default or an opportunity to cure before termination "after three material breaches of a franchise agreement occurring with a twelve-month period, for which the franchisee has been given notice and an opportunity to cure, the franchisor may terminate upon any subsequent material breach within the twelve-month period without providing an opportunity to cure, provided that the action is not arbitrary or capricious."[42] The 2000 Act is a bit more ambiguous, stating that notice and an opportunity to cure are not required if "the franchisee repeatedly fails to comply with one or more material provisions of the franchise agreement, when the enforcement of such material provisions is not arbitrary or capricious, whether or not the franchisee cures after receiving notice of the failure to comply."[43]

b. Annotations

There is no case law addressing this issue under the Iowa Acts.

4. Grounds for Termination

a. Commentary

The Iowa Acts permit early terminations of franchise agreements in certain circumstances.[44] Under Iowa Code sections 523H.7 and 537A.10(7), it is unlawful for a franchisor to terminate a franchise agreement before expiration of the franchise except for good cause. Under the Iowa Acts, "good cause" is defined as

---

41. *Id.* §§ 523H.7(3), 537A.10(7)(c).
42. *Id.* § 523H.7(3)(f).
43. *Id.* § 537A.10(7)(c)(6).
44. *Id.* §§ 523H.7, 537A.10(7).

"cause based upon a legitimate business reason."[45] The Iowa Acts go on to provide that "good cause" may include "the failure of the franchise to comply with any material lawful requirements of the franchise agreement, provided that the termination by the franchisor is not arbitrary or capricious."[46] The franchisee carries the burden of showing that the franchisor's action is arbitrary or capricious under both the Iowa Acts.[47] However, the 1992 Act sets forth guidance that the measure of whether the franchisor has acted arbitrarily or capriciously can be determined by comparing the actions of the franchisor in other similar circumstances.[48]

The Iowa Acts provide that a franchisor may terminate the franchise agreement for a "legitimate business reason."[49] A "legitimate business reason" is defined to include the failure of the franchisee to comply with the requirements of the franchise.[50] Such broad language suggest that a franchisor may terminate a franchise agreement for any legitimate business reason; however, one could argue that such a reading or interpretation would invalidate the notice and opportunity to cure provisions, rendering them superfluous. Perhaps a better reading, which gives meaning to all parts of the Iowa Acts, is that termination may only occur as a result of a franchisee's noncompliance or nonperformance with the franchise agreement.

b. Annotations

There is no case law addressing this issue under the Iowa Acts.

D. Restrictions on Nonrenewal

1. What Constitutes Nonrenewal

a. Commentary

Not applicable.[51]

b. Annotations

Not applicable.

2. Notice Requirements

a. Commentary

The Iowa Acts prohibit nonrenewal of a franchise agreement unless the franchisee has been given at least six months' notice of the franchisor's intention to not renew.[52]

---

45. *Id.* §§ 523H.7(1), 537A.10(7)(a).
46. *Id.*
47. *Id.*
48. *Id.* § 524H.7(1).
49. *Id.* §§ 523H.7, 537A.10(7).
50. *Id.*
51. *Id.* §§ 523H.8, 537A.10(8).
52. *Id.* §§ 523H.8(1), 537A.10(8)(a).

b. Annotations

There is no case law addressing this issue under the Iowa Acts.

3. Grounds

a. Commentary

Under the Iowa Acts, one of the following must occur in order for a franchisor to exercise nonrenewal: (1) good cause, as defined in the termination section of each statute, based upon a legitimate business reason, exists and the refusal of the franchisor to renew cannot be arbitrary or capricious; (2) the parties agree to not renew; or (3) the franchisor completely withdraws from directly, or indirectly, distributing its products or services in the geographic market served by the franchisee and agrees to not seek enforcement of any covenant not to compete.[53] A franchisor may require, as a condition of renewal, that the franchisee meet the franchisor's current requirements for franchisees and require the franchisee to execute the franchisor's current agreement.[54]

A franchisee may recover damages, costs, and attorneys' fees, or obtain injunctive relief, for wrongful nonrenewal.[55]

b. Annotations

There is no case law addressing this issue under the Iowa Acts.

4. Repurchase Obligations

a. Commentary

The 1992 Act, but not the 2000 Act, contains a provision wherein the franchisor may not prohibit a franchisee, after termination or nonrenewal, from engaging in any lawful business, unless such business is one that depends upon a marketing program "substantially similar" to that of the franchisor, or unless the franchisor purchases the assets of the franchisee at "fair market value."[56] This, essentially, acts as a limited prohibition on covenants not to compete. However, the asset-purchase provision of the statutory language is very limited and includes only assets that the franchisee has purchased from the franchisor or "its agent."[57] Further, the definition of "fair market value" excludes the value imparted to the business by the franchisor's trademarks.[58] Alternatively, in the context of the nonrenewal of a franchise, if the franchisor's reason for nonrenewal is that the franchisor is withdrawing from distributing its products or services in the geographic market served by the franchisee, then the franchisor cannot seek to enforce a covenant prohibiting competition.[59]

---

53. *Id.*
54. *Id.* §§ 523H.8(2), 537A.10(8)(b).
55. *Id.* §§ 523H.13, 537A.10(13).
56. *Id.* §§ 523H.5(1), 523H.8(b)(3).
57. *Id.*
58. *Id.*
59. *Id.* § 523H.8(b)(3).

b. Annotations
There is no case law addressing this issue under the Iowa Acts.

E. Transfers and Succession
a. Commentary
Transfers of franchised businesses are also governed by the Iowa Acts.

Under the 1992 Act, a "transfer" of a franchise is defined as "any change in ownership or control of a franchise, franchised business, or a franchisee."[60] However, several circumstances are not considered transfers, and do not require the franchisor's consent or implicate a franchisor's right of first refusal under the 1992 Act. This includes, with restrictions, (1) succession of ownership upon the death or disability of a franchisee to the surviving spouse or heirs, or to the partner(s) in the management of the franchisee; (2) incorporation of a proprietorship franchisee; (3) transfer within an existing ownership group; (4) transfer of less than a controlling interest in the franchise to the franchisee's spouse or child; (5) transfer of less than a controlling interest in the franchise to an employee stock ownership plan or incentive plan; and/or (6) grant or retention of a security interest in the franchise business or assets or the ownership interest in the franchise.[61] The 2000 Act provides for similar exceptions as to transfers.[62] Pursuant to the 1992 Act only, a franchisor is prohibited from interfering or attempting "to interfere with any disposition of an interest in a franchise or franchised business" under the same circumstances.[63]

As set forth earlier, one of the circumstances included as an exception to the definition of "transfer" is the succession of ownership of the franchise upon the death or disability of a franchisee, or the owner of a franchise, to the surviving spouse, heir, or a partner active in the management of the franchise. However, under the 1992 Act, if such successors fail to meet the franchisor's reasonable qualifications within one year, and the enforcement of such qualifications is not arbitrary or capricious, then such transfer is not allowed.[64] Under the 2000 Act, succession transfers upon the death of a franchisee owner are not expressly exempted; however, the 2000 Act does, similarly, provide:

> A franchisor shall not deny the surviving spouse or a child or children of a deceased or permanently disabled franchisee the opportunity to participate in the ownership of a franchise under a valid franchise agreement for a reasonable period, which need not exceed one year, after the death or disability of the franchisee. During such reasonable period, the surviving spouse or the child or children of the franchisee shall either meet all of the qualifications which the franchisee was subject to at the time of the death or disability of the franchisee, or sell,

---

60. *Id.* § 523H.5(11).
61. *Id.* § 523H.5(12).
62. *Id.* § 537A.10(5).
63. *Id.* § 523H.5(13).
64. *Id.* § 523H.5(1).

transfer, or assign the franchise to a person who meets the franchisor's current qualifications for a new franchisee. The rights granted pursuant to this subsection are subject to the surviving spouse or the child or children of the franchisee maintaining all standards and obligations of the franchise.[65]

Accordingly, pursuant to the Iowa Acts, a transfer of less than a controlling interest upon death or disability of the franchisee to the franchisee's child(ren) or spouse is permitted, so long as the controlling interest is held by those who meet the franchisor's reasonable qualifications.[66]

The 1992 Act sets forth that the incorporation of a proprietorship franchisee is not a transfer, so long as the incorporation does not prohibit the franchisor from requiring or being able to require a personal guaranty by the franchisee of or for obligations related to the franchise.[67] Similarly, under the 2000 Act, such incorporation is allowed as a nontransfer only after 60 days' prior written notice to the franchisor and does not prohibit a franchisor from requiring or being able to require a personal guaranty of or for obligations related to the franchise. Further, the 2000 Act requires the owners of the corporation to meet the franchisor's reasonable current qualifications for franchisees.[68]

Under the 1992 Act, a transfer of equity within an existing ownership group of a franchise is not a transfer requiring consent of the franchisor, if more than 50 percent of the franchise is owned by persons who meet the franchisor's reasonable current requirements for franchisees.[69] However, if less than 50 percent of the franchise owners meet the franchisor's then-current reasonable qualifications, the franchisor may refuse to approve the transfer so long as such enforcement of the reasonable qualifications, and therefore refusal, is not arbitrary or capricious.[70] The 2000 Act similarly provides that such transfers are permitted, but with the additional requirement that the franchisor must be given 60 days' prior written notification of the transfer.[71]

The 1992 Act provides that a transfer of less than a controlling interest of a franchise to an employee's stock ownership plan or employee incentive plan is not considered a transfer requiring the franchisor's consent so long as more than 50 percent of the entire franchise is held by persons who meet the franchisor's reasonable current qualifications for franchisees.[72] However, the franchisor may refuse such transfer if less than 50 percent of the equity would be owned by such qualified persons, providing enforcement of the reasonable current qualifications is not arbitrary or capricious.[73] In the 2000 Act, franchisees may make such transfers only so long as they are approved by the franchisor;

---

65. *Id.* § 537A.10(5)(h).
66. *Id.* §§ 523H.5(12)(d), 537A.10(5)(g).
67. *Id.* § 523H.5(12)(b).
68. *Id.* § 537A.10(5)(i).
69. *Id.* § 523H.5(12)(c).
70. *Id.*
71. *Id.* § 537A.10(5)(j).
72. *Id.* § 523H.5(12)(e).
73. *Id.*

however, such approval shall not be unreasonably withheld.[74] As with the 1992 Act, under the 2000 Act, if such a transfer would result in less than 50 percent of the entire franchise being owned by qualified persons, the franchisor may refuse to approve the transfer, if enforcement of the then current reasonable qualifications would not be arbitrary or capricious.[75] The 2000 Act also helpfully clarifies that "participation by an employee in an employee stock ownership plan or employee incentive plan established pursuant to this subsection does not confer upon such employee any rights to access trade secrets protected under the franchise agreement which access the employee would not otherwise have the right if the employee did not participate in such plan."[76]

Finally, under the 1992 Act, a franchisee need not obtain the franchisor's consent for:

> a grant or retention of a security interest in a franchised business or its assets, or an ownership interest in the franchisee, provided the security agreement establishes an obligation on the part of the secured party enforceable by the franchisor to give the franchisor notice of the secured party's intent to foreclose on the collateral simultaneously with notice to the franchisee, and a reasonable opportunity to redeem the interests of the secured party and recover the secured party's interest in the franchisee or franchised business by paying the secured obligation.[77]

There is no corresponding provision under the 2000 Act.

With regard to transferring of a franchise, the 1992 Act prohibits a franchisor from enforcing a covenant in the franchise agreement that effectively prohibits the transferring franchisee from engaging in any lawful occupation or enterprise.[78]

b. Annotations

The Iowa Acts' provisions concerning circumstances under which franchisees can transfer their franchises, as applied to existing franchise agreements at the time the statute was enacted (retroactive application), was found unconstitutional under the contract clauses of both United States and Iowa Constitutions, and therefore the transfer restrictions were deemed unenforceable as applied retroactively to already existing franchise agreements.[79]

---

74. *Id.* § 537A.10(5)(b)(1).
75. *Id.* § 537A.10(5)(b)(2).
76. *Id.* § 537A.10(5)(b)(3).
77. *Id.* § 523H.5(12)(f).
78. *Id.* § 523H.5(10).
79. Holiday Inns Franchising, Inc. v. Branstad, 29 F.3d 383 (8th Cir. 1994) (affirming district court decision finding retroactive application of sections 523H.5–523H.8 was unconstitutional), *cert. denied*, 115 S. Ct. 613, 513 U.S. 1032, 130 L. Ed. 2d 522 (1994).

F. Other Regulations of the Franchise Relationship

1. Right of Free Association

a. Commentary

Franchisors may not restrict franchisees from associating with one another or from participating in trade associations.[80] Likewise, franchisors may not retaliate against franchisees for engaging in such activities.[81]

b. Annotations

There is no case law addressing this issue under the Iowa Acts.

2. Exclusive Territory and Encroachment

a. Commentary

The Iowa Acts both address encroachment with minor differences. The Iowa Acts provide that a franchisee has a cause of action for monetary damages if a franchisor develops, or grants a franchisee a right to develop, a new franchise, if the new location developed or granted adversely affects gross sales of the franchisee's existing outlet. However, under the 2000 Act, this cause of action only accrues if the new location is in "unreasonable proximity" to the existing franchisee's location(s).[82]

The Iowa Acts provide exceptions to the franchisor's liability for the consequences of encroachment. Under both, encroachment is excused if the franchisor first offered the new franchise location to the existing franchisee on the same terms as offered to the new franchisee.[83] The 2000 Act adds the requirement that the existing franchisee must meet the franchisor's reasonable current qualifications, including any financial requirements.[84] Under the 1992 Act, if the adverse impact suffered by the existing franchise is less than 5 percent or, under the 2000 Act, less than 6 percent during the first 12 months of operation of the new outlet or location, the franchisor is not liable for the consequences of encroachment.[85]

A third exception under the Iowa Acts is if the existing franchisee, at the time the new location is developed, is not in compliance with the franchisor's then-current reasonable criteria for a new franchise.[86] The 2000 Act further expands that this requirement does not encompass financial requirements.[87] The 1992 Act, but not the 2000 Act, provides that if a franchisee does not meet the then-current reasonable criteria, the franchisee may seek other compensation

---

80. Iowa Code §§ 523H.9, 537A.10(10).
81. Id.
82. Id. §§ 523H.6(1), 5327A.10(6)(a).
83. Id. §§ 523H.6(1)(a), 537A.10(6)(a)(1).
84. Id. § 537A.10(6)(a)(1).
85. Id. §§ 523H.6(1)(b), 537A.10(6)(a)(2).
86. Id. §§ 523H.6(1)(c), 537A.10(6)(a)(3).
87. Id. § 537A.10(6)(a)(3).

pursuant to a formal procedure, as its exclusive remedy.[88] Under the 1992 Act, the franchisee may select one of the following procedures:

> (a) A panel, comprised of an equal number of members selected by the franchisee and the franchisor, and one additional member to be selected unanimously by the members selected by the franchisee and the franchisor.
>
> (b) A neutral third-party mediator or an arbitrator with the authority to make a decision or award in accordance with the formal procedure. The procedure shall be deemed reasonable if approved by a majority of the franchisor's franchisees in the United States, either individually or by an elected representative body.
>
> (c) Arbitration of any dispute before neutral arbitrators pursuant to the rules of the American Arbitration Association. The award of an arbitrator pursuant to this subparagraph division is subject to judicial review pursuant to chapter 679A.[89]

An additional exception exists under the 1992 Act if the franchisor has established "a formal procedure for hearing and acting upon claims by an existing franchisee with regard to a decision by the franchisor to develop, or grant to a franchisee the right to develop, a new outlet or location, prior to the opening of the new outlet or location."[90] However, the franchisor must also have established a reasonable formal procedure for awarding compensation or other form of consideration to a franchisee to offset all or a portion of the franchisee's lost profits caused by the establishment of the new outlet or location in order for such exception to arise.

Similarly, the 2000 Act provides that the franchisor must establish both (1) a formal procedure for hearing and acting upon such claims, and (2) a "reasonable formal procedure for mediating a dispute resulting in an award of compensation or other form of consideration to a franchisee to offset all or a portion of the franchisee's lost profits caused by the establishment of the new outlet or location."[91] This process must involve a neutral third-party mediator, and it will "be deemed reasonable if approved by a majority of the franchisor's franchisees in the United States."[92] Unlike the 1992 Act, under the 2000 Act, if the formal procedure for acting on claims before opening the new outlet does not result in settlement, the franchisor or the franchisee may still bring an action for encroachment.[93]

The 2000 Act includes a fourth exception, not included in the 1992 Act, to liability for encroachment, where: "[t]he existing franchisee has been granted reasonable territorial rights and the new outlet or location does not violate those

---

88. *Id.* § 523H.6(1)(c).
89. *Id.* § 523H.6(1)(d)(2).
90. *Id.* § 523H.6(d)(1).
91. *Id.* § 537A.10(6)(b)(1)(b).
92. *Id.*
93. *Id.* § 537A.10(6)(b)(2).

territorial rights."[94] The 1992 Act specifically provides that injunctive relief is available to preserve the status quo pending the outcome of a formal procedure.[95] However, the 2000 Act has no corresponding provision, although it does permit franchisors and franchisees to seek injunctive and other equitable relief generally.[96]

b. Annotations

The 1992 Act's encroachment provision only applies to encroaching franchise-related stores, new outlets, company-owned stores, or carry-out stores located within Iowa.[97] The court in *Holiday Inns Franchising, Inc. v. Branstad* determined that the language of section 523H.6(1) was ambiguous, finding that the 1992 Act did not define "outlet," "company-owned store," or "carry-out store," nor was it clear whether the territorial limitation of section 523H.2 applied to new outlets, company-owned stores, or carry-out stores.[98] The court determined that the legislature intended, and so held, that the terms "outlet," "company-owned store," and "carry-out store" as stated in section 523H.6(1) meant such outlets or stores located within the borders of the state of Iowa.[99] Accordingly, "unreasonable proximity" was found not to encompass any outlets or stores operated outside of the borders of the state of Iowa.[100] Given the similar language in the 2000 Act, the court would likely make the same finding under the 2000 Act.

3. Restrictions on Sources of Supply

a. Commentary

The 2000 Act contains a provision stating that "a franchisor shall not require that a franchisee purchase goods, supplies, inventories, or services exclusively from the franchisor or from a source or sources of supply specifically designated by the franchisor where such goods, supplies, inventories, or services of comparable quality are available from sources other than those designated by the franchisor."[101] However, this does not apply to principal goods, supplies, inventories, or services manufactured by the franchisor, or such goods, supplies, inventories, or services entitled to protection as a trade secret.[102]

Similarly, the 1992 Act provides, "[a] franchisor shall allow a franchisee to obtain equipment, fixtures, supplies, and services used in the establishment and operation of the franchised business from sources of the franchisee's choosing, provided that such goods and services meet standards as to their nature and quality promulgated by the franchisor."[103] Again, this is not applicable

---

94. *Id.* § 537A.10(6)(a)(4).
95. *Id.* § 523H.6(5).
96. *Id.* § 537A.10(13).
97. Holiday Inns Franchising, Inc. v. Branstad, 537 N.W.2d 724, 731 (Iowa 1995).
98. *Id.*
99. *Id.*
100. *Id.* at 732.
101. Iowa Code § 537A.10(9)(a).
102. *Id.* § 537A.10(9)(b).
103. *Id.* § 523H.12(1).

to "reasonable quantities of inventory goods or services, including display and sample items, that the franchisor requires the franchisee to obtain from the franchisor or its affiliate, but only if the goods or services are central to the franchised business and either are actually manufactured or produced by the franchisor or its affiliate, or incorporate a trade secret owned by the franchisor or its affiliate."[104]

b. Annotations

There is no case law addressing this issue under the Iowa Acts.

4. No-Waiver Clauses and Releases

a. Commentary

Both the 1992 and 2000 Acts provide that "a condition, stipulation, or provision requiring a franchisee to waive compliance with or relieving a person of a duty or liability imposed by or right provided by" the Iowa Acts is void.[105] Provisions of franchise agreements requiring that disputes be resolved in a venue outside of the state of Iowa are expressly void,[106] as are provisions choosing the law of another state in lieu of the Iowa Acts.[107]

b. Annotations

There is no case law addressing this issue under the Iowa Acts.

5. Good Faith

a. Commentary

The Iowa Acts impose a duty of good faith (and fair dealing) on both parties, meaning "honesty in fact and the observance of reasonable commercial standards of fair dealing in the trade."[108] This provision mirrors the common law duty articulated in the Restatement (Second) of Contracts.

The 2000 Act also provides, "[t]he duty of good faith is imposed in situations including, but not limited to, where the franchisor opens a new outlet or location that has an adverse impact on an existing franchisee. A determination of whether the duty of good faith with respect to a new outlet or location has been met shall be made pursuant to the procedures set forth" in the encroachment subsection.[109]

b. Annotations

There is no case law addressing this issue under the Iowa Acts.

---

104. *Id.* § 523H.12(2).
105. *Id.* §§ 523H.4, 537A.10(4).
106. *Id.* §§ 523H.3.1, 537A.10(3)(a).
107. *Id.* §§ 523H.14, 537A.10(14).
108. *Id.* §§ 523H.10, 537A.10(11).
109. *Id.* § 537A.10(11)(b).

G. Remedies and Administrative Action

1. Restrictive Covenants

a. Commentary

The 1992 Act, but not the 2000 Act, contains a provision under which the franchisor may not prohibit a franchisee, after termination or nonrenewal, from engaging in any lawful business unless it is one that depends upon a marketing program "substantially similar" to that of the franchisor, or unless the franchisor purchases the assets of the franchisee at "fair market value."[110]

In conjunction with transferring a franchise, while a franchisor may not enforce a covenant that prohibits the transferring franchisee from engaging in any lawful occupation or enterprise under the 1992 Act, the franchisor may enforce covenants in the franchise agreement that prohibit the transferring franchisee from misusing the franchisor's trade secrets or intellectual property.[111] In the context of the nonrenewal of a franchise, if the franchisor's reason for nonrenewal is that the franchisor is withdrawing from distributing its products or services in the geographic market served by the franchisee, then the franchisor cannot seek to enforce a covenant not to compete in a franchise agreement.[112]

The 2000 Act contains a provision identical to the prohibition of a covenant not to compete in the instance of nonrenewal of a franchise agreement as just set forth.[113] However, as previously noted, the 2000 Act does not include the general prohibition against covenants not to compete or transfers of the franchise, suggesting enforceability of covenants against competition in franchise agreements entered July 1, 2000, and after for transferred or terminated franchise agreements.[114]

b. Annotations

Applying Iowa common law rather than either of the Iowa Acts, the Federal District Court for the Northern District of Iowa found that the covenant not to compete in a franchise agreement that prohibited the franchisee (a financial services advisor) from conducting business in the "same geographic area" for one year following termination was enforceable as reasonably necessary to protect the franchisor's financial planning business, including customer lists and trade secrets. The court enjoined the former franchisee from competing for one year. *American Express Financial Advisors, Inc. v. Yantis*.[115]

Applying Iowa common law, the Federal District Court for the Southern District of Iowa held, in *Medicap Pharmacies, Inc. v. Kennedy*, that, although the noncompete clause technically had expired, it was in the interest of justice to extend the restraint period for an additional 18 months because it was the franchisee that

---

110. *Id.* §§ 523H.5(1), 523H.8(b)(3).
111. *Id.* § 523H.5(10).
112. *Id.* § 523H.8(b)(3).
113. *Id.* § 537A.10.
114. *See, e.g.*, Am. Express Fin. Advisors, Inc. v. Yantis, 358 F. Supp. 2d 818, 828–29 (N.D. Iowa 2005) (enforcing one year noncompete in a franchise agreement).
115. *Id.*

was primarily responsible for the prolonged litigation and who continued to violate the noncompete clause throughout the majority of the two years following his unilateral termination.[116] The court recognized that refusal to enforce the legal and valid covenant that had yet to be enforced since the action was commenced over two years earlier "would eliminate all force and effect of the covenant."[117]

2. Damages and Remedies

a. Commentary

Under the Iowa Acts, "[a] person who violates a provision of [the Act] . . . is liable for damages caused by the violation, including, but not limited to, costs and reasonable attorneys' and experts' fees, and subject to other appropriate relief including injunctive and other equitable relief."[118]

b. Annotations

There is no case law addressing this issue under the Iowa Acts.

3. Rescission

a. Commentary

Not applicable.

b. Annotations

Not applicable.

4. Injunctive Relief

a. Commentary

Not applicable.

b. Annotations

Not applicable.

5. Control Person Liability

a. Commentary

Not applicable.

b. Annotations

Not applicable.

6. Attorneys' Fees

a. Commentary

Not applicable.

---

116. Medicap Pharmacies, Inc. v. Kennedy, Bus. Franchise Guide (CCH) ¶ 11,973 (S.D. Iowa 2000), aff'd, Bus. Franchise Guide (CCH) ¶ 12,187 (6th Cir. 2001).
117. Id.
118. IOWA CODE §§ 523H.13, 537A.10(13).

b. Annotations
Not applicable.

7. Limitations on Damages Waivers
a. Commentary
Not applicable.

b. Annotations
Not applicable.

8. Administrative Action
a. Commentary
Not applicable.

b. Annotations
Not applicable.

H. Dispute Resolution

1. Limitations on Franchisors' Ability to Restrict Venue
a. Commentary
Pursuant to both the 1992 and 2000 Acts, any provision in a franchise agreement that requires the application of the law of another state instead of Iowa law is void.[119] The statutes do not expressly state whether such is applicable only to statutory law or both statutory and common law.[120]

Both the 1992 and 2000 Acts provide that any provision in a franchise agreement restricting jurisdiction to a forum outside of the state of Iowa is void with respect to any claim enforceable under the Iowa Acts.[121] However, in an unreported case, this prohibition was found to violate the supremacy clause because it would have voided an arbitration clause that was enforceable under the FAA (due to a forum selection outside of Iowa for the arbitration), thus, because it directly conflicted with section 2 of the FAA, it violated the supremacy clause and the FAA would preempt Iowa Code section.[122] Ultimately, the court dismissed the case in favor of arbitration but did not discuss the forum of the arbitration.[123]

b. Annotations
Even if Iowa law applies under conflict-of-laws analysis, the Iowa Franchise Act "shall never apply to a franchise operated beyond the borders of the state of

---

119. *Id.* §§ 523H.14, 537A.10(14).
120. *Id.*
121. *Id.* §§ 523H.3, 537A.10(3).
122. Cahill v. Alternatives Wines, Inc., 2013 WL 427396, at *3, *5 (N.D. Iowa Feb. 4, 2013).
123. *Id.* at *6.

Iowa."[124] This would be true even if the franchise agreement includes an Iowa choice of law provision.[125] However, the Iowa Acts are applicable when there is an Iowa franchisor and an out of state franchise operating a franchise within the borders of Iowa.[126]

A choice of law provision indicating that the franchise agreement is to be interpreted under the laws of another state is void under the Iowa Franchise Act.[127] The court went on to apply Iowa law to the petition for injunction as well as the breach of contract, misappropriation of confidential information, conversion, and unfair competition claims when considering whether to grant an injunction.[128]

Section 537A.10(3) of the Iowa Franchise Act provides that "[a] provision in a franchise agreement restricting jurisdiction to a forum outside this state is void with respect to a claim otherwise enforceable under this section."[129] As this applies to franchise agreements specifically and not to contracts generally, it "violates the Supremacy Clause because it directly conflicts with Section 2 [of] the FAA."[130] Accordingly, the court found that section 537A.10(3), as it relates to arbitration provisions, is preempted by the FAA (Federal Arbitration Act).[131] Because the parties agreed to binding arbitration, the case was dismissed.[132]

In, *S & G Janitschke, Inc. et al. v. Cottman Transmission Systems, LLC*, though decided by a Minnesota federal court, Iowa Code section 537A.10(3)(a) was found to void the forum selection clause as to the six Iowa franchisee plaintiffs and the motion to dismiss for improper venue (i.e., not being brought within the venue set forth in the void forum selection clause) was denied as the six Iowa plaintiffs were not bound by such clause.[133]

2. Limitations Period

a. Commentary

The Iowa Acts do not contain an express statute of limitations. Actions for violation of the Iowa Acts are likely governed by the five-year period for injuries to property and cases not otherwise provided for under Iowa law.[134]

b. Annotations

Not applicable.

---

124. Holiday Inns Franchising, Inc. v. Branstad, 537 N.W.2d 724, 730 (Iowa 1995).
125. *Id.*
126. *Id.*
127. Am. Express Fin. Advisors, Inc. v. Yantis, 358 F. Supp. 2d 818, 827 (2005).
128. *Id.* at 827–37.
129. Cahill v. Alternatives Wines, Inc., 2013 WL 427396, at *3 (N.D. Iowa Feb. 4, 2013).
130. *Id.* at *5.
131. *Id.*
132. *Id.* at *6.
133. S & G Janitschke, Inc. v. Cottman Trans. Sys., LLC, No. Civ. 05-2806(DSD/SRN), 2006 WL 1662892, at *4 (D. Minn. June 8, 2006).
134. Iowa Code § 614.1(5).

Michigan

Mark Burzych

I. Introduction

The Franchise Investment Law (Michigan Franchise Investment Law, the Act, or the MFIL) was enacted in 1974. Among franchise practitioners, the MFIL is considered both a disclosure and a relationship statute. The Act has not been updated since 1989 and does not reflect any changes as result of the significant revisions in 2007 to the Federal Trade Commission Franchise Rule, or any of the subsequent commentary published by the North American Securities Administrators Association (NASAA). The statute is generally cited as Michigan Compiled Laws sections 445.1501 through 445.1546, or Michigan Statutes Annotated sections 19.854(1) through 19.854(46). For the purposes of this chapter, it will be cited in the formal format, Michigan Compiled Laws.

The Michigan legislature stated the purpose of the MFIL is to "[R]egulate the offer, sale and purchase of franchises; to prohibit fraudulent practices in relation thereto; to prohibit pyramid and chain promotions;[1] to impose regulatory duties upon certain state departments and agencies; and to provide penalties."[2]

Several court decisions discuss the MFIL's purpose. In *In re: Dynamic Enterprises, Inc. v. Fitness World of Jackson*, the court found that, in general, the MFIL plays an important role in determining the rights and duties of parties to a franchise agreement in Michigan.[3] Courts have also found that the Act's purpose is to address perceived inequalities in the bargaining positions between the franchisor and franchisee.[4] A large majority of courts have found that the Act's

---

1. Michigan Franchise Investment Law, 1974 Mich. Pub. Acts 269 (defining a pyramid or chain promotion as any plan or scheme or device by which (a) a participant provides consideration for the right to receive compensation in return for inducing others to participate; or (b) a participant is entitled to receive compensation when he or she is able to induce others to cause additional parties to participate in the scheme). *See also* Phipps v. Ward, Bus. Franchise Guide (CCH) ¶ 10,357 (W.D. Mich. 1993).
2. 1974 Mich. Pub. Acts 269.
3. *In re* Dynamic Enters., Inc., 32 B.R. 509 (Bankr. Tenn. 1983); *see also* Gen. Aviation, Inc. v. The Cessna Aircraft Co., 915 F.2d 1038 (6th Cir. 1990).
4. Geib v. Amoco Oil Co., 29 F.3d 1050 (6th Cir. 1994).

clear purpose is to protect the public through this "fundamental public policy."[5] However, a few courts have reached a contrary result.[6]

II. Commentary

A. Definition of Franchise

To meet the MFIL's definition of a franchise, there must be a contract or agreement, whether express or implied, and whether oral or written, between two or more persons, to which each of three elements apply:

(1) A franchisee is granted the right to engage in the business of offering, selling, or distributing goods or services under a marketing plan or system prescribed in substantial part by a franchisor;
(2) A franchisee is granted the right to engage in the business of offering, selling, or distributing goods or services substantially associated with the franchisor's trademark, services mark, trade name, logotype, advertising, or other commercial symbol designating the franchisor or its affiliate; and
(3) The franchisee is required to pay, directly or indirectly, a franchise fee.[7]

A contract or agreement that does not possess all three of these elements is not a "franchise" under Michigan law and is thus not subject to the requirements imposed by the MFIL.[8]

"Whether a contract or agreement constitutes a franchise for purposes of the MFIL must be determined from the circumstances present at the time of the offer or sale," and "[s]ubsequent market developments cannot transform an agreement that was not subject to the MFIL at its inception into a franchise."[9]

In *Hamade v. Sunoco*, the Michigan Court of Appeals rejected a distributor's argument that market conditions occurring after it executed a distribution agreement with its supplier could create a franchise agreement.[10] The distributor argued the supplier's inventory quota was so high under the present market that it rendered his store illiquid, and thus established a franchise fee, a required element of a franchise under the MFIL. However, the court noted that such market conditions were not present "at the time of the offer or sale," which, the court held, is the relevant time for assessing whether an agreement constitutes a

---

5. The Maids Int'l, Inc. v. Saunders, Inc., 569 N.W.2d 857 (Mich. Ct. App. 1997); Martino v. Cottman Transmission Sys., 554 N.W.2d 17, 20 (Mich. Ct. App. 1996); Cherry Invs., Inc. v. Yogurt Ventures USA, Inc., No. 2:92-CV-72428, 1992 WL 12916473 (E.D. Mich. Nov. 16, 1992).

6. *See* Banek Inc. v. Yogurt Ventures U.S.A., Inc., 6 F.3d 357 (6th Cir. 1993); JRT Inc., v. TCBY Sys. Inc., No. LR- C-93-076, 1994 WL 17092057 (E.D. Ark. July 7, 1994); *see also* Cottman Transmission Sys., LLC v. Dale Kershner., 492 F. Supp. 2d 461, 468–69 (E.D. Pa. 2007) (stating in dictum that Michigan's franchise law is "not as strongly worded as Minnesota law and therefore did not evince public policy strong enough to void choice-of-law provisions").

7. Mich. Comp. Laws § 445.1502.

8. SPX Corp. v. Shop Equip. Specialists, Inc., No. 4:00cv 49, 2001 WL 36512993 (W.D. Mich. Mar. 28, 2001) ("Michigan law requires three general perquisites for the finding of a franchise.").

9. Hamade v. Sunoco, 721 N.W.2d 233, 243 (Mich. Ct. App. 2006).

10. *Id.*

franchise agreement.[11] Subsequent courts have cited this principle from *Hamade* to reject other arguments attempting to establish a franchise under the MFIL.[12] However, none of the Michigan courts have ruled on whether executed amendments to an agreement are considered when assessing whether a franchise was offered or sold under the MFIL.

1. Trademark Element

a. Commentary

As a core element of a franchise, the MFIL requires that the franchisee be granted the right to offer or sell services "substantially associated" with the franchisor's trademark.[13] The Michigan franchise regulations clarify that a business is "substantially associated" with the franchisor's trademark when "circumstances permit or require the franchisee to identify its business to its customers primarily under that trademark" or "to otherwise use the franchisor's mark in a manner likely to convey to the public that it is an outlet of or represents directly or indirectly the franchisor."[14] In naming factors that, among others, indicate a business of a franchisee is substantially associated with the franchisor's mark, the regulations include: "The identification of the franchisor's mark is utilized . . . to enhance the chances of the franchisee's success in respect to . . . the franchisor's products or services."[15]

The requirement that a franchise relationship be associated with the franchisor's marks serves to increase the goodwill of the franchisee's business, as well as that of the entire franchise system. The absence of a requirement that the purchaser identify the business with the seller's marks negates any argument that the relationship was a franchise. In *Joseph James v. Whirlpool Corp.*, for example, the plaintiffs owned an appliance parts distribution center that sold the equipment of several name brands.[16] The plaintiffs entered into an agreement with Whirlpool to distribute its parts (Whirlpool Agreement). In fact, a majority of the plaintiffs' business was selling the Whirlpool branded goods. The plaintiffs entered into a contract to sell the business to a third party, which was subject to Whirlpool's approval pursuant to the Whirlpool Agreement. Whirlpool rejected the proposed purchaser, and the plaintiffs sued, claiming the Whirlpool Agreement was a franchise under Michigan law, which forbade the franchisor from denying the transfer without good cause.[17] The court rejected

---

11. *Id.*
12. *See* Bye v. Nationwide Mut. Ins. Co., 733 F. Supp. 2d 805, 829 (E.D. Mich. 2010) (rejecting plaintiff's argument that a profit from selling his business to a new agent established a franchise fee because such profit occurred after the parties' agreement terminated); Kello v. Wireless Toyz Franchise, LLC, No. 299128, 2011 WL 5604685 (Mich. Ct. App. Nov. 17, 2011) (rejecting plaintiff's argument that there was an implied franchise created through the parties' subsequent course of dealing, though the court did not explain the nature of such "implied franchise").
13. MICH. COMP. LAWS § 445.1502.
14. MICH. ADMIN. CODE r. 445.101(5).
15. *Id.*
16. Joseph James v. Whirlpool Corp., 806 F. Supp. 835 (E.D. Mo. 1992).
17. *See* MICH. COMP. LAWS § 445.1527.

the plaintiffs' position, finding that, even though a majority of the plaintiffs' business involved the sale of the branded products, they also sold the branded parts of other major name brands. Instead, the plaintiffs "had [their] own independent identity separate from the many distributor lines that [they] carried."[18]

b. Annotations[19]

A subscription agreement between a car dealer and an internet referral service did not create a franchise within the meaning of the MFIL as argued by JDI, the purported franchisee, since the agreement did not require the dealer to distribute goods substantially associated with the purported franchisor's trademark. Rather than a franchise agreement, the agreement was as it was titled, a subscription agreement that allowed the dealer to fill internet orders.[20]

A "purchase option" agreement between plaintiff and defendant wherein the plaintiff had the right to purchase discount coupon books at wholesale for resale to the public was not a franchise because the agreement did not permit the plaintiff to use the defendant's marks.[21]

2. Franchise Fee Element

a. Commentary

The Act defines a "franchise fee" as [a] fee or charge that a franchisee or subfranchisor is required to pay or agrees to pay for the right to enter into a business under a franchise agreement, including but not limited to payments for goods and services. The following are not the payment of a franchise fee:

(a) The purchase or agreement to purchase goods, equipment, or fixtures directly or on consignment at a bona fide wholesale price.

(b) The payment of a reasonable service charge to the issuer of a credit card by an establishment accepting or honoring the credit card.

(c) Amounts paid to a trading stamp company by a person issuing trading stamps in connection with the retail sale of merchandise or service.

(d) Payments made in connection with the lease or agreement to lease of a franchised business operated by a franchisee on the premises of a franchisor as long as the franchised business is incidental to the business conducted by the franchisor at such premises.[22]

While courts have developed certain rules pertaining to specific types of alleged indirect franchise fees, some rules apply to all franchise fees, regardless of the alleged form. To constitute a franchise fee, there must generally be (1) a transfer of wealth from the alleged franchisee to the alleged franchisor, (2) it

---

18. *Joseph James*, 806 F. Supp. at 842.
19. The MFIL is not often litigated. The cases cited throughout reflect the current state of the law in Michigan as of the writing of this chapter.
20. Jerome-Duncan, Inc. v. Auto-by-Tel, LLC, 176 F.3d 904 (E.D. Mich. 1999).
21. Rzepka v. Michael, 431 N.W.2d 441 (Mich. Ct. App. 1988).
22. MICH. COMP. LAWS § 445.1503(1).

must be required under the parties' agreement, and (3) the fee is for the right to engage in the alleged franchisee's business.[23]

Initially, a franchise fee must involve some "transfer of wealth" from the alleged franchisee to the alleged franchisor.[24] In *Hamade*, the owner of a Sunoco gas station alleged he had paid indirect franchise fees to Sunoco, in part, through the cost of certain required improvements to its store.[25] However, the costs of the improvements were not paid to Sunoco, but instead were paid to the contractor who was hired to apply the improvements.[26] Thus, the court held that such payments could not have been franchise fees under the MFIL.

One example of when the necessary transfer of wealth from franchisee to franchisor is absent occurs when a "franchisee" repays a loan principal to a "franchisor."[27] In *Hamade*, a gas station owner alleged that it paid a franchise fee to Sunoco by repaying a loan.[28] However, the Michigan Court of Appeals held that such payments could not constitute a franchise fee because "repayment of a loan principal is not a transfer of wealth from the franchisee to the franchisor."[29] The payment of market-rate interest on a loan is also not a franchise fee. In *Boeve*, an insurance agent argued that receiving and paying on a loan from the insurance provider constituted a franchise fee.[30] There, the Federal Eastern District of Michigan, following the Michigan Court of Appeals' reasoning in *Hamade*, reiterated that repayment of a loan cannot be a franchise fee because it does not constitute "a necessary 'transfer of wealth'" and held that because the insurance agent only alleged franchise fees through her payment of "money and interest" to the insurance provider, she had not "alleged a specific payment she made which would constitute a 'franchise' fee."[31]

The language of the MFIL restricts potential franchise fees to payments that the franchisee is required to pay to the franchisor.[32] Thus, courts have rejected

---

23. *See* Hamade v. Sunoco, 721 N.W.2d 233 (Mich. Ct. App. 2006), Watkins & Son Pet Supplies v. Iams Co., No. 94-70379, 1995 WL 871235, at *4 (E.D. Mich. Apr. 5, 1995); MICH. ADMIN. CODE r. 445.101 (while defining "bona fide wholesale price," the regulation states, "[a] payment made directly or indirectly to *or for the benefit* of the franchisor in excess of the bona fide wholesale price constitutes a franchise fee") (emphasis added). It is possible, for example, that franchisee payments made to a supplier that pays kickbacks or rebates to a franchisor could constitute a franchise fee if the supplier charges more than a bona fide wholesale price.

24. *See Hamade*, 721 N.W.2d at 243; *see also* Implement Serv., Inc. v. Tecumseh Prods. Co., 726 F. Supp. 1171, 1179 (S.D. Ind. 1989) (interpreting Indiana law, "that the good or service must be rendered to the 'franchisor' in order to qualify as a franchise fee"); Boat & Motor Mart v. Sea Ray Boats, Inc., 825 F.2d 1285, 1289 (9th Cir. 1987) (referring generally to holdings of states interpreting the meaning of franchise fee, "Payments made to parties other than the franchisor have regularly been regarded as not constituting fees.").

25. *Hamade*, 721 N.W.2d at 243.

26. *Id.*

27. *See id.*; Boeve v. Nationwide Mut. Ins. Co, No. 08-CV-12213, 2008 WL 3915011 (E.D. Mich. Aug. 20, 2008).

28. *Hamade*, 721 N.W.2d at 246 (Mich. Cit. App. 2006).

29. *Id.*

30. *Boeve*, 2008 WL 3915011, at *5.

31. *Id.* at *6.

32. MICH. COMP. LAWS § 445.1502(2)(c).

allegations of franchise fees when the subject payments were not required under the parties' agreement.[33] In *Hamade*, the Michigan Court of Appeals held that a gas station owner's purchase of toys, signs, and other articles bearing Sunoco's trademark was not a franchise fee, in part, because the gas station owner could not show he was required to purchase such items.[34] Likewise, the *Hamade* court also rejected the gas station owner's argument that payment of a loan was a franchise fee, partially because there was no evidence that the owner was required to take the loan from Sunoco.[35]

Similarly, in *Bucciarelli*, an insurance agent elected to receive a loan from the insurance provider to finance his agency's start-up.[36] The Eastern District Court of Michigan held that because the parties' agreement did not require the agent to accept the loan (the agent could have financed starting his agency with different funds), it was not a franchise fee under the MFIL.[37]

"Under the plain language of the MFIL, a payment will not constitute a franchise fee unless the payment was for the right to enter into a business under a franchise agreement."[38] Courts have distinguished payments "for the right to do business," from payments that are merely "ordinary business expense[] incurred during the course of business."[39]

In *Watkins*, a distributor of pet supplies argued that it incurred a number of franchise fees under the MFIL pursuant to its agreement with its supplier, including (1) representing the distributor's products at dog and cat shows, (2) ensuring that retail customers rotated their stock of supplier's products, (3) engaging in certain sales promotions directed by the supplier, (4) preparing reports that tracked results of product promotions, (5) expanding warehouse facilities to comply with supplier's inventory requirements, and (6) installing a computer system to prepare paperwork and reports required by the supplier.[40] The Eastern District Court of Michigan rejected each of these expenses as a franchise fee because they were "easily classified as ordinary business expenses," even though a number of them were required expenses under the parties' agreement.[41] The court further clarified that none of the expenses were paid for the right to engage in business

---

33. *See* Hamade v. Sunoco, 721 N.W.2d 233, 243 (Mich. Cit. App. 2006), Bucciarelli v. Nationwide Mut. Ins. Co., 662 F. Supp. 2d 809, 818 (E.D. Mich. 2009).

34. *Hamade*, 721 N.W.2d at 243–44.

35. *Id.* at 246.

36. *Bucciarelli*, 662 F. Supp. 2d at 819.

37. *Id.*

38. Hamade v. Sunoco, 721 N.W.2d 233, 245–46 (Mich. Cit. App. 2006) (holding that repaying a loan was not a franchise fee, in part, because the "franchisee" accepting the loan was not a condition of entering into the parties' agreement).

39. Watkins & Son Pet Supplies v. Iams Co., No. 94-70379, 1995 WL 871235, at *4 (E.D. Mich. Apr. 5, 1995); *see also* Schultz v. Onan Corp., 737 F.2d 339 (8th Cir. 1984) (interpreting Minnesota law, "[t]he expenditure of funds for travel, lodging, food and other business expenses does not constitute a franchise fee").

40. *Watkins & Son*, 1995 WL 871235, at *3.

41. *Id.* at *4.

because none of them "constitute an unrecoverable firm-specific investment" that would have given the supplier "a superior bargaining position."[42]

When determining whether a franchise fee existed between parties, some courts have noted that franchise fees are usually paid when the relevant parties enter into their agreement.[43] In *Bye*, the Eastern District Court of Michigan rejected an insurance agent's theory that the insurance provider's profit from selling his book of business to a new insurance agent constituted a franchise fee.[44] There, "although the logic of this alleged business theory escape[d] the court," any profit the insurance provider would have made occurred after the parties' agreement ended, precluding it from being a franchise fee because, according to the court, a fee paid "for the right to enter into [an] agreement, [] of necessity would have to be paid at the inception of the agreement."[45] Similarly, the Eastern District Court in *Boeve* found that an insurance agent's payments to an insurance provider pursuant to a promissory note were not franchise fees in part because the note was executed two years after the parties' agency agreement.[46]

Although the Eastern District Court in *Bye* stated that a franchise fee would need to be paid at a franchise agreement's inception, such view arguably contradicts the franchise regulations' inclusion of deferred payments, royalty payments, and "payments as a condition to maintaining the franchise relationship" among other possible forms of franchise fees.[47] It also arguably contradicts situations where courts have analyzed whether payments for goods above the bona fide wholesale price or substantial and unrecoverable costs to receive training constituted franchise fees when those payments were not made at the agreements' inceptions.[48] However, the aforementioned courts' concerns with the timing of alleged franchise fees, relative to when the alleged franchisee began its business operations under the relevant agreement, suggest that timing is a factor in determining whether a particular payment was made for the right to engage in the business.

---

42. *Id.* (citing to Wright-Moore Corp. v. Ricoh Corp., 908 F.2d 128, 136 (7th Cir. 1990) (discussing how costs incurred in training can result in indirect franchise fees under Indiana franchise law because "[t]raining can be highly firm-specific. Technicians trained to services [franchisor's] copiers may not be able to service other copiers.").

43. *See* Bye v. Nationwide Mut. Ins. Co., 733 F. Supp. 2d 805 (E.D. Mich. 2010); SPX Corp. v. Shop Equip. Specialists, Inc., No. 4:00cv 49, 2001 WL 36512993, at *11 (W.D. Mich. Mar. 28, 2001) ("It is undisputed that, at the time the parties entered into the Service Center Agreement, no franchisee fee was paid.").

44. *Bye*, 733 F. Supp. 2d at 828.

45. *Id.* at 829.

46. Boeve v. Nationwide Mut. Ins. Co, No. 08-CV-12213, 2008 WL 3915011 (E.D. Mich. Aug. 20, 2008).

47. *See* MICH. ADMIN. CODE r. 445.101(2)(a) (emphasis added); *but see* Little Ceasars Enters. v. Dep't of Treasury, 575 N.W.2d 562 (Mich. Ct. App. 1997) (rejecting the franchise regulations' inclusion of royalty payments as franchise fees as being a "clearly wrong" interpretation of the MFIL).

48. *See* Kenaya Wireless, Inc. v. SSMJ, LLC, No. 281649, 2009 WL 763496 (Mich. Ct. App. Mar. 24, 2009); Watkins & Son Pet Supplies v. Iams Co., No. 94-70370, 1995 WL 871235, at *4 (E.D. Mich. Apr. 5, 1995).

Lastly, franchise fees may have to be payments for which the parties' know the amount at the time the agreement is entered into.[49] In *Little Caesars*, the Michigan Court of Appeals held that royalty payments were not "franchise fees" under the MFIL after consulting section 6 of the MFIL, which exempts from the MFIL's notice and disclosure requirements sales of franchises that require franchise fees of $500 or less.[50] According to the court, royalty payments are not franchise fees under the MFIL because, in part, with respect to the $500 exemption, "[i]f royalties are encompassed within the definition of 'franchise fee,' then a franchisor would be unable to determine whether the exemption applied because a franchisor cannot predict a prospective franchisee's royalties and thereby determine, with any certainty, whether the franchise fee exceeds $500."[51] Thus, franchise fees must arguably be those that the parties can determine with some degree of certainty will exceed $500.

Apart from the general franchise rules just discussed, the franchise regulations and courts have developed rules applicable to specific types of indirect franchise fees. These rules apply when an alleged franchise fee involves payments for training, purchasing goods at bona fide wholesale prices, and interest rates on loans taken from the putative franchisor.[52]

The MFIL and franchise regulations include payments made to receive training as potential franchise fees.[53] Under the franchise regulations, payments to a franchisor for services presumptively constitute franchise fees, and training is included among such services.[54] Thus, payments made for receiving training may potentially constitute a franchise fee.

However, "[t]raining expenses do not per se constitute an indirect franchise fee."[55] The Eastern District Court of Michigan has held that only payments for training that are "substantial and unrecoverable, locking the franchisee into the franchisor" are franchise fees.[56] At least one court has held that without such a limitation, "any distributor who spent money training its employees with regard to the products it distributed, and promoting, marketing, and stocking those products, would be a franchisee."[57] For example, in *Watkins*, an alleged franchisee listed several expenses that it argued constituted a franchise fee under a distributor agreement, including "sending its employees to training seminars conducted by [the alleged franchisor]."[58] Although the agreement generally required the alleged franchisee to pay such costs, the court found that it

---

49. *See Little Ceasars Enters.*, 575 N.W.2d 562.
50. *Id.* at 630.
51. *Id.*
52. *See* Watkins & Son Pet Supplies v. Iams Co., No. 94-70379, 1995 WL 871235, at *4 (E.D. Mich. Apr. 5, 1995), Kenaya Wireless, Inc. v. SSMJ, LLC, 2009 WL 763496 (Mich. Ct. App. 2009).
53. MICH. COMP. LAWS § 445.1503; MICH. ADMIN. CODE r. § 445.101.
54. MICH. ADMIN. CODE r. § 445.101(2)(c).
55. *Watkins & Son Pet Supplies*, 1995 WL 871235, at *4.
56. *Id.* at 4; *see also* Live Cryo, LLC v. CryoUSA Import & Sales, LLC, No. 17-CV-11888, 2017 WL 4098853 (E.D. Mich. Sept. 15, 2017) (training fee was likely not a franchise fee when the amount was only $250, and thus likely not substantial and unrecoverable).
57. *Watkins & Son Pet Supplies*, 1995 WL 871235, at *4.
58. *Id.* at *3.

did not create a franchise fee because the alleged franchisee failed to show "that the costs were so substantial as to lock it into the franchisor."[59] In *Tractor and Farm Supply, Inc.*,[60] on the other hand, the court applied the MFIL when it found that, even though the plaintiff did not pay a fee called a "franchisee fee," it paid for employee training, online computer services, and advertising and that these payments rose to the level of a franchisee fee.[61] In making its ruling, the court delved into the administrative interpretations of the MFIL, at Rule 445.101(2)(c) of the Michigan Administrative Code Rule, in which the Michigan Attorney General stated that:

> [T]he words "fee or charge". . . include, but are not limited to: . . . payments for services. These payments are presumed to be in part for the right granted to the franchisee to engage in the franchise business.

The MFIL explicitly excludes from the definition of "franchise fee" purchases or agreements to purchase "goods, equipment, or fixtures directly or on consignment at a bona fide wholesale price."[62] The franchise regulations further develop this exclusion by clarifying that "bona fide wholesale price," "refers to a price which constitutes a fair payment for goods purchased at a comparable level of distribution, and no part of which constitutes a payment for the right to enter into, or continue in, the franchise business."[63] Under the franchise regulations, such goods sold at a bona fide wholesale price may include (but are not limited to) "goods sold to the franchisee for resale, . . . equipment, . . . supplies, and other goods used by the franchisee in the conduct of the franchise business."[64] To determine whether the price of such goods, equipment, or supplies is a bona fide wholesale price, the regulations encourage courts to consider "relevant cost, marketing, pricing, or payment information, among other factors."[65]

In *Bucciarelli v. Nationwide*, an insurance agent alleged that it paid franchise fees by purchasing certain office furniture and supplies.[66] Although the Eastern District of Michigan allowed the agent to proceed to discovery, it noted that it was doubtful such supplies were purchased above a bona fide wholesale price, and so it was unlikely those payments were franchise fees.[67]

Charging for "out-of-pocket" costs with regard to certain goods falls under the "bona fide wholesale price" exception to franchise fees under the MFIL.[68] In *Kenaya Wireless*, a supplier of wireless phones entered into an Independent Retail

---

59. *Id.*
60. Tractor & Farm Supply, Inc. v. Ford New Holland, 898 F. Supp. 1198 (W.D. Ky. 1995).
61. *See Watkins & Son Pet Supplies*, 1995 WL 871235, at *4 (holding that for an expense to qualify as a franchise fee, it must be substantial and unrecoverable).
62. MICH. COMP. LAWS § 445.1503.
63. MICH. ADMIN. CODE r. 445.101(6).
64. *Id.*
65. *Id.*
66. Bucciarelli v. Nationwide Mut. Ins. Co., 662 F. Supp. 2d 809 (E.D. Mich. 2009).
67. *Id.* at 818.
68. *See* Kenaya Wireless, Inc. v. SSMJ, LLC, No. 281649, 2009 WL 763496 (Mich. Ct. App. Mar. 24, 2009).

Partner and License Agreement with the plaintiff.[69] Pursuant to such agreement, plaintiff-licensee purchased from the defendant numerous cell phones for $105/phone, which defendant had purchased from the manufacturer at a price of $95/phone.[70] However, defendant testified that the minimal mark-up on each phone was to cover defendant's "shipping and general overhead expenses, including rent, insurance, handling charges and labor costs."[71] Because plaintiff could produce no evidence to the contrary, the Michigan Court of Appeals held that the price paid for the cell phones was not a franchise fee because plaintiff's costs were a "fair payment for goods purchased at a comparable level of distribution."[72] In *SPX Corporation v. Shop Equipment Specialists, Inc., aka Shop Equipment Service, Inc.*,[73] the court decided that the mere fact that a purchaser paid an "inflated" price (over the bona fide wholesale price) for its equipment did not create a franchise fee, because the nexus between the price paid and the statutory franchise fee definition was too vague and conclusory to raise a triable issue of fact. In *Laethem Equipment Co. v Deere & Co.*,[74] the court found that the franchisee's payment of costs for services (as opposed to goods as used in the MFIL) that the franchisor delivered could be deemed a franchise fee even though they were charged at a wholesale or "cost" basis to the franchisee.[75] [76]

When an alleged franchisee pays an amount exceeding the alleged franchisor's actual costs, a court may find that such payment is a franchise fee because it is more than the bona fide wholesale price.[77] For example, in *Lofgren v. Canada*, the franchisor charged the franchisee for certain upgraded equipment necessary for delivering new services franchisor began offering. Particularly, the franchisor invoiced the franchisee $20,000 for equipment that cost the franchisor $13,500.[78] The Eastern District Court of Michigan found that because the franchisee was charged more for the equipment than what the franchisor paid, the cost of the equipment was "at or above bona fide wholesale prices for the same goods."[79] This case suggests that any time a party derives a profit by charging

---

69. *Id.* at *1.
70. *Id.*
71. *Id.* at *2.
72. *Id.*
73. SPX Corp. v. Shop Equip. Specialists, Inc., No. 4:00CV 49, 2001 WL 36512993 (W.D. Mich. Mar. 28, 2001).
74. Laethem Equip. Co. v. Deere & Co., No. 05-10113, 2008 WL 4056359 (E.D. Mich. Aug. 26, 2008).
75. JJCO v. Isuzu Motors, No. 08-00419 SOM/LEK, 2009 WL 1444103 (D. Haw. May 22, 2009) ("*Laethem* relied on a rule promulgated by the Michigan Attorney General, providing: The words 'fee or charge' . . . include, but are not limited to: . . . payments for services. These payments are presumed to be in part for the right granted to the franchisee to engage in the franchise business.") (citing MICH. ADMIN. CODE r. 445.101(2)(c)); *see also Laethem Equip. Co.*, 2008 WL 4056359.
76. Shaheen Hyundai Motors, Inc. v. Hyundai Motor Am., No. 1-92-CV-327, 1993 WL 13937614 (W.D. Mich. Sept. 17, 1993) (holding that an automobile dealership was not a franchise within the meaning of the act because the dealer never paid a franchise fee, directly or indirectly, to the manufacture).
77. *See* Lofgren v. AirTrona Canada, No. 2:13-13622, 2016 WL 25977 (E.D. Mich. Jan. 4, 2016).
78. *Id.* at *8.
79. *Id.*

franchisees for goods, that party runs the risk of deriving a "franchise fee" for purposes of the MFIL.

Interest payments on a loan paid to a franchisor may constitute franchise fees if the interest rate exceed fair market value.[80]

In *Bucciarelli*, the Eastern District of Michigan rejected an insurance agent's argument that her interest payments on a loan she claimed to have been required to take from the insurance provider constituted a franchise fee. *Id.* at 819. In so holding, the court stated, "there are no allegations . . . that the interest payable on the loan exceeded a fair market rate, and therefore the loan itself cannot constitute a franchise fee."[81]

b. Annotations

The plaintiff bought a franchise from a sales representative of the franchisor company's predecessor. The sales representative, representing the franchisor, subsequently approached the plaintiff with a new business model involving new technologies. The court found that a new franchise agreement was created after the original sale as evidenced by an invoice from the franchisor company sent to the plaintiff that stated the later agreement was for "1 Franchise Michigan location" and that the plaintiff had paid a franchise fee as a result of being charged more than the value of the equipment that neither the sales representative nor franchisor company could account for.[82]

In a lease between an optometrist and manufacturers of prescription lenses, where the tenant-optometrist paid a percentage of rent based upon sales of services, the mere payment of rent was not a payment of a franchise fee within the meaning of the statute.[83]

The purported franchisee's payments for employee training, an online computer service, and the use of the franchisor's advertising, promotion, and sales materials rose to the level of a franchisee fee within the MFIL.[84]

A "purchase option" agreement between plaintiff and defendant, whereby the plaintiff had the right to purchase discount coupon books at wholesale for resale to the public, was not a franchise. Though the plaintiff would have liked the transaction to be considered a franchise, the court refused the invitation by finding that the agreement did not require the payment of a franchise fee.[85]

Plaintiff never paid a direct franchise fee, and the court found that the purported franchisee's requirements to both make payments for replacement parts

---

80. *See* Hamade v. Sunoco, 721 N.W.2d 233, 246 (2006) ("[T]he payment of interest in excess of a fair market rate on a loan that the franchisor required of the franchisee might arguably constitute the indirect payment of a franchise fee."); Boeve v. Nationwide Mut. Ins. Co, No. 08-CV-12213, 2008 WL 3915011 (E.D. Mich. Aug. 20, 2008) ("Interest payments 'might arguably' constitute the indirect payment of a franchise fee if the interest rate exceeded a fair market loan rate."); Bucciarelli v. Nationwide Mut. Ins. Co., 662 F. Supp. 2d 809 (E.D. Mich. 2009).

81. *Id.*

82. Lofgren v. AirTrona Canada, 677 Fed. App'x 1002 (6th Cir. 2017).

83. Galper v. U.S. Shoe Corp., 815 F. Supp. 1037 (E.D. Mich. 1993).

84. Tractor & Farm Supply, Inc. v. Ford, Inc., 898 F. Supp. 1198 (W.D. Ky. 1995).

85. Rzepka v. Michael, 431 N.W.2d 441 (Mich. Ct. App. 1988).

during off seasons and to maintain a continuous 45-day stock of inventory were not an indirect franchise fee under the MFIL.[86]

A franchisee's payment of costs for services delivered by the franchisor could be deemed a franchise fee even though such services were charged at a wholesale or "cost" basis to the franchisee, because the MFIL's bona fide wholesale price exception only applies to "goods," not services.[87]

An insurance agent's allegations that he was required to purchase overpriced used furniture and equipment from his insurance company principal was sufficient to allege the franchise fee element, thereby surviving a motion for judgment on the pleadings. In the same matter, however, the court also found that the payments of principal and interest on a loan made by the agent to the insurance company principal did not constitute a franchise fee even though the insurance company allegedly induced the agent to undertake the loan.[88]

A gasoline service station operator's agreement with distributor was not a "franchise" for purposes of MFIL because the operator was not required to pay, directly or indirectly, a franchise fee; mandatory minimum gasoline purchases did not constitute "franchise fee," absent a showing that the purchases made were in excess of a bona fide wholesale price.[89]

3. Community of Interest; Significant Degree of Control; Joint Marketing Plan

a. Commentary

The Michigan franchise regulations clarify that "[a] marketing plan may be determined to be prescribed if the franchise or other written or oral agreement, the nature of the franchise business, or other circumstances permit or require the franchisee to follow an operating plan or standard operating procedure, or their substantial equivalent, promulgated by or for the franchisor."[90] "An operating plan or standard operating procedure includes required procedures, prohibitions against certain business practices, or recommended or offered practices, whether or not enforceable with economic sanctions."[91]

The Eastern District Court of Michigan has turned to Black's Law Dictionary to define "prescribe" and has applied it to the MFIL.[92] In *Vaughn*, for example, the Eastern District Court noted that, according to Black's Law Dictionary (6th ed), "prescribe" means "[t]o lay down authoritatively as a guide, direction, or rule; to impose as a peremptory order; to dictate; to point, to direct; to give as a guide, direction, or rule of action; to give law. To direct; define; mark out."[93]

---

86. James v. Whirlpool Corp., 806 F. Supp. 835 (E.D. Mo. 1992).
87. Laethem Equip. Co. v. Deere & Co., No. 05-10113, 2008 WL 4056359 (E.D. Mich. Aug. 26, 2008).
88. Bucciarelli v. Nationwide Mutual Ins., 662 F. Supp. 2d 809 (E.D. Mich. 2009).
89. Partner & Partner, Inc. v. ExxonMobil Oil Corp., 326 Fed. Appx. 892 (6th Cir. 2009).
90. MICH. ADMIN. CODE r. 445.101(4).
91. *Id.*
92. *See, e.g.*, Vaughn v. Digital Message Sys. Corp., No. 96-CV-70533-DT, 1997 WL 115821 (E.D. Mich. Mar. 10, 1997); Buist v. Digital Message Sys. Corp., No. 229256, 2002 WL 31957703 (Mich. Ct. App. Dec. 27, 2002).
93. *Vaughn*, 1997 WL 115821, at *4.

The *Buist* court, in agreeing with Vaughn's use of that definition, further noted that because the MFIL is a "remedial" statute, it should be construed liberally to achieve its intended goals.[94] Accordingly, the *Buist* court concluded that "prescribe," as used in the MFIL, "encompasses a situation in which a franchisee follows a set marketing plan developed by the franchisor because that plan was [1] proffered as a suggested guide . . . as well as [2] one in which the franchisee was specifically required to adopt the franchisor's marketing plan."[95] In *Vaughn*, the court explained how strongly recommending guidelines for selling a product pursuant to a license agreement could constitute a prescription, and thus create a franchise.[96]

When determining whether a marketing plan or system was prescribed, courts will consider any relevant portion of the parties' contract; no one single item or contractual provision dispositively establishes a prescribed marketing plan or system.[97]

Under the franchise regulations, one factor indicating a prescribed marketing plan or system is "representations by, or requirements of, the franchisor that the franchisor aid or assist the franchisee . . . in marketing the franchisor's products or service."[98]

The Eastern District of Michigan has found that providing advertising materials and reserving ultimate control over such materials is a factor supporting a finding of a prescribed marketing plan or system.[99] In *Buist* and *Vaughn*, licensees were provided the right to sell messaging while on-hold systems to certain distributors. The Eastern District Court of Michigan found relevant that the supplier both "reserve[d] the right to approve all promotional and advertising methods and materials" and agreed to provide all marketing materials and certain marketing supplies to the distributor.[100] According to the court, the aforementioned provisions, taken together with other relevant provisions identified later, "make it perfectly clear that, under MFIL and its regulations," licensor prescribed in substantial part a marketing plan or system for licensees.[101]

Similarly, the Eastern District Court of Michigan in *Lofgren v. AirTrona Canada* found a prescribed marketing plan or system, in part, from a franchisor requiring a franchisee to purchase a van that exhibited franchisor's trademarks and, at one point, asking for franchisee's list of customers to send out promotional materials.[102]

Finally, the Eastern District Court of Michigan has identified factors as "helpful" in determining whether a marketing system or plan had been prescribed in

---

94. *Buist*, 2002 WL 31957703, at *5.
95. *Id.* at *6.
96. *Vaughn*, 1997 WL 115821, at *4.
97. *See* MICH. ADMIN. CODE r. 445.101(4) (considering the nature and circumstances surrounding the business and contract, as well as factors that may, among others, indicate a prescribed marketing plan or system).
98. *Id.*
99. *See, e.g., Vaughn*, 1997 WL 115821; *Buist*, 2002 WL 31957703.
100. *Buist*, 2002 WL 31957703, at *7; *Vaughn*, 1997 WL 115821, at *6.
101. *Vaughn*, 1997 WL 115821, at *6.
102. *See* Lofgren v. AirTrona Canada, 2016 WL 25977 (E.D. Mich. Jan. 4, 2016).

substantial part. Those factors include a franchisee advertising the franchisor's business.[103]

Also relevant are any contractual provisions that "require the franchisee to follow an operating plan or standard operating procedure" involving certain mandatory procedures or prohibited practices.[104] One indication of a prescribed marketing plan or procedure under the franchise regulations includes:

> Representations by, or requirements of, the franchisor that the franchisee follow an operating plan, standard procedure, training manual, or its substantial equivalent promulgated by the franchisor in the operation of the franchise, violations of which may, under the terms of the agreement, permit the franchisor to terminate or refuse to renew the agreement.[105]

In *Buist* and *Vaughn*, the Eastern District Court of Michigan found a prescribed marketing plan or system in part because the parties' contract provided that the franchisor would provide franchisee with a "training/operating manual."[106] The *Buist* court additionally noted that franchisee was required to "at all times . . . abide by such reasonable rules, regulations and policies as the [Licensor] may from time to time establish."[107]

In *Lofgren v. Canada*, the court found that a franchisor requiring franchisee to report weekly sales numbers was probative to the question of whether a prescribed marketing plan or system existed.[108]

The Eastern District Court of Michigan has also looked to factors laid out by the Second Circuit when considering whether a relationship constituted a franchise.[109] Among those factors were the franchisor's control over the franchisee's hours and days of operation, lighting at the franchisee's place of business, and the requirement by the franchisor that the franchisee's employees wear uniforms. According to the *Jerome-Duncan* court, "[t]he key element [of a franchise] is control over a large majority of the franchisee's day-to-day operations."[110] There, the alleged franchisor owned a website directing car purchasers to car dealerships and the alleged franchisee was a Ford dealership in the Detroit area; the parties agreement gave the website control over:

- Specific guidelines of when dealerships could contact customers,
- What the dealers should say in those encounters, and
- The length of time that offers of prices must stay open.

---

103. Jerome-Duncan, Inc. v. Auto-By-Tel, LLC, 989 F. Supp. 838 (E.D. Mich. 1997).
104. MICH. ADMIN. CODE r. 445.101(4).
105. *Id.* r. 445.101(4)(ii).
106. *Buist*, 2002 WL 31957703, at *7, *Vaughn*, 1997 WL 115821, at *6.
107. *Buist*, 2002 WL 31957703, at *7.
108. Lofgren v. AirTrona Canada, No. 2:13-cv-13622, 2016 WL 25977 (E.D. Mich. May 12, 2016).
109. Jerome-Duncan, Inc. v. Auto-By-Tel, LLC, 989 F. Supp. 838 (E.D. Mich. 1997).
110. *Id.*

The court concluded that the putative franchisor in that case did not have the "key element" of control.[111] The *Jerome-Duncan* court also identified certain factors as relevant to the question of whether a franchisor exerted sufficient control to determining whether a franchise relationship existed. These include whether the franchisor offers to provide financial support; has the right to audit the franchisee's books; has the right to inspect the franchisee's business premises; and can issue sales quotas.

A franchisor supplying a franchisee with supplies used in its daily operations is also probative of a prescribed marketing plan or system.[112] For example, in *Buist* and *Vaughn*, the Eastern District Court of Michigan found a marketing plan or system, in part, because the franchisor would provide the franchisee with all supplies, reasonable quantities of selling supplies, brochures, demonstration tapes, supply order/price forms, and such other materials as the supplier would make available from time to time.[113]

Training a franchisee or assisting the franchisee in training its employees indicates a marketing plan or system was prescribed in substantial part.[114] In *Buist* and *Vaughn*, the Eastern District Court of Michigan found a marketing plan or system in part because the franchisor supplied the franchisee with a training/operating manual.[115] Similarly, in *Lofgren*, the Eastern District Court of Michigan found a prescribed marketing plan or system, in part, because the franchisor provided franchisee the technical training necessary to run the business and promised franchisee training in sales techniques.[116]

The franchise regulations provide that an operating plan may include certain recommended practices.[117] Among such practices commonly cited by courts as being probative of a prescribed marketing plan or system is setting or recommending prices that a franchisee will charge customers for the relevant services.[118] For example, in *Buist* and *Vaughn*, the franchisor provided franchisee with order/price forms and up-to-date pricing products that the distributor was selling.[119] Similarly, the franchisor in *Lofgren* "prescribed, or at least suggested" the prices that the franchisee would charge customers for its services.[120] Finally, the Eastern District of Michigan in *Jerome-Duncan* noted that one of the helpful

---

111. *Id.*
112. *See, e.g.,* Vaughn v. Digital Message Sys. Corp., No. 96-CV-70533-DT, 1997 WL 115821 (E.D. Mich. Mar. 10, 1997); *Buist,* 2002 WL 31957703; *Lofgren,* 2016 WL 25977.
113. *Buist,* 2002 WL 31957703, at *7; *Vaughn,* 1997 WL 115821, at *6.
114. *See* MICH. ADMIN. CODE r. 445.101(4) (Listing "[r]epresentations by, or requirements of, the franchisor that the franchisor aid or assist the franchisee in training" as an indication of a prescribed marketing plan or system").
115. *Buist,* 2002 WL 31957703, at *7; *Vaughn,* 1997 WL 115821, at *6.
116. *See Lofgren,* 2016 WL 25977.
117. MICH. ADMIN. CODE r. 445.101(4).
118. *See Vaughn,* 1997 WL 115821; *Buist,* 2002 WL 31957703; *Lofgren,* 2016 WL 25977; Jerome-Duncan, Inc. v. Auto-By-Tel, LLC, 989 F. Supp. 838 (E.D. Mich. 1997).
119. *Buist,* 2002 WL 31957703, at *7; *Vaughn,* 1997 WL 115821, at *6.
120. *See Lofgren,* 2016 WL 25977.

factors in determining whether a marketing plan or system had been prescribed was whether a franchisor had control over the setting of franchisee's prices.[121]

b. Annotations

The authority to offer (but not sell) insurance plans for sale to the public by an insurance agent was sufficient for finding a marketing plan existed. The court found that even though the agent could not bind the insurance company and was, in some sense, a mere order taker, the MFIL should be read broadly to include relationships where the franchisee solicits insurance business with the intent and expectation that the insurance company will accept the client.[122]

A subscription agreement between a car dealer and an internet referral service did not create a franchise within the meaning of the MFIL as the agreement did not require the dealer to conform to a marketing plan or system and the referral service did not have any meaningful control over the day-to-day operation of the business.[123]

A multiline appliance parts distributorship was not a "franchise" within the meaning of the MFIL in part because the business was not subject to any meaningful marketing plan or system created by the manufacturer as distributor was also a distributor of other parts.[124]

A "purchase option" agreement between plaintiff and defendant wherein the plaintiff had the right to purchase discount coupon books at wholesale for resale to the public was not a franchise because it did not provide a marketing plan or system as required by the MFIL.[125]

A plaintiff bought a franchise from a sales representative of the franchisor company's predecessor then later the sales representative now representing the franchisor, approached the plaintiff with a new business model involving new technologies. The court found that while the franchisee had relative day-to-day autonomy the franchisor still prescribed a marketing plan that the plaintiff relied on for training, business and equipment, and business relationships to sustain the upgraded business model. Further, the new franchise sanitization technology and process was materially different from the original marketing plan under which plaintiff operated and was considered a new franchise instead of an extension of the past franchise relationship.[126]

B. Scope and Jurisdiction

1. Commentary

The Act applies to all such arrangements that meet the definition of a "franchise," including but not limited to (1) franchise agreements; (2) contracts for the sale of goods or services; (3) leases and mortgages or real or personal

---

121. *Jerome-Duncan*, 989 F. Supp. 838.
122. Bucciarelli v. Nationwide Mutual Ins., 662 F. Supp. 2d 809 (E.D. Mich. 2009).
123. Jerome-Duncan, Inc. v. Auto-by-Tel, LLC, 176 F.3d 904 (E.D. Mich. 1999).
124. James v. Whirlpool, 806 F. Supp. 835 (E.D. Mo. 1992).
125. Rzepka v. Michael, 431 N.W.2d 441 (Mich. Ct. App. 1988).
126. Lofgren v. AirTrona Canada, No. 16-1804, 2017 WL 384876 (6th Cir. Jan. 27, 2017).

property; (4) promises to pay; (5) security interests; (6) pledges; (7) insurance;[127] (8) advertising; (9) construction or installation contracts; (10) servicing contracts; and (11) all other arrangements in which the franchisor has an interest. An offer or sale is made in Michigan: (1) when the offer to sell is made in the state; (2) if the prospective purchaser is domiciled in the state; or (3) if the business will be operated in the state.

In *Joseph James, Darrell Woods and St. Louis Appliance Parts, Inc. v. Whirlpool Corp.*,[128] the court, applying Michigan law, found that an appliance dealership was not a franchise because the written distributorship agreement: (1) characterized it as a "distributorship"; (2) did not contain the word "franchise" or its derivatives; (3) failed to describe a marketing plan or system by which the plaintiff was to operate; (4) failed to require the plaintiffs to pay a direct or indirect franchise fee; and (5) did not require or permit defendant to have significant control over plaintiffs' operations. In *Khamis v. Atlas Oil Co.*,[129] a franchise relationship was found where a purported franchisee entered into a Product Supply Agreement with one party, wherein the purported franchisee agreed to follow a third party's operating conditions and appearance standards.

Remarkably, the MFIL did not apply to a contract that had been negotiated and signed in Indiana between parties domiciled in Indiana, even though the franchise would be located in Michigan.[130]

2. Annotations

A contract was not subject to the Act when it was not made in Michigan, neither party was domiciled in Michigan and the business was not located in Michigan.[131]

The MFIL did not apply to a contract negotiated and then signed in Indiana between parties domiciled in that state. There was, therefore, no offer, sale, or acceptance "made in this state," even though the franchise was located in Michigan.[132]

C. Termination

1. What Constitutes Termination or Cancellation

a. Commentary

The Act prohibits a franchisor from terminating a franchise prior to the expiration of its term except for good cause.[133] Good cause is defined as the failure of the franchisee to comply with any lawful provision of the franchise agreement

---

127. *Bucciarelli*, 662 F. Supp. 2d 809.
128. *James*, 806 F. Supp. 835.
129. Khamis v. Atlas Oil Co., No. 04-CV-73750, 2015 WL 2319001 (E.D. Mich. Sept. 21, 2015).
130. Hacienda Mexican Rests. v. Hacienda Franchise Grp., 489 N.W.2d 108 (Mich. Ct. App. 1992).
131. Ward's Equip., Inc., v. New Holland N. Am., Inc., 254 S.E.2d 516 (Va. 1997).
132. *Hacienda*, 489 N.W.2d 108.
133. MICH. COMP. LAWS § 445.1527(c).

and the failure to cure that default after at least 30 days' written notice.[134] Thus, once a franchisor (1) provides a franchisee written notice of default, (2) provides a reasonable opportunity to cure, and (3) the franchisee fails to cure the default, termination is permitted under the Act.

b. Annotations

While no Michigan cases have discussed constructive termination under the MFIL, *TRBR, Inc v. Americredit* discussed constructive termination in the context of the Michigan Motor Vehicle Franchise Act.[135] TRBR alleged that requirements to continue a particular discount constituted constructive termination of a "dealer agreement" under the Motor Vehicle Franchise Act because it caused TRBR's sales to decline. In response to this, the court said "Plaintiffs cite to authorities outside this jurisdiction that have recognized constructive termination of franchise agreements in other states. But Plaintiffs do not identify any authority to support this constructive termination theory under the Michigan Motor Vehicle Franchise Act or Michigan law generally. (Plaintiffs do cite to several employment cases addressing constructive termination, but this Court will not venture to expand the application of the Michigan Motor Vehicle Franchise Act by analogy to employment disputes—that is a question for Michigan law for Michigan Courts.)"[136]

In *Marathon Petroleum Co., Ltd. Partnership v. Future Fuels of America, Ltd. Liability Co.*, the Eastern District of Michigan stated, "The Sixth Circuit has recognized a cause of action under the PMPA for the constructive termination of a franchise."[137]

2. Restrictions on Termination or Cancellation

a. Commentary

Pursuant to the Act, any provision of a franchise agreement that permits a franchisor to terminate without good cause is void and unenforceable.[138] A franchisor cannot unilaterally terminate or fail to renew its franchisee's contract in the absence of good faith legitimate reason which would be uniformly applied across the entire franchise system.[139] Moreover, termination of a franchisee is not permissible if based solely upon an extreme downturn of the market.[140]

---

134. *Id.*
135. TRBR, Inc v. Americredit, No. 20-11269, 2021 U.S. Dist. LEXIS 57959, at *24 (E.D. Mich. Mar. 26, 2021).
136. *Id.* (citations omitted).
137. Marathon Petroleum Co., Ltd. P'ship v. Future Fuels of Am., Ltd. Liab. Co., No. 10-14068, 2012 U.S. Dist. LEXIS 71814, at *6 (E.D. Mich. May 23, 2012); *see also* Clark v. BP Oil Co., 137 F.3d 390–91 (6th Cir. 1998) (finding that constructive termination PMPA claim arose where the franchisor breached the franchise agreement).
138. MICH. COMP. LAWS § 445.1527(c).
139. Gen. Aviation, Inc. v. The Cessna Aircraft Co., 915 F.2d 1038 (6th Cir. 1990).
140. Karl Wendt Farm Equip. v. Int'l Harvester Co., 931 F.2d 1112 (6th Cir. 1991).

In *7-Eleven, Inc. v. CJ-Grand, LLC*,[141] the convenience store franchisor brought an action against a franchisee seeking declaratory judgment that the franchisor was entitled to terminate the franchise agreement in accordance with the termination provision. Specifically, the franchise agreement stated that the franchisee could be immediately terminated, without opportunity to cure, if the franchisee received a fourth breach notice within two years of the first breach notice's delivery, regardless of if any of the prior breaches were cured. Although the franchise agreement allowed termination after four breaches, this franchisee committed ten. The court noted that "the MFIL has been drafted broadly compared to a number of other statutes which proscribe specific situations which constitute 'good cause'" and held that 7-Eleven's four-strikes provision satisfied the MFIL's good cause requirement. In so holding, the court listed some of the other material breaches that would have satisfied the good cause requirement, such as: failing to properly maintain the store premises; discontinuing using franchisor issued video recording equipment without prior written consent; failing to comply with inventory requirements and foodservice standards; failing to maintain required minimum net worth; and failing to record or submit cash reports and other financial records.[142]

b. Annotations

Under the Michigan Farm and Utility Equipment Act, MCL 445.1457a(1), which provides, "[a] supplier shall not terminate, cancel, fail to renew, or substantially change the competitive circumstances of an agreement without good cause," it was considered a wrongful termination for a franchisor of farm equipment to unilaterally terminate a dealer agreement based solely upon an extreme downturn of the market. Such market downturn cannot be viewed as a permissible reason to terminate the contract under the theory of impracticability of performance.[143]

3. Notice Requirement

a. Commentary

To terminate under an enforceable termination provision for good cause requires the franchisor to provide the franchisee written notice of termination, specifying the franchisee's default and providing an opportunity to cure, which need not be more than 30 days.[144]

In *Rockne's Inc. v. Dan Mazzola, Inc.* (In re Dan Mazzola, Inc.),[145] a franchisor sent numerous memos to all locations informing them of an E. coli recall of the supplier's romaine lettuce and directed all franchisees to cease serving and immediately discard the contaminated lettuce. Defendant franchisee continued

---

141. 7-Eleven, Inc. v. CJ-Grand, LLC, 517 F. Supp. 3d 688 (E.D. Mich. 2021).
142. *Id.* at 693.
143. *Karl Wendt*, 931 F.2d 1112.
144. Mich. Comp. Laws § 445.1527(c).
145. Rockne's Inc. v. Dan Mazzola, Inc., No. 19-8007, 2020 Bankr. LEXIS 238, at *12 (B.A.P. 6th Cir. Jan. 28, 2020).

to serve the lettuce despite the franchisor's notice. A few months after the franchisee's service of the contaminated lettuce, the franchisor terminated the franchisee without notice or opportunity to cure pursuant, in part, to the franchise agreement provision which stated, "Franchisor may, at its option, terminate this Agreement . . . without affording Franchisee any opportunity to cure the default, effective immediately upon notice by Franchisor to Franchisee, upon the occurrence of any of the following events: . . . If a threat or danger to public health or safety results from the construction, maintenance, or operation of the Franchised Business." Although this case addressed a bankruptcy dispute, the court held that the termination without notice was improper. A franchisor can only terminate a franchisee immediately and without notice or an opportunity to cure for their use of potentially contaminated lettuce if the danger to the public health and safety was ongoing.[146]

However, termination does not require an opportunity to cure if the reason underlying termination is good cause under the statute. MCL 445.1527(c) provides that the following provision in a Franchise Agreement is void and unenforceable: "[a] provision that permits a franchisor to terminate a franchise prior to the expiration of its term except for good cause. Good cause shall include the failure of the franchisee to comply with any lawful provision of the Franchise Agreement and to cure such failure after being given written notice thereof and a reasonable opportunity, which in no event need be more than 30 days, to cure such failure."[147] In *7-Eleven, Inc. v. CJ-Grand, LLC*[148] the court considered a franchisor's termination of a franchisee under a franchise agreement "four strikes" default provision, that provided that "the franchise could be terminated, immediately and without any opportunity to cure, if after the [franchisee] received three separate notices of breaches of the [franchise] agreement, a fourth notice of breach was delivered within two years after delivery of the first breach notice, regardless whether any of the breaches were cured."[149] The court found that a franchisor could terminate without notice or an opportunity to cure so long as the franchisor had good cause to terminate. "Certainly, a Franchise Agreement that allows termination for a single breach that remains uncured for 30 days after notice would fall within the [MFIL]'s safe harbor. But that does not mean other provisions also could not satisfy the good-cause requirement. In both an ordinary grammatical sense, and in customary legislative use, '[t]he word "includes" is usually a term of enlargement, and not of limitation.'"[150] Court held that the four strikes provision satisfied the good cause requirement, as that provision was clearly intended to address the problem of serial breaches.[151]

b. Annotations

Not applicable.

---

146. *Id.*
147. MICH. COMP. LAWS § 445.1527(c).
148. 7-Eleven, Inc. v. CJ-Grand, LLC, 517 F. Supp. 3d 688, 693 (E.D. Mich. 2021).
149. *Id.* at 691.
150. *Id.* at 694.
151. *Id.*

4. Grounds for Termination

a. Commentary

It is illegal for a franchisor to terminate a franchise agreement on grounds other than good cause.[152] The MFIL defines "good cause" as "include[ing] the failure of the franchisee to comply with any lawful provision of the franchise agreement and to cure such failure after being given written notice thereof and a reasonable opportunity, which in no event need be more than 30 days."[153] Failure of the franchisee to pay fees has been held to be good cause for termination, even though the franchisee complained that it was not receiving the support it deserved.[154] A market withdrawal in the form of a phase-out of an entire line of automobiles and subsequent termination of the franchise agreement can also be good cause.[155]

b. Annotations

Failure of the franchisee to pay advertising fees to franchisor is a material breach of the franchise for which termination would be permitted if not cured, even in light of the fact that the franchisee complained that it was not receiving the level of advertising support promised in the agreement.[156]

Interpreting a contract pursuant to Michigan law, the court found that market withdrawal in the form of a phase-out of an entire line of automobiles and the subsequent termination of the franchise agreement is deemed to be a termination for good cause upon which no cause of action could be pled.[157]

Under the MFIL, franchisee's ten material breaches of convenience store franchise agreement within two years gave rise to good cause for termination of agreement, which contained a "four strikes" provision, even though franchisee subsequently cured breaches; the breaches were material as defined by terms of franchise agreement.[158]

Under the MFIL, franchisees' failure to comply with lawful provisions in franchise agreements by failing to pay royalties and advertising fees and failing to file monthly sales reports constituted "good cause" for franchisor's termination of agreements, where franchisor gave notice of termination in writing and franchisees made no effort to cure.[159]

---

152. MICH. COMP. LAWS § 445.1527(c).
153. *Id.*
154. *See* Gregory v. Popeyes Famous Fried Chicken, 857 F.2d 1474 (6th Cir. 1988).
155. Hubbard Auto Ctr., Inc. v. Gen. Motors Corp., 422 F. Supp. 2d 999 (D. Ind. 2006).
156. *Gregory,* 857 F.2d 1474.
157. *Hubbard,* 422 F. Supp. 2d 999.
158. 7-Eleven, Inc. v. CJ-Grand, LLC, 517 F. Supp. 3d 688 (E.D. Mich. 2021).
159. Two Men & a Truck/International Inc. v. Two Men and a Truck/Kalamazoo, Inc., 955 F. Supp. 784 (W.D. Mich. 1997).

5. Required Cure Period

a. Commentary

In addition to notice, the Act requires that the franchisee be provided with a reasonable opportunity to cure the default. Although the Act does not outline a minimum cure period, it does clarify that a reasonable opportunity to cure need never be for a time greater than 30 days.[160]

b. Annotations

Not applicable.

6. Repurchase Obligations

a. Commentary

The MFIL generally does not require that a franchisor buy back a franchise, inventory, equipment, or other property when the franchise is terminated for good cause. The Act does, however, hold void and unenforceable any provision that requires the franchisee to resell to the franchisor items not uniquely identified with the franchisor. That prohibition specifically does not include provisions that either give the franchisor a right of first refusal to purchase assets or allow the franchisor to acquire the franchise assets if the franchisee breaches a lawful provision and then fails to cure the default.[161]

b. Annotations

Not applicable.

D. Restrictions on Nonrenewal

1. What Constitutes Nonrenewal

a. Commentary

The MFIL does not provide a right to renew a franchise agreement. However, the MFIL prohibits a franchisor from refusing to renew a franchise upon expiration of its term without good cause.[162]

b. Annotations

Not applicable.

2. Restrictions on Nonrenewal

a. Commentary

The Act makes void any provision that permits the franchisor to refuse to renew on terms generally available to other franchisees under similar circumstances.[163]

---

160. MICH. COMP. LAWS § 445.1527(c).
161. *Id.* § 445.1527(h).
162. *Id.* § 445.1527(c).
163. *Id.* § 445.1527(e).

b. Annotations

In *General Aviation, Inc. v. Cessna Aircraft Co.*, the Sixth Circuit considered whether section 27(e) of the MFIL (the MFIL's nondiscrimination provision) requires Cessna to have a legitimate reason for refusing to renew General Aviation's franchise agreement while renewing contracts with other, similarly situated franchisees, or whether Cessna may lawfully refuse to renew its franchise agreements at will as long as it offers the same terms to those franchisees it does renew.[164] The court held that the MFIL requires a legitimate, nondiscriminatory reason for nonrenewal.[165]

3. Notice Requirement

a. Commentary

The Act does not set requirements for effective notice of nonrenewal. However, if, the term of the franchise agreement is less than five years and the franchisee is prohibited from continuing to conduct substantially the same business under another trademark, service mark, trade name, logotype, advertising, or commercial symbol in the same area subsequent to the expiration of the franchise or the franchisee receives at least six months advance notice of franchisor's intent not to renew the franchise, MCL 445.1527(d) requires a franchisor to fairly compensate a nonrenewed franchisee by repurchasing at fair market value the franchisee's inventory, supplies, equipment, fixtures, and furnishings.[166] While there is no notice requirement for nonrenewal, a franchisor's failure to provide at least six months' notice of its intent not to renew will require franchisor to repurchase the franchisee's inventory, supplies, equipment, fixtures, and furnishings at fair market value (if the franchise agreement is less than five years in duration and has restrictive covenants that prohibit the franchisee from continuing business in the area).

b. Annotations

There is no case law addressing this issue.

4. Grounds for Nonrenewal

a. Commentary

The Act prohibits a franchisor from refusing to renew a franchise upon expiration of its term except for good cause.[167] "Good cause" is specifically defined in the Act with regard to termination, as "the failure of the franchisee to comply with any lawful provision of the franchise agreement and to cure such failure after being given written notice thereof and a reasonable opportunity, which in no event need be more than 30 days, to cure such failure."[168] Since "good cause" is also used in the renewal section, presumably the same definition

---

164. Gen. Aviation, Inc. v. Cessna Aircraft Co., 13 F.3d 178 (6th Cir. 1993).
165. *Id.*
166. MICH. COMP. LAWS § 445.1527(d).
167. *Id.* § 445.1527(c).
168. *Id.*

would apply. Case law confirms that a business undergoing a market withdrawal in the form of a phase-out of an entire line of products is good cause for nonrenewal and the franchisee is left with no claim or action to plead.[169] In contrast, discrimination of a suspect class is never good cause for nonrenewal of a franchise.[170] Good cause can be good faith legitimate reason that is uniformly applied across the entire system.[171] A franchisor also cannot refuse to renew a franchise on terms generally available to other franchisees of the same class or type under similar circumstances.[172]

b. Annotations

Interpreting a contract pursuant to Michigan law, an Indiana court found that market withdrawal in the form of a phase-out of the Oldsmobile line of automobiles and the subsequent termination of the franchise agreement is deemed to be a termination for good cause upon which no cause of action can be pled.[173]

While not decided under the MFIL, unilateral nonrenewal of a franchise agreement to an African American franchisee for discriminatory reasons can be actionable under 42 U.S.C. § 1981.[174]

An airplane manufacturer franchisor cannot unilaterally terminate or fail to renew its franchisee's contract in absence of a good faith legitimate reason (and good cause) that would be uniformly applied across its entire franchise system. Although the airline manufacturer argued that it could refuse to renew for any or no reason, the court held that the MFIL required Cessna to renew its franchise with General Aviation in accord with the renewal terms Cessna offered to other, similarly situated franchisees and absent good cause, it could not elect to not renew.[175]

In *7-Eleven, Inc. v. CJ-Grand, LLC*, the Eastern District noted that "the MFIL has been drafted broadly compared to a number of other statutes which prescribe specific situations which constitute 'good cause'" and held that 7-Eleven's four-strikes provision satisfied the MFIL's good cause requirement.[176] In so holding, the court listed some of the other material breaches that would have satisfied the good cause requirement, such as failing to properly maintain the store premises; discontinuing using franchisor issued video recording equipment without prior written consent; failing to comply with inventory requirements and foodservice standards; failing to maintain required minimum net worth; and failing to record or submit cash reports and other financial records.[177]

---

169. Hubbard Auto Ctr., Inc. v. Gen. Motors Corp., 422 F. Supp. 2d 999 (N.D. Ind. 2006).
170. Fair v. Prime Sec., 134 F.3d 371 (6th Cir. 1997).
171. Gen. Aviation, Inc. v. The Cessna Aircraft Co., 915 F.2d 1038 (6th Cir. 1990).
172. MICH. COMP. LAWS § 445.1527(e).
173. *Hubbard*, 422 F. Supp. 2d 999.
174. *Fair*, 134 F.3d 371.
175. *Gen. Aviation*, 13 F.3d 178.
176. 7-Eleven, Inc. v. CJ-Grand, LLC, 517 F. Supp. 3d 688 (E.D. Mich. 2021).
177. *Id.* at 693.

5. Required Cure Period

a. Commentary
Not applicable.

b. Annotations
Not applicable.

6. Limitations on Franchisors' Right to Impose Conditions for Renewal

a. Commentary
The MFIL deems void and unenforceable any provision that permits a franchisor to refuse to renew a franchise on terms generally available to other franchisees of the same class or type under similar circumstances.[178]

b. Annotations
Not applicable.

7. Repurchase Obligations

a. Commentary
The MFIL declares void and unenforceable any provision that permits the franchisor to refuse to renew without buying back the franchisee's inventory, supplies, equipment, fixtures, and furnishings if (1) the franchise term is for less than five years and (2) the franchisee is contractually prohibited from competing after the term or did not receive six months' notice of the franchisor's intent to not renew, even if franchisor has good cause not to renew. Otherwise, there is no buyback requirement placed on the franchisor. In any instance, personalized materials that have no value to the franchisor and inventory, supplies, equipment, fixtures, and furnishings not reasonably required in the conduct of the franchise business are not subject to compensation.[179]

b. Annotations
Not applicable.

E. Transfers and Successions

1. Commentary
The MFIL declares void and unenforceable a provision that permits the franchisor to refuse to allow a transfer without good cause. Good cause includes, but is not limited to, failure of the proposed transferee to meet the franchisor's then-current reasonable qualifications, the fact that the proposed transferee is a competitor of the franchisor, the unwillingness of the proposed transferee to agree to comply with lawful obligations, or the failure of the franchisee or proposed

---

178. MICH. COMP. LAWS § 445.1527(e); *see also Gen. Aviation*, 13 F.3d 178.
179. MICH. COMP. LAWS § 445.1527(d).

transferee to pay any sums owing to the franchisor or cure any default.[180] A court did enforce a franchise agreement provision that required the franchisee to sign a general release as a condition precedent to permitting a transfer.[181] The MFIL does not, however, restrict the franchisor's right to object to transfers on death.

2. Annotations

Franchisees' failure to provide release of their claims other than those under the MFIL provided good cause for franchisor not to approve transfer of the franchise; it was commercially reasonable for franchisor to require franchisees to resolve all non-MFIL disputes between the parties before franchisor approved the transfer.[182]

A franchise agreement that contained language requiring the transferor to sign a release form releasing the franchisor of any previously known or unknown violation of the franchise agreement was enforceable as it did not also seek release of any violations of the MFIL.[183]

Under the Michigan Motor Vehicle Franchise Act[184] the manufacturer's refusal to approve a contract to transfer the dealership where the contract was contingent upon the dealership relocating to a less profitable site was a reasonable exercise of the manufacturer's rights.[185]

A plaintiff, who had received a pizza restaurant franchise from a previous franchisee, was subject to the arbitration clause the previous franchisee had entered into with the franchisor and was required to arbitrate its four claims against the franchisor because the transfer agreement between the two franchisees unambiguously provided that the assignee assumed all obligations, covenants, and agreements arising under the franchise agreement.[186]

The MFIL did not support a claim by a franchisee that the franchisor breached a franchise agreement by not approving the transfer of a franchise; franchise agreement provided that it was governed by law of Massachusetts, and in any event franchisor did not disapprove proposed new franchisee by exercise of contractual veto power made unenforceable by statute in question, but rather on grounds that franchisee was terminated for misconduct prior to making transfer request and consequently had nothing to transfer.[187]

---

180. *Id.* § 445.1527(g).
181. Franchise Mgmt. Unlimited Inc. v. America's Favorite Chicken, 561 N.W.2d 123 (Mich. Ct. App. 1997).
182. *Id.*
183. *Id.*
184. MICH. COMP. LAWS §§ 445.1561, *et seq.*
185. Ed Koehn Nissan, Inc. v. Nissan Motor Corp in U.S.A., No. 1:93:cv:415, 1994 WL 17092047 (W.D. Mich. 1994) (Dealership failed to produce any factual support for its claim that the manufacturer's refusal to consent to the sale was unreasonable, whereas the manufacturer provided adequate evidence for its denial, including survey results showing that the proposed site lacked an adequate market.).
186. Braverman Props., LLC v. Boston Pizza Rests., LP, No. 1:10-CV-941, 2011 WL 2551189 (W.D. Mich. June 27, 2011).
187. Dunkin' Donuts Inc. v. Taseski, 47 F. Supp. 2d 867 (E.D. Mich. 1999).

F. Other Regulation of the Franchise Relationship

1. Commentary

Section 27 of the MFIL holds discriminatory provisions found in franchise documents void and unenforceable. Courts have determined that that discrimination against a suspect class is never permissible as a grounds for nonrenewal.[188] Additionally, at least one court recognized that a franchisee's claim of discriminatory nonrenewal was sufficiently stated based on the alleged animosity between the franchisee's son and the manufacturer.[189]

The Act prohibits a franchise agreement's restrictions on a franchisee joining an association of franchisees.[190]

2. Annotations

Franchisees are permitted to associate with other franchisees to discuss a myriad of issues, including the joint termination of the franchise, without being in violation of the law.[191]

G. Remedies and Administrative Action

1. Restrictive Covenants

a. Commentary

The Act does not directly address the enforceability of covenants against competition in the franchising context.[192] However, the MFIL references covenants against competition in section 27(d), which provides that a provision in a franchise agreement that permits a franchisor to refuse to renew a franchise without fairly compensating the franchisee for the fair market value of certain inventory, supplies, equipment, fixtures, and furnishings is void and unenforceable.[193] Section 27(d) only applies if the term of the franchise is less than five years and (1) *the franchisee is prohibited from continuing to conduct substantially the same business in the same area subsequent to the expiration of the franchise*, or (2) the franchisee does not receive at least six months advance notice of the franchisor's intent not to renew the franchise agreement.[194]

For franchise agreements entered into prior to 1985, the Michigan Supreme Court applied the rule of reason to determine the enforceability of covenants against competition even before the enactment of statutes regulating antitrust practices.[195]

---

188. Fair v. Prime Sec., 134 F.3d 371 (6th Cir. 1997).
189. Tractor & Farm Supply Inc. v. Ford New Holland, Inc., 898 F. Supp. 1198 (W.D. Ky. 1995).
190. MICH. COMP. LAWS § 445.1527(a).
191. McAlpine v. AAMOCO, 461 F. Supp. 1232 (E.D. Mich. 1978).
192. *See* MICH. COMP. LAWS § 445.1501 to 445.1546.
193. *Id.* § 445.1527.
194. *Id.*
195. *See* Bristol Windows v. Hoogenstyn, 650 N.W.2d 670, 677 (Mich. Ct. App. 2002).

b. Annotations

The resulting harm of loss of customer goodwill and loss of fair competition that would occur to the franchisor if the court did not grant its request for injunctive relief barring the franchisee from its continued violation of a noncompete covenant outweighed any harm to the franchisee from the enforcement of the covenant because the franchisee should have anticipated such harm because it specifically agreed to the covenant.[196]

The use of a Michigan franchisor's marks by a former franchisee that was terminated for cause was a trade dress infringement and a breach of the non-competition agreement between the parties.[197]

A covenant not to compete in a franchise agreement that was declared to be void under an antitrust statute that was later repealed was not revived upon the declaration of invalidity of the statute.[198]

An in-term covenant not to compete in a franchise agreement did not violate the Michigan antitrust prohibition against restraint on trade as it prevented only competition during the term of the contract.[199]

A covenant restricting a franchisee from engaging in a competing business during the terms of the franchise is valid, and the franchisor may terminate the franchisee's license if the franchisee violates the covenant by opening a similar business during the life of the franchise and fails promptly to cure such failure to observe the covenant.[200]

2. Damages

a. Commentary

The MFIL contains a private right of action.[201] The aggrieved party, however, must make an election of remedies between rescission of the franchise opportunity or a right to damages suffered as a result of the violation of the disclosure sections of the Act.[202] Section 31 of the Act was cited in *In re Dynamic Enterprises, Inc.*,[203] in which the court affirmed that the remedy permitted by this section was either the right to rescission or the right to actual damages.[204] This limita-

---

196. Allegra Network LLC v. Cormack, No. 11-13087, 2012 WL 3583618 (E.D. Mich. Aug. 20, 2012).
197. Little Caesar Enter., Inc., v. Little Caesar's Va., Inc., No. 2:09-CV-112, 2009 WL 10459862 (E.D. Va. Aug. 27, 2009).
198. Lansing-Lewis Servs., Inc., v. Schmitt, 470 N.W.2d 405 (Mich. Ct. App. 1990).
199. Banek Inc. v. Yogurt Ventures U.S.A., Inc., 6 F.3d 357 (6th Cir. 1993).
200. 5620 Mich. Op. Att'y Gen. 531 (1980).
201. Geib v. Amoco Oil, 163 F.3d 329 (6th Cir. 1995); *but see* Franchise Mgmt. Unlimited Inc. v. America's Favorite Chicken, 561 N.W.2d 123 (Mich. Ct. App. 1997) (ruling that there is no private right of action for a non-purchaser of a franchise).
202. *See* Lofgren v. AirTrona Canada, No. 16-1804, 2017 WL 384876 (6th Cir. Jan. 27, 2017) (where the court concluded that, under section 8 of the MFIL, there was no fraud requirement or causal requirement that the disclosure failure must directly cause financial damage in order for rescission or damages to be sought).
203. *In re* Dynamic Enters., Inc., 32 B.R. 509 (Bankr. Tenn. 1983).
204. Interstate Automatic Transmission Co., Inc. v. Harvey, 350 N.W.2d 907 (Mich. Ct. App. 1984).

tion, however, will not prevent the aggrieved party from applying for multiple remedies, including both rescission and damages if such damages are specifically permitted by any statute or the common law.[205] In *Abbo v. Wireless Toyz Franchise, L.L.C.*,[206] the trial court's judgment notwithstanding the verdict of the jury's award for rescission damages was improper when the plaintiff was required to choose between either seeking rescission or other types of damages.

b. Annotations

Not applicable.

3. Rescission

a. Commentary

Under the Act, rescission is an available remedy to an aggrieved franchisee.[207]

b. Annotations

Not applicable.

4. Injunctive Relief

a. Commentary

When bringing an action on behalf of the people of the state (see the discussion in subsection II.G.8 concerning administrative actions), the Department may enjoin the acts or practices of a party that attempts to enforce an otherwise void and unenforceable provisions termination listed under section 27. Thus, the Department may, among other things, grant injunctive relief.[208]

b. Annotations

Not applicable.

5. Control Person Liability

a. Commentary

Section 32 of the MFIL provides for personal liability for any person who "directly or indirectly controls a person liable under this act, a principal executive officer or director of a corporation so liable, . . . an employee of a person so liable who materially aids in the act or transaction constituting the violation . . . unless the other person who is so liable had no knowledge of or reasonable grounds to believe in the existence of facts by reason of which the liability is alleged to exist."[209] This officer, director, and employee joint and

---

205. MICH. COMP. LAWS § 445.1534 (1984); *see also* Toyz, Inc. v. Wireless Toyz, Inc., 799 F. Supp. 2d 737 (E.D. Mich. 2011) (concluding that the MFIL's civil liability provision did not limit any other cause of action brought under common law).

206. Abbo v. Wireless Toyz Franchise, LLC, No. 2007-082804-CK, 2014 WL 1978185 (Mich. Ct. App., May 13, 2014).

207. MICH. COMP. LAWS § 445.1534.

208. *Id.* § 445.1535(1).

209. *Id.* § 445.1532.

several liability combined with the felony nature of these violations are serious consequences for violations of the MFIL.[210]

In terms of criminal culpability, the MFIL provides that a person who violates the Act shall be fined not more than $10,000 or imprisoned for not more than seven years, or both.[211] Additionally, the MFIL expressly states that it does not limit or constrict the state's power to punish a person for conduct considered criminal under any other statute.[212] Although no case law addresses or enforces these types of potential criminal liability for franchisors under the MFIL, the opportunity exists for the state to initiate criminal proceedings against those liable for MFIL violations involving conduct that is otherwise criminal in nature. Further, because the MFIL provides that officers, executives, and persons who directly or indirectly control a person so liable, among others, may be jointly and severally liable for MFIL violations, a scenario, such as where the franchisor has since become insolvent, may present itself where rescission or damages are not or cannot be offered as a remedy and the state seeks to enforce the criminal provisions stated earlier. In *People v. Cooper and Attaway*,[213] the antipyramid language of the Act, Michigan Compiled Laws section 445.1528, was criminally enforced. Although this case involved sales of securities, it does illuminate the potential criminal liability that may befall a franchisor involved in fraudulent conduct connected to the selling or offering of a franchise, among other activities.

b. Annotations

Section 28 of the MFIL was broadly interpreted to prohibit any plan, scheme, or device that falls under either of the two delineated definitions and was further interpreted to not be restricted to just franchises.[214]

The MFIL at section 445.1532 clearly indicates that the officers and shareholders of the franchisor were jointly and severally liable for the failure to register or issue the disclosure.[215]

Additionally, after the court found him to be an employee of the franchisor, a sales representative did not qualify for the employee safe harbor provision within section 32 of the MFIL after failing to show why he "had no knowledge of or reasonable grounds to believe in the existence of the facts" of the franchise transaction of which he played a fundamental part. Thus, under the meaning of the MFIL, he could be held liable for failing to provide a required disclosure statement to a prospective franchisee.[216]

The civil liability provision of the MFIL did not limit any other cause of action brought under common law. Therefore, the claims for intentional fraud

---

210. *Id.* § 445.1538 (providing that "[a] person who violates a provision of this act shall be fined not more than $10,000, or imprisoned for not more than 7 years, or both").
211. *Id.*
212. *Id.*
213. People v. Cooper & Attaway, 421 N.W.2d 177 (Mich. Ct. App. 1987).
214. *Id.*
215. Kohr v. Gropp and Lehman Enters., 718 F.2d 1099 (6th Cir. 1983).
216. Lofgren v. AirTrona Canada, No. 16-1804, 2017 WL 384876 (6th Cir. Jan. 27, 2017).

and negligent misrepresentation brought by several wireless phone store franchisees against a franchisor were not preempted by the civil liability section of the MFIL.[217]

6. Attorneys' Fees

a. Commentary

A person who offers or sells a franchise in violation of the MFIL at section 445.1508 is liable to the person purchasing the franchise for damages or rescission, with interest at 12 percent per year and reasonable attorney fees and court costs.[218] The same provisions do not apply to the relationship sections of MFIL.

b. Annotations

In accordance with the terms of the franchise agreement and in keeping with the MFIL, the franchisor was entitled to attorney's fees in enforcing the termination of the agreement.[219]

Only the anti-fraud provisions of the MFIL permit the aggrieved franchisee to collect reasonable attorney's fees as well as other damages.[220]

7. Limitations on Damage Waivers

a. Commentary
Not applicable.[221]

b. Annotations
Not applicable.

8. Administrative Actions

a. Commentary

The Michigan Franchise Investment Law expressly provides the Department of the Attorney General the authority to bring an action in the appropriate circuit court in the name of the people of the state of Michigan for a violation, including those of disclosure, of any provision or any rule established under the Act. In such actions, the Department may seek restitution on behalf of the franchisee, order specific performance, or injunctive relief.[222] The Department is also provided the discretion to make private or public investigations, within or outside of the state, in order to determine either the veracity of a violation or simply to enforce the Act.[223]

---

217. Toyz, Inc. v. Wireless Toyz, Inc., 799 F. Supp. 2d 737 (E.D. Mich. 2011).
218. MICH. COMP. LAWS § 445.1531(1) (1984).
219. Dunkin' Donuts, Inc., v. Taseski, 47 F. Supp. 2d 867 (E.D. Mich. 1999).
220. Gen. Aviation, Inc., v. Cessna, 13 F.3d 178 (6th Cir. 1993).
221. MICH. COMP. LAWS § 445.1527.
222. Id. § 445.1535(1).
223. Id. § 445.1536.

b. Annotations
Not applicable.

H. Dispute Resolution
1. Limitations on Franchisors' Ability to Restrict Venue
a. Commentary
Section 445.1527(f) of the Act renders void and unenforceable any provision in a franchise agreement "requiring that arbitration or litigation be conducted outside of [Michigan]."[224] However, if properly disclosed by franchisor, section 445.1527(f) is preempted by the Federal Arbitration Act (FAA) and the venue dictated in the agreement will prevail.[225] A franchisor must disclose its intent to rely on the FAA's preemption or otherwise disclose to a franchisee the FAA's preemptive effect in its disclosure document to avoid an argument of fraud in the inducement, since virtually all franchisors disclose the MFIL's void and unenforceable provisions listed in MFIL section 445.1527.[226]

b. Annotations
A court-ordered arbitration of the dispute between a pharmacy franchisee, its two guarantors, and a franchisor to be held at the American Arbitration Association (AAA) office in Southfield, Michigan, after severing the voidable venue provision of an arbitration clause in a parties' franchise agreement that required disputes to be arbitrated by the AAA in St. Louis, Missouri. The franchisor had misrepresented its intention to invoke FAA preemption in order to compel arbitration outside of Michigan, and that plaintiff's relied on these assertions contained in the Uniform Franchise Offering Circular that a provision that required arbitration outside the state of Michigan was void when they signed the agreement. The severance of the Missouri venue provision and the court's order to arbitrate in Michigan effectively precluded arbitration outside of the state, thus, the only alternative was to hold the arbitration proceedings at a AAA office in-state.[227]

Even though the court recognized the federal preemption issues related to the Federal Arbitration Act (FAA), the court nevertheless refused to enforce the Arizona venue provision for arbitration finding that the franchisor's failure to disclose the preemptive effect of the FAA amounted to fraud when franchisor disclosed the MFIL's void and enforceable provisions in its disclosure document. The court refused to enforce the venue clause and ordered future arbitration proceedings to take place in Michigan.[228]

Forum-selection clause in putative franchise agreement between Michigan-based fabricator of stone countertops and Minnesota-based supplier of stone

---
224. *Id.* § 445.1527(f).
225. Flint Warm Air Supply Co., Inc. v. York Int'l Corp., 115 F. Supp. 2d 820 (E.D. Mich. 2000).
226. Binder v. Medicine Shoppe Intern., Inc., No. 09-14046, 2010 WL 2854308 (E.D. Mich. July 20, 2010); Alphagraphics Franchising, Inc. v. Whaler Graphics, Inc., 840 F. Supp. 708 (D. Ariz. 1993).
227. *Id.*
228. *Alphagraphics*, 840 F. Supp. 708.

slabs, designating Minnesota as forum, violated a strong public policy reflected in Michigan Franchise Investment Law (MFIL), which voided out-of-state forum-selection clauses contained in franchise agreements, and thus, supplier could not enforce putative franchise agreement's forum-selection clause, warranting dismissal under doctrine of forum non conveniens in diversity action brought by fabricator in Michigan federal district court, relating to supplier's termination of putative franchise agreement.[229]

2. Limitations Period

a. Commentary

The Act contains a four-year statute of limitations pursuant to which no action, civil or criminal, may be brought more than four years after the act or transaction constituting the violation.[230] However, nothing in the MFIL prohibits the tolling of the limitations period for reasons consistent with the Revised Judicature Act of 1961.[231]

b. Annotations

The claims asserted by several wireless phone store franchisees against a franchisor for violation of the MFIL were not barred by the Act's four-year statute of limitations because the majority of the alleged misconduct was not known until one of the franchisees examined the franchisor's books and records and the filing of another lawsuit revealed more information. Therefore, the tolling provisions of the Michigan statute that permitted an action to be commenced at any time within two years from the date of discovery in cases where the existence of the claim was fraudulently concealed applied.[232]

---

229. Lakeside Surfaces, Inc. v. Cambria Co., LLC, 16 F.4th 209 (6th Cir. 2021).
230. MICH. COMP. LAWS § 445.1533.
231. *Toyz, Inc.*, 799 F. Supp. 2d 737.
232. *Id.*

Minnesota

Kirsten Nordstrom and Henry Pfutzenreuter

I. Introduction

A. Commentary

The Minnesota Franchise Act (MFA) was enacted in 1973 in response to the growing franchise industry and concerns that lack of regulation could expose franchisees to abuse,[1] particularly with respect to misleading sales practices by unregistered franchisors,[2] but also inequitable terminations and other unfair practices in the franchise relationship.[3] The MFA thus governs both franchise sales and relationships.

At the time, Minnesota was one of only a dozen or so states to enact a law governing franchising, preceding the Federal Trade Commission's entry to the regulatory field in 1979. Today, Minnesota is home to many major franchise brands and thousands of franchisees who contribute billions to its economy.[4]

Minnesota's available legislative history and the MFA itself do not provide much insight to its policy rationale and intent.[5] Soon after the MFA's enactment, the Minnesota Supreme Court described it as "remedial legislation designed to protect potential franchisees within Minnesota from unfair contracts and other

---

1. Clapp v. Peterson, 327 N.W.2d 585, 586 (Minn. 1982) ("Chapter 80C was adopted in 1973 as remedial legislation designed to protect potential franchises within Minnesota from unfair contracts and other prevalent and previously unregulated abuses in a growing national franchise industry.").

2. *Id.* ("Chapter 80C seeks to protect potential franchisees by requiring any person offering or selling a franchise within the state to register with the Commissioner of Securities a proposed public offering statement making full disclosure of all facts required by statute or rules of the commissioner.").

3. Pac. Equip. & Irrigation, Inc. v. Toro Co., 519 N.W.2d 911, 917 (Minn. Ct. App. 1994) ("The Minnesota Franchise Act is an attempt to protect the franchisee from undue usurpation of the franchise relationship and to establish balance of bargaining power.") (Amundson, J., concurring).

4. Ashley Rogers et al., Int'l Franchise Ass'n, 2024 Franchising Economic Outlook 26, appx. (2024), https://www.franchise.org/wp-content/uploads/2025/03/2024-Franchising-Economic-Report.pdf.

5. 1973 Minn. Laws 612 (describing the MFA as "[a]n act relating to commerce; providing for the registration and regulation of franchises by the commissioner of securities;—requiring certain disclosures; defining and prohibiting unfair practices; providing penalties").

prevalent and previously unregulated abuses in a growing national franchise industry."[6] The characterization held, with courts continuing to interpret the MFA's remedial protections "broadly to better effectuate its purpose" while construing "exceptions contained within . . . narrowly."[7]

B. Annotations

Franchisees were not required to show they justifiably relied on franchisor's representations regarding prospective earnings in signing their respective franchise agreements in order to bring suit against franchisor for misrepresentations under the MFA. *Randall v. Lady of America Franchise Corp.*, 532 F. Supp. 2d 1071, 1088 (D. Minn. 2007) ("Minnesota courts have repeatedly observed that the Minnesota Franchise Act is a remedial statute designed to favor franchisees over franchisors.").

The MFA establishes public policy in favor of providing special protection to franchisees leading to a presumption of irreparable harm when applying factors for injunctive relief. *Pacific Equipment & Irrigation, Inc. v. Toro Co.*, 519 N.W.2d 911, 917 (Minn. Ct. App. 1994) ("Following World War II, there was a massive growth in franchising. This economic phenomenon has continued through to the present. The unfettered growth in franchising has brought about many abuses in the system. Thus, regulatory supervision has been attempted at both the state and federal levels. As the majority opinion notes, Chapter 80C of the Minnesota Statutes was adopted in 1973 as remedial legislation designed to protect franchises within Minnesota from unfair contracts and other prevalent and unregulated abuses. The Minnesota Franchise Act is an attempt to protect the franchisee from undue usurpation of the franchise relationship and to establish balance of bargaining power.") (Amundson, J., concurring).

The rule promulgated under the public offering statement requirement provision in the MFA that "good cause" is required to terminate a franchise arrangement cannot be applied retroactively to agreements executed before the rule was created on January 13, 1975. *Bitronics Sales Co., Inc. v. Microsemiconductor Corp.*, 610 F. Supp. 550, 556 (D. Minn. 1985) ("Like most other franchise regulation acts, the Minnesota statute required registration by any person offering or selling a franchise within the state with the Commissioner of Securities and full disclosure in a proposed public offering statement.").

The Minnesota Supreme Court has acknowledged that Chapter 80C was enacted for the purpose of protecting potential franchisees within Minnesota from unfair and other abuses. *Martin Investors, Inc. v. Vander Bie*, 269 N.W.2d 868, 872 (Minn. 1978) ("Chapter 80C was adopted in 1973 as remedial legislation designed to protect potential franchisees within Minnesota from unfair contracts and other prevalent and previously unregulated abuses in a growing national franchise industry.").

A statement from an unidentified senator describing the bill as giving "the commissioner of securities some control over the franchising business in the

---

6. Martin Invs., Inc. v. Vander Bie, 269 N.W.2d 868, 872 (Minn. 1978) (citing Editorial Board, *Regulation of Franchising*, 59 MINN. L. REV. 1027, 1036 (1975)).

7. Current Tech. Concepts, Inc. v. Irie Enters., Inc., 530 N.W.2d 539, 544 (Minn. 1995).

state of Minnesota." Hearing on the Minnesota Franchise Act Before the Minnesota Senate, 68th Legis., Reg. Sess. (Minn.1973).

II. Commentary and Annotations

A. Definition of Franchise

The MFA's definition of "franchise" involves three elements: (1) the franchisee is granted the right to engage in business using the franchisor's trademark or other commercial symbol; (2) the franchisee and the franchisor share a "community of interest" in the marketing of goods or services; and (3) the franchisee pays a franchise fee, directly or indirectly.[8] All three elements must be present for a franchise to exist. Minnesota, however, expands on this definition and also defines certain business opportunities or other distribution relationships as "franchises." Those include motor vehicle fuel franchises,[9] vending machine or similar display or currency machine business opportunities,[10] and security system business opportunities.[11]

Minnesota specifically excludes from its definition of franchise: (1) businesses that are operated under a lease or license on the premises of the lessor or licensor that are incidental to the business conducted by the lessor or licensor, such as concession stands;[12] (2) any relationship that would otherwise qualify as a franchise, but the franchisee pays the franchisor less than $100 per year, except in the case of motor vehicle fuel franchises;[13] agreements to market motor vehicles;[14] and agreements between air carriers.[15]

1. Trademark Element

a. Commentary

The MFA's trademark element is satisfied when a franchisor grants a franchisee "the right to engage in the business of offering or distributing goods or services using the franchisor's trade name, trademark, service mark, logotype, advertising, or other commercial symbol or related characteristics."[16] It is not necessary that the franchisor's trademark or other commercial symbol be registered; any allowed use of a franchisor's mark, symbol, or advertising is sufficient to satisfy this element.[17] For example, it is clearly satisfied when a franchisee is granted a license to use the mark in a written agreement.[18] It is not necessary for the

---

8. MINN. STAT. § 80C.01 subdiv. 4(a)(1).
9. *Id.* subdiv. 4(a)(2).
10. *Id.* subdiv. 4(a)(3).
11. *Id.* subdiv. 4(a)(4).
12. *Id.* subdiv. 4(b).
13. *Id.* subdiv. 4(c).
14. *Id.* subdiv. 4(d).
15. *Id.* subdiv. 4(e).
16. *Id.* subdiv. 4(a)(1)(i).
17. *See* Martin Invs. v. Vander Bie, 269 N.W.2d 868, 874 (Minn. 1978) ("[t]he statute requires only that the franchisee be granted the right to use the franchiser's name").
18. Coyne's & Co. v. Enesco, LLC, 565 F. Supp. 2d 1027, 1048 (D. Minn. 2008).

franchisee to be granted the right to hold itself out as the franchisor.[19] Instead, courts have held that the right to use the mark in marketing a manufacturer's product is sufficient to satisfy this element.[20]

b. Annotations

To satisfy the trademark element of the MFA, all that is necessary is for the franchisor to grant the franchisee the right to use its name. It is not necessary that the franchisee be granted the right to hold itself out as the franchisor or that it be granted a license. For example, the trademark element is satisfied when the franchisee is given the right to use marketing and sales materials provided by the franchisor. *Martin Investors v. Vander Bie*, 269 N.W.2d 868, 874 (Minn. 1978).

The trademark element was satisfied when a written distributor agreement granted the distributor the right to use the manufacturer's trademarks to market the manufacturer's products offered by the distributor in the territory. *Coyne's & Co. v. Enesco, LLC*, 565 F. Supp. 2d 1027, 1048 (D. Minn. 2008).

It is not necessary for the franchisee to be granted the right to hold itself out as the franchisor to satisfy the trademark element. *RJM Sales & Marketing, Inc. v. Banfi Products Corp.*, 546 F. Supp. 1368, 1373 (D. Minn. 1982).

The trademark element is satisfied when the franchisee is given the right to use the franchisor's name in marketing the franchisor's product. *Unlimited Horizon Marketing, Inc. v. Precision Hub, Inc.*, 533 N.W.2d 63, 66 (Minn. Ct. App. 1995).

2. Franchise Fee Element

a. Commentary

The MFA defines "Franchise Fee" as:

> Any fee or charge that a franchisee . . . is required to pay or agrees to pay for the right to enter into a business or to continue a business under a franchise agreement, including, but not limited to, the payment either in a lump sum or by installments of an initial capital investment fee, any fee or charges based upon a percentage of gross or net sales whether or not referred to as royalty fees, any payment for goods or services, or any training fees or training school fees or charges[.][21]

The definition goes on to exempt several types of payments from the otherwise broad definition. Those include the purchase of goods at a bona fide wholesale price or other arrangements in which the franchisee ultimately pays the wholesale price of the goods, repayment of any bona fide loan, the purchase of supplies or fixtures at their fair market value necessary to enter into or continue the business, and the purchase or lease of property, at its fair market value, necessary to enter into or continue the business.[22]

---

19. RJM Sales & Mktg., Inc. v. Banfi Prod. Corp., 546 F. Supp. 1368, 1373 (D. Minn. 1982).
20. Unlimited Horizon Mktg., Inc. v. Precision Hub, Inc., 533 N.W.2d 63, 66 (Minn. Ct. App. 1995).
21. MINN. STAT. § 80C.01 subdiv. 9.
22. *Id.*

The MFA does not require a direct, up-front payment to satisfy the franchise fee element.[23] A minimum purchase requirement can constitute a franchise fee if the franchisee purchases amounts or items they would not purchase otherwise.[24] Additionally, price markups on goods above a bona fide wholesale price can constitute an indirect franchise fee.[25] When determining if a minimum purchase requirement or prices for products constitute a franchise fee, courts will consider if the requirements were unreasonable.[26] An indirect franchise fee can also be found in payments for required training.[27]

On the other hand, ordinary business expenses do not qualify as franchise fees under the MFA unless they are unreasonable and lack a valid business purpose.[28] Nonmonetary consideration, similarly, does not meet the statutory definition of franchise fee.[29] Additionally, if the purported franchisee can choose to purchase goods or services or otherwise make payments that may otherwise qualify as a franchise fee, these payments will not be considered a franchise fee because they are optional and therefore not necessary for the right to enter into or continue the business.[30]

b. Annotations

Payments for services can qualify as a franchise fee. However, when a contract involves mixed payments for goods and services, such as a contract to sell finished countertops and a fabrication fee associated with finishing those countertops, the predominant purpose of the contract will determine if the contract is primarily for goods or services and thus if the services payment constitutes a franchise fee. When the predominant purpose of the contract is a contract for the sale of goods, and the goods are sold at a wholesale price, then the related service fee does not constitute a franchise fee. *Cambria Co., LLC v. M&M Creative Laminants, Inc.*, 995 N.W.2d 426, 437 (Minn. Ct. App. 2023).

A distributor's purchase of goods above wholesale price does not qualify as a franchise fee if there is no threat of termination if the distributor does not purchase the goods. *Louis DeGidio, Inc. v. Industrial Combustion, LLC*, 66 F.4th 707, 713 (8th Cir. 2023).

A minimum purchase requirement can qualify as a franchise fee under the MFA if a franchisee is required to purchase amounts or items that it otherwise would not. This, however, is not a subjective standard. To determine if

---

23. Coyne's & Co. v. Enesco, LLC, 553 F.3d 1128, 1131 (8th Cir. 2009).
24. Twin Cities Galleries, LLC v. Media Arts Grp., Inc., 476 F.3d 598, 601 (8th Cir. 2007).
25. OT Indus., Inc. v. OT-tehdas Oy Santasalo-Sohlberg Ab, 346 N.W.2d 162, 166 (Minn. Ct. App. 1984).
26. Upper Midwest Sales Co. v. Ecolab, Inc., 577 N.W.2d 236, 242 (Minn. Ct. App. 1998).
27. MINN. STAT. § 80C.01 subdiv. 9; *see, e.g.*, Hogin v. Barnmaster, Inc., No. C3–02–1880, 2003 WL 21500044, at *4–5 (Minn. Ct. App. July 1, 2003) (payment of 80 percent markup for training fee was not a franchise fee because training, although highly recommended, was not mandatory).
28. RJM Sales & Mktg., Inc. v. Banfi Prod. Corp., 546 F. Supp. 1368, 1373 (D. Minn. 1982); *see also* Day Distrib. Co. v. Nantucket Allserve, Inc., No. 07-1132 (PJS/RLE), 2008 WL 2945442, at *5 (D. Minn. July 25, 2008) (collecting cases).
29. *Upper Midwest Sales Co.*, 577 N.W.2d at 243.
30. Bitronics Sales Co. v. Microsemiconductor Corp., 610 F. Supp. 550, 558–59 (D. Minn. 1985).

a minimum purchase requirement qualifies as a franchise fee, courts apply an objective test to examine if the purchase requirement was reasonable. *Coyne's & Co. v. Enesco, LLC*, 553 F.3d 1128, 1131 (8th Cir. 2009).

A minimum purchase requirement is a franchise fee when the quantity of goods purchased were so unreasonably large that they acted as a fee to enter into the business. Minimum purchase requirements are not franchise fees when the commitment is within the reasonable requirements of the business, not unreasonable, and have a valid business purpose. *Twin Cities Galleries, LLC v. Media Arts Group, Inc.*, 476 F.3d 598, 601 (8th Cir. 2007).

Minimum purchase requirements can qualify as franchise fees in two ways. First, a minimum purchase requirement constitutes a franchise fee if the sales are at prices exceeding bona fide wholesale prices. Second, a minimum purchase requirement is a franchise fee if the franchisee is directed to purchase amounts or items that it otherwise would not. *OT Industries, Inc. v. OT-tehdas Oy Santasalo-Sohlberg Ab*, 346 N.W.2d 162, 166 (Minn. Ct. App. 1984).

Courts will consider if a minimum purchase requirement is reasonable when determining if it qualifies as a franchise fee. However, when the sales price for the goods is the ordinary, wholesale price of the goods and franchisees are not required to purchase unreasonable amounts of inventory, a minimum purchase requirement does not qualify as a franchise fee. *Upper Midwest Sales Co. v. Ecolab, Inc.*, 577 N.W.2d 236, 242 (Minn. Ct. App. 1998).

A wine distributor contended that it paid a franchise fee when purchasing wine samples and jackets from the manufacturer, purchasing signs from third parties, and receiving a commission that was a lower percentage than industry average. The court found that the first two expenditures were ordinary business expenses that did not qualify as a franchise fee. The court also found that the lower commission than industry average was not a franchise fee because nothing in the agreement suggested that was the parties' intent, the commission rate was the manufacturer's standard rate for that product, and the distributor did not pay any amounts to the manufacturer by accepting the lower rate. *RJM Sales & Marketing, Inc. v. Banfi Products Corp.*, 546 F. Supp. 1368, 1373 (D. Minn. 1982).

Optional payments do not qualify as franchise fees under the MFA. For example, when a distributor, at its own initiative, created a wholly owned subsidiary to offer the manufacturer's products in a given territory, it did not pay a franchise fee in the form of nonpayment of commissions on sales to its subsidiary and necessary training and other expenses, as it would not have incurred such costs absent its decision to delegate tasks to the subsidiary. *Bitronics Sales Co. v. Microsemiconductor Corp.*, 610 F. Supp. 550, 558–59 (D. Minn.1985).

3. Community of Interest; Significant Degree of Control; Joint Marketing Plan

a. Commentary

The MFA requires that "the franchisor and franchisee have a community of interest in the marketing of goods or services at wholesale, retail, by lease, agreement, or otherwise."[31] Minnesota courts have interpreted "community of

---

31. MINN. STAT. § 80C.01 subdiv. (4)(a)(ii).

interest" broadly, so that any common financial interest is likely sufficient to satisfy the element. For example, the Minnesota Supreme Court has held that any sharing of fees from a common source constitutes a community of interest.[32]

b. Annotations

A company that sold a computer service in which potential borrowers were matched to potential lenders was found to have a community of interest with the lenders because it took a fee of 1 percent of the loan proceeds. The court rejected the company's argument that 1 percent of the proceeds was too insignificant to create a community of interest, finding that the MFA did not contain a substantiality requirement. *Martin Investors, Inc. v. Vander Bie*, 269 N.W.2d 868, 875 (Minn. 1978).

B. Scope and Jurisdiction

1. Commentary

A frequently litigated issue is the scope and jurisdiction of the MFA. In some cases, residents of states without franchise relationship laws seek to avail themselves of the MFA's protections. In other cases, franchisors are surprised to learn the parties' contractual choice-of-law may not override the MFA's applicability.

These are threshold issues practitioners should analyze and address as early as possible. Unfortunately, as discussed later, the answers are not always clear at first. The most important facts are where the offer is made from, the location of the franchise, the residency of the franchisee, and the franchise agreement's choice of law.

a. Statutory Scope

Much of the uncertainty regarding the MFA's territorial scope comes from its section plainly titled "Scope," which states that its provisions "concerning sales and offers to sell" apply: (1) "when a sale or offer to sell is made in this state," (2) "when an offer to purchase is made and accepted in this state," or (3) "when the franchise is to be located in this state."[33] This section also attempts to define when an offer is "made" or "accepted" in Minnesota, which unfortunately does not conclusively answer all questions concerning the MFA's scope.

An offer is "made" in Minnesota when it either originates from there or is directed at and received there, regardless of whether either party is then present.[34] An offer is "accepted" in Minnesota when acceptance is communicated to the offeror there, and was not previously communicated elsewhere, regardless of whether either party is then present, so long as the offeree reasonably believes the offeror received acceptance there.[35]

These definitions attempt to impose some territorial limitations, but it is difficult to apply them in practice. The section defining the MFA's scope expressly

---

32. Martin Invs., Inc. v. Vander Bie, 269 N.W.2d 868, 875 (Minn. 1978).
33. MINN. STAT. § 80C.19 subdiv. 1.
34. *Id.* subdiv. 2.
35. *Id.* subdiv. 3.

states that it applies to "provisions . . . concerning sales and offers to sell," so they may not even apply to the territorial scope of its other provisions governing the franchise relationship.[36]

As a result of the ambiguity, courts and practitioners have struggled to apply these definitions in connection with the MFA's territorial scope, particularly to issues surrounding the franchise relationship. The various outcomes have led one court to describe the issue as "murky water."[37] The Minnesota Supreme Court recently resolved some of the ambiguity, but as discussed next, the territorial scope of the MFA's relationship provisions must still be analyzed on a case-by-case basis.

b. Residents and Nonresidents

Issues regarding the MFA's territorial scope typically arise when an aggrieved franchisee who is a resident of a state without a franchise relationship law purchases a franchise from a Minnesota franchisor. The franchisee, lacking a similar remedy under its own state's laws, seeks to avail itself of the MFA's franchise relationship provisions regarding unfair practices, such as termination without cause, discrimination, encroachment, or unreasonable standards.

Early decisions by the Minnesota Supreme Court interpreting the MFA suggested it only applied to franchisees "within Minnesota."[38] The Eighth Circuit followed suit.[39] More recently, however, courts noted how these earlier cases did not involve nonresident franchisees seeking to invoke the MFA's protections.[40] As a result of the lack of controlling precedent, courts split on the issue.

The Minnesota Supreme Court has now weighed in, holding the MFA "does not categorically preclude an out-of-state company from enforcing a claim for

---

36. *Id.* subdiv. 1.; *see also* Cambria Co., LLC v. M&M Creative Laminates, Inc., 2024 WL 4139394, *5 (Minn. Sept. 11, 2024) ("The Legislature *did* include express territorial limitations in other provisions contained within the Act. For example, . . . section 80C.19 . . . ."); Klosek v. Am. Express Co., 2008 WL 4057534, at *21 (D. Minn. Aug. 26, 2008) ("As the statute indicates, the geographic limits do not apply to the entire MFA, but only to '[t]he provisions concerning sales and offers to sell [.]'"), *aff'd*, 370 F. App'x 761 (8th Cir. 2010)).

37. Mainstream Fashions Franchising, Inc. v. All These Things, LLC, 453 F. Supp. 3d 1167, 1188 (D. Minn. 2020).

38. Clapp v. Peterson, 327 N.W.2d 585, 586 (Minn. 1982) (citing Martin Invs., Inc. v. Vander Bie, 269 N.W.2d 868,

872 (Minn. 1978)).

39. Modern Comput. Sys., Inc. v. Modern Banking Sys., Inc., 871 F.2d 734, 739 (8th Cir. 1989) (stating the MFA "protects franchisees *in Minnesota* from unreasonable or abusive treatment by powerful franchisors") (emphasis added), *superseded by statute on other grounds as acknowledged by*, Com. Prop. Invs., Inc. v. Quality Inns Int'l, Inc., 938 F.2d 870, 874 (8th Cir. 1991).

40. Mainstream Fashions Franchising, Inc. v. All These Things, LLC, 453 F. Supp. 3d 1167, 1188 (D. Minn. 2020) ("[T]he Minnesota Court of Appeals has recently noted that the application of the MFA to an out-of-state franchisee is 'a question without controlling precedent' because the Martin and Clapp decisions did not explicitly address the extraterritorial scope of the MFA."); Cambria Co. LLC v. M&M Creative Laminants Inc., 2019 WL 3543602, at *2 (Minn. Ct. App. Aug. 5, 2019) ("However, *Martin Inv'rs, Inc.*, does not address the issue now raised by the parties on the scope of the MFA.").

unfair practices."[41] The court, however, did not go so far as to hold that the MFA "is enforceable by *every* out-of-state company."[42] And unfortunately, it did not establish a bright line test for determining when a nonresident franchisee can assert a claim for unfair practices under the MFA.

Instead, the court explained that "an out-of-state company must show that [the MFA] is otherwise applicable, and companies without a connection to Minnesota may face jurisdictional or other hurdles."[43] The court then narrowed its analysis to the facts of the case before it, holding that the MFA applied "here" because the putative franchisee "engaged in continuous business" with a Minnesota franchisor "for eight years," their "business agreements were drafted in Minnesota," and the putative franchisee "sent personnel to Minnesota for training and certifications."[44] Perhaps most importantly, the court observed that the parties' contact included "a Minnesota choice-of-law provision."[45] As a result, determining whether a nonresident can assert a claim for unfair practices under the MFA must still be analyzed on a case-by-case basis.

The existence of an agreement between the parties to apply Minnesota law is likely an important factor because most cases have held the MFA does not apply to nonresident franchisees who do not operate franchises in Minnesota when there is a contractual choice of law applying another state's law. The MFA's anti-waiver provision expressly only applies to residents, so nonresidents may waive its applicability by agreeing to apply another state's law.[46] Furthermore, Minnesota courts generally apply a presumption that state statutes do not apply extraterritorially for the benefit of nonresidents.[47]

Courts declining to apply the MFA to nonresident franchisees have done so citing the aforementioned precedent suggesting its legislative intent was to protect only Minnesota franchisees, although the "tension between the language of the statute and what courts have deemed to be legislative intent" has been noted by courts, and now clarified by the Minnesota Supreme Court as already discussed.[48] In these cases, an offer was made by a Minnesota franchisor's agent outside Minnesota,[49] the franchisees were either not located nor operating in

---

41. Cambria Co., LLC v. M&M Creative Laminates, Inc., 2024 WL 4139394, at *5 (Minn. Sept. 11, 2024).
42. *Id.* (emphasis original).
43. *Id.*
44. *Id.*
45. *Id.*
46. MINN. STAT. § 80C.21.
47. Harrington v. Nw. Airlines, Inc., 2003 WL 22016032, at *2 (Minn. Ct. App. Aug. 26, 2003) (declining to apply Minnesota statute for the protection of nonresidents because of "presumption against a state statute having extraterritorial application").
48. Wave Form Sys. v. AMS Sales Corp., 73 F. Supp. 3d 1052, 1058 (D. Minn. 2014); Hockey Enters., Inc. v. Total Hockey Worldwide, LLC, 762 F. Supp. 2d 1138, 1146 (D. Minn. 2011) (holding MFA did not apply to nonresident franchisee because "it is . . . construed in favor of protecting Minnesota franchisees"); Healy v. Carlson Travel Network Assocs., Inc., 227 F. Supp. 2d 1080, 1087 (D. Minn. 2002) (declining to apply MFA to nonresident franchisee because it is "the policy of the MFA to guard against abuses of franchisees in Minnesota").
49. Healy v. Carlson Travel Network Assocs., Inc., 227 F. Supp. 2d 1080 (D. Minn. 2002) ("Healy urges that the statute applies because the offer to sell the franchise came from an agent of Carlson,

Minnesota[50] and contractually chose not to apply Minnesota law,[51] or at least "the Minnesota nexus" was "very minimal."[52]

Fewer cases have held the MFA applies to nonresident franchisees. These courts analyzed the MFA's definition of its "Scope" and held nonresident franchisees could assert claims under the MFA, albeit sometimes for divergent reasons and outcomes.[53] In one case, the court held the MFA applied to a nonresident franchisee because the franchisor made the offer from and received its acceptance in Minnesota, although the court also relied on the franchise agreement's choice of Minnesota law, which may have been the dispositive factor.[54] In another case, the court held the MFA applied to a nonresident franchisee because any "geographic limits" imposed by the MFA's broad definition of its

---

a Minnesota corporation. No authority is cited for the proposition that the MFA applies merely because the franchisor is a Minnesota corporation."); Bixby's Food Sys., Inc. v. McKay, 193 F. Supp. 2d 1053, 1059 (N.D. Ill. 2002) ("The McKays have not proven or even alleged that they were or are residents of Minnesota or that their franchise was to be operated in Minnesota. Therefore, they have not shown that the waiver contained in the Franchise Agreement was void or otherwise unenforceable in this case. The McKays allege no facts demonstrating that the franchise at issue here was offered or sold in Minnesota.").

50. Johnson Bros. Liquor Co. v. Bacardi U.S.A., Inc., 830 F. Supp. 2d 697, 703 (D. Minn. 2011) ("[E]ven where a party to a 'franchise agreement' is a Minnesota corporation, the agreement is not within the purview of the MFA if the franchisee is not located in and does not operate in Minnesota."); In re Ne. Express Reg'l Airlines, Inc. v. Nw. Airlines, Inc., 228 B.R. 53, 59 (Bankr. D. Me. 1998) ("Clearly, the intent is to protect Minnesotans."); Sound of Music Co. v. Minn. Mining & Mfg. Co., 389 F. Supp. 2d 988 (N.D. Ill. 2005) ("It is undisputed that Sound of Music is neither a Minnesota resident nor a "franchise to be operated" in Minnesota. Based on this straightforward reading of the statute, this anti-waiver provision does not apply here, and Sound of Music therefore waived any rights under the Act."), aff'd, 477 F.3d 910 (7th Cir. 2007).

51. *Hockey Enters., Inc.*, 762 F. Supp. at 1146 ("Plaintiffs have provided no relevant support for the notion that the statute is intended or has been held to extend to non-Minnesota franchisees that do not operate in Minnesota. Accordingly, the Court concludes that the parties' choice-of-law provision is not void under Minnesota law and that the MFA does not apply to Plaintiffs' claims."); Novus Franchising, Inc. v. Superior Entrance Sys. Inc., 2012 WL 3542451, at *3 (W.D. Wis. Aug. 15, 2012) ("As mentioned, however, the choice of law provision in the parties' contract expressly rejects the application of the Minnesota Franchise Act to franchises located outside that state. Even without the choice of law provision, that Act is inapplicable to defendants, who are not Minnesota residents and who operate a franchise territory located entirely outside of Minnesota.").

52. *Wave Form Sys.*, 73 F. Supp. 3d at 1058.

53. In a series of identical rulings, the court observed, "There is nothing in the language of the statute suggesting that the MFA cannot apply to a foreign franchisee when the offer, in this case a solicitation, 'originates' from Minnesota." Dolphin Kickboxing Co. v. FranChoice, Inc., 2019 WL 7598649, at *8 (D. Minn. Dec. 19, 2019); Hamilton v. FranChoice, Inc., 2019 WL 7598651 (D. Minn. Dec. 19, 2019); Rise Above Fitness, Inc. v. FranChoice, Inc., 2019 WL 7598652 (D. Minn. Dec. 19, 2019); Xiaolin Li v. FranChoice, Inc., 2019 WL 7598656 (D. Minn. Dec. 19, 2019); Van Saders v. Franchoice, Inc., 2019 WL 7598665, at *8 (D. Minn. Dec. 19, 2019); Johnson v. FranChoice, Inc., 2019 WL 7598623 (D. Minn. Dec. 19, 2019).

54. Candleman Corp. v. Farrow, Bus. Franchise Guide (CCH) ¶ 11,635 (D. Minn. Feb. 1, 1999) ("Therefore, the MFA applies in this case because: (1) Candleman's offer to sell the franchise to Farrow originated from Candleman's Minnesota offices; and (2) Farrow's acceptance of the offer was received by Candleman in Minnesota. Further, the franchise agreement's choice of law provision provides for Minnesota law.").

"Scope" applied only to provisions "concerning sales and offers to sell," and not the MFA's relationship provisions.[55]

2. Annotations

Despite Minnesota precedent suggesting that the MFA's relationship provisions apply exclusively to franchisees who reside or operate within the state of Minnesota, the Minnesota Supreme Court has held the MFA "does not categorically preclude an out-of-state company from enforcing a claim for unfair practices," although the MFA is not "enforceable by *every* out-of-state company." *Cambria Co., LLC v. M&M Creative Laminants, Inc.*, WL 4139394, at *5 (Minn. Sept. 11, 2024) (emphasis original). As a result of this recent decision, prior cases holding that the MFA only applies to franchisees who are Minnesota residents are not authoritative, but other cases may still aid in identifying factors relevant to whether there is a sufficient "connection" between the nonresident and Minnesota for the MFA to apply.

Courts have "split on the issue," and the outcome often depends on the facts and circumstances of each case. *Mainstream Fashions Franchising, Inc. v. All These Things, LLC*, 453 F. Supp. 3d 1167 (D. Minn. 2020) (listing cases for the observation that "several courts have concluded that the MFA does not apply to out-of-state franchisees" and "other judges in this district have reached the opposite conclusion.").

There is no express limitation to in-state franchisees contained within the MFA despite precedent suggesting its legislative intent was to protect Minnesota franchisees. *Johnson v. FranChoice, Inc.*, 2019 WL 7598623 (D. Minn. Dec. 19, 2019) ("There is nothing in the language of the statute suggesting that the MFA cannot apply to a foreign franchisee when the offer, in this case a solicitation, 'originates' from Minnesota."); *Dolphin Kickboxing Co. v. FranChoice, Inc.*, 2019 WL 7598649 (D. Minn. Dec. 19, 2019); *Hamilton v. FranChoice, Inc.*, 2019 WL 7598651 (D. Minn. Dec. 19, 2019); *Rise Above Fitness, Inc. v. FranChoice, Inc.*, 2019 WL 7598652 (D. Minn. Dec. 19, 2019); *Xiaolin Li v. FranChoice, Inc.*, 2019 WL 7598656 (D. Minn. Dec. 19, 2019); *Van Saders v. Franchoice, Inc.*, 2019 WL 7598665 (D. Minn. Dec. 19, 2019).

Courts have struggled in defining what type of "Minnesota nexus" warrants the MFA's extraterritorial application. *Wave Form Systems v. AMS Sales Corp.*, 73 F. Supp. 3d 1052 (D. Minn. 2014) ("While a construction of the language of the statute does support Wave Form's position, the Minnesota nexus with the factual predicate is very minimal. Other than receiving an offer transmitted from Minnesota and then remitting acceptance back to Minnesota, Wave Form has had no contact with Minnesota. Wave Form has never had a single sale in this state nor does it have any physical presence here. While Wave Form does conduct business in states outside of Oregon, it is undisputed that Minnesota is not

---

55. Klosek v. Am. Express Co., 2008 WL 4057534 at *21 (D. Minn. Aug. 26, 2008) ("As the statute indicates, the geographic limits do not apply to the entire MFA, but only to '[t]he provisions concerning sales and offers to sell [.]'"), *aff'd*, 370 F. App'x 761 (8th Cir. 2010)).

one of them. To construe the MFA broadly enough to apply here given the facts currently of record in this case is a stretch.").

The existence of a Minnesota choice-of-law provision is an important consideration for the MFA's extraterritorial application because franchisees who are not Minnesota residents may waive its application. The MFA did not apply to nonresidents who did not operate in Minnesota when there was an express waiver of the MFA in the choice-of-law provision. *Novus Franchising, Inc. v. Superior Entrance Systems Inc.*, 2012 WL 3542451 (W.D. Wis. Aug. 15, 2012) ("As mentioned, however, the choice of law provision in the parties' contract expressly rejects the application of the Minnesota Franchise Act to franchises located outside that state. Even without the choice of law provision, that Act is inapplicable to defendants, who are not Minnesota residents and who operate a franchise territory located entirely outside of Minnesota.").

The MFA's anti-waiver provision, however, prevents franchisees who are Minnesota residents from agreeing to the application of another state's law. *Long John Silver's Inc. v. Nickleson*, 923 F. Supp. 2d 1004 (W.D. Ky. 2013) ("However, as this Court has already noted in a prior decision, the MFA anti-waiver provision 'has been interpreted to invalidate any binding out-of-state choice-of-law provision imposed on a Minnesota resident-franchisee and any other provision purporting to diminish rights granted to Minnesota franchisees pursuant to the Act.'").

As a court sitting in diversity jurisdiction, the New Jersey court opted to apply the MFA's provision voiding choice of law provisions in franchise agreements where a franchisee is a Minnesota resident. *Red Roof Franchising LLC v. AA Hospitality Northshore LLC*, 877 F. Supp. 2d 140 (D.N.J. 2012) ("Under Minnesota law, if a franchisee is a Minnesota resident, partnership, or corporation, any choice of law clause contained in the franchise agreement is void. Since Minnesota law applies to the franchise agreement and voids the choice of law provision, Texas law does not apply.").

Courts have refused to apply the MFA's prevention of choice-of-law provisions in franchise agreements against non-Minnesotan franchisees that do not operate in Minnesota. *Hockey Enterprises v. Total Hockey Worldwide, LLC*, 762 F. Supp. 2d 1138 (D. Minn. 2011) ("Plaintiffs have provided no relevant support for the notion that the statute is intended or has been held to extend to non-Minnesota franchisees that do not operate in Minnesota. Accordingly, the Court concludes that the parties' choice-of-law provision is not void under Minnesota law and that the MFA does not apply to Plaintiffs' claims.").

Minnesota cannot regulate franchise agreements that are formed and performed in other states. *Johnson Brothers Liquor Co. v. Bacardi U.S.A, Inc.*, 830 F. Supp. 2d 697 (D. Minn. 2011) ("[E]ven where a party to a 'franchise agreement' is a Minnesota corporation, the agreement is not within the purview of the MFA if the franchisee is not located in and does not operate in Minnesota.").

Provisions relating to sales and offer to sell a franchise are subject to geographical restrictions relating to where the subject sale or offer occurs. These restrictions do not apply to the entire MFA; rather, the restrictions apply exclusively to the provisions regarding offers and sales. *Klosek v. American Express Co.*,

2008 WL 4057534, at *21 (D. Minn. Aug. 26, 2008) ("As the statute indicates, the geographic limits do not apply to the entire MFA, but only to "[t]he provisions . . . concerning sales and offers to sell [.]"), *aff'd*, 370 F. App'x 761 (8th Cir. 2010).

An agreement containing a provision stating that the plaintiff is not a franchisee is not prohibited by the anti-waiver provision of the MFA. *Sound of Music Co. v. Minnesota Mining & Manufacturing Co.*, 389 F. Supp. 2d 988 (N.D. Ill. 2005) ("It is undisputed that Sound of Music is neither a Minnesota resident nor a 'franchise to be operated' in Minnesota. Based on this straightforward reading of the statute, this anti-waiver provision does not apply here, and Sound of Music therefore waived any rights under the Act."), *aff'd*, 477 F.3d 910 (7th Cir. 2007).

The MFA is inapplicable in a case where an offer to sell the franchise came from an agent of a Minnesota corporation. There is no authority for the proposition that the MFA applies merely because the franchisor is located in Minnesota. The franchise agreement was signed and presented in Illinois. *Healy v. Carlson Travel Network Associates, Inc.*, 227 F. Supp. 2d 1080 (D. Minn. 2002) ("Healy urges that the statute applies because the offer to sell the franchise came from an agent of Carlson, a Minnesota corporation. No authority is cited for the proposition that the MFA applies merely because the franchisor is a Minnesota corporation.").

The anti-waiver restriction of the MFA held inapplicable when the franchise agreement contains a waiver provision applicable only to franchisees that are not residents of Minnesota and where the franchise was not located in Minnesota. The offer and sale were also not in the state of Minnesota. Therefore, the MFA was not applicable. *Bixby's Food Systems, Inc. v. McKay*, 193 F. Supp. 2d 1053, 1059 (N.D. Ill. 2002) ("The McKays have not proven or even alleged that they were or are residents of Minnesota or that their franchise was to be operated in Minnesota. Therefore, they have not shown that the waiver contained in the Franchise Agreement was void or otherwise unenforceable in this case. The McKays allege no facts demonstrating that the franchise at issue here was offered or sold in Minnesota.").

The MFA applies where the offer to sell the franchise originated out of the Minnesota office, the acceptance of the offer was accepted by the franchisor in Minnesota, and the agreement's choice of law provision selected the application of Minnesota law. *Candleman Corp. v. Farrow*, Bus. Franchise Guide (CCH) ¶ 11,635 (D. Minn. Feb. 1, 1999) ("Therefore, the MFA applies in this case because: (1) Candleman's offer to sell the franchise to Farrow originated from Candleman's Minnesota offices; and (2) Farrow's acceptance of the offer was received by Candleman in Minnesota. . . . Further, the franchise agreement's choice of law provision provides for Minnesota law.").

The purpose of prohibiting certain choice-of-law provisions is to ensure Minnesota franchisees are protected by the MFA. *Van Dusen Airport Services Co., L.P. v. Allied Signal, Inc.*, 1991 WL 151377 (Minn. Ct. App. 1991) ("Prohibiting choice of law clauses ensures that Minnesota franchisees will be protected by the Minnesota franchise act.").

The MFA's protections do not extend to franchisees not within Minnesota. The court held the MFA's intent is to protect Minnesotans and not to apply the MFA's relationship laws extraterritorially. *In re Northeast Express Regional*

Airlines, Inc. v. Northwest Airlines, Inc., 228 B.R. 53 (Bankr. D. Me. 1998) ("We agree with Northwest that the Debtors cannot claim the protections afforded under the MFA because they are not franchisees within Minnesota.").

Similarly, courts have questioned if the MFA is sufficiently strong enough of a governmental interest to preclude enforcement of the parties' contractual choice of law provision that would apply the contractually designated franchise laws from a different jurisdiction. Where the application of the contractually chosen law would not be repugnant to the public policy of Minnesota because of the comparable bargaining power of the parties, the anti-waiver provision of the MFA will not be enforced. Therefore, New York law was applied. *Carlock v. Pillsbury Co.*, 719 F. Supp. 791 (D. Minn. 1989) ("That Act, codified at Minn. Stat. § 80C.01 et seq., was adopted in 1973 to protect franchisees within Minnesota from unfair contracts and other previously unregulated abuses in the then-burgeoning franchise industry.").

C. Termination

1. What Constitutes Termination or Cancellation

a. Commentary

Minnesota has yet to recognize a claim for de facto or constructive termination of the franchise agreement.[56] The only cases addressing the issue, however, have found that the franchisee has failed to plead factors that would support a finding of a de facto termination, if the cause of action was viable. Thus, while only an actual termination constitutes termination or cancellation currently, the issue has not been tested against a well-pled complaint.

b. Annotations

The Eighth Circuit noted that courts have yet to recognize de facto termination as a violation of the MFA. The court further reasoned that if de facto termination was a viable theory under the MFA, the plaintiff failed to properly plead facts to support the theory as it did not allege that its franchisor intended to put them out of business or that the franchisor's actions resulted in a substantial decline in the value of their franchises. *Klosek v. American Express Co.*, No. CIV. 08-426 JNE/JJG, 2008 WL 4057534, at *22 (D. Minn. Aug. 26, 2008), *aff'd*, 370 F. App'x 761 (8th Cir. 2010).

The MFA does not actually recognize de facto termination as a cause of action, but even if it did, the franchisee's pleading was insufficient to state a claim for de facto termination as it failed to allege that the franchisor made it effectively impossible for the franchisee to do business. *Healy v. Carlson Travel Network Assocs., Inc.*, 227 F. Supp. 2d 1080, 1090 (D. Minn. 2002).

---

56. *Id.* at *22; Healy v. Carlson Travel Network Assocs., Inc., 227 F. Supp. 2d 1080, 1090 (D. Minn. 2002).

2. Restrictions on Termination or Cancellation

a. Commentary

The MFA limits a franchisor's ability to terminate a franchisee absent good cause and without first giving proper notice.[57]

b. Annotations

There is no case law addressing this issue.

3. Notice Requirement

a. Commentary

In general, the MFA requires that franchisors provide written notice setting forth all reasons for termination of a franchise at least 90 days in advance of any termination.[58] The MFA, however, does set forth certain circumstances where the franchisor is able to terminate immediately upon notice, or on only 24 hours' notice.[59]

Courts generally require that any notice provided to the franchisee state all the applicable reasons for termination with particularity and, in cases where a cure period is required, state the exact actions the franchisee must take in order to avoid termination. For example, a notice for termination citing nonpayment of amounts due must state the exact amount the franchisee must pay in order to cure the default.[60]

b. Annotations

A franchisor's termination notice was inadequate because it did not make mention of the exact amount the franchisee owed. The court held that this notice was "particularly necessary" in cases where the franchisee is being terminated for nonpayment of amounts owed, as the franchisor may be the only party that can accurately calculate how much the franchisee owes at any time. *Culligan International Co. v. Culligan Water Conditioning of Carver County, Inc.*, 563 F. Supp. 1265, 1270 (D. Minn. 1983).

4. Grounds for Termination

a. Commentary

A franchisor may not terminate a franchise agreement except for good cause.[61] Good cause is defined as the "failure by the franchisee to substantially comply with the material and reasonable franchise requirements imposed by the franchisor."[62] It includes, but is not limited to, the franchisee's bankruptcy or insolvency;[63] the franchisee assigning the franchise agreement for the benefit of

---

57. MINN. STAT. § 80C.14.
58. *Id.* § 80C.14 subdiv. 3.
59. *Id.*
60. Culligan Int'l Co. v. Culligan Water Conditioning of Carver Cnty., Inc., 563 F. Supp. 1265, 1270 (D. Minn. 1983); *but see* Novus Franchising, Inc. v. Taylor, 795 F. Supp. 122, 130 (M.D. Pa. 1992) (finding no need to state the exact amounts due when the amount owed was clear).
61. MINN. STAT. § 80C.14 subdiv. 3(b).
62. *Id.*
63. *Id.* subdiv. 3(b)(1).

creditors or a similar disposition;[64] the franchisee's voluntary abandonment of the franchise;[65] the franchisee's conviction, guilty plea, or no contest plea to a charge of violating any law relating to the franchise business;[66] or the franchisee's acts or conduct that materially impairs the goodwill associated with the franchisor's trade name, trademark, service mark, or commercial symbol.[67]

Examples of circumstances where a court has found good cause include a franchisee's repeated failure to timely pay amounts due under the contract[68] and a franchisees' repeated failures of quality control evaluations or inspections.[69]

There is no good cause to terminate, however, when a franchisee fails to comply with unreasonable requirements of a franchise agreement. For example, a franchisee's failure to rebuild or remodel its location was unreasonable, when the franchisor did not impose the same remodeling requirements on the three closest corporate-owned locations.[70]

b. Annotations

A distributor's repeated failure, over an extended period of time, to pay amounts due to the manufacturer constituted good cause to terminate. The distributor's untimely cure of the indebtedness after the termination was final did not entitle the distributor to reinstatement. *OT Industries, Inc. v. OT-tehdas Oy Santasalo-Sohlberg Ab*, 346 N.W.2d 162, 167 (Minn. Ct. App. 1984).

A hotel franchisee's repeated quality control evaluation failures were good cause for the franchisor to terminate the agreements, despite the franchisee's argument that the termination was retaliation against the franchisees for filing an unrelated lawsuit against the franchisor. *Pooniwala v. Wyndham Worldwide, Corp.*, No. CIV. 14-778 DWF/LIB, 2014 WL 1772323, at *6 (D. Minn. May 2, 2014).

Upon the renewal and to maintain consistency with other locations, a franchisor required a franchisee to install a drive thru service lane and separate customer restrooms. To do this, the franchisee would be required to relocate or entirely rebuild its location. The franchisee failed to rebuild or relocate by the deadline set in the agreement, and the franchisor terminated the franchise agreement. In issuing a preliminary injunction stopping the termination, the court found that the requirements were unreasonable, in part because the three closest corporate-owned locations did not have separate restrooms or drive thru lanes, and thus could not form the basis for termination. *Delaria v. KFC Corp.*, No. CIV. 4-94-116, 1995 WL 17079305, at *6 (D. Minn. Jan. 13, 1995).

---

64. *Id.* subdiv. 3(b)(2).
65. *Id.* subdiv. 3(b)(3).
66. *Id.* subdiv. 3(b)(4).
67. *Id.* subdiv. 3(b)(5).
68. OT Indus., Inc. v. OT-tehdas Oy Santasalo-Sohlberg Ab, 346 N.W.2d 162, 167 (Minn. Ct. App. 1984).
69. Pooniwala v. Wyndham Worldwide, Corp., No. CIV. 14-778 DWF/LIB, 2014 WL 1772323, at *6 (D. Minn. May 2, 2014).
70. Delaria v. KFC Corp., No. CIV. 4-94-116, 1995 WL 17079305, at *6 (D. Minn. Jan. 13, 1995).

5. Required Cure Period

a. Commentary

For most breaches, franchisors must provide franchisees with a 60-day cure period prior to terminating the franchise.[71] No cure period is required if the alleged grounds for termination or cancellation are the franchisee's voluntary abandonment of the franchise or the franchisee's conviction of an offense directly related to the franchised business.[72] A 24-hour cure period is required if the franchisee commits a default under the franchise agreement that materially impairs the good will associated with the franchisor's trade name or other commercial symbol.[73]

Some courts have also allowed franchisors to terminate immediately upon notice when any potential cure would be impossible. For example, the Minnesota Supreme Court has ruled that the franchisor's failure to provide a 24-hour cure period to remedy conduct involving consumer fraud did not preclude the termination of a franchise, as any attempted cure under those circumstances would be futile.[74]

b. Annotations

After numerous customers of an auto repair franchisee reported the franchisee to the Minnesota attorney general, the franchisor and the attorney general jointly investigated the complaints and determined that the franchisee was defrauding consumers by telling them that their vehicles, which generally needed only nominal repairs, required expensive transmission repairs. The franchisor then terminated the franchisee immediately, without providing 24 hours' notice. The court determined that notice was not required in this instance as any of the franchisee's attempts to cure would have been futile. *AAMCO Industries, Inc. v. DeWolf*, 312 Minn. 95, 103, 250 N.W.2d 835, 840 (1977).

A factual dispute existed as to whether a franchisor had good cause to terminate its franchisee when the franchisor only provided the franchisee with 30 days to implement a new POS system prior to terminating, instead of the 60 days required under the MFA, but then asserted that it was terminating the franchisee due to the franchisee's abandonment of the franchise. *Mainstream Fashions Franchising, Inc. v. All These Things, LLC*, 453 F. Supp. 3d 1167, 1191 (D. Minn. 2020).

A franchisor was justified in terminating a franchise only five days after its franchisee voluntarily abandoned its franchise, as the MFA does not require any cure period in cases of voluntary abandonment. *Red Roof Franchising, LLC v. AA Hospitality Northshore, LLC*, 877 F. Supp. 2d 140, 158 (D.N.J. 2012), *aff'd sub nom.* Red Roof Franchising, LLC v. Patel, 564 F. App'x 685 (3d Cir. 2014).

A sandwich shop franchisor terminated eight franchisees who were officers or members of its franchisee association after the association published a former

---

71. MINN. STAT. § 80C.14 subdiv. 3.
72. *Id.*
73. *Id.*
74. AAMCO Indus., Inc. v. DeWolf, 312 Minn. 95, 103, 250 N.W.2d 835, 840 (1977).

franchisee's suicide note that attributed the suicide to the franchisor. The termination letters sent to the franchisees did not identify any specific misconduct or violations but instead stated that the franchisees were terminated for engaging in conduct that, in the franchisor's judgment, impaired the goodwill associated with the franchisor's marks. Some of the letters sent did not provide for a cure period, while others provided a 24-hour cure period. The court granted a preliminary injunction preventing the terminations, finding among other things that the MFA mandated notice and an opportunity to cure, even in cases where the franchisor was exercising its judgment. The court did not consider that the MFA allows for a 24-hour cure period when the franchisee commits an act that materially impairs the franchisor's goodwill. *Bray v. QFA Royalties LLC*, 486 F. Supp. 2d 1237, 1254 (D. Colo. 2007).

A franchisor was able to terminate its franchisee immediately without an opportunity to cure when the franchisee failed to pay taxes and mismanaged funds and was able to show that the franchisee's actions materially impaired the franchisor's goodwill. *Video Update, Inc. v. Malaske*, No. C6-94-787, 1994 WL 523837, at *3 (Minn. Ct. App. Sept. 27, 1994).

6. Repurchase Obligations

a. Commentary
Not applicable.

b. Annotations
Not applicable.

D. Restrictions on Nonrenewal

1. What Constitutes Nonrenewal

a. Commentary
Under the MFA, a franchise agreement cannot expire on its own terms absent notice of the franchisor's intent to not renew or nonrenewal for cause, even if the agreement does not provide for renewal.[75] However, as Minnesota courts have yet to recognize a claim for constructive termination of a franchise agreement,[76] it is likely courts would also not recognize a claim for constructive nonrenewal of a franchise agreement.

b. Annotations
If the MFA applied to the relationship, a manufacturer's nonrenewal of manufacturing agreement would not be effective absent proper notice of at least 180 days in advance of the termination date, even though agreement did not

---

75. Wave Form Sys., Inc. v. AMS Sales Corp., 73 F. Supp. 3d 1052, 1062 (D. Minn. 2014).
76. Klosek v. Am. Express Co., No. CIV. 08-426 JNE/JJG, 2008 WL 4057534, at *22 (D. Minn. Aug. 26, 2008), *aff'd*, 370 F. App'x 761 (8th Cir. 2010); Healy v. Carlson Travel Network Assocs., Inc., 227 F. Supp. 2d 1080, 1090 (D. Minn. 2002).

call for renewal. *Wave Form Systems, Inc. v. AMS Sales Corp.*, 73 F. Supp. 3d 1052, 1062–63 (D. Minn. 2014).

2. Restrictions on Nonrenewal

a. Commentary

Except in situations where the franchisor has good cause to terminate a franchisee and has complied with the requisite notice and cure period, the MFA limits a franchisor's ability to refuse to renew a franchise to situations where (1) the franchisor provided the franchisee with notice of its intent not to renew at least 180 days before the franchise agreement expired and (2) the franchisee has had the opportunity to recover the fair market value of the franchise during the life of the franchise.[77] Franchisors are expressly prohibited from refusing to renew a franchise agreement for the purpose of converting the franchise into a company-owned location.[78]

In determining if a franchisee has had sufficient opportunity to recoup the fair market value of the franchise, courts do not require that the franchisee be debt-free at the time of renewal.[79]

b. Annotations

A franchisee had sufficient time to recover the fair market value of the franchise, even though the franchisee still had significant debt related to equipment purchases he made for the franchise. The court found that the franchisee operated the business for over 16 years and found it notable that the franchisor had offered to purchase the franchisee's business for over $20 million. *McCabe v. AIR-serv Group, LLC*, No. CIV. 07-4553 RHK/JSM, 2007, WL 4591932, at *4 (D. Minn. Dec. 28, 2007).

3. Notice Requirement

a. Commentary

If a franchisor refuses to renew a franchisee for good cause, then the franchisor must comply with the notice and cure requirements of section 80C.14 subdivision 3. Therefore, when nonrenewing for cause and except in cases of abandonment, conviction of a crime related to the franchise, or actions that materially impact the franchisor's good will the franchisor must provide notice 90 days prior to the nonrenewal and 60 days to cure the default.

If the franchisor refuses to renew for any other reason, it must provide the franchisee with written notice of its intent at least 180 days prior to the termination of the franchise agreement and the franchisee must have had sufficient time to recoup the value of the franchise.[80] The franchisor's notice should explicitly state that the franchisor intends to not renew the franchise, not merely that

---

77. Minn. Stat. § 80C.14 subdiv. 4.
78. *Id.*
79. McCabe v. AIR-serv Grp., LLC, No. CIV. 07-4553 RHK/JSM, 2007 WL 4591932, at *4 (D. Minn. Dec. 28, 2007).
80. Minn. Stat. § 80C.14 subdiv. 4.

the franchise agreement is set to expire.[81] Unfortunately for franchisors, it is unclear how long a franchisee must operate to recoup the value of their investment. From a practical standpoint, franchisors should consider factors such as the franchisee's profitability, if the franchisee is likely to have outstanding debt remaining from its initial investment, and the length of time the franchisee has been operating before refusing to renew absent good cause.

b. Annotations

The court found that there was an issue of material fact if notice that franchise agreement would expire was sufficient to satisfy the MFA's nonrenewal notice requirements. The court noted that the expiration notices did not use the words "renewal," "nonrenewal," or any similar variant. *Rogers Family Foods, LLC v. DFO, LLC*, No. CV 19-1476 (DWF/ECW), 2020 WL 5816589, at *9 (D. Minn. Sept. 30, 2020).

A franchise agreement cannot expire on its own terms, even if the agreement does not have a renewal option. Instead, the franchisor must provide the requisite notice of nonrenewal and satisfy the other conditions, either sufficient time to recoup the value of the investment or good cause for termination, in order to avoid renewal of the franchise agreement. *Wave Form Systems, Inc. v. AMS Sales Corp.*, 73 F. Supp. 3d 1052, 1063 (D. Minn. 2014).

4. Grounds for Nonrenewal

a. Commentary

Except in cases where the franchisor wishes to fail to renew a franchise in order to replace it with a company-owned unit, the MFA does not limit the reasons for which a franchisor can refuse to renew a franchise, so long as it either has good cause to terminate or the franchisee has operated for a sufficient amount of time and the franchisor has provided 180 days' notice of nonrenewal.[82]

Legitimate business reasons, such as a manufacturer's decision to terminate its distribution program, support the nonrenewal of a franchise.[83] However, nonrenewals based on business reasons would not constitute good cause for termination, and thus the 180-day notice requirement and opportunity to recoup the value of the franchise requirements must be met.

b. Annotations

A manufacturer had legitimate business reasons to not renew a distribution agreement when the distributor was changing its business model, discontinuing its distributor system, and would no longer be manufacturing the products its former distributors sold. The court found the franchisor complied with

---

81. Rogers Fam. Foods, LLC v. DFO, LLC, No. CV 19-1476 (DWF/ECW), 2020 WL 5816589, at *9 (D. Minn. Sept. 30, 2020) (issue of material fact if notice that franchise agreement would expire was sufficient to satisfy the nonrenewal notice requirement precluded summary judgment).

82. Minn. Stat. § 80C.14 subdiv. 4.

83. McCabe v. AIR-serv Grp., LLC, No. CIV. 07-4553 RHK/JSM, 2007 WL 4591932, at *4 (D. Minn. Dec. 28, 2007).

the MFA's requirements for nonrenewal in that it provided approximately ten months' notice, and the franchisee had sufficient time to recoup the franchise's value. *McCabe v. AIR-serv Group, LLC*, No. CIV. 07-4553 RHK/JSM, 2007 WL 4591932, at *4 (D. Minn. Dec. 28, 2007).

5. Required Cure Period

a. Commentary

Franchisors must comply with the notice and cure periods applicable to termination when not renewing a franchisee for cause, meaning that the franchisor must provide at least 90 days' notice of nonrenewal, and 60 days to cure the default upon which the nonrenewal is based.[84]

b. Annotations

Not applicable.

6. Limitations on Franchisors' Right to Impose Conditions for Renewal

a. Commentary

The MFA does not place any restrictions on a franchisor's right to impose conditions for renewal. However, one court recently questioned, without deciding, if a franchisor could offer a franchisee a successor agreement with different terms than the original agreement, and thus it appears that this may be an open question in Minnesota.[85]

b. Annotations

Court questioned, without deciding, if offering a renewal agreement with different terms than the original agreement would constitute a "failure to renew" under the MFA. The franchise agreement at issue in the case stated that the franchisee had no right to renew the agreement, but expressly incorporated the terms of the MFA. *Rogers Family Foods, LLC v. DFO, LLC*, No. CV 19-1476 (DWF/ECW), 2020 WL 5816589, at *6 (D. Minn. Sept. 30, 2020).

7. Repurchase Obligations

a. Commentary

The MFA does not impose repurchase obligations on franchisors.

b. Annotations

Not applicable.

---

84. MINN. STAT. § 80C.14 subdiv. 3.
85. Rogers Fam. Foods, LLC v. DFO, LLC, No. CV 19-1476 (DWF/ECW), 2020 WL 5816589, at *6 (D. Minn. Sept. 30, 2020).

E. Transfers and Succession

1. Commentary

The MFA prohibits franchisors from unreasonably withholding consent to a transfer when the franchisee to be substituted meets the franchisor's then-current qualifications for new franchisees.[86] The MFA does not explicitly address transfers in cases of death or permanent disability.

2. Annotations

There was sufficient evidence for a jury to find that a franchisor's failure to consent to a transfer violated the MFA when the proposed transferee had greater financial ability than the majority of the franchisees that the franchisor had recently approved and that rejecting the proposed transferee on the grounds that the transferee did not have retail experience was not a valid reason for rejection when the franchisor had approved other franchisees with no retail experience. *BASCO, Inc. v. Buth-Na-Bodhaige, Inc., et al.*, 198 F.3d 1053 (8th Cir. 1999).

F. Other Regulation of the Franchise Relationship

The MFA also prohibits other "unfair or inequitable practices" specified in the Minnesota Administrative Rules, which are state administrative agency regulations issued to implement the law.[87] The MFA delegates authority to the Minnesota Commissioner of Commerce to adopt rules defining its prohibited unfair and inequitable practices.[88] The Commissioner's rules establish both the rights of franchisees and the limits of their protections from unfair and inequitable practices prohibited under the MFA, suggesting there are no other unenumerated rights or prohibited practices.[89]

1. Discrimination

a. Commentary

The MFA prohibits franchisors from discriminating between franchisees without a reasonable basis. The Commissioner's rule defines it as an unfair and inequitable practice for a franchisor "to discriminate between franchisees in the charges offered or made for royalties, goods, services, equipment, rentals, advertising services, or in any business dealing."[90]

A franchisor, however, may discriminate between franchisees "based on franchises granted at different times, geographic, market, volume, or size differences, costs incurred by the franchisor, or other reasonable grounds considering the purposes" of the MFA.[91] These exceptions may require fact-intensive

---

86. MINN. STAT. § 80C.14 subdiv. 5.
87. MINN. R. 2860.4400.
88. MINN. STAT. § 80C.18.
89. Rittmiller v. Blex Oil, Inc., 624 F.2d 857, 862 (8th Cir. 1980) ("Plaintiffs' statutory protection could go no farther than may be prescribed by administrative regulation.").
90. MINN. R. 2860.4400.B.
91. *Id.*

inquiries that make early dismissal unlikely.[92] While it might appear a franchisor would bear the burden of proving the existence of an exception, one court placed it on the franchisee to prove discrimination by establishing differential treatment between only "similarly situated" franchisees "under similar financial and marketing conditions," which the franchisee failed to do.[93]

A franchisee's remedy for discrimination is likely limited to money damages and not injunctive relief, at least insofar as the practice is not ongoing and causing irreparable harm. While unfair and inequitable practices may be enjoined under the MFA, one court has noted that a franchisee's "appropriate remedy" for a claim alleging a discriminatory practice "would be money damages rather than injunctive relief."[94]

b. Annotations

Regardless of what an agreement is called, it may establish a franchise relationship prohibiting differential treatment under the MFA, provided that the relationship meets the statutory requirements that were held to be plausible under the allegations to survive a motion to dismiss. *Newpaper LLC v. Party City Corp.*, 2014 WL 2986653 (D. Minn. 2014) (denying motion to dismiss even though "[t]he facts may later demonstrate" justification for differential treatment).

Nonrenewal of franchise agreement was held not discriminatory when franchisor was changing its business model and not converting the franchisee's business premises to an operation owned by the franchisor for its own account. *McCabe v. AIR-serv Group LLC*, 2007 WL 4591932 (D. Minn. Dec. 28, 2007) ("This is not evidence of a discriminatory intent to take over McCabe's business, but rather is evidence of AIR-serv's intent to execute a change in its business model.").

Franchisee alleged that franchisor's waiver of royalty fees and purchasing requirements for certain franchisees was discriminatory. Citing precedent from the Seventh Circuit, the court dismissed franchisee's claims for failing to establish the franchisees were similarly situated. *Kieland v. Rocky Mountain Chocolate Factory, Inc.*, 2006 WL 2990336 (D. Minn. 2006) ("Here, Plaintiffs do not allege and there is no evidence in the record that Plaintiffs are similarly situated to the franchises whose fees were waived. In fact, Mr. Kieland testified that his franchise's performance never dropped to the level where Rocky Mountain would typically consider waiving royalty fees.").

2. Association Rights

a. Commentary

Franchisees under the MFA have the right to freely associate with each other and form franchisee associations. The Commissioner's rule defines it as an unfair and inequitable practice for a franchisor to "restrict or inhibit, directly

---

92. Newpaper LLC v Party City Corp., 2014 WL 2986653 (D. Minn. 2014) (denying motion to dismiss even though "[t]he facts may later demonstrate" justification for differential treatment).
93. Kieland v. Rocky Mountain Chocolate Factory, Inc., 2006 WL 2990336 (D. Minn. 2006).
94. McCabe v. AIR-serv Grp. LLC, 2007 WL 4591932 (D. Minn. Dec. 28, 2007).

or indirectly, the free association among franchisees for any lawful purpose."[95] The rule, however, does not prohibit franchise agreements from including class action waivers.[96]

b. Annotations

A waiver of the right to proceed as a class action in a unit franchise agreement was enforceable and did not violate the rules promulgated under the MFA. *Green v. SuperShuttle International, Inc.*, 2010 WL 3702592 (D. Minn. Sept. 13, 2010) ("Plaintiffs cite to no legal authority that rule 2860.4400 also prohibits class action waiver provisions."), *aff'd in part, rev'd in part*, 653 F.3d 766 (8th Cir. 2011).

3. Exclusive Territory and Encroachment

a. Commentary

While the MFA does not address the issue of encroachment generally, it does protect franchisees' rights to exclusive territory granted by franchisors. The Commissioner's rule defines it as an unfair or inequitable practice for a franchisor to "compete with the franchisee in an exclusive territory or grant competitive franchises in the exclusive territory."[97]

The exclusive territory, however, must be "specifically granted to a franchisee" in "the terms of the franchise agreement."[98] Consequently, practitioners must carefully review the franchise agreement's terms and any addenda defining the franchisee's exclusive territory. One court held that a franchisor's online sales did not violate the franchisee's exclusive territory where it only "contemplate[d] the sale of . . . merchandise from 'store premises'" and excepted "sale of products online."[99]

The MFA also prohibits a franchisor from failing to renew a franchisee for the "purpose of converting the franchisee's business premises to an operation that will be owned by the franchisor for its own account."[100] There is no authority interpreting the meaning of the phrase "business premises" and whether it might be construed so broadly as to include a franchisee's territory. One court, however, has held that a franchisor may decline to renew a franchise when "legitimate business reasons" supported "a change in its business model" that might include servicing the former franchisee's accounts.[101]

---

95. MINN. R. 2860.4400.A.

96. Green v. SuperShuttle Int'l, Inc., 2010 WL 3702592 at *3 (D. Minn. Sept. 13, 2010) ("Plaintiffs cite to no legal authority that rule 2860.4400 also prohibits class action waiver provisions."), *aff'd in part, rev'd in part*, 653 F.3d 766 (8th Cir. 2011).

97. MINN. R. 2860.4400(C).

98. *Id.*

99. Newpaper LLC v. Party City Corp., 2014 WL 2986653 (D. Minn. 2014) ("Newpaper further agreed in the Internet Addendum that Party City was 'not prohibited from selling any products over the Internet, to any customers regardless of location, and in any manner whatsoever.'").

100. MINN. STAT. § 80C.14, subdiv. 4.

101. McCabe v. AIR-serv Grp., LLC, 2007 WL 4591932, at *4 (D. Minn. Dec. 28, 2007) ("Thus, McCabe is unlikely to show that AIR-serv's decision of nonrenewal was for the purpose of taking over his business, in violation of the MFA.").

b. Annotations

The franchise agreement granted the franchisee an exclusive right to operate stores within several states excluding preexisting stores. The franchisor's online sales did not violate the franchisee's exclusive territory regardless of location. *Newpaper LLC v. Party City Corp.*, 2014 WL 2986653 (D. Minn. 2014) ("Newpaper is correct that the Agreement prohibits Party City from operating Halloween Stores in the Territory. But the language of the Agreement emphasizes that this prohibition addresses physical stores: the Agreement contemplates the sale of Halloween merchandise from 'store premises.'").

Franchisor did not intend to convert franchisee's business premises for its own account when its nonrenewal was for legitimate business reasons. Franchisor's business model had changed from manufacturing and sales to servicing existing equipment. *McCabe v. AIR-serv Group, LLC*, 2007 WL 4591932 (D. Minn. Dec. 28, 2007) ("[T]he record shows that AIR-serv's decision not to renew was for legitimate business reasons and not for the purpose of taking over McCabe's business. Thus, McCabe is unlikely to show that AIR-serv's decision of nonrenewal was for the purpose of taking over his business, in violation of the MFA.").

4. Standards of Conduct

a. Commentary

The MFA generally prohibits franchisors from imposing unreasonable standards of conduct, although like other states with similar prohibitions, there is little guidance on how to determine the reasonableness of a particular standard. The Commissioner's rule defines it as an unfair and inequitable practice for a franchisor to "impose on a franchisee by contract or rule, whether written or oral, any standard of conduct that is unreasonable."[102]

Despite the rule's potential breadth, courts have noted the "dearth of authority"[103] on the issue and that "[g]uidance . . . is limited."[104] Whether a standard of conduct is reasonable is obviously a fact-intensive inquiry.[105] And it is equally obvious that a franchisor must impose some brand standards, which franchisees reasonably agree to follow as a condition to operating the franchise.

Courts have avoided the issue by narrowly interpreting the phrase "standards of conduct." One court has held that "standards of conduct" refers only to "the conduct of the franchisee while operating the franchise, rather than any rights that the franchisee has under the franchise agreement," and a mere "disparity between the rights of the parties . . . does not seem to be enough to render a franchise agreement unreasonable."[106] Another court has held that a franchisee's general claims about a franchisor's unreasonable conduct did not

---

102. MINN. R. 2860.4400.G.
103. Klosek v. Am. Express Co., 2008 WL 4057534 (D. Minn. Aug. 26, 2008), *aff'd*, 370 F. App'x 761 (8th Cir. 2010).
104. *Newpaper, LLC*, 2014 WL 2986653, at *9.
105. Mainstream Fashions Franchising, Inc. v. All These Things, LLC, 453 F. Supp. 3d 1167, 1190 (D. Minn. 2020) (denying motion to dismiss because "the reasonableness of this mandate is itself in dispute").
106. *Klosek*, 2008 WL 4057534.

state a claim when it "fail[ed] to identify any standard of conduct" and instead "accuse[d] [the franchisor] of frustrating [its] ability to perform," which was more appropriately considered and dismissed under the franchisee's implied covenant of good faith and fair dealing claim.[107] And another court has held that a practice was not "imposed" on a franchisee when it was free to decline participation in the program requiring it, even though the program represented "30–40% of [the franchisee's] revenue."[108]

b. Annotations

The court noted a lack of authority providing guidance on the "standard of conduct" provision as it relates to the prohibition of unfair and inequitable standards of conduct imposed upon a franchisee by rule or contract. *Newpaper LLC v. Party City Corp.*, 2014 WL 2986653 (D. Minn. 2014) ("Six of the alleged violations fail to identify any standard of conduct whatsoever, let alone identify how the alleged standard is unreasonable.").

Franchisee argued noncompete and assignability terms imposed unreasonable standards of conduct. The court determined that whether a contractual provision imposes such a "standard of conduct" is in reference to the conduct of the franchisee when operating the franchise as opposed to any general rights that a franchisee has under the franchise agreement. *Klosek v. American Express Co.*, 2008 WL 4057534 (D. Minn. Aug. 26, 2008) ("With this caveat, this Court thinks the phrase 'standard of conduct' is likely to refer the conduct of the franchisee when operating the franchise, rather than any rights that the franchisee has under the franchise agreement."), *aff'd*, 370 F. App'x 761 (8th Cir. 2010).

Franchisee argued that depreciation schedule permitting franchisor to acquire equipment without paying fair value was unfair and inequitable standard of conduct. Because franchisee was permitted to decline participation and franchisor was not enforcing the provision, the court determined that franchisee was unlikely to succeed on the merits on motion for preliminary injunction. *McCabe v. AIR-serv Group, LLC*, 2007 WL 4591932 (D. Minn. Dec. 28, 2007) ("The Court determines that McCabe is unlikely to show that AIR-serv violated the MFA here because there is no evidence that AIR-serv 'imposed' this depreciation schedule on McCabe. Indeed, McCabe was free to decline participation in the servicing of the chain accounts. Furthermore, AIR-serv is not enforcing the provision because it is allowing McCabe to remove the machines. Thus, it is unlikely McCabe will succeed on the merits of this claim.").

5. Restriction on Releases or Waivers

a. Commentary

The MFA includes an anti-waiver provision voiding "[a]ny condition, stipulation or provision, including any choice of law provision, purporting to . . .

---

107. *Newpaper, LLC*, 2014 WL 2986653, at *9.
108. McCabe v. AIR-serv Grp., LLC, 2007 WL 4591932, at *5 (D. Minn. Dec. 28, 2007).

waive compliance" with the MFA.[109] This provision, however, only applies to Minnesota residents and businesses formed under Minnesota law.[110]

As a result, a Minnesota franchisor may not require a franchisee who is a Minnesota resident or business to prospectively waive compliance with the MFA, including through a choice-of-law provision.[111] A Minnesota franchisor may, however, preclude the MFA from applying to a nonresident franchisee operating outside the state through a contractual choice-of-law provision by selecting the law of a state other than Minnesota.[112]

The Commissioner's rule further defines it as an unfair and inequitable practice for a franchisor to "require a franchisee to assent to a release, assignment, novation, or waiver that would relieve any person from liability imposed by" the MFA.[113] This rule, however, "shall not bar the voluntary settlement of disputes."[114] As a result, the rule prohibits only prospective waivers and not releases of past or present claims.[115]

b. Annotations

Court in Tennessee applied Tennessee choice-of-law principles in order to determine whether MFA's anti-waiver provision precluded a Tennessee choice-of-law provision. The plaintiffs argued the MFA should apply to the extent they operated a franchise within Minnesota. The court held the stores' physical location should be controlling at least on the question of whether the MFA applied

---

109. MINN. STAT. § 80C.21. The Minnesota legislature amended the MFA's anti-waiver statute in 1989 to explicitly apply to choice-of-law provisions. Com. Prop. Inv., Inc. v. Quality Inns Int'l, Inc., 938 F.2d 870, 874 (8th Cir. 1991). As a result, decisions prior to this amendment analyzed the issue based on common law choice-of-law principals that no longer apply. See, e.g., Carlock v. Pillsbury Co., 719 F. Supp. 791, 810–11 (D. Minn. 1989); Modern Comput. Sys., Inc. v. Modern Banking Sys., Inc., 871 F.2d 734, 738 (8th Cir. 1989).

110. MINN. STAT. § 80C.21.

111. Long John Silver's Inc. v. Nickleson, 923 F. Supp. 2d 1004, 1010 (W.D. Ky. 2013) ("The MFA's anti-waiver provision voids anything in a franchise agreement or contract that explicitly waives or has the effect of waiving compliance with the MFA."); Red Roof Franchising LLC v. AA Hospitality Northshore LLC, 877 F. Supp. 2d 140, 147–48 (D.N.J. 2012) ("Here, as stated, Minnesota law, which governs the franchise agreement, nullifies any choice of law provision."); Van Dusen Airport Servs. Co., LP v. Allied Signal, Inc., 1991 WL 151377 (Minn. Ct. App. 1991) ("Prohibiting choice of law clauses ensures that Minnesota franchisees will be protected by the Minnesota franchise act.").

112. Hockey Enters. v. Total Hockey Worldwide, LLC, 762 F. Supp. 2d 1138, 1146 (D. Minn. 2011) ("The plain language of MINN. STAT. § 80C.21 prohibits the waiver of rights secured by the MFA through a choice-of-law provision if the waiver purports to bind a person who is a Minnesota resident (or a corporation incorporated under Minnesota law) at the time that person/organization acquired a franchise or a person (regardless of residence) who is acquiring a franchise that will operate in Minnesota.").

113. MINN. R. 2860.4400.D.

114. Id.

115. Schmitt-Norton Ford, Inc. v. Ford Motor Co., 524 F. Supp. 1099, 1105 (D. Minn. 1981), aff'd, 685 F.2d 438 (8th Cir. 1982) ("The release at issue in the present case, however, did not prevent suit until after the cause of action arose and only after the plaintiffs signed a separate contract and received additional consideration for the contract. Unlike the waiver of defense provision in Clusiau, the franchise agreement itself did not prevent suit.").

to the franchises operated within Minnesota and denied the franchisor's motion to dismiss without prejudice. *Sugarlips Bakery, LLC v. A&G Franchising, LLC*, 2022 WL 210135, at *6–8 (M.D. Tenn. Jan. 24, 2022) ("This court is inclined to conclude that physical location of the actual store being regulated should win out, at least on the question of whether other states' franchising statutes apply to franchises within their borders.").

The MFA's anti-waiver provision did not apply to release included in amendment to franchise agreement. The court held the MFA's anti-waiver provision only prohibited waivers at the time the franchisee obtained the franchise, and not to a subsequent amendment. *Tim-Minn, Inc. v. Tim Hortons USA, Inc.*, Case No. 19-cv-409 (D. Minn. Aug. 19, 2020) (holding that anti-waiver provision did not bar voluntary release).

The court held that the MFA does not expressly prohibit franchisors from requiring franchisees to litigate outside of Minnesota, and therefore the anti-waiver provision did not apply to forum selection clauses. The court likewise held that franchisor's decision to commence litigation outside of Minnesota was not inherently unfair or inequitable. Similarly, the court rejected franchisee's argument that the MFA's anti-waiver provision invalidated the forum selection clause, noting that nothing in the contract prevented defendants from availing themselves of the protections afforded by Minnesota law. *Allegra Holdings LLC v. Davis*, 2014 WL 1652221 (E.D. Mich. Apr. 24, 2014) ("Defendants do not, however, argue that commencing litigation outside Minnesota is an unfair or inequitable practice, and nothing in the cited provisions of the MFA so provide.").

The MFA's anti-waiver provision did not invalidate franchise agreement's forum selection clause, as the franchise agreement did not diminish franchisee's rights under MFA. The court applied Kentucky law to the franchisee's common law fraud counterclaim against the franchisor under the forum selection clause but the franchisee could still pursue MFA claims in Kentucky. *Long John Silver's Inc. v. Nickleson*, 923 F. Supp. 2d 1004, 1010 (W.D. Ky. 2013) ("Since the Franchise Agreement's forum selection provision does not diminish Defendants' rights under the MFA, the MFA's anti-waiver provision does not result in the invalidation of Franchise Agreement's forum selection clause.").

The MFA's anti-waiver provision nullified the franchise agreement's Texas choice-of-law provision. As a result, the federal court in New Jersey applied New Jersey choice-of-law principles to apply New Jersey law to franchisee's common law implied covenant of good faith and fair dealing claim. *Red Roof Franchising LLC v. AA Hospitality Northshore LLC*, 877 F. Supp. 2d 140, 147–48 (D.N.J. 2012) ("Here, as stated, Minnesota law, which governs the franchise agreement, nullifies any choice of law provision.").

The MFA's anti-waiver provision did not invalidate jury trial waiver where the franchise agreement's Minnesota choice-of-law provision expressly did not apply to franchises located outside the state and franchisees were not Minnesota residents and the franchise was not operated in Minnesota. *Novus Franchising, Inc. v. Superior Entrance Systems, Inc.*, 2012 WL 3542451, at *2 (W.D. Wis. Aug. 16, 2012) ("As mentioned, however, the choice of law provision in the parties' contract expressly rejects the application of the Minnesota Franchise Act to franchises located outside that state.").

The MFA's anti-waiver provision did not invalidate the franchise agreement's Florida choice of law provision when franchisee did not reside in Minnesota, organize or incorporate in Minnesota, or operate the franchises in Minnesota. *Hockey Enterprises, Inc. v. Total Hockey Worldwide, LLC*, 762 F. Supp. 2d 1138 (D. Minn. 2011) ("Here, Comeau is not a resident of Minnesota, HEI is not organized or incorporated in Minnesota, and HEI's franchises were to be operated in Florida not Minnesota.").

On review of arbitrator's decision that California choice of law applied notwithstanding MFA's anti-waiver provision, and that plaintiff did not pay a franchise fee as required to establish a franchise under the MFA, plaintiff challenged the decision as violating Minnesota's fundamental public policy. Court affirmed the award due to the absence of conflict in the states' standards and fundamental public policies. *Twin Cities Galleries, LLC v. Media Arts Group, Inc.*, 476 F.3d 598 (8th Cir. 2007) ("Because the Minnesota and California standards are virtually identical, Twin Cities cannot demonstrate that the arbitrator's application of California law frustrated a fundamental policy of Minnesota.").

Putative franchisee sought summary judgment on claim under MFA in adversary proceeding before bankruptcy court. Putative franchisor argued that the parties' contractual choice of law prevented the MFA from applying. The court held that summary judgment materials were insufficient to allow choice of law determination. *In re Patterson*, 375 B.R. 652, 665 (Bankr. D. Kan. 2007) ("Sellner's summary judgment materials are insufficient to enable the Court to determine the choice of law question, even assuming he will be able to establish the contract qualified as the sale of a franchise under the MFA.").

The MFA anti-waiver provision does not apply when the franchisee is neither a Minnesota resident nor is it a franchise that was to be operated in Minnesota. *Sound of Music Co. v. Minnesota Mining and Manufacturing Co.*, 389 F. Supp. 2d 988, 1003 (N.D. Ill. 2005) ("It is undisputed that Sound of Music is neither a Minnesota resident nor a 'franchise to be operated' in Minnesota. Based on this straightforward reading of the statute, this anti-waiver provision does not apply here, and Sound of Music therefore waived any rights under the Act."), *aff'd*, 477 F.3d 910 (7th Cir. 2007).

Franchisee argued that the MFA applied based on the franchise agreement's Minnesota choice of law. Franchisor argued that the Illinois Franchise Disclosure Act's anti-waiver provision voided the franchise agreement's Minnesota choice of law. The court applied Illinois law because franchisee was an Illinois resident, franchise was operated in Illinois, and found no support for the proposition that the MFA should apply simply because the franchisor is a Minnesota entity. *Healy v. Carlson Travel Network Associates, Inc.*, 227 F. Supp. 2d 1080 (D. Minn. 2002) ("The instant case, like *Hengel* and *Bixby's*, presents the curious and potentially inequitable position of the Defendant franchisor seeking to void its own governing law provision by way of an anti-waiver clause of another state's statute. This produces the result that the IFDA, enacted to protect franchisees, avoids application of the analogous MFA, which would provide the

Plaintiff with additional remedies. This, however, is the current state of the case law, and upon further analysis, makes sense in the present case in light of the relationship between the parties and the states involved.").

The court applied the Illinois Franchise Disclosure Act and dismissed claims asserted under the MFA. Despite a Minnesota choice of law provision, the IFDA's nonwaiver provision controlled where the Illinois residents opened a franchise in Illinois. *Bixby's Food Systems, Inc. v. McKay*, 193 F. Supp. 2d 1053, 1059 (N.D. Ill. 2002) ("The McKays have not proven or even alleged that they were or are residents of Minnesota or that their franchise was to be operated in Minnesota. Therefore, they have not shown that the waiver contained in the Franchise Agreement was void or otherwise unenforceable in this case. The McKays allege no facts demonstrating that the franchise at issue here was offered or sold in Minnesota.").

The MFA's anti-waiver provision does not void otherwise valid forum selection clause. *Van Dusen Airport Services Co., L.P. v. Allied Signal, Inc.*, 1991 WL 151377 (Minn. Ct. App. 1991) ("Prohibiting choice of law clauses ensures that Minnesota franchisees will be protected by the Minnesota franchise act. It is not necessary to also prohibit choice of forum clauses to achieve this goal. If necessary, courts in other jurisdictions may apply Minnesota law to disputes litigated in their forums.").

The MFA's anti-waiver provision does not apply retroactively. *TCBY Systems, Inc. v. RSP Co., Inc.*, 33 F.3d 925, 930 (8th Cir. 1994) ("Although a clarifying amendment states the antiwaiver statute applies to choice-of-law provisions . . . , the amendment does not apply to agreements signed before the amendment's effective date.").

Acceptance of subsequent sales agreement following improper termination of franchise agreement did not constitute waiver of rights under the MFA. While the MFA permits voluntary settlements of disputes, the evidence did not establish that the subsequent sales agreement was a waiver or voluntary settlement of a dispute, novation, or release of claims under the improperly terminated franchise agreement. *Culligan International Co. v. Culligan Water Conditioning of Carver County, Inc.*, 563 F. Supp. 1265, 1271 (D. Minn. 1983) ("The plaintiff argues that the 1981 Sales Agreement was entered into voluntarily as a settlement of any disputes between the parties. The evidence does not support this argument. The plaintiff argues further that the 1981 Sales Agreement constituted a novation and, as such, it extinguished the defendants' rights concerning the 1972 Franchise Agreement. . . . There is no evidence that Mayer viewed the 1981 agreement as a substitute for the prior agreement.").

The MFA did not constitute sufficient evidence of public policy to void release supported by consideration that did not constitute a prospective waiver of rights. *Schmitt-Norton Ford, Inc. v. Ford Motor Co.*, 524 F. Supp. 1099, 1105 (D. Minn. 1981) ("Thus, since the defendant gave the plaintiffs consideration and the release was not a prospective waiver of rights, the release is not invalid as a matter of state public policy under the Minnesota Franchise Act."), *aff'd*, 685 F.2d 438 (8th Cir. 1982).

Waiver of defense provision included in lease made part of franchise agreement held invalid under the MFA. *Chase Manhattan Bank, N.A. New York, N.Y. v.*

Clusiau Sales & Rental, Inc., 308 N.W.2d 490, 494 (Minn. 1981) ("As the trial court pointed out, enforcement of waiver of defense provision against Minnesota residents who have entered franchise agreements with franchisors who failed to comply with the franchise statute would adversely affect the remedial reach of that statute.").

G. Remedies and Administrative Action

The MFA is enforced through private causes of action brought by franchisees as well as criminal penalties and civil enforcement actions brought by Minnesota's attorney general.[116] Many types of relief are available for violations of the MFA, including damages, rescission, injunctive relief, and attorneys' fees.[117] The MFA also imposes joint and several liability on those who control franchisors' violations.[118] The MFA thus affords broad remedies to franchisees.

These remedies must be carefully considered when addressing issues that arise during the franchise relationship, ideally prior to taking any actions that could give rise to claims. Long before the time to award any remedy, franchisors and franchisees must understand the potential outcomes, however remote or likely, to assess the value and risks of their claims and defenses and make the most optimal decisions not only in litigation and settlement but also their practices in the franchise relationship itself.

1. Restrictive Covenants

a. Commentary

While the MFA does not prohibit franchise agreements from containing restrictive covenants, it does impose some nominal regulations on noncompetes. The Commissioner's rule defines it as an unfair and inequitable practice for a franchisor to enforce any "unreasonable" post-termination noncompete.[119] Franchisors must also disclose the conditions of any noncompete in their franchise disclosure document (FDD).[120]

The prohibition on enforcing "unreasonable" post-termination noncompetes simply codifies Minnesota's common law treatment of them. Since the MFA does not define an unreasonable noncompete, courts have applied Minnesota's common law standard.[121] Under it, a noncompete is enforceable so long

---

116. MINN. STAT. §§ 80C.16, 80C.17. Personal guarantors of the franchise agreement, however, may not bring claims under the MFA. Long John Silver's Inc. v. Nickleson, 923 F. Supp. 2d 1004, 1012 (W.D. Ky. 2013) ("Regarding standing under the MFA, Nickleson does not gain standing as a de facto franchisee by virtue of being a guarantor or sole shareholder."); Hockey Enters., Inc. v. Total Hockey Worldwide, LLC, 762 F. Supp. 2d 1138, 1151 (D. Minn. 2011) ("Plaintiffs have not cited to any law in support of that proposition that Comeau, as a shareholder of HEI and a guarantor for each of the Franchise Agreements, is a de facto franchisee.").
117. MINN. STAT. § 80C.17 subdiv. 1.
118. *Id.* subdiv. 2.
119. MINN. R. 2860.4400.I.
120. *Id.* 2860.3500 subpt. 8.N.
121. Adcom Express, Inc. v. EPK, Inc., 1996 WL 266412, at *4 (Minn. Ct. App. May 21, 1996) ("Based on these principles, we hold that the noncompete provisions in both agreements are not

as it serves a legitimate business purpose and is reasonable, based on the circumstances, in scope, time, and geographic area.[122] This standard, akin to that applied in business and property transfers, is broader than the more restrictive one for noncompetes in the employment context.[123] While both facts and law differ, Minnesota courts analyzing restrictive covenants in franchise disputes still sometimes cite cases involving other, non-franchise relationships, like employment or commercial disputes.[124]

Courts applying Minnesota law have found that franchisors have legitimate business interests in enforcing noncompetes, not only since "a franchisor has invested its training, good will, and resources,"[125] and "[i]t is difficult to attract a new franchisee when a former franchisee is improperly competing within the same area,"[126] but also to protect the entire system and "its franchisees from unfair competition."[127] Franchisors' interests may be even greater in connection with other considerations such as confidentiality, misuse of intellectual property, and in-term violations.[128]

With respect to scope, courts typically uphold durations as long as two years and geographic areas equivalent to the franchisee's territory.[129] Particular circumstances may even support a broader geographic scope covering other franchisees' territory.[130] Although rare, courts may apply the "blue pencil" doctrine under Minnesota law to save an otherwise unenforceable noncompete,

---

unreasonably in restraint of trade because (1) a franchisor has a legitimate interest in protecting itself or one of its franchisees from the individual competition of another franchisee already operating in a different market, and (2) the restrictions were reasonable in light of the franchisees' option of ending the contracts (and the restrictions) at any time with advance written notice.").

122. Bennett v. Storz Broadcasting Co., 134 N.W.2d 892 (Minn. 1965) ("Where the restraint is for a just and honest purpose, for the protection of a legitimate interest of the party in whose favor it is imposed, reasonable as between the parties, and not injurious to the public, the restraint has been held valid.").

123. TENA Cos., Inc. v. Ellie Mae, Inc., 2022 WL 624644, at **3–4 n.4. (D. Minn. Mar. 3, 2022) (discussing distinction).

124. Anytime Fitness, Inc. v. Fam. Fitness of Royal, LLC, 2010 WL 145259, at *4 (D. Minn. Jan. 8, 2010) (citing standard for "employment contract").

125. Novus Franchising, Inc. v. AZ Glassworks, LLC, 2013 WL 1110838 (D. Minn. Mar. 18, 2013).

126. Novus Franchising, Inc. v. Livengood, 2012 WL 38580, at *5 (D. Minn. Jan. 9, 2012).

127. Anytime Fitness, Inc. v. Fam. Fitness of Royal, LLC, 2010 WL 145259 (D. Minn. Jan. 8, 2010).

128. Anytime Fitness, LLC v. Edinburgh Fitness LLC, 2014 WL 1415081 (D. Minn. Apr. 11, 2014) ("AF has shown irreparable harm through unfair competition, through misuse of the AF franchise membership information and other AF operational and development information, through loss of goodwill, and through other misuse of its Names and Marks because customers are now either with Fit 12 and not ANYTIME FITNESS® or are no longer fitness center customers at all.").

129. *Id.* (two years and within five miles from franchise location); Wakeman v. Aqua2 Acquisition, Inc., 2011 WL 1667926, at *3 (D. Minn. May 3, 2011) (two years and within franchise territory); *Fam. Fitness of Royal, LLC*, 2010 WL 145259, at *4 (two years and within six miles from franchise location); Anytime Fitness, Inc. v. Rsrv. Holdings, LLC, 2008 WL 5191853 (D. Minn. Oct. 8, 2008) (two years and within five miles from franchise location).

130. *AZ Glassworks, LLC*, 2013 WL 1110838 ("As for the operation of a competing business throughout Florida, which was not within Hersh's area of primary responsibility but is within the area of primary responsibility for other Novus franchisees or within 10 miles of a Novus

narrowing their unreasonable scope by making their reasonable aspects severable, and enforcing them to the extent reasonable under the circumstances.[131]

Other common types of restrictive covenants, such as in-term noncompetes, nonsolicitation, nondisclosure, and confidentiality terms, are generally enforceable under Minnesota common law.[132] While facts may differ, Minnesota law would likely apply the same principles to both in-term and post-term covenants not to compete.[133] Minnesota does not have any unique statutes or common law principles prohibiting the enforcement of covenants not to compete nor restrictive covenants more generally.

b. Annotations

Distributor enjoined from violating noncompete notwithstanding argument that distribution agreement was improperly terminated. The court found that the manufacturer had a substantial likelihood of prevailing on its claim that distributor breached the agreement as well as its defense that termination was proper where distributor violated restrictive covenants prior to termination. *Powerlift Door Consultants, Inc. v. Shepard*, 2021 WL 2911177 (D. Minn. July 12, 2021) ("Turning to the breach-of-contract claim itself, the allegations in Powerlift's complaint demonstrate that Powerlift has a fair chance of prevailing on the merits of this claim.").

Franchisee enjoined from violating post-term restrictive covenants, including noncompete and nondisclosure. Franchisor properly terminated franchise agreement after discovering franchisee had diverted products and failed to pay fees, after which franchisee held over. *Rpc Acquisition Corp. v. J & D World Corp.*, 2013 WL 3338784 (D. Minn. July 2, 2013) ("Defendants are continuing to operate hair salons in four of their former franchise locations in violation of the post-term covenants not to compete. Defendants further continue to use PRO–CUTS Marks and materials in violation of the franchise agreements.").

Franchisee permanently enjoined from violating restrict covenants, including noncompete and nondisclosure. Franchisee failed to respond to complaint and the court held that franchisor was likely to succeed and would suffer irreparable harm from trademark infringement and unfair competition. The court awarded attorney's fees. *Novus Franchising, Inc. v. AZ Glassworks, LLC*, 2013 WL 1110838 (D. Minn. Mar. 18, 2013) ("Here, Capital One wholly appropriated

---

franchisee, the Court finds that, under the particular facts of this case, in which Defendants have offered no response, the covenant not to compete is reasonably applied to this conduct, as well.").

131. Bess v. Bothman, 257 N.W.2d 791 (Minn. 1977) ("The rationale of the blue pencil doctrine is that a court is merely enforcing the legal parts of a divisible contract rather than making a new contract for the parties."); Waxing the City Franchisor LLC v. Katularu, 2024 WL 3887109, at *6 (D. Minn. Aug. 20, 2024) ("[A] court is likely to the [sic] limit the geographic scope of the in-term non-compete clause at issue. Specifically, a court is likely to blue pencil the non-compete so it is limited to the market that WTC is actively targeting.").

132. Anytime Fitness, LLC v. Edinburgh Fitness LLC, 2014 WL 1415081 (D. Minn. Apr. 11, 2014) (enforcing nondisclosure and confidentiality restrictive covenants).

133. Adcom Express, Inc. v. EPK, Inc., 1996 WL 266412, at *4 (Minn. Ct. App. May 21, 1996) ("Courts apply this reasonableness standard to both in-term and post-term covenants not to compete.").

Novus's trademarks for a directly competing business, clearly with the intent to mislead consumers into choosing Capital One based on the mistaken belief that they were choosing a Novus franchisee.").

Franchisee enjoined from violating post-term noncompete. Franchisor was likely to succeed notwithstanding franchisee's argument that amendment allowing franchisee to continue property ownership and management business also permitted operation of competitive business. *Anytime Fitness, LLC v. Edinburgh Fitness LLC*, 2014 WL 1415081 (D. Minn. Apr. 11, 2014) ("The Court finds unpersuasive Defendants' arguments that the Amendment is to be read to essentially nullify the provision relating to competition. The evidence before the Court supports AF's view that the Amendment was intended to allow Ravich to continue to engage in his primary business of commercial property ownership and management. . . . This is different, however, from Ravich's and Edinburgh's current conduct of owning and operating a competitor's fitness center in the same location as the previous franchise—this is precisely the type of conduct a non-compete agreement is intended to prohibit.").

Franchisor failed to establish irreparable harm required to enjoin franchisee's alleged violations of noncompete. One franchise agreement had expired while three remained in effect. The court found the franchisor's allegations of irreparable harm speculative because the franchisee's new business, while offering similar services, was sufficiently separate and the franchisee was continuing to perform obligations under the franchise agreements that remained in effect. *Anytime Fitness, Inc. v. Family Fitness of Royal, LLC*, 2010 WL 145259 (D. Minn. Jan. 8, 2010) ("Therefore, Anytime Fitness has not established irreparable harm. While this finding suffices to deny Anytime Fitness's motion for a TRO, the court nevertheless considers the remaining Dataphase factors.").

Franchisee enjoined from violating noncompete. The court found the franchisor's evidence of ongoing violations outweighed franchisee's claims to have ceased using the franchisor's marks and confidential information. *Anytime Fitness, Inc. v. Reserve Holdings, LLC*, 2008 WL 5191853 (D. Minn. Oct. 8, 2008) ("The threat of irreparable injury on all three of AFI's asserted claims weighs in favor of granting the requested injunction. . . . AFI faces a number of significant potential harms, including loss of the opportunity to refranchise, injury to its good will, and damage to its entire franchise system.") (applying New Jersey law).

Franchisor's termination of franchise agreements based on violations of in-term noncompete was proper notwithstanding lack of geographic and temporal restrictions. The restrictions were reasonable in light of franchisee's right to terminate on notice. *Adcom Express, Inc. v. EPK, Inc.*, 1996 WL 266412, at *4 (Minn. Ct. App. May 21, 1996) ("Appellants argue that the noncompete covenants in both agreements are unenforceably overbroad and vague. The absence of a territorial limit in the interim agreement is permissible, however, in light of EPK's right to cancel the agreement at will in order to pursue another such business.").

Franchisee enjoined from violating in-term noncompete when it purchased similar businesses including from a competing franchisor. Lack of geographic and temporal restrictions did not invalidate in-term noncompete. *Casey's General Stores, Inc. v. Bowen*, Bus. Franchise Guide (CCH) ¶ 7976 (D. Minn. 1983) ("The non-competition clause in question protected a legitimate business interest of the franchisor in that it prevented confidential information supplied to franchisees from being used by its competitor. The franchisee's contention that none of the information received by franchisees was confidential was without merit.").

Franchisor's motion for preliminary injunction denied when franchisor failed to establish irreparable harm with evidence of customer confusion and inability to re-franchise its territory. The court found that franchisor may have contributed to any customer confusion the franchisor was not registered to sell franchises in Minnesota, it was speculative whether other franchisees would disregard their obligations, and the franchise agreement provided for liquidated damages. The court also held that franchisor had not established likelihood of success on the merits based on reasonableness of noncompete's geographic scope and duration. *Cookie Dough Bliss Franchising, LLC v. Feed Your Soul Minnesota, LLC*, 2023 WL 4901292, at *3 (D. Minn. Aug. 1, 2023).

Franchisor's motion for preliminary injunction granted to enforce in-term noncompete against franchisee. The court held that the franchisor's "ability to re-franchise is a protectable interest" and limited the geographic scope of the in-term noncompete "to the market that the franchisor is actively targeting." *Waxing the City Franchisor LLC v. Katularu*, 2024 WL 3887109, at *6 (D. Minn. Aug. 20, 2024) ("Non-competes in franchise agreements, including in-term non-competes, are generally enforceable if they serve 'a just and honest purpose,' and are 'for the protection of a legitimate interest of the party in whose favor it is imposed, reasonable as between the parties, and not injurious to the public.'").

2. Damages

a. Commentary

Under the MFA, a franchisee may recover "actual damages" caused by violations of the MFA and the Commissioner's rules. The MFA imposes liability for violating "any provision of this chapter or any rule or order thereunder" and provides that "[a]ny suit authorized under this section may be brought to recover the actual damages sustained by the plaintiff."[134] The nature and extent of recoverable damages depends on the type of violation at issue.

For alleged violations of the MFA's "unfair practices" concerning wrongful termination, nonrenewal, and the other unfair and inequitable practices defined by the Commissioner's rule, franchisees may seek damages for actual out-of-pocket losses or lost profits, depending again on the type of injuries they suffered. Lost profits is an appropriate measure of damages for wrongful termination or nonrenewal.[135] As with most jurisdictions, lost profits must be proven with "reasonable certainty," not "absolute certainty."[136]

---

134. Minn. Stat. § 80C.17.
135. Hughes v. Sinclair Mktg., Inc., 389 N.W.2d 194, 199 (Minn. 1986) ("We hold that, under the circumstances of this case, lost future profits may be recovered by the respondents as 'actual damages' for misrepresentation under the act.").
136. *Id.*

Another potential measure of damages for a franchisor's wrongful termination or nonrenewal may be recoupment of the franchisee's investment.[137] Recoupment must be offset by the value of any benefits or profits expected or received from the relationship[138] and cannot include loss of future profits.[139] As a practical matter then, recoupment is typically only sought where an agreement is terminated or nonrenewed without cause early in a relationship or shortly after a subsequent investment, before the franchisee has an opportunity to recover its investment, and when the agreement does not include a fixed term over which to project lost profits.[140]

Franchisors may also seek damages for lost profits for wrongful termination or breach of the franchise agreement by the franchisee.[141] The Commissioner's rule, however, defines it as an unfair and inequitable practice for a franchisor to require a franchisee to consent to liquidated damages.[142]

b. Annotations

Appropriate remedy for discrimination in violation of the MFA is money damages, not injunctive relief. *McCabe v. AIR-serv Group LLC*, 2007 WL 4591932 (D. Minn. Dec. 28, 2007) ("McCabe argues that AIR-serv discriminated against him by refusing to turn over newly-acquired locations within his exclusive

---

137. Clausen & Sons, Inc. v. Theo. Hamm Brewing Co., 395 F.2d 388, 391 (8th Cir. 1968) ("Thus we feel that under Minnesota law where an exclusive franchise dealer under an implied contract, terminable on notice, has at the instance of a manufacturer or supplier invested his resources and credit in establishment of a costly distribution facility for the supplier's product, and the supplier thereafter unreasonably terminates the contract and dealership without giving the dealer an opportunity to recoup his investment, a claim may be stated.").

138. Ag-Chem Equip. Co. v. Hahn, Inc., 480 F.2d 482, 489 (8th Cir. 1973) ("Thus it appears irrefutable that Ag-Chem itself derived substantial benefits both in the years prior to and after termination of the Hahn distributorship from those operating expenses attributable to future development. Therefore, in the event of another trial, evidence of unamortized capital expenses should be confined to that portion which served to promote and develop the Hahn distributorship alone.").

139. Schultz v. Onan Corp., 737 F.2d 339, 348 (3d Cir. 1984) ("'[U]nrecouped expenditures' refers to the initial or continuing investment required of the franchisee, reduced to the extent that profits were earned by the distributorship as a fruit of the investment."); McGinnis Piano & Organ Co. v. Yamaha Int'l Corp., 480 F.2d 474, 481 (8th Cir. 1973) ("We read these instructions as permitting the jury to add McGinnis' unrecouped investment and future profits in computing damages, and this is clearly error.").

140. *Ag-Chem Equip. Co.*, 480 F.2d at 487 (8th Cir. 1973) ("Recoupment has traditionally been confined to the recovery of preliminary expenses incurred in setting up a distributorship system, such as sums expended for initial promotion and renting a facility. Thus the doctrine has envisioned a distributorship requiring one, large, initial investment."); Gilderhus v. Amoco Oil Co., 1980 WL 1955, at *1 (D. Minn. Apr. 23, 1980) ("That theory is designed to protect franchisees who invest substantial money to distribute the franchisor's products, then are terminated without cause before they have the opportunity to recoup their investment.").

141. Holiday Hospitality Franchising, Inc. v. H-5, Inc., 165 F. Supp. 2d 937, 940 (D. Minn. 2001) ("However, there is no provision of Minnesota law or the contract between the parties which prevents Holiday from seeking other contractual damages, such as damages for lost profits.").

142. MINN. R. 2860.4400.J.

territory even though it turned over new locations to other distributors. The appropriate remedy for such a violation would be money damages rather than injunctive relief that would force AIR-serv to renew the Distributor Agreements.").

Franchisor brought an action against franchisee for breach of contract seeking lost profits for early termination of a franchise license agreement; the franchisee brought a counterclaim seeking declaration that lost profits were barred by the MFA's restriction on liquidated damages clauses. However, the court held that the MFA's liquidated damages restriction did not prevent a franchisor's claim for lost profits. *Holiday Hospitality Franchising, Inc. v. H-5, Inc.*, 165 F. Supp. 2d 937 (D. Minn. 2001) ("However, there is no provision of Minnesota law or the contract between the parties which prevents Holiday from seeking other contractual damages, such as damages for lost profits.").

Franchisees brought claims against a franchisor for damages resulting from nonrenewal. The court held that relief for improper nonrenewal is not limited to injunctive relief and franchisees may recover actual damages. *Hughes v. Sinclair Marketing, Inc.*, 389 N.W.2d 194 (Minn. 1986) ("Since Minn. Rule 2860.5500 was explicitly promulgated under section 80C.18, the actual damages provision of section 80C.17, subdivision 3 applies and the respondents were not limited to injunctive relief in their suit for improper nonrenewal.").

Distributor sought to recoup an investment based upon a premature termination. Recoupment only applies to franchises terminable at will, which is a theory designed to protect franchisees who invest substantial money to distribute the franchisor's products and then are terminated without cause before they have an opportunity to recoup their original investment. It does not apply when the franchise agreement is not terminable at will. *Gilderhus v. Amoco Oil Co.*, 1980 WL 1955 (D. Minn. Apr. 23, 1980) ("That theory is designed to protect franchisees who invest substantial money to distribute the franchisor's products, then are terminated without cause before they have the opportunity to recoup their investment.").

Under the recoupment doctrine in Minnesota, distributor is entitled to damages to the amount of its unrecouped expenditures. An unrecouped expenditure means the initial and continued investment required of a franchisee that reduces the extent of profits earned by the distributorship. *Schultz v. Onan Corp.*, 737 F.2d 339, 348 (3d Cir. 1984) ("'[U]nrecouped expenditures' refers to the initial or continuing investment required of the franchisee, reduced to the extent that profits were earned by the distributorship as a fruit of the investment.").

Franchisee sought out-of-pocket expenses, lost profits, damages to reputation, and other incidental and consequential damages; or, in the alternative, rescission. Recoupment, however, was not available when the franchisee's "investment" consisted entirely of employee expenses and did not have to hire any additional employees. *RJM Sales & Marketing, Inc. v. Banfi Products Corp.*, 546 F. Supp. 1368 (D. Minn. 1982) ("RJM incurred no such 'preliminary expenses' when it became Banfi's broker. RJM was a going brokerage organization with an existing staff of employees. Significantly, RJM did not hire any additional employees when it took on the Banfi account. For these reasons, RJM cannot take advantage of the recoupment doctrine.").

Recoupment held only available when an agreement is terminable at will. Operational expenses attributable to future development may be considered part of the initial capital investment, but it requires more proof than mere assertion. *Ag-Chem Equipment Co. v. Hahn, Inc.*, 480 F.2d 482 (8th Cir. 1973) ("Recoupment has traditionally been confined to the recovery of preliminary expenses incurred in setting up a distributorship system, such as sums expended for initial promotion and renting a facility. Thus the doctrine has envisioned a distributorship requiring one, large, initial investment.")

Recoupment is measured by the length of time reasonably necessary for a dealer to recoup its investment. As a result, a jury instruction may not permit the jury to find that the relationship could continue for as long as performance was satisfactory. *McGinnis Piano & Organ Co. v. Yamaha Int'l Corp.*, 480 F.2d 474, 481 (8th Cir. 1973) ("We read these instructions as permitting the jury to add McGinnis' unrecouped investment and future profits in computing damages, and this is clearly error.")

Recoupment is available for termination of at-will franchise agreement before opportunity to recover investment. *Clausen & Sons, Inc. v. Theo. Hamm Brewing Co.*, 395 F.2d 388, 391 (8th Cir. 1968) ("Thus we feel that under Minnesota law where an exclusive franchise dealer under an implied contract, terminable on notice, has at the instance of a manufacturer or supplier invested his resources and credit in establishment of a costly distribution facility for the supplier's product, and the supplier thereafter unreasonably terminates the contract and dealership without giving the dealer an opportunity to recoup his investment, a claim may be stated.").

3. Rescission

a. Commentary

Under the MFA, a franchisee may seek to rescind a franchise agreement for a franchisor's violation of the MFA and the Commissioner's rules. The MFA permits a franchisee to "sue for . . . rescission . . . or other relief as the court may deem appropriate." Rescission is an equitable remedy and with it comes a variety of attendant considerations.

Rescission provides the franchisee with "the right to have his agreements with the franchisor treated as entirely void and to be restored to the position he occupied prior to his involvement with the franchisor."[143] In doing so, a franchisee may obtain "restitution of sums expended in setting up a business under the contract in order to place both parties at status quo ante the contract."[144] The

---

143. Chase Manhattan Bank, N.A. New York, N.Y. v. Clusiau Sales & Rental, Inc., 308 N.W.2d 490, 494 (Minn. 1981).
144. Martin Invs., Inc. v. Vander Bie, 269 N.W.2d 868, 876 (Minn. 1978).

equitable theories of recission and restitution are thus distinct from legal damages and their causal requirements.[145]

The question of whether a technical violation of the MFA permits rescission is closely related to the equitable defenses available to the franchisor for such a claim. For example, a technical violation may arise if a franchisor fails to register or disclose information and the franchisee would have bought the franchise anyway, or continues to perform instead of rescinding notwithstanding the fact she knew or should have known of the violation. In such circumstances, a franchisor may assert equitable estoppel as a defense to prevent a franchisee from obtaining rescission and restitution.[146] A franchisee is not "allowed to use the franchise laws as an escape hatch to undo a business decision they now regret."[147]

b. Annotations

In action to enforce franchise agreement's noncompete, franchisee could not avoid enforcement based on allegations that franchisor failed to register franchise. Technical violations of the MFA will not result in a franchisee's absolute right to rescind the franchise agreement. *Bonus of America, Inc. v. Angel Falls Services, LLC*, 2010 WL 2734218 (D. Minn. July 6, 2010) ("Bonus of America responds that the August 20, 2007, Master Franchisor Agreements superseded the expedited agreement, and that Hart, Sanchez and Bonus in Minneapolis have ratified the Master Franchisor Agreements. Bonus of America further argues that Hart's unclean hands bars rescission. The court finds this registration violation to be the type of 'technical violation' that concerned the Clapp court.").

4. Injunctive Relief

a. Commentary

Under the MFA, a franchisee may seek injunctive relief to enjoin violations of the MFA and the Commissioner's rules. The MFA's private cause of action generally permits franchisees to "sue for . . . other relief as the court may deem appropriate" and specifically provides that certain unfair and inequitable practices are "enjoinable by a court of competent jurisdiction."[148] Such practices include wrongful termination, nonrenewal, and withholding of consent

---

145. *Id.* ("Some confusion was generated by the mischaracterization of this award as damages. CCC argues that Martin Investors must be put to an election of remedies and may not have both rescission of its contract and damages. In effect, Martin Investors was not granted damages but rather rescission of its contract with restitution of sums expended in setting up a business under the contract in order to place both parties at status quo ante the contract.").

146. U-Bake Rochester, LLC v. Utecht, 2014 WL 223439, at *6 (D. Minn. Jan. 21, 2014) ("Therefore, Defendants are not precluded from asserting the defense of equitable estoppel."); Dr. Performance of Minnesota, Inc. v. Dr. Performance Mgmt., LLC, 2002 WL 31628440, at *6 (D. Minn. Nov. 12, 2002) ("Both state and federal courts applying Minnesota law have held that franchisees seeking rescission and restitution under the MFA must first overcome any equitable defenses to rescission."); Bonus of Am., Inc. v. Angel Falls Servs., LLC, 2010 WL 2734218 (D. Minn. July 6, 2010) ("Equitable defenses are available, however, in an action for rescission under the MFA.").

147. *U-Bake Rochester, LLC*, 2014 WL 223439, at *6.

148. Minn. Stat. §§ 80C.14 subdiv. 1, 80C.17 subdiv. 1.

to transfer, as well as the other unfair and inequitable practices defined by the Commissioner's rule.[149]

A franchisee seeking to enjoin a violation of the MFA in federal court must establish the ordinary factors required to obtain injunctive relief: likelihood of success on the merits, irreparable injury, favorable balance of harm, and public interest.[150] Under Minnesota procedure, the factors are stated differently and require consideration of the parties' background and the court's administrative burden as well.[151] While no one factor is dispositive, courts generally focus the most on the movant's likelihood of success and relative irreparable harm in the absence of an injunction.[152]

The MFA provides that "[i]rreparable harm to the franchisee will be presumed" for an unregistered franchisor's wrongful termination, nonrenewal, or withholding of consent to transfer, which presumption may tend to support other factors as well.[153] As a result, courts have that the MFA's applicability is a central issue, because if it applies, all of the factors for injunctive relief are more likely to be satisfied.[154]

Absent a presumption, a court is unlikely to find an improper termination causes irreparable harm based solely on lost profits, which even if they are difficult to prove, are compensable by money damages and thus an adequate legal remedy.[155] When franchisees have argued that improper termination

---

149. MINN. R. 2860.4400.
150. Wave Form Sys., Inc. v. AMS Sales Corp., 73 F. Supp. 3d 1052, 1057 (D. Minn. 2014) (listing "*Dataphase*" factors).
151. Pac. Equip. & Irrigation, Inc. v. Toro Co., 519 N.W.2d 911, 915 (Minn. Ct. App. 1994) (listing "*Dahlberg*" factors).
152. *Wave Form Sys., Inc.*, 73 F. Supp. 3d at 1057 ("No single factor is determinative. Instead, the court considers the particular circumstances of each case, with the focus on the primary question of whether the 'balance of equities so favors the movant that justice requires the court to intervene to preserve the status quo until the merits are determined.'"); *Pac. Equip. & Irrigation, Inc.*, 519 N.W.2d at 915 ("The key factor in our analysis is the likelihood that [the franchisee] will prevail on the merits.").
153. MINN. STAT. § 80C.14 subdiv. 1.
154. *Pac. Equip. & Irrigation, Inc.*, 519 N.W.2d at 915 ("The applicability of the franchise act is important because if the franchise act applies, the analysis of the Dahlberg factors may change substantially."); Unlimited Horizon Mktg., Inc. v. Precision Hub, Inc., 533 N.W.2d 63, 67 (Minn. Ct. App. 1995) ("Applicability of the Franchise Act will increase UHM's likelihood of success on the merits because of the presumption of irreparable harm. In addition, public policy considerations will favor UHM, since it is entitled to special protections under the law as a franchisee."); Louis DeGidio, Inc. v. Indus. Combustion, LLC, 2019 WL 6894437, at *2 (D. Minn. Dec. 18, 2019) ("If DeGidio were a franchise, it would be entitled to a presumption of irreparable harm, and furthermore would be likely to succeed on the merits, given the various protections of the MFA. DeGidio would thus likely be entitled to a preliminary injunction.").
155. *Wave Form Sys., Inc.*, 73 F. Supp. 3d at 1058 ("Harm to reputation and goodwill, on the other hand, can form sufficient irreparable harm to grant a preliminary injunction."); *Pac. Equip. & Irrigation, Inc.*, 519 N.W.2d at 917 ("Although the district court stated that it is 'arguable' whether Pacific will suffer irreparable harm if the temporary injunction is denied, the court noted that the availability of money damages negates any presumption of irreparable harm."); Upper Midwest Sales Co. v. Ecolab, Inc., 577 N.W.2d 236, 244 (Minn. Ct. App. 1998) ("Because the franchise act does not apply, there will be no irreparable harm to respondents, and they will have a remedy at law for damages.").

would cause irreparable harm to their reputation or goodwill, to the extent they remain in business distributing other products or at other franchised locations, courts have held that such claims are speculative when unsupported by sufficient evidence.[156] On a motion to enjoin a franchise agreement's termination, a court will balance the franchisee's harm in light of the remaining term against a franchisor's harm in being forced to remain in "an undesirable business relationship."[157] If the MFA applies, it serves as a public policy consideration likely favoring injunctive relief to a franchisee.[158]

Practitioners seeking or opposing preliminary injunctive relief face the challenge of presenting as much evidence to support their claims or defenses as possible early in the case and under expedited procedures. A "close factual dispute" or uncertainty about the MFA's applicability, whether due to its territorial scope or the existence of a franchise, will preclude injunctive relief.[159] An "undeveloped" record likewise may not convince a judge to order the extraordinary remedy of injunctive relief.[160] When injunctive relief is at issue, an early win or loss at the minimum sets important momentum and at the most may practically dispose of the entire case.

The most common scenario where franchisees seek injunctive relief is to enjoin franchisors' termination or nonrenewal of the franchise agreement. The most likely scenario where a franchisee will succeed is the wrongful termination of an "accidental franchise." In this scenario, irreparable harm is presumed under the MFA, and the likelihood of success is high due to the unregistered franchisor's failure to appreciate the MFA's requirements for notice and cause, which can tip the balance of harm in favor of the franchisee and advance the MFA's public policy of protecting franchisees.[161]

---

156. *Wave Form Sys., Inc.*, 73 F. Supp. 3d at 1058 ("Similarly, Wave Form's evidence of irreparable harm to its reputation, goodwill, and customer relationships is insufficient to warrant injunctive relief."); Delaria v. KFC Corp., 1995 WL 17079305, at *3 (D. Minn. Jan. 13, 1995) ("The court finds that these allegations of irreparable harm are purely speculative."); Watkins Inc. v. Lewis, 2002 WL 31319491, at *10 (D. Minn. Oct. 11, 2002) ("There is insufficient evidence to support a finding that the termination of their Watkins distributorship has had or will have any meaningful impact on the Lewises ability to sell other product lines to these businesses."), *aff'd*, 346 F.3d 841 (8th Cir. 2003); Modern Comput. Sys., Inc. v. Modern Banking Sys., Inc., 871 F.2d 734 (8th Cir. 1989) ("The district court did not err in denying preliminary injunctive relief in this case because MB's actions caused no irreparable injury to MC.").

157. *Wave Form Sys., Inc.*, 73 F. Supp. 3d at 1058.

158. *Pac. Equip. & Irrigation, Inc.*, 519 N.W.2d at 917.

159. *Upper Midwest Sales Co.*, 577 N.W.2d at 241; *Wave Form Sys., Inc.*, 73 F. Supp. 3d at 1058 ("At present, whether Wave Form will likely succeed on the merits of its claim is uncertain.").

160. Mainstream Fashions Franchising, Inc. v. All These Things, LLC, 453 F. Supp. 3d 1167, 1202 (D. Minn. 2020) ("Mainstream's contention that the mere operation of a purportedly competing business constitutes irreparable harm to its entire franchise system is too speculative, at this stage in the proceedings, because the record remains undeveloped on this issue.").

161. Pool Concepts, Inc. v. Watkins, Inc., Bus. Franchise Guide (CCH) ¶ 12,249 (D. Minn. 2002) ("Because plaintiff is entitled to the protections of the Minnesota Franchise Act, plaintiff has demonstrated that it will probably succeed on the merits."); Unlimited Horizon Mktg., Inc. v. Precision Hub, Inc., 533 N.W.2d 63, 67 (Minn. Ct. App. 1995) ("Applicability of the Franchise Act will increase UHM's likelihood of success on the merits because of the presumption of irreparable harm.").

Franchisors, on the other hand, will typically seek to enjoin a franchisee's violation of restrictive covenants, misappropriation of trade secrets, or trademark infringement. A franchisor's delay in seeking an injunction[162] or taking action to advance its interests can be grounds for denial.[163] A franchisor may enjoin nonsignatories who are "in active concert and participation" with the franchisee in violating a franchise agreement's restrictive covenants.[164]

b. Annotations

Franchisor brought claims against franchisees for breach of the franchise agreement claiming they failed to comply with post-termination obligations requiring franchisees to purchase assets. The court enjoined the franchisees' trademark infringement and use of exclusive products; however, the court did not enforce the franchise agreement's noncompete and other post-termination obligations based on insufficient evidence of irreparable harm. *Mainstream Fashions Franchising, Inc. v. All These Things, LLC*, 453 F. Supp. 3d 1167 (D. Minn. 2020) (applying North Carolina law) ("Accordingly, Mainstream has proven its right to a preliminary injunction with respect to its claims regarding its Marks and exclusive products. . . . Mainstream is not entitled to a preliminary injunction barring Defendants from continuing to operate their businesses, or requiring performance at this time of other post-termination obligations.").

Franchisees sought to enjoin franchise agreements' termination. The court held the franchisor was likely to prevail on whether it properly terminated the agreements due to compliance failures. The court held the franchisees' showing of irreparable harm due to loss of business did not outweigh franchisor's harm due to trademark infringement. *Pooniwala v. Wyndham Worldwide, Corp.*, 2014 WL 1772323 (D. Minn. May 2, 2014) ("In this case, both parties are being significantly harmed by the conduct alleged by the parties. However, the Court concludes that in considering the balance of harms, the scales do not 'tip[] decidedly toward' the moving party.").

Franchisor's 17-month delay in seeking injunctive relief supported lack of irreparable harm. *Novus Franchising, Inc. v. Dawson*, 725 F.3d 885, 895 (8th Cir. 2013) ("After considering all of the arguments made by both parties for and against the need for a preliminary injunction to enforce the noncompete clause, we conclude the district court did not abuse its discretion when it

---

162. Novus Franchising, Inc. v. Dawson, 725 F.3d 885, 895 (8th Cir. 2013) ("At a minimum, Novus's failure to seek injunctive relief for a period of seventeen months after Dawson quit paying royalties 'vitiates much of the force of [Novus's] allegations of irreparable harm.'").

163. Bonanza Int'l, Inc. v. Double "B," 331 F. Supp. 694, 697 (D. Minn. 1971) ("The nature and location of defendant's restaurant coupled with the seeming lack of interest plaintiff has shown in commercially developing this area vitiate any conclusion that plaintiff would be irreparably harmed if his request for a temporary injunction is denied.").

164. Bonus of Am., Inc. v. Angel Falls Servs., LLC, 2010 WL 2734218, at *6 (D. Minn. July 6, 2010) ("[B]ased on the present record, the court finds that Diaz and Patron are in active concert and participation with Hart and Bonus in Minneapolis, and may properly be bound by the preliminary injunction.").

determined Novus failed to show irreparable harm under the particular facts involved in this case.").

Those in active concert and participation with franchisee's violation of restrictive covenants may be enjoined. Nonparty affidavits supported the court's finding of concerted activity. *Bonus of America, Inc. v. Angel Falls Services, L.L.C.*, 2010 WL 2734218 (D. Minn. July 6, 2010) ("[B]ased on the present record, the court finds that Diaz and Patron are in active concert and participation with Hart and Bonus in Minneapolis, and may properly be bound by the preliminary injunction.").

Franchisee's delay in seeking injunctive relief and availability of damages negated the MFA's presumption of irreparable harm for improper nonrenewal. *McCabe v. AIR-serv Group LLC*, 2007 WL 4591932 (D. Minn. Dec. 28, 2007) ("Irreparable harm is presumed for violations of the MFA. That presumption, however, may be negated if a party delays in seeking injunctive relief. . . . Indeed, any concession that damages are a sufficient remedy would negate his assertion of irreparable harm. Accordingly, the Court finds that McCabe is unlikely to succeed on the merits of his claims.").

Balance of harms weighed in favor of dealer because, in the event of termination, the dealer would lose business, customer contacts, and goodwill, while the manufacturer would suffer little irreparable harm if it was ordered to maintain its long-standing relationship with the dealer. The court presumed irreparable harm for improper termination under the MFA. *Pool Concepts, Inc. v. Watkins, Inc.*, Bus. Franchise Guide (CCH) ¶ 12,249 (D. Minn. 2002) ("Because plaintiff is entitled to the protections of the Minnesota Franchise Act, plaintiff has demonstrated that it will probably succeed on the merits.").

Injunction not warranted where the MFA held not to apply, the elements of a franchise were not satisfied, and thus irreparable harm and likelihood of success factors were not met. Regardless, improper nonrenewal under the MFA did not warrant injunctive relief because at most the remedy would be 180 days continued operations under the distributorship, which could be compensated by monetary damages. *Upper Midwest Sales Co. v. Ecolab, Inc.*, 577 N.W.2d 236, 244 (Minn. Ct. App. 1998) ("If the franchise act applies, irreparable injury is presumed, and a court likely would find that analysis of the Dahlberg factors compels the issuance of an injunction.").

On cross motions for preliminary injunction to enjoin termination and operation of franchise, the court found both the franchisor and franchisee failed to satisfy the required factors. The court held that the franchisee's harm was speculative and could be compensated by monetary damages. The court found the franchisor was not harmed because the franchisee was not violating standards or improperly using trademarks. *Delaria v. KFC Corp.*, 1995 WL 17079305, at *5 (D. Minn. Jan. 13, 1995) ("The court concludes that DeLaria has failed to meet its burden of showing the irreparable harm necessary to justify injunctive relief. This failure is sufficient grounds for the court to deny a preliminary injunction.").

Franchisee may satisfy requirement for irreparable harm by establishing likelihood of success on claim for violation of the MFA, since it creates a presumption of irreparable harm. *Unlimited Horizon Marketing, Inc. v. Precision Hub, Inc.*, 533 N.W.2d 63, 67 (Minn. Ct. App. 1995) ("Applicability of the Franchise Act will increase UHM's likelihood of success on the merits because of the presumption of irreparable harm.").

Distributor who only established a close factual dispute regarding the MFA's applicability was not entitled to preliminary injunction. *Pacific Equipment & Irrigation, Inc. v. Toro Co.*, 519 N.W.2d 911, 918 (Minn. Ct. App. 1994) ("We hold that where the parties legitimately dispute whether a product distributor is actually a franchisee under the Minnesota Franchise Act, the district court is not required to grant a temporary injunction where the court merely finds that the party claiming the existence of a franchise agreement is more likely than not to prevail on the merits of that claim. If there is a close factual dispute which could go either way at a trial on the merits, a court should be reluctant to issue a preliminary injunction.").

Distributor threatened with termination was entitled to temporary injunction to maintain the status quo, but only as to lease agreement, and not dealer agreement, which could be compensated through monetary damages. *Pickerign v. Pasco Marketing, Inc.*, 228 N.W.2d 562, 564 (Minn. 1975) ("The 'status quo' of the parties on that date was that plaintiff was a tenant of defendant who had a potential claim at law for damages based on defendant's breach of the dealer agreement.").

Franchisor was not entitled to injunctive relief when the nature and location of the franchisee's location coupled with franchisor's lack of interest in developing the area vitiated did not support a finding of irreparable harm. Franchisee, however, was previously enjoined from continued use of the franchisor's trademarks. *Bonanza International, Inc. v. Double "B"*, 331 F. Supp. 694, 697 (D. Minn. 1971) ("The nature and location of defendant's restaurant coupled with the seeming lack of interest plaintiff has shown in commercially developing this area vitiate any conclusion that plaintiff would be irreparably harmed if his request for a temporary injunction is denied.").

5. Control Person Liability

a. Commentary

The MFA imposes liability not only on franchisors but also those who control them. Under the MFA, joint and several liability exists for a person who "directly or indirectly controls" a franchisor or "materially aids in the act or transactions constituting the violation," unless she "had no knowledge of or reasonable grounds to know of the existence of the facts by which reason of the liability is alleged to exist."[165] The MFA specifically lists a "partner in a firm," a "principal executive officer or director of a corporation," "a person occupying a similar status or performing similar functions," and an "employee," as persons who may be subject to joint and several liability.[166] Although most of the reported cases on control person liability involve alleged sales misrepresentations, franchisees

---

165. MINN. STAT. § 80C.17 subdiv. 2.
166. Id.

have alleged claims against control persons for violations of the MFA's relationship provisions as well.[167]

Due to the structure of the MFA's joint and several liability provision, it is not readily apparent whether the "materially aids" requirement applies just to an "employee" or all control persons.[168] Courts, however, have generally resolved the apparent ambiguity in favor of the requirement applying to all control persons,[169] even though there is grammatical support for the contrary interpretation under the "last antecedent rule."[170] One court has held that a parent corporation with a 40 percent interest in the franchisor is not liable absent evidence it participated in the franchisors "general operations" or "had the power to control the fraudulent statements [the franchisor] allegedly made."[171]

Franchisees have faced personal jurisdiction issues attempting to join nonresident control persons as defendants in actions with their franchisors. Courts have held that personal liability under the MFA does not automatically confer personal jurisdiction.[172] A control person must have his or her own sufficient minimum contacts to satisfy due process, besides contacts made solely in a corporate official capacity, since a corporation's contacts will not be imputed to its officers.[173] Consequently, merely signing a franchise agreement[174] or sending

---

167. *See, e.g.*, Randall v. Lady of Am. Franchise, 2005 WL 2709641, at *2 (D. Minn. Oct. 21, 2005) (alleging control person liability for franchisor's failure "to fulfill its obligations under the franchise agreements").

168. MINN. STAT. § 80C.17 subdiv. 2.

169. Cherrington v. Wild Noodles Franchise Co., 2006 WL 1704301 (D. Minn. June 15, 2006) ("[F]or [the defendant] to be liable, he must have been a control person at the time of the alleged violations or must have materially participated in the violation—his status as COO, alone, does not establish liability."); Randall v. Lady of Am. Franchise, 2005 WL 2709641, at *2 (D. Minn. Oct. 21, 2005) ("A principal executive officer of a corporation may be jointly and severally liable for the corporation's violations of the MFA if the officer 'materially aids in the act or transaction constituting the violation.'"); Dr. Performance of Minn., Inc. v. Dr. Performance Mgmt., LLC, 2002 WL 31628440 (D. Minn. Nov. 12, 2002) ("In order for personal liability to attach to controlling persons under the Minnesota Franchise Act, they must have been in positions of control at the time of the alleged violation, or actively participated in the violation."); Avery v. Solargizer Int'l, Inc., 427 N.W.2d 675, 681 (Minn. Ct. App. 1988) ("[A]ny executive officer, director, or person occupying a similar status or performing similar functions, and all employees who materially aid in the act or transaction are jointly and severally liable.").

170. United States v. Hayes, 555 U.S. 415, 425, (2009) (describing "the 'rule of the last antecedent,' under which 'a limiting clause or phrase . . . should ordinarily be read as modifying only the noun or phrase that it immediately follows'").

171. Berglund v. Cynosure, Inc., 502 F. Supp. 2d 949, 958 (D. Minn. 2007).

172. *Dr. Performance of Minn.*, 2002 WL 31628440, at *5 ("[T]he officer liability section of the Minnesota Franchise Act cannot alone provide a basis for personal jurisdiction."); Sanford v. Maid-Rite Corp., 2014 WL 1608301, at *3 (D. Minn. Apr. 21, 2014) ("Defendants' potential MFA liability does not obviate the requirement that minimum contacts must be established.").

173. Sanford v. Maid-Rite Corp., 2014 WL 1608301, at *3 (D. Minn. Apr. 21, 2014) ("[T]he corporate shield doctrine, also known as the fiduciary-shield doctrine, holds that an individual's actions performed solely as a corporate officer do not create personal jurisdiction over that officer as an individual but may be used to subject the corporation to jurisdiction.").

174. S&G Janitschke, Inc. v. Cottman Transmission Sys., LLC, 2006 WL 1662892, at *11 (D. Minn. June 8, 2006) ("Plaintiffs merely allege that Leff, as a controlling officer of Cottman, executed the

or receiving communications[175] on behalf of a franchisor are insufficient. Practically speaking, this makes it difficult to identify purposeful, claim-related contacts necessary to subject nonresident control persons to personal jurisdiction since they will typically be acting in their corporate official capacities on behalf of franchisors when engaging in forum activities that could give rise to a claim.

b. Annotations

Personal jurisdiction over a controlling person under the MFA can be established where there is liability under the MFA coupled with sufficient minimum contact with the forum state. However, potential liability under the MFA does not obviate the requirement to establish minimum contacts with the forum state. *Sanford v. Maid-Rite Corp.*, 2014 WL 1608301 (D. Minn. Apr. 21, 2014) ("Defendants' potential MFA liability does not obviate the requirement that minimum contacts must be established.").

The MFA's control person liability provision includes an "escape clause" allowing the controlling person to avoid liability if he or she could not have known of the violation. *MSaxon, Inc. v. Holmes*, 2013 WL 12142590 (S.D. Iowa Aug. 2, 2013) ("In support of their position, Plaintiffs point out that the Minnesota Franchise Act ("MFA") and the Minnesota Uniform Securities Act ("MUSA") both impose controlling-person liability and include an escape clause allowing the controlling person to avoid liability by proving that he or she did not know and could not have known that the primary violator committed a wrongdoing.").

Owner held not a control person of franchisor under the MFA despite 40 percent ownership interest, guarantee of lease, supply contract, and shared management. The court found the owner did not participate in the franchisor's alleged misrepresentations or general operations. *Berglund v. Cynosure, Inc.*, 502 F. Supp. 2d 949, 958 (D. Minn. 2007) ("The Amended Complaint asserts Cynosure controlled Sona because: (1) Cynosure owned a 40% interest in Sona; (2) Cynosure guaranteed some of Sona's leases; (3) Cynosure had an exclusive purchasing contract with Sona; and (4) Furumoto, Cynosure's founder, served on Sona's board of directors. However, assuming these facts are true, they do not suggest Cynosure participated in Sona's general operations or that Cynosure had the power to control the fraudulent statements Sona allegedly made to the Minnesota Plaintiffs in connection with the sale of a franchise from SLC to LTS. Therefore, the MFA claim in Count 8 of the Amended Complaint must be dismissed.").

Officer's role alone was insufficient to establish control person liability under the MFA. The relevant inquiry focuses on actual control, not titles, and there was no evidence the officer was involved in the marketing of the franchise or making representations. *Cherrington v. Wild Noodles Franch. Co.*, 2006 WL 1704301 (D. Minn. June 15, 2006) ("[F]or [the defendant] to be liable, he

---

license agreements between Cottman and the Minnesota plaintiffs. The Court finds that this allegation is not enough to confer personal jurisdiction over Leff as an individual defendant.").

175. *Dr. Performance of Minn.*, 2002 WL 31628440, at *5 ("It is well-settled in this circuit that phone calls and mailings between residents of diverse jurisdictions alone are insufficient to establish minimum contacts with the forum state.").

must have been a control person at the time of the alleged violations or must have materially participated in the violation—his status as COO, alone, does not establish liability.").

Franchisee did not allege facts supporting officer's material aid to franchisor's alleged violations of the MFA. As a result, the franchisee failed to state a claim for control person liability under the MFA. *Randall v. Lady of America Franchise*, 2005 WL 2709641 (D. Minn. Oct. 21, 2005) ("A principal executive officer of a corporation may be jointly and severally liable for the corporation's violations of the MFA if the officer 'materially aids in the act or transaction constituting the violation.'").

Control person liability under the MFA does not automatically establish personal jurisdiction. Franchisor's managers did not have sufficient minimum contacts with Minnesota. *Dr. Performance of Minnesota, Inc. v. Dr. Performance Management, LLC*, 2002 WL 31628440 (D. Minn. Nov. 12, 2002) ("In order for personal liability to attach to controlling persons under the Minnesota Franchise Act, they must have been in positions of control at the time of the alleged violation, or actively participated in the violation. . . . Plaintiff cannot establish personal jurisdiction over Baldwin and Atkins based on violations it alleges the L.L.C. committed several months before they took an active role in the L.L.C.").

Genuine dispute of material fact precluded summary judgment on franchisor's defense under the MFA's exception to control person liability where there is "no knowledge" of wrongdoing. Alleged control persons had little involvement with franchisor and no sales or marketing responsibilities, but they did not offer evidence rebutting allegation of actual knowledge. *Avery v. Solargizer Int'l, Inc.*, 427 N.W.2d 675, 681 (Minn. Ct. App. 1988) ("However, the question whether the Andersons had actual knowledge, or should have known about the failure to provide the distributors with the appropriate documentation, is one of fact. The trial court did not err when it found a disputed material fact question exists, and denied the Andersons' motions for summary judgment on this issue.").

Control person liability under the MFA does not establish personal jurisdiction, and the alleged control person's minimum contacts must be personal and separate from his or her activities on behalf of the franchisor. *S&G Janitschke, Inc. v. Cottman Transmission Systems, LLC*, 2006 WL 1662892 (D. Minn. June 8, 2006) ("Plaintiffs merely allege that Leff, as a controlling officer of Cottman, executed the license agreements between Cottman and the Minnesota plaintiffs. The Court finds that this allegation is not enough to confer personal jurisdiction over Leff as an individual defendant.").

6. Attorneys' Fees

a. Commentary

The MFA permits awards of attorneys' fees for prevailing franchisees. Under the MFA, a franchisee may recover "costs and disbursements plus reasonable attorney's fees" in connection with a "suit authorized under this section . . . to recover the actual damages sustained by the plaintiff."[176] Despite how this

---

176. MINN. STAT. § 80C.17 subdiv. 3.

would appear to limit recovery of attorneys' fee only to suits for damages, the Minnesota Supreme Court has held that a franchisee may also recover attorneys' fees in suits for recission and restitution, since such suits are authorized under the same section as suits for damages.[177]

One court, however, has held that a franchisee must be awarded some relief under the MFA to recover its attorneys' fees, and so a franchisee who prevails only on breach of contract claim in the same action will not suffice.[178] Continuing the logic, one could argue that an attorneys' fee award must be limited to only those fees incurred in connection with an MFA claim in a case where a franchisee prevailed on other claims as well, although no court has decided this issue.

b. Annotations

Franchisee was not entitled to attorneys' fees where jury verdict did not clearly award some form of relief under the MFA. *Dunn v. National Beverage Corp.*, 745 N.W.2d 549, 554 (Minn. 2008) ("Because we conclude that the jury's special verdict form answers can be reconciled, we agree with the court of appeals that Twin City did not receive relief under the Minnesota Franchise Act and is, therefore, not entitled to recover attorney fees under the Act.").

Franchisee entitled to recover attorneys' fees for rescission and restitution under the MFA. *Martin Investors, Inc. v. Vander Bie*, 269 N.W.2d 868, 876 (Minn. 1978) ("We do not interpret that provision as limiting the recovery of attorneys' fees to damage actions. Rather, it specifically permits a claim for costs and disbursements plus reasonable attorneys' fees in '(a)ny suit authorized under this section,' which plainly includes a suit for rescission and restitution.").

Franchisee sought 1.5 multiplier of attorneys' fees awarded under the MFA. Trial court's denial of multiplier affirmed. *Hughes v. Sinclair Marketing, Inc.*, 389 N.W.2d 194, 200 (Minn. 1986) ("We find that the trial court did not commit an abuse of discretion in denying the request for a multiplier.").

7. Limitations on Damages

a. Commentary

The MFA does not expressly impose any limitations on damages waivers. As discussed earlier, however, the MFA does more generally prohibit the parties' from prospectively waiving compliance with it, which a franchisee might argue limits prospective waivers of remedies such as actual damages.[179]

---

177. Martin Invs., Inc. v. Vander Bie, 269 N.W.2d 868, 876 (Minn. 1978) ("We do not interpret that provision as limiting the recovery of attorneys' fees to damage actions. Rather, it specifically permits a claim for costs and disbursements plus reasonable attorneys' fees in "(a)ny suit authorized under this section," which plainly includes a suit for rescission and restitution.").

178. Dunn v. Nat'l Bev. Corp., 745 N.W.2d 549, 554 (Minn. 2008) ("The franchise statute is not a "strict liability" statute. Consequently, where, as here, the sole relief sought under the franchise act was damages, the party seeking attorney fees must have sustained 'actual damages' under the statute to qualify for attorney fees as a matter of law."), *aff'd*, 745 N.W.2d 549 (Minn. 2008).

179. MINN. STAT. § 80C.21.

One court has held that a franchisee may not recover punitive damages under the MFA since it only authorizes a suit to recover the actual damages sustained by the plaintiff.[180] In the same case, however, the franchisee was permitted to plead a claim seeking punitive damages for common law fraud.[181]

Minnesota has a unique procedural law prohibiting plaintiffs from alleging punitive damages in their initial complaint and requiring a subsequent motion to amend the complaint to include punitive damages, which may be granted upon a showing of sufficient legal basis and prima facie evidence.[182] The same procedural rule does not apply in Minnesota federal court, so a franchisee need not wait to seek punitive damages, but Minnesota's substantive standard of proof for punitive damages does still apply.[183]

b. Annotations

Franchisee was not entitled to punitive damages under the MFA because it only permits recovery of "damages caused" by violations and only allows recovery for "actual damages." *Cherrington v. Wild Noodles Franch. Co.*, Bus. Franchise Guide (CCH) ¶ 13,349 (D. Minn. Apr. 28, 2006) ("[P]unitive damages are not available under the Minnesota Franchise Act.").

8. Administrative Action

a. Commentary

The MFA authorizes both criminal penalties and civil enforcement actions by the Minnesota attorney general. In practice, however, investigations and contested cases are typically handled administratively by the Minnesota Department of Commerce.[184] Investigations of significant violations may be referred to the Minnesota Attorney General's Office for further legal action, which is rare, but not unprecedented.[185]

The Minnesota Department of Commerce's contested cases are governed by the Minnesota Administrative Rules.[186] The most common investigations relate to registration issues, with penalties in contested cases settled through consent decrees generally ranging from $1,000 to $10,000, depending on the nature and number of violations at issue.[187] Other penalties include orders to cease and

---

180. Cherrington v. Wild Noodles Franchise Co., Bus. Franchise Guide (CCH) ¶ 13,349 (D. Minn. Apr. 28, 2006) ("[P]unitive damages are not available under the Minnesota Franchise Act.").

181. *Id.*

182. Minn. Stat. §§ 549.191, .549.20.

183. Orange Rabbit, Inc. v. Franchoice, Inc., 2020 WL 2191947, at *3 (D. Minn. May 6, 2020) ("The large majority of these courts now apply Rule 15 instead of Minn. Stat. § 549.191 when considering motions to add punitive damage claims.").

184. Minn. Stat. §§ 45.027, 80C.12.

185. Settlement Agreement Between the States of Massachusetts, California, Illinois, Iowa, Maryland, Minnesota, New Jersey, New York, North Carolina, Oregon, Pennsylvania, Rhode Island, Vermont, and the District of Columbia and Burger King Corporation, Bus. Franchise Guide (CCH) ¶16,609 (Mar. 2, 2020).

186. Minn. R. 1400.5010–.8400.

187. Commerce Actions and Regulatory Documents Search, https://www.cards.commerce.state.mn.us/ (last visited Mar. 28, 2025).

desist unlawful practices, submit required registration materials, offer franchisees an option to rescind, and pay restitution.

Those who violate the MFA's registration, disclosure, advertising, prohibited, and unfair practices requirements are subject to a fine not exceeding $2,000 for each violation.[188] Those who fail to comply with a court order for a violation of the MFA are subject to a fine not exceeding $25,000.[189] The MFA also imposes criminal penalties for willful violations, with fines not to exceed $10,000 and imprisonment not to exceed five years.[190]

When the Minnesota attorney general investigates a matter, it may also settle through a consent decree. For example, the Minnesota attorney general along with other states settled with a group of four major national franchisors to stop using and enforcing "no-poach" agreements that restrict franchisees' employees from moving to other franchises.[191]

b. Annotations

In a settlement of attorneys general of several states along with major franchisors, the franchisors agreed to stop enforcing no-poach agreements as contained within their franchise agreements. "No-poach" provisions refer to provisions containing language that purports to restrict, limit, or prevent the franchisee or restaurant from hiring, recruiting, or soliciting employees of the franchisors or any other franchisee. Settlement Agreement Between the States of Massachusetts, California, Illinois, Iowa, Maryland, Minnesota, New Jersey, New York, North Carolina, Oregon, Pennsylvania, Rhode Island, Vermont, and the District of Columbia and Burger King Corporation, Bus. Franchise Guide (CCH) ¶ 16,609 (Mar. 2, 2020).

H. Dispute Resolution

Disputes between franchisors and franchisees over claims alleging violations of the MFA may be resolved through civil actions in state or federal court, arbitrations, and negotiated settlements.[192] The MFA, however, imposes some limitations on where and when claims must be brought.

1. Limitations on Franchisors' Ability to Restrict Venue

a. Commentary

Under the MFA, franchisors may not use mandatory forum selection clauses to prevent franchisees to whom the MFA applies from bringing their claims under the MFA in Minnesota. The Commissioner's rule defines it as an unfair

---

188. Minn. Stat. § 80C.16 subdiv. 2.
189. Id.
190. Id. subdiv. 3.
191. Settlement Agreement Between the States of Massachusetts, California, Illinois, Iowa, Maryland, Minnesota, New Jersey, New York, North Carolina, Oregon, Pennsylvania, Rhode Island, Vermont, and the District of Columbia and Burger King Corporation, Bus. Franchise Guide (CCH) ¶16,609 (Mar. 2, 2020).
192. Minn. R. 2860.4400.D, .J, ("[T]his part shall not bar the voluntary settlement of disputes; . . . [T]his part shall not bar an exclusive arbitration clause.").

and inequitable practice for a franchisor to "require a franchisee . . . to waive rights to any procedure, forum, or remedies provided for by the laws of the jurisdiction."[193]

The rule refers vaguely to "the jurisdiction," not explicitly Minnesota, but practically speaking it can only mean Minnesota.[194] If a franchisor uses a foreign forum selection clause and matching choice of law, and they would always match to preserve the common law requirement of rationality, then the MFA will not apply to a nonresident franchisee, who is not barred from waiving its applicability.[195]

Thus, the rule only prohibits a franchisor from using a mandatory forum selection clause to prevent a franchisee to whom the MFA applies from bringing their claims under the MFA in Minnesota.[196] It does not require all types of claims between franchisors and franchisees to be litigated in Minnesota.[197] A franchisor may first sue a franchisee in any court with jurisdiction to hear its

---

193. *Id.* at J.
194. Ramada Worldwide Inc. v. SB Hotel Mgmt. Inc., 2015 WL 758536, at *3 (D.N.J. Feb. 23, 2015) ("Essentially, under the Act and Minnesota Rule 2860.440J, a franchisor cannot prevent a Minnesota franchisee from filing suit in its 'home' court in Minnesota.").
195. Sound of Music Co. v. Minn. Mining & Mfg., Co., 389 F. Supp. 2d 988, 1003 (N.D. Ill. 2005) ("It is undisputed that Sound of Music is neither a Minnesota resident nor a "franchise to be operated" in Minnesota. Based on this straightforward reading of the statute, this anti-waiver provision does not apply here, and Sound of Music therefore waived any rights under the Act."), *aff'd sub nom.*, 477 F.3d 910 (7th Cir. 2007).
196. Moxie Venture LLC v. UPS Store, Inc., 156 F. Supp. 3d 967, 971 (D. Minn. 2016) ("Accordingly, the anti-waiver provision does not invalidate the forum-selection clause as applied to Moxie's common-law claims, and those claims will be transferred to the Southern District of California."); Family Wireless #1 LLC v Auto. Techs. Inc., 2015 WL 5142350, at *5 (E.D. Mich. Sept. 1, 2015) ("Because, as the franchise agreement states, Minnesota law prohibits Defendant 'from requiring litigation to be conducted outside of Minnesota,' . . . , the forum-selection clauses in these agreements are invalid."); *Ramada Worldwide Inc.*, 2015 WL 758536, at *2–3 (D.N.J. Feb. 23, 2015) ("Essentially, under the Act and Minnesota Rule 2860.440J, a franchisor cannot prevent a Minnesota franchisee from filing suit in its 'home' court in Minnesota"); S & G Janitschke v. Cottman Transmission Sys., LLC, 2006 WL 1662892 (D. Minn. June 8, 2006) ("Therefore, the Court finds that the Cottman forum selection clause is void as applied to the three Minnesota plaintiffs."); Blaske v. Burger King Corp., 1991 WL 238998, at *3 (D. Minn. 1991) ("Under the terms of the addendum, which is clearly not part of the standard Burger King franchise agreement, plaintiffs have retained the privilege of submitting those claims to a Minnesota court."); *but see* Zutz v Scottsdale Models LLC, 2016 WL 1019393, at *5–6 (D. Minn. Jan. 25, 2016) (transferring action from Minnesota to Arizona based on mandatory forum selection clause notwithstanding the fact the franchise was located in Minnesota).
197. *Ramada Worldwide Inc.*, 2015 WL 758536, at *2–3 (D.N.J. Feb. 23, 2015) (rejecting Minnesota franchisee's argument that foreign forum selection clause was invalid where franchisor sued first); Allegra Holdings LLC v. Davis, 2014 WL 1652221, at *3 (E.D. Mich. Apr. 24, 2014) (same); Ramada Worldwide Inc. v. Grand Rios Inv. LLC, 2013 WL 5773085, at *3 (D.N.J. Oct. 23, 2013) ("[Franchisees] would have the Court read the Minnesota statute to preclude all cases and controversies stemming from sales of franchises operated in Minnesota from litigating in any forum other than Minnesota. However, a plain reading of the statute's language indicates that . . . a Minnesota franchisee cannot be prevented from filing suit in its 'home' court in Minnesota by a franchisor."); Long John Silver's Inc. v. Nickleson, 923 F. Supp. 2d 1004, 2–3 (W.D. Ky. 2013) (rejecting Minnesota franchisee's argument that foreign forum selection clause was invalid where franchisor sued first and franchisee alleged MFA counterclaims).

claims, who then may need to assert compulsory counterclaims under the MFA, with the result that they will be litigated in the first filed forum.[198]

The MFA's limitations on forum selection clauses expressly do not prohibit arbitration agreements.[199] The Federal Arbitration Act would preempt the contrary.[200] The MFA does not limit arbitration venue.[201]

b. Annotations

Franchisee brought an action against a franchisor alleging fraudulent inducement into the franchise agreement and claims for violations of the MFA along with other claims. After dismissing the MFA claim, the court enforced the forum-selection clause which selected California. *Moxie Venture L.L.C. v. UPS Store, Inc.*, 156 F. Supp. 3d 967 (D. Minn. 2016) ("Accordingly, the anti-waiver provision does not invalidate the forum-selection clause as applied to Moxie's common-law claims, and those claims will be transferred to the Southern District of California.").

Motion to dismiss and transfer granted pursuant to a forum selection clause. The court found there was no language in the forum selection clause that waived compliance with the MFA. *Zutz v. Scottsdale Models LLC*, 2016 WL 1019393 (D. Minn. Jan. 25, 2016) (transferring action from Minnesota to Arizona based on mandatory forum selection clause notwithstanding the fact the franchise was located in Minnesota).

The MFA only prohibits forum selection clauses preventing Minnesota franchisees from filing suit in Minnesota. The court denied franchisee's motion to transfer despite the fact the franchise was located in Minnesota because the plaintiff-franchisor's choice of forum outweighed the franchisee's inconvenience. *Ramada Worldwide Inc. v Grand Rios Investments LLC*, 2013 WL 5773085 (D.N.J. Oct. 23, 2013) ("[Franchisees] would have the Court read the Minnesota statute to preclude all cases and controversies stemming from sales of franchises operated in Minnesota from litigating in any forum other than Minnesota. However, a plain reading of the statute's language indicates that . . . a Minnesota franchisee cannot be prevented from filing suit in its 'home' court in Minnesota by a franchisor.").

Before addressing the merits of the claims, the court addressed standing with respect to the application of the MFA in a Kentucky court. Citing the MFA's

---

198. Long John Silver's Inc. v. Nickleson, 923 F. Supp. 2d 1004, 1010 (W.D. Ky. 2013) ("Since the Franchise Agreement's forum selection provision does not diminish Defendants' rights under the MFA, the MFA's anti-waiver provision does not result in the invalidation of Franchise Agreement's forum selection clause.").

199. MINN. R. 2860.4400.J; Nolan v. HairColorExpress Int'l, LLC, Bus. Franchise Guide (CCH) ¶ 13,049 (D. Minn. 2005).

200. Mahnke v. Executive Tans USA, LLC, 2007 WL 2340056, at *2 (D. Minn. Aug. 13, 2007) ("Based on the history of the FAA, the Court determined that Congress intended to foreclose any state legislative attempts to foreclose arbitration agreements.").

201. Nolan v. HairColorExpress Int'l, LLC, Bus. Franchise Guide (CCH) ¶ 13,049 (D. Minn. 2005) ("That Defendants agreed in Exhibit D that 'litigation' must be conducted in Minnesota conforms to the distinction made elsewhere in the franchise agreement between 'litigation' and 'arbitration.'").

anti-waiver provision, the court found that it only applied to the franchisee whose franchise is located in Minnesota. The Court determined that the forum selection clause in the franchise agreement does not diminish the defendant's rights under the MFA and the Kentucky court will enforce the MFA accordingly. *Long John Silver's Inc. v. Nickleson*, 923 F. Supp. 2d 1004, 1010 (W.D. Ky. 2013) ("Since the Franchise Agreement's forum selection provision does not diminish Defendants' rights under the MFA, the MFA's anti-waiver provision does not result in the invalidation of Franchise Agreement's forum selection clause.").

In group action brought by franchisees located in multiple states, exclusive forum selection clause in Minnesota franchisees' agreements was held unenforceable under the MFA. The FDDs' citation to the MFA's provision prohibiting such clauses supported denial of transfer. *Family Wireless #1 LLC v. Automotive Technologies Inc.*, 2015 WL 5142350 (E.D. Mich. Sept. 1, 2015) ("Because, as the franchise agreement states, Minnesota law prohibits Defendant 'from requiring litigation to be conducted outside of Minnesota,' . . . , the forum-selection clauses in these agreements are invalid.").

Nonexclusive forum selection clause held not invalid under the MFA. The court denied franchisee's motion to transfer after the franchisor filed a lawsuit in New Jersey for failing to establish that convenience and justice factors warranted transfer. *Ramada Worldwide Inc. v. SB Hotel Management Inc.*, 2015 WL 758536 (D.N.J. Feb. 23, 2015) ("Essentially, under the Act and Minnesota Rule 2860.440J, a franchisor cannot prevent a Minnesota franchisee from filing suit in its 'home' court in Minnesota.").

The MFA's anti-waiver provision did not prohibit franchisor from bringing suit against franchisee outside Minnesota. Franchise agreement did not have exclusive Minnesota forum selection clause and franchisee could still avail itself of rights under the MFA. *Allegra Holdings LLC v. Davis*, 2014 WL 1652221 (E.D. Mich. Apr. 24, 2014) ("First, there is nothing in the contractual language limiting Defendants' selection of a Minnesota court as a forum should they, as Franchisors, choose to file suit. Second, there is nothing in the contractual language or in the referenced Minnesota statutes or rule precluding parties to a franchise agreement from agreeing to a forum selection.").

The MFA prohibited franchisor from enforcing exclusive Pennsylvania forum selection clause after a lawsuit was brought by franchisees in Minnesota. *S & G Janitschke v. Cottman Transmission Systems, LLC*, 2006 WL 1662892 (D. Minn. June 8, 2006) ("The Court finds that the text of § 80C.21 expressly authorizes the Commissioner of Commerce to promulgate rules interpreting 'unfair and inequitable' practices. The Commissioner has, in turn, prohibited forum selection clauses like the one in the Cottman license agreement. Therefore, the Court finds that the Cottman forum selection clause is void as applied to the three Minnesota plaintiffs.").

The MFA did not prohibit arbitration agreement's exclusive Florida forum selection clause. The court distinguished "litigation" and "arbitration" and held that valid arbitration agreements must be enforced according to their terms. *Nolan v. HairColorExpress International, LLC*, Bus. Franchise Guide (CCH) ¶ 13,049 (D. Minn. 2005) ("That Defendants agreed in Exhibit D that 'litigation' must be conducted in Minnesota conforms to the distinction made elsewhere in the franchise agreement between 'litigation' and 'arbitration.'").

Transfer factors did not support franchisor's motion to transfer case from Minnesota to Kansas based on plaintiff's choice of forum, the proposed transfer would only serve to shift the inconvenience between the parties, and the dispute was likely to require the testimony from witnesses located in multiple states. An earlier action between the parties was filed in Minnesota and the settlement agreement resulting from that suit provided that Minnesota law governed its terms. In addition, the settlement agreement provided that certain types of actions would be brought exclusively in that state. *Home Owners Management Services, Inc. v. ProHome International, LLC*, Bus. Franchise Guide (CCH) ¶ 12,948 (D. Minn. 2004) ("The Former Franchisees have chosen Minnesota as the forum in which to bring this suit. The first action between these parties was filed in Minnesota and the Settlement Agreement that was negotiated as a result of that suit provided that Minnesota law governs its terms and the interpretation of those terms. In addition, the Settlement Agreement provided that certain types of actions would be brought exclusively in the courts of this state.").

Franchisee's motion to transfer denied in favor of franchisor-plaintiff's choice of forum, which was not outweighed by choice of another state's law or the convenience of witness and parties. *Grow Biz International, Inc. v. MNO Inc.*, 2002 WL 113849 (D. Minn. 2002) ("In short, none of the factors raised by the Defendants, either individually or in totality, justify this Court ignoring the Plaintiff's choice of forum in favor of transferring this action to North Carolina.").

Franchisee was not fraudulently induced to include a Minnesota forum selection clause in its franchise agreement. The franchisee's attorney had read the franchise agreement and altered the choice of law provision immediately preceding the forum selection clause. It could reasonably be inferred that the attorney had reviewed the entire document. *Candleman Corp. v. Farrow*, Bus. Franchise Guide ¶ 11,635 (D. Minn. Feb. 1, 1999) ("Focusing on the franchise agreement language, Farrow argues that because he could be denied removal, the forum selection clause violates the mandate set forth in Rule § 2860.4400. The Court disagrees. Because 'the law of the jurisdiction' is Minnesota law, and removal is purely a federal procedure—not a procedure or remedy in Minnesota law—the Court finds that the forum selection agreement does not violate section 80C.14 of the MFA.").

Despite the Florida forum selection clause contained in 20 of the parties' franchise agreements, the court denied transfer based on more recent addendum reserving the franchisee's right to litigate in Minnesota. *Blaske v. Burger King Corp.*, 1991 WL 238998, at *3 (D. Minn. 1991) ("In this Court's view, the addendum clauses reflect the most recent expression of the parties' intent. These newer contracts were crafted after nearly seven years of commercial affiliation between the parties, and clearly constitute a knowing addition to an otherwise standard franchise agreement.").

The MFA does not invalidate forum selection clause entered into before the effective date of administrative rule preserving Minnesota franchisees' right to litigate in Minnesota. *Van Dusen Airport Services Co., L.P. v. Allied Signal, Inc.*,

1991 WL 151377 (Minn. Ct. App. 1991) ("This rule clearly prohibits choice of forum clauses.").

The MFA did not prohibit arbitration agreement that required venue outside Minnesota. *Mahnke v. Executive Tans USA, LLC*, 2007 WL 2340056, at *2 (D. Minn. Aug. 13, 2007) ("Based on the history of the FAA, the Court determined that Congress intended to foreclose any state legislative attempts to foreclose arbitration agreements.").

2. Limitations Period

a. Commentary

The MFA has a three-year statute of limitations. It provides, "No action may be commenced pursuant to this section more than three years after the cause of action accrues."[202] When a claim accrues depends on the nature of the claim and the facts.

For violations of the MFA's relationship provisions, such as wrongful termination, it is typically easier to ascertain when claims accrue. For example, when a franchisee alleges wrongful termination more than three years after the parties ceased to do any business, it may be possible to obtain dismissal for failure to state a claim based on the MFA's statute of limitations despite the fact it usually operates as an affirmative defense.[203]

A statute of limitations is typically a defendant's affirmative defense. When the discovery rule applies, however, the plaintiff bears the burden of alleging and proving facts supporting his or her discovery of the misrepresentation within the statute of limitations.[204]

One court has upheld a contractual limitations period of just one year notwithstanding the MFA's three-year statute of limitations.[205] Under Minnesota common law, a contractually shortened limitations period is valid if not unreasonably short under the circumstances.[206]

---

202. Minn. Stat. § 80C.17(5).

203. Louis Degidio, Inc. v. Indus. Combustion, LLC, 2020 WL 4676289, at *2–3 (D. Minn. Aug. 12, 2020) ("Although statute-of-limitations assertions are usually an affirmative defense, dismissal for failure to state a claim based on statute of limitations can be appropriate if 'the complaint itself establishes the defense.'").

204. Novus Franchising, Inc. v. Dawson, 2013 WL 4483205, at *2 (D. Minn. Aug. 20, 2013) ("When the discovery rule applies, 'the burden is on the plaintiff to allege and prove that he did not discover the facts constituting the fraud until within [three] years before the commencement of the action.'"); Counter Active, Inc. v. Tacom, LP, 2008 WL 781922, at *6 (D. Minn. Mar. 21, 2008) ("Plaintiffs do not allege facts in the Second Amended Complaint relating to when they learned of any of the alleged violations. Therefore, the discovery rule does not apply and Plaintiffs do not receive the benefit of a tolling of the statute of limitations.").

205. Berglund v. Re/Max N. Cent., Inc., ¶ 13,735 (Minn. Dist. Ct. Oct. 29, 2007) ("Minnesota law does not preclude parties from agreeing contractually upon a shortened limitations period, and Section 80C.17(5) does not guaranty a franchisee a minimum period within which to make claims.").

206. Sportmart, Inc. v. Hargesheimer, 1997 WL 406386, at *3 (Minn. Ct. App. July 22, 1997) ("The first inquiry is whether a specific statute prohibits the use of a different limitation period; if no such statute exists, the contract limitation will be upheld if reasonable in length.").

b. Annotations

The MFA's three-year statute of limitations applied to claims seeking declaration of rights thereunder. *Louis DeGidio, Inc. v. Industrial Combustion, LLC*, 2020 WL 4676289 (D. Minn. Aug. 12, 2020) ("DeGidio does not dispute that Louis DeGidio, Inc., ceased to have any relationship with Defendants after 2010, but instead argue that certain responses in Defendants' Answer indicate that, despite the SAC's allegations, perhaps Louis DeGidio, Inc. did continue to have a contractual relationship. But the Defendants' Answer does not establish such facts. Instead, it is clear on the face of the SAC that Louis DeGidio, Inc., ceased to have any relationship with Defendants in 2010, and accordingly, whatever claims that entity may have had under the Minnesota Franchise Act are now time barred.").

The parties may contractually agree to a shorter limitations period than that provided by the MFA. The court upheld a contractual one-year limitations period, shorter than the three-year period imposed by the MFA. *Berglund v. Re/Max North Central, Inc.*, ¶ 13,735 (Minn. Dist. Ct. Oct. 29, 2007) ("Minnesota law does not preclude parties from agreeing contractually upon a shortened limitations period, and Section 80C.17(5) does not guaranty a franchisee a minimum period within which to make claims.").

Mississippi

Benjamin L. Mitchell

I. Introduction

Mississippi has one statute regulating franchises, which primarily addresses the franchise relationship, although there is a section that applies to the sale of franchises.[1] The Mississippi franchise statute has been referred to by the Fifth Circuit Court of Appeals as the "Mississippi Franchise Cancellation Statute"[2] and the "Mississippi Franchise Act,"[3] but it has no formal name or statutorily prescribed citation.

The Mississippi franchise statute became effective on July 1, 1975. There is no specific legislative intent or rationale mentioned in the statute. As enacted, the statute included a prohibition on "pyramid promotional schemes" and existed as a combined "franchise" and "pyramid scheme" law until July 1, 2018, when, as a result of the passage of Mississippi Senate Bill No. 2805, the pyramid scheme provisions of the statute were separated out from the franchise provisions. However, as an apparent oversight, there remains one sentence addressing pyramid sales schemes embedded in the franchise portion of the statute.[4]

As a franchise relationship law, the statute essentially restricts a franchisor's ability to terminate or not renew a franchise agreement on less than 90 days advance notice to the franchisee, except in certain situations. This is purely a notice requirement, meaning that the statute does not provide the franchisee with a period in which to cure any default of the franchise agreement serving as the basis of termination or nonrenewal. A harmed franchisee has the right to institute legal proceedings against a franchisor that violates the 90-day notice requirement and, if the franchisee prevails, recover certain damages and obtain equitable relief. The statute also empowers the Mississippi attorney general to bring an action in the name of the state to enjoin violations of the statute.

The statute does not provide for the promulgation of any regulations. In addition, compared to some other states with franchise relationship laws, there

---

1. Miss. Code Ann. §§ 75-24-51 *et seq.*
2. Crosthwait Equip. Co. v. John Deere Co., 992 F.2d 525 (5th Cir. 1993).
3. McDonald's Corp. v. Watson, 69 F.3d 36, 44 (5th Cir. 1995).
4. Miss. Code Ann. § 75-24-57.

is relatively little case law addressing the Mississippi franchise statute or interpreting its provisions.

II. Commentary and Annotations

A. Definition of Franchise

1. Trademark Element

a. Commentary

In order to meet the definition of a franchise, the Mississippi statute requires, among other things, that the franchisor grant the franchisee "a license to use a trade name, trademark, service mark, or related characteristic."[5] A typical business format franchise would meet this requirement, since a trademark license is inherent to the arrangement. However, certain distribution and other arrangements that do not involve an actual trademark license may not meet this requirement of the definition. The language of the trademark element of the Mississippi statute is more narrowly tailored than what is found in some other state franchise statutes that require the franchisee's business be "substantially associated with the franchisor's trademark."[6] Under the Mississippi statute, a license agreement—more than just "substantial association" with a mark—is required. Although not defined in the statute, the licensing of a "related characteristic" is likely a reference to other types of commercial symbols that share the characteristics of a trademark, such as trade dress and certification marks.

b. Annotations

In *Crosthwait Equipment Co., Inc.*, the Crosthwaits owned and operated an authorized John Deere dealership selling agricultural and consumer products and equipment. John Deere terminated the dealership agreement after learning that the dealer had prepared and submitted falsified sales and credit documents to John Deere. The dealer filed suit in state court, but the case was subsequently removed to the federal district court. The district court ordered that the dealer could stay in business for 90 days under Mississippi law. A jury returned a verdict in favor of the dealer, but the district court then granted John Deere's motion for judgment as a matter of law on the applicable claims. On appeal, the dealer claimed, among other things, that it was entitled to damages under the Mississippi franchise statute as a result of the termination of the dealership by John Deere. The Fifth Circuit stated that it was "arguable" as to whether the relationship between the dealer and John Deere qualified as a franchise under the Mississippi franchise statute. However, even if the relationship was a franchise, the court noted that the 90-day notice period prior to termination does not apply where the basis of the termination is fraud, which, in this case, was plainly evident. The court went on to say that even if fraud was not the basis of the termination, the district court's order that the dealer could stay in business

---

5. *Id.* § 75-24-51.
6. *See* Ill. Comp. Stat. § 705/3(1); R.I. Gen. Laws § 19-28.1-3(g)(l)(C).

for 90 extra days satisfied the statutory notice requirement. In elaborating on whether the relationship qualified as a franchise, the Fifth Circuit asserted that consideration was the only element of the definition of a franchise under the statute that may not have been clearly met, implying that the trademark element was clearly met under the circumstances. The court did not address the trademark element and, presumably, the underlying dealership agreement contained a license by John Deere to Crosthwait to use the John Deere trademarks in the operation of the dealership.[7]

In *Snacks R Plenty, LLC v. Travelbee Snacks LLC*, the plaintiff entered into a distributorship agreement with two of the defendants in the lawsuit, S-L Distribution Company and its subsidiary S-L Routes, LLC, for the right to distribute Snyder's-Lance products in an exclusive territory in Mississippi. Under the arrangement, the defendants would sell the products to the plaintiff, who would pick up the orders at the defendant's warehouse and further distribute the products to gas stations for retail sale. Another defendant in the lawsuit was Richard Grabert, an employee of S-L Distribution. Less than a year after entering into the distribution agreement, the plaintiff received a letter terminating the agreement. The plaintiff filed suit in Mississippi state court alleging, among other things, violation of the Mississippi franchise statute for failing to provide 90 days written notice of termination of the distributorship. The defendants removed the case to federal court based on diversity of citizenship. The plaintiff then filed a motion to remand. One of the issues considered by the court in deciding the motion to remand was whether the plaintiff was able to establish a cause of action against Grabert under the Mississippi franchise statute. Applying Mississippi law in interpreting the plaintiff's claims against Grabert, the court found that there was no cognizable claim. The plaintiff, in its motion to remand, argued that Grabert should be personally liable for violation of the statute as S-L Distribution's "agent." However, the court pointed out that Grabert was not a party to the distributorship agreement and further noted that, as an employee acting within the scope of his employment, Grabert's actions constituted the actions of S-L Distribution. As a result of these findings, the court agreed with Grabert that the plaintiff would not be able to establish a cause of action against him individually for violation of the Mississippi franchise statute. Essentially, the court concluded that Grabert did not meet the definition of a franchisor under the statute because he did not receive consideration in exchange for granting the plaintiff a license to use a trademark. For this and other reasons, the plaintiff's motion to remand was denied.[8]

In the same case, the plaintiff argued that the relationship between it and the supplier met the definition of a franchise under the Mississippi statute. In support of this argument, the plaintiff stated that it paid a fee in exchange for an exclusive territory, paid a weekly fee for other benefits, and was granted the right to use the Snyder's-Lance trademarks on certain materials. The plaintiff further argued that it did not engage in sales from warehouses (which would

---
7. Crosthwait Equip. Co. v. John Deere Co., 992 F.2d 525 (5th Cir. 1993).
8. Snacks R Plenty, LLC v. Travelbee Snacks LLC, 2012 WL 12884480 (S.D. Miss. Oct. 31, 2012).

have excluded the relationship from the definition of a "franchise" under the statute) but rather received product from the defendant's warehouse and delivered those products to customers. However, the court noted that, contrary to the plaintiff's contention that it was granted the right to use a trademark, the distribution agreement explicitly prohibited the plaintiff from using the Snyder's-Lance marks. Therefore, the arrangement did not meet the definition of a franchise under the statute because the underlying distributor agreement did not include the necessary element of a grant of a "license to use a trade name, trademark, service mark, or related characteristic." In addition, the court noted that the agreement provided for the plaintiff to pick up orders for the product from the defendant's warehouse and the Mississippi franchise statute expressly excludes from the definition of a franchise "persons engaged in sales from warehouses or like places of storage." The plaintiff contended that the arrangement did not constitute "sales from warehouses" under the statute because the plaintiff only picked up product at the defendant's warehouse and did not sell products from the warehouse. However, the district court concluded that the plaintiff receiving product orders at the defendant's warehouse excluded the arrangement from the definition of a franchise under the Mississippi statute. Ultimately, in ruling on the defendants' motion, the district court dismissed the plaintiff's claim for violation of the Mississippi franchise statute.[9]

2. Franchise Fee Element

a. Commentary

The Mississippi statute also requires that the franchisor receive "a consideration" for the grant of the license to the franchisee.[10] One commentator has said that any good consideration is equivalent to a "franchise fee" under Mississippi law.[11] However, the statute expressly excludes from the definition of consideration (1) "payment for sales demonstration equipment and materials furnished at cost for use in making sales and not for resale" and (2) "payments amounting to less than One Hundred Dollars ($100.00) when computed on an annual basis."[12]

b. Annotations

In *Crosthwait Equipment Co.*, the terminated John Deere dealer claimed that it was entitled to damages under the Mississippi franchise statute as a result of the termination. The Fifth Circuit stated that it was "arguable" whether the dealership relationship qualified as a franchise under the statute because the element of consideration was not clearly met. The court noted that Mississippi does not necessarily require any sort of "payments" as consideration for a franchise. However, the court did not have to determine whether the consideration

---

9. Snacks R Plenty, LLC v. Travelbee Snacks LLC, 2013 WL 12123364 (S.D. Miss. Jan. 28, 2013).
10. Miss. Code Ann. § 75-24-51.
11. *Crosthwait Equip. Co.*, 992 F.2d at 529, n.4 (citing Kenneth H. Slade, *Applicability of Franchise and Business Opportunity Laws to Distribution and Licensing Agreements*, 15 Am. Intell. Prop. L.J. 1 (1987)).
12. Miss. Code Ann. § 75-24-51.

element was met because, even if it was, and the relationship was a franchise under the Mississippi statute, there was no violation of the statute under the facts of the case.[13] The requirement to provide 90 days' notice prior to termination does not apply when fraud is the basis for termination and, in this case, the dealer was terminated for falsifying sales and credit documents.

3. Community of Interest; Significant Degree of Control; Joint Marketing Plan

a. Commentary

To be a franchise under the Mississippi statute, the arrangement must be one "in which there is a community of interest in the marketing of goods or services at wholesale, retail, by lease, agreement or otherwise."[14] The term "community of interest" is not defined in the Mississippi statute and the author was unable to find any case law addressing the issue. However, a "community of interest" element is found in the definition of a franchise in other state franchise statutes, such as the New Jersey Franchise Practices Act and Minnesota Franchise Act.[15] Mississippi courts may look to jurisdictions such as these for instruction on this issue, since these other jurisdictions have guiding case law. For example, under New Jersey law, courts have found the community of interest element met "when the terms of the agreement between the parties or the nature of the franchise business requires the licensee, in the interest of the licensed business's success, to make a substantial investment in goods or skills that will be of minimal utility outside the franchise."[16] And under Minnesota law, a relationship involving the sharing of fees from a common source have been held to have created a community of interest.[17]

b. Annotations

In *Crosthwait Equipment Co.*, the terminated John Deere dealer claimed it was entitled to damages under the Mississippi franchise statute as a result of the termination. In determining whether the relationship between John Deere and the dealer constituted a franchise under the statute, the Fifth Circuit noted that the only open issue was whether there was consideration, thereby implying that the "community of interest" element was met under the circumstances. However, the court did not explain the basis for determining that the community of interest element was met in the case.[18]

---

13. *Crosthwait Equip. Co.*, 992 F.2d at 525.
14. MISS. CODE ANN. § 75-24-51.
15. N.J. STAT. ANN. §§ 56:10-1 *et seq.*; MINN. STAT. §§ 80C.01 *et seq.*
16. Lawmen Supply Co. of New Jersey, Inc. v. Glock, Inc., 330 F. Supp. 3d 1020, 1033 (D.N.J. 2018) (citing Cassidy Podell Lynch, Inc. v. SnyderGeneral Corp., 944 F.2d 1131, 1142 (3d Cir. 1991)).
17. Martin Invs., Inc. v. Vander Bie, 269 N.W.2d 868, 875 (Minn. 1978).
18. *Crosthwait Equip. Co.*, 992 F.2d at 525.

B. Scope and Jurisdiction

1. Commentary
The Mississippi franchise statute does not expressly address any geographic, residency, or jurisdictional requirements. Neither does it address whether parties can waive its applicability.

2. Annotations
In *McDonald's Corp. v. Joe L. Watson & Lashon Enterprises, Inc.*, the franchisees operated McDonald's franchises in Mississippi under license agreements that permitted the franchisees to use McDonald's trademarks on the condition that they comply with their obligations under the agreements. However, the franchisees failed to make required payments to the franchisor. Over the course of 18 months, the franchisor sent several default notices to the franchisees following events of default, warning the franchisees that the agreements would be terminated if they did not stay current on their payment obligations. The franchisor eventually decided to terminate the franchise agreements, but did not provide a formal notice of termination to the franchisees. Instead, about two months after having decided to terminate the agreements, the franchisor filed a lawsuit against the franchisees and, in its complaint, alleged that the franchise agreements were terminated and sought the surrender of the restaurants, an injunction against further interference by the franchisees, and damages for, among other things, trademark infringement. The franchisee defendants received the complaint via personal service. The franchisees continued to operate the restaurants for a few weeks following their receipt of the complaint when they surrendered one restaurant to the franchisor and the other to the IRS. The franchisee defendants filed a motion for summary judgment, claiming that they never received effective notice of termination of the agreements and, therefore, did not infringe on McDonald's trademarks. The district court initially agreed with the defendants that the agreements had never been terminated but, on the franchisor's motion for reconsideration, the court reversed itself, holding that service of the complaint was effective notice. The district court then held that the franchisor terminated the agreements for cause and that the franchisees infringed upon the McDonald's trademarks during the time between the franchisor's complaint being served and the restaurants being surrendered. On appeal, the franchisee defendants asserted that the franchisor did not terminate the franchises in compliance with the requirements of the Mississippi franchise statute, which entitled them to 90 days' advance notice of termination. However, the Fifth Circuit refused to address this issue because the franchise agreement expressly provided that Illinois law would be used to construe the contract and held that the defendants acquiesced to the district court's ruling that Illinois law governed the case. Had the franchisees properly preserved this issue for appeal, it may have changed the outcome of the case. Also, it is worth mentioning that the Mississippi franchise statute does not have an anti-waiver provision, which could otherwise have affected the outcome of this case.[19]

---

19. McDonald's Corp. v. Watson, 69 F.3d 36 (5th Cir. 1995).

In ruling on the defendants' motion to dismiss or transfer, the district court in *Snacks R Plenty* dismissed the plaintiff's claim of violation of the Mississippi franchise statute. The plaintiff argued that the relationship between the parties was a franchise under the statute. However, the district court determined that the defendants could not meet the definition of a franchise under the statute because the underlying distributor agreement did not include a grant of a "license to use a trade name, trademark, service mark, or related characteristic." Although the plaintiff argued that the defendant gave it the right to use the defendant's trademark on invoice sheets, rack displays, and other items, the agreement expressly prohibited the plaintiff from using the defendants' trademarks. In addition, the court noted that the agreement provided for the plaintiff to pick up orders for product from the defendant's warehouse and the Mississippi franchise statute expressly excludes from the definition of a franchise "persons engaged in sales from warehouses or like places of storage."[20]

C. Termination

1. What Constitutes Termination or Cancellation

a. Commentary

The Mississippi statute regulates a franchisor's ability to "cancel or otherwise terminate" a franchise agreement under certain circumstances.[21] What specifically constitutes termination is not addressed in the statute, leaving that issue, including the statute's applicability to constructive termination, open to interpretation.

b. Annotations

In *Walker v. U-Haul*, Walker agreed to operate a U-Haul franchise pursuant to a "moving center agreement" on premises owned by U-Haul and leased to Walker under a lease. The moving center agreement provided that it would automatically and simultaneously terminate with the lease. The lease had a fixed term of one year. After Walker refused to recognize a rent increase under the lease, U-Haul decided not to renew the lease and, upon expiration of the lease term, wrote Walker a letter stating that the lease had expired. However, Walker did not vacate the premises or cease operation of the franchise until six months following expiration of the lease term when Walker received a notice to quit from U-Haul's attorney. Walker sued U-Haul for violation of the Mississippi franchise statute, claiming that U-Haul failed to comply with the statute's 90-day advance notice requirement for termination or nonrenewal of a franchise. The district court entered summary judgment in favor of U-Haul on all claims and Walker appealed. In determining whether U-Haul violated the Mississippi franchise statute, the Fifth Circuit pointed out that, by entering into the moving center agreement, Walker had agreed that the franchise would terminate upon termination or expiration of the lease. According to the court, this alone may have satisfied the statutory notice requirement, because Walker agreed from the

---

20. Snacks R Plenty, LLC v. Travelbee Snacks LLC, 2013 WL 12123364 (S.D. Miss. Jan. 28, 2013).
21. Miss. Code Ann. § 75-24-53.

outset that the franchise would terminate if the lease was not renewed. However, the fact that Walker was not required to cease operation of the franchise until six months following his receipt of notice of expiration of the lease from U-Haul made the court feel "confident" that Walker had actual notice of termination of the franchise well in advance of 90 days. The Fifth Circuit said that to require U-Haul to provide a separate notification of termination of the franchise would be to interpret the Mississippi franchise statute "with dogged literal- mindedness." In the court's eyes, the objectives of the statute had been met and there was no indication that U-Haul attempted to circumvent the statute's requirements.[22]

2. Restrictions on Termination or Cancellation

a. Commentary

The Mississippi franchise statute does not contain any restrictions on termination or cancellation of a franchise, provided that the franchisor complies with the applicable notice requirements set forth in the statute. Generally, the franchisor must notify the franchisee of the cancellation or termination of the franchise agreement in writing at least 90 days in advance of the cancellation or termination.[23] However, the 90-day notice requirement does not apply if the basis or grounds for the cancellation or termination of the franchise agreement is "criminal misconduct, fraud, abandonment, bankruptcy or insolvency of the franchisee, or the giving of a no account or insufficient funds check."[24] Any other restrictions on termination or cancellation of a franchise agreement would be determined based on the terms of the parties' contractual arrangement and common law principles.

b. Annotations

In *Crosthwait Equipment Co., Inc., et al.*, John Deere Company terminated one of its farm equipment dealers, without advanced notice or an opportunity to cure, after the dealer submitted falsified sales and credit documents. The dealership agreement gave John Deere Company the right to cancel the agreement by giving notice "at any time" upon the dealer's "falsification of records, contracts reports or any other documents" submitted by the dealer to John Deere Company. The dealer claimed, among other things, that John Deere terminated the dealer agreement in "bad faith" retaliation for the dealer's sales outside of its designated area, and this "bad faith" termination constituted an affirmative defense to the dealer's fraud. The district court referred to this claim as a "novel idea" and agreed with the trial court's finding that there was insufficient evidence to raise a jury issue on that claim.[25]

---

22. Walker v. U-Haul Co. of Miss., 734 F.2d 1068 (5th Cir. 1984).
23. Miss. Code Ann. § 75-24-53.
24. *Id.*
25. Crosthwait Equip. Co. v. John Deere Co., 992 F.2d 525 (5th Cir. 1993).

3. Notice Requirement

a. Commentary

Under the Mississippi franchise statute, the franchisor must notify the franchisee of the cancellation or termination of the franchise agreement in writing at least 90 days in advance of the cancellation or termination.[26] The statute does not specify the method for calculating the 90-day period and courts have not interpreted that issue. However, courts have interpreted the method of notice, finding notice to have been provided under the statute by way of service of a complaint to a franchisee[27] as well as by way of notice of expiration of a lease (where termination of the franchise agreement was tied to termination of the lease).[28] The 90-day notice requirement does not apply if the basis or grounds for the cancellation or termination of the franchise agreement is "criminal misconduct, fraud, abandonment, bankruptcy or insolvency of the franchisee, or the giving of a no account or insufficient funds check."[29] In such situations, the franchisor may terminate the franchise agreement immediately without violating the statute. Notably, while the statute does not require 90 days' notice where the franchisee's failure to pay amounts owed arises in connection with the "giving a no account or insufficient funds check," it is unclear whether 90 days' notice is required where the franchisee simply fails to remit timely payment of amounts owed although on a plain reading, the notice would still be required. The author was unable to locate any cases specifically addressing that issue.

b. Annotations

In *Walker v. U-Haul*, Walker asserted that U-Haul violated the Mississippi franchise statute by failing to provide 90 days' notice of termination of his franchise. The Fifth Circuit stated that the franchise agreement providing for automatic and simultaneous termination with the related lease for the premises was a fact that alone might satisfy the notice requirement under the Mississippi statute. In addition, Walker was provided with notice of expiration of the lease and continued to operate the franchise for six months, which made the court "confident" that Mississippi courts would hold that Walker had actual written notice of termination of the franchise agreement well in advance of 90 days. The court went further to say that requiring U-Haul to provide a separate notice of termination of the franchise agreement "would be to construe the statute with dogged literal-mindedness."[30]

In *McDonald's Corp. v. Joe L. Watson & Lashon Enterprises, Inc.*, the franchisees claimed that they never received effective notice of termination of the franchise agreements. Although the Fifth Circuit refused to consider the issue of whether the franchisor complied with the 90-day notice period required under the Mississippi franchise statute, the court held that service of a complaint, stating that

---

26. Miss. Code Ann. § 75-24-53.
27. McDonald's Corp. v. Watson, 69 F.3d 36, 44 (5th Cir. 1995).
28. Walker v. U-Haul Co. of Miss., 734 F.2d 1068 (5th Cir. 1984).
29. *Id.*
30. *Id.*

the franchise agreements had been terminated satisfied the notice of termination requirements under the agreements and applicable law (and effectively terminated the agreements).

In *Crosthwait Equipment Co., Inc., et al.*, the dealership agreement gave John Deere Company the right to cancel the agreement by giving notice "at any time" upon the dealer's "falsification of records, contracts reports or any other documents" submitted by the dealer to John Deere Company. Upon removal of the case from state court, the district court ordered that the dealer could stay in business for 90 days under Mississippi law. The dealer claimed, among other things, that it was entitled to damages under the Mississippi franchise statute as a result of the termination. In denying the dealer's claim, the Fifth Circuit pointed out that 90-day notice prior to termination is not required under the Mississippi statute when fraud is the basis of termination and, even if the 90-day notice was required, the trial court permitted the dealer to continue its day-to-day operations for 90 days after John Deere Company's notice of termination. Therefore, there was no violation of the statute.[31]

4. Grounds for Termination

a. Commentary

Other than generally requiring 90 days' advance written notice of cancellation or termination of the franchise agreement, the Mississippi statute does not address permitted or prohibited grounds for cancellation or termination. Presumably, a franchisor may cancel or terminate a franchise agreement for any reason (or no reason) without violating the statute, so long as the franchisor complies with the 90-day notice requirement if the grounds for such cancellation or termination warrant such notice under the statute. Of course, franchisors should also make sure that any termination complies with the franchise agreement.

b. Annotations

Not applicable.

5. Required Cure Period

a. Commentary

Not applicable.

b. Annotations

Not applicable.

6. Repurchase Obligations

a. Commentary

Not applicable.

---

31. Crosthwait Equip. Co. v. John Deere Co., 992 F.2d at 525 (5th Cir. 1993).

D. Restrictions on Nonrenewal

1. What Constitutes Nonrenewal

a. Commentary

The Mississippi statute regulates a franchisor's ability to "cancel or otherwise terminate" a franchise agreement under certain circumstances.[32] A "failure to renew" is expressly contemplated as a means of cancelling or otherwise terminating a franchise agreement. However, what specifically constitutes a failure to renew is not addressed in the statute, nor does the statute address what conditions a franchisor may impose for a renewing franchisee. The Mississippi statute does not specify whether it creates an affirmative right to renew even if the franchise agreement does not contain any express renewal right.

b. Annotations

In *Walker v. U-Haul*, Walker's franchise agreement provided that it would automatically and simultaneously terminate upon termination of U-Haul's lease of the premises to Walker. The lease had a fixed term of one year. After Walker refused to recognize a rent increase under the lease, U-Haul decided not to renew the lease and, upon expiration of the lease term, wrote Walker a letter stating that the lease had expired. However, Walker did not vacate the premises or cease operation of the franchise until six months following expiration of the lease term when Walker received a notice to quit from U-Haul's attorney. In determining whether U-Haul violated the Mississippi franchise statute's 90-day notice requirement for termination or nonrenewal of a franchise, the Fifth Circuit found no violation because Walker had agreed to the cross-termination language in the franchise agreement and did not cease operation of the franchise for six months following expiration of the lease.[33]

2. Restrictions on Nonrenewal

a. Commentary

The Mississippi franchise statute does not contain any restrictions on nonrenewal of a franchise, provided that the franchisor complies with any applicable notice requirements set forth in the statute.

b. Annotations

Not applicable.

---

32. Miss. Code Ann. § 75-24-53.
33. Walker v. U-Haul Co. of Miss., 734 F.2d 1068 (5th Cir. 1984).

3. Notice Requirement

a. Commentary

Under the Mississippi statute, the franchisor must notify the franchisee of the nonrenewal of the franchise agreement in writing at least 90 days in advance of the nonrenewal.[34] However, the 90-day notice requirement does not apply if the basis or grounds for nonrenewal of the franchise agreement is "criminal misconduct, fraud, abandonment, bankruptcy or insolvency of the franchisee, or the giving of a no account or insufficient funds check."[35]

b. Annotations

In *Walker v. U-Haul*, the Fifth Circuit found no violation of the 90-day notice requirement where the franchise agreement provided for termination upon expiration of the franchisee's lease and the franchisee continued operating the franchise for six months following expiration of the lease.[36]

4. Grounds for Nonrenewal

a. Commentary

Other than generally requiring 90 days' advance written notice of nonrenewal of the franchise agreement, the Mississippi statute does not address permitted or prohibited grounds for nonrenewal. Presumably, a franchisor may decline to renew a franchise agreement for any reason (or no reason) without violating the statute, so long as the franchisor complies with the notice requirement under the statute. Of course, the franchisor should also make sure that any nonrenewal complies with the franchise agreement.

b. Annotations

Not applicable.

5. Required Cure Period

a. Commentary

Not applicable.

b. Annotations

Not applicable.

6. Repurchase Obligations

a. Commentary

Not applicable.

b. Annotations

Not applicable.

---

34. MISS. CODE ANN. § 75-24-53.
35. *Id.*
36. *Walker*, 734 F.2d at 1068.

7. Limitations on Franchisor's Right to Impose Conditions for Renewal

a. Commentary

Not applicable.

b. Annotations

Not applicable.

E. Transfers and Succession

1. Commentary

The Mississippi statute does not expressly address the franchisee's ability to transfer the franchise or franchise agreement. However, since unauthorized transfers are typically grounds for termination of a franchise agreement, a franchisor desiring to terminate a franchise agreement in such circumstances should consider the statute's 90-day advance written notice requirement.

2. Annotations

Not applicable.

F. Other Regulations of the Franchise Relationship

1. Commentary

Although not addressed in the Mississippi franchise statute, the Mississippi Supreme Court has recognized that contractual arrangements can give rise to fiduciary relationships outside the conventional boundaries traditionally recognized as creating fiduciary relationships,[37] and the Fifth Circuit has applied this principle to the contractual arrangement between franchisor and franchisee.[38]

2. Annotations

In *Carter v. John Deere*, a John Deere franchisee located in Mississippi claimed to have expended large sums to build a dealership facility based on John Deere's promises to its dealers regarding future product offerings and calls for its franchisees to aggressively participate in such offerings. The building project created financial difficulties for the franchisee, who fell behind on his payment obligations to suppliers. After John Deere notified the franchisee that it was terminating the franchise, the franchisee was forced to sell his business at a substantial loss. The franchisee claimed that a fiduciary relationship existed between the parties and that John Deere had breached its fiduciary duty. The jury agreed and returned a verdict and substantial damages award in favor of the franchisee. On appeal, John Deere contended that a fiduciary duty could not exist between the parties because the franchise agreement controlled the parties' relationship in its entirety. The Fifth Circuit noted that "Mississippi applies a broad

---

37. *See* Risk v. Risher, 197 Miss. 155, 19 So. 2d 484 (1944); Parker v. Lewis Grocer Co., 246 Miss. 873, 153 So. 2d 261 (1963).
38. Carter Equip. Co. v. John Deere Indus. Equip. Co., 681 F.2d 386 (1982).

brush to the equitable doctrine of the fiduciary and does not preclude a jury's finding a fiduciary relationship exists between a franchisor and franchisee."[39] However, the court determined that the district court erred in failing to provide any guidance to the jury regarding what might constitute a breach of the fiduciary duty. As a result, the court reversed the district court's judgment as it related to whether a fiduciary duty existed or was breached and remanded the case for a new trial on those issues.

G. Remedies and Administrative Action

1. Restrictive Covenants

a. Commentary

The Mississippi franchise statute does not address restrictive covenants or their enforceability. In addition, no Mississippi case has addressed a restrictive covenant in a franchise agreement. In other contexts, Mississippi courts have required that covenants against competition be ancillary to a lawful contract, reasonable, and consistent with the public interest.[40]

b. Annotations

Not applicable.

2. Damages

a. Commentary

A franchisee who prevails in an action against the franchisor for failure to give notice of termination or cancellation of a franchise as required under the Mississippi franchise statute may be awarded "a recovery of damages sustained to include loss of goodwill, costs of the suit, and any equitable relief that the court deems proper."[41] However, because the harm arises from failure to provide required notice under the statute, it is likely that damages related to loss of business or revenue would be limited to the 90-day notice period.

b. Annotations

The author was unable to locate any published cases addressing this issue.

3. Rescission

a. Commentary

Not applicable.

---

39. *Id.*
40. LDDS Commc'ns, Inc. v. Automated Commc'ns, Inc., 35 F.3d 198, 199 (5th Cir. 1994) (covenants not to compete, which are ancillary to sale of business and constitute a reasonable protection of what was sold, are enforceable as general proposition, despite hostility toward most collusive carvings of markets); Union Nat'l Life Ins. Co. v. Tillman, 143 F. Supp. 2d 638, 646 (N.D. Miss. 2000) (noncompetition covenant enforced against ex-employee, as the public would not allow parties to a contract to "unilaterally breach binding contracts and disclose trade secrets").
41. Miss. Code Ann. § 75-24-57.

b. Annotations
Not applicable.

4. Injunctive Relief
a. Commentary
The Mississippi franchise statute expressly provides that, in addition to damages, a franchisee who prevails in an action against the franchisor for failure to give notice of termination or cancellation of a franchise as required under the Mississippi franchise statute may be awarded "a recovery of damages sustained to include loss of goodwill, costs of the suit, and any equitable relief that the court deems proper."[42] The author was unable to locate any cases in which this provision of the statute has been addressed or interpreted by Mississippi courts. Therefore, it is unclear whether "any equitable relief that the court deems proper" would include injunctive relief.

b. Annotations
The author was unable to locate any published cases addressing this issue.

5. Control Person Liability
a. Commentary
The notice requirement under the Mississippi franchise statute applies to any "person who has granted a franchise."[43] Furthermore, the statute permits the franchisee to institute legal proceedings against "the franchisor."[44] The Mississippi statute does not specifically address whether a franchisee may bring an action against officers, directors, or other individuals associated with the franchisor, or whether any such individuals may be personally liable, under the statute.

b. Annotations
In *Snacks R Plenty, LLC v. Travelbee Snack LLC et al.*, the plaintiff entered into a distributorship agreement with S-L Distribution Company and its subsidiary S-L Routes, LLC, for the plaintiff to distribute Snyder's-Lance products in an exclusive territory. Less than a year later, the plaintiff received a letter terminating the agreement. In its complaint, the plaintiff alleged, among other things, that a certain individual, as an agent of S-L Distribution, violated the Mississippi franchise statute by failing to provide 90 days written notice of termination of the distributorship. In ruling on the plaintiff's motion to remand, the court had to determine whether any of the plaintiff's allegations represented a claim for which a Mississippi state court may grant relief. The court noted that the individual was not a party to the distributorship agreement and, as a result, agreed with the defendants that the plaintiff would not be able to establish a

---

42. *Id.*
43. *Id.* § 75-24-53.
44. *Id.* § 75-24-57.

cause of action against the individual for violation of the Mississippi franchise statute. Essentially, the individual could not meet the definition of a franchisor under the statute, which would have required him to have received consideration in exchange for granting the plaintiff a license to use a trademark.[45]

6. Attorneys' Fees

a. Commentary

The Mississippi franchise statute expressly provides that a franchisee who prevails in an action against the franchisor for failure to give notice of termination or cancellation of a franchise as required under the Mississippi franchise statute "may be awarded a recovery of damages sustained to include . . . costs of the suit[.]"[46]

b. Annotations

The author was unable to locate any published cases addressing this issue.

7. Limitations on Damage Waivers

a. Commentary

Not applicable.

b. Annotations

Not applicable.

8. Administrative Action

a. Commentary

In addition to affording a franchisee a private right of action, the Mississippi statute empowers the attorney general of Mississippi to bring an action in the name of the state to enjoin any act or practice that appears to violate any of the provisions of the statute.[47]

A person found to have willfully violated the advance written notice requirements under the Mississippi statute is guilty of a misdemeanor under the statute. If convicted, the statute provides for punishment by a fine of up to $500 or imprisonment of up to six months in county jail (or both).[48]

b. Annotations

The author was unable to locate any published cases addressing this issue.

---

45. Snacks R Plenty, LLC v. Travelbee Snacks LLC, 2012 WL 12884480, (S.D. Miss. Oct. 31, 2012).
46. MISS. CODE ANN. § 75-24-57.
47. Id. § 75-24-59.
48. Id. § 75-24-61.

H. Dispute Resolution

1. Limitations on Franchisor's Ability to Restrict Venue

a. Commentary

If a franchisee suffers damage as a result of a franchisor's failure to give notice of the cancellation or termination of a franchise as required under the Mississippi statute, the statute provides the franchisee with the right to institute legal proceedings against the franchisor.[49] The franchisee has a statutory right to bring the action in the county in which the franchisor, or the franchisor's agent resides (or can be located) or in the county where the franchisee resides.[50] The Mississippi statute does not address the enforceability of a forum selection clause in the franchise agreement that may conflict with the statute. Neither does it address the parties' ability to contract away the applicability of the statute by a contractual choice of law or otherwise.

b. Annotations

The author was unable to locate any published cases addressing this issue.

2. Limitations Period

a. Commentary

The Mississippi statute does not include any express limitations period. Under Mississippi law, actions for which no other period of limitations is prescribed must be brought within three years after the cause of such action accrues.[51] Therefore, a franchisee would likely need to bring the action within three years of the franchisor's failure to cancel, terminate, or renew in accordance with the statute, but may still only be able to recover 90 days' worth of damages.

b. Annotations

Not applicable.

---

49. *Id.* § 75-24-57.
50. *Id.*
51. *Id.* § 15-1-49.

Missouri

David Gusewelle

I. Introduction to Statute

Generally, the Missouri Franchise Act (Act) requires franchisors to provide franchisees with 90 days' written notice, except in certain circumstances, before cancelling, terminating, or not renewing a franchisee's franchise agreement.

The Act appears in its entirety within chapter 407 of the Missouri Revised Statues, which is commonly known by Missouri lawyers as the Missouri Merchandising Practices Act (MMPA). The MMPA collectively contains a broad range of consumer protection laws enacted to regulate and protect consumers from various types of consumer fraud and schemes.[1] The Act is contained in subchapter 400, which is described in its heading as governing "Pyramid Sales Schemes" but makes no mention of franchises.[2] Despite the heading not advising the reader of franchise regulations, within subchapter 400, both pyramid sale schemes and franchises are regulated.

The legality of the Act has been challenged on the basis that connecting two separate areas of regulation (pyramid sales schemes and franchises) is unconstitutional because article III, section 23 of the Missouri Constitution requires that a bill only contain one subject.[3] A Missouri court has noted this confusion, stating that the MMPA is "not a model of legislative clarity."[4] However, courts have upheld the validity of the Act, holding that the coupling of pyramid sales and franchise regulations together within the Act did not violate the Missouri Constitution.[5]

The definition of a "franchise" under the Act is different from (and, arguably, much more expansive than) the federal definition of a franchise.[6] Under the Act, a "franchise" could be found in relationships that practitioners might not think of as a traditional "franchise." As a result, practitioners must proceed cautiously and consider the Act's definition of a "franchise" prior to any

---

1. *See generally* Mo. Rev. Stat. §§ 407 *et seq.*
2. *See id.* § 407.400.
3. Mo. Const. art. III, § 23.
4. ABA Distribs., Inc. v. Adolph Coors Co., 542 F. Supp. 1272, 1286 (W.D. Mo. 1982).
5. *See* Brown-Forman Distillers Corp. v. McHenry, 566 S.W.2d 194, 196 (Mo. 1978).
6. *Compare* 16 C.F.R. § 436.1(h) *with* Mo. Rev. Stat. § 407.400(1).

attempt to cancel, terminate, or not renew contracts in Missouri where those contracts contain a licensing component.

The Act is "paternalistic" and designed to "protect those who could not otherwise protect themselves."[7] The 90-day notice requirement before termination of a franchise is "strong public policy" in Missouri.[8] Missouri courts have consistently held that the protections under the Act cannot be waived as a fundamental policy to "protect a person against the oppressive use of superior bargaining power."[9] Courts have also found that the portions of the Act that "are remedial in nature are to be given a liberal construction."[10] The Act's 90-day notice requirement for termination, cancellation, or nonrenewal of a franchise is such a fundamental policy of state law that a Missouri court did not apply a South Carolina choice of law provision to all claims between parties to a franchise agreement because South Carolina does not have a similar notice requirement.[11] In drafting the Act, "[t]he Missouri Legislature created a legislative presumption that franchisees are in an inferior bargaining position with respect to franchisors and thus are entitled to protection from the oppressive use of the franchisor's superiority. The Legislature has further decreed that allowing franchisors to terminate franchise agreements on less than 90 days' notice is an oppressive use of bargaining strength. Franchisees are entitled to rely on these presumptions and take advantage of the statute's protection regardless of their true economic power."[12] The policy is significant enough that willful violations of 90-day notice requirement are a class E felony, which cannot be bypassed by a choice of law provision.[13]

II. Commentary and Annotations

A. Definition of Franchise

The Act's definition of a "franchise" is located in Annotated Missouri Statutes section 407.400(1). Missouri's definition is notable in comparison with other states' definitions of "franchise" in several respects: (1) it includes oral relationships; (2) it has no fee or other form of consideration as a required element; and (3) it uses the "community of interest" test.[14] Because of this, Missouri's

---

7. High Life Sales Co. v. Brown-Forman Corp., 823 S.W.2d 493, 498 (Mo. 1992).
8. Id.
9. Id.
10. C & J Delivery, Inc. v. Emery Air Freight Corp., 647 F. Supp. 867, 871 (E.D. Mo. 1986).
11. Elec. Magneto Serv. Co. v. AMBAC Int'l Corp., 941 F.2d 660 (8th Cir. 1991).
12. Id. at 663, n.3.
13. Id.; see also Mo. Rev. Stat. § 407.420.
14. A "franchise" is defined under the Act as a "written or oral arrangement for a definite or indefinite period, in which a person grants to another person a license to use a trade name, trademark, service mark, or related characteristic, and in which there is a community of interest in the marketing of goods or services at wholesale, retail, by lease, agreement, or otherwise . . . except that, the term 'franchise' shall not apply to persons engaged in sales from warehouses or like places of storage, other than wholesalers as above described, leased departments of retail stores, places of original manufacture, nor shall the term 'franchise' apply to a commercial relationship

definition is relatively expansive when compared with other states. Relationships that might not meet the definition of a franchise in other states by avoiding the fee element, not having a written agreement, or not having significant control could still be a franchise in Missouri and thereby trigger the Act's notice requirements. For example, an oral distribution agreement of indefinite duration could be a franchise under the Act.[15]

The "community of interest" definitional element is also used in Hawaii,[16] Minnesota,[17] Mississippi,[18] Nebraska,[19] New Jersey,[20] and Wisconsin.[21] Missouri courts frequently look to New Jersey when guidance or further interpretation of the definition of "franchise" is needed.[22] Because of this, counsel unable to find supportive case law analyzing the Missouri Act, would be wise to look to New Jersey case law.

1. Trademark Element

a. Commentary

The licensing of a trademark, trade name, or related characteristic is a required element in the Act's definition of a franchise. The Act specifically requires that "a person grants to another person a license to use a trade name, trademark, service mark, or related characteristic."[23]

In determining whether a license exists, courts analyze whether one party licenses the right to use the mark or a related characteristic to another, whether one party receives permission to be named an authorized dealer or distributor of the other, whether the selling party relies on the goodwill of another's name to sell products or services, and whether the marks are used in marketing efforts.[24]

A trademark license exists where the fact finder determines that the permission to use the trademark, trade name, or related characteristics would create a reasonable belief to the customer or public that the licensor vouches for the activity of the licensee in connection with the goods or services sold by the licensee.[25]

---

that does not contemplate the establishment or maintenance of a place of business within the state of Missouri[.]" Mo. Rev. Stat. § 407.400(1).

15. *See, e.g.*, Major Brands, Inc. v. Mast-Jägermeister US, Inc., No. 4:18CV423 HEA, 2019 WL 6050731 (E.D. Mo. Nov. 15, 2019) (litigating a long-standing oral agreement of continuing indefinite duration based on the ongoing pattern and practice of the parties).

16. Haw. Rev. Stat. § 482-E-2.

17. Minn. Stat. § 80C.01(4).

18. Miss. Code Ann. § 75-24-51(6).

19. Neb. Rev. Stat. § 87-402(1).

20. N.J. Stat. Ann. § 56:10-3.

21. Wis. Stat. § 135.02(3)(a).

22. *See* Mo. Beverage Co. v. Shelton Bros., Inc., 669 F.3d 873, 878–79 (8th Cir. 2012); (quoting Am. Bus. Interiors, Inc. v. Haworth, Inc., 798 F.2d 1135, 1139 (8th Cir. 1986) (citing McHenry, 566 S.W.2d at 196) (relying on interpretation of New Jersey Franchise Practices Act).

23. Mo. Rev. Stat. § 407.400(1).

24. Mo. Beverage Co. v. Shelton Bros., Inc., 669 F.3d 873, 879 (8th Cir. 2012).

25. Major Brands, Inc. v. Mast-Jägermeister US, Inc., 4:18CV423 HEA, 2022 WL 3585606, at *10 (E.D. Mo. Aug. 22, 2022).

Courts in Missouri have looked to New Jersey in analyzing the trademark element. For example, the Eighth Circuit noted that a "hallmark of the franchise relationship is the use of another's trade name in such a manner as to create a reasonable belief on the part of the consuming public that there is a connection between the trade name licensor and licensee by which the licensor vouches, as it were, for the activity of the licensee in respect of the subject of the trade name."[26] As a result, not every relationship involving the license of a trademark was contemplated in the Act's definition. Rather, "[t]he license contemplated by the [New Jersey] Act is one in which the franchisee wraps himself with the trade name of the franchisor and relies on the franchisor's goodwill to induce the public to buy."[27] This ruling suggests that a mere trademark license to display or use trademarks may be insufficient absent a meaningful commercial affiliation in the eyes of the public and customers.

b. Annotations

An authorized dealer relationship between a furniture manufacturer and dealer met the trademark element under the Act where the dealer was allowed to hold itself out as an authorized dealer but not use the name in its own business operations.[28] The furniture manufacturer argued that the trademark element did not exist because the dealer did not operate under the name and was not in possession of a license to use the name and the relationship was not a franchise under the Act.[29] Because the dealer was entitled to call itself an "authorized dealer" of the manufacturer, was required to present the manufacturer's products to the public in a certain manner, and had to send its employees to a two-day training seminar held by the manufacturer, the trademark element was satisfied.[30] The court looked to New Jersey for guidance and ultimately found that "a hallmark of the franchise relationship is the use of another's trade name in such a manner as to create a reasonable belief on the part of the consuming public that there is a connection between the trade name licensor and licensee by which the licensor vouches, as it were, for the activity of the licensee in respect of the subject of the trade name" and that these facts are sufficient to create a franchise relationship.[31]

A nonexclusive privilege to identify oneself as an authorized dealer and to display trademarks and service marks in the conduct of dealership operations was sufficient to meet the trademark element of a franchise under the Act.[32]

---

26. *Mo Beverage Co.*, 669 F.3d at 879 (quoting Neptune T.V. & Appliance Serv., Inc. v. Litton Microwave Cooking Prods. Div., 190 N.J. Super. 153, 462 A.2d 595, 599 (N.J. App. Div. 1983).

27. *Id.* (quoting Liberty Sales Assocs., Inc. v. Dow Corning Corp., 816 F. Supp. 1004, 1009–10 (D.N.J. 1993)) (quoting and citing Instructional Sys., Inc. v. Comput. Curriculum Corp., 130 N.J. 324, 614 A.2d 124, 138–40 (1992)).

28. Am. Bus. Interiors v. Haworth, Inc., 798 F.2d 1135 (8th Cir. 1986).

29. *Id.* at 1140.

30. *Id.*

31. *Id.* (quoting Neptune T.V. v. Litton Microwave, 190 N.J. Super. 153, 462 A.2d 595, 599 (1983)).

32. Lift Truck Lease & Serv., Inc. v. Nissan Forklift Corp., No. 4:12-CV-153 CAS, 2012 WL 3891615, at *6 (E.D. Mo. Sept. 7, 2012).

A trademark license was not found between a Missouri beverage distributor and an out of state beer supplier where no license was granted to use the trademark or a related characteristic (such as trade dress or service mark) of the beer supplier. The distributor never used the beer supplier's name in marketing efforts, never requested permission to use the beer supplier's name, and never received permission to call itself an authorized dealer or otherwise use the name of the beer supplier and where the beverage distributor relied on its own reputation to sell the beer supplier's products.[33]

Evidence that a liquor wholesaler had access to a liquor manufacturer's trademarks, logos, images, password-protected website, and restricted database for use in creating custom promotional materials was sufficient to support a jury's decision that the relationship met the trademark element of a franchise.[34] This was despite the arguments by the manufacturer that the wholesaler had worked to build an independent reputation and that the wholesaler's logos were also included on the business cards and promotional materials.[35] The court noted that the wholesaler's use of both its logos and the manufacturer's logos demonstrated that they were working together and that no permission was required from the manufacturer prior to the wholesaler using the manufacturer's trademarks.[36] The specific jury instruction to determine whether there was a trademark license stated: "The term 'license,' . . . means permission to use [the liquor manufacturer's] trade names, trademarks, or related characteristics in such a manner as to create a reasonable belief on the part of alcohol retailers or the consuming public that there was a connection between [manufacturer] and [wholesaler] by which [manufacturer] vouched for the activity of [wholesaler] relating to the [manufacturer] brand(s) of spirits."[37]

2. Franchise Fee Element

a. Commentary
Not applicable.

b. Annotations
Not applicable.

3. Community of Interest; Significant Degree of Control; Joint Marketing Plan

a. Commentary
The final element of a "Franchise" under the Act is a "community of interest in the marketing of goods or services at wholesale, retail, by lease, agreement, or otherwise[.]"[38] The Act does not specify how or at what point in a license

---

33. Mo. Beverage Co. v. Shelton Bros., Inc., 669 F.3d 873, 878–79 (8th Cir. 2012).
34. Major Brands, Inc. v. Mast-Jägermeister US, Inc., 4:18CV423 HEA, 2022 WL 3585606, at *8–9 (E.D. Mo. Aug. 22, 2022).
35. Id.
36. Id.
37. Id. at *10.
38. Mo. Rev. Stat. § 407.400(1).

relationship two parties have a "community of interest," leaving courts to provide their own interpretation. In Missouri, courts have generally considered it to mean, at a minimum, either (1) the franchisor benefits from the franchisee's marketing of the franchisor's product or service, or (2) the franchisee benefits from the franchisor's marketing of the product or service.[39]

Notably, the "community of interest" standard is a significant departure from the "significant assistance" or "significant control" element that is used in the federal definition of a franchise and must be carefully analyzed in determining whether the relationship between a licensor and licensee has created a franchise. Courts in Missouri have looked to New Jersey and Wisconsin for guidance in interpreting the "community of interest" element due to their similar definitions of a franchise.

b. Annotations

A community of interest was sufficiently pled by a wholesaler alleging it made specific investments in a liquor manufacturer's brand in an oral distribution agreement including hiring a brand specialist, training employees specific to the brand, and purchasing brand-specific products.[40] A jury's determination that the liquor wholesaler was in a franchise relationship was not set aside, and the court noted sizeable and specialized investments in the liquor manufacturer, which were required by the nature of the parties' relationship, were sufficient to satisfy the community of interest element.[41] The specific jury instruction to ascertain a community of interest in the case stated: "The phrase 'community of interest,' . . . means [wholesaler's] investments in the [manufacturer] brand(s) of spirits were substantially specific to the brand(s), and [wholesaler] was required to make those investments by the parties' agreement or the nature of the business."[42]

A community of interest existed between a national package delivery service and a local delivery company used to deliver packages because the quality of the services by the local delivery company benefited the national package company, while the volume of business generated by the national package company benefited the local delivery company. This relationship was sufficient to show the parties' interests were aligned such that a community of interest existed.[43]

However, no community of interest existed where a Missouri beverage distributor's sale of products was a small percentage of overall sales during the relationship, the out-of-state beer supplier's name was not used in marketing by the distributor, and the distributor was not required to make and did not make a sizeable investment particular to the manufacturer. Because of this, the

---

39. C & J Delivery, Inc. v. Emery Air Freight Corp., 647 F. Supp. 867, 872 (E.D. Mo. 1986).
40. Major Brands, Inc. v. Mast-Jägermeister US, Inc., 4:18CV423 HEA, 2019 WL 6050731, at *17 (E.D. Mo. Nov. 15, 2019).
41. Major Brands, Inc. v. Mast-Jägermeister US, Inc., 4:18CV423 HEA, 2022 WL 3585606, at *6–7 (E.D. Mo. Aug. 22, 2022).
42. *Id.* at *9.
43. *C & J Delivery Inc.*, 647 F. Supp. at 872–73.

distributor could not be found to be economically dependent on or in a position of unequal bargaining power with the manufacturer.[44]

Because case law in Missouri is not well developed on the issue, courts analyzing the Act often will look to case law in New Jersey and Wisconsin—states that also use the community of interest element. Given the strong similarities between the "franchise" definitions in Missouri, New Jersey, and Wisconsin, it is likely, in the opinion of one federal court, that the Missouri Supreme Court would determine the existence of a "community of interest" under a standard commensurate with those articulated by the Third Circuit in *Cooper Distributing* and by the Seventh Circuit in *Frieburg*.[45] In *Cooper Distributing*, New Jersey's Franchise Practices Act created a two-part test for determining whether a community of interest exists: "(1) the distributor's investments must have been substantially franchise-specific, and (2) the distributor must have been required to make these investments by the parties' agreement or the nature of the business."[46] In *Frieburg*, Wisconsin created two circumstances under the Wisconsin Fair Dealership Law in which a community of interest exists: (1) "when a large proportion of an alleged dealer's revenues are derived from the dealership," or (2) "when the alleged dealer has made sizable investments (in, for example, fixed assets, inventory, advertising, training) specialized in some way to the grantor's goods or services, and hence not fully recoverable upon termination."[47]

B. Scope and Jurisdiction

1. Commentary

The Act excludes any "commercial relationship that does not contemplate the establishment or maintenance of a place of business within the state of Missouri."[48] However, a business that is established or maintained by the *franchisor* in Missouri is sufficient to fall within the Act—the business established does not necessarily need to be operated by the *franchisee*.[49] Therefore, the Act could be applied if either party maintains a business in Missouri regardless of whether the business is established by the franchisor or the franchisee, including a business operated by a franchisee outside of Missouri if the franchisor maintains a business in Missouri.

While the definition of the Act is relatively expansive when compared with similar statutes from other states, its scope is relatively narrow. It is also notable that the definition of a "place of business" is "a fixed, geographical location at which goods, products or services are displayed or demonstrated for sale." The

---

44. Mo. Beverage Co. v. Shelton Bros., 669 F.3d 873, 879–80 (8th Cir. 2012).
45. Major Brands, Inc. v. Mast-Jägermeister US, Inc., 4:18CV423 HEA, 2022 WL 3585606, at *5–6 (E.D. Mo. Aug. 22, 2022).
46. Cooper Distrib. Co. v. Amana Refrigeration, Inc., 63 F.3d 262, 269 (3d Cir.1995).
47. Frieburg Farm Equip., Inc. v. Van Dale, Inc., 978 F.2d 395, 399 (7th Cir. 1992) (citations omitted).
48. Mo. Rev. Stat. § 407.400(1).
49. *C & J Delivery Inc.*, 647 F. Supp. at 867.

Act predates internet commerce and virtual businesses having been enacted in 1974. It is written in a way that makes it specific to businesses that involve storefronts, warehouses, and other physical locations. Because of this, a mobile business, a digital or virtual business, and other forms of online commerce—even those based in Missouri—might not be considered a "place of business" under the Act.[50]

Because the Act is remedial, it is given a liberal construction when determining which relationships it governs.[51] Nonetheless, the Act expressly excludes certain relationships from its application. For example, a business relationship that otherwise constitutes a franchise is excepted if it is specifically governed by other parts of the MMPA. Thus, for example, a relationship between a mutual life insurance company and a general insurance agent was found to not be a franchise because the regulation of insurance practices is instead governed by chapters 374–385.[52]

Missouri courts would likely not apply the Act to contracts entered into before the Act's effective date. However, if the contracts were renewed or substantially amended after the Act's effective date, Missouri courts would likely apply the remedial portions of the Act to the relationship.[53] For example, amending a contract annually with new price terms was deemed to be such an annual renewal.[54]

The geographic scope of the Act is distinguishable from the New Jersey relationship law. New Jersey requires that a place of business be established specifically by the franchisee within New Jersey. Missouri similarly requires that a place of business be established within Missouri but does not specify that it must be the franchisee that establishes the business.[55]

Despite the definition of a franchise in section 407.400 of the Act specifically referencing wholesalers who sell intoxicating liquor (alcoholic content above 1.5 percent ABV) to retailers, the Act's franchise protections also apply to protect a beer distributor from termination by a beer manufacturer. The Act merely uses intoxicating liquor as an example of a relationship that is covered but does not limit the relationship to specific forms of alcohol beverages.[56]

2. Annotations

A package forwarding business maintained by a franchisor in Missouri was sufficient to meet the physical location requirement even though the franchisee did not establish a place of business in Missouri.[57]

---

50. The author could not locate any specific case that analyzes the "place of business" language under the act.
51. *C & J Delivery, Inc.*, 647 F. Supp. at 871.
52. Emerick v. Mutual Benefit Life Ins. Co., 756 S.W.2d 513, 526 (Mo. 1988); *see also* Mo. Rev. Stat. §§ 407.374–407.385-(1).
53. *See C & J Delivery, Inc.*, 647 F. Supp. at 871 (citing Arnott v. Am. Oil Co., 609 F.2d 873 (8th Cir. 1979); and Reinders Bros. v. Rain Bird E. Sales Corp., 627 F.2d 44 (7th Cir. 1980)).
54. *C & J Delivery, Inc.*, 647 F. Supp. at 871.
55. *Id.* at 873–74.
56. ABA Distribs., Inc. v. Adolph Coors Co., 542 F. Supp. 1272, 1291 n.27 (W.D. Mo. 1982).
57. *Id.* at 874.

C. Termination

1. What Constitutes Termination or Cancellation

a. Commentary

While termination, cancellation, or nonrenewal of a franchise is required to trigger the Act's 90-day notice requirement, the franchisor's conduct should be reviewed and considered because the Act may apply to scenarios that fall short of traditional termination. If the franchisor, for example, were to stop providing services required under a license agreement but not formally terminate the agreement, this conduct could be sufficient to create a constructive termination requiring a 90-day notice.

b. Annotations

Evidence that a distributor stopped providing leads and made sales directly to the customers of the local tractor equipment company during the 90-day notice period, after terminating an oral agreement between the parties that designated the local tractor equipment company as its exclusive distributor in Missouri, was sufficient to find that the distributor/franchisor may have violated the Act's 90-day notice period requirement through an effective termination and set aside a summary judgment motion in favor of the franchisor/distributor.[58] The court found that the distributor/franchisor's sales directly to customers in Missouri during the notice period could be deemed constructive termination and a breach of the required notice period under the Act.

When a distributor filed suit under an oral franchise agreement with a pool table manufacturer alleging improper notice under the Act, the manufacturer claimed that the dispute was subject to arbitration pursuant to the parties' subsequent e-commerce agreement relating to installation and servicing pool tables sold by the manufacturer. The manufacturer sent a 60-day notice of cancelation to the distributor demanding that it cease promoting their pool tables under the oral agreement. The court held that the agreements were to be treated independently and that the arbitration clause under the e-commerce agreement was inapplicable to the oral franchise agreement, despite the e-commerce agreement containing an integration clause, and the case was not dismissed.[59]

2. Notice Requirement

a. Commentary

Generally, the Act requires the franchisor to provide 90 days' notice prior to termination, cancellation, or nonrenewal of a franchise agreement. However, the Act allows for immediate termination, cancellation, or nonrenewal upon (1) criminal misconduct; (2) fraud; (3) abandonment; (4) bankruptcy or insolvency of the franchisee; or (5) the giving of a no account or insufficient funds

---

58. Cole v. Homier Distrib. Co., 599 F.3d 856, 868 (8th Cir. 2010).
59. Suburban Leisure Ctr. v. AMF Bowling Prods., Inc., Case No. 4:06CV188-DJS, 2006 WL 680964 (E.D. Mo. Mar. 13, 2006).

check.⁶⁰ As a best practice, when one of these scenarios exists, the franchisor should provide written notice specifying the basis for termination, cancellation, or nonrenewal. This is, in part, because courts have disallowed a franchise termination based on subsequently available information.⁶¹ Doing so can help avoid or defeat an argument that the franchise was terminated on a pretextual basis.⁶² Absent grounds for immediate action under the Act, the franchisor should provide at least 90 days' written notice to the franchisee of termination, cancellation, or nonrenewal.

In addition to complying with the Act's notice requirements, the notice should comply with the applicable requirements under the contract between the parties. This includes method of delivery, delivery receipts, addressee(s), what specific grounds for termination exist, and any appropriate contractual or statutory notice period.

b. Annotations

The author was not able to locate any published cases addressing this issue.

3. Grounds for Termination

a. Commentary

The Act, unlike other franchise relationship laws, does not require good cause to terminate a franchise relationship.⁶³ However, the prudent franchisor should not solely rely on statutory language and, instead, must always be cognizant of both the contractual terms upon which termination can be made and the implied covenant of good faith and fair dealing. Just because the Act does not limit the franchisor's grounds for termination does not mean the franchisor can ignore the terms of its contract. A termination must be in compliance with both the Act and the termination provisions under the franchise agreement in order to be lawful. Otherwise, it would still be subject to a breach of contract claim. Similarly, pursuant to Missouri statutory and common law, the covenant of good faith and fair dealing is implicit in all contracts.

Unless the contract calls for a longer notice period, a franchisor can immediately terminate or cancel a franchise agreement and no advance written advance notice must be given under the Act if the grounds for termination are (1) criminal misconduct; (2) fraud; (3) abandonment; (4) bankruptcy or insolvency of the franchisee; or (5) the giving of a no account or insufficient funds check. Other than these situations, 90 days' advance written notice must be given in all situations in which a franchisor terminates or cancels a franchise.⁶⁴

Failure to give notice can result in the terminated or cancelled franchisee having a private right of action under the Act. Dring the 90-day notice period, a

---

60. Mo. Rev. Stat. § 407.405.
61. *ABA Distribs., Inc.*, 542 F. Supp. at 1275.
62. *Id.*
63. While not an element under the Act, good cause is a specific element to terminate a wholesale liquor franchise relationship under the portion of the MMPA that specifically prohibits discrimination of wholesale liquor franchises. *See* Mo. Rev. Stat. § 407.413.
64. Am. Bus. Interiors v. Haworth, Inc., 798 F.2d 1135, 1139–40 (8th Cir. 1986).

franchisor cannot refuse to do business with the franchisee (or the 90-day notice provision is rendered "meaningless").[65]

When a franchisor attempts to terminate a franchisee without providing the requisite 90-day written notice, the notice of termination can be set aside and the franchisor can be required to reinstate the franchise relationship with the franchisee and give new appropriate notice.[66] In addition, a pretextual termination is likely to be unwound by a court because the franchisor may not use subsequently discovered evidence in support of avoiding the requisite 90-day written notice.[67]

(i) Criminal Misconduct

The Act does not specify when or how behavior rises to the level of "criminal misconduct." For example, whether a charge of criminal behavior is sufficient or whether conviction is required.

(ii) Fraud

A donut franchisor required a franchisee to remove two unapproved owners of the franchisee entity formed to operate one of its restaurants until they were approved by the franchisor for ownership. The franchisee submitted documents purporting to show the individuals' removal but actually concealed from the franchisor that they had not removed the unapproved owners and instead had continued with the original ownership structure. The entity information showing the unapproved owners was subsequently discovered through an audit of the franchisee's tax returns. The franchisor ultimately terminated the franchise agreements without providing the franchisee with any cure period. The court held that no opportunity to cure was required because the termination was based on fraudulent misrepresentations of the franchisee's ownership and fraud is an exception that does not require 90 days' written notice under the Act.[68]

(iii) Abandonment

Where a franchisee "could not come up with the monies which were demanded by the seller" for a premises it intended to purchase and the subsequent bankruptcy of the owner of the premises stalled the franchisee's ability to purchase the premises, the court refused to find an abandonment by the franchisee under the Act.[69] The court noted that the franchisee continued to actively pursue the premises and dealership opportunity until ultimately obtaining the premises.[70] The court determined that abandonment is a question of intention and there was nothing in the record to infer that the franchisee intended to stop pursuing the opportunity. A finding of abandonment due to the franchisee's temporary

---

65. *Id.* at 1141.
66. *ABA Distribs., Inc.*, 542 F. Supp. at 1272.
67. *Id.* at 1275.
68. Dunkin' Donuts Franchising LLC v. Sai Food Hospitality, LLC, No. 4:11CV01484 AGF, 2013 WL 6885339 (E.D. Mo. Dec. 31, 2013).
69. Maude v. Gen. Motors Corp., 626 F. Supp. 1081, 1086 (W.D. Mo. 1986).
70. *Id.*

impossibility to proceed due to outside circumstances (seller's bankruptcy) would be inconsistent with the remedial purpose of the Act.[71]

(iv) Bankruptcy / Insolvency

A bankruptcy filing is grounds to accelerate termination under the Act. However, in practice, franchisors will likely need to obtain relief from the bankruptcy court stay before terminating a franchisee that has filed for bankruptcy.

Insolvency is not defined in the Act.

(v) No Account / Insufficient Funds Check

A no account or insufficient funds check is sufficient to avoid a 90-day written notice of default. In practice, failure to pay amounts owed may be more common but the failure to pay amounts owed is not expressly included in the Act as grounds for immediate termination.

b. Annotations

While insolvency is not defined in the Act, the definition of insolvency used to terminate a franchise agreement has been litigated in Missouri. In *LC Franchisor, LLC v. Valley Beef, LLC*, a roast beef sandwich franchisor terminated its franchisee following notice based on receipt of a balance sheet showing a negative net worth. The franchise agreement did not define "insolvency," and the parties argued whether the definition should be the inability of a party to pay its debts as they fall due or having debts that exceed the entity's property at fair market value. The franchisee argued that although its debts exceeded its assets, it could pay its debts as they came due. It contended that termination under the insolvency clause in the franchise agreement and the Act was wrongful. The court held that both the franchise agreement (under the reasoning that it contained a separate default ground and event for being unable to pay one's debts as they come due) and applicable law treat insolvency as liabilities exceeding assets (a negative net worth). The court also did not accept the franchisee's estoppel argument that the franchisor should be unable to proceed because it was aware of insolvency at the time it entered into a franchise agreement.[72]

In *ABA Distributors, Inc. v. Adolph Coors Co.*, a manufacturer's immediate termination of a beer distributor based on a third party's report that it had been distributing beer outside of its territory was found to be a violation of the Act.[73] Further, because the manufacturer lacked actual knowledge of facts to support the grounds of termination in its notice, it was found to have acted in violation of the covenant of good faith and fair dealing and was enjoined from further attempts to carry out the termination. As a result, the termination was invalidated, and the distribution agreement was reinstated.[74]

---

71. *Id.* at 1085–86.
72. LC Franchisor, LLC v. Valley Beef, LLC, No. 4:15-CV-838-JCH, 2016 WL 5689792, at *4 (E.D. Mo. Oct. 3, 2016).
73. ABA Distribs., Inc. v. Adolph Coors Co., 542 F. Supp. 1272 (W.D. Mo. 1982).
74. *Id.*

4. Required Cure Period

a. Commentary

As discussed earlier, except for certain enumerated circumstances, the Act requires that the franchisor give the franchisee 90 days' advance written notice prior to the termination, cancellation, or nonrenewal of the franchise. However, franchisees do not have a statutory right to cure the default on which the termination is based. Because the failure to provide proper notice can result in courts requiring a new notification, effectively restarting the 90-day clock, practitioners should be careful to ensure that the 90-day period is based on receipt (or contractually deemed receipt) of the applicable notice. However, during the 90-day notice period, the franchisor must continue to comply with its contractual obligations and allow the franchisee to continue to operate its franchised business. Otherwise, the franchisor can be found to have effectively terminated the franchisee during the notice period. The only cure period to which a franchisee is entitled will be any contractual cure period because although notice of termination is required, the Act does not impose any required cure period.

b. Annotations

A bankruptcy court in Kansas held that the 90-day termination notice of a pizza franchise by a national franchisor following separate shorter default notices with shorter cure periods was in compliance with the Act and, following the passage of the 90-day cure period, the franchise agreement was deemed terminated by passage of time.[75] Continued receipt of royalties during the notice period by the franchisor is not a waiver of any right under the Act. A waiver would require the intentional waiver of a known right under Missouri law, and therefore, the franchisor should expressly reserve all rights in its termination notice.[76]

5. Repurchase Obligations

a. Commentary

Not applicable.

b. Annotations

Not applicable.

D. Restrictions on Nonrenewal

1. What Constitutes Nonrenewal

a. Commentary

The Act expressly regulates the failure to renew a franchise in the same manner as termination. However, there is no case law specifically imposing a requirement that a franchisor offer to renew its relationship with a franchisee absent a contractual right to do so. Therefore, a franchisee likely cannot use the act to create a renewal right where none would otherwise exist.

---

75. *In re* Tornado Pizza, LLC, 431 B.R. 503, 518 (Bankr. D. Kan. 2010).
76. *Id.* at 518–19.

b. Annotations

Notwithstanding a contractual provision that provides for automatic renewal, for a finding that the franchisee has perpetual renewal rights the agreement must "unequivocally express an intent of the parties to create a perpetual, never-ending franchise agreement."[77]

2. Notice Requirement

a. Commentary

Franchisors must provide 90 days' advance written notice of their intent to not renew a franchisee.

b. Annotations

A notice informed the dealer that the forklift manufacturer did not intend to renew the dealer's agreement days before expiration and also claimed to serve as a 90-day notice of nonrenewal, albeit sent less than 90 days before the agreement's expiration date. Ultimately, however, the court found that the notice met the statutory requirements despite providing only 60 days to cure certain deficiencies, because the notice indicated that termination would not go into effect for at least 90 days, and no cure period was required by the Act.[78]

3. Grounds for Nonrenewal

a. Commentary

As discussed earlier, nonrenewal requires the same notice period as termination.

b. Annotations

The author was unable to locate any published cases addressing this issue.

4. Required Cure Period

a. Commentary

As discussed earlier, nonrenewal is treated the same as termination and no cure period is required in connection with nonrenewal.

b. Annotations

Not applicable.

5. Limitations on Franchisors' Right to Impose Conditions for Renewal

a. Commentary

Not applicable.

---

77. H & R Block Tax Servs. LLC v. Franklin, 691 F.3d 941, 944 (8th Cir. 2012) (quoting Armstrong Bus. Servs., Inc. v. H & R Block, 96 S.W.3d 867, 877 (Mo. Ct. App. 2002)).

78. Lift Truck Lease & Serv., Inc. v. Nissan Forklift Corp., No. 4:12-CV-153 CAS, 2013 WL 2642951, at *6 (E.D. Mo. June 12, 2013).

b. Annotations
Not applicable.

6. Repurchase Obligations
a. Commentary
Not applicable.

b. Annotations
Not applicable.

E. Transfers and Succession
1. Commentary
The Act does not address transfers of franchises. However, a franchisee's right to transfer has been analyzed under the common law doctrine of recoupment.[79]

2. Annotations
At least one Missouri court has held that the franchisor cannot unreasonably withhold its approval of a prospective transferee under Missouri's recoupment law, holding that when a franchisor attempted to terminate a franchise in violation of the Act, the franchisee was entitled to a stay of further termination attempts, to restore the franchise, and be permitted time to recoup its investment.[80]

F. Other Regulation of the Franchise Relationship
1. Commentary
The MMPA covers several other areas of the law, and certain types of industries and businesses are subject to differing provisions under the MMPA. Claims that the Act does not apply to franchisors who are subject to other areas of the MMPA have generally been denied, and attempted repeals of scope of the Act by implication are disfavored.[81] For example, the Act applied to a motor vehicle franchisor notwithstanding its claim that the termination of an automobile dealer was subject to the Motor Vehicle Franchise Practices Act,[82] to a power equipment dealer arguing that its rights in terminating a forklift and transportation dealer was governed exclusively by the Power Equipment Act,[83] and to a liquor manufacturer arguing that it does not apply to a liquor wholesaler.[84]

---

79. The doctrine of recoupment is discussed further in Section III.G.2.
80. ABA Distribs., Inc. v. Adolph Coors Co., 542 F. Supp. 1272, 1294 (W.D. Mo. 1982).
81. Maude v. Gen. Motors Corp., 626 F. Supp. 1081, 1084 (W.D. Mo. 1986) ("Such repeals by implication are disfavored.") (citing Wright v. Martin, 674 S.W.2d 238, 242–43 (Mo. Ct. App. 1984)).
82. *Maude*, 626 F. Supp. 1081, 1084 (W.D. Mo. 1986).
83. Lift Truck Lease & Serv., Inc. v. Nissan Forklift Corp., No. 4:12-CV-153 CAS, 2012 WL 3891615, at 4–5 (E.D. Mo. Sept. 7, 2012).
84. Major Brands, Inc. v. Mast-Jägermeister United States, Inc., No. 4:18CV423 HEA, 2019 WL 1130294, at *9 (E.D. Mo. Mar. 12, 2019); *see also* High Life Sales Co. v. Brown-Forman Corp., 823 S.W.2d 493 (Mo. 1992).

Thus, these provisions of the Act provide additional protections to franchisees in certain industry-specific areas.

Franchisors should take care in what they communicate to third parties concerning cancellations, renewals, and terminations. Public statements that a franchisee has been terminated before the 90-day period has lapsed may give rise to claims by the franchisee for wrongful termination.[85]

A franchise relationship under the Act does not create a fiduciary relationship between the franchisor and franchisee under Missouri law.[86] Instead, the rights and duties of the parties are governed by the contract.[87] Claims for breach of fiduciary duty between parties in a franchise relationship have not succeeded in Missouri without an independent fiduciary obligation. Evidence that the franchisor ran the franchisee's business or was involved in the franchisee's management decisions supports a fiduciary relationship.[88] However, evidence that a franchisee was free in its management decisions, had owners with business experience, and no profit sharing with the franchisor would support a lack of a fiduciary relationship.[89] Mere evidence of a royalty payment structure between the franchisor and franchisee is not sufficient to create a fiduciary relationship.[90]

The Missouri Court of Appeals outlined the elements necessary for a franchisee to succeed on a claim that the franchisor owes it a fiduciary obligation: "(1) as between the parties, one must be subservient to the dominant mind and will of the other as a result of age, state of health, illiteracy, mental disability, or ignorance; (2) things of value such as land, monies, a business, or other things of value which are the property of the subservient person must be possessed or managed by the dominant party; (3) there must be a surrender of independence by the subservient party to the dominant party; (4) there must be an automatic or habitual manipulation of the actions of the subservient party by the dominant party; and (5) there must be a showing that the subservient party places a trust and confidence in the dominant party."[91]

2. Annotations

Because a franchisee/dealer relationship creates economic interests between the franchisee/dealer and the franchisor/distributor, communication to customers of the franchisee/dealer by the franchisor/distributor that it had terminated prior to expiration of the 90-day notice period could be found to be tortious interference with a business expectancy.[92]

---

85. *See generally* Lift Truck Lease & Serv., Inc. v. Nissan Forklift Corp., No. 4:12-CV-153 CAS, 2012 WL 3891615, at *10 (E.D. Mo. Sept. 7, 2012).
86. *See* C & J Delivery, Inc. v. Emery Air Freight Corp., 647 F. Supp. 867, 875 (E.D. Mo. 1986) (citing Bain v. Champlin Petroleum Co., 692 F.2d 43, 47–48 (8th Cir. 1982) and Chmieleski v. City Prods. Corp., 660 S.W.2d 275, 295 (Mo. Ct. App. 1983)).
87. *Chmieleski*, 660 S.W.2d at 292.
88. Bunzl Distrib. USA, Inc. v. Schultz, Cause No. 4:05CV605 JCH, 2006 WL 2265274, at *16 (E.D. Mo. Aug. 7, 2006). *See also Chmieleski*, 660 S.W.2d at 294.
89. *Id.*
90. State *ex rel.* Domino's Pizza, Inc. v. Dowd, 941 S.W.2d 663, 666–67 (Mo. Ct. App. 1997).
91. *Chmieleski*, 660 S.W.2d at 294.
92. *See* Lift Truck Lease & Serv., Inc. v. Nissan Forklift Corp., No. 4:12-CV-153 CAS, 2012 WL 3891615, at *10 (E.D. Mo. Sept. 7, 2012).

There was no fiduciary relationship between the franchisor and franchisee of a Ben Franklin's retail store. The franchisee's owners had 15 years of past retail business and experience in banking, there was no profit sharing, and the franchisee was free in its management decisions creating an arm's-length bargained for contract and a cooperative business relationship.[93]

G. Remedies and Administrative Action

1. Restrictive Covenants

a. Commentary

The Act does not interpret or otherwise impact restrictive covenants in Missouri. Missouri courts typically enforce noncompetes that are reasonable with respect to time and geographic scope and where the enforcing party has a legitimate interest in enforcement. Legitimate interests can include possible harm to a franchisor's reputation and goodwill, as well as the protection of confidential information and trade secrets. The "geographic reasonableness" of the covenants is fact-specific, but Missouri courts tend to enforce noncompetition covenants that have a time limitation of less than three years.[94]

b. Annotations

A two-year, 25-mile radius noncompete imposed by a national tax franchisor was enforceable against the franchisee and was reasonably tailored to serve the franchisor's interests.[95]

2. Damages

a. Commentary

A franchisee that prevails on claims under the Act can be awarded damages, including loss of goodwill, costs of the suit, and any equitable relief that the court deems proper such as an injunction to reinstate the relationship temporarily until termination is made properly under the Act and contract.[96] Franchisors do not have a statutory right to recover costs, notwithstanding prevailing on a claim brought by the franchisee.

In addition, franchisees who are wrongfully terminated under the Act before they have an opportunity to recoup their investment may have a common law claim for recoupment. The recoupment doctrine in Missouri imputes into a contract a length of time reasonably necessary for a dealer or franchisee to recoup their investment. If a franchisor terminates a franchisee in violation of the Act before its franchisee has had the opportunity to recoup its investment, the franchisee may be entitled to a stay of termination in order to restore the franchise

---

93. *Id.*
94. For information on the impact of restrictive covenants in Missouri franchises, *see* Covenants Against Competition in Franchise Agreements, 4th ed. (Michael Gray, Natalma M. McKnew & William Sentell, eds. 2022).
95. H&R Block Tax Servs. LLC v. Clayton, Case No. 4:16-cv-00185-SRB, 2016 WL 1247205, at *5 (W.D. Mo. Mar. 24, 2016).
96. Mo. Rev. Stat. § 407.410.

and sell the business to another company to recoup its investment.[97] Moreover, in some circumstances, a franchise agreement that is otherwise terminable at will may be extended to allow the franchisee to recoup or be compensated on a quantum merit basis for its initial investment. Courts will review whether the franchisee was induced to enter into the agreement, incurred expenses in good faith, and devoted sufficient time and labor into the relationship without having an opportunity to recoup those expenditures.[98] However, where the franchisor does not actually terminate the franchisee, recoupment is not an available remedy.[99]

Because the statute expressly limits the grounds for termination, which will operate to shorten the 90-day notice requirement, franchisors looking to terminate a franchise agreement for cause could find themselves choosing between the risk of a franchisee's claim it violated the Act or a painfully long waiting period. For example, virtually all franchise agreements allow the franchisor to immediately terminate a franchise agreement where the franchisee's conduct reflects materially and unfavorably upon the entire franchise system or for repeated defaults of the same nature. However, in Missouri this would still require 90 days' advance written notice.

b. Annotations

One Missouri court held that the Act did not limit damages to loss of "goodwill, costs of the suit and any equitable relief the court deems equitable," noting the statute allows for all damages sustained, which may include any other actual damages that the franchisee has sustained.[100]

If a franchisee prevails in a wrongful termination claim under the Act, under the recoupment doctrine, a franchisee would be entitled to recoup the amount of their investment less the current value of the business and the profits realized.[101] While the recoupment doctrine only applies to agreements that are terminable at will, an agreement with no specific duration can be treated as being terminated at will, regardless of whether there is a provision requiring notice or cause for termination.[102]

Attempts to terminate a distribution agreement in violation of the Act deprive the distributor of its right to recoup its investment and cause irreparable injury.[103] Failure to comply with the Act's notice requirement does not entitle a franchisee to punitive damages.[104]

---

97. ABA Distribs., Inc. v. Adolph Coors Co., 542 F. Supp. 1272, 1294 (W.D. Mo. 1982).

98. Ernst v. Ford Motor Co., 813 S.W.2d 910, 919 (Mo. Ct. App. 1991) (citing Lockewill, Inc. v. United States Shoe Corp., 547 F.2d 1024, 1028–29 (8th Cir. 1976) cert. denied, 431 U.S. 956, 97 S. Ct. 2678, 53 L. Ed. 2d 272 (1977) (applying Missouri law)). See also Armstrong Bus. Serv. v. H & R Block, 96 S.W.3d 867, 878 (Mo. Ct. App. 2003); Bain v. Champlin Petroleum Co., 692 F.2d 43, 48 (8th Cir. 1982).

99. Rolscreen Co. v. Pella Prods. of St. Louis, 64 F.3d 1202, 1212 (8th Cir. 1995) (citing A.H. Gibbs v. Bardahl Oil Co., 331 S.W.2d 614, 621–22 (Mo. 1960)).

100. Saey v. Xerox Corp., 31 F. Supp. 2d 692, 702 (E.D. Mo. 1998).

101. Dunkin' Donuts Franchising LLC v. SAI Food Hospitality, LLC, No. 4:11CV01484 AGF, 2013 WL 6885339, at *4 (E.D. Mo. July 16, 2013).

102. Ernst v. Ford Motor Co., 813 S.W.2d 910, 919 (Mo. Ct. App. 1991).

103. ABA Distribs., Inc. v. Adolph Coors Co., 542 F. Supp. 1272, 1297 (W.D. Mo. 1982).

104. Ridings v. Thoele, Inc., 739 S.W.2d 547 (Mo. banc.).

Costs granted to a prevailing party bringing a claim for wrongful termination that were approved included court reporter fees, witness fees, and clerk fees. However, copying costs were disallowed due to insufficient documentation being provided.[105]

A court's decision to award 18 years of lost profits for a wrongful termination claim was a misapplication of the Act. Claims under the Act are limited to lost profit damages for a 90-day period based on the expectation that the relationship would continue for at least a 90-day period from the date proper notice is given under the Act, together with the costs of filing suit, assuming the notice period applies.[106] Further amounts would give "unintended breadth" to the damages obtainable under the Act.[107]

When an award of lost future profits was based on an expert witness's erred calculations, the damage calculation was found to be too speculative and overturned.[108] A court will only award lost profits when supported by accurate evidence, not speculation, and the recovery of them is viewed cautiously by Missouri courts.[109]

3. Rescission

a. Commentary
Not applicable.

b. Annotations
Not applicable.

4. Injunctive Relief

a. Commentary
A franchisee terminated in violation of the Act may be afforded any equitable relief that a court deems proper.[110] The proper remedy for a failure to provide proper notice of termination under the Act would be an order requiring the violating party to comply with the procedural requirements of the contract or Missouri law.[111] Missouri courts can set aside a termination, cancellation, or nonrenewal and require that the relationship be reinstated until such time as the violating party gives proper notice under the Act.[112]

In addition to setting aside a termination, at least one court has prohibited the franchisor from granting a franchise in the same territory to anyone

---

105. Major Brands, Inc. v. Mast-Jägermeister US, Inc., 4:18CV423 HEA, 2022 WL 4646061, at *1 (E.D. Mo. Sept. 30, 2022).
106. Sun Aviation, Inc. v. L-3 Commc'ns Avionics Sys., Inc., 533 S.W.3d 720, 730 (Mo. 2017).
107. Id.
108. Chmieleski v. City Prods. Corp., 660 S.W.2d 275, 297 (Mo. Ct. App. 1983).
109. Id. at 298 (citing Jack L. Baker Co. v. Pasley Mfg. Distrib. Co., 413 S.W.2d 268, 270 (Mo. 1967); Coonis v. Rogers, 429 S.W.2d 709, 714 (Mo. 1968); Morrow v. Missouri Pacific Railway Co., 140 Mo. Ct. App. 200, 123 S.W. 1034, 1038 (1909)).
110. Mo. Rev. Stat. § 407.410.
111. ABA Distribs., Inc. v. Adolph Coors Co., 661 F.2d 712, 715 (8th Cir. 1981).
112. Maude v. Gen. Motors Corp., 626 F. Supp. 1081, 1082 (W.D. Mo. 1986).

other than the aggrieved franchisee until such time as the franchisor had given required notice of termination.[113]

b. Annotations

Where a beer manufacturer terminated a distributor without providing proper notice under the distribution agreement or the Act, a preliminary injunction was appropriate pending resolution of claims that the termination was wrongful under the Act.[114]

Where a wine manufacturer provided notice that it would no longer accept orders from a wholesale distributor, a temporary restraining order and preliminary injunction were issued to enjoin the manufacturer from prematurely terminating the distribution relationship absent good cause by the manufacturer together with an order requiring that the manufacturer subsequently comply with the Act's 90-day advance notice requirement for termination.[115]

5. Control Person Liability

a. Commentary

Willful failure to give notice under the Act is a Class E felony to be brought by the Missouri Attorney General's Office.[116]

b. Annotations

The author was not able to locate any case in which a franchisor was prosecuted for violation of the Act.

6. Attorneys' Fees

a. Commentary

There is no statutory authority for attorneys' fees created under the Act. However, the Act does provide for a recovery of costs.

b. Annotations

An oral franchise agreement did not contain a clause for or otherwise contemplate an award of attorneys' fees. Because there is no statutory authority for an award of attorneys' fees under the Act, a franchisee that was terminated without the proper 90-day notice under the Act was unable to recoup its attorneys' fees.[117]

7. Limitations on Damage Waivers

a. Commentary

Not applicable.

---

113. *Id.* at 1087.
114. ABA Distribs., Inc., 496 F. Supp. at 1202–05.
115. Garco Wine Co. v. Constellation Brands, Inc., No. 4:13CV00661 ERW, 2013 WL 5433480 (E.D. Mo. Sept. 27, 2013).
116. Mo. Rev. Stat. § 407.420.
117. Suburban Leisure Ctr., Inc. v. AMF Bowling Prods., No. 4:06CV188-DJS, 2008 WL 695394, at *4 (E.D. Mo. Mar. 12, 2008).

b. Annotations
Not applicable.

8. Administrative Action
a. Commentary
Not applicable.

b. Annotations
Not applicable.

H. Dispute Resolution
1. Limitations on Franchisors' Ability to Restrict Venue
a. Commentary
The Act does not restrict venue. Generally, forum selection clauses that would prevent courts within the state of Missouri from exercising jurisdiction over actions brought by Missouri citizens are void as against the strong Missouri public policy of providing Missouri citizens with access to courts within the State of Missouri.[118] Forum selection clauses that designate a particular court in Missouri as the exclusive forum are enforceable as long as they are not unfair and not unreasonable.[119]

b. Annotations
Not applicable.

2. Limitations Period
a. Commentary
The Act makes clear that claims involving pyramid sales schemes must be brought within a five-year statute of limitations.[120] However, the Act does not specifically create a limitations period in which claims must be brought by franchisees.[121] Missouri does, however, establish a five-year statute of limitations on claims created by statute other than penalty and forfeiture.[122]

b. Annotations
Not applicable.

---

118. *Id.* (citing Reichard v. Manhattan Life Ins. Co., 31 Mo. 518 (1862); State *ex rel.* Gooseneck Trailer Mfg. Co. v. Barker, 619 S.W.2d 928, 930 (Mo. Ct. App. 1981); State *ex rel.* Marlo v. Hess, 669 S.W.2d 291, 293–94 (Mo. Ct. App. 1984)).

119. Medicine Shoppe Intern., Inc. v. Browne, 683 F. Supp. 731, 732 (E.D. Mo. 1988) (citing Osage Homestead, Inc. v. City of New Florence, 713 S.W.2d 51, 52 (Mo. Ct. App. 1986); State *ex rel.* Marlo v. Hess, 669 S.W.2d 291, 293–94 (Mo. Ct. App. 1984); Gibson v. Gibson, 687 S.W.2d 274, 276 (Mo. Ct. App. 1985)).

120. Mo. Rev. Stat. § 407.410(1).

121. The author was unable to locate any cases specifically analyzing the statute of limitations under the act for franchises.

122. Mo. Rev. Stat. § 516.120.

3. Discrimination

a. Commentary

Section 407.413 prohibits discrimination by suppliers of wholesalers in the context of liquor franchise relationships.[123]

b. Annotations

The author was not able to locate any cases addressing this issue.

4. Preemption

a. Commentary

The Act is likely to apply notwithstanding a choice of law provision in the franchise agreement that calls for contract interpretation under a different state's law.

b. Annotations

A South Carolina choice of law provision between a Delaware franchisor located in South Carolina and a franchisee with a principal office located in Missouri was preempted by the Act when the franchisor attempted to terminate the franchisee without complying with the notice requirement under the Act because South Carolina did not have a similar notice requirement.[124]

A Missouri choice-of-law provision in a contract between a Missouri franchisor and an Illinois franchisee was not preempted by the Illinois Franchise Disclosure Act because the Illinois Franchise Disclosure Act did not address the choice of law as to claims between franchisors and Illinois franchisees, other than as to jurisdiction and venue.[125]

---

123. Mo. Rev. Stat. § 407.413.
124. Elec. Magneto Serv. Co. v. AMBAC Int'l Corp., 941 F.2d 660 (8th Cir. 1991).
125. Hardee's Food Sys., Inc. v. Hallbeck, 776 F. Supp. 2d 949, 7–8 (E.D. Mo. 2011).

Nebraska

Theresa D. Koller

I. Introduction to Statute

The Nebraska Franchise Practices Act, Neb. Rev. Stat. §§ 87-401 to 87-410 (Nebraska Act, or the Act), was passed by the state's Unicameral Legislature in 1978 after it determined that "distribution and sales through franchise arrangements in the state vitally affect the general economy of the state, the public interest and public welfare."[1] The Act was closely modeled after the New Jersey Franchise Practices Act (New Jersey Act).[2]

The Nebraska Act significantly modifies how applicable franchise relationships are treated. For example, prior to the Act's passage, franchisors were able to terminate or not renew a franchise agreement for practically any reason.[3] The Act regulates key franchise relationship issues including, without limitation, termination, nonrenewal, transfer, noncompetition covenants, and unreasonable standards of performance. The Act does not retroactively apply to contracts executed before the Act was enacted.[4] The Act also does not address franchise disclosures, nor does any other Nebraska law. And although the Nebraska Act has, for the most part, remained unchanged since it was enacted in 1978, there is a scarcity of interpretive case law.[5]

---

1. Neb. Rev. Stat. § 87-401.
2. *See* N.J. Stat. Ann. §§ 56:10-1 *et seq.*
3. *See, e.g.*, McArtor v. Mobil Oil Corp., 212 Neb. 592, 593, 324 N.W.2d 399, 400 (1982) (holding that "prior to the enactment of the Nebraska Franchise Practice Act . . . the law of Nebraska generally was that any person might do or refuse to do business with whomsoever he desired"); McDonald's Corp. v. Markim, Inc., 209 Neb. 49, 56, 306 N.W.2d 158, 162 (1981) (noting that prior to the Nebraska Act, the common law in Nebraska relating to franchise agreements was that "[a]ny person may do business with whomsoever he desires. Also, he may refuse business relations with any person whomsoever, whether the refusal is based on reason, whim or prejudice. And where, by the terms of a contract, it is specified that either party may terminate the agreement at any time, such termination may likewise be had as stipulated and upon the conditions in such contract contained.") (internal quotations and citation omitted).
4. *See McArtor*, 324 N.W.2d at 400; *Markim*, 306 N.W.2d at 162 (refusing to retroactively apply the Act and rejecting the argument that the Act's passage established a public policy of the state.).
5. The most significant revisions to the Act took place in 2016 and 2018. Both amendments pertain to noncompetition agreements in franchise agreements. See Section II.G.1.

II. Commentary and Annotations

A. Definition of Franchise

The Nebraska Act defines a franchise as "a written arrangement for a definite or indefinite period, in which a person grants to another person for a franchisee fee a license to use a trade name, trademark, service mark, or related characteristics and in which there is a community of interest in the marketing of goods or services."[6] Additionally, the Act's definition of franchise broadly encompasses "any arrangement, agreement, or contract, either expressed or implied, for the sale, distribution, or marketing of nonalcoholic beverages,"[7] but excludes arrangements "for the sale, distribution, or marketing of petroleum products."[8]

Accordingly, except for franchises involving nonalcoholic beverages, four elements must be satisfied for an arrangement to constitute a franchise under the Act: (1) a written arrangement for a definite or indefinite period; (2) the payment of a franchise fee; (3) a license to use a trade name, trademark, service mark, or related characteristics; and (4) a community of interest in the marketing of goods or services between the parties to the arrangement.[9] Courts have generally not discussed the "written arrangement" element under the Nebraska Act, other than to conclude, based on the plain language of the statute, that where there is no written agreement to use a franchisor's trademarks, it is not a franchise under the Nebraska Act.[10] One court also held that when a written agreement contains a clause stating, "[t]his Agreement is not, nor is it to be construed as, a franchise agreement," the Nebraska Act will not apply in the absence of a showing of the statutory elements required to establish a franchise.[11] The remaining three elements are discussed next.

1. Trademark Element

a. Commentary

As just noted, for a franchise to exist under the Nebraska Act, the franchisor must grant "a license to use a trade name, trademark, service mark, or related characteristics" in exchange for a franchise fee.[12] No court has yet interpreted the trademark license element of the Nebraska Act. But because the New Jersey

---

6. NEB. REV. STAT. § 87-402(1)(a).
7. *Id.* § 87-402(1)(b).
8. *Id. See also* Regnev, Inc. v. Shasta Beverages, Inc., 215 Neb. 230, 232, 337 N.W.2d 783, 784–85 (1983) (confirming that under the Act, a franchise agreement involving nonalcoholic beverages does not need to be written); Western Convenience Stores, Inc. v. Burger King, Corp., No. 8:07CV270, 2007 WL 2682245, at *6 (D. Neb. Sept. 7, 2007) (discussing the narrow holding in *Regnev*).
9. NEB. REV. STAT. § 87-402(1). *But see* NEB. REV. STAT. § 87-403, discussed later, for limitations on applicability of the Act.
10. Western Convenience Stores, Inc. v. Burger King Corp., No. 8:07CV270, 2007 WL 2682245, at *5 (D. Neb. Sept. 7, 2007).
11. Home Pest & Termite Control, Inc. v. Dow Agrosciences, LLC, No. 8:02CV406, 2004 WL 240556, at *2–3 (D. Neb. Feb. 6, 2004).
12. NEB. REV. STAT. § 87-402(1)(a). *See* discussion of the franchise fee element later in the chapter.

Act also includes the grant of a trademark license in its definition of a franchise, one can look to cases interpreting the New Jersey Act for guidance.[13]

In *Neptune T.V. and Appliance Services, Inc. v. Litton Microwave Cooking Products Division, Litton Systems, Inc.*, the court held that "a hallmark of the franchise relationship is the use of another's trade name in such a manner as to create a reasonable belief on the part of the consuming public that there is a connection between the trade name licensor and licensee by which the licensor vouches, as it were, for the activity of the licensee in respect to the subject of the trade name."[14] As another court explained, the term "license" means "to use as if it is one's own, [which] implies a proprietary interest."[15] The New Jersey Act's license requirement contemplates an "obligation of the franchisee to promote the [franchisor's] [trade]mark itself, as distinct from merely using it to make sales."[16]

Subsequent cases have affirmed and expanded the scope of *Neptune T.V.*'s holding, finding that contractual language concerning use of the franchisor's trademarks, directed and approved marketing activities, print and social media guidelines, and the relationship of the parties, among other factors, should be considered in determining the existence of a license.[17] Such courts have recognized that approved use of a franchisor's trade name or trademarks in advertisements and marketing materials, such as, without limitation, uniforms, logoed attire, automobile decals and wraps, billboards, and point of sale materials, could be viewed by the consuming public as creating a special relationship between the parties and thus constitute a "license" under the New Jersey Act.[18] Importantly, however, courts have refused to find the existence of a license under the New Jersey Act where a manufacturer merely furnishes advertising materials to a distributor and allows the distributor to place its name next to the manufacturer's name on the materials.[19]

b. Annotations

Not applicable.

---

13. N.J. STAT. ANN. § 56:10-3(a). Notably, the New Jersey Act does not require the payment of a franchise fee as an element of a franchise. The cases discussed in this section focus solely on the trademark license element.

14. 190 N.J. Super. 153, 160, 462 A.2d 595, 599 (Super. Ct. App. Div. 1983).

15. Finlay & Assocs., Inc. v. Borg-Warner Corp., 146 N.J. Super 210, 219, 369 A.2d 541, 546 (Super. Ct. 1976), *aff'd*, 155 N.J. Super. 331, 382 A.2d 933 (Super. Ct. App. Div. 1978).

16. Liberty Sales Assocs., Inc. v. Dow Corning Corp., 816 F. Supp. 1004, 1011 (D.N.J. 1993).

17. *See, e.g.*, Golden Fortune Import & Export Corp. v. Mei-Xin (Hong Kong) Ltd., No. 22-01369, 2022 WL 1002626, at *11–12 (D.N.J. Apr. 4, 2022); Cooper Distrib. Co. v. Amana Refrigeration, Inc., 63 F.3d 262, 272–73 (3d Cir. 1995); Cassidy Podell Lynch, Inc. v. SnyderGeneral Corp., 944 F.2d 1131, 1138–40 (3d Cir. 1991); Atlantic City Coin & Slot Serv. Co. v. IGT, 14 F. Supp. 2d 644, 644–45 (D.N.J. 1998); Instructional Sys., Inc. v. Comput. Curriculum Corp., 614 A.2d 124, 138–40 (N.J. 1992).

18. *See, e.g., Golden Fortune*, 2022 WL 1002626, at *11–12; *Cassidy Podell Lynch, Inc.*, 944 F.2d at 1138–40.

19. *See Finlay*, 146 N.J. Super at 219–21, 369 A.2d at 545–47, Colt Indus., Inc. v. Fidelco Pump & Compressor Corp., 844 F.2d 117, 119–20 (3d Cir. 1998); *Liberty Sales*, 816 F. Supp. at 1009–11.

2. Franchise Fee Element

a. Commentary

A franchise fee is broadly defined in the Nebraska Act as "any payment made by the franchisee to the franchisor, other than a payment for the goods or services, for a surety bond, for a surety deposit, or for security for payment of debts due."[20] No franchise is established under the Nebraska Act without the payment of a franchise fee.[21]

The question of whether certain "indirect" expenses constitute payment of a "franchise fee" under the Act was a key issue in *Jones Distributing Co. Inc. v. White Consolidated Industries, Inc.*[22] In that case, the defendant manufacturer sought summary judgment on the plaintiff distributor's claims for violation of the franchise laws of several states, including Nebraska.[23] The manufacturer argued that it was entitled to judgment as a matter of law on such claims because the distributor could not satisfy the franchise fee requirement. Specifically, the manufacturer argued that the undisputed evidence established that the distributor never paid a direct franchise fee to the manufacturer, and the "indirect" fees paid by the distributor were simply routine business expenses.[24] The alleged "indirect" fees included (1) paying higher prices for product than certain dealers were paying; (2) paying to train employees at approved training facilities; (3) paying for advertising; (4) having to maintain certain excess amounts of inventory; and (5) having to maintain offices and warehouses within the states of Nebraska, Iowa, and South Dakota, where it had to rent or lease showroom space.[25] The court agreed with the manufacturer, holding that the distributor failed to show that each indirect fee was "anything but a normal business expense."[26] Accordingly, the court granted the manufacturer's motion for summary judgment on the franchise law claims.[27]

Another court held, despite the broad definition of "franchise fee" under the Nebraska Act, that the franchise fee requirement could not be met by demonstrating the payment of royalty fees to the franchisor.[28] In *Western Convenience Stores, Inc. v. Burger King Corp.*, the original franchisee transferred its rights under the franchise agreement without receiving approval from the franchisor. The buyer applied to become a franchisee, and began paying monthly royalty fees to the franchisor pursuant to the original franchise agreement, which

---

20. NEB. REV. STAT. § 87-402(5).
21. *See* Home Pest & Termite Control, Inc. v. Dow Agrosciences, LLC, No. 8:02CV406, 2004 WL 240556, at *2 (D. Neb. Feb. 6, 2004) (refusing to find a franchise under the Nebraska Act when the parties' arrangement did not include any payments other than for basic goods and services).
22. 943 F. Supp. 1445, 1457–58 (N.D. Iowa 1996).
23. *Jones Distrib. Co. Inc.*, 943 F. Supp. at 1457.
24. *Id.*
25. *Id.*
26. *Id.* at 1458.
27. *Id.*
28. Western Convenience Stores, Inc. v. Burger King Corp., No. 8:07CV270, 2007 WL 2682245, at *5.

the franchisor accepted.[29] When the franchisor denied the buyer's application to become a franchisee and refused to consent to the assignment of franchise rights, the buyer initiated a lawsuit claiming, among other things, violation of the Nebraska Act.[30] The court held that the buyer could not succeed on a claim under the Act because there was no written agreement between the buyer and the franchisor granting a license to use the franchisor's marks and because the buyer had not paid a franchisee fee.[31] Regarding the franchise fee element, the court noted that under the express terms of the franchise agreement, the payment of an initial franchise fee and payment of royalties were "separate and distinct obligations" owed to the franchisor, and that although there was no dispute that the buyer had paid some royalties to the franchisor, there was no evidence that the buyer paid an initial franchise fee.[32]

b. Annotations

If the parties' written agreement creates an obligation to pay a franchisee fee and a separate and distinct obligation to make royalty payments, evidence of royalty payments does not satisfy the Nebraska Act's requirement of a franchise fee. *Western Convenience Stores, Inc. v. Burger King Corp.*, No. 8:07CV270, 2007 WL 2682245, at *5 (D. Neb. Sept. 7, 2007).

If there is no written agreement granting a party the right to use the franchise trademark and no payment of a franchise fee, there is no franchise under the Nebraska Franchise Practices Act. *Western Convenience Stores, Inc. v. Burger King Corp.*, No. 8:07CV270, 2007 WL 2682245, at *5 (D. Neb. Sept. 7, 2007).

A franchise will not be found under the Nebraska Act without the payment of a franchise fee in exchange for a license to use the franchisor's name or mark. *Home Pest and Termite Control, Inc. v. Down Agrosciences, LLC*, No. 8:02CV406, 2004 WL 240556, at *2 (D. Neb. Feb. 6, 2004). Under the Nebraska Act, a plaintiff must show that it has paid a franchisee fee to the franchisor, which does not include payments for normal business expenses. *Jones Distributing Co. Inc. v. White Consolidated Industries, Inc.*, 943 F. Supp. 1445, 1457–58 (N.D. Iowa 1996).

3. Community of Interest; Significant Degree of Control; Joint Marketing Plan

a. Commentary

Neither the Nebraska Act nor any courts have defined the Nebraska Act's "community of interest" element. Several courts have, in contrast, interpreted this same element under the New Jersey Act, characterizing it as "broad, elastic, and elusive."[33]

The "community of interest" element focuses on the inequality of bargaining power between a franchisor and a franchisee, and is an important factor in

---

29. *Id.* at *3.
30. *Id.* at *1–6.
31. *Id.* at *5.
32. *Id.*
33. Neptune T.V. & Appliance Serv., Inc. v. Litton Microwave Cooking Products Div., Litton Sys., Inc., 190 N.J. Super. at 165, 462 A.2d at 601.

distinguishing franchises from other types of business arrangements.[34] A "community of interest" exists only "when the terms of the agreement between the parties or the nature of the franchise business requires the licensee, in the interest of the licensed business's success, to make a substantial investment in goods or skills that will be of minimal utility outside the franchise."[35]

Some courts have evaluated the community of interest element using a balancing test considering the following four factors: "(1) licensor's control over the licensee, (2) the licensee's economic dependence on the licensor[,] (3) disparity in bargaining power, and (4) the presence of a franchise-specific investment by the licensee."[36] Others have reformulated the test to find that for a community of interest to exist, two requirements must be met: "(1) the distributor's investments must have been 'substantially franchise-specific,' and (2) the distributor must have been required to make these investments by the parties' agreement or the nature of the business."[37] Courts have further held that the most important factor to consider in determining whether a "community of interest" exists is the franchisee's economic dependence on the franchisor.[38]

b. Annotations
Not applicable.

B. Scope and Jurisdiction

1. Commentary
The Nebraska Act only applies to a franchise that (1) establishes or maintains a place of business in Nebraska; (2) had gross sales exceeding $35,000 over 12 months preceding the institution of a suit under the Nebraska Act; and (3) derives or intends to derive more than 20 percent of the franchisee's gross sales from the franchise.[39] Each of these elements is discussed next.

a. Place of Business
Under the Nebraska Act, a "place of business" in Nebraska is defined as "a fixed geographical location at which the franchisee displays for sale and sells the franchisor's goods or offers for sale and sells the franchisor's services."[40] The statute excludes from this definition "an office, a warehouse, a place of storage,

---

34. Instructional Sys., Inc. v. Comput. Curriculum Corp., 130 N.J. 324, 356, 614 A.2d 124, 140 (1992).
35. *Id.* at 130 N.J. at 359, 614 A.2d at 142 (internal quotations and citation omitted).
36. Orologio of Short Hills Inc. v. The Swatch Group (U.S.) Inc., 653 Fed. App'x 134, 139 (3d Cir. 2016) (internal citations omitted) (quoting Cassidy Podell Lynch, Inc. v. SynderGeneral Corp., 944 F.2d 1131, 1140 (3d Cir. 1991)).
37. Lawmen Supply Co. of N.J., Inc. v. Glock, Inc., 330 F. Supp. 3d 1020, 1033 (D.N.J. 2018) (quoting Cooper Distrib. Co. v. Amana Refrigeration, Inc., 63 F.3d at 269 (3d Cir. 1995)).
38. McPeak v. S-L Distribution Co., Inc., Civ. No. 12-348, 2014 WL 320074, at *5–7, (D.N.J. Jan. 29, 2014) (citing *Cooper*, 63 F.3d at 272); *see also Instructional*, 130 N.J. at 360–64, 614 A.2d at 142–45.
39. NEB. REV. STAT. § 87-403.
40. *Id.* § 87-402(7).

a residence or a vehicle."[41] Based on the plain language of the Nebraska Act, at least one court has opined that "Nebraska has declined to take any interest in regulating franchises outside of Nebraska."[42] Courts have not, however, analyzed the Act's definition of a "place of business" to determine whether certain types of franchises are excluded from the Act, such as franchises that operate as wholesale distributors or service industry franchises that sell their services out of an office and perform the services at customers' homes.

The New Jersey Act similarly requires that the franchise agreement contemplate or require the franchisee to maintain a place of business within the state, but in 2010 the New Jersey Act's definition of "place of business" was amended to add that "[p]lace of business shall not mean an office, a warehouse, a place of storage, a residence or a vehicle, *except that with respect to persons who do not make a majority of their sales directly to consumers, 'place of business' means a fixed geographical location at which the franchisee displays for sale and sells the franchisor's goods or offers for sale and sells the franchisor's services, or an office or a warehouse from which franchisee personnel visit or call upon customers or from which the franchisor's goods are delivered to customers.*"[43] Thus, unlike Nebraska, there is no question that distributorship franchisees in New Jersey, which meet all the other applicability requirements, are governed by the New Jersey Act.

Courts interpreting the New Jersey Act have also recognized new and different franchising arrangements, including marketing facilities for technology demonstrations[44] and showrooms.[45] But the New Jersey Act's requirement that the parties contemplate or require a physical location in the state still stands.[46]

In 2020, a court was faced with the question of whether the New Jersey Act applied to franchised locations outside of the state under circumstances where the franchisee was operating franchised locations in New Jersey as well. In *Crest Furniture, Inc. v. Ashley Homestores, Ltd.*, a New Jersey-based furniture store franchisee entered into multiple Trademark Usage Agreements (TUAs) to operate 11 stores in New Jersey and neighboring Pennsylvania.[47] The franchisor attempted to not renew the TUAs for the Pennsylvania stores only, and the plaintiff filed suit for, among other things, breach of the New Jersey Act.[48]

In opposition to the franchisor's motion to dismiss, the franchisee argued that rather than constituting multiple independent franchises, the parties' conduct demonstrates that their arrangement actually constituted a single "unified

---

41. *Id.*
42. *See* Modern Comput. Sys. Inc. v. Modern Banking Sys. Inc., 871 F.2d 734, 741 (8th Cir. 1989) (Heaney, dissenting) (superseded on other grounds).
43. N.J. STAT. ANN. § 56:10-3(f) (emphasis added); *see also* the New Jersey chapter for further discussion on the New Jersey Act's definition of "place of business."
44. *Instructional Systems*, 614 A.2d at 137–38.
45. *Cooper*, 63 F.3d at 274.
46. *See, e.g., id.* at 275 ("Apart from requiring Cooper to establish that the showroom was a [place of business], the statute also obligated Cooper to show that the parties contemplated or required that the [place of business] be located in New Jersey.").
47. Crest Furniture, Inc. v. Ashley Homestores, Ltd., No. 1:20CV01383, 2020 WL 6375808, at *1 (D.N.J. Oct. 30, 2020).
48. *Id.*

multi-state franchise" operated out of its New Jersey headquarters.[49] The court agreed, holding that the franchisee had "alleged sufficient facts that they operate a New Jersey-based, unified multi-state franchise to which the [New Jersey Act] is applicable, and that through the nonrenewal of four TUAs [the franchisor had] terminated, in part and effectively in whole, their franchise without good cause."[50] In reaching this conclusion, the court looked to the factual allegations of the complaint, which included that the franchisor required the franchisee to service its Pennsylvania stores from the franchisee's New Jersey warehouse; the purchase order and stock order forms submitted to the franchisor were single unified documents that did not differentiate between the New Jersey and Pennsylvania stores; the franchisor treated the Southern New Jersey and Eastern Pennsylvania market as a consolidated market; and the franchisor lumped together the New Jersey and Pennsylvania stores in documents the franchisee was required to sign during the renewal process.[51] Accordingly, at least under the New Jersey Act, and potentially under the similar language of the Nebraska Act, there may be circumstances where the Acts are applied to franchises located outside of the state.

b. Gross Sales During Year Prior to Litigation

The second required element for jurisdiction under the Nebraska Act is that the franchisee must have realized gross sales of products or services in excess of $35,000 for the 12 months directly preceding the institution of suit pursuant to the Act.[52] No court has interpreted this element of the Nebraska Act.

c. Anticipated Gross Sales from Franchise

Finally, the Nebraska Act only applies "when more than twenty percent of the franchisee's gross sales are intended to be or are derived from such franchise."[53] Once again, no court has interpreted this element of the Nebraska Act. But the plain language indicates that even if a franchisee does not realize gross sales of more than 20 percent from the franchise, the Nebraska Act may still apply if the franchisee can prove that the parties intended such sales to be derived from the franchise.

2. Annotations

The Nebraska Act only extends to franchisees within the state of Nebraska. *Modern Computers Systems, Inc. v. Modern Banking Systems, Inc.*, 871 F.2d 734, 742 (8th Cir. 1989) (superseded on other grounds).

Nebraska has not shown an interest in regulating franchises outside of the state. *Modern Computer Systems, Inc., v. Modern Banking Systems, Inc.*, 871 F.2d 734, 741 (8th Cir. 1989) (Heaney, dissenting) (superseded on other grounds).

---

49. *Id.*
50. *Id.* at *7.
51. *Id.* at *4.
52. NEB. REV. STAT. § 87-403(2).
53. *Id.* § 87-403(3).

C. Termination

1. What Constitutes Termination or Cancellation?

a. Commentary

The Nebraska Act prohibits the direct or indirect termination, cancellation, or nonrenewal of a franchise unless the franchisor first provides written notice stating all the reasons for termination, cancellation, or nonrenewal.[54] The franchisor must also have good cause, which is limited to failure by the franchisee to substantially comply with the requirements imposed upon it by the franchise.[55] No court has interpreted or dealt at length with the Nebraska Act's definition of good cause, including what it means to "substantially comply" with the requirements of a franchise agreement.

b. Annotations

Prior to enactment of the Nebraska Franchise Practices Act, "the law of Nebraska generally was that any person might do or refuse to do business with whomsoever he desired." *McArtor v. Mobil Oil*, 212 Neb. 592, 593, 324 N.W.2d 399, 400 (1982). The Nebraska Act may not be applied retroactively to agreements executed before 1978. *McArtor v. Mobil Oil Corp.*, 212 Neb. 592, 593, 324 N.W.2d 399, 400 (1982). *See also McDonald's Corp. v. Markim, Inc.*, 209 Neb. 49, 55, 306 N.W.2d 158, 162 (1981) (same).

Nebraska has statutorily regulated the termination of all franchise contracts. *Consumer International, Inc. v. SYSCO, Inc.*, 191 Ariz. 32, 34, 951 P.2d 897, 899 (Ariz. Ct. App. 1998) (citing the Nebraska Franchise Practices Act, NEB. REV. STAT. §§ 87-401 *et seq.*).

2. Restrictions on Termination or Cancellation

a. Commentary

Not applicable.

b. Annotations

Not applicable.

3. Notice Requirement

a. Commentary

With few exceptions, discussed next, notice under the Nebraska Act must be written and be provided "at least sixty days in advance of such termination, cancellation, or intent not to renew."[56] The written notice must give "all the reasons" for such termination or nonrenewal, but the Nebraska Act does not require that the franchisee be given an opportunity to cure the identified defaults.[57] Courts have not interpreted the Nebraska Act's notice requirement.

---

54. *Id.* § 87-404(1).
55. *Id.* §§ 87-404(1), 402(8).
56. *Id.* § 87-404(1).
57. *Id.*

Courts interpreting this same requirement under the New Jersey Act have held that a franchisor's termination must comply with the statute's plain language.[58]

The Nebraska Act allows for a shorter notice period if a franchisee voluntary abandons the franchise, in which case written notice is required only 15 days in advance of termination.[59] There is no case law establishing the requirements to prove voluntary abandonment under the Nebraska Act.

Finally, the Nebraska Act allows for immediate termination, effective upon the delivery and receipt of written notice, in any of the following cases: (1) the franchisee's conviction of an "offense directly related to the business conduct pursuant to the franchise"; (2) insolvency or the institution of bankruptcy or receivership proceedings; (3) default in payment or "failure to account for the proceeds of a sale of good by the franchisee" to the franchisor or its subsidiary; (4) falsification of records or reports required by the franchisor; (5) an imminent danger to public health or safety; or (6) loss of the right to occupy the premises from which the franchise is operated by either the franchisee or franchisor.[60]

b. Annotations
Not applicable.

4. Grounds for Termination

a. Commentary
Termination is only permitted when the franchisor has good cause, which is limited to failure by the franchisee to substantially comply with the requirements imposed upon it by the franchise.[61] In addition, the franchisor is generally required to provide the franchisee with 60 days' written notice prior to termination except under certain circumstances specified in the Nebraska Act.[62]

b. Annotations
Not applicable.

5. Required Cure Period

a. Commentary
Not applicable.

b. Annotations
Not applicable.

---

58. *See* Carlo C. Gelardi Corp. v. Miller Brewing Co., 421 F. Supp. 233, 236 (D.N.J. 1976) (issuing a preliminary injunction requiring the defendant's compliance with the 60-day notice language in the New Jersey Act, which is equivalent to NEB. REV. STAT. § 87-404(1)).

59. NEB. REV. STAT. § 87-404(1).

60. *Id.*

61. See Section II.C.1.a.

62. See Section II.C.3.a.

6. Repurchase Obligations

a. Commentary
Not applicable.

b. Annotations
Not applicable.

D. Restrictions on Nonrenewal

1. What Constitutes Nonrenewal

a. Commentary
The same requirements of written notice and good cause, discussed earlier in connection with termination, also apply to nonrenewal.[63] Additionally, the Nebraska Act expressly states that it does not "prohibit a franchise from providing that the franchise is not renewable or that the franchise is only renewable if the franchisor or franchisee meets certain reasonable conditions."[64] No court has construed this statutory language, including reaching a determination as to whether the language should be construed to mean that a franchise agreement must be renewed if the agreement itself is silent on whether it is renewable. Moreover, one cannot look to cases interpreting the New Jersey Act for guidance on this issue because the preceding quoted statutory language is unique to the Nebraska Act.[65]

b. Annotations
Not applicable.

2. Restrictions on Nonrenewal

a. Commentary
Not applicable.

b. Annotations
Not applicable.

---

63. See Sections II.C.1.a and C.3.a.
64. NEB. REV. STAT. § 87-404(1).
65. Under the New Jersey Act, "good cause" for nonrenewal is limited to failing to substantially comply with the requirements imposed by the franchise agreement. N.J. STAT. ANN. § 56:10-5. Thus, courts in New Jersey have held that where a franchisee does not violate its franchise agreement, the franchisee has the benefit of an "infinite" franchise. Dunkin' Donuts of Am., Inc. v. Middletown Donut Corp., 100 N.J. 166, 185, 496 A.2d 66, 75–76 (1985). Even if a franchisor has a good faith and bona fide reason for nonrenewal, absent the franchisee breaching the franchise agreement, the franchisor has no ability not to renew. Westfield Ctr. Serv., Inc. v. Cities Serv. Oil Co., 86 N.J. 453, 469, 432 A.2d 48, 57 (1981).

3. Notice Requirement

a. Commentary

See the preceding discussion pertaining to notice requirements for termination, which applies equally to nonrenewal under the Nebraska Act.[66]

b. Annotations

Not applicable.

4. Grounds for Nonrenewal

a. Commentary

See the preceding discussion pertaining to grounds for termination, which applies equally to nonrenewal under the Nebraska Act.[67] Additionally, the franchise agreement may expressly provide that the agreement is nonrenewable or only renewable if certain reasonable conditions are met.[68]

b. Annotations

Not applicable.

5. Required Cure Period

a. Commentary

Not applicable.

b. Annotations

Not applicable.

6. Limitations on Franchisor's Right to Impose Conditions for Renewal

a. Commentary

The Nebraska Act permits franchise agreements to contain "reasonable conditions," which franchisees must satisfy as a precondition to renewal.[69] Additionally, franchise agreements that expressly state that the agreement is not renewable do not violate the Nebraska Act.[70]

b. Annotations

Not applicable.

7. Repurchase Obligations

a. Commentary

Not applicable.

---

66. See Section II.C.3.a.
67. See Section II.C.1.a.
68. NEB. REV. STAT. § 87-404(1).
69. Id.
70. Id.

b. Annotations
Not applicable.

E. Transfers and Succession

1. Commentary

The only prohibition imposed on franchisees by the Nebraska Act is the prohibition against franchisees transferring, assigning, or selling a franchise interest, or any interest therein, without first notifying the franchisor in writing.[71] The written notice must contain the "prospective transferee's name, address, statement of financial qualification and business experience during the previous five years," and must be delivered by certified mail.[72] Following receipt of such notice, the franchisor has 60 days to either approve or deny the transfer in writing.[73] If denying the transfer, the franchisor must detail in the written rejection notice "the unacceptability of the proposed transferee setting forth material reasons relating to the character, financial ability or business experience of the proposed transferee."[74] A lack of response from the franchisor within the 60-day period is deemed as approval of the transfer.[75] Finally, the proposed transferee must agree in writing to fully comply with the franchise agreement.[76]

No court has interpreted this provision of the Nebraska Act. The New Jersey Act's transfer provision,[77] which is identical to the Nebraska Act, has been interpreted to give effect to the plain language of the statute. For example, in at least one case, an unapproved transfer without written notice to the franchisor was deemed a material breach of the franchisee's obligations under the Act and the franchise agreement, resulting in the transfer being deemed invalid and providing grounds for termination under the New Jersey Act.[78] Additionally, the court in that case held that the unapproved transferee had no standing to assert the rights of a franchisee under New Jersey law.[79] Finally, courts have held that under the New Jersey Act, the franchisor's review of a proposed transferee is subject to a "reasonable exercise of discretion" standard.[80] Among the factors a franchisor may consider when analyzing a possible transferee are whether there has been a material misrepresentation of fact, failure to reveal criminal proceedings against the proposed transferee, and the actual or perceived dishonesty of the proposed transferee.[81]

---

71. *Id.* § 87-405.
72. *Id.*
73. *Id.*
74. *Id.*
75. *Id.*
76. *Id.*
77. N.J. STAT. ANN. § 56:10-6.
78. Simmons v. Gen. Motors Corp., Oldsmobile Div., 180 N.J. Super. 522, 540–41, 435 A.2d 1167, 1177–78 (Super. Ct. App. Div. 1981).
79. 180 N.J. Super at 543, 435 A.2d at 1178–79.
80. 180 N.J. Super at 540, 435 A.2d at 1177.
81. Horn v. Mazda Motor of Am., Inc., 265 N.J. Super. 47, 61, 625 A.2d 548, 556 (Super. Ct. App. Div. 1993) (holding a misrepresentation of material facts in a notice of intent to transfer, whether

2. Annotations
Not applicable.

F. Other Regulation of the Franchise Relationship
1. Commentary
The Nebraska Act does not regulate discrimination, exclusive territory and encroachment, pricing restrictions, sources of supply, or ad funds. The Act does, however, make it a violation for a franchisor to directly or indirectly engage in any of the following:

(1) To require a franchisee at the time of entering into a franchise arrangement to assent to a release, assignment, novation, waiver or estoppel which would relieve any person from liability imposed by [the Nebraska Act];
(2) To prohibit . . . the right of free association among franchisees for any lawful purpose;
(3) To require or prohibit any change in management of any franchisee unless such requirement or prohibition of change shall be for good cause, which cause shall be stated in writing by the franchisor;
(4) To restrict the sale of any equity or debenture issue or the transfer of any securities of any franchisee or in any way prevent or attempt to prevent the transfer, sale, or issuance of shares of stock or debentures to employees, personnel of the franchisee, or heirs of the principal owner, as long as basic financial requirements of the franchisor are complied with and any such sale, transfer, or issuance does not have the effect of accomplishing a sale of the franchise;
(5) To impose unreasonable standards of performance upon a franchisee; and
(6) To provide any term or condition in any lease or other agreement ancillary or collateral to a franchise, which term or condition directly or indirectly violates sections 87-401 to 87-410.[82]

Of the preceding statutory prohibitions, the only one that has been somewhat addressed by a court, albeit in a cursory manner, is the prohibition against requiring a franchisee, at the time of entering into the franchise agreement, "to assent to a release, assignment, novation, waiver or estoppel which would relieve any person from liability" under the Act. In *Servicemaster Residential/ Commercial Services, L.P. v. Proctor*, in an unpublished opinion, the U.S. District Court for the District of Nebraska enforced a Tennessee choice-of-law provision in a franchise agreement involving a Nebraska franchisee.[83] The choice-of-law provision stated, in relevant part, that Tennessee law would apply, except that:

---

intentional or inadvertent, will toll the franchisor's 60-day response period pending the franchisor's investigation); 265 N.J. Super at 62–63, 625 A.2d at 557 (holding that a franchisor properly rejected a proposed transferee based on his criminal indictments, perceived dishonesty from nondisclosure of material facts, and implicit admission of serious crimes, which the franchisor reasonably concluded were material to the proposed transferee's character).

82. NEB. REV. STAT. §87-406.
83. Case No. 4:01CV3089, Bus. Franchise Guide (CCH) ¶ 12,251 (D. Neb. Oct. 31, 2001).

if the state in which the Franchised Business is located has enacted legislation regulating franchising which requires that the law of that state shall apply to the relationship created by this Agreement, it is agreed that this Agreement shall be interpreted and construed under the laws of the state in which the Franchised Business is located.[84]

Without discussing section 87-406(1), the court concluded that the Nebraska Act contains no provision requiring application of the Nebraska Act to Nebraska franchisees. The court further held that the contractual choice of Tennessee law should be upheld because: (1) the choice-of-law provision was in a written commercial contract agreed upon by the parties; (2) contacts in Nebraska and Tennessee were about evenly divided between the parties; (3) there was no convincing evidence that the franchisor's bargaining strength was substantially greater than the franchisee's; and (4) the public policy of Nebraska supports enforcement of such provisions.[85] As such, the court allowed waiver of the Nebraska Act through the contractual choice-of-law provision.

The Nebraska federal court relied upon *Modern Computer Systems, Inc. v. Modern Banking Systems, Inc.*[86] in reaching its conclusion.[87] In *Modern Computer Systems, Inc.*, the U.S. Court of Appeals for the Eighth Circuit found that the anti-waiver provision of the Minnesota Franchise Act (MFA) did not outweigh Minnesota's interest in enforcing choice-of-law provisions.[88] There, a Minnesota distributor brought an action alleging a violation of the MFA even though the parties agreed in the distributorship agreement that disputes would be governed by the laws of Nebraska.[89] At the time of contracting, the MFA included an anti-waiver provision providing that: "Any condition, stipulation or provision purporting to bind any person acquiring any franchise to waive compliance with any provision of [the MFA] or any rule or order thereunder is void."[90] Nevertheless, the Eighth Circuit found that the freedom to contract for a particular law outweighed the public policy backing the MFA.[91] Additionally, the court held that the choice-of-law provision should be upheld because the parties agreed to the law to be applied to future disputes, the contacts between the parties and the two forum states were fairly evenly divided, and the parties were not of unequal bargaining power.[92]

---

84. *Id.*
85. *Id.*
86. 871 F.2d 734, 738–40 (8th Cir. 1989).
87. *Servicemaster*, Case No. 4:01CV3089 at ¶ 12,251. The court also cited section 187 of the Restatement (Second) of Conflict of Laws, although it provided no express analysis under the section.
88. *Modern Comput. Sys., Inc.*, 871 F.2d at 738.
89. *Id.* at 739.
90. MINN. STAT. § 80C.21 (1988).
91. *Modern Comput. Sys., Inc.*, 871 F.2d at 740 ("The Minnesota Franchise Act undeniably does evince a policy in favor of offering franchisees in Minnesota remedies greater than those available under traditional common law, but we also see a powerful countervailing policy: Minnesota's traditional willingness to enforce parties' choice of law agreements.").
92. *Id.* at 738–39 (relying on Tele-Save Merch. Co. v. Consumers Distrib. Co., 814 F.2d 1120, 1123 (6th Cir. 1987)).

Notably, in response to the *Modern Computer Systems, Inc.* case the Minnesota Legislature amended the MFA to explicitly provide that the act could not be waived through a choice-of-law provision.[93] The Nebraska Legislature has made no such amendment to the Nebraska Act.[94]

2. Annotations

Despite a choice-of-law provision designating Nebraska law in the parties' franchise agreement, the court utilized Colorado law given Colorado's greater material interest in the controversy and the fact that the franchisee did not satisfy the applicability requirements of the Nebraska Act (i.e., the franchisee did not have a "place of business" in Nebraska). *Colorado Security Consultants, LLC v. Signal 88 Franchise Group, Inc.*, 8:16cv439, 2017 WL 1047260, at *4–5 (D. Neb. Mar. 17, 2017).

Choice-of-law provisions in franchise agreements should be enforced when the parties agree to a choice-of-law provision; the contacts between the parties are relatively evenly divided between the two forums; and there is no convincing evidence that one party's bargaining strength was substantially greater than the other's. *Servicemaster Residential/Commercial Services, L.P. v. Proctor*, Bus. Franchise Guide (CCH) ¶ 12,251 (D. Neb. Oct. 31, 2001). Due to the commercial nature of a franchise agreement, Nebraska public policy does not find choice-of-law provisions in such agreements repugnant. *Servicemaster Residential/Commercial Services, L.P. v. Proctor*, Bus. Franchise Guide (CCH) ¶ 12,251 (D. Neb. Oct. 31, 2001).

Application of the Nebraska Act to a franchisee whose business is located outside of Nebraska, based on the parties' contractual choice of Nebraska law, would leave the franchisee without the remedies available under the potentially applicable state franchise act for the state in which the franchise is located. *Modern Computers Systems, Inc. v. Modern Banking Systems, Inc.*, 871 F.2d 734, 742 (8th Cir. 1989) (superseded on other grounds).

G. Remedies and Administration Action

1. Restrictive Covenants

a. Commentary

In 2016 and 2018, the Nebraska Act was substantially modified to address noncompete agreements in the franchising context and applicability of the Act when it comes to enforcing such noncompete agreements.[95]

Nebraska courts have long enforced noncompete agreements, in both the franchising context and otherwise, but only if they are reasonable. The reasonableness analysis consists of three factors, namely that the agreement or covenant: (1) is not injurious to the public; (2) is not greater than necessary to protect legitimate business interests; and (3) is not unduly harsh or oppressive on the restricted

---

93. MINN. STAT. § 80C.21 (1989) (amended by Laws 1989, c. 198, § 2 eff. May 20, 1989).
94. NEB. REV. STAT. § 87-406.
95. *Id.* §§ 87-402(9), 87-404(2).

party.[96] Nebraska courts have also consistently held that as a matter of public policy, it is not the function of the courts to reform or "blue pencil" noncompetition covenants that fail the reasonableness analysis to make them enforceable.[97]

In 2015, the Nebraska Supreme Court refused to enforce a post-term noncompetition covenant contained in a franchise agreement. In *Unlimited Opportunity, Inc. v. Waadah*, Jani-King sought to enforce a post-term noncompetition covenant against a former franchisee. Among other things, the covenant prohibited the franchisee from competing with the franchisor for one year after termination in any territory in which another Jani-King franchisee operated.[98] The court determined that because the franchisor operated on a multistate and international basis, such a restriction was tantamount to having no territorial restriction at all, which rendered the noncompetition covenant an unreasonable restraint on competition.[99] Accordingly, because under Nebraska common law courts do not reform noncompetition covenants, the noncompetition covenant was deemed invalid.[100]

The following year, in response to *Waadah*, the Nebraska Legislature deviated from Nebraska's long-held public policy by amending the Nebraska Act to allow courts and arbitrators to reform otherwise unenforceable noncompete agreements in the franchise context.[101] Specifically, section 87-404(2) was added to the Nebraska Act, which provides in relevant part:

> If restrictions in a noncompete agreement are found by an arbitrator or a court to be unreasonable in restraining competition, the arbitrator or court shall reform the terms of the noncompete agreement to the extent necessary to cause the restrictions contained therein to be reasonable and enforceable. The arbitrator or court shall then enforce the noncompete agreement against the franchisee, the guarantor, or any person with a direct or indirect beneficial interest in the franchise in accordance with the reformed terms of the noncompete agreement.[102]

Importantly, however, to reform a noncompetition agreement under the 2016 amended Act, the franchisee must have a "place of business" within the state of Nebraska and satisfy the other applicability requirements of the Nebraska

---

96. H & R Block Tax Servs., Inc. v. Circle A Enters., Inc., 269 Neb. 411, 417, 693 N.W.2d 548, 553–54 (2005).

97. 269 Neb. at 415–17, 693 N.W.2d at 552–53. *See also* Unlimited Opportunity, Inc. v. Waadah, 290 Neb. 629, 634–36, 861 N.W.2d 437, 441–42 (2015).

98. 290 Neb. at 631–32, 861 N.W.2d at 439–40.

99. 290 Neb. at 639, 861 N.W.2d at 444.

100. *Id.*

101. The term "noncompete agreement" is defined as "any agreement between a franchisor and a franchisee, a guarantor, or any person with a direct or indirect beneficial interest in the franchise that restricts the business activities in which such persons may engage during or after the term of the franchise. Noncompete agreement includes any stand-alone agreement or any covenant not to compete provision within a franchise agreement or ancillary agreement." Neb. Rev. Stat. § 87-402(9).

102. Neb. Rev. Stat. § 87-404(2) (2016).

Act, discussed previously.[103] In 2018, section 87-404(2) was further amended to state that the subsection applies to any noncompete agreement entered into by a franchisor headquartered in Nebraska, even if the franchisee's place of business is outside of Nebraska, unless otherwise agree to by the parties.[104] Furthermore, the subsection applies to any noncompete agreement entered into before, on, or after April 8, 2016, which was the effective date of the 2016 amendment.[105]

b. Annotations

The U.S. District Court for the District of Nebraska held that because the franchise in question was located outside of Nebraska, the 2016 amended Act, which allowed for reformation of unreasonable noncompetition covenants in franchise agreements, did not apply. *Colorado Security Consultants, LLC v. Signal 88 Franchise Group*, 8:16cv439, 2017 WL 1047260, at *4 n.2 (D. Neb. 2017).

Prior to the 2016 legislative changes to the Nebraska Act, which allowed court or arbitrator reformation of noncompete provisions in franchise agreements, Nebraska courts would not sever, reform, or blue pencil unenforceable noncompete agreements as a matter of public policy. *Unlimited Opportunity, Inc. v. Waadah*, 290 Neb. 629, 634–36, 861 N.W.2d 437, 441–42 (2015).

Nebraska courts enforce reasonable noncompete agreements. Reasonableness is analyzed using the following factors: (1) whether the covenant is injurious to the public; (2) whether the covenant is greater than necessary to protect the employer's legitimate business interest; and (3) whether the covenant is unduly harsh or oppressive on the party against whom it operates. *H & R Block Tax Services, Inc. v. Circle A Enterprises, Inc.*, 269 Neb. 411, 417, 693 N.W.2d 548, 553–54 (2005).

2. Damages

a. Commentary

The Nebraska Act allows franchisees "to recover damages sustained by reason of any violation of [the Act]."[106] Although there is no case law interpreting the measure of damages under the Nebraska Act, courts have interpreted similar language under the New Jersey Act. Such courts have held that if a franchisor violates the Act by improperly terminating a franchise without good cause, the franchisor is liable to the franchisee for the actual or reasonable value of the franchisee's business when the franchise is cut off.[107] The actual or reasonable value of the franchisee's business should be reduced by the net liquidating

---

103. *See* Colorado Sec. Consultants, LLC v. Signal 88 Franchise Grp., Inc., No. 8:16CV439, 2017 WL 1047260, at *4 n.2 (D. Neb. Mar. 17, 2017).
104. NEB. REV. STAT. § 87-404(2) (2018).
105. *Id.*
106. NEB. REV. STAT. § 87-409.
107. Westfield Ctr. Serv., Inc. v. Cities Serv. Oil Co., 86 N.J. 453, 465–66, 432 A.2d 48, 55 (1981). *See also* Ocean City Express Co., Inc. v. Atlas Van Lines, Inc., 194 F. Supp. 3d 314, 325 (D.N.J. 2016) (holding that damages under the New Jersey Act should be measured by the present value of lost future earnings or the present market value of the lost business, plus any actual expenses from the termination).

worth of any assets retained by the franchisee.[108] However, a franchisee who was properly terminated is not entitled to any compensation because the Act "sensibly authorizes damages only to aggrieved franchisees and does not compensate those franchisees who have lost their franchises as a result of their own neglect or misconduct[.]"[109]

b. Annotations
Not applicable.

3. Rescission

a. Commentary
Not applicable.

b. Annotations
Not applicable.

4. Injunctive Relief

a. Commentary
The Nebraska Act provides that injunctive relief is available "when appropriate."[110] This language in the Nebraska Act has not been interpreted by any court. The New Jersey Act similarly provides for injunctive relief "where appropriate."[111] Courts have interpreted the New Jersey Act broadly to allow for injunctive relief to prevent violations of the Act, to maintain the status quo during litigation, to provide a franchisee with additional time to close the franchised business, or for other equitable purpose.[112]

b. Annotations
Not applicable.

5. Control Person Liability

a. Commentary
Not applicable.

b. Annotations
Not applicable.

---

108. *Id.*
109. Dunkin' Donuts Franchised Rests., LLC v. JF-Totowa Donuts, Inc., Civ. No. 2:09CV02636, 2013 WL 5574522, at *5 (D.N.J. Oct. 9, 2013).
110. Neb. Rev. Stat. § 87-409.
111. N.J. Stat. Ann. § 56:10-10.
112. *See, e.g., Westfield,* 86 N.J. at 466–67, 432 A.2d at 55; Alboyacian v. BP Prods. N. Am., Inc., Civ. No. 9-5143, 2012 WL 3862549, at *3–4 (D.N.J. Sept. 5, 2012).

6. Attorneys' Fees

a. Commentary

The Nebraska Act provides that the prevailing party shall be entitled to "costs of the action including but not limited to reasonable attorney's fees."[113]

b. Annotations

Not applicable.

7. Limitations on Damage Waivers

a. Commentary

Not applicable.

b. Annotations

Not applicable.

8. Administrative Action

a. Commentary

Not applicable.

b. Annotations

Not applicable.

H. Dispute Resolution

1. Limitations on Franchisor's Ability to Restrict Venue

a. Commentary

Not applicable.

b. Annotations

Not applicable.

2. Limitations Period

a. Commentary

Not applicable.

b. Annotations

Not applicable.

---

113. NEB. REV. STAT. § 87-409.

New Jersey

Peter G. Siachos

I. Introduction to Statute[1]

The New Jersey Franchise Practices Act (NJFPA), N.J.S.A. sections 56:10-1 *et seq.*, is among the earliest and most franchisee-friendly state franchise protection statutes. Enacted in 1971, the statute seeks to protect franchisees who have "conscientiously striven to carry out their obligations under the franchise agreement" while simultaneously permitting "the severance of those who deliberately disregard reasonable requirements contained in their contract with the franchisor."[2] The legislature enacted the NJFPA in large part due to the perceived unfair practices of automobile manufacturers and oil companies and "to prevent arbitrary or capricious actions by the franchisor who generally has vastly greater economic power than the franchisee."[3] In the decades since the 1970s, the NJFPA's scope has broadened to include the full spectrum of franchises operating within the state.

The hallmark of the NJFPA is its stringent limitations on the right of a franchisor to terminate a franchise. The NJFPA grants a nearly indefeasible property right to the franchisee given that "once a franchise relationship begins, all that a franchisee must do is comply substantially with the terms of the agreement in return for which he receives the benefit of an 'infinite' franchise—he cannot be terminated or refused renewal."[4] The only basis for termination is "good cause" and such good cause is typically found only when a franchisee has not substantially performed its obligations under the franchise agreement.[5]

The NJFPA also contains provisions intended to prohibit "the inclusion in the contract of provisions that would relieve franchisors of liability."[6] Accordingly, the NJFPA prohibits franchisors from imposing unreasonable conditions

---

1. Thanks to my partner Jennifer A. Guidea for her extensive work on this chapter, along with our law clerks John Manos and Delaney Tyson.
2. Amerada Hess Corp. v. Quinn, 143 N.J. Super. 237, 362 A.2d 1258 (Law Div. 1976).
3. Franchise Practices Act: Hearing on A. 2063 Before the Assembly Judiciary Comm., 194th Leg., 2d Sess. 136 (1971) (Hearing on A. 2036) (Statement of Charles W. Davis, Executive Vice-President New Jersey Hotel/Motel Ass'n).
4. Dunkin' Donuts of Am., Inc. v. Middletown Donut Corp., 100 N.J. 166, 495 A.2d 66, 76 (1985).
5. N.J. STAT. ANN. § 56:10-16 to 56:10-29.
6. Kubit & Persse Assoc., Inc. v. Sun Microsystems, Inc., 146 N.J. 176, 680 A.2d 618, 628 (1996).

on their franchisees, from requiring franchisees to sign releases or other exculpatory documents as a condition of franchise establishment or renewal, and from otherwise using their superior bargaining power to the detriment of franchisees.[7] The NJFPA also imposes obligations on franchisees, including prohibiting the transfer of a franchise unless the franchisee first notifies the franchisor of such intention by written notice setting forth in any notice of intent the prospective transferee's name, address, statement of financial qualification, and business experience during the previous five years.

II. Commentary and Annotations

A. Definition of Franchise

Pursuant to the NJFPA, "franchise" means:

> a written arrangement for a definite or indefinite period, in which a person grants to another person a license to use a trade name, trade mark, service mark or related characteristics, and in which there is a community of interest in the marketing of goods or services at wholesale retail, by lease, agreement or otherwise.[8]

To constitute a franchise under the NJFPA, there must be both the grant of a license and a community of interest.[9] Further, two additional requirements must be met for a franchise to fall within the protection of the NJFPA. First, its gross sales must exceed $35,000 in the 12 months prior to initiation of the lawsuit and more than 20 percent of gross sales must derive from the franchise. Further, the franchisee must contemplate or maintain a physical place of business in New Jersey.[10]

Oral agreements or arrangements are insufficient to establish a franchise relationship. However, under certain circumstances, discussed later, a franchise relationship may be established through the parties' course of conduct, even in the absence of a written agreement.[11] "Prospective franchisees" have no standing to sue under the NJFPA.[12]

---

7. While the NJFPA does primarily impose obligations on franchisors for the protection of franchisees, it should be noted that the act does, on occasion, impose obligations on franchisees as well. For example, the act restricts the ability of a franchisee to transfer, assign, or sell its franchise without the franchisor's approval, imposing a notice and approval requirement on the franchisee for such transfers.

8. N.J. STAT. ANN. § 56:10-3(a).

9. Cassidy Podell Lynch, Inc. v. SnyderGeneral Corp., 944 F.2d 1131 (3d Cir. 1991).

10. N.J. STAT. ANN. § 56:10-3(a), 4(a).

11. Finlay & Assoc., Inc. v. Borg-Warner Corp., 146 N.J. Super. 210, 369 A.2d 541, 546 (Law Div. 1976), aff'd on other grounds, 155 N.J. Super 331 (App. Div. 1978); see also Am. Bus. Interiors, Inc. v. Haworth, Inc., 798 F. 2d 1135, 1140 n.3 (8th Cir. 1986) (noting that NJFPA does not include oral arrangements); Fanizzi v. Exxon Co., 572 F. Supp. 716 (D.N.J. 1983) (NJFPA requires a written contract for the creation of a franchise).

12. Tynan v. Gen. Motors Corp., 428 N.J. Super. 654 (App. Div. 1991).

In *Atlantic City Coin & Slot Services Co. v. IGT*, the district court stated that the elements of a franchise under NJFPA are "a community of interest between the franchisor and franchisee; the franchisor's grant of a license to the franchisee; and the parties contemplation that the franchisee would maintain a place of business in New Jersey."[13] In 2018, the district court again affirmed these elements in *Lawmen Supply Co. of New Jersey, Inc. v. Glock Inc.*, holding that a franchise exists and NJFPA applies if the following criteria are met: (1) there is a community of interest between the franchisor and franchisee; (2) the franchisor granted a license to the franchisee; and (3) the parties contemplated that the franchisee would maintain a place of business in New Jersey.[14]

In applying these elements, the court in *Windsor Card Shops, Inc. v. Hallmark Cards Inc.* held that the plaintiff could not state a claim under the NJFPA because it failed to satisfy all of the section 56:10-4(a) requirements.[15] Similarly, in *LLC, B-Jays USA, Inc. v. Red Wing Shoe Co., Inc.* and *Bella & Rosie Rock, LLV v. We Rock the Spectrum, LLC*, the district court held that all elements set forth in NJFPA section 56:10-4(a) must be met for a franchise to fall within the statute's purview.[16]

The Third Circuit held in *Cassidy Podell Lynch, Inc. v. SnyderGeneral Corp.* that the NJFPA did not apply because although distributor had been granted a license, there was no community of interest.[17] Similarly, the court in *Neptune T.V. & Appliance Service, Inc. v. Litton Microwave Cooking Products Division, Litton Systems, Inc.* held that a licensed service center was not a franchisee even though it satisfied the license requirement because it did not satisfy the NJFPA's community of interest requirement.[18] Additionally, in *Achieve 24 Fitness Limited Liability Co., v. Alloy Personal Training Solutions, LLC* the court found that even if the NJFPA's definitional criteria of a license and community of interest are met, the NJFPA does not apply unless the franchise meets the monetary threshold and place of business requirements.[19] Similarly, in *APFA, Inc. v. UATP Management* the court held that because the complaint did not allege any information as to the monetary threshold or location of the franchisees, plaintiff could not state a claim under the NJFPA.[20]

Finally, in *Colt Industries, Inc. v. Fidelco Pump & Compressor Corp.* the district court found that the relationship and contact between the parties was insufficient to create a franchise, holding that the fact that two parties share in the profits realized from the sale of a product to the ultimate consumer is

---

13. Atl. City Coin & Slot Serv. Co., Inc. v. IGT, 14 F. Supp. 2d 644 (D.N.J. 1988).
14. Lawmen Supply Co. of N.J., Inc. v. Glock, Inc., 330 F. Supp. 3d 1020 (D.N.J. 2018).
15. Windsor Card Shops, Inc. v. Hallmark Cards, Inc., 957 F. Supp. 562, 569 n.11 (D.N.J. 1997).
16. B-Jays USA, Inc. v. Red Wing Shoe Co., 2015 WL 5896151, at *4 (D.N.J. Oct. 6, 2015); Bella & Rosie Rock, LLC v. We Rock the Spectrum, LLC, 2018 WL 844398 (D.N.J. Feb. 13, 2008).
17. Cassidy Podell Lynch, Inc. v. SnyderGeneral Corp., 944 F.2d 1131 (3d Cir. 1991).
18. Neptune T.V. & Appliance Serv., Inc. v. Litton Microwave Cooking Prod. Dev., 190 N.J. Super. 153, 462 A.2d 595 (App. Div. 1983).
19. Achieve 24 Fitness LLC v. Alloy Personal Training Solutions, LLC, 2023 WL 2264129, *8 (D.N.J. Feb. 28, 2023).
20. APFA, Inc. v. UATP Mgmt., 2021 WL 323474, at * 3 (D.N.J. Jan. 31, 2021).

insufficient to create a franchise under the NJFPA.[21] Additionally, the court in *Finlay & Associates, Inc. v. Borg-Warner Corp.* held that without more, a sale or distribution agreement does not constitute a franchise arrangement.[22]

1. Trademark Element

a. Commentary

As is typically the case, under the NJFPA the "hallmark of the franchise relationship is the use of another's trade name in such a manner as to create a reasonable belief on the part of the consuming public that there is a connection between the trade name licensor and licensee by which the licensor vouches, as it were, for the activity of the licensee in respect of the subject of the trade name."[23] Compared to the law in most non-franchise contexts, the NJFPA takes a much narrower view of what constitutes "license to use" a trademark—here, it implies a proprietary interest in a trademark and the authority to use the mark as one's own.[24] This requires more than just the display of the franchisor's marks; in addition, the franchisee must benefit from the goodwill associated with the franchisor's trade name.[25]

This characterization of license to use can create an "inadvertent franchise" where a license may be found even in the absence of a formal contract between the parties. Even where there is a written agreement between the parties, the court must examine their overall relationship to determine whether a license exists.[26] Elements suggesting an implied grant of a license are exclusivity of the licensee's relationship to the licensor and the obligation to promote the mark itself, rather than merely promoting the goods or services being offered.[27]

b. Annotations

In *Lawmen Supply Co.*, the district court interpreted the NJFPA to contemplate a license under which "the franchisee wraps himself with the trade name of the franchisor and relies on the franchisor's goodwill to induce the public to buy."[28] The Third Circuit found this determination of whether a license had been granted to be a question of fact for the jury in *Cassidy Podell Lynch* where the manufacturer (1) designated the sales representative as authorized seller and repair center for its climate control systems; (2) required representative to maintain facilities and equipment, perform services in workmanlike manner,

---

21. Colt Indus., Inc. v. Fidelco Pump & Compressor Corp., 700 F. Supp. 1330 (D.N.J. 1987).
22. Finlay & Assoc., Inc. v. Borg-Warner Corp., 146 N.J. Super. 210, 369 A.2d 541 (Law Div. 1976).
23. Instructional Sys., Inc. v. Comput. Curriculum Corp., 130 N.J. 324, 352–53, 614 A.2d 124, 139 (1992) (internal quotations omitted); *see also* Lawmen Supply Co. of N.J., Inc. v. Glock, Inc., 330 F. Supp. 3d 1020 (D.N.J. 2018) (quoting Neptune T.V. & Appliance Serv., Inc., 190 N.J. Super. 153, 462 A.2d 595 (App. Div. 1983)).
24. *Finlay & Assoc., Inc.*, 369 A.2d at 546.
25. Cooper Distrib. Co. v. Amana Refrigeration, Inc., 63 F.3d 262, 272–73 (3d Cir. 1995).
26. *Neptune TV & Appliance Serv., Inc.*, 462 A.2d at 599.
27. *Cooper Distrib. Co.*, 63 F.3d at 272–73.
28. *Lawmen Supply Co.*, 330 F. Supp. 3d at 1034.

and follow detailed inspection, repair, and invoicing procedures; (3) allowed representative to maintain signs bearing manufacturer's trade name at its repair facility; and, (4) allowed representative's servicemen to wear uniforms bearing its trade name and to drive trucks with decals provided by manufacturer.[29]

In several cases, New Jersey courts have held that use of the manufacturer's name, insignia, or mark, without more, does not create a license to use under the NJFPA.[30] For example, in *Finlay & Assoc., Inc.*, the court held that simply selling goods or distributing materials bearing a manufacturer's name or trade mark is insufficient to create a license to use trademarks; there must also be a "holding out to the public of some special relationship or connection," such as use of manufacturer's name in the business title of the franchisee.[31] Similarly, in *Cooper Distributing Co., Inc. v. Amana Refrigeration, Inc.*, the court stated that mere use of a manufacturer's insignia by a distributor was not, by itself, sufficient to satisfy the "license to use" required by the NJFPA.[32] However, coupled with other facts, such as the length of the relationship between the manufacturer and distributor, the display of the manufacturer's sign in the distributor's showroom, the distributor's employees wearing the manufacturer's uniforms, and the exclusivity of the distributor in a four-state territory for over 30 years, the distributor established the requisite license.[33] Finally, the court in *Neptune T.V. & Appliance Services, Inc.* held that an independent contractor's use of another's trade name in the contractor's own advertising did not, by itself, create a license under the NJFPA—but such a license was found where the manufacturer "gave its imprimatur" to a service center with regard to its product and induced the consuming public to expect a quality-controlled service endorsed by the manufacturer.[34]

The extent to which a special relationship can be perceived between a manufacturer and distributor has also been considered in determining whether a license exists. In *Instructional Systems, Inc. v. Computer Curriculum Corp.*, the court found that a license existed under NJFPA where an exclusive regional distributor had exclusive rights to distribute a producer's products, training of customers on the products occurred through the distribution, and "any purchaser could have reasonably perceived a special relationship between the distributor and the producer."[35] In contrast, the court in *Liberty Sales Associates, Inc. v. Dow Corning Corp.*, found that although a distributor may have created some good will for itself and the manufacturer, there was no license granted where the agreement required the distributor to promote the products as distinct from the manufacturer's name or trademark.[36]

---

29. Cassidy Podell Lynch, Inc. v. SnyderGeneral Corp., 944 F.2d 1131 (3d Cir. 1991).
30. *See, e.g.*, Finlay & Assoc., Inc., 146 N.J. Super. 210, 369 A.2d 541 (Law Div. 1976); *Cooper Distrib. Co.*, 63 F.3d at 272–73; *Neptune T.V. & Appliance Serv., Inc.*, 190 N.J. Super. at 164.
31. *Finlay & Assoc., Inc.*, 146 N.J. Super. 210.
32. *Cooper Distrib. Co., Inc.*, 63 F.3d at 272–73.
33. *Id.*
34. *Neptune T.V. & Appliance Serv., Inc.*, 190 N.J. Super. at 164.
35. Instructional Sys., Inc. v. Comput. Curriculum Corp., 130 N.J. 324, 614 A.2d 124 (1993).
36. Liberty Sales Assoc., Inc. v. Dow Corning Corp., 816 F. Supp. 1004 (D.N.J. 1993).

2. Franchise Fee Element

a. Commentary
Not applicable.

b. Annotations
Not appliable.

3. Community of Interest; Significant Degree of Control; Joint Marketing Plan

a. Commentary

The NJFPA does not define the term "community of interest." However, the New Jersey Supreme Court has held that community of interest exists where "the terms of the agreement between the parties or the nature of the franchise business requires the licensee, in the interest of the licensed business's success, to make a substantial investment in goods or skills that will be of minimal utility outside the franchise."[37] The key to finding community of interest is that the franchisee's investment must be "substantially franchise specific" and not generally applicable to goods or services that could be promoted outside the franchise system. Further, the franchisee must have been required to make these investments by the parties' agreement or the nature of the business.[38]

While "community of interest" is a broad and "elastic" concept, it does not include an arrangement lacking "both the symbiotic character of a true franchise arrangement and the consequent vulnerability of the alleged franchisee to an unconscionable loss of his tangible and intangible equities."[39] Most significantly, there must be a high degree of interdependence between the franchisee and the franchisor given that once a franchisee has made a significant franchise-specific investment, it loses virtually all of its bargaining power. There is a potential for abuse by the franchisor when "the reputation and good will of the network, created primarily by the efforts of each of the individual franchisees passes back to the franchisor without compensation to the franchisee."[40] Thus, community of interest requires more than the fact that the parties share in profits generated by sale of the franchisor's goods or services.[41]

Community of interest may be established by the economic dependence of the franchisee upon the franchisor, as demonstrated by a high percentage of the franchisee's sales deriving from the franchisor's product.[42] Additionally, the substantial investment required to find a community of interest may include investments in intangible assets, such as business goodwill associated with the

---

37. *Instructional Sys., Inc.*, 614 A.2d at 141.
38. Cooper Distrib. Co. v. Amana Refrigeration, Inc., 63 F.3d 262, 269 (3d Cir. 1995).
39. *Neptune TV & Appliance Serv., Inc.*, 190 N.J. Super. at 165.
40. *Id.* at 164.
41. Colt Indus. Inc. v. Fidelco Pump & Compressor Corp., 844 F.2d 117, 120 (3d Cir. 1988).
42. Atl. Cty. Coin & Slot Servs. Co., v. IGT, 14 F. Supp. 2d 644, 663 (D.N.J. 1998) (community of interest found where franchisee derived 76 percent of its revenue from sales of franchisor's product); *Instructional Sys.*, 130 N.J. at 365 (community of interest demonstrated where 97 percent of franchisee's sales came from sale of the franchisor's products).

franchisor's name. However, as with tangible assets, such goodwill must be useful to the franchisee only in the context of its relationship to the franchisor.[43]

b. Annotations

The Third Circuit held in *Cooper Distributing, Inc.* that the "community of interest" required by NJFPA was satisfied where (1) wholesale distribution was required to make franchise-specific investments; (2) nature of business required distributor to acquire manufacturer-specific knowledge, since without such knowledge, it would have been unable to educate retail dealers about manufacturer's productions; and (3) distributor was required to implement marketing strategies that were dictated by the manufacturer and designed to breach brand goodwill.[44] In *Lawmen Supply Co. of New Jersey, Inc.*, the distributor adequately alleged a community of interest with a firearm manufacturer where it alleged that sales pursuant to the distribution agreement constituted over 21 percent of its overall business, it had exclusively distributed the manufacturer's pistols for at least four years, and the distribution agreement required the distributor to use best efforts to market manufacturer's products.[45] However, in *Colt Industries Inc. v. Fidelco Pump & Compressor Corp.*, the court held that even where manufacturer granted distributor a trademark license, no franchise was created because there was no community of interest, as the parties relationship was cooperative and not based on interdependency or control.[46]

The extent to which the franchisee has invested in the franchise, along with the type of investment, are also considered as part of the community of interest analysis. In *Atlantic City Coin & Slot Services Co.*, the court held that when the terms of the agreement between the parties or the nature of the franchise business requires the licensee, "in the interest of the licensed business's success, to make a substantial investment in goods and services that will be of minimal utility outside the franchise," a community of interest exists.[47] The court concluded that community of interest existed where exclusive distributor of slot machines established that it made numerous franchise-specific investments and was subject to manufacturer's competitive restraints.[48] In contrast, the Third Circuit, in *Cassey Podell Lynch, Inc.*, found that the investment was not franchise specific and thus there was no community of interest where the representative obtained knowledge of an air-conditioning business that could be used to sell and repair other brands of heating and refrigeration equipment.[49] Similarly, in *New Jersey America, Inc. v. Allied Corp.*, the court found that community of interest did not exist because the distributor dealt with many brake manufacturers and there was no requirement that it undertake substantial specific investments

---

43. *Instructional Sys.*, 614 A2d at 141.
44. Cooper Distrib., Co. v. Amana Refrigeration, Inc., 63 F.3d 262 (3d Cir. 1995).
45. Lawmen Supply Co. of N.J. v. Glock, Inv., 330 F. Supp. 3d 1020 (D.N.J. 2018).
46. *Colt Indus. Inc.*, 844 F.2d 117.
47. *Atl. Cty.*, 14 F. Supp. 2d 644.
48. *Id.*
49. Cassidy Podell Lynch, Inc. v. SnyderGeneral Corp., 944 F.2d 1131 (3d Cir. 1991).

in manufacturer's products.[50] Finally, in *Boyle v. Vanguard Car Rental USA, Inc.*, the court found that the investment of time and effort in developing franchise-specific goodwill can constitute a sufficient investment to find community of interest. The court noted that "[d]evelopment of customer goodwill can be a franchise-specific investment sufficient to find a community of interest," and held that the putative franchisee's allegations that she invested time and effort establishing a customer base for the franchisee were sufficient for a finding of community of interest under the NJFPA.[51]

The percentage of revenue that a franchisee derives from the sale of the franchisor's products is also an important factor in the community of interest analysis. In *Neptune T.V. & Appliance Service, Inc.* the court found that no community of interest existed where the purported franchisee derived only 38 percent of its revenue from sale of franchisor's products.[52] Similarly, in *Orologio of Short Hills, Inc. v. The Swatch Group (U.S.), Inc.*, the Third Circuit found that there was no community of interest where the retailer obtained watches from another supplier in addition to brand owner, it was not economically dependent on brand owner as only 25 percent of its revenue derived from sale of brand owner's watches, the retailer made no specific investment in marketing and advertising of brand owner's watches, and there was no significant level of control exerted by brand owner over retailer.[53]

B. Scope and Jurisdiction

1. Commentary

a. Place of Business Within New Jersey

The NJFPA applies only where the parties contemplated, or the franchisor required, that the franchisee maintain a "place of business" in New Jersey.[54] The NJFPA defines "place of business" as "a fixed geographical location at which the franchisee displays for sale and sell's the franchisor's goods or offers for sale and sells the franchisor's services." The statute explicitly excludes from the definition, a business's office, warehouse, place of storage, residence, or vehicle.[55] With regard to persons "who do not make a majority of their sales directly to consumers, 'place of business' means 'a fixed geographical location at which the franchisee displays for sale and sells the franchisor's goods or offers for sale and sells the franchisor's services, or an office or a warehouse from which franchisee personnel visit or call upon customers or from which the franchisor's goods are delivered to customers.'"

---

50. N.J. Am., Inc. v. Allied Corp., 875 F.2d 58 (3d Cir. 1989).
51. Boyle v. Vanguard Car Rental USA, Inc., 2009 WL 3208310 (D.N.J. Sept. 30, 2009).
52. Neptune T.V. & Appliance Serv., Inc. v. Litton Microwave Cooking Prods. Div., 190 N.J. Super. 153 (App. Div. 1983).
53. Orologio of Short Hills, Inc. v. The Swatch Group (U.S.), Inc., 653 Fed. App'x 134 (3d Cir. 2016).
54. N.J. STAT. ANN. § 56:10-3(a), 4(a).
55. *Id.* § 56:10-3(f).

There is some authority suggesting that this requirement is met where the parties *contemplated* that the franchisee would have a place of business in New Jersey, even if such plans never came to fruition.[56] These courts have explained that if the franchisor *required* a place of business in New Jersey, that would be an express term of the parties' written agreement. Otherwise the question is whether the parties "reasonably anticipated" that the franchisee would establish a place of business in New Jersey.[57]

b. Annotations

In *Ocean City Express Co., Inc. v. Atlas Van Lines, Inc.*, the court held that complaint properly alleged that agent had a "place of business" within New Jersey where it alleged that its New Jersey place of business was (1) the hub of its day-to-day business and marketing operations; (2) the location of all sales personnel; (3) the retail address identified in advertisements directed at its customers; and (4) the location at which it displayed and distributed carrier's signage.[58] The court in *Cassidy Podell Lynch* held that in order for a New Jersey place of business to be "contemplated" within the meaning of the NJFPA, the franchisee must produce evidence sufficient to show that the parties "had in mind the type of business facility the statute defines, either initially or later as their relationship evolved" and not simply that it was "possible" that the franchisee would establish such a facility.[59] In *Strassle v. Bimbo Foods Bakeries Distribution, Inc.*, the court found that the distribution agreement indicated that the parties contemplated establishment of a place of business in New Jersey where it included language suggesting that sales to customers could be made at distributor's facility.[60] Additionally, the court in *Carlo C. Gelardi Corp. v. Miller Brewing Co.* noted that the NJFPA explicitly states that it applies to franchisee wholesalers, and that place of business requirement is satisfied if the wholesaler-franchisee's place of business reflects "normal characteristics of a wholesale business."[61]

New Jersey courts have held that in order to be a place of business, the location must in some way operate as a sales facility, excluding locations operating solely as warehouses or places of solicitation. In *Fischer Thompson Beverages, Inc. v. Energy Brands, Inc.*, the court found that the place of business requirement was not satisfied where Fischer Thompson maintained a warehouse in New Jersey but did not show that selling was a "major activity" at the facility—onsite sales activity was "miniscule," as only 17 out of over 1,000 customers visited the facility during the preceding three years and product was stored but

---

56. *See* Strassle v. Bimbo Foods Bakeries Distrib., Inc., 2013 WL 1007289, at *3 (D.N.J. Mar. 13, 2013).
57. Cassidy Podell Lynch, Inc. v. SnyderGeneral Corp., 944 F.2d 1131, 1145 (3d Cir. 1991) ([T]he term "contemplates" is construed to mean "consideration of a fixed business location for the sale of the franchisor's products.").
58. Ocean City Exp. Co., Inc. v. Atlas Van Lines, Inc., 46 F. Supp. 3d 503 (D.N.J. 2014).
59. *Cassidy Podell Lynch*, 944 F.2d 1131.
60. *Strassle*, 2013 WL 1007289.
61. Carlo C. Gelardi Corp. v. Miller Brewing Co., 421 F. Supp. 233 (D.N.J. 1976).

not displayed at the facility.[62] Similarly, in *Liberty Sales Associates, Inc.*, the court held that the home of distributor's president was not a "place of business" even though president used a home office for telephone sales calls because the house was essentially an office and warehouse for customer orders.[63] In *Lithuanian Commerce Corp. Ltd. v. Sara Lee Hosiery*, the "place of business" requirement was not established where distributor maintained a New Jersey office to store product distributed in Lithuania, visited a New Jersey location on one occasion to view product samples, and was not authorized to do business in New Jersey.[64] Likewise, in *Watchung Spring Water Co., Inc. v. Nestle Waters North America, Inc.*, the distributor failed to establish a place of business in New Jersey because the distribution agreement required only that the distributor maintain a warehouse and the New Jersey facility is primarily used as a warehouse.[65] In the same vein, the court in *Lawmen Supply Co. of New Jersey, Inc.* found the distributor failed to allege that selling constituted a major activity at its place of business and therefore failed to state a claim under the NJFPA, but, allowed the distributor to amend the complaint to add facts establishing that the New Jersey location was a sales facility and not merely a distribution site.[66] Additionally, the court in *Greco Steam Cleaning Inc. v. Associated Dry Goods Corp.* held that the NJFPA's requirement of a "fixed geographic location where franchisee both offers for sale and sells franchisor's goods or services" does not include locations used for solicitation only.[67] However, in *Cooper Distributing Co., Inc.*, the distributor's showroom/marketing center constituted a place of business where it regularly used this facility for activities, such as product demonstration and inspection, that were "an integral part of the sales process" despite the fact that no sales were ever consummated there.[68] Similarly, in *Instructional Systems, Inc.*, the "place of business" requirement was satisfied where distributor maintained a marketing facility in New Jersey where its customers could inspect its products and receive sales demonstrations of the product's operation.[69]

2. Monetary Threshold

a. Commentary

The NJFPA applies only to franchises where gross sales stemming from the franchise agreement exceeded $35,000 in the 12 months preceding initiation of the lawsuits and where more than 20 percent of the gross sales are intended to

---

62. Fischer Thompson Beverages, Inc. v. Energy Brands, Inc., 2007 WL 3349746 (D.N.J. Nov. 9, 2007).
63. Liberty Sales Assoc., Inc. v. Dow Corning Corp., 816 F. Supp. 1004 (D.N.J. 1993).
64. Lithuanian Commerce Corp. Ltd. v. Sara Lee Hosiery, 23 F. Supp. 2d 509 (D.N.J. 1998).
65. Watchung Spring Water Co., Inc. v. Nestle Waters N. Am., Inc., 588 Fed. App'x 197 (3d Cir. 2014).
66. Lawmen Supply Co. of N.J. v. Glock, Inc., 330 F. Supp. 3d 1020 (D.N.J. 2018).
67. Greco Steam Cleaning Inc. v. Associated Dry Goods Corp., 257 N.J. Super. 594, 608 A.2d 1010 (Law Div. 1992).
68. Cooper Distrib. Co. v. Amana Refrigeration, Inc., 63 F.3d 262 (3d Cir. 1995).
69. Instructional Sys., Inc. v. Comput. Curriculum Corp., 130 N.J. 324, 614 A.2d 124 (1992).

be or are derived from the franchise. Failure to satisfy these requirements will result in dismissal of an NJFPA claim.[70]

b. Annotations

In *Tynan v. General Motors Corp.*, the court stated that the purpose of the $35,000 requirement was intended "to restrict the application of the Act to franchises that [are] sufficiently consequential to the franchisee to merit protection."[71] The court in *B-Jays USA, Inc. v. Red Wing Shoe Co.* held that this $35,000 threshold applies to gross sales between franchisor and franchisee, not franchisee's total gross sales.[72] In *Boyle v. Vanguard Car Rental USA, Inc.*, the court held that the franchisee met the $35,000 threshold, and thus could invoke application of the NJFPA, where her sole form of revenue was comprised of commissions paid by the franchisor.[73] On the other hand, in *Dunkin' Donuts of America, Inc. v. Middletown Donut Corp.*, the NJFPA did not apply where it was undisputed that franchisee's gross sales of product did not meet the $35,000 threshold during the 12-month period prior to institution of the lawsuit.[74] Similarly, in *Achieve 24 Fitness Limited Liability Co. v. Alloy Personal Training Solutions*, the court dismissed the NJFPA claim where the franchisee failed to allege gross sales stemming from the franchise agreement that exceeded $35,000 in the 12 months preceding initiation of the action, and that more than 20 percent of gross sales came from the franchise relationship.[75] Additionally, the court in *Windsor Card Shops, Inc.* held that where alleged franchisee had stopped selling the alleged franchisor's products for over 12 months before the action was initiated, the NJFPA did not apply because its gross sales over the last 12 months were zero.[76]

In *Ocean City Express Co.*, the court held that the inclusion of the phrase "intended to be" in the NJFPA's 20 percent threshold for gross revenue, "compels, on its face, an inquiry into the scope of intended revenues, in addition to actual revenues."[77] However, the court in *Bella and Rose Rock LLC* found no authority to support franchisee's claim that projected gross sales are sufficient to meet the $35,000 threshold and thus did not apply the NJFPA.[78] Additionally, in *New Jersey American*, the court held that "by excluding from the Act's reach a franchisee that derives 20% or less of gross sales from its franchisor, [the Act] implies that a firm may be a franchisee even if only 21% of its gross sales are

---

70. N.J. STAT. ANN. § 56:10-4(a)(2); Am. Estates, Inc. v. Marietta Cellars, Inc., 2011 WL 1560923, at *3 (D.N.J. Feb. 25, 2011).
71. Tynan v. Gen. Motors Corp., 127 N.J. 269, 270, 604 A.2d 99 (1992) (citing partial dissent in Tynan v. Gen. Motors Corp., 248 N.J. Super. 654, 591 A.2d 1024 (App. Div. 1991), *judgment rev'd in part*, 127 N.J. 269, 604 A.2d 99 (1992)).
72. B-Jays USA, Inc. v. Red Wing Shoe Co., 2015 WL 5896151 (D.N.J. Oct. 6, 2015).
73. Boyle v. Vanguard Car Rental USA, Inc., 2009 WL 3208310, at *5 (D.N.J. Sept. 30, 2009).
74. Dunkin' Donuts of Am., Inc. v. Middletown Donut Corp., 100 N.J. 166 (1985).
75. Achieve 24 Fitness Ltd. Liab. Co. v. Alloy Pers. Training Sols., LLC, 2023 WL 2264129, at *8 (D.N.J. Feb. 28, 2023).
76. Windsor Card Shops, Inc. v. Hallmark Cards, Inc., 957 F. Supp. 562 (D.N.J. 1997).
77. Ocean City Express Co. v. Atlas Van Lines, Inc., 194 F. Supp. 3d 314 (D.N.J. 2016).
78. Bella & Rose Rock LLC v. We Rock the Spectrum, LLC, 2018 WL 844398 (D.N.J. Feb. 13, 2018).

derived from the franchisor."[79] Finally, in *Engines, Inc. v. MAN Engines & Components, Inc.*, the court stated that the fact that franchisee also sold competitors' products was irrelevant where sale of franchisor's product exceeds the 20 percent threshold for gross sales.[80]

C. Termination
1. What Constitutes Termination or Cancellation
a. Commentary
Under the NJFPA, termination by the franchisor constitutes a violation of the NJFPA unless the termination is for good cause and the applicable notice requirements are met.[81] Termination in this context refers to both express and constructive termination.[82] Express termination must be via written communication setting forth the reasons for the termination (discussed later in connection with notice requirements).

The NJFPA expressly contemplates constructive termination, providing that "a franchisor is not permitted to accomplish a termination by indirect means that it would not be permitted to accomplish by direct means."[83] The inclusion of constructive termination in the NJFPA's provisions was intended to ensure that franchisors do not circumvent the "good cause" requirement for direct termination by engaging in "a course of conduct geared to forcing out [the franchisee]." While the franchisee need not formally withdraw from the franchise arrangement to bring a claim for constructive termination,[84] there can be no NJFPA claim for constructive termination where the franchise is still in operation."[85] Notably, the courts have repeatedly held that constructive termination requires something more than a change in the franchisor's business model that negatively impacts the franchisee's operations or revenue—there must be evidence that the franchisor had some intent to drive the franchisee completely out of business.

b. Annotations
In *Maintainco, Inc. v. Mitsubishi Caterpillar Forklift America, Inc.*, the court found that a forklift manufacturer constructively terminated a forklift dealership in violation of the NJFPA where manufacturer (1) attempted to establish a second dealer as the only viable dealer in the territory; (2) let second dealer begin operating on the strength of just a letter agreement; (3) blanketed existing dealership's

---

79. N.J. Am., Inc. v. Allied Corp., 875 F.2d 58 (3d Cir. 1989).
80. Engines, Inc. v. MAN Engines & Components, Inc., 2010 WL 3021871 (D.N.J. July 29, 2010).
81. N.J. STAT. ANN. § 56:10-5 ("It shall be a violation of this act for a franchisor to terminate . . . without good cause. For the purposes of this act, good cause . . . shall be limited to failure by the franchisee to substantially comply with those requirements imposed upon him by the franchise.").
82. Maintainco, Inc. v. Mitsubishi Caterpillar Forklift Am., Inc., 408 N.J. Super. 461, 975 A.2d 510 (App. Div. 2009).
83. Carlo C. Gelardi Corp. v. Miller Brewing Co., 502 F. Supp. 637 (D.N.J. 1980).
84. *Id.*
85. Pai v. DRX Urgent Care LLC, 2014 WL 837158, at *13 (D.N.J. Mar. 4, 2014) (citing Mac's Shell Serv., Inc. v. Shell Oil Prods. Co., 559 U.S. 175 (2010) (holding that "a claim for constructive termination by a franchisee requires that a franchise no longer be in operation")).

territory with the message that second dealer was its favored dealer; (4) provided discounts, rebates, and other subsidies that let second dealer undercut existing dealership's prices; and (5) let second dealer buy forklifts without paying for them and even allowed the second dealer to steal forklifts from manufacturer.[86] The court also found that the manufacturer developed a platform strategy in response to realization that New Jersey law forbade termination of a dealer with satisfactory performance, proposed various arrangements to many other dealers, pursued the platform strategy without the existing dealership for years with little progress until admitting it was not feasible, and told the existing dealership in a letter that it would sell parts to dealership for only one year after appointing new dealer.[87] On these facts, the court found there to be constructive termination in violation of the NJFPA.[88]

On the other hand, the court in *Fabbro v. DRX Urgent Care, LLC* found no constructive termination where, although franchisor made changes to their business model that harmed franchisees, there were no allegations "from which to reasonably infer that franchisor wanted to terminate the franchises, and in fact, franchisees remained in good standing."[89] Similarly, in *Naik v. 7-Eleven, Inc.*, despite being harmed by franchisor's requirements, including control over "all aesthetic aspects of their stores, including radio volume, television channel and level of heat and air conditioning, which causes [franchisees] to lose customers," the court found there was no claim for constructive termination where the franchisees were still operating and gaining a profit from their stores.[90] Likewise, the court in *SAT Agiyar, LLC v. 7-Eleven, Inc.* held that the claim for constructive termination failed as a matter of law because, although franchisee alleged it was harmed by franchisor's alteration of its profit distribution scheme, franchisee's store remained open and in business.[91] Finally, in *Pai v. DRK Urgent Care LLC*, there was no finding of constructive termination where there was no allegation regarding any threat by franchisor to termination franchise or force franchisee to resign and the franchisee remained in business and earned enough revenue to cover costs and earn a small profit.[92]

2. Restrictions on Termination or Cancellation

a. Commentary

The NJFPA's restrictions on termination are stringent. The act has essentially eliminated the ability of a franchisor to terminate a franchise agreement at will, instead requiring "good cause" for termination. In turn, the only grounds for "good cause" is the franchisee's failure to substantially comply with the terms of the franchise agreement.[93] Substantial compliance "is something less than

---

86. *Maintainco, Inc.*, 408 N.J. Super. 461, 975 A.2d 510 (App. Div. 2009).
87. *Id.*
88. *Id.*
89. Fabbro v. DRX Urgent Care, LLC, 616 Fed. App'x 485, 490 (3d Cir. 2015).
90. Naik v. 7-Eleven, Inc., 2014 WL 3844792 (D.N.J. Aug. 5, 2014).
91. SAT Agiyar, LLC v. 7-Eleven, Inc., 2021 WL 5205941 (D.N.J. Nov. 8, 2021).
92. Pai v. DRK Urgent Care LLC, 2014 WL 837158 (D.N.J. Mar. 4, 2014).
93. N.J. STAT. ANN. § 56:10:5.

absolute adherence to every nuanced term of an agreement, but, at a minimum, requires that the franchisee refrain from acting in direct defiance of a term of the franchise agreement."[94]

Even if the franchisor "acts in good faith and for a bona fide reason," it is a violation of the NJFPA to terminate the franchise agreement on any basis other than lack of substantial compliance.[95] Additionally, even if a franchise agreement provides for termination "at will," the NJFPA will supersede that provision and require a showing of good cause for termination.[96]

Litigants have turned to a variety of preemption arguments in an attempt to avoid the restrictive termination provisions of the NJFPA. These attempts have been largely unsuccessful, as courts have found that the NJFPA is not preempted by the Commerce Clause, the Federal Aviation Administrative Authorization Act (FAAAA), the Lanham Act, or the Federal Automobile Dealers' Day in Court Act, 15 U.S.C.A. §§ 1221–1225.[97]

b. Annotations

In *Maintainco, Inc.*, the court held that the NJFPA requirement of good cause prohibits a franchisor from terminating a franchisee agreement, even for sound and nondiscriminatory business reasons, absent a substantial failure of franchisee compliance.[98] The court held in *Instructional Systems, Inc.* that "good cause" does not include bona fide business reasons for discontinuing the franchise relationship—if the franchisee was in substantial compliance with its obligations,

---

94. Maple Shade Motor Corp. v. Kia Motors of Am., Inc., 384 F. Supp. 2d 770 (D.N.J. 2005), *aff'd*, 260 Fed. App'x 517 (3d Cir. Jan. 11, 2008).
95. Simmons v. Gen. Motors Corp., 180 N.J. Super. 522 (App. Div. 1981).
96. N.J. Am., Inc. v. Allied Corp., 875 F.2d 58 (3d Cir. 1989).
97. Gen. Motors Corp. v. Gallo GMC Truck Sales, Inc., 711 F. Supp. 810 (D.N.J. 1989) (NJFPA did not conflict with Commerce Clause because there was only an incidental burden on interstate commerce if franchisee was allowed to recover monetary damages for manufacturer's good faith cancellation of the franchise); Westfield Centre Serv., Inc. v. Cities Serv. Oil Co., 158 N.J. Super. 455, 386 A.2d 448 (1978) (requirement that a franchisor compensate a franchisee for the value of the franchise when termination is made in compliance with the parties' agreement and in good faith does not violate constitutional due process, "as the economic effect of compensating the franchisee for the reasonable value of its business when balanced against the evil that the legislature sought to eliminate is a reasonable accommodation of the rights of the franchisor and the general public in franchise arrangements"); Ocean City Exp. Co., Inc. v. Atlas Van Lines, Inc., 46 F. Supp. 3d 503 (D.N.J. 2014) (claim that motor carrier improperly terminated its agent in violation of the NJFPA was not preempted by the Federal Aviation Administration Authorization Act (FAAAA) where application of the NJFPA "would not significantly impact rates, routes, or services of carrier with respect to transportation of property, given that it merely erected procedural mechanism to protect franchisees from terminations that occurred at franchisors' convenience and expressly preserved franchisors' autonomy to terminate franchise agreements under certain conditions"); *Gen. Motors Corp.*, 711 F. Supp. 810 (NJFPA's termination provisions were not preempted by Federal Automobile Dealers' Day in Court Act, 15 U.S.C.A. §§ 1221–1225); Ispahani v. Allied Domecq Retailing USA, 320 N.J. Super. 494, 727 A.2d 1023 (App. Div. 1999) (NJFPA's termination provisions are not preempted by Lanham Act or any other federal law).
98. Maintainco, Inc. v. Mitsubishi Caterpillar Forklift Am., Inc., 408 N.J. Super. 461, 975 A.2d 510 (App. Div. 2009).

termination was prohibited by the NJFPA.[99] Similarly, in *General Motors Corp. v. Gallo Truck Sales, Inc.*, the court held that a franchisor does not have a defense to a suit under the NJFPA even if it acted in good faith and for bona fide reasons in terminating a franchise agreement where there was no "cause" to support termination.[100] In applying this principle, the court in *Westfield Centre Service, Inc.* held that the franchisor violated NJFPA where it terminated the franchisee for bona fide business reasons to dispose of property.[101]

In *Simmons v. General Motors Corp.*, the court held that termination was proper where the franchisee committed a substantial breach of its franchise agreement by failing to give proper notice to the franchisor before selling its franchise to a new owner.[102] The court in *Dunkin' Donuts of America, Inc. v. Middletown Donut Corp.* also found good cause for termination where the franchisee attempted to defraud franchisor as to amount of gross sales in contravention of express anti-fraud provision in franchise agreement.[103] Similarly, in *Amerada Hess Corp. v. Quinn*, the court found termination to be proper where franchised dealer deliberately violated federal pricing regulations in connection with the sale of gasoline, in contravention of the franchise agreement's prohibition against illegal activities.[104] Termination for good cause was also found in *General Motors Corp. v. New A.C. Chevrolet, Inc.*, where automobile dealership failed to substantially comply with its obligations under the franchise agreement because the dealership insisted on adding a second manufacturer to the dealership despite provision requiring written authorization before making any change in premises, including the addition of other vehicle lines.[105] In the same vein, the court in *Dunkin' Donuts Franchising LLC v. C3WAIN Inc.* found good cause for termination where franchisees breached an express anti-fraud provision in the franchise agreement by misrepresenting their involvement with a competing business.[106] Additionally, termination was held to be proper in *Dunkin' Donuts Franchised Restaurants, LLC v. Strategic Ventures Group, Inc.*, where the franchisee failed to comply with tax and wage laws under provision of franchise agreement requiring compliance with all applicable laws.[107] Finally, the court in *Jiffy Lube International, Inc. v. Weiss Brothers, Inc.* held that termination was proper where franchisee failed to make timely payments of royalties owed to franchisor and knowingly underreported sales in violation of the franchise agreement.[108] Similarly, in *Red Roof Franchising LLC v. Patel*, there was

---

99. Instructional Sys., Inc. v. Comput. Curriculum Corp., 826 F. Supp. 831 (D.N.J. 1993).
100. *Gen. Motors Corp.*, 711 F. Supp. 810.
101. *Westfield Centre Serv., Inc.*, 158 N.J. Super. 455.
102. Simmons v. Gen. Motors Corp., 180 N.J. Super. 522, 435 A.2d 1167 (App. Div. 1981), *cert. denied*, 88 N.J. 498, 443 A.2d 712 (1981).
103. Dunkin' Donuts of Am., Inc. v. Middletown Donut Corp., 100 N.J. 166, 495 A.2d 66 (1985).
104. Amerada Hess Corp. v. Quinn, 143 N.J. Super. 237, 362 A.2d 1258 (Law Div. 1976).
105. Gen. Motors Corp. v. New A.C. Chevrolet, Inc., 263 F.3d 296 (3d Cir. 2001).
106. Dunkin' Donuts Franchising LLC v. C3WAIN Inc., 677 Fed. App'x 779 (3d Cir. 2017).
107. Dunkin' Donuts Franchised Rests., LLC v. Strategic Ventures Grp., Inc., 2010 WL 4684738 (D.N.J. Nov. 10, 2010).
108. Jiffy Lube Int'l Inc. v. Weiss Bros., Inc., 834 F. Supp. 683 (D.N.J. 1993).

good cause for termination where franchisee failed to make payments owed to franchisor under franchise agreement.[109]

3. Notice Requirement

a. Commentary

A franchisor must give written notice to the franchisee, at least 60 days in advance, of any termination, cancellation, or failure to renew. The termination notice must be in writing and must set forth "all the reasons" for such termination, cancellation, or failure to renew. Termination for reasons not specifically enumerated in the franchisor's notice is a violation of the NJFPA. If the franchisee does not cure the defaults listed in the termination notice within the 60-day period, the franchisor may immediately proceed with termination.

There are only two, very limited exceptions to the 60-day notice requirement. First, a 15-day notice period applies where the franchisee has voluntarily abandoned the franchise relationship. Additionally, if the franchisee is convicted of an indictable offence *directly related to the business conduct pursuant to the franchise*, termination, cancellation, or failure to renew will be effective immediately upon the delivery and receipt of written notice.[110]

b. Annotations

In *Red Roof Franchising LLC*, the court held that the franchisor's letter advising that it was a "written notice of default and termination" and setting forth that the reason for termination was nonpayment of amounts due under the franchise agreement was sufficient under the NJFPA, although it stated that the failure to cure the past due amount by the given date would result in termination of the franchise agreement "without further notice to you effective immediately on the Termination Date."[111] Additionally, the court in *Dunkin' Donuts Franchising LLC* found that written notice to franchisee advising that he had breached the franchise agreement by fraudulently misrepresenting the franchise owner's involvement with a competing business was adequate notice of termination under the NJFPA.[112] Similarly, the franchisor's "supplemental notice of material breach" was held to be adequate notice of termination under the NJFPA in *7 Eleven Inc. v. Sodhi*.[113] Finally, the court in *Carlo C. Gelardi Corp.* held that the beer manufacturer's telegram stating reasons for termination was adequate written notice under the NJFPA.[114]

In contrast, the court in *Carlos v. Philips Business Systems, Inc.* held that a memorandum did not show cause for termination of distributorship because it did not inform the distributor of any failure to substantially comply with the terms of the distribution agreement but instead stated that the sales organization

---

109. Red Roof Franchising LLC v. Patel, 877 F. Supp. 2d 124 (D.N.J. 2012).
110. N.J. STAT. ANN. § 56:10-5.
111. *Red Roof Franchising LLC*, 877 F. Supp. 2d 124.
112. Dunkin' Donuts Franchising LLC v. C3WAIN Inc., 677 F. App'x 779 (3d Cir. 2017).
113. 7-Eleven Inc. v. Sodhi, 706 Fed. App'x 777 (3d Cir. 2017).
114. Carlo C. Gelardi Corp. v. Miller Brewing Co., 421 F. Supp. 237 (D.N.J. 1976).

was being restructured.[115] Additionally, in *Lawmen Supply Company of New Jersey*, the court held that an NJFPA claim was proper where distributor alleged that manufacturer attempted to terminate distribution agreement immediately, in contravention of the 60-day notice required by the NJFPA.[116]

4. Grounds for Termination

a. Commentary

The only grounds for "good cause" is the franchisee's failure to substantially comply with the terms of the franchise agreement.[117] Substantial compliance "is something less than absolute adherence to every nuanced term of an agreement, but, at a minimum, requires that the franchisee refrain from acting in direct defiance of a term of the franchise agreement."[118]

b. Annotations

In *Maintainco, Inc.*, the court held that the NJFPA requirement of good cause prohibits a franchisor from terminating a franchisee agreement, even for sound and nondiscriminatory business reasons, absent a substantial failure of franchisee compliance.[119]

5. Required Cure Period

a. Commentary
Not applicable.

b. Annotations
Not applicable.

6. Repurchase Obligations

a. Commentary
Not applicable.

b. Annotations
Not applicable.

---

115. Carlos v. Philips Bus. Sys., Inc., 556 F. Supp. 769 (E.D.N.Y. 1983), *aff'd*, 742 F.2d 1432 (2d Cir. 1983).
116. Lawmen Supply Co. of N.J., Inc. v. Glock, Inc., 330 F. Supp. 3d 1020 (D.N.J. 2018).
117. N.J. STAT. ANN. § 56:10:5.
118. Maple Shade Motor Corp. v. Kia Motors of Am., Inc., 384 F. Supp. 2d 770 (D.N.J. 2005), *aff'd*, 260 Fed. App'x 517 (3d Cir. Jan. 11, 2008).
119. Maintainco, Inc. v. Mitsubishi Caterpillar Forklift Am., Inc., 408 N.J. Super. 461, 975 A.2d 510 (App. Div. 2009).

D. Restrictions on Nonrenewal

1. What Constitutes Nonrenewal

a. Commentary

The NJFPA's restrictions on nonrenewal are identical to those for termination of a franchise. Under the NJFPA, nonrenewal by the franchisor constitutes a violation of the act unless the nonrenewal is for good cause and the applicable notice requirements are met.[120]

b. Annotations

There must be good cause, defined as failure to substantially comply with the terms of the franchise agreement, for a franchisor to refuse to renew a franchise agreement.[121] Additionally, the same notice requirements apply, under which the franchisor must provide written notice 60 days in advance of the failure to renew stating the grounds for nonrenewal.[122] As with a termination notice (discussed earlier), if the franchisee does not cure the defaults listed in the nonrenewal notice within the 60-day period, the franchisor may decline to renew.

2. Restrictions on Nonrenewal

a. Commentary

The NJFPA's restrictions on nonrenewal are stringent, requiring "good cause" for nonrenewal. As with termination, the only grounds for "good cause" is the franchisee's failure to substantially comply with the terms of the franchise agreement.[123] Substantial compliance "is something less than absolute adherence to every nuanced term of an agreement, but, at a minimum, requires that the franchisee refrain from acting in direct defiance of a term of the franchise agreement."[124] A franchisor violates the NJFPA if it non-renews on any basis other than lack of substantial compliance, even if the franchisor is acting in good faith or for a bona fide reason.[125]

b. Annotations

In *Dunkin' Donuts of America, Inc. v. Middletown Donut Corp.*, the court stated that a franchisee cannot be refused renewal if there is substantial compliance

---

120. N.J. STAT. ANN. § 56:10-5 ("It shall be a violation of this act for a franchisor to . . . fail to renew without good cause. For the purposes of this act, good cause . . . shall be limited to failure by the franchisee to substantially comply with those requirements imposed upon him by the franchise.").

121. Westfield Centre Serv., Inc. v. Cities Oil Co., 86 N.J. 453, 432 A.2d 48 (1981) (termination was improper where franchisor lacked good cause for failing to renew the franchise).

122. N.J. STAT. ANN. § 56:10-5 ("It shall be a violation of this act for any franchisor . . . to terminate, cancel, *or fail to renew* a franchise without having first given written notice setting forth all the reasons for such termination, cancellation, or intent not to renew to the franchisee at least 60 days in advance of such termination, cancellation, or failure to renew[.]") (emphasis added).

123. N.J. STAT. ANN. § 56:10:5.

124. Maple Shade Motor Corp. v. Kia Motors of Am., Inc., 384 F. Supp. 2d 770 (D.N.J. 2005), *aff'd*, 260 Fed. App'x 517 (3d Cir. Jan. 11, 2008).

125. Simmons v. Gen. Motors Corp., 180 N.J. Super. 522 (App. Div. 1981).

with the terms of the franchise agreement.[126] Similarly, the court in *Westfield Centre Service, Inc.* stated that nonrenewal for any reason other than good cause is a violation of the NJFPA and the franchisor is liable to the franchisee for the loss caused.[127] The court further stated that while the NJFPA did not entirely preclude nonrenewal for a good faith business reason, unless there was good cause for the nonrenewal, the franchisor would be required to pay the franchisee the reasonable value of its business.[128]

3. Notice Requirement

a. Commentary

A franchisor must give written notice to the franchisee at least 60 days in advance of any nonrenewal. The termination notice must be in writing and must set forth "all the reasons" for failure to renew. Nonrenewal for reasons not specifically enumerated in the franchisor's notice is a violation of the NJFPA. If the franchisee does not cure the defaults listed in the nonrenewal notice within the 60-day period, the franchisor may elect not to renew upon the natural expiration of the franchise agreement.

b. Annotations

Save for two very limited exceptions that may shorten the notice period for termination under the NJFPA, a franchisee must be given 60 days to cure the defaults in any nonrenewal notice.[129]

4. Grounds for Nonrenewal

a. Commentary

Good cause is required for nonrenewal. "[G]ood cause" is the franchisee's failure to substantially comply with the terms of the franchise agreement.[130] Substantial compliance "is something less than absolute adherence to every nuanced term of an agreement, but, at a minimum, requires that the franchisee refrain from acting in direct defiance of a term of the franchise agreement."[131]

b. Annotations

The NJFPA requirement of good cause prohibits a franchisor from not renewing a franchisee agreement, even for sound and nondiscriminatory business reasons, absent a substantial failure of franchisee compliance.[132] Failure to pay monies due under a franchise agreement,[133] a franchisee's fraudulently misrepresenting

---

126. Dunkin' Donuts of Am., Inc. v. Middletown Donut Corp., 100 N.J. 166, 495 A.2d 66 (1995).
127. Westfield Centre Serv., Inc., 86 N.J. at 465–69.
128. *Id.*
129. Lawmen Supply Co. of N.J., Inc. v. Glock, Inc., 330 F. Supp. 3d 1020 (D.N.J. 2018).
130. N.J. STAT. ANN. § 56:10:5.
131. Maple Shade Motor Corp. v. Kia Motors of Am., Inc., 384 F. Supp. 2d 770 (D.N.J. 2005), *aff'd*, 260 Fed. App'x 517 (3d Cir. Jan. 11, 2008).
132. Maintainco, Inc. v. Mitsubishi Caterpillar Forklift Am., Inc., 408 N.J. Super. 461, 975 A.2d 510 (App. Div. 2009).
133. *Red Roof Franchising LLC*, 877 F. Supp. 2d at 124.

the franchise owner's involvement with a competing business,[134] and failure to construct facilities as required by an addendum to a franchise agreement[135] have all been held to be good cause under the NJFPA. Similarly, the franchisor's "supplemental notice of material breach" was held to be adequate notice of termination under the NJFPA in *7 Eleven Inc. v. Sodhi*.[136]

The court found that grounds for a valid claim existed under the NJFPA for nonrenewal in *Carlos*, where failure to renew agreement was driven by manufacturer's intent to streamline its marketing system by eliminating exclusive dealerships.[137] Additionally, in *Goldwell of New Jersey, Inc. v. KPSS, Inc.*, the court held that the franchisee had a claim under the NJFPA where a franchisor provided notice of intent not to renew the franchise and the franchisee treated such notice as a repudiation.[138] In contrast, the court in *Maple Shade Motor Corp. v. Kia Motors of America, Inc.* found that termination was supported by good cause and thus proper under the NJFPA, where an addendum to franchise agreement specifically provided that the franchisee would construct a separate showroom for the franchisor's line of vehicles, and the franchisee failed to do so.[139]

5. Required Cure Period

a. Commentary

Not applicable.

b. Annotations

Not applicable.

6. Limitations on Franchisors' Right to Impose Conditions for Renewal

a. Commentary

Not applicable.

b. Annotations

Not applicable.

7. Repurchase Obligations

a. Commentary

Not applicable.

b. Annotations

Not applicable.

---

134. Dunkin' Donuts Franchising LLC v. C3WAIN Inc., 677 F. App'x 779 (3d Cir. 2017).
135. *Maple Shade*, 384 F. Supp. 2d at 770.
136. 7-Eleven Inc. v. Sodhi, 706 Fed. App'x 777 (3d Cir. 2017).
137. Carlos v. Phillips Bus. Sys., Inc., 556 F. Supp. 769 (D.N.J. 1983).
138. Goldwell of N.J., Inc. v. KPSS, Inc., 622 F. Supp. 2d 168 (D.N.J. 2009).
139. Maple Shade Motor Corp. v. Kia Motors of Am., Inc., 384 F. Supp. 2d 770 (D.N.J. 2005), *aff'd sub nom.* Maple Shade Motor Corp. v. Kia Motors Am., Inc., 260 F. App'x 517 (3d Cir. 2008).

E. Transfers and Succession

1. Commentary

The NJFPA restricts the ability of a franchisee to transfer, assign, or sell its franchise without the franchisor's approval. The franchisee must notify the franchisor of the proposed transfer in writing and include the prospective transferee's name, address, statement of financial qualifications, and business experience during the past five years. The transferee must also agree in writing to comply with the requirements of the franchise then in effect. The franchisor then has 60 days to approve the proposed transfer or set forth in writing the unacceptability of the proposed transferee setting forth material reasons relating to the character, financial ability or business experience of the proposed transferee. Thus, the standard is different from the good cause standard for termination or nonrenewal. The franchisor may base its rejection of the proposed transfer on a bona fide business decision by showing that there is substantial objective evidence showing that the proposed transferee is material deficient.

If the franchisor fails to respond to the intent to transfer within 60 days, it is deemed approved.[140] If the franchisee submits incomplete or inadequate information for the franchisor to make a decision as to the acceptability of the franchisee, the 60-day period is tolled until such information is supplied.[141] Specific performance is appropriate to compel a transfer where a franchisor has unreasonably withheld its consent to the transfer.[142]

2. Annotations

The court in *VW Credit, Inc. v. Coast Automotive Group Ltd.* stated that the test for reasonableness of a franchisor's withholding consent to transfer a franchise is an objective test requiring substantial evidence showing that the proposed franchisee is materially deficient.[143] The court held that the failure to consent was unreasonable because the transferee's principals had extensive prior experience as automobile dealers.[144] In *Maple Shade Motor Corp.*, the court found that rejection of proposed transferee did not violate NJFPA where the transferee did not agree to meet all the requirements of the existing franchise agreement.[145] Additionally, in *Simmons*, the court held that termination of a franchise was justified where the franchisee transferred its dealership, without prior notice to the franchisor, to a purchaser who the franchisor found to be justifiably unacceptable.[146]

---

140. N.J. STAT. ANN. § 56:10-6.
141. Mercedes-Benz of N. Am. v. Dep't of Motor Vehicles, 455 So. 2d 404 (Fla. Ct. App. 1984).
142. VW Credit, Inc. v. Coast Auto. Grp. Ltd., 346 N.J. Super. 326, 787 A2d. 957 (App. Div. 2002).
143. Id.
144. Id.
145. Maple Shade Motor Corp. v. Kia Motors Am., Inc., 260 Fed. App'x 517 (3d Cir. 2008).
146. Simmons v. Gen. Motors Corp., 180 N.J. Super. 522 (App. Div. 1981).

F. Other Regulations of the Franchise Relationship

1. Prohibited Practices

a. Commentary

In addition to the provisions regarding termination and nonrenewal, the NJFPA enumerates several prohibited practices that give rise to a claim under the act.

The majority of litigation as to these provisions focuses on the prohibition against imposing "unreasonable standards of performance upon a franchisee." The NJFPA does not define the term, and the courts have not provided much guidance as to what type of requirements impose "unreasonable standards." However, the findings of unreasonable performance standards typically involve "arbitrariness, bad intent or economic ruin."[147] In the absence of such obvious factors, the question of whether a performance standard is "unreasonable" is an issue for the finder of fact and is not suitable for determination on summary judgment.[148]

b. Annotations

In *Dunkin' Donuts, Inc. v. Dough Boy Management, Inc.*, the court held that whether standards imposed by franchisor constituted an unreasonable standard of performance was a question for the jury.[149] In *Beilowitz v. General Motors Corp.*, it was determined that the franchisor imposed an unreasonable performance requirement when it required the franchisee to sustain a loss of $11 million or 40 percent of sales by implementing a new marketing program.[150] Similarly, in *Gelardi Corp. v. Miller Brewing Co.*, the franchisor's standards were unreasonable where they "made [franchisee's] business life sufficient[ly] miserable that [the franchisee] was forced to quit its distribution of [franchisor's] products in its primary area of responsibility."[151] However, in *King v. GNC Franchising Inc.*, the franchisee did not demonstrate "unreasonable standards of performance" under the NJFPA when its complaints were that (1) they were required to comply with GNC's store appearance and product placement guidelines, which caused them to sustain an economic loss; (2) that they were required to purchase a certain amount of product from GNC and relegate more popular products to less-preferred store space, causing decreased cash flow; and (3) they were forced to buy GNC products that do not sell well, resulting in reduced sales and discarded expired product.[152] The court found that there was no nexus between the poor products sales and GNC's policies, and the franchisees' complaints were not within the scope

---

147. King v. GNC Franchising, Inc., 2006 WL 3019551, at *4 (D.N.J. Oct. 23, 2006).
148. Carlo C. Gelardi Corp. v. Miller Brewing Co., 502 F. Supp. 637, 653 (D.N.J. 1980) (denying summary judgment where fact issue existed as to whether unreasonable standards of performance were imposed upon distributor).
149. Dunkin' Donuts, Inc. v. Dough Boy Mgmt., Inc., 2006 WL 20521, at *11 (D.N.J. Jan. 3, 2006).
150. *See, e.g.*, Beilowitz v. Gen. Motors Corp., 233 F. Supp. 2d 631, 643–44 (D.N.J. 2002).
151. *Carlo C. Gelardi Corp.*, 502 F. Supp. at 652–53.
152. King v. GNC Franchising Inc., 2006 WL 3019551, at *4 (D.N.J. Oct. 23, 2006).

of the NJFPA, as they were primarily in disagreement with the standards imposed by the franchise agreement that they voluntarily entered.[153]

2. Complete Defense

a. Commentary

The NJFPA provides that it is a "complete defense" to any action brought under the statute where the franchisee "has failed to substantially comply with requirements imposed by the franchise and other agreements ancillary or collateral thereto."[154] Thus, where a franchisee has committed a material breach of the franchise agreement, a franchisor may properly terminate the agreement or impose conditions that would otherwise violate the NJFPA.[155]

Substantial noncompliance has been found to include material breach of the franchise agreement, disregard for the franchise agreement's "reasonable requirements," the franchisee's "deliberate illegal behavior," and willful violation of the statutes and regulations governing the operation of the franchised business.[156]

b. Annotations

In *Goldsworthy v. Browndorf*, the court held that it is "incontrovertible" that a franchisee's violation of the law and regulations pertaining to the business has failed to substantially perform.[157] Similarly, the court in *Amerada Hess Corp. v. Quinn* stated that "a franchisee who has willfully violated the statute and regulations governing the operation of his business contra the terms of the franchise agreement, has failed to substantially perform his franchise obligations within the intendment of the Franchise Practices Act."[158] Additionally, in *Coast Auto Group Limited v. VW Credit, Inc.*, the Third Circuit held that the NJFPA provides a complete defense to a franchisor in any action under the NJFPA where the franchisee has committed a material breach of the franchise agreement.[159]

G. Remedies and Administrative Action

1. Restrictive Covenants

a. Commentary

The New Jersey courts have not specifically opined as to the enforceability of restrictive covenants contained in franchise agreements, nor are such covenants expressly addressed in the NJFPA. Generally, under New Jersey law, restrictive

---

153. *Id.*
154. N.J. STAT. ANN. § 56:10-9.
155. Coast Auto. Grp. Ltd. v. VW Credit, Inc., 199 Fed. App'x 419, 423 (3d Cir. 2005).
156. *Id.; see also* Amerada Hess Corp. v. Quinn, 143 N.J. Super. 237 (Law Div. 1976); Goldsworthy v. Browndorf, 2011 WL 3687401, at *4 (App. Div. Aug. 24, 2011); Gen. Motors Corp. v. New A.C. Chevrolet, Inc., 263 F.3d 296 (2d Cir. 2001); Mall Chevrolet v. Gen. Motors LLC, 2021 WL 426193 (D.N.J. Feb. 8, 2021).
157. *Goldsworthy*, 2011 WL 3687401.
158. *Amerada Hess Corp.*, 143 N.J. Super. at 252.
159. *Coast Auto Grp. Ltd.*, 199 Fed. App'x at 419.

covenants are enforceable only if they are reasonable under the circumstances. Historically, the "reasonableness" inquiry arose in the context of employment litigation where restrictive covenants were found reasonable if they (1) protected a legitimate interest of the employer; (2) imposed no undue hardship on the employee, and (3) did not impair the public interest.[160] Even if a covenant is found enforceable, the court may "blue pencil" or limit its application as to geographic area, period of enforceability, or scope of activity.[161]

In the context of sales of businesses, restrictive covenants are afforded more latitude because parties to a business transaction typically have more bargaining power than employees. Further, the good will established by the seller is one of the components of the sale, and restrictive covenants are designed to protect this good will.[162] In a case decided by the District of New Jersey, the court predicted that "the New Jersey Supreme Court would rule that covenants not to compete in franchise agreements are closer to agreements ancillary to the sale of a business." The rationale is that, not only are the franchisee and franchisor in a more equitable bargaining situation than the typical employer-employee relationship, but also that, in the franchise context, restrictive covenants are designed to protect the goodwill that attaches to the entire business of the seller.[163] While the *Solari* three-factor test applies in the franchise context, the covenant must be examined under the more liberal standards applicable to the same of a business.

Under this analysis, the court has the ability to blue pencil covenants not to compete. However, the actual length or geographic limits to these noncompete covenants varies widely according to the specific facts at issue.

b. Annotations

The court in *HouseMaster SPV LLC v. Burke* granted preliminary injunction restricting franchisee from operating a competing business within a 25-mile radius of the former franchise location for an 18-month period.[164] Similarly, in *Jackson Hewitt, Inc. v. Dupree-Roberts*, the court enforced a covenant not to compete that was geographically restricted to five zip codes plus a ten-mile radius and limited to two years as written.[165] Additionally, in *Lawn Doctor v. Rizzo*, the court enforced a restrictive covenant lasting 18 months and prohibiting former franchise from providing "lawn care service" within 50 miles of franchisee's former territory or within any territory granted by Lawn Doctor to another franchisee.[166] A covenant not to compete was found enforceable given New Jersey's "legitimate interests" in ensuring protection of trade secrets, confidential information, and customer relationships, along with goodwill developed in the area,

---

160. Solari Indus. v. Malady, 55 N.J. 571, 264 A.2d 53 (1970).
161. Id.
162. Jiffy Lube Int'l v. Weiss Bros., Inc., 834 F. Supp. 683 (D.N.J. 1993).
163. Id. at 691.
164. HouseMaster SPV LLC v. Burke, 2022 WL 2373874 (D.N.J. June 30, 2022).
165. Jackson Hewitt, Inc. v. Dupree-Roberts, 2013 WL 4039021 (D.N.J. Aug. 7, 2013).
166. Lawn Doctor, Inc. v. Rizzo, 2012 WL 6156228 (D.N.J. Dec. 11, 2012).

in *Jackson Hewitt Inc. v. Childress*.[167] Finally, in *Athlete's Foot Marketing Assoc. v. Athlete's Foot Brands, LLC*, the court enforced a three-year, nation-wide noncompete in a franchise agreement via an injunction.[168]

On the other hand, in *Dunkin' Donuts Franchising LLC v. C3WAIN Inc.*, the court refused to enforce a restrictive covenant against other franchise locations where only one location violated the terms of the franchise agreement.[169] Additionally, in *Jiffy Lube International, Inc. v. Weiss Bros., Inc.*, the court limited enforcement of a restrictive covenant to a five-mile radius around franchised location and a term of three years.[170]

2. Damages

a. Commentary

The NJFPA explicitly authorizes any franchisee to "bring an action for violation of this act in the Superior Court of the State of New Jersey to recover damages sustained by reason of any violation of this act."[171] Damages are typically calculated as "the reasonable value of the business less the amount realizable on liquidation."[172] For example, in interpreting this provision New Jersey courts have found a franchisee who has violated the franchise agreement by failing to pay royalties or fees liable to the franchisor for the amounts outstanding.[173] Additionally, it has been held that a franchisee may be required to pay liquidated damages if the franchise agreement is terminated for cause prior to the expiration of its term.[174]

Liquidated damages are only appropriate where they "reasonably forecast the harm resulting from the breach."[175] However, in franchise agreements, liquidated damages clauses are presumptively valid and the party who will be required to pay such damages bears the burden of proof of a contractually acceptable excuse to avoid application of the clause.[176]

b. Annotations

The court in *Cooper Distributing Co. v. Amana Refrigeration, Inc.* held that the measure of damages for wrongful termination of franchise agreement was "fair market value to a hypothetical buyer and seller, minus the value of assets that

---

167. Jackson Hewitt, Inc. v. Childress, 2008 U.S. Dist. LEXIS 24460, at *21 (D.N.J. Mar. 27, 2008).
168. Athlete's Foot Mktg. v. Athlete's Foot Brands, LLC, 2007 U.S. Dist. LEXIS 32995 (D.N.J. May 4, 2007).
169. Dunkin' Donuts Franchising LLC v. C3WAIN Inc., 2018 WL 4688335 (D.N.J. Sept. 28, 2018).
170. Jiffy Lube Int'l, Inc. v. Weiss Bros., Inc., 834 F. Supp. 683 (D.N.J. 1993).
171. N.J. STAT. ANN. § 56:10-10.
172. Maintainco, Inc. v. Mitsubishi Caterpillar Forklift Am., Inc., 408 N.J. Super. 461, 975 A.2d 510 (App. Div. 2009).
173. Dunkin' Donuts of Am., Inc. v. Middletown Donut Corp., 100 N.J. 166, 495 A.2d 66 (1985).
174. Red Roof Franchising LLC v. AA Hospitality Northshore LLC, 937 F. Supp. 2d 537 (D.N.J. 2013).
175. Wasserman's Inc. v. Township of Middletown, 137 N.J. 238, 249 (1994).
176. Knights Franchise Sys., Inc. v. First Value RC, LLC, 2017 WL 1170849 (D.N.J. Mar. 29, 2017).

could be liquidated by franchisee."[177] Additionally, in *Knights Franchise Systems, Inc. v. First Value RC, LLC*, the court held that a liquidated damages provision was enforceable as a reasonable estimate of the harm resulting from the breach where such damages were calculated by multiplying the combined monthly fees due from the franchisee by the lesser of 12 or the number of full calendar months remaining in the current term.[178] Similarly, in *Days Inns Worldwide, Inc. v. Evergreen Lodging, LLC*, the court awarded liquidated damages based on formula set forth in franchise agreement which multiplied monthly fees by the number of guest rooms.[179]

3. Rescission

a. Commentary

While the NJFPA does not explicitly provide for rescission as a remedy, under New Jersey common law, rescission is available where a party proves, by clear and convincing evidence, "(1) a material misrepresentation of a presently existing or past fact; (2) the makers intent that the other party rely on it; and (3) detrimental reliance."[180] The element of detrimental reliance requires the moving party to demonstrate damages.[181]

Notably, rescission is an equitable remedy, not a recognized cause of action under New Jersey law.[182] A court may only utilize the rescission remedy under extraordinary circumstances and where the court can return the parties to the "ground upon which they originally stood."[183]

b. Annotations

In *Mercedes-Benz, U.S.A. L.L.C. v. Coast Automotive Group, Ltd.*, the court held that rescission was not available where it would be an exercise in futility to attempt to return the parties to where they "originally stood."[184] The court found that the parties had expended large amounts of capital and that unmaking the transactions spanning many years would be impossible and thus recission was not appropriate.[185] Similarly, in *Windsor Card Shops, Inc. v. Hallmark Cards, Inc.*, the court found that rescission was not an appropriate remedy for alleged equitable fraud when the retailer of greeting cards indebted itself to the manufacturer in order to acquire inventory based upon the manufacturer's alleged promise not to open competing stores within retailer's trade area.[186] The court noted that

---

177. Cooper Distrib. Co. v. Amana Refrigeration, Inc., 180 F.3d 542 (3d Cir. 1999).
178. *Knights Franchise Sys., Inc.*, 2017 WL 1170849.
179. Days Inns Worldwide, Inc. v. Evergreen Lodging, LLC, 2023 WL 179953 (D.N.J. Jan. 13, 2023).
180. First Am. Title Ins. v. Lawson, 798 A.2d 661, 667 (App. Div. 2002).
181. *Id.*
182. Silva v. Fed. Nat'l Mortgage Corp., No 150514, 2015 WL 9460559, at *3 (D.N.J. Dec. 23, 2015).
183. Hilton Hotels Corp. v. Piper Co., 214 N.J. Super. 328, 336 (Ch. Div. 1986).
184. Mercedes-Benz, U.S.A. LLC v. Coast Auto. Grp., Ltd., 2006 WL 2830962 (D.N.J. Sept. 29, 2006).
185. *Id.*
186. Windsor Card Shops, Inc. v. Hallmark Cards, Inc., 957 F. Supp. 562 (D.N.J. 1997).

the retailer could not offer back to manufacturer inventory that it had acquired by use of credit, as cards had been sold and thus recission was not an available remedy.[187] Finally, in *Achieve 24 Fitness Limited Liability Co. v. Alloy Personal Training Solutions, LLC*, the court dismissed a claim for rescission because it is not a recognized cause of action under New Jersey or federal law.[188]

4. Injunctive Relief

a. Commentary

The NJFPA expressly provides franchisees with the right to seek injunctive relief against the franchisor for violation of the act.[189] Under New Jersey law, the party seeking injunctive relief must show (1) a reasonable probability of success on the merits; (2) irreparable harm that will occur without the issuance of injunctive relief; (3) that the injunctive relief will not result in even greater harm to the nonmoving party; and (4) that granting injunctive relief will be in the public interest.[190]

To establish reasonable likelihood of success on the merits, the party seeking a preliminary injunction must demonstrate a "reasonable probability of eventual success in the litigation."[191] The moving party does not need to show with full certainty that its claims will be successful, but it does bear the burden to make a prima facie case showing a reasonable probability of success.[192]

In most franchise cases, the primary focus is on the irreparable harm element. To prove irreparable harm, the moving party must "demonstrate potential harm which cannot be redressed by a legal or an equitable remedy following a trial."[193] The Third Circuit has established that "grounds for irreparable injury include loss of control of reputation, loss of trade, loss of goodwill," and "the possibility of confusion."[194] The New Jersey courts require a specific showing of each grounds for irreparable harm—requiring the moving party, for example, to provide evidence of the loss or the imminent possibility that the loss will occur.

Where a party demonstrates both likelihood of success on the merits and irreparable harm, "it almost always will be the case that the public interest will favor the issuance of an injunction."[195] In most franchise cases, particularly those involving restrictive covenants, the public interest will be met by issuance of injunctive relief.[196]

---

187. *Id.*
188. Achieve 24 Fitness LLC v. Alloy Personal Training Solutions, LLC, 2023 WL 2264129 (Feb. 28, 2023).
189. N.J. STAT. ANN. § 56:10-10.
190. Allegheny Energy, Inc. v. DQE, Inc., 171 F.3d 153, 158 (3d Cir. 1999); North v. Rooney, 2003 U.S. Dist. LEXIS 11299, at *16 (D.N.J. June 18, 2003); ACLU of N.J. v. Black Horse Pike Reg'l Bd. of Educ., 84 F.3d 1471, 1477 (3d Cir. 1996); Scholastic Funding Grp., LLC v. Kimble, 2007 U.S. Dist. LEXIS 30333, at *3 (D.N.J. Apr. 24, 2007).
191. Bennington Foods LLC v. St. Croix Renaissance Grp., LLP, 528 F.3d 176, 179 (3d Cir. 2008).
192. Oburn v. Shapp, 521 F.2d 142, 148 (3d Cir. 1975).
193. Acierno v. New Castle Cnty., 40 F.3d 645, 653 (3d Cir. 1994).
194. Pappan Enters., Inc. v. Hardee's Food Sys., Inc., 143 F.3d 800, 805 (3d Cir. 1998).
195. Marsellis-Warner Corp. v. Rabens, 51 F. Supp. 2d 508, 532–33 (D.N.J. 1999).
196. *See* SK & F, Co. v. Premo Pharm. Labs., 625 F.2d 1055, 1057 (3d Cir. 1980).

b. Annotations

The court in *VW Credit, Inc. v. Coast Automotive Group, Ltd.* held that the trial court properly granted a preliminary injunction enjoining franchisor from terminating franchise because franchisee demonstrated (1) a reasonable probability of success on the merits of its claim that termination was without good cause in violation of the NJFPA, and (2) that it would suffer irreparable injury if relief was not granted.[197] Similarly, in *Beilowitz v. General Motors Corp.*, the court found that the balance of harms and public interest favored granting of preliminary injunction in distributor's suit alleging that the manufacturer's unilateral imposition of territorial limitations violated NJFPA because it was not clear that manufacturer would suffer any harm from granting of relief, and public interest was served by protection of franchises from abuse.[198]

In *Jackson Hewitt, Inc. v. Barnes*, the court stated that "where a party is in possession of another party's confidential information and is poised to use or disclose such information . . . there is a likelihood of irreparable harm."[199] Additionally, the court in *Jiffy Lube International, Inc. v. Weiss Brothers, Inc.* held that loss of reputation constitutes irreparable harm.[200] The court recognized loss of goodwill as grounds to establish irreparable injury in *S & R v. Jiffy Lube International, Inc.*,[201] and in *Mister Softee, Inc. v. Amanollahi*, the court found irreparable harm and granted a preliminary injunction enjoining violation of a noncompete in the franchise agreement where plaintiff established harm to goodwill.[202]

On the other hand, in *Central Jersey Freightliner, Inc. v. Freightliner Corp.*, the court denied injunctive relief where the franchisee failed to prove probability of success in litigation.[203] The court noted that the franchisee submitted no evidence to support its contentions that the franchise agreement was terminated without good cause or that franchisor otherwise violated the NJFPA.[204] Similarly, in *Ispahani v. Allied Domecq Retailing USA*, the court found that the donut shop franchisor failed to carry the burden of establishing that it would likely prevail on merits of its claim that franchisees breached franchises—thereby terminating franchises—where facts bearing on issue of franchisor's right to terminate franchise agreements were sparse and contested.[205]

---

197. VW Credit, Inc. v. Coast Auto. Grp., Ltd., 346 N.J. Super. 326, 787 A.2d 951 (App. Div. 2002).
198. Beilowitz v. Gen. Motors Corp., 233 F. Supp. 3d 631 (D.N.J. 2002).
199. Jackson Hewitt, Inc. v. Barnes, 2011 WL 181431 (D.N.J. Jan. 18, 2011).
200. Jiffy Lube Int'l, Inc. v. Weiss Bros., Inc., 834 F. Supp. 683 (D.N.J. 1993).
201. S & R v. Jiffy Lube Int'l, Inc., 968 F.2d 371, 378 (3d Cir. 1992).
202. Mister Softee, Inc. v. Amanollahi, 2014 WL 3110000, at *14 (D.N.J. July 1, 2014).
203. Central Jersey Freightliner, Inc. v. Freightliner Corp., 987 F. Supp. 289 (D.N.J. 1997).
204. *Id.*
205. Ispahani v. Allied Domecq Retailing USA, 320 N.J. Super. 494, 727 A.2d 1023 (App. Div. 1999).

5. Attorneys' Fees

a. Commentary

A franchisee who is "successful" on a claim for violation of the NJFPA, "shall also be entitled to the costs of the action including but not limited to reasonable attorneys' fees."[206] The attorneys' fees provision is meant to encourage "private enforcement of the Act by franchisees who might otherwise be deterred from instituting meritorious suits and further the legislative intent to make franchisees economically whole."[207] Franchisors who successfully obtain injunctive relief are considered "successful" and may recover fees and costs incurred.[208]

b. Annotations

In *Westfield Service Centre, Inc. v. Cities Service Oil Co.*, the court held that the franchisor was entitled to attorneys' fees and costs where it successfully obtained an injunction preventing the sale of the franchised property.[209] Additionally, the court in *Alboyacian v. BP Products North America, Inc.*, held that where the franchisees successfully sued to prevent nonrenewal of their Commissioner Marketer Agreements, they were entitled to recover attorneys' fees because "a plain reading of the statute allows that a 'successful' franchisee is a franchisee that is successful in *any* action he brought pursuant to the private right of action created in the first sentence of the statute."[210] The court concluded that because the franchisees prevented a violation of the NJFPA, they were "successful" in their suit.[211]

However, in *Maintainco, Inc. v. Mitsubishi Caterpillar Forklift America, Inc.*, the court held that although a forklift dealership was successful in its action against the manufacturer and entitled to recover "the costs of the action," such costs did not include an award of expert witness fees.[212] Rather, the court limited recover to reasonable attorneys' fees and "those costs that have been traditionally included as reasonable out-of-pocket expenses incurred by the attorney that are normally charged to a fee-paying client, such as photocopying, paralegal expenses, travel and telephone costs, and the like."[213]

---

206. N.J. STAT. ANN. § 56:10-10.
207. Westfield Centre Serv., Inc. v. Cities Serv. Oil Co., 86 N.J. 453, 471–72, 432 A.2d 48 (1981).
208. *Id.*; *see also* Alboyacian v. BP Prods. N. Am., Inc., 2012 WL 3862549, at *4 (D.N.J. Sept. 5, 2012).
209. *Westfield Centre Serv. Inc.*, 86 N.J. 453.
210. *Alboyacian*, 2012 WL 3862549, at *4 (emphasis in original).
211. *Id.*
212. Maintainco, Inc. v. Mitsubishi Caterpillar Forklift Am., Inc., 408 N.J. Super. 461, 975 A.2d 510 (App. Div. 2009).
213. *Id.*

H. Dispute Resolution

1. Limitations on Franchisors' Ability to Restrict Venue

a. Commentary

The New Jersey Franchise Practices Act prohibits enforcement of forum selection clauses unless the franchisor can satisfy the burden of proving that the clause was not imposed on the franchisee unfairly. The Supreme Court of New Jersey has held such clauses to be "presumptively invalid because they fundamentally conflict with the basic legislative objectives of protecting franchisees from the superior bargaining power of franchisors and providing swift and effective judicial relief against franchisors that violate the Act."[214] This position was further driven by the view that "the policies of the NJFPA are best served by ensuring that New Jersey franchisees have the benefit of a local forum."[215]

Franchisors cannot overcome the presumption merely by showing that the forum selection clause was included as part of the standard franchise agreement. On the other hand, "evidence of specific negotiations over the inclusion of the forum selection clause and that it was included in exchange for specific concessions to the franchisee" would overcome the presumption of non-enforceability.[216]

The presumption of invalidity only applies to franchises within the purview of the NJFPA. If a franchisee has not reached the $35,000 threshold amount, it is not entitled to the protection of the statute.[217] Similarly, the presumption of invalidity does not extend to out-of-state franchisees, as such an extension "would have no basis in New Jersey public policy, would not further the purpose of the statute and would be unwarranted."[218]

An additional caveat is that a federal statute, such as the Federal Arbitration Act (FAA), will preempt the presumptive invalidation of a forum selection clause under the NJFPA.[219] However, the court will consider whether the arbitration clause was unconscionable or whether the agreement was a contract of adhesion.[220]

b. Annotations

In *Kubis & Perszyk Associates, Inc. v. Sun Microsystems, Inc.*, the court held that "forum selection clause[s] in franchise agreements are presumptively invalid and should not be enforced unless the franchisor can satisfy the burden of

---

214. Kubis & Perszyk Assocs., Inc. v. Sun Microsystems, Inc., 146 N.J. 176, 192–93 (1996).
215. Park Inn Intern. LLC v. Mody Enters., Inc., 105 F. Supp 2d. 370, 374 (D.N.J. 2000).
216. *Kubis*, 146 N.J. at 195.
217. Bella & Rosie Rock LLC v. We Rock the Spectrum, LLC, 2018 WL 844398, at *5 (D.N.J. Feb. 13, 2018).
218. Crest Furniture, Inc. v. Ashley Homestores, Ltd., 2020 WL 6375808, at *7 (D.N.J. Oct. 30, 2020).
219. B&S Ltd., Inc. v. Elephant & Castle Int'l, Inc., 906 A.2d 511, 514, 388 N.J. Super. 160, 164 (Ch. Div. 2006); Allen v. World Inspection Network Int'l, Inc., 389 N.J. Super. 115 (App. Div. 2006); Alpert v. Alphagraphics Franchising Inc., 731 F. Supp. 685 (D.N.J. 1990).
220. *Allen*, 389 N.J. Super. at 118, 129; Brooks v. Fetch! Pet Care, Inc., 2011 WL 2374808 (App. Div. May 13, 2011).

proving that such a clause was not imposed on the franchisee unfairly on the basis of its superior bargaining position."[221] Similarly, the court in *Goldwell of New Jersey, Inc. v. KPSS, Inc.* held that forum selection clauses in contracts subject to the NJFPA are presumptively invalid and found that the franchisee did not attempt to rebut the presumption.[222] In contrast, the court in *Park Inn International, L.L.C. v. Mody Enterprises, Inc.* found that the forum selection clause was enforceable. The court held that although the clause itself was not negotiated, other aspects of the franchise agreement were, showing that the franchisees "had the ability to exact those concessions that were important to them" and were "sufficiently competent business people to read [the] fairly straightforward contract."[223]

In *Cadapult Graphic Systems, Inc v. Tektronix, Inc.*, the court held that the presumption against forum selection clauses did not apply where a purported franchisee failed to assert a valid NJFPA claim.[224] Similarly, the court in *Bella and Rosie Rock, LLC v. We Rock the Spectrum*, held that the presumption against enforceability of forum selection clauses did not apply where franchisee failed to meet the monetary threshold for application of the NJFPA.[225] Additionally, in *Crest Furniture, Inc. v. Ashley Homestores, Ltd.*, the court stated that the presumption against forum selection clauses does not apply to out-of-state franchises.[226] However, the court noted that where a unified, multistate franchise operates out of New Jersey, the presumption will still bar enforcement of forum-selection provisions.[227]

In *Allen v. World Inspection Network International, Inc.*, the court held that the presumption that forum selection clause in a franchise agreement is invalid is preempted by the FAA with respect to forum-selection clauses in agreements governed by FAA.[228] Similarly, in *Navraj Restaurant Group, LLC v. Panchero's Franchise Corp.*, the arbitration clauses between franchisor and franchisee were deemed enforceable based on a finding that federal FAA preempts the NJFPA.[229] Finally, in *B&S Ltd. Inc. v. Elephant & Castle International, Inc.*, the court held that an arbitration clause in the franchise agreement preempted the NJFPA where the clause was not the product of unconscionability.[230] The court found that the franchisee did not demonstrate that it was an unsophisticated entity or of limited financial means, there was no proof of unfair bargaining tactics during

---

221. Kubis & Perszyk Assoc., Inc. v. Sun Microsystems, Inc., 146 N.J. 176 (1996).
222. Goldwell of N.J., Inc. v. KPSS, Inc., 622 F. Supp. 2d 168 (D.N.J. 2009).
223. Park Inn Int'l, LLC v. Mody Enters., Inc., 105 F. Supp. 2d 370 (D.N.J. 2000).
224. Cadapult Graphic Sys., Inc v. Tektronix, Inc., 98 F. Supp. 2d 560 (D.N.J. 2000).
225. Bella & Rosie Rock, LLC v. We Rock the Spectrum, LLC, 2018 WL 844398 (D.N.J. Feb. 13, 2018).
226. Crest Furniture, Inc. v. Ashely Homestores, Ltd., 2020 WL 6375808 (D.N.J. Oct. 30, 2020).
227. Id.
228. Allen v. World Inspection Network Int'l, Inc., 389 N.J. Super. 115, 911 A.2d 484 (App. Div. 2006).
229. Navraj Rest. Grp., LLC v. Panchero's Franchise Corp., 2013 WL 4430837 (D.N.J. Aug. 15, 2012).
230. B&S Ltd, Inc. v. Elephant & Castle Intern., Inc., 906 A.2d 511, 399 N.J. Super. 160 (Ch. 2006).

negotiations of the agreement, and that the obligations imposed on the franchisee were not "so one-sided it shocks the conscience."[231]

On the other hand, the court in *Red Roof Franchising LLC v. Patel* found that a franchisee located in New Jersey benefits from the protections of the NJFPA regardless of the Texas choice-of-law provision contained in the franchise agreement.[232] Additionally, in *Instructional Systems, Inc. v. Computer Curriculum Corp.*, the court held that the NJFPA applied to a dispute between the producer of learning systems and its distributor even though choice-of-law provision provided that California law governed because (1) the franchisee's principal place of business was in New Jersey, (2) New Jersey had a strong policy interest in protecting its franchisees, and (3) franchise-specific investments related to assets located in New Jersey and goodwill had been developed by New Jersey residents.[233]

2. Limitations Period

a. Commentary

The New Jersey Franchise Practices Act does not contain its own statute of limitations. Rather, the applicable limitations period is determined by the nature of the claims. Most actions under the NJFPA are for breach of contract and therefore governed by the four-year statute of limitations applicable to such claims.[234] To the extent that fraud or misrepresentation is asserted, New Jersey courts will apply a six-year statute of limitations to such claims.[235]

b. Annotations

Under New Jersey law, the statute of limitations begins to run when the claim has "accrued" or when the potential plaintiff "knows of his or her injuries and of facts sufficient to attribute those injuries to the fault of another."[236]

---

231. *Id.*
232. Red Roof Franchising LLC v. Patel, 877 F. Supp. 2d 124 (D.N.J. 2012).
233. Instructional Sys., Inc. v. Comput. Curriculum Corp., 130 N.J. 324, 614 A.2d 124 (1992).
234. N.J. STAT. ANN. § 2A:14-1.
235. *Id.*
236. Cruz v. City of Camden, 898 F. Supp. 1100, 1106 (D.N.J. 1995) (citing Viviano v. CBS, Inc., 101 N.J. 538, 546, 503 A.2d 296, 200 (1986)).

Puerto Rico

Rossell Barrios

I. Introduction to the Statute

The Puerto Rico Dealers' Contracts Act of 1964 (Law 75) is a relationship statute that applies to a broad class of "dealers," and prohibits expiration, termination, nonrenewal, or "impairment" of the dealer-principal relationship without "just cause."

Prior to the enactment of Law 75, there was no statute restricting the termination, expiration, renewal, or impairment of dealer/distribution agreements. The only applicable laws existing prior to the enactment of Law 75 were the general contract provisions of the Puerto Rico Civil Code, which require the parties to comply with any agreement according to its terms. Thus, prior to Law 75, dealer/distribution agreements would terminate according to their expiration provisions or could be terminable at will if the parties had agreed to it. Until the enactment of Law 75, restrictions on such matters as expiration, termination, renewal, and impairment of a dealer agreement were those contained in the provisions of the agreement itself.

The word "dealer," as used in Law 75, has been held to include a broad range of commercial relationships, including distributorships, dealerships, franchises, and other arrangements including, it appears, retailers.[1]

Law 75 was primarily focused on the protection of distributors and dealers. Although the word "franchise" is used in section 278(b) of Law 75—concerning "dealer contracts"—the statute does not provide any definition of that word. The statute does not refer to the traditional requirements of business format franchises such as, for instance, the trademark element; requirement of an operational system; "significant degree of control"; "significant assistance"; "community of interest"; and/or franchise fee. Some federal decisions, however, have assumed that Law 75 applies to business format franchises and licenses.[2] In this sense, Law 75 is different from the typical franchise statute.

---

1. J. Soler Motors Inc. v. Kaiser Jeep Int'l Corp., 108 D.P.R. 138, 139–40 (1978) (car retailer that sells to consumers is considered covered by Act 75 without discussion).
2. Caribbean Rests. v. Burger King Corp., 23 F. Supp. 3d 70 (D.P.R. 2014); Marpor Corp. v. DFO, LLC, 2010 WL 4922693 (D.P.R. Dec. 2, 2010); BMJ Foods P.R. Inc. v. Metromedia Steakhouses Co., LP, 562 F. Supp. 2d 229 (D.P.R. 2008); Tatan Mgmt. v. Jacfran Corp., 270 F. Supp. 2d 197 (D.P.R.

Law 75 defines "dealer" as "[a] person actually interested in a dealer's contract because of his having effectively in his charge in Puerto Rico the distribution, agency, concession or representation of a given merchandise or service."[3] However, Law 75 does not necessarily protect every actor or intermediary in the chain of distribution.[4] For instance, the Puerto Rico Supreme Court and the U.S. District Court for the District of Puerto Rico have held that Law 75 affords no protection to commissioned sales agents or representatives that do not meet the criteria to be considered "dealers" developed in the case law.[5] In any analysis of the potential merits of a Law 75 claim, therefore, a review of the specific facts of the case in light of the pertinent statutory definition of "dealer" is appropriate.

Law 75 does not require registration or disclosure of the franchisor's offering and there are no other registration or disclosure laws or regulations under Puerto Rico law for "dealers" or franchisees. However, federal law requiring disclosure applies to Puerto Rico.[6]

Law 75 was expressly enacted to protect dealers, who had developed the local market, by principals with significantly greater bargaining power. The court in *Medina & Medina v. Country Pride Foods*[7] held that arbitrary terminations of Puerto Rican dealers who had created Puerto Rico markets for a supplier's product or service "frustrat[ed] the legitimate expectations and interests of those who so efficiently carried out their responsibilities."[8] Puerto Rico territorial[9] courts and the federal district court, sitting in diversity in Puerto Rico, have relied on this legislative intent when applying Law 75.[10] The Puerto Rico Supreme Court has often cited the Statement of Motives of Law 75, which states as follows:

> The Commonwealth of Puerto Rico cannot remain indifferent to the growing number of cases in which domestic and foreign enterprises, without just cause, eliminate their dealers, concessionaires or agents, as soon as these have created a favorable market and without taking into account their legitimate interests.

2003). Note that, in order to be governed by Law 75, business format franchises must meet enough of the criteria enumerated here to qualify as a dealer.

3. P.R. Laws Ann. tit. 10, § 278(a).

4. Triangle Trading Co. v. Robroy Indus., Inc., 1998 U.S. Dist. LEXIS 16841, Bus. Franchise Guide (CCH) ¶ 11,563 (D.P.R. 1998).

5. *See* Roberco, Inc. v. Oxford Indus., Inc., 122 D.P.R. 115, 130–32 (1988); *see also* Euromotion, Inc. v. BMW of N. Am., Inc., 136 F.3d 866, 870 (1st Cir. 1998) (interpreting language of Law 75 "in the light of the ends sought by the statute," and affirming district court's summary judgment that plaintiff could not support a Law 75 termination claim against BMW); *J. Soler Motors*, 108 D.P.R. 134 (1978) (Law 75 language forces courts to interpret the statute in light of its legislative goals).

6. *See* Disclosure Requirements and Prohibitions Concerning Franchising, 16 C.F.R. § 436.

7. 858 F.2d 817 (1st Cir.1988).

8. *Id.* at 820.

9. Puerto Rico is an unincorporated territory of the United States although its official name is the Commonwealth of Puerto Rico. Sovereignty over Puerto Rico resides in the U.S. Congress since Spain surrendered its sovereignty over Puertó Rico to the United States through the Treaty of Paris that ended the Spanish American War of 1898.

10. *See, e.g., Roberco, Inc.*, 122 D.P.R. at 121.

The Legislative Assembly of Puerto Rico declares that the reasonable stability in the dealer's relationship in Puerto Rico is vital to the general economy of the country, to the public interest and to the general welfare, and in the exercise of its police power, it deems it necessary to regulate, insofar as pertinent, the field of said relationship, so as to avoid the abuse caused by certain practices.[11]

The U.S. Court of Appeals for the First Circuit has also cited the Statement of Motives in, among others, *R.W. International Corp. v. Welch Foods, Inc.*[12] In *Welch*, the court affirmed the district court's holding that a fruit juice manufacturer, Welch, had just cause to terminate its relationship with its Puerto Rico dealer.[13] The court found that the dealer's conduct in continuing to sell products that competed directly with the Welch fruit juice line, during a trial period, precluded it from recovering any compensation under Law 75. Because Law 75 is remedial in nature, its provisions are construed to further its legislative purpose and prevent its application in cases where the legislative intent is not furthered.[14]

Since the enactment of Law 75 in 1964, the U.S. District Court for the District of Puerto Rico has published more opinions under Law 75 than the Puerto Rico Supreme Court. As a practical matter, because Puerto Rico Supreme Court's decisions are reported in Spanish, they are not as easily accessed by English-speaking practitioners except when the decisions have been officially translated into English. Moreover, many cases that call into question the applicability of Law 75 and other issues under the statute are routinely removed to the U.S. District Court for the District of Puerto Rico under the court's diversity jurisdiction.

Law 75's purpose has been to "remedy the abusive practices of suppliers who arbitrarily terminated distributors after the latter had invested in the business and had successfully established a market for the supplier's product or service."[15] Law 75 "regulates the termination of a supplier's relationship with a dealer providing that, regardless of any unilateral right to terminate present in a contract, 'no principal or grantor may directly or indirectly perform any act detrimental to the established relationship [. . .] without just cause.'"[16]

"Law 75's main interest is to prevent unfair usurpation by the supplier of the distributor's hard-won clientele and goodwill."[17] In other words, the main purpose of Law 75 is to "level the contractual conditions between two groups that are economically unequal," recognizing that the supplier, typically a more powerful company, has leverage over the Puerto Rico dealer who lacks bargaining power when negotiating dealer contracts.[18]

---

11. 18-3 Diario de Sesiones 1531 (1954), cited in *Roberco, Inc.*, 122 D.P.R. at 121.
12. 88 F.3d 49, 51 (1st Cir. 1996).
13. *Id.* at 50.
14. *See Roberco, Inc.*, 122 D.P.R. at 120.
15. Re-Ace, Inc. v. Wheeled Coach Indus., Inc, 363 F.3d 51, 54 (1st Cir. 2004) (internal citation and quotation omitted).
16. *Id.* at 54 (quoting P.R. LAWS ANN. tit. 10, § 278a).
17. V. Suarez & Co. v. Dow Brands, Inc, 337 F.3d 1, 7 (1st Cir. 2003).
18. Next Step v. Biomet, Inc.,190 D.P.R. 474, 488 (2014); *V. Suarez & Co.*, 337 F.3d at 7 (discussing Borg Warner Int'l Corp. v. Quasar Co., 138 D.P.R. 60 (1995)).

Law 75 was enacted with the purpose of protecting dealers, especially after having invested considerable resources in creating a favorable market for the manufacturer's products.[19]

Another reason for the enactment of Law 75 is Puerto Rico's long-standing policy of promoting the formation and enforcement of dealer agreements.[20]

The underlying public policy of Law 75 is to prevent termination of a dealership agreement without just cause.[21] The Puerto Rico Legislature enacted Law 75 because traditional contract-law principles did not afford dealers adequate protection from arbitrary contract terminations by principals that normally enjoy a superior bargaining position.[22]

II. Commentary and Annotations

A. Definition of Franchise and Its Elements

No such definition exists under Law 75. Federal law applies as indicated in preceding text.

1. Trademark Element

a. Commentary

Not applicable.

b. Annotations

Not applicable.

2. Franchise Fee Element

a. Commentary

Not applicable.

b. Annotations

Not applicable.

3. Community of Interest; Significant Degree of Control; Joint Marketing Plan

a. Commentary

Not applicable.

b. Annotations

Not applicable.

---

19. Triangle Trading Co. v. Robroy Indus., Inc., 1998 U.S. Dist. LEXIS 16841, Bus. Franchise Guide (CCH) ¶ 11,563 (D.P.R. 1998).

20. Patterson v. Ford Motor Co., 931 F. Supp. 98, 101 (D.P.R. 1996).

21. *Id.*

22. R.W. Int'l Corp. v. Welch Foods, Inc., 88 F.3d 49, 51 (1st Cir. 1996). In *Welch Foods*, however, the Commerce Code provision requiring written corroboration was not raised.

4. Definition of "Dealer" Under Law 75

a. Commentary

In *Roberco Inc., v. Oxford Industries, Inc.*,[23] the Puerto Rico Supreme Court enumerated several factors to be considered in evaluating whether Law 75 protects a claimant. As held in *Roberco*, a claimant is a "dealer" under Law 75 if it:

(a) actively creates a market for the product or service of the principal;
(b) closes its own contracts with customers;
(c) keeps inventory;
(d) has a say or control in determining the price to its customers;
(e) has discretion to fix the sales terms with its customers;
(f) has delivery, billing and collection responsibilities;
(g) has authority to extend credit or incurs credit risk;
(h) independently or jointly embarks on promotional, advertising and marketing campaigns;
(i) has assumed the risks and responsibilities for the activities it performs; and
(j) has facilities and offers product-related services to its clients.[24]

Not all of the foregoing criteria need be present to qualify a claimant as a dealer and no criterion is more important than the others.[25] Those two caveats together make it difficult to determine coverage under Law 75 when some criteria are present and others are not.

In *Roberco*, the court found that the plaintiff had not "assumed the responsibilities or risks attached to a 'dealer' . . . [because the court] cannot consider that it actually and effectively was in charge in Puerto Rico of the 'distribution . . . of a given merchandise.'"[26] In reaching its decision, the court held that the dealer/supplier relationship "is characterized by cooperation, stability, mutual trust . . . geared to create, develop and coordinate a market and to obtain new clients."[27] In response to *Roberco*'s seemingly limiting holding, the Puerto Rico Legislature enacted the Puerto Rico Sales Representatives Act, Law 21 (normally, sales representatives are commission-paid, independent contractors who solicit customers for the principal's product or service).[28] Law 21 governs only exclusive sales agents and representatives who enter into agreements with principals after December 5, 1990.[29] Its provisions are very similar to those of Law 75 and are similarly interpreted by courts.

Both the Supreme Court of Puerto Rico (which is normally the only precedent setting court in the territorial court system) and the U.S. District Court

---

23. 122 D.P.R. 115 (1988).
24. *Id.* at 131.
25. Sudouest Import Sales Corp. v. Union Carbide Corp., 732 F.2d 14 (1st Cir. 1984).
26. *Roberco Inc.*, 122 D.P.R. at 132 (citing Law 75 (emphasis in original)).
27. *Id.* at 133.
28. P.R. Laws Ann. tit. 10, § 279–279(h).
29. *See* Triangle Trading Co., Inc. v. Robroy Indus., Inc., 1998 U.S. Dist. LEXIS 16841, Bus. Franchise Guide (CCH) ¶ 11,563 (D.P.R. 1998).

for the District of Puerto Rico have applied the *Roberco* analysis and holding.[30] In another early case prior to *Roberco*, the Puerto Rico federal district court held that, in determining a party's potential status as a "dealer" under Law 75, the ultimate matter to be determined is whether all activities performed, be they warehousing, delivery, or advertising, add up to the development of a market through promotion and closing of sales contracts.[31]

In *Mario R. Franceschini, Inc. v. Riley Co.*,[32] the court further held that no particular factor was determinative of the status of dealer.[33] The distributor in *Franceschini* did create a small market in Puerto Rico for the principal's products, but because the distributor did not have any authority to set prices or to fix the contract terms with customers, the court found that the relationship was not within the scope of Law 75.[34]

Because the analysis of dealer status is fact-intensive, some courts have been reluctant to make this determination based solely on the pleadings filed in the case. In *Jorge Rivera Surillo & Co., Inc. v. Cerro Copper Products Co.*,[35] the court denied the defendant manufacturer's motion for summary judgment of the Law 75 termination claim, stating that there existed "documentary evidence tending to establish that the dealer created a favorable market in Puerto Rico for [defendant's products] by promoting and closing sales contracts."[36] Thus, the *Cerro Copper* court chose to allow the jury to evaluate the evidence in the case in light of the factors enumerated in Law 75 and in the controlling cases.[37]

b. Annotations

To determine whether a relationship is subject to Law 75, it does not matter how the parties refer to each other, nor does it depend on whether there is a written contract. What matters are the actual functions performed by the purported dealer on behalf of the principal and whether the dealer actually and effectively takes charge of the distribution of the principal's products. Thus, even though a dealer did not actually sell any of the defendant's boats, this fact was not dispositive in determining whether the relationship was subject to Law 75 if the dealer promoted and attempted to sell the products.[38]

---

30. *See* Inst. of Innovative Medicine, Inc. v. Laboratorio Unidos de Bioquimica Functional, Inc., 613 F. Supp. 2d 181 (D.P.R. 2009) (holding that several of the *Roberco* factors must be present to deem an actor a "dealer").

31. Mario R. Franceschini, Inc. v. Riley Co., 591 F. Supp. 414, 418 (D.P.R. 1984).

32. *Id.*

33. *Id.; accord* Re-Ace, Inc. v. Wheeled Coach Indus., Inc., 363 F.3d 51, 56–57 (1st Cir. 2004); *see also* Triangle Trading Co., 200 F.3d 1, 5 (1st Cir. 1999).

34. *Mario R. Franceschini, Inc.*, 591 F. Supp. at 420.

35. 885 F. Supp. 358 (D.P.R. 1995).

36. *Id.* at 362.

37. *See also* Innovation Mktg. v. Tuffcare Inc., 31 F. Supp. 2d 218, 221 (D.P.R. 1998) (stating that "the determination of whether a particular plaintiff is a 'dealer' under Act 75, or a salesperson . . . is essentially a fact-specific one, which can rarely be rendered based on the pleadings alone").

38. Yacht Caribe Corp. v. Carver Yacht LLC, 270 F. Supp. 3d 547 (D.P.R. Aug. 23, 2017).

A party still in the process of negotiating the final terms of a dealer's contract might fall under the protective aegis of Law 75 if, for some time, it has acted as a dealer authorized by the principal, not by a third party.[39]

Unilateral efforts to sell a product and develop a market are not sufficient to create a dealer relationship within the purview of Law 75.[40]

The determination of whether a distributor is a "dealer" for purposes of Law 75 is a fact-specific one, which can rarely be rendered based on the pleadings alone.[41]

Responsibilities taken by a participant in a joint venture, as opposed to the responsibilities of the joint venture as a whole, were insufficient to qualify the participant, who did not operate his own enterprise, assume his own risks, or pursue his own profits, as a dealer under Law 75.[42]

Where an alleged distributor was not an independent entrepreneur effectively in charge of closing sales, and where the distributor's relationship with its supplier had a "hierarchical subordination quality," the alleged distributor was not a dealer under Law 75.[43]

A commissioned salesperson is not a dealer within the scope of section 278(a) of Law 75 when the salesperson does not have an obligation to purchase inventory, does not maintain warehouse facilities, does not extend credit to customers, cannot approve or reject orders, and does not engage in any form of advertising.[44]

Although "dealer" status under Law 75 is not limited to distributors of merchandise and may be extended to providers of services, a provider of services is not a dealer under Law 75 when it cannot be reasonably credited for the creation of a favorable market nor for gaining customers of a supplier's products.[45]

A determination that a distributor was a "dealer" under Law 75 was not clearly erroneous when the distributor did not acquire title over the relevant products because a distributor's purchase of a product is merely one factor to be considered.[46] In that case, the dealer did not acquire title because the products were manufactured to meet the precise specifications of each customer. However, the dealer closed its own contracts with customers to sell those products.

When a seller of ambulances did not advertise or receive the vehicles, and did not acquire title to or maintain an inventory of the ambulances, numerous fact issues remained concerning whether the seller was a dealer—and thus entitled to statutory protection from the allegedly wrongful termination of its dealership agreement by the provider of the ambulances. These fact issues included that the seller maintained sales and service facilities, invested in working

---

39. Euromotion, Inc. v. BMW of N. Am., Inc.,136 F.3d 866, 870 (1st Cir. 1998).
40. *Id.*
41. *Innovation Mktg.*, 31 F. Supp. 2d at 221.
42. Kolthoff v. Fernandez, 1996 U.S. Dist. LEXIS 7433, Bus. Franchise Guide (CCH) ¶ 10,985 (D.P.R. 1996).
43. Patterson v. Ford Motor Co., 931 F. Supp. 98, 104 (D.P.R. 1996).
44. An-Port, Inc. v. MBR Indus., Inc.,772 F. Supp. 1301 (D.P.R. 1991).
45. Accessories & Commc'n Sys., Inc. v. Nortel Cala, Inc., 85 F. Supp. 2d 95, 98–99 (D.P.R. 2000).
46. Re-Ace, Inc. v. Wheeled Coach Indus., Inc., 363 F.3d 51, 56–57 (1st Cir. 2004).

capital, maintained lines of credit, delivered numerous accounting and administrative records, established prices paid by purchasers, and contributed to the establishment of the ambulance market.[47]

A distributor's unilateral efforts to sell a product and develop a market area are not sufficient alone to create a dealer relationship.[48]

The decisions from the Puerto Rico and federal courts have consistently held that a mere commissioned-paid sales representative is not a dealer for purposes of Law 75 when the representative is not engaged in the activities enumerated in the case law, even when a representative's activities result in increased sales and expanded market because of the solicitation of customers in Puerto Rico. To be covered by Law 75, dealers who sell services must show that they meet the *Roberco* criteria, except that some of the factors are, by their nature, inapplicable, such as warehousing and inventory.[49]

5. Definition of "Dealer Contract" Under Law 75

a. Commentary

The entire statutory scheme of Law 75 also rests upon the definition of a "dealer's contract," from which the definition of "dealer" is derived. A "dealer's contract" is defined as:

> [The] relationship established between a dealer and a principal or grantor whereby and irrespectively of the manner in which the parties may call, characterize or execute such relationship, the former actually and effectively takes charge of the distribution of merchandise, or of the rendering of a service, by concession or franchise, on the market of Puerto Rico.[50]

Much of the litigation under Law 75 has centered on the issue of precisely which contracts—and, as a consequence, which dealers—are protected under Law 75. The cases instruct that not every relationship between a supplier, principal, or grantor of a dealership, franchise, or concession is intended to come under the aegis of Law 75.

b. Annotations

The lack of a formal agreement is not a legal obstacle to a finding that plaintiff is entitled to the protective cloak of Law 75.[51]

Despite the intent of the legislature to protect dealers, the statutory definition of a dealer encompasses a wide range of actors within the distribution process and threatens to extend Act 75's protective sweep well beyond the end that the statute sought to achieve.[52] This is why the Puerto Rico Supreme Court has

---

47. Id.
48. Xavier Garcia v. Duron, Inc.,175 F. Supp. 2d 135, 139–40 (D.P.R. 2001).
49. *See* EBI, Inc. v. Gator Indus., Inc., 807 F.2d 1, 2 (1st Cir. 1986); *but see Accessories & Commc'n Sys., Inc.*, 85 F. Supp. 2d at 98–99.
50. P.R. Laws Ann. tit. 10, § 278(b) (emphasis added).
51. Homedical Inc. v. Sarns/3M Health Care, Inc., 875 F. Supp. 947 (D.P.R. 1995).
52. B. Fernandez & Hnos., Inc. v. Kellogg USA, Inc., 2005 U.S. Dist. LEXIS 60554 (D.P.R. 2005).

established several criteria that a claimant must prove to acquire the protection of Law 75 and to be considered a "dealer."[53]

B. Scope and Jurisdiction

1. Commentary

There is no reference to jurisdiction in Law 75. In addition to limiting the application of Law 75 based upon the nature of distributors' efforts to create a market for suppliers' products or services, the case law has also clarified the requisite physical operation or presence in Puerto Rico when determining dealer status. In *A.M. Capen's v. American Trading & Production Corp.*,[54] the First Circuit reviewed the matter of physical presence. The plaintiff distributor in *A.M. Capen's* had its principal place of business in New Jersey, from which it took orders and shipped products to Puerto Rican customers, as well as customers throughout the Caribbean region.[55] The plaintiff did not advertise or maintain any physical presence in Puerto Rico, nor was the plaintiff authorized to conduct business in Puerto Rico.[56] The First Circuit held that the distributor's tenuous links with the local economy indicated that the distributor did not operate "in Puerto Rico" for purposes of the application of Law 75.[57] Relying primarily on legislative history, the First Circuit's ruling in *A.M. Capen's* further restricted the definition of "dealer" within the Law 75 framework by interpreting a requirement, perhaps previously assumed, that "[a] Law 75 dealer be located in, be a resident of, or be authorized to do business in Puerto Rico."[58]

2. Annotations

Law 75 does not apply outside Puerto Rico and its protections are limited to dealers in Puerto Rico.[59]

As to a dealer's business dealings outside Puerto Rico, the court stated that it was "mindful that Puerto Rico's Law 75 may not have extraterritorial effect."[60]

In determining whether Law 75 applied to the relationship between the parties, the First Circuit noted that "[a]lthough the [statute] does not explicitly require a dealer to be a resident of Puerto Rico, to be authorized to do business in the Commonwealth, or to have a place of business such as an official showroom or warehouse in Puerto Rico, as do comparable statutes in New Jersey and Missouri . . . it does strongly suggest that the dealer must operate in Puerto Rico under similar requirements."[61]

---

53. Garcia v. Duron, Inc., 175 F. Supp. 2d 135 (D.P.R. 2001).
54. 202 F.3d 469, 473–74 (1st Cir. 2000).
55. Id.
56. Id.
57. Id.
58. Id.
59. Velez v. Palladio Beauty Grp., 2012 U.S. Dist. LEXIS 204396, at *14, 2012 WL 12995633 (D.P.R. 2012).
60. Goya de P.R., Inc. v. Rowland Coffee, 206 F. Supp. 2d 211, 215 n.4 (D.P.R. 2002).
61. A.M. Capen's Co. Inc. v. Am. Trading & Prod. Corp., 202 F.3d 469, 473–74 (1st Cir. 2000).

C. Termination

1. What Constitutes Termination or Cancellation

a. Commentary

Law 75 does not apply to sales made outside Puerto Rico by a Puerto Rico dealer. See *M30 Brands LLC v. Riceland Foods Inc.*[62]

Law 75 does not define the word "termination." However, the case law implies or assumes that a termination is the cessation or end of a dealer/distribution agreement.[63]

Business relationships that are governed by Law 75 cannot be terminated by the principal absent "just cause" as defined in the statute:

> Notwithstanding the existence in a dealer's contract of a clause reserving to the parties the unilateral right to *terminate the existing relationship*, no principal or grantor may directly or indirectly perform any act detrimental to the established relationship or refuse to renew said contract on its normal expiration, *except for just cause*.[64]

There is no specific definition of "termination" in Law 75. Termination, however, is assumed to be the total severance of the dealer from the line of products that it used to distribute.[65]

b. Annotations

Reading constructive termination into Law 75's potential causes of action strays from the statute's terms.[66]

2. Restrictions on Termination or Cancellation

a. Commentary

Grantors may only terminate dealers for "just cause." Just cause under Law 75, however, requires more than a breach on the part of the dealer. In addition to a breach, a grantor seeking to terminate a dealer must show that the dealer's acts or omissions serving as the basis for termination arose from a failure to perform "essential obligations" or that such acts or omissions "adversely and substantially affect the interests of the principal or grantor in promoting the marketing or distribution of the merchandise or service."[67]

---

62. 2020 U.S. Dist. LEXIS 192252 (D.P.R. 2020).
63. *E.g.*, Freightliner LLC v. Puerto Rico Truck Sales, Inc., 399 F. Supp. 2d 57, 71 (D.P.R. 2005).
64. P.R. Laws Ann. tit. 10, § 278(a) (emphasis added).
65. *See* Matosantos Com. Corp. v. SCATissue N. Am., LLC, 369 F. Supp. 2d 191, 196–97 (D.P.R. 2005).
66. Casco, Inc. v. John Deere Constr. Co. & Forestry Co., 2014 WL 4233241, at *3 n.2 (D.P.R. Aug. 26, 2014).
67. P.R. Laws Ann. tit. 10, § 278(d).

Withdrawal from the market, despite not being listed in Law 75 as just cause for termination or nonrenewal, has been held to be a sufficient basis for avoiding liability under Law 75 if certain criteria are met.[68]

b. Annotations

In *La Playa Santa Marina v. Chris-Craft Corp.*, defendant Chris-Craft Corp. terminated certain nonexclusive dealership agreements with one of its Puerto Rico dealers after less than two years of operation on the grounds that the dealer provided unsatisfactory service to customers and failed with respect to signage requirements and inventory levels.[69] The trial court found that Chris-Craft had not established "just cause" for the termination. The First Circuit affirmed, noting that there was no "just cause" for termination because there was no evidence that the dealer's alleged breaches adversely affected the defendant's interest in promoting the marketing or distribution of its products.

Similarly, in *Yacht Caribe Corp. v. Carver Yacht LLC*, the grantor terminated one of its boat dealers on the grounds that the dealer failed to sell the grantor's boats. The court, however, held that the selling of a grantor's product in a given period is not necessarily an "essential obligation," particularly where the agreement did not specifically require it. The terminated dealer also presented evidence that there was a significant market downturn in the relevant time period and the grantor failed to specify whether or not it adjusted sales expectations based on the overall market decline.[70]

3. Notice Requirement

a. Commentary

There is no specific notice requirement under Law 75. However, some sort of notice of the termination or change in the commercial relationship could avoid the implication of bad faith. Bad faith could bolster the allegations of the dealer that the principal did not have "just cause" for the termination.

The only notice requirement established by the Puerto Rico Supreme Court is when the principal intends to totally withdraw from the Puerto Rico market. See *Medina & Medina v. Country Pride Foods Ltd.*[71]

The adequacy or usefulness of the pre-withdrawal notice depends on "the closeness of the relationship, the dependency of the dealer on the principal's product line, the age of the ties broken by the dealer, market conditions, and the dealer's relationship with other suppliers and with the clientele. The determination is one of reasonableness under the circumstances."[72]

Negotiation in good faith is also normally required to withdraw from the market but not always.[73]

---

68. Medina & Medina v. Country Pride Foods Ltd., 901 F.2d 181 (1st Cir. 1990).
69. 597 F.2d 1 (1st Cir. 1979).
70. 270 F. Supp. 3d 547, 554 (D.P.R. 2017).
71. 122 D.P.R. 172 (P.R. 1988).
72. *See* V. Suarez & Co. v. Dow Brands, Inc., 2002 WL 731759 (D.P.R. Apr. 24, 2002).
73. *Id.*

b. Annotations

As parties spent six weeks discussing the price, and this period constituted one-third of the duration of the contract between supplier and distributor, and it was implied in the negotiations that, if no agreement were reached, there would be no contract, the termination (even when there was no withdrawal from the market) was sufficient.[74] When distributorship agreement contains no specific provision on the length of time for its duration, termination *by distributor* of commercial relationship with manufacturer without alleging cause or justification and without any notice in advance to the manufacturer did not constitute a breach of said agreement. *Castillo v. Smart Products, Inc.*[75]

4. Grounds for Termination

a. Commentary

The Puerto Rico Legislature defined "just cause," as follows:

> Nonperformance of any of the essential obligations of the dealer's contract, on the part of dealer, or any action or omission on his part that adversely and substantially affects the interests of the principal or grantor in promoting the marketing or distribution of the merchandise or service.[76]

The statute affirmatively seeks to protect Puerto Rico dealers.[77] The general rule is that just cause is based on the principal proving that the dealer violated the essential obligations of the agreement or proving that the dealer's act or omission had an adverse and substantial impact on the principal's interest in the distribution of its product or service or the development of the Puerto Rico market. The burden of proving just cause is on the supplier or principal.[78] This aspect of Puerto Rico's relationship law has the practical effect of preventing enforcement of certain contractual provisions that contravene or fail to factor in the just cause standard, including, without limitation, those relating to the expiration, termination, nonrenewal, and the transfer of ownership or change in managerial control through threat of termination or other sanction.

In *La Playa Santa Marina v. Chris-Craft Corp.*,[79] defendant Chris-Craft Corp. terminated certain nonexclusive dealership agreements with one of its Puerto Rico dealers after less than two years of operation, alleging, inter alia, unsatisfactory service to customers and failures with respect to signage requirements and inventory levels.[80] The trial court found that Chris-Craft had not established "just cause" for the termination.[81] The First Circuit affirmed, noting that:

---

74. *Medina & Medina*, 901 F.2d 181.
75. 289 F. Supp. 138 (D.P.R. 1968).
76. P.R. Laws Ann. tit. 10, § 278(d).
77. *See* Action Corp. v. Toshiba Am. Consumer Prods., 975 F. Supp. 170, 171–73 (D.P.R. 1997).
78. Yacht Caribe Corp. v. Carver Yacht LLC, 270 F. Supp. 3d 547 (D.P.R. 2017).
79. 597 F.2d 1 (1st Cir. 1979).
80. *Id.* at 3.
81. *Id.*

the district court here expressly found that the evidence clearly showed that any alleged violations of the agreements did not in any way *adversely affect* the interest of the defendant "*in promoting the marketing or distribution*" *of its products.*[82]

Other courts have noted the weighty evidentiary burden placed upon principals who terminate their relationships with Puerto Rico distributors or franchisees. In *R.W. International Corp. v. Welch Foods, Inc.*,[83] the First Circuit Court of Appeals stated that "once a dealer demonstrates that its principal unilaterally terminated their contract, the principal must carry the burden of persuasion on the factual elements of the 'just cause' showing."

Notwithstanding the statutory limitations on the meaning of "just cause," courts have found "just cause" in various circumstances.[84] In *An-Port, Inc. v. MBR Industries, Inc.*,[85] plaintiff An-Port was the defendant's sales representative[86] in Puerto Rico and imported the defendant's plastics and electronics product lines into Puerto Rico.[87] The evidence in the case established that An-Port was also buying these products directly from the defendant's suppliers and selling them in direct competition with the defendant.[88] The evidence also showed that some of the products purchased from the defendant's suppliers directly by An-Port utilized labeling artwork that was identical to defendant's packaging and, in fact, had been designed by defendant.[89] The *An-Port* court granted the defendant's motion for summary judgment dismissing An-Port's wrongful termination claim, finding that the standard for just cause had been met. Specifically, the court stated that the dealer's actions "adversely and substantially affected the interest of

---

82. *Id.* at 4 (emphasis added); *accord* Newell P.R., Ltd. v. Rubbermaid Inc., 20 F.3d 15, 22–24 (1st Cir. 1994) (weighing competing evidence on issue of "just cause" and stating, "supplier bears the burden of showing that the dealer's violations or nonperformance of the contract adversely affected the suppliers [sic] interests").

83. 88 F.3d 49, 52 (1st Cir. 1996).

84. Casco Sales v. Maruyama U.S. Inc., 901 F. Supp. 2d 311 (D.P.R. 2012) (nine overdue payments; and the failure to provide sales reports, participate in a planning program, and hire and train sales personnel as required by the distributor agreement); PPM Chem. Corp. v. Saskatoon Chems., Ltd., 931 F.2d 138, 140 (1st Cir. 1991) (dealer's consistent violation of established payment terms); Tatan Mgmt. v. Jacfran Corp., Bus. Franchise Guide (CCH) ¶ 12,577 (D.P.R. 2003) (dealer's failure to pay past-due royalties or past-due balance for delivered merchandise); Jordan K. Rand Ltd. v. Lazoff Bros., 537 F. Supp. 587 (D.P.R. 1982) (dealer infringement of principal's trademarks); *but see* Biomedical Instrument & Equip. Corp. v. Cordis Corp., 797 F.2d 16, 17 (1st Cir. 1986) (reversing district court's grant of supplier's partial motion for summary judgment when genuine factual issue existed about whether the dealer's duty to pay on time was considered by the principal to be an essential element of the contract); Luis Rosario Inc. v. Amana Refrigeration Inc., 733 F. 2d 172, 173 (1st Cir. 1984) (dealer's poor performance).

85. 772 F. Supp. 1301 (D.P.R. 1991).

86. Although the sales representative was covered by Law 21, not Law 75, courts very often interpret both statutes in a similar fashion. *See* IOM Corp. v. Brown Forman Corp., 627 F.3d 440, 445 n.2 (1st Cir. 2010).

87. 772 F. Supp. at 1302.

88. *Id.*

89. *Id.*

[defendant] in promoting and marketing its products in Puerto Rico."[90] Likewise, the determination of just cause may be predicated upon a finding that "the contracting parties considered the particular contract obligation allegedly breached by the dealer to be 'essential.'"[91] One practical consequence of this essentiality requirement is that the principal or franchisor should consistently require the dealer or franchisee to comply with its obligations. A lax enforcement of such an obligation could be used to argue that it is not essential.[92]

Courts interpreting Law 75 generally have held that the "just cause" language of section 278(d) "applies only to acts and/or omissions of the distributor."[93] The only exception to this rule is the total withdrawal of the principal from the Puerto Rico market as explained earlier.[94] In *R.W. International Corp. v. Welch Foods, Inc.*,[95] the court indicated that, during a trial period while negotiations of a dealer agreement ensue, a supplier has just cause under Law 75 to terminate the engagement if it has bargained in good faith but has not been able "to reach an agreement as to price, credit, or some other essential element of the dealership." The court analogized the total withdrawal of the market under *Medina & Medina* with an impasse after a trial period that the principal affords the dealer while negotiations ensue to enter into a stable dealer agreement. It remains to be seen whether the Puerto Rico Supreme Court agrees with the First Circuit's conclusion.

Law 75 provides that any sales or purchase quotas or rules of conduct must be reasonable in light of the circumstances of the Puerto Rico market at the time of their violation by the dealer. Otherwise, no sanction such as termination, nonrenewal, or the elimination of exclusivity may be imposed upon the dealer. Law 75 provides:

> The violation or nonperformance by the dealer of any provision included in the dealer's contract fixing *rules of conduct or distribution quotas or goals because it does not adjust to the realities of the Puerto Rican market at the time of the violation or nonperformance by the dealer* shall not be deemed just cause. The burden of proof to show the reasonableness of the rule of conduct or the quota or goal fixed shall rest on the principal or grantor.[96]

The burden of proving that the quotas or rules "adjust" to the Puerto Rico market rests on the principal who always has the burden of proving just cause.[97]

---

90. *Id.*
91. R.W. Int'l Corp. v. Welch Foods, Inc., 88 F.3d 49, 51 (1st Cir. 1996) (citing Biomedical Instrument & Equip. Corp. v. Cordis Corp., 797 F.2d 16, 18 (1st Cir. 1986) and *PPM Chem. Corp.*, 931 F.2d at 140).
92. *Welch Foods, Inc.*, 88 F.3d at 51.
93. An-Port, Inc. v. MBR Indus., Inc.,772 F. Supp. 1301, 1302 (D.P.R. 1991); *but see Welch Foods*, 88 F.3d at 52 (following Medina & Medina v. Country Pride Foods, Ltd., 858 F.2d 817, 822-23 (1st Cir. 1988) (stating that "Puerto Rico Supreme Court has read a 'third' 'just cause' into [Law 75]")).
94. *See* Medina & Medina v. Country Pride Foods Ltd., 122 D.P.R. 172 (1988).
95. 13 F.3d 478, 484 n.4 (1st Cir. 1996).
96. P.R. Laws Ann. tit. 10, § 278a-1 (emphasis added).
97. *See* Casas Office Machs. v. Mita Copystar Machs., 847 F. Supp. 981, 1993 (D.P.R. 1993), *vacated* 42 F.3d 668 (1st Cir. 1994).

b. Annotations

When the supplier did not establish that dealer's failures relating to signage and inventory levels adversely and substantially affected the supplier's interests, just cause for termination was absent.[98]

Plaintiff dealer's lawsuit against defendant supplier that sought damages resulting from the termination of an exclusive distribution agreement failed under summary judgment standard, inter alia, because of the dealer's repeated late payments. *Casco Sales Co. v. Maruyama U.S., Inc.*[99]

Nonpayment of invoices is ordinarily considered a breach of an essential obligation of a dealer contract, but when the supplier does not insist on timely payment, it could be interpreted that timely payment is not considered essential by the principal.[100]

Where a dealer had abandoned the dealership, there was just cause for termination.[101]

The failure of a purported dealer to actually sell (as opposed to promoting sales) the principal's product did not necessarily constitute just cause for termination under Law 75.[102]

Supplier was entitled to summary judgment on the distributor's counterclaim for violation of Law 75 as the record amply showed just cause for terminating the parties' relationship: it was undisputed that distributor began exceeding its credit limit soon after distribution agreement was executed, and that situation persisted in the following months.[103]

Where a manufacturer terminated a distribution agreement with a distributor due in part to the breach by the distributor in timely paying its obligations, the manufacturer was prevented from terminating the agreement with the distributor because the manufacturer historically had exhibited a lack of concern with the overdue payments of the distributor. The court could not conclude that the district court judgment was clearly erroneous.[104]

Where a manufacturer terminated a distribution agreement with a distributor in part on the basis that the distributor had wrongfully endorsed and deposited a check payable jointly to the manufacturer and the distributor, the manufacturer was enjoined from terminating the agreement with the distributor under Law 75 because it was not clear that the check had to be endorsed by both parties, and there was nothing in the parties' agreement that prohibited dealer's conduct.[105]

---

98. Playa Santa Marina v. Chris-Craft Corp., 597 F.2d 1, 4 (1st Cir. 1979).
99. 901 F. Supp. 2d 311 (D.P.R. 2012).
100. GPS Distrib., Inc. v. Powermax Battery (U.S.A.), Inc., 2016 WL 5376232 (D.P.R. Aug. 8, 2016).
101. Mueller Streamline Co. v. Rafael Rodriguez Barril, Inc., 2014 WL 2946023 (D.P.R. June 27, 2014).
102. Yacht Caribe Corp. v. Carver Yacht LLC, 270 F. Supp. 3d 547 (D.P.R. 2017).
103. Greenville Funeral Supply, LLC v. Rockvale, Inc., 597 F. Supp. 2d 241 (D.P.R. 2008).
104. Waterproofing Sys. v. Hydro-Stop, Inc., 440 F.3d 24 (1st Cir. 2006).
105. *Id.*

The defendant title insurance company had just cause for terminating its relationship with the plaintiff when (1) under their agreement, the defendant retained the right to terminate the agreement if, during any calendar year, claims expense exceeded 25 percent of annual net premium remittance, and (2) in the year preceding the termination, claims expense exceeded 250 percent of annual net premiums.[106]

A supplier had just cause to terminate its relationship with a distributor when (1) from the beginning of the distributorship relationship, the distributor repeatedly failed to make timely payments to the distributor, and (2) despite repeated efforts by the supplier to set reasonable payment schedules, the distributor continued to make untimely payments.[107]

Unjustified delay on the part of distributor in conveying to principal the amounts owing in accordance with contract constitute just cause for termination.[108]

There is an exception to the rule that paying for goods on time normally is one of the essential obligations of the dealer's contract, the nonfulfillment of which can constitute just cause, namely, the "[u]nusual, abnormal circumstance in which a supplier does not care about late payments."[109]

When there is an impasse between distributor and its supplier regarding, for instance, prices, when the parties have agreed that such prices must be mutually agreed, supplier may withdraw completely from the Puerto Rico market after prior sufficient notice and negotiating in good faith.[110]

Jeans manufacturer had just cause to terminate distributorship or license agreement where Puerto Rico distributor violated provisions thereof by not paying royalties for use of trademark and for using said trademark on other garments without permission.[111]

Although plaintiffs seeking to invoke the protections of Law 75 bear the burden of proof on the ultimate issue of liability, once a dealer demonstrates that its principal unilaterally terminated its contract, the principal must carry the burden of persuasion on the factual elements of the "just cause" showing.[112]

Under section 278a-1(a) of Law 75, in order to show "just cause," the supplier bears the burden of showing that the dealer's violations or nonperformance of the contract adversely affected the supplier's interests.[113]

Under Law 75's section on termination of distribution contracts, said contracts are extended indefinitely, regardless of the expiration date, unless just cause exists for termination of the contract or unless the principal is willing to pay damages.[114]

---

106. Sheils Title Co. v. Commonwealth Land Title Ins. Co., 184 F.3d 10 (1st Cir. 1999).
107. Dyno Nobel, Inc. v. Amotech Corp., 63 F. Supp. 2d 140 (D.P.R. 1999).
108. PPM Chem. Corp. v. Saskatoon Chem., Ltd., 931 F.2d 138 (1st Cir. 1991).
109. *Id.* at 140.
110. Medina & Medina v. Country Pride Foods, Ltd., 122 D.P.R. 172 (1986); *see also* B.W.A.C. Int'l v. Quasar Co., 138 D.P.R. 60 (P.R. 1995).
111. Jordan K. Rand Ltd. v. Lazoff Bros., 537 F. Supp. 587 (D.P.R. 1982).
112. R.W. Int'l Corp. v. Welch Foods, Inc., 88 F.3d 49, 52 (1st Cir. 1996).
113. Newell P.R., Ltd. v. Rubbermaid Inc., 20 F.3d 15, 22 (1st Cir. 1994).
114. Picker Int'l v. Kodak Caribbean, Ltd., 826 F. Supp. 610 (D.P.R. 1993).

When a dealer delegated to a subagent the essential responsibility of rendering maintenance services in violation of his dealership contract, and, moreover, assigned said rights and responsibilities to a known worldwide competitor of its principal, more than one statutory ground existed to have its dealer contract terminated.[115]

A plaintiff-distributor was barred from pursuing an action against a principal under Law 75 when the contract was rejected by the debtor in bankruptcy because such rejection constitutes a breach of contract, and the rejected contract is no longer part of the bankruptcy estate.[116]

Even in the absence of contract language requiring payment for licensed merchandise, legal and policy considerations dictate that payment for licensed merchandise constitutes an "essential obligation" under a license or franchise agreement, whereby failure to make payment under a dealer's contract constitutes "just cause" for termination under Law 75.[117]

5. Required Cure Period

a. Commentary
Not applicable.

b. Annotations
Not applicable.

6. Repurchase Obligations

a. Commentary
See the damages section. Repurchase obligations may be part of the remedy to the dealer.

b. Annotations
See Section G.2, Damages.

D. Nonrenewal

1. What Constitutes Nonrenewal

a. Commentary
Nonrenewal is not defined by Law 75. However, the only definition implied in the case law is failure to continue the agreement after expiration.[118]

b. Annotations
Not applicable.

---

115. Pan Am. Comput. Corp. v. Data Gen. Corp., 652 F.2d 215 (1st Cir. 1981).
116. Am. Healthcare Corp. v. Beiersdorf, Inc., 2006 WL 753001 (D.P.R. Mar. 23, 2006).
117. Tatan Mgmt. v. Jacfran Corp., 270 F. Supp. 2d 197 (D.P.R. 2003).
118. *E.g., id.*

2. Restrictions on Nonrenewal

a. Commentary

Nonrenewal is prohibited unless "just cause" exists.[119] "Just cause" for nonrenewal is treated the same as "just cause" for termination. See also the commentary on termination under Section C.3.a, regarding withdrawal from the Puerto Rico market.

b. Annotations

In *Tatan Management v. Jacfran Corp.*, 270 F. Supp. 2d 197 (D. P.R. 2003), the court held that there was "just cause" not to renew a franchisee where the franchisee never submitted the renewal fee, refused to perform agreed-upon renovations, and was in default of its payment obligations.

3. Notice Requirement

a. Commentary

Not applicable.

b. Annotations

Not applicable.

4. Grounds for Nonrenewal

a. Commentary

Law 75 prohibits nonrenewal absent "just cause" and treats "just cause" for nonrenewal the same as it treats "just cause" for termination.

b. Annotations

In *Fornaris v. Ridge Tool Co.*, 423 F.2d 563 (1st Cir. 1970), the court held that the phrase "just cause" for nonrenewal is not unconstitutionally vague and unspecific.

5. Required Cure Period

a. Commentary

Not applicable.

b. Annotations

Not applicable.

6. Limitations on Franchisor's Right to Impose Conditions for Renewal

a. Commentary

Some renewal requirements might pass muster while others might not.[120] Some requirements would likely contradict Law 75 such as requiring a liability waiver

---

119. P.R. Laws Ann. tit. 10, § 278a.
120. *Tatan Mgmt.*, 270 F. Supp. 2d at 205–06.

or the execution of the current standard form of the franchise agreement.[121] Anticipatory waivers are certainly prohibited by the statute. However, the case law is not altogether definitive regarding some of those issues.[122] On the other hand, a reasonable renewal fee would likely pass muster under Law 75.[123]

b. Annotations

In *Tatan Management v. Jacfran Corp.*, 270 F. Supp. 2d 197, 206–06 (D. P.R. 2003), the court noted that Law 75 does not preclude parties from agreeing on conditions for renewal, as long as the conditions are not contrary to law, morals, or policy. Law 75 has a nonwaiver provision declaring that the rights granted by Law 75 are a matter of public policy and, thus, are not waivable.[124] Releases and compelling the execution of the current standard form of the franchise agreement as a condition for renewal could be considered a waiver of rights in the absence of consideration other than the renewal itself, which is mandated by Law 75, unless there is just cause for nonrenewal.

7. Repurchase Obligations

a. Commentary

See the damages section. Repurchase obligations may be part of the remedy to the dealer.

b. Annotations

See Section G.2, Damages.

E. Transfers and Succession

1. Commentary

Law 75 provides that

> the violation or nonperformance by a dealer of any provision included in the dealer's contract to prevent or restrict *changes in the capital structure of the dealer's business, or changes in the managerial control of said business, or the manner or form of financing the operation, or to prevent or restrict the free sale, transfer,* or encumbrance of any corporate action, participation, right, or interest that any person could have in said distribution business, *shall not be considered as being just cause unless the principal or grantor shows that such nonperformance may affect, or has truly and effectively affected, the interests of such principal or grantor in an adverse or substantial manner in the development of the market,* distribution of the merchandise, or rendering of services.[125]

---

121. *Id.*
122. *Id.*
123. *Id.*
124. P.R. LAWS ANN. tit. 10, § 278c.
125. *Id.* § 278a-1(a) (emphasis added).

The foregoing does not include the assignment of the dealer contract itself. There is a difference between transferring a business and assigning a contract. Dealer contracts may be assigned, but an effective assignment requires that all interested parties (the assignor, the assignee, and the obligor) concur in the act of the assignment.[126]

2. Annotations

Under Puerto Rico law, the assignment of a contract is "the transfer by one of the contracting parties to a third-party, of the exact and integral position occupied by the former in the assigned contract. (citation omitted) For an effective assignment to occur, the three interested parties must concur in the act of the assignment: the party that transfers its position in the contract (the assignor), the assignee party that will acquire it and the obligor that will be affected by the change of the person with whom he had contracted."[127]

F. Other Regulations of the Dealer Relationship

1. Commentary

a. Impairment

Impairment is an action or omission of the principal that is detrimental to the dealer's contract rights, but the dealer continues to distribute or market the principal's product or service.[128]

The definition of just cause for impairment is the same definition applicable to terminations or nonrenewal, but the protection afforded to dealers is ultimately dependent on the specific terms of their distribution contract.[129]

In *Irvine v. Murad Skin Research Labs., Inc.*,[130] the First Circuit found impairment of a Law 75 dealer contract when, after the principal was put on notice by its exclusive Puerto Rico distributor that the principal's products were reaching Puerto Rico through the internet, the principal failed to take action to curtail the practice.[131]

In other cases, no impairment has been found depending on the terms of the contract.[132] In *Caribe Industrial Systems, Inc. v. National Starch & Chemical Co.*,[133] the court held that:

---

126. Unilever Home & Personal Care v. Puerto Rico Beauty Supply, 162 Fed. App'x 22, 25 (1st Cir. 2006.
127. *Id.*
128. *See* Caribbean Wholesales & Serv. Corp. v. U.S. JVC Corp., 101 F. Supp. 2d 236, 241–42 (S.D.N.Y. 2000).
129. *See* Irvine v. Murad Skin Rsch. Labs., Inc., 194 F.3d 313, 318 (1st Cir. 1999).
130. *Id.*
131. *Id.*
132. *See, e.g.*, Graphics Supply, Inc. v. Polychrome Corp., 116 F.3d 464 (1st Cir. 1997) (affirming district court's denial of Law 75 protection where principal offered justifiable reasons for delivery delays to counter dealer's claim of impairment of the parties' contract); Vulcan Tools of P.R. v. Makita U.S.A., Inc., 23 F.3d 564 (1st Cir. 1994) (affirming district court's decision in favor of supplier where parties' contract was not exclusive).
133. 36 F. Supp. 2d 448 (D.P.R. 1999).

Law 75 does not prevent a supplier from establishing a wholly owned subsidiary as an additional distributorship in Puerto Rico where a *non-exclusive* distributor was already operating *even if the existing distributor suffered an economic harm as a consequence of such action*.[134]

As in termination cases, courts construing Law 75 are in accord that an action for impairment will lie only when evidence of the impairment is proffered by the party seeking to apply Law 75. Moreover, courts have scrutinized the specific allegations of impairment, with the "central focus [being] whether the terms of an agreement between two parties have been breached short of a termination."[135]

In *Graphics Supply, Inc. v. Polychrome Corp.*,[136] the court reviewed the relationship between two corporations that were parties to a "Dealer's Agreement" involving the distribution of lithographic supplies.

The parties' relationship deteriorated, with the Puerto Rico dealer contending that its supplier had approached the dealer's clients directly, in violation of what the distributor claimed was an exclusive relationship with the principal. The Puerto Rico dealer sued its principal under Law 75, alleging that the principal's acts, which the distributor claimed were in violation of the parties' exclusive relationship, had the effect of impairing the parties' contract.[137] The First Circuit Court of Appeals, on de novo review, found that much of the evidence proffered by the Puerto Rico dealer as to exclusivity was barred by Puerto Rico law and case law.[138] The *Graphics Supply* court further held that the parties' agreement, which was unambiguous, did not contemplate an exclusive relationship.[139] Consequently, the court found that the supplier's actions in approaching Puerto Rico clients directly did not impair the parties' agreement in violation of Law 75. If the dealer is not exclusive, direct sales by the principal are allowed.

b. Discrimination

There is no specific provision regarding discrimination between dealers in Law 75. However, discriminating between competing distributors by imposing sanctions (i.e., termination) on one distributor but not the other(s) for the same conduct could be considered as evidence that the "just cause" posited by the principal is pretextual.[140]

---

134. *Id.* at 451 (citation omitted; emphasis added).
135. *Murad*, 194 F.3d at 318; *Graphics Supply*, 116 F.3d 464 (citing *Vulcan Tools*, 23 F.3d at 569).
136. 1997 U.S. App. LEXIS 15368 (1st Cir. 1997).
137. *Id.*
138. *Id.*
139. *Id. See also* Innovation Mktg. v. Tuffcare Inc., 31 F. Supp. 2d 218, 221 (D.P.R. 1998) (stating that "[u]nder Puerto Rico law, an agreement is 'clear' when it can 'be understood in one sense alone, without leaving any room for doubt, controversies or difference of interpretation . . .'"); Borshow Hosp. & Med. Supplies, Inc. v. Cesar Castillo Inc., 96 F.3d 10, 16 (1st Cir. 1996) (holding that integration clause in contract nullifies oral or written understandings between the parties).
140. *Cf.* Casco Sales Co. v. Maruyama U.S., Inc., 901 F. Supp. 2d 311 (D.P.R. 2012); M30 Brands, LLC v. Riceland Foods, Inc., 2020 WL 6084138 (D.P.R. Oct. 15, 2020).

c. Unjustified Delays in Shipments

Law 75 establishes a rebuttable presumption that unjustified delays in shipping products constitutes an "impairment."[141] Law 75 presumes (iuris tantum) that a violation of Law 75 has occurred:

> when the principal or grantor *unjustifiably refuses or fails to fill the order* for merchandise sent to him by the dealer *in reasonable amounts and within a reasonable time.*[142]

When activated, the presumption shifts the burden to dispute the occurrence of the impairment to the principal as provided by Puerto Rico Rule of Evidence 302. 32A L.P.R.A. Ap.VI R. 302. In federal diversity jurisdiction cases, however, if Federal Rule of Evidence (FRE) 301 were applied, the principal would have to come forward with evidence, but the burden of persuasion regarding the occurrence of the impairment would remain on the dealer. Of course, the burden of proving just cause for the impairment, once it is found to have occurred, remains on the principal.

d. Unreasonable Changes in Payment and Shipping Terms

Law 75 establishes another rebuttable presumption that unreasonable modifications in payment and/or shipping terms is an impairment. Law 75 presumes (iuris tantum) that a violation of Law 75 has occurred:

> when the principal or grantor *unilaterally and in an unreasonable manner varies the shipping methods or the manner, conditions, or terms of payment* for the merchandise ordered, to the prejudice of the dealer.[143]

When activated, the presumption shifts the burden to dispute the occurrence of the impairment to the principal as provided by Puerto Rico Rule of Evidence 302. 32A L.P.R.A. Ap.VI R. 302. In federal diversity jurisdiction cases, however, if FRE 301 were applied, the principal would have to come forward with evidence, but the burden of persuasion regarding the occurrence of the impairment would remain on the dealer. Of course, the burden of proving just cause for the impairment, once it is found to have occurred, remains on the principal.

e. Impairment of Exclusivity

Law 75 further establishes a rebuttable presumption that adding distributors when the existing distributor has exclusive contract rights is an impairment. Law 75 presumes (iuris tantum) that a violation of Law 75 has occurred:

---

141. Irvine v. Murad Skin Rsch. Labs., Inc., 194 F.3d 313, 318 (1st Cir. 1999); Casco, Inc. v. John Deere Constr. Co. & Forestry Co., 2014 WL 4233241 (D.P.R. Aug. 26, 2014) (enumerating the rebuttable presumptions under Law 75).

142. P.R. Laws Ann. tit. 10, § 278a-1(b)(3) (emphasis added); *see also* Graphics Supply, Inc. v. Polychrome Corp., 116 F.3d 464 (1st Cir. 1997) (shipment delays were justified, among other reasons, because of the renovation of the principal's manufacturing plant); *M30 Brands, LLC*, 2020 WL 6084138 (defendant's summary judgment denied because of controversy over whether shipment delays were justified).

143. P.R. Laws Ann. tit. 10, § 278a-1 (emphasis added).

when the principal or grantor establishes a distribution relationship with one or more additional dealers for the area of Puerto Rico or any part of said area in conflict with the contract existing between the parties.[144]

In the absence of a grant of exclusivity to the distributor, the principal may appoint other distributors without impediment under Law 75.[145]

When activated, the presumption shifts the burden to disprove the existence of exclusivity to the principal as provided by Puerto Rico Rule of Evidence 302. 32A L.P.R.A. Ap.VI R. 302. In federal diversity jurisdiction cases, however, if FRE 301 were applied, the principal would have to come forward with evidence, but the burden of persuasion regarding the occurrence of the impairment would remain on the dealer. Of course, the burden of proving just cause for the impairment, once it is found to have occurred, remains on the principal.

Also, Law 75 creates a presumption that, when a principal establishes facilities in Puerto Rico while having a local distributor, there is an impairment. Law 75 reads as follows:

> when the principal or grantor *establishes facilities in Puerto Rico* for the direct distribution of merchandise or the rendering of services that were previously in the charge of the dealer[.][146]

This presumption is also dependent on whether the claimant has exclusive rights. In the absence of exclusivity, the principal may sell directly to customers within certain parameters. In *Caribbean Wholesales*,[147] for example, the court held that no impairment existed because the principal did not undertake any affirmative act to induce a particular customer of the nonexclusive distributor to stop buying from the latter.

2. Annotations

When the evidence in a case failed to show that a supplier's delivery delays were "unjustifiable," the appellate court found that the district court's dismissal of the dealer's Law 75 claim of impairment was proper.[148]

Where a supplier reserved the right to appoint additional nonexclusive distributors within a dealer's territory in the parties' dealer contract, such appointment of additional distributors did not constitute an impairment of the existing dealer's contract for purposes of Law 75.[149]

There was an impairment when (1) the plaintiff was the exclusive distributor of the defendant's products in Puerto Rico; (2) the defendant broadcast an infomercial on various cable television stations as part of its advertising

---

144. *Id.* (emphasis added).
145. *See* Caribbean Wholesales & Serv. Corp. v. U.S. JVC Corp., 101 F. Supp. 2d 236, 241–42 (S.D.N.Y. 2000) (appointment of other dealers is not an impairment if the plaintiff is nonexclusive; direct sales by the principal to customers of the nonexclusive dealer are not necessarily an impairment either).
146. P.R. LAWS ANN. tit. 10, § 278a-1 (emphasis added).
147. *Id.*
148. Graphics Supply, Inc. v. Polychrome Corp., 116 F.3d 464 (1st Cir. 1997).
149. Vulcan Tools of P.R. v. Makita USA, Inc., 23 F.3d 564, 568–69 (1st Cir. 1994).

campaign; and (3) unbeknownst to the defendant, a New York station relayed the infomercial to Puerto Rico and the products were thereby made available in Puerto Rico through telemarketing.[150]

Principal's assignment of dealer contract to a general distributor did not, in and of itself, constitute impairment of the dealer contract when principal contractually reserved right to assign. Other specific hardships on the dealer caused by the assignment, however, might qualify as impairment under certain circumstances.[151]

Although Law 75 may not directly restrict the sale of goods by a stateside reseller to Puerto Rico customers, the suppliers of the stateside reseller could be compelled—under Law 75—to restrict the latter from selling products in Puerto Rico because such sales violate the exclusivity of the Puerto Rico distributor appointed by those suppliers. However, it would first be necessary to ascertain if the scope of the Puerto Rico distributor's exclusivity extended to sales by third parties located outside Puerto Rico.[152]

G. Remedies and Administration Action[153]

1. Restrictive Covenants

a. Commentary

Regulation of restrictive covenants is not part of Law 75. The limitations on such covenants are exclusively judicially created based on the "public policy" of free competition.[154] The P.R. Supreme Court has imposed geographic, time, and functional limits to restrictive covenants.[155]

b. Annotations

In the case of business format franchises, the period of the covenant not to compete cannot exceed two years. The specific time limit depends on the circumstances. In *Franquicias Martin's BBQ, Inc v. García de Gracia*, the court considered that the franchisee could still operate a restaurant at the site of the franchised restaurant, albeit with a different menu.[156]

Geographic limitations *normally* should not exceed the area granted as "operational" territory or, perhaps, the "protected" territory, if applicable, unless the franchisor can show a specific and legitimate interest that demands more territorial protection.[157]

Functional limits are those based on criteria such as, for instance, clientele and the type and scope of the restricted economic activity.[158]

---

150. Irvine v. Murad Skin Rsch. Lab., 194 F.3d 313 (1st Cir. 1999).
151. J. Soler Motors, Inc. v. Kaiser Jeep Int'l Corp., 108 D.P.R. 134 (1978).
152. Twin Cnty. Grocers, Inc. v. Méndez & Co., 81 F. Supp. 2d 276 (D.P.R. 1999).
153. Law 75 does not address rescission or directors and officer's liability.
154. 178 D.P.R. 978 (P.R. 2010).
155. Id.
156. Id.
157. Id.
158. Id.

All restrictive covenants must be designed not to exceed whatever restrictions are reasonably required to protect the reasonable interests of the principal or franchisor in protecting, inter alia, its franchise system and confidential business information.[159]

Restrictive covenants should always be in writing and the restricted party should receive consideration in return for the covenant.[160]

Restrictive covenants may not be blue penciled by the courts if such covenants exceed reasonable time, geographic, and/or functional limitations.[161]

2. Damages

a. Commentary

Law 75 provides guidance with respect to the calculation of damages when a violation of Law 75 is found. Under section 278(b) of the statute, a court may consider several factors in determining the amount of damages, inter alia, (1) the loss of goodwill of the business attributable to the dealer's efforts; and (2) lost benefit (profits) of the last five years or, if the commercial relationship has had less than five years duration, the average annual profit multiplied by five.[162] Other items include the value of the dealer's stock or inventory and the value of any investment in assets that cannot be used for any endeavor other than the terminated line of business. Those factors are not mandatory or exclusive of others but operate as guidelines for the trier of fact to measure actual damages. Courts have treated evidence of damages as an essential element of a Law 75 violation as to which plaintiff bears the burden of proof.[163]

In calculating lost profits, some courts postulate that the only allowed deduction from the gross profits are the expenses incurred by the dealer that are directly related to the sales of the product line in question. This generally means deducting only the expenses that the dealer would have had to incur if the manufacturer had not terminated the contract.[164]

Puerto Rico law does not allow recovery of gross profits because those would constitute a windfall. It has not been completely settled, however, if only direct expenses may be subtracted from the gross profit. See *El Coqui Landfill v. Municipio de Gurabo*, which although not a Law 75 case, discusses the categories of expenses that may be subtracted from gross profits to arrive at the net profit in a loss of income claim.[165]

Recovery under Law 75 is pre-tax because the compensation received under Law 75 is not tax exempt and, thus, pre-tax recovery does not constitute a

---

159. *Id.*
160. Franquicias Martín's BBQ, Inc. v. García de Gracia, 178 D.P.R. 978 (P.R. 2010).
161. *Id.*
162. P.R. Laws Ann. tit. 10, § 278b.
163. Irvine v. Murad Skin Rsch. Lab., 194 F.3d 313, 319–20 (1st Cir. 1999).
164. Ballester Hermanos, Inc. v. Campbell Soup Co., 1993 WL 269656, at *6 (D.P.R. 1993).
165. 186 D.P.R. 688, 701 (2012) (this is not a Law 75 case); *see also* La Playa Santa Marina, Inc. v. Chris-Craft Corp., 597 F.2d 1, 6 (1st Cir. 1979); *Ballester Hermanos, Inc.*, 1993 WL 269656, at *6.

windfall when compared to the income that the dealer would have received in the normal course of business if the termination had not occurred.[166]

If the fact finder concludes that the principal or grantor impaired the agreement without just cause, damages for any lost profits are to be determined based on the net profit that the dealer would have received in distributing the products had the impairment not occurred, less the expenses of making that net profit.[167]

Evidence of damages is an essential element of a Law 75 violation as to which plaintiff bears the burden of proof. Therefore, in order to prevail, a Law 75 plaintiff must submit sufficient evidence of damages to meet the preponderance of the evidence standard.[168]

b. Annotations

In *La Playa Santa Marina, Inc. v. Chris-Craft Corp.*,[169] the appellate court reviewed the district court's calculation of damages. The First Circuit upheld the district court's finding that there was no specific evidence to support a request for reimbursement of investment capital in the amount of "around $60,000–$80,000."[170] With respect to goodwill, the First Circuit applied the factors set forth in Law 75 and sustained an award for goodwill in the amount of $10,000, rather than plaintiff's claim of "at least $75,000."[171] There are various ways to calculate the loss of goodwill subject to expert testimony.[172]

An award of compensation for lost profits and loss of goodwill is not duplicative (punitive).[173] However, in *A.M. Capen's Co. v. American Trading & Production Corp.*,[174] the Puerto Rico district court engaged in a detailed analysis of the underlying facts and concluded that the plaintiff's impairment lasted only 18 months and that, in fact, "[t]he earnings of [plaintiff] . . . were higher than any year prior to the date of the impairment."[175] The court also held that, under the language of section 278(b) authorizing recovery for lost profits, "[the statute] already includes compensation for the portion of those future profits that constitute goodwill. Therefore, . . . a distributor would be receiving a double compensation for loss of goodwill if it were to receive an award under both 278b(c) [goodwill] and 278b(d) [loss of profit]."[176] The court did not award goodwill damages to plaintiff.[177]

---

166. *Ballester Hermanos, Inc.*, 1993 WL 269656, at *6; Casas Office Machines Inc. v. Mita Copystar Am., Inc., 961 F. Supp. 353, 359 (D.P.R. 1997).

167. *Casas Office Machines Inc.*, 961 F. Supp. 360–61; *see also* Matosantos Com. Corp. v. SCATissue N. Am., LLC, 369 F. Supp. 2d 191, 196–98 (D.P.R. 2005).

168. *See Irvine*, 194 F.3d at 319–20; Sun Blinds, Inc. v. S.A. Recasens, 11 Fed. App'x 617, 619 (1st Cir. 2004).

169. *La Playa Santa Marina, Inc.*, 597 F.2d at 3–6.

170. *Id.*

171. *Id.*

172. *See also Ballester Hermanos, Inc.*, 1993 U.S. Dist. LEXIS 9619; Goya de P.R. Inc. v. Rowland Coffee Roasters, 2004 U.S. Dist. LEXIS 30649 (D.P.R. 2004).

173. *Ballester Hermanos, Inc.*, 1993 U.S. Dist. LEXIS 9619, at *9; *see also* Thomas Diaz, Inc. v. Colombina S.A, 831 F. Supp. 2d 528, 536 (D.P.R. 2011).

174. 12 F. Supp. 2d 222 (D.P.R. 1998).

175. *Id.* at 228.

176. *Id.* at 229.

177. *Id.* at 229–30.

The factors enumerated in Law 75 for the measure of damages are not mandatory or exclusive of other factors.[178] Those are guidelines to be utilized contingent upon the presentation of adequate proof in each case.[179] Adequate proof means that the party claiming damages must prove "their existence, their relationship to the act complained of and their value."[180] Once the existence of damages and the relation to the act complained of has been established, the amount of damages can be estimated on a reasonable basis and there is no need for mathematical certainty.[181]

3. Rescission

a. Commentary

There is no specific rescission remedy under Law 75. Such remedy is unnecessary given the remedies provided by Law 75 to the dealer. Normally, the dealer will not request the cancellation of its distribution agreement because, when the principal has breached the agreement, the dealer will simply bring a claim for unlawful termination under Law 75. Moreover, if the contract does not have a definite duration, the dealer would not need such a remedy to terminate the agreement. Finally, rescission would be inconsistent with Law 75 if requested by the principal, supplier, or franchisor. A contract termination by the principal must be based on just cause.

b. Annotations

Not applicable.

4. Injunctive Relief

a. Commentary

In furtherance of the protections it affords to statutory dealers, Law 75 contains a section authorizing courts or arbitrators[182] to grant preliminary or *pendente lite* injunctive relief to preserve the status quo (prior to the alleged violation) pending litigation or arbitration based on the balance of equities and the dictates of Law 75's public policy.[183] While courts have applied the traditional criteria for injunctions in Law 75 cases, such criteria must be applied to achieve the intent of Law 75 by considering the injunction's potential effects on statutory policies.[184]

b. Annotations

In *A.M. Capen's Co. v. American Trading and Production Corp.*,[185] a Puerto Rico dealer with an exclusive distribution contract sought an injunction to prevent

---

178. Marina Indus., Inc. v. Brown Boveri Corp., 14 D.P.R. 64 (1983).
179. Irvine v. Murad Skin Rsch. Lab., 194 F.3d 313, 319–20 (1st Cir. 1999).
180. Computec Sys. Corp. v. Gen. Automation, Inc., 599 F. Supp. 819, 825 (D.P.R. 1984).
181. *Id.* at 825.
182. For instance, Rule 38 of the Commercial Rules of the American Arbitration Association allows parties to seek emergency relief from an "emergency arbitrator." *See* Encore Benefit Mgmt. v. Phoenix Benefits Mgmt., LLC, 2019 WL 5957174 (D.P.R. Nov. 12, 2019).
183. *See* P.R. Laws Ann. tit. 10, § 278(b)(1) (titled "Provisional remedy").
184. Freightliner, LLC v. P.R. Truck Sales, Inc., 399 F. Supp. 2d 57, 72 (D.P.R. 2005).
185. 892 F. Supp. 36 (D.P.R. 1995).

its supplier from engaging in direct sales within its territory, in violation of Law 75.[186] The court granted the dealer's motion for provisional relief, stating that "[u]pon solving a request for provisional remedy under [Law 75], the district court need not rely on the criteria of 'probability of success' ... notwithstanding, nothing in [the statute] prevents a district court from using this criteria."[187] The court noted that the language of Law 75 requires an analysis of the parties' interests and the public policy of the law:

> The strength of the parties' interests also may depend upon the likelihood that "just cause" will be found. Thus, in *Pan American Computer Corp. v. Data General Corp.*, 652 F.2d 215, 217 (1st Cir. 1981) we stated: "While the statute does not require a finding of likelihood of success as a prerequisite to issuance of an injunction, the court's view of the merits would certainly affect it's [sic] judgment of the parties' interests and of the injunction's effect on the statutory policies."[188]

As part of its ruling, the court ordered the defendant supplier to "cease and desist from any and all actions in prejudice and/or diminishment of the exclusive relation established ... between [plaintiff] as dealer and [defendant] as principal."[189] On appeal, the injunction was affirmed.[190]

In *José Santiago Inc. v. Smithfield Foods, Inc.*,[191] the Court expressed that "(a)lthough Law 75 does not require us to find irreparable harm or a likelihood of success on the merits, our thoughts on these will affect how we view the parties' interests and the question of whether an injunction would further Law 75's public policy."

In *P.R. Hospital Supply, Inc. v. Boston Scientific Corp.*,[192] the First Circuit held that a district court has jurisdiction to issue preliminary injunctions, pending arbitration, to preserve the status quo prior to the alleged termination or impairment. Moreover, it held that the district court may "make a preliminary judgment regarding which law to apply for the purpose of injunctive relief."

In *Next Step Medical Co. Inc. v. Bromedicon Inc.*,[193] the Puerto Rico Supreme Court vowed to clarify how traditional injunction criteria should be applied in the context of Law 75. However, the court uses vague indications such as not "rigorously" applicable and not "necessarily" applicable when referring to the "irreparable harm" and "probability of prevailing on the merits" criteria. With respect to the "probability of prevailing" factor, the court focuses on whether the distributor meets the *Roberco* factors and/or whether the agreement is exclusive when exclusivity is at issue. However, it asserts that the distributor does not "necessarily" have to prove absence of just cause in the injunction context.

---

186. *Id.*
187. *Id.* at 38 n.2 (citations omitted).
188. *Id.* at 38.
189. *Id.* at 41.
190. A.M. Capens Co. v. Am. Trading & Prod. Corp., 74 F.3d 317 (1997).
191. 2022 WL 2155023 (D.P.R. June 15, 2022).
192. 426 F.3d 503, 505–06 (1st Cir. 2005).
193. 190 D.P.R. 474 (2014).

Interestingly, the court admonishes that a preliminary injunction should issue only when there "is a clear and unambiguous violation" of the distributorship agreement. It also reiterated that any injunction criteria must be applied as necessary to effectuate the purposes of Law 75.

There is no *permanent* injunction remedy in the text of Law 75 to compel the principal to do business with the dealer indefinitely. Such a permanent injunction would suffer from constitutional infirmities.

5. Control Person Liability

a. Commentary
Not applicable.

b. Annotations
Not applicable.

6. Attorneys' Fees

a. Commentary
Law 75 was amended on September 1, 2000, to allow for the grant of attorneys' and experts' fees to the prevailing party. It provides as follows:

In every action filed pursuant to the provisions of this chapter, the court may allow the granting of *attorneys'* fees to *the prevailing party*, as well as a reasonable reimbursement of the *expert's* fees.[194]

With respect to the issue of attorneys' fees, before the foregoing amendment to Law 75, courts deciding Law 75 cases applied the body of statutory and case law authority that recognizes the award of attorneys' fees under Puerto Rico law in case of obstinacy.[195] The amendment to Law 75, however, expressly allows courts discretion to award attorneys' fees, as well as expert witness fees, in actions filed pursuant to Law 75 regardless of obstinacy. It bears noting that recovery of such fees is not limited to Law 75 dealers, but any "prevailing party."[196] According to the Legislature's Statement of Motives, Law 75's fee-shifting provision is patterned after the provision in the federal Civil Rights Act authorizing recovery of attorneys' fees to the prevailing party.

b. Annotations
The Statement of Motives for Act No. 288 of September 1, 2000 (Puerto Rico Senate Bill 1371) of the fee shifting amendment, states that the "Legislature deem[ed] it necessary to allow the granting of attorneys' fees to the prevailing party under parameters similar to those under Title VII of the Civil Rights Act of 1964, as amended."[197]

---

194. P.R. Laws Ann. tit. 10, § 278(e) (emphasis added).
195. P.R. Rule Civ. P. 44.1(d); P.R. Laws Ann. tit. 32, App. III.
196. P.R. Laws Ann. tit. 10, § 278(e).
197. Act No. 288 of Sept. 1, 2000, S.B. 1371, at 1 (2000).

7. Limitations of Damage Waivers

a. Commentary

Law 75 also contains a section declaring that its "provisions cannot be waived."[198] The broad language of the anti-waiver provision reflects the policy underlying Law 75, that is, to protect local dealers. Section 278c states:

> The provisions of this chapter are of a public order and therefore the rights determined by such provisions cannot be waived. This chapter being of a remedial character, should, for the most effective protection of such right, be liberally interpreted; in the adjudgment of the claims that may arise hereunder, the courts of justice shall recognize the right in favor of whom may, effectively, have at his charge the distribution of activities, notwithstanding the corporate or contractual structures or mechanisms that the principal or grantor may have created or imposed to conceal the real nature of the relationship established.[199]

The prohibition against waiver extends to all of a dealer's rights under Law 75.

The most reasonable interpretation of this nonwaiver provision is that it prohibits anticipatory waivers but does not prohibit settlement of existing disputes. Otherwise, Law 75 litigation could never be settled, and all such litigation would have to proceed to final judgment.

b. Annotations

In *Walborg Corp. v. Superior Court*,[200] the court held that the rights conferred by Law 75, including the right to litigate Law 75 claims in Puerto Rico, could not be waived.[201]

8. Administrative Action

a. Commentary

Not applicable.

b. Annotations

Not applicable.

H. Dispute Resolution

1. Limitations on Franchisor's Ability to Restrict Venue

a. Commentary

Law 75 voids any choice of judicial forum outside Puerto Rico:

---

198. *Id.* § 278(c).
199. *Id.*
200. 104 D.P.R. 184 (1975).
201. *Id.*

Any stipulation that obligates a dealer to adjust, arbitrate, or *litigate any controversy that comes up regarding his dealer's contract outside of Puerto Rico* or under foreign law or rule of law shall be likewise considered as violating the public policy set forth by this chapter and *is therefore null and void.*[202]

Thus, if the litigation is filed in a Puerto Rico (territorial) court involving a resident distributor covered by Law 75, the forum will likely be Puerto Rico despite the existence of a forum selection clause in the contract.

If the litigation is filed in or removed to federal district court, other considerations apply given that 28 U.S.C. § 1404(a) will come into play. When there is *no* forum selection clause, actions brought under Law 75 by local distributors could be transferred to a federal district outside Puerto Rico if the transfer factors under section 1404(a) are met. However, given the strong Puerto Rico public policy against such a transfer, this is very unlikely to happen.[203]

However, if the federal case involves a forum selection clause agreed by the parties, other considerations come into play. Even before the U.S. Supreme Court decided *Atlantic Marine Construction Co. v. United States District Court*,[204] the U.S. District Court for the District of Puerto Rico routinely enforced judicial forum selection clauses that required the transfer of a Law 75 litigation to federal courts outside Puerto Rico. The basis for those decisions was that forum selection criteria under Puerto Rico case law set forth in *Unisys P.R. Inc. v. Ramallo Brothers Printing Inc.*[205] are essentially undistinguishable from the federal criteria under section 1404. These federal court cases so held despite that *Unisys* was not a Law 75 case. In any event, *Atlantic Marine* has, for all practical purposes, probably settled the matter. Forum selection clauses must be enforced except in the most exceptional circumstances. The application of Law 75 does not appear to be an exceptional circumstance according to *Caribbean Restaurant LLC v. Burger King Corp.*[206]

Moreover, despite the public policy of Law 75, the First Circuit has enforced a forum selection clause selecting a judicial forum outside the United States based on the forum non conveniens doctrine. In *Royal Bed & Spring Co. v. Famossul Industria e Comercio de Moveis Ltda.*,[207] the court dismissed the Law 75 complaint so that it could be filed in a foreign country (Brazil) if the plaintiff so chose. The public policy of Law 75 was merely one of the factors to be considered under the forum non conveniens doctrine and did not appear to be dispositive. The court found that said doctrine required the enforcement of the forum selection clause after weighing all the relevant factors to foster international trade.

---

202. P.R. Laws Ann. tit. 10, § 278b-3 (emphasis added).
203. Caguas Lumber Yard, Inc. v. Ace Hardware Corp., 2011 WL 5837808 (D.P.R. Nov. 21, 2011).
204. 571 U.S. 49, 61–62 (2013).
205. 128 D.P.R. 842 (1991).
206. 23 F. Supp. 3d 70, 76 (2014).
207. 906 F.2d 45 (1st Cir. 1990).

b. Annotations

The U.S. District Court for the District of Puerto has consistently upheld mandatory forum selection clauses in cases brought under Law 75, despite the statute's language rendering such contractual provisions null and void.[208]

Where a defendant presented evidence that tended to show that the parties' relationship was not within the scope of Law 75 in that the Puerto Rico distributor was not a statutory dealer, Law 75 would have no effect on the choice of forum clause and enforcing such clause would be required.[209]

Despite the language of Law 75 declaring void any provision in a dealer's contract mandating that controversies be arbitrated or litigated in a forum other than Puerto Rico, transfer of a case to a forum outside Puerto Rico chosen in the parties' dealer contract was permissible under federal law, 28 U.S.C. § 1404(a).[210]

Where a clause in a dealer contract regarding forum selection was permissive in that it did not specify a particular court but rather the "courts of Puerto Rico," the district court held that the federal district court situated within the Commonwealth of Puerto Rico was a proper forum.[211]

Transferring venue out of Puerto Rico does not violate the public policy justification of Law 75, nor does it "present any *Erie*-type difficulties."[212]

2. Limitations Period

a. Commentary

Law 75 has a three-year statute of repose that starts running from the time the dealer is put on notice of the violation of the statute. Dealer agreements are commercial contracts ruled by the provisions of the Puerto Rico Commerce Code on matters of repose. Such a commercial statute of repose cannot be tolled by a demand letter. Filing in court (or arbitration) or a formal recognition of liability (and renewal of the debt document) are the only ways to toll the repose period.[213]

b. Annotations

In *Basic Controlex Corp. v. Klockner Moeller Corp.*,[214] the court held that a letter from the principal to its alleged exclusive distributor expressing its intent to appoint additional distributors was considered an act of impairment despite

---

208. BMJ Foods P.R. Inc. v. Metromedia Steakhouses Co., 562 F. Supp. 2d 229 (D.P.R. 2008) (upholding transfer to Texas); Antilles Cement Corp. v. Aalborg Portland A/S, 526 F. Supp. 2d 205 (D.P.R. 2007) (upholding England forum selection clause); D.I.P.R. Mfg., Inc. v. Perry Ellis Intern., Inc., 472 F. Supp. 2d 151 (D.P.R. 2007) (upholding Florida forum selection clause); Díaz-Rosado v. Auto Wax Co., Inc., 2005 WL 2138794 (D.P.R. Aug. 26, 2005) (upholding Texas forum-selection clause); Outek Caribbean Distribs., Inc. v. Echo, Inc., 206 F. Supp. 2d 263, 270 (D.P.R. 2002) (upholding the Illinois forum selection clause).
209. Triangle Trading Co. v. Robroy Indus., Inc., 1998 U.S. Dist. LEXIS 16841, Bus. Franchise Guide (CCH) ¶ 11,563 at 314 (D.P.R. 1998).
210. Maxon Eng'g Servs., Inc. v. United Sciences, Inc., 34 F. Supp. 2d 97, 99–100 (D.P.R. 1998).
211. Action Corp. v. Toshiba Am. Consumer Prods., Inc., 975 F. Supp. 170, 171 (D.P.R. 1997).
212. Marpor Corp. v. DFO, LLC, 2010 U.S. Dist. LEXIS 127616 (D.P.R. 2010).
213. *See* Pacheco v. Nat'l W. Life Ins. Co., 122 D.P.R. 55 (1988); Quality Cleaning Prods. v. SCA Tissue N. Am. LLC, 794 F. 3d 200, 206–07 (1st Cir. 2015).
214. 202 F.3d 450 (1st Cir. 2000).

the fact that no such appointment had occurred at the time the letter was sent. Thus, the three-year statute of repose started to run from the date of the letter in which the plaintiff was put on notice of defendant's intent.[215]

3. Arbitration

a. Commentary

Federal courts applying Puerto Rico law have also consistently upheld forum selection clauses in arbitration agreements.[216]

Arbitration provisions in Law 75 contracts are construed under the standard set forth in the Supreme Court's decision in *Prima Paint Corp. v. Flood & Conklin Manufacturing*.[217] In *Carro Rivera v. Parade of Toys, Inc.*,[218] the Puerto Rico federal district court stated that under *Prima Paint*, "fraud in the inducement of an entire contract containing a broad arbitration clause is for the arbitrators to decide."[219] The court further stated that "where the arbitration clause is broad, federal courts should only adjudicate claims of fraud in the inducement of the arbitration clause itself."[220] In *Carro*, the court found the arbitration clause to be narrow, "reflect[ing] an intent to arbitrate only a limited range of disputes."[221] Thus, the court decided that the Law 75 claim was not arbitrable.[222]

Section 278(b)(3) of Law 75, added by amendment in 2000, states in part that:

> Before any agreement or clause that would compel the parties to resolve through arbitration any controversy arising under a distribution contract granted pursuant to the present chapter may be invoked or made effective, it shall be an indispensable requirement before said controversy may be submitted to arbitration, at the request of any of the parties, that a court with jurisdiction in Puerto Rico determine that said clause or arbitration agreement was subscribed freely and voluntarily by both parties. There shall exist [a] controvertible presumption that any arbitration agreement or clause contained in a distribution contract was included or subscribed at the request of the principal or grantor, and that any agreement or clause that compels the parties to resolve through arbitration any controversy arising under said contract is an adhesion contract to be interpreted and made effective as such.[223]

---

215. *See also* Trafon Grp., Inc. v. Butterball, LLC, 820 F.3d 490, 494–95 (1st Cir. 2016); Medina & Medina, Inc. v. Hormel Foods Corp., 840 F.3d 26, 42 (1st Cir. 2016).
216. *See, e.g.*, Mitsubishi Motors Corp. v. Soler Chrysler-Plymouth, Inc., 723 F.2d 155, 158 (1st Cir. 1983) (holding that Federal Arbitration Act superseded local law invalidating arbitration outside Puerto Rico), *rev'd in part on other grounds*, 473 U.S. 614 (1985); *accord* KKW Enters., Inc. v. Gloria Jean's Gourmet Coffees Franchising Corp., 184 F.3d 42, 51 (1st Cir. 1999).
217. 388 U.S. 395 (1967).
218. 950 F. Supp. 449 (D.P.R. 1996).
219. *Id.* at 451.
220. *Id.*
221. *Id.* at 452.
222. *Id.*; *but see* Gemco Latinoamerica, Inc. v. Seiko Time Corp., 623 F. Supp. 912 (D.P.R. 1985) (since only claim by principal against dealer derived strictly from the terms of dealership contract and was, by its very nature, arbitrable, dealer had to submit to arbitration).
223. P.R. Laws Ann. tit. 10, § 278(b)(3).

Law 75 does not void an arbitration clause covered by the Federal Arbitration Act.[224] However, Law 75 purports to require a court determination that the arbitration clause was voluntarily and freely agreed by both parties.[225] It also presumes that any agreement to arbitrate is an adhesion contract. These limitations appear to collide with the Federal Arbitration Act because they single out arbitration agreements to impose burdens that do not apply to other contracts. This possible contradiction remains to be determined by a precedent setting court in Puerto Rico. Notably, however, the Puerto Rico Supreme Court has held that "whenever art. 3b of the Dealers' Act, 10 L.P.R.A. § 278(b)(2), is in conflict with the Federal Arbitration Act, the latter shall prevail."[226]

b. Annotations

The Federal Arbitration Act preempts section 278b-2 of Law 75 inasmuch as it precludes arbitration outside of Puerto Rico under foreign law or rule of law. The arbitrator decides which law to apply to the substantive dispute in the arbitration even if there is a choice-of-law clause in the contract.[227]

Provisions of Law 75 regarding arbitration are superseded when the Federal Arbitration Act applies, which empowers courts to stay any action involving an arbitrable dispute, provided parties agreed in writing concerning arbitration.[228]

Notwithstanding contractual clause establishing arbitration for any dispute arising from insurance general agency contract, when the principal answered the court complaint and stipulated speedy judicial solution, it waived its contract right to arbitration.[229]

Pursuant to Convention on the Recognition and Enforcement of Foreign Arbitral Awards, ordering arbitration under the Convention does not violate provisions of Law 75. The court held that the "null and void" provision of the Convention was not intended to incorporate Law 75.[230]

4. Limitations on Choice of Law Clauses

a. Commentary

Law 75 expressly voids choice-of-law clauses requiring the application of any law other than Law 75:

> The dealer's contracts referred to in this chapter shall be interpreted pursuant to and ruled by the laws of the Commonwealth of Puerto Rico, and *any other stipulation to the contrary shall be void*.[231]

---

224. *See* Mitsubishi Motors Corp. v. Soler Chrysler-Plymouth, Inc., 723 F.2d 155, 158 (1st Cir. 1983), *aff'd in part, rev'd in part*, 473 U.S. 614 (1985); Audiovisual Concepts, Inc. v. Smart Techs., 2011 U.S. Dist. LEXIS104304 (D.P.R. 2011).
225. 10 L.P.R.A. section 278b-3.
226. World Films, Inc. v. Paramount Pictures Corp., 125 D.P.R. 352 (1990).
227. Medika Intern., Inc. v. Scanlan Intern., Inc., 830 F. Supp. 81, 84 (D.P.R. 1993).
228. Michael v. NAP Consumer Elecs. Corp., 574 F. Supp. 68, 69 (D.P.R. 1983).
229. Caribbean Ins. Servs., Inc. v. Am. Bankers Life Assurance Co., 715 F.2d 17 (1st Cir. 1983).
230. Ledee v. Ceramiche Ragno, 684 F.2d 184, 187 (1st Cir. 1982).
231. *See* P.R. Laws Ann. tit. 10, § 278b-2 (emphasis added).

In cases in which the case is subject to arbitration, the arbitrator has authority to decide which substantive law to apply, whether it be the law chosen by the parties or Law 75.[232]

b. Annotations

If the litigation is filed in a Puerto Rico local court or in the U.S. District Court for the District of Puerto Rico, Law 75 will likely be applied rather than the law chosen by the parties insofar as the dominant contacts with the controversy—including the strong Puerto Rico public policy protecting local distributors—would likely favor the application of Puerto Rico law.[233]

---

232. *See* Medika Intern., Inc. v. Scanlan Intern., Inc., 830 F. Supp. 81, 84 (D.P.R. 1993).
233. *See* Caribbean Rest. LLC v. Burger King Corp., 23 F. Supp. 3d 70, 79–80 (2014); Autogermana, Inc. v. BMW of N. Am., Inc., 38 F. Supp. 3d 230, 235 n.5 (D.P.R. 2014); Beatty Caribbean, Inc. v. Viskase Sales Corp., 241 F. Supp. 2d 123 (D.P.R. 2003).

Rhode Island

Nicole Liguori Micklich

I. Introduction to Statute

The state of Rhode Island has enacted both a franchise relationship law and a franchise investment act. The relationship law is known as the Rhode Island Fair Dealership Act (RIFDA). The investment act is called the Rhode Island Franchise Investment Act (RIFIA). The Rhode Island Department of Business Regulation has also promulgated a franchise regulation that applies to franchises offered or sold in Rhode Island pursuant to the RIFIA.[1]

The RIFDA was enacted on June 14, 2007, and it requires written notice and cure periods for termination, cancellation, and nonrenewal except for certain types of dealer defaults and, although not explicit, implies a good cause requirement.

The "underlying purposes and policies" of the RIFDA are "To promote the compelling interest of the public in fair business relations between dealers and grantors and in the continuation of dealerships on a fair basis; To protect dealers against unfair treatment by grantors; To provide dealers with rights and remedies in addition to those existing by contract or common law; [and] To govern dealerships, including any renewals or amendments, to the full extent consistent with the constitutions of this state and the United States."[2] The RIFDA is to be "liberally construed and applied to promote its underlying remedial purposes and policies."[3] However, it is not a remedial statute because the obligations created and rights defined by the statute make it a substantive act.[4] Therefore, it must only be applied to relationships entered into after its enactment in 2007.[5]

Although the RIFIA is primarily a registration and disclosure statute, it is relevant to any discussion of Rhode Island franchise relationship laws because it also provides for a right of free association for franchisees, forbids certain false and misleading practices by franchisors, and grants aggrieved franchisees a private right of action to enforce the provisions of the act.

---

1. 230-RICR-50-10-1.
2. R.I. GEN. LAWS § 6-50-3.
3. *Id.* § 6-50-3.
4. Pascale Serv. Corp. v. Int'l Truck & Engine Corp., 558 F. Supp. 2d 217 (D.R.I. 2008).
5. *Id.* at 221–22.

The legislative intent of the RIFIA is set forth in the statute.[6] "The act seeks to ensure that each offeree receives the information necessary to make an informed decision about the offered franchise. Further, it is the intent of this chapter to prohibit the sale of franchises when there is a likelihood that the franchisor's promises will not be fulfilled."[7] The legislature determined that "many franchisees lack bargaining power" and are unfamiliar with "operating a business, the franchised business and with industry practices in franchising" and sought to even the playing field.[8]

II. Commentary and Annotations

The RIFDA was enacted in 2007. At the time, the enactment ended a 17-year drought in which no state in the United States enacted a generally applicable franchise relationship law.[9] It was met with opposition from franchisors, in part because it included a 90-day notice period for termination or change in dealership and afforded franchisees a 60-day cure period.[10] The act was amended in 2008.[11]

The original act required franchisors to give franchisees 90-day notice before making "substantial change in competitive circumstances" or terminating, cancelling, or nonrenewal. The 2008 amendments included a reduction in the notice period to 60 days and reduced the cure period to 30 days.[12] The 2008 amendments also deleted the terms "substantial change in competitive circumstances."[13]

---

6. R.I. GEN. LAWS § 6-50-3(b).

7. Id.

8. Id. § 19-28.1-2. See also DeRosa v. Boston Bakery & Italian Food Specialty, Inc., 103 B.R. 382 (Bankr. D.R.I. 1989) (reciting similar intent behind R.I. GEN. LAWS § 19-28-2).

9. Iowa passed such a law in 1992. Iowa Franchise Act, IOWA CODE §§ 523H.1 et seq. In 2000, Iowa passed a second relationship law that applies to franchise agreements entered into after July 1, 2000. Iowa Franchise Act, IOWA CODE § 537A.10.

10. R.I. GEN. LAWS § 6-50-4. Notice of termination or change in dealership. —Except as provided in this section, a grantor shall provide a dealer at least ninety (90) days' prior written notice of termination, cancellation, nonrenewal or substantial change in competitive circumstances. The notice shall state all the reasons for termination, cancellation, nonrenewal or substantial change in competitive circumstances and shall provide that the dealer has sixty (60) days in which to rectify any claimed deficiency. If the deficiency is rectified within sixty (60) days the notice shall be void. The notice provisions of this section shall not apply if the reason for termination, cancellation or nonrenewal is insolvency, the occurrence of an assignment for the benefit of creditors or bankruptcy. If the reason for termination, cancellation, nonrenewal or substantial change in competitive circumstances is nonpayment of sums due under the dealership, the dealers shall be entitled to written notice of such default, and shall have ten (10) days in which to remedy such default from the date of delivery or posting of such notice. Commercial Law—General Regulatory Provisions—Rhode Island Fair Dealership Act, 2007 R.I. Pub. Laws 07-28 (07–S 540); Legal Briefs, FRANCHISE TIMES (Sept. 1, 2007), https://www.franchisetimes.com/article_archive/legal-briefs/article_d5315e68-8114-5cb1-abf1-5e1e9a5892f1.html.

11. Commercial Law—General Regulatory Provisions—Rhode Island Fair Dealership Act, 2008 R.I. Pub. Laws 08-347 (08–H 8150A).

12. Id.

13. Id.

The 2008 amendments clarified whether "good cause" was required for termination and nonrenewal. Originally, the act defined "good cause" as "(i) Failure by a dealer to comply substantially with essential and reasonable requirements imposed upon the dealer by the grantor, or sought to be imposed by the grantor, which requirements are not discriminatory as compared with requirements imposed on other similarly situated dealers either by their terms of in the matter of their enforcement; or (ii) bad faith by the dealer in carrying out the terms of the dealership."[14] The 2008 amended law defined "good cause" and stated that, "for purposes of this act, good cause for terminating, canceling or nonrenewal shall include, but not be limited to, failure by the dealer to comply with the reasonable requirements imposed by the grantor or any of the reasons listed in subdivisions 6-50-4(a)(1) through (a)(6)."[15] Those six reasons were: the dealer "(1) voluntarily abandons the dealership relationship; (2) is convicted of a felony offense related to the business conducted pursuant to the dealership; (3) engages in any substantial act which tends to materially impair the goodwill of the grantor's trade name, trademark, service mark, logotype or other commercial symbol; (4) makes a material misrepresentation of fact to the grantor relating to the dealership; (5) attempts to transfer the dealership (or a portion thereof) without authorization of the grantor; or (6) is insolvent, files or suffers to be filed against it any voluntary or involuntary bankruptcy petition, or makes an assignment for the benefit of creditors or similar disposition of assets of the dealer business."[16] The six reasons remain in the act 15 years later.[17]

A. Definition of Franchise

1. Trademark Element

a. Commentary

The definition of "dealership" under the RIFDA requires that a person is granted the right to sell or distribute goods or services, *or* use a trade name, trademark, service mark, logotype, advertising, or other commercial symbol, but not both.[18]

b. Annotations

In a New York case, a franchisee alleged that the franchisor terminated the franchise, including by constructively terminating the franchise without good cause, in violation of various state's laws, including Rhode Island's. The parties' arrangement was called a "Dealership/License Agreement," which made the defendant the "exclusive licensee" of the plaintiff's trademark.[19] In preliminary pleadings, the plaintiff franchisor presented the relationship as licensor-licensee,

---

14. *Id.*
15. The word "inclusive" at the end of this sentence in the current act was added in 2014. 2014 R.I. Pub. Laws 14-528 (14-H 8104A).
16. The only subsequent amendment to these six reasons was to capitalize the first word of each listed reason in 2014. 2014 R.I. Pub. Laws 14-528 (14-H 8104A).
17. R.I. Gen. Laws § 6-50-4.
18. *Id.* § 6-50-2(3) (emphasis added).
19. Safe Step Walk in Tub Co. v. CKH Indus., Inc., 242 F. Supp. 3d 245, 261 (S.D.N.Y. 2017).

while the defendant franchisee alleged that the parties' agreements constituted franchise agreements.[20] The court held that the defendant's operations qualified as a franchise under the RIFIA.[21] It later also found that the defendant stated a plausible claim for violation of the act.[22] It is unclear why the court did not refer to the RIFDA, since the franchisee's counterclaim alleged wrongful termination. But the court wrote, "Whatever protections are available under the New York and Rhode Island franchise statutory schemes for the alleged wrongful termination or failure to renew the agreements will have to suffice."[23]

2. Franchise Fee Element

a. Commentary

The definition of a dealership under RIFDA does not explicitly require the payment of a franchise fee; however, as discussed later, the community of interest element requires a continuing financial interest.

Notably, while the RIFDA does not include a franchise fee requirement, the RIFIA requires a marketing plan, a franchise fee, and association with a trademark.[24]

b. Annotations

Like the RIFDA, the Connecticut Franchise Act[25] does not have a franchise fee element. The lack of a franchise fee element in the RIFDA leaves open the possibility that a grantor may be an inadvertent or accidental franchisor, as the Connecticut federal court once held.[26] An inadvertent franchisor in Rhode Island may have additional liability in circumstances where the grantor believes that it is not a franchisor and does not register in accordance with the RIFIA.

3. Third Element (Community of Interest; Significant Degree of Control; Joint Marketing Plan; Other)

a. Commentary

As already described, the RIFDA only has two elements, the second of which is a "community of interest in the business of offering, selling, or distributing goods or services." The RIFDA defines "community of interest" as "a continuing

---

20. *Id.*
21. *Id.*
22. Safe Step Walk in Tub Co. v. CKH Indus., Inc., 2018 WL 4539656, 2018 U.S. Dist. LEXIS 161082, at *15 (S.D.N.Y. Sept. 20, 2018).
23. *Safe Step*, 242 F. Supp. 3d 245 at 262 *citing* N.Y. GEN. BUS. LAW § 687 and R.I. GEN. LAWS § 19-28.1-17. The court did not cite to R.I. GEN. LAWS § 6-50-4, requiring notice of termination and implicitly requiring good cause for termination, nor any other provision of the RIFDA.
24. R.I. GEN. LAWS. § 19-28.1-3.
25. CONN. GEN. STAT. § 42-133e *et seq.*
26. *See* Charts v. Nationwide Mut. Ins. Co., 397 F. Supp. 2d 357 (D. Conn. 2005) (holding that defendant insurance company violated the Connecticut Franchise Act when it terminated its contracts with independent insurance agent) *rev'd on other grounds* Chartschlaa v. Nationwide Mut. Ins. Co., 583 F.3d 116 (2d Cir. 2008).

financial interest between the grantor and the grantee in either the operation of the dealership business or the marketing of such goods or service."[27]

b. Annotations

There are no cases interpreting the definition of "community of interest," in the RIFDA.

With respect to the requirement of a contract or agreement,[28] a Florida federal court held that a plaintiff manufacturer did not have an ongoing obligation to provide a defendant distributor of hair care products with its products as the RIFDA "requires a 'dealership' and 'does not create a binding contract where one does not exist.'"[29] The court found that, "As a matter of law and undisputed fact, there was no dealership business arrangement between the parties was not the result of a binding oral contract or other agreement imposing an ongoing obligation upon the Plaintiff."[30]

B. Scope and Jurisdiction

1. Commentary

The RIFDA applies to "dealerships," which are defined as written, oral, or implied agreements by which a person or entity "is granted the right to sell or distribute goods or services, or use a trade name, trademark, service mark, logotype, advertising, or other commercial symbol, in which there is a community of interest in the business of offering, selling, or distributing goods or services at wholesale, retail, by lease, agreement, or otherwise."[31] Where a business arrangement between parties is not the result of a binding agreement there is no dealership.[32] The RIFDA applies only to dealers "situated in" Rhode Island.[33]

The RIFDA's protections do not extend to "malt beverage dealerships; motor vehicle dealerships; insurance agency relationships; any relationship relating to the sale or administration of insurance or any similar contract with an entity organized under chapters 19 or 20 of title 27; fuel distribution dealerships; and door-to-door sales dealerships."[34]

2. Annotations

Courts have not interpreted the phrase "situated in this state" as used in the RIFDA.

---

27. R.I. GEN. LAWS § 6-50-2(1).
28. *Id.* § 6-50-2(3).
29. It's a New 10, LLC v. Masello Salon Services of New England, LLC, No. 18-61073-CIV, 2019 WL 4691777, at *4 (S.D. Fla. Aug. 13, 2019).
30. *Id.* at n.4.
31. R.I. GEN. LAWS § 6-50-2.
32. *It's a New 10, LLC*, No. 18-61073-CIV, 2019 WL 4691777, at n.4.
33. R.I. GEN. LAWS § 6-50-2.
34. *Id.* § 6-50-9.

The "effect of" the RIFDA "may not be varied by contract or agreement," and any "contract or agreement purporting to do so is void and unenforceable to that extent only."[35]

Pursuant to the act, "if the criteria for determining whether good cause existed for a termination, cancellation, or nonrenewal and the relief provided is no less than that provided for in [the Act]," the act "shall not apply to provisions for the binding arbitration of disputes contained in a dealership agreement."[36] No court has interpreted this provision.

Defendant franchisor Cold Stone Creamery, Inc. succeeded in transferring an action against it by a franchisee in Rhode Island to Maricopa County, Arizona, pursuant to an enforceable and reasonable choice of venue provision in the parties' franchise agreement.[37]

C. Termination

1. What Constitutes Termination or Cancellation

a. Commentary

The RIFDA does not define termination or cancellation, nor does it distinguish between termination, cancellation, or nonrenewal. It does not define or include the idea of constructive termination.

b. Annotations

In *Safe Step Walk-In Tub Co. v. CKH Industries, Inc.*, the defendant alleged that it was a franchisee protected by the RIFDA and other state franchise protection laws and that, inter alia, the plaintiff intentionally escalated its costs in order to constructively terminate the alleged franchise without good cause in violation of the RIFDA. The allegations survived plaintiff's motion to dismiss.[38]

2. Restrictions on Termination or Cancellation

a. Commentary

The 2008 amendments to the RIFDA just described implied in the act a requirement that a franchisor have good cause to terminate a franchise under the RIFDA.

---

35. *Id.* § 6-50-3.
36. *Id.* § 6-50-6.
37. Fowler v. Cold Stone Creamery, Inc., No. CA 13-662 S, 2013 WL 6181817, at *3 (D.R.I. Nov. 25, 2013) ("As noted earlier, Plaintiffs not only agreed to the terms of the franchise agreement, but also reviewed a franchise offering circular that clearly and unequivocally warned of additional costs associated with litigating in Arizona as opposed to the franchisee's home state. While it is regrettable that Plaintiffs may indeed incur certain additional costs in litigating this matter in Arizona, these costs were (or should have been) contemplated as part of Plaintiffs' decision to enter into the franchise agreement.").
38. Safe Step Walk In Tub Co. v. CKH Indus., Inc., No. 15 CIV. 7543 (NSR), 2018 WL 4539656 (S.D.N.Y. Sept. 20, 2018); Safe Step Walk In Tub Co. v. CKH Indus., Inc., No. 15 CIV. 7543 (NSR), 2023 WL 1383678 (S.D.N.Y. Jan. 1, 2023).

b. Annotations

At least one court has found that the RIFDA prohibits a franchisor from terminating the franchise relationship with a franchisee without good cause.[39]

3. Notice Requirement
a. Commentary

As just set forth, regardless of any contractual provision to the contrary, the RIFDA requires a franchisor to provide a franchisee with 60 days' prior written notice of termination, cancellation, or nonrenewal.[40] "The notice shall state all the reasons for termination, cancellation, or nonrenewal and shall provide that the dealer has thirty (30) days in which to cure any claimed deficiency; provided that a dealer has a right to cure only three (3) times in any twelve-month (12) period during the period of the dealership agreement."[41] The cure period is reduced to ten days, "if the reason for termination, cancellation, or nonrenewal is nonpayment of sums due under the dealership."[42] It is further reduced to only 24 hours, "if the reason for termination, cancellation, or nonrenewal is for violation of any law, regulation, or standard relating to public health or safety."[43]

The notice provisions of the RIFDA do not apply and "the termination, cancellation, or nonrenewal may be made effective immediately upon written notice if the reason for termination, cancellation, or nonrenewal is in the event the dealer: (1) voluntarily abandons the dealership relationship; (2) is convicted of a felony offense related to the business conducted pursuant to the dealership; (3) engages in any substantial act that tends to materially impair the goodwill of the grantor's trade name, trademark, service mark, logotype, or other commercial symbol; (4) makes a material misrepresentation of fact to the grantor relating to the dealership; (5) attempts to transfer the dealership (or a portion thereof) without authorization of the grantor; or (6) is insolvent, files, or suffers to be filed against it, any voluntary or involuntary bankruptcy petition or makes an assignment for the benefit of creditors or similar disposition of assets of the dealer business."[44]

b. Annotations

The RIFDA imposes notice obligations on any attempted termination.[45] Interpreting the June 14, 2007 Act, in a case involving a notice of intent to terminate

---

39. Faxon Sales, Inc. v. U-Line Corp., No. 17-CV-872-JPS, 2017 WL 4990617, at *2 (E.D. Wis., Oct. 31, 2017) ("Among other requirements, the CFA and RIFDA prohibit a franchisor from terminating a franchise relationship without good cause and impose notice and inventory repurchasing obligations on any attempted termination.") (citing CONN. GEN. STAT. § 42–133f; R.I. GEN. LAWS § 6-50-4(a)).
40. R.I. GEN. LAWS § 6-50-4(a).
41. *Id.*
42. *Id.* § 6-50-4(b).
43. *Id.* § 6-50-4(c).
44. *Id.* § 6-50-4(a).
45. Faxon Sales, Inc. v. U-Line Corp., No. 17-CV-872-JPS, 2017 WL 4990617, at *2 (E.D. Wis. Oct. 31, 2017) ("Among other requirements, the CFA and RIFDA prohibit a franchisor from terminating a

issued on April 9, 2007, the federal court for the District of Rhode Island found that the notice provisions in the RIFDA govern notice of termination, but not the termination or cancellation of the dealership agreement itself, and do not impose a good cause requirement, and specifically noted that the notice requirement is not "phrased to require that no termination may be effectuated without notice being given in accordance with the terms of the statute."[46]

4. Grounds for Termination

a. Commentary

As stated earlier, the RIFDA requires written notice and cure periods for termination, cancellation, and nonrenewal except for certain types of dealer defaults and, although not explicit, implies a good cause requirement. Good cause is defined broadly in section 6-50-2(4) and then more specifically in section 6-50-4 where the six specific subdivisions that the act indicates are good cause for termination, cancellation, or nonrenewal are set forth. The definitions provided by the RIFDA make the act stronger than those laws of other states, such as Virginia, which requires reasonable cause for termination but does not define the term. For example, the RIFDA defines good cause as "(i) The failure by the dealer to comply with the reasonable requirements imposed by the grantor; or (ii) any of the reasons listed in § 6-50-4(a)(1)–(a)(6)."[47] Those reasons are (1) voluntarily abandons the dealership relationship; (2) is convicted of a felony offense related to the business conducted pursuant to the dealership; (3) engages in any substantial act that tends to materially impair the goodwill of the grantor's trade name, trademark, service mark, logotype, or other commercial symbol; (4) makes a material misrepresentation of fact to the grantor relating to the dealership; (5) attempts to transfer the dealership (or a portion thereof) without authorization of the grantor; or (6) is insolvent, files, or suffers to be filed against it, any voluntary or involuntary bankruptcy petition or makes an assignment for the benefit of creditors or similar disposition of assets of the dealer business.

---

franchise relationship without good cause and impose notice and inventory repurchasing obligations on any attempted termination.") (citing Conn. Gen. Stat. § 42–133f; R.I. Gen. Laws § 6-50-4(a)).

46. Pascale Serv. Corp. v. Int'l Truck & Engine Corp., 558 F. Supp. 2d 217, 220 (D.R.I. 2008) ("Applying tried and true principles of statutory interpretation, and giving the words of Section 6–50–4 their plain and ordinary meaning, it is clear that the terms of the FDA govern *notice* of termination, not the termination or cancellation of the dealership agreement itself. Section 6–50–4 does not impose a good or just cause requirement for termination, nor is it phrased to require that no termination may be effectuated without notice being given in accordance with the terms of the statute. Rather, Section 6–50–4 speaks only to notice itself—when it should be given, what it should contain, and how it may be rendered void by the dealer. However, nothing in the FDA indicates that Section 6–50–4 regulates anything but conduct (i.e.—notice) occurring after its effective date. Thus, while the question remains open of whether actions violating the statute and occurring after June 14, 2007 might be prohibited where the contract at issue was entered into prior to June 14, 2007, conduct which occurred before June 14, 2007 unquestionably falls outside the scope of the FDA.") (internal quotations omitted).

47. R.I. Gen. Laws § 6-50-2(5).

b. Annotations
Not applicable.

5. *Required Cure Period*
a. Commentary
As discussed earlier, a franchisor must provide a franchisee with written notice at least 60 days before any termination, cancellation, or nonrenewal. The franchisor must state all the reasons for its action in the notice and provide the franchisee with 30 days in which to cure the alleged deficiencies, "provided that a dealer has a right to cure three (3) times in any twelve-month (12) period during the period of the dealership agreement."[48]

The notice and cure periods do not apply, and the termination, cancellation, or nonrenewal "may be made effective immediately upon written notice," if the reason for the termination, cancellation, or nonrenewal is that the franchisee (1) voluntarily abandons the dealership relationship; (2) is convicted of a felony offense related to the business conducted pursuant to the dealership; (3) engages in any substantial act that tends to materially impair the goodwill of the grantor's trade name, trademark, service mark, logotype, or other commercial symbol; (4) makes a material misrepresentation of fact to the grantor relating to the dealership; (5) attempts to transfer the dealership (or a portion thereof) without authorization of the grantor; or (6) is insolvent, files, or suffers to be filed against it any voluntary or involuntary bankruptcy petition, or makes an assignment for the benefit of creditors or similar disposition of assets of the dealer business.[49]

There are also certain statutory grounds for termination, cancellation, or nonrenewal with shortened notice and cure periods. First, if the reason for termination, cancellation, or nonrenewal is the franchisee's failure to pay an amount due, the franchisor must provide written notice of the default, and the franchisee will have ten days "from the date of such notice" to cure the default.[50] Under these circumstances, the franchisee has the right to cure a payment default three times in any 12-month period during the dealership agreement.[51] Second, if "the reason for termination, cancellation, or nonrenewal is for violation of any law, regulation, or standard relating to public health or safety," the dealer is entitled to immediate written notice and has 24 hours to cure the violation.[52] While the cure period for a health or safety violation is shorter than other cure periods in the RIFDA, there is no restriction on the number of times a franchisee may violate such a law or regulation and cure the same in a 12-month period. It is unclear from the act whether a franchisee might continuously violate such a law and avoid termination, or whether after a certain number of or type of violations a franchisor might successfully argue that the franchisee has materially impaired its goodwill or caused harm to its brand or system such that good cause exists to terminate the franchise agreement immediately.

---

48. *Id*. § 6-50-4.
49. *Id*.
50. *Id*.
51. *Id*.
52. *Id*. § 6-50-4.

b. Annotations

It is also unclear what happens if the franchisee has defaulted on a payment obligation more than three times in any 12-month period. Arguably the franchisor has grounds for immediate termination. On the other hand, as the *Pascale* court wrote regarding the 2007 version of the RIFDA, "it is clear that the terms of the FDA govern *notice* of termination, not the termination or cancellation of the dealership agreement itself."[53]

6. Repurchase Obligations

a. Commentary

If a franchisor terminates the franchise or dealership, the RIFDA requires the franchisor to repurchase all inventory sold by the franchisor to the franchisee at wholesale market value, at the option of the franchisee.[54] If the franchisee opts for the repurchase, the franchisor must repurchase all inventory that bears the franchisor's name, trademark, label, or other identifying mark that the franchisor sold to the franchisee for resale under the dealership agreement "at the fair, wholesale market value."[55] The franchisor's obligation under the RIFDA to repurchase branded inventory and merchandise sold to the franchisee applies even when there is good cause for termination.[56]

b. Annotations

Not applicable.

D. Restrictions on Nonrenewal

1. What Constitutes Nonrenewal

a. Commentary

The RIFDA does not define nonrenewal. Whenever the terms are used in the RIFDA, the words "termination, cancellation, or nonrenewal" appear together, so presumably, courts will look to the case law that addresses termination when addressing cases relating to nonrenewal.

b. Annotations

Not applicable.

2. Restrictions on Nonrenewal

a. Commentary

The restrictions on nonrenewal in the RIFDA are identical to the restrictions on termination or cancellation set forth earlier in the chapter.

---

53. Pascale Serv. Corp. v. Int'l Truck & Engine Corp., 558 F. Supp. 2d 217, 220 (D.R.I. 2008).
54. R.I. GEN. LAWS § 6-50-5.
55. *Id.*
56. *Id.*; *cf.* ARK. CODE ANN. § 4-72-209.

3. Notice Requirements

a. Commentary

The notice requirements for nonrenewal of a franchise agreement under the RIFDA are identical to the notice requirements for termination of a franchise agreement under the act.

b. Annotations

Not applicable.

4. Grounds for Nonrenewal

a. Commentary

The grounds for nonrenewal under the RIFDA are the same as the grounds for termination and cancellation described previously.

b. Annotations

Not applicable.

5. Required Cure Period

a. Commentary

The cure periods related to nonrenewal are the same as the cure periods relating to termination and cancellation described earlier.

b. Annotations

Not applicable.

6. Limitations on Franchisors' Rights to Impose Conditions for Renewal

a. Commentary

Not applicable.

b. Annotations

Not applicable.

7. Repurchase Obligations

a. Commentary

As is discussed previously with respect to termination, if a franchisor refuses to renew the franchise or dealership agreement, the RIFDA requires the franchisor to repurchase all inventory sold by the franchisor to the franchisee at wholesale market value, at the option of the franchisee.[57] If the franchisee opts for the repurchase, the franchisor must repurchase all inventory that bears the

---

57. R.I. GEN. LAWS § 6-50-5.

franchisor's name, trademark, label, or other identifying mark that the franchisor sold to the franchisee for resale under the dealership agreement "at the fair, wholesale market value."[58]

The franchisor's obligation under the RIFDA to repurchase branded inventory and merchandise sold to the franchisee applies even when there is good cause for the nonrenewal.[59]

b. Annotations
Not applicable.

E. Transfers and Succession

1. Commentary
The RIFDA protects the franchisor's right to approve the franchisee's transfer of all or any portion of the dealership. The act provides that the 60-day notice provision giving the dealer the right to notice and cure prior to termination, cancellation, or nonrenewal shall not apply if the dealer attempts to transfer the dealership (or a portion thereof) without authorization of the franchisor.[60] This protects the franchisor's right to terminate the franchise agreement or declare a transfer void if the franchisee attempts to transfer without the franchisor's approval.

2. Annotations
Not applicable.

F. Other Regulations on the Franchise Relationship

1. Commentary
As noted earlier, although primarily a disclosure and registration act, the RIFIA addresses certain aspects of the franchise relationship. While the RIFDA does not contain a no-waiver provision, the RIFIA voids waivers of duties of liability or rights under the RIFIA and specifies that integration clauses or similar provisions do not "negate or remove from judicial review any statement, misrepresentations, or action that would violate" that act.[61]

A choice of law provision in the parties' agreement that chooses another state's law is void "with respect to a claim otherwise enforceable under [the RIFIA]."[62] The RIFIA also prohibits any "condition, stipulation or provision requiring a franchisee to waive compliance with or relieving a person of a duty of liability imposed" by the act.[63] In particular, any "acknowledgement provision, disclaimer or integration clause or a provision having a similar effect in a

---

58. *Id.*
59. *Id.*; *cf.* ARK. CODE ANN. § 4-72-209.
60. R.I. GEN. LAWS § 6-50-4.
61. *Id.* § 19-28.1-15.
62. *Id.* § 19-28.1-14; *see also* Honey Dew Assocs., Inc. v. M&K Food Corp., 81 F. Supp. 2d 352 (D.R.I. 2000) (discussing absence of clear Rhode Island precedent on a choice-of-law issue), *vacated on other grounds*, 241 F.3d 23 (1st Cir. 2001).
63. R.I. GEN. LAWS § 19-28.1-14.

franchise agreement does not negate or act to remove from judicial review any statement, misrepresentations or action that would violate" the act.[64]

The RIFIA makes void any provision or clause in a franchise agreement that "negate[s] or act[s] to remove from judicial review any statement, misrepresentations or action that would violate" the act, and specifically prohibits disclaimers and integration clauses.[65]

Under the RIFIA, a franchisor "shall not restrict a franchisee from associating with other franchisees or from participating in a trade association, or retaliate against a franchisee for engaging in these activities."[66]

2. Annotations

In a case in New York that included claims under the RIFIA, the defendant franchisor argued that the plaintiff franchisee's fraudulent inducement claim was barred by a nonreliance disclaimer in the franchise agreement.[67] Although the New York court was "extremely reluctant" to decide a Rhode Island question of first impression, it found the RIFIA to be explicit (more so than the comparable New York law) and specific in its prohibition of such contractual disclaimers, and thus the court declined to dismiss the franchisee's fraudulent inducement claim.[68]

Although the New York court believed this was a question of first impression under Rhode Island law, in a 2010 case, the District of Rhode Island granted summary judgment to the defendant franchisor based on an integration clause in the franchise agreement, which disclaimed representations and reliance and required the plaintiff franchisee to release claims against the defendant.[69] The court noted that the plaintiff initialed those provisions and was represented by counsel, and there was no ambiguity in the contract language.[70] This decision appears to overlook the RIFIA provision that voids such clauses.[71]

In *Sandonato v. Days Inn Worldwide, Inc.*, the U.S. District Court of Rhode Island noted that the RIFIA prohibits fraudulent or deceptive practices in connection with the sale of a franchise, including making untrue or misleading statements, but, without commenting on R.I. General Laws section 19-28.1-15, concluded that the plaintiff's attestations that he was the victim of fraudulent misrepresentations were not colorable in light of unambiguous integration clauses in the franchise agreement.[72] However, a court in New York faced with claims under the RIFIA found the prohibition of integration clauses to be specific and clear.[73]

---

64. *Id.*
65. *Id.* § 19-28.1-15.
66. *Id.* § 19-28.1-16.
67. EV Scarsdale Corp. v. Engel & Voelkers N.E. LLC, 13 N.Y.S.3d 805, 820 (N.Y. Sup. Ct. 2015).
68. *Id.*
69. Sandonato v. Days Inn Worldwide, Inc., C.A. No. 07-451S, 2010 WL 8461122, at *6 (D.R.I. July 21, 2010) report and recommendation adopted CA 07-451 S, 2012 U.S. Dist. LEXIS 28589, 2012 WL 718720 (D.R.I. Mar. 5, 2012).
70. *Id.*
71. R.I. GEN. LAWS § 19-28.1-15.
72. *Sandonato*, 2010 WL 8461122 at *16, *18.
73. *EV Scarsdale Corp.*, 13 N.Y.S.3d at 820.

G. Remedies and Administration Action

1. Restrictive Covenants

a. Commentary
The RIFIA and RFDA are silent with respect to restrictive covenants.

b. Annotations
Rhode Island law largely prohibits employers from entering into noncompete agreements with their employees.[74] Generally, Rhode Island courts have adopted the doctrine of reasonableness in the determination of the validity of restrictive covenants.[75] No Rhode Island case applying Rhode Island law addresses restrictive covenants in franchise agreements.

2. Damages

a. Commentary
If a franchisor violates the RIFDA, "a dealer may bring an action against such [franchisor] in any court of competent jurisdiction for damages sustained by the dealer as a consequence of the [franchisor's] violation, together with the actual costs of the action, including reasonable, actual attorneys' fees."[76]

An aggrieved franchisee has a private right of action under the RIFIA. A franchisee may sue for damages, attorneys' and expert fees, and costs pursuant to the RIFIA.[77] "The franchisee" may sue for (1) damages for any violation of the act, or (2) rescission as a result of a violation of the registration, disclosure, or anti-fraud sections of the act.[78] A person who violates the RIFIA is liable only to the franchisee for damages.[79] Attorneys' fees, expert fees, and costs are recoverable by a franchisee.[80]

The limitations period under the RIFIA is (1) four years from the act or transaction constituting the violation, or (2) 90 days after receipt by the franchisee of a rescission offer by the franchisor in the form approved by the director of business regulation.[81]

b. Annotations
Future royalties may be considered in a damages calculation for breach of a franchise agreement.[82]

---

74. *See* Rhode Island Noncompetition Agreement Act, R.I. GEN. LAWS §§ 28-59-1, *et seq.*
75. *See* Max Garelick, Inc. v. Leonardo, 105 R.I. 142, 250 A.2d 354, 356 (1969).
76. R.I. GEN. LAWS § 6-50-5.
77. *Id.* § 19-28.1-21(a); *see* DeRosa v. Boston Bakery & Italian Food Specialty, Inc., 98 B.R. 644 (Bankr. D.R.I. 1989); *see also* DeRosa v. Boston Bakery & Italian Food Specialty, Inc., 103 B.R. 382 (Bankr. D.R.I. 1989) (detailing $36,342.24 of damages awarded).
78. R.I. GEN. LAWS § 19-28.1-21(a).
79. *See id.* § 19-28.1-23 (except as expressly provided in the act "no civil liability arises from a violation" of the act).
80. *Id.*
81. *Id.* § 19-28.1-22.
82. In *United Consumers Club, Inc. v. Bledsoe*, the U.S. District Court for the Northern District of Indiana concluded that where franchise agreement contained choice of law provisions electing

3. Rescission

a. Commentary
Not applicable.

b. Annotations
Not applicable.

4. Injunctive Relief

a. Commentary
Under the RIFDA, if any franchisor violates the act, a dealer may "be granted injunctive relief against unlawful termination, cancellation, or nonrenewal."[83] In any action brought by a franchisee against a franchisor under the RIFDA, any violation of that act by the franchisor "is deemed an irreparable injury to the dealer in determining if temporary injunctions should issue."[84]

b. Annotations
Not applicable.

5. Control Person Liability

a. Commentary
The RIFDA does not specifically apply to officers or directors of an entity.

The RIFIA permits a private civil action to be brought against any person who violates any of its provisions and specifically provides that every officer and director is jointly and severally liable for the actions or omissions of the person liable for the violation of the statute.[85]

b. Annotations
Not applicable.

6. Attorneys' Fees

a. Commentary
Under the RIFDA, damages include "reasonable, actual attorneys' fees."[86] A person who violates the RIFIA is liable to the franchisee for attorneys' and expert fees.[87]

Rhode Island law, lost future profits were an appropriate element of contract damages "if the profits can be calculated with reasonable certainty." 441 F. Supp. 2d 967, 987 (N.D. Ind. 2006) (*citing* Sweet v. Pace Membership Warehouse, Inc., 795 A.2d 524, 529 (R.I. 2002)).

83. R.I. GEN. LAWS § 6-50-7.
84. *Id.* § 6-50-8.
85. *Id.* § 19-28.1-21.
86. *Id.*
87. *Id.* § 19-28.1-21(a); *see* DeRosa v. Boston Bakery & Italian Food Specialty, Inc., 98 B.R. 644 (Bankr. D.R.I. 1989); DeRosa v. Boston Bakery & Italian Food Specialty, Inc., 103 B.R. 382 (Bankr. D.R.I. 1989) (detailing $36,342.24 of damages awarded).

b. Annotations

In a case where the defendant franchisor and its alter ego committed fraud under the RIFIA and breached their franchise agreement the court properly awarded attorneys' fees.[88]

7. Limitations on Damage Waivers

a. Commentary

The RIFDA does not contain a no-waiver provision.

The RIFIA prohibits any "condition, stipulation or provision requiring a franchisee to waive compliance with or relieving a person of a duty of liability imposed" by that law.[89]

b. Annotations

Not applicable.

8. Administrative Action

a. Commentary

The RIFDA does not include administrative remedies.

Under the RIFIA, the director of business regulation may take various actions including bringing a civil action against any person whom it appears to the director has violated a provision of the law or a rule or order under the act and seeking to recover a penalty from such person.[90] When the director prevails in such an action, the director is entitled to recover the costs, expenses, and experts' fees incurred incident to the action.[91]

b. Annotations

Not applicable.

H. Dispute Resolution

1. Limitations on Franchisors' Ability to Restrict Venue

a. Commentary

The RIFDA is silent with respect to a franchisor's ability to restrict venue.

Under the RIFIA, a choice of law provision in the parties' agreement that chooses another state's law is void "with respect to a claim otherwise enforceable."[92] However, under the RIFIA, a contract provision requiring disputes to be litigated

---

88. Guzman v. Jan-Pro Cleaning Sys., Inc., 839 A.2d 504, n.3 (R.I. 2003) ("The defendants do not claim, nor is there any evidence in the record, that the trial justice erred in calculating attorney's fees; consequently, we will not disturb that component of the award.").

89. R.I. GEN. LAWS § 19-28.1-15.

90. *Id.* § 19-28.1-18(c).

91. *Id.* § 19-28.1-18(e).

92. *Id.* § 19-28.1-14; *see also* Honey Dew Assocs., Inc. v. M&K Food Corp., 81 F. Supp. 2d 352 (D.R.I. 2000) (discussing absence of clear Rhode Island precedent on a choice-of-law issue), *vacated on other grounds*, 241 F.3d 23 (1st Cir. 2001).

outside of Rhode Island is void.[93] But a contract provision requiring a franchisee to arbitrate outside of Rhode Island may be enforced because the Federal Arbitration Act preempts contrary state law.[94]

b. Annotations

In *KKW Enterprises v. Gloria Jean's Gourmet Coffees, Franchising Corp.*, the First Circuit Court of Appeals held that the bar of all arbitration outside Rhode Island imposed by the RIFIA violates the Federal Arbitration Act (FAA) and was preempted.[95] The franchisee in the case would have to arbitrate in Chicago, Illinois, because Gloria Jean's choice of arbitral forum should be "honored" by the court.[96] The court wrote, "Writ simple, because § 19-28.1-14 is not a generally applicable contract defense, it is, if applied to arbitration agreements, preempted by § 2 of the FAA."[97]

2. Limitations Period

a. Commentary

The RIFDA does not contain a statutory limitations period. In Rhode Island, all civil actions not otherwise limited have a ten-year statute of limitations; this generally includes claims for breach of contract.[98]

The limitations period under the RIFIA is (1) four years from the act or transaction constituting the violation, or (2) 90 days after receipt by the franchisee of a rescission offer by the franchisor in the form approved by the director of business regulation.[99]

b. Annotations

A one-year contractual limitations period was enforced by a Wisconsin court, which dismissed as untimely a terminated distributor's claims against the dealer for violation of various states' statutes, including the RIFDA.[100]

---

93. R.I. GEN. LAWS § 19-28.1-14.
94. KKW Enters., Inc. v. Gloria Jean's Gourmet Coffees, Franchising Corp., 184 F.3d 42 (1st Cir. 1999).
95. *Id.*
96. *Id.* at 52.
97. *Id.* at 51.
98. R.I. GEN. LAWS § 9-1-13.
99. *Id.* § 19-28.1-22.
100. Faxon Sales, Inc. v. U-Line Corp., Docket No. 17-CV-872-JPS, 2017 U.S. Dist. LEXIS 179811 (E.D. Wis. Oct. 31, 2017) ("Plaintiff filed the action more than a year from the date of the termination letter, but within a year of the effective date of the termination. Faxon's claims accrued either on the date of U-Line's notice of termination or its June 7, 2016, email, which renders Faxon's complaint untimely under the applicable one-year limitations period provided in the parties' agreement. As a result, the Court must dismiss this action.").

U.S. Virgin Islands

John R. Gotaskie, Jr.[1]

I. Introduction to Statute

The United States Virgin Islands (USVI) has one franchise law, the Virgin Islands Franchise Business Act (VIFBA). The USVI has not enacted any industry-specific franchise laws, and the VIFBA is the only source of law regulating the franchise relationship for most industries. The only two exceptions are (1) automobile dealerships, which are also governed by the federal Automobile Dealer's Day in Court Act, and (2) petroleum retailers who are governed solely by the federal Petroleum Marketing Practices Act, which preempts the Virgin Islands Franchise Business Act.

II. Commentary and Annotations

A. Definition of Franchise

1. Commentary

The VIFBA defines a franchise using five elements:

(1) a contract or an agreement, express or implied, whether oral or written, involving a commercial relationship;
(2) the franchisee is granted the right to offer, sell, and distribute goods or services manufactured, processed, or distributed by the franchisor;
(3) the franchisee's independent business is a component of the franchisor's distribution system;
(4) the operation of the franchised business is substantially associated with the franchisor's trademark, service mark, trade name, advertising, or other commercial symbol designating the franchisor; and
(5) the franchisee is substantially reliant on the franchisor for a continued supply of goods or services.[2]

---

1. The author wishes to thank his colleague Blake Jacobs for his assistance in the preparation of this chapter.
2. V.I. CODE ANN. tit. 12A, § 130(2).

2. Annotations

Courts applying USVI law have explicitly held that the VIFBA applies to implied contracts.[3] The VIFBA does not require that a franchisee pay a franchise fee or that there be community of interest, or a marketing plan.[4] Additionally, there is no published case law defining what constitutes substantial association with the franchisor's trademark under the VIFBA.[5]

B. Scope and Jurisdiction

1. Commentary

The VIFBA governs almost all franchise disputes in the USVI.[6] The USVI lacks any industry-specific distribution laws for car dealerships, alcohol distributors, farm equipment, or petroleum retailing.[7] USVI automobile dealers are governed by both the Automobile Dealer's Day in Court Act (Dealer's Act) and the VIFBA.

The Dealer's Act allows an automobile dealer to bring suit against any automobile manufacturer who fails to act in good faith in performing or complying with any of the terms or provisions of a franchise, or in terminating, cancelling, or not renewing a franchise with the dealer.[8] The Dealer's Act is a remedial statute enacted to redress the economic imbalance between automobile manufacturers and local dealerships, which protects the dealerships from unfair termination and other coercive practices.[9]

To bring a claim under the Dealer's Act a plaintiff must establish that (1) they are an automobile dealer; (2) the defendant is an automobile manufacturer engaged in commerce; (3) there is a manufacturer-dealer relationship embodied in a written franchise agreement; and (4) the defendant manufacturer

---

3. *See* Fleming v. Orange Crush of P.R., Inc., 30 V.I. 268, 272 (D.V.I. July 11, 1994).
4. *See* 1 Franchise & Distrib. L. & Prac. § 5:36, Virgin Islands (2023).
5. *Id.*
6. *See* Spenceley Off. Equip. v. Ricoh Latin Am., Inc., 48 V.I. 848, 850 (D.V.I. Feb. 28, 2007) (applying the VIFBA to a franchise dispute between an office supply company and a distributor); *Fleming*, 30 V.I. at 270 (applying the VIFBA to a franchise dispute between soda manufacturer and a distributor); Gassett v. Nissan N.A., Inc., 877 F. Supp. 974, 986 (D.V.I. 1994), *aff'd*, 66 F.3d 311 (3d Cir. 1995) (applying the VIFBA to a franchise dispute between an auto dealership and manufacturer); United States v. Topa Equities (V.I.), Ltd., 1995 WL 481368, at *2 (D.V.I. July 14, 1995) (citing the VIFBA when discussing an alcohol manufacturer's relationship with its distributor); Luma Enterprises, Inc. v. Richemont Int'l, S.A., No. CV 2005-177, 2008 WL 11380419, at *2 (D.V.I. Mar. 19, 2008) (applying the VIFBA when discussing a luxury brand accessory manufacturer's relationship with its distributor).
7. *See* Legal Aspects of Selling & Buying, App'x N., State Motor Vehicle Dealer Laws (3d ed. 2021) (survey on automobile dealership distribution laws does not include any statutes from the USVI); *see also* 3 Franchise & Distrib. L. & Prac. § 16:4 (2023); W. Michael Garner, 3 Franchise & Distrib. L. & Prac. § 16:4 Beer, Wine, and Liquor Distributorships—Summary of Beer, Wine, and Liquor Statutes (2023) (survey on alcohol distribution statutes does not include any statutes from the USVI); Franchise & Distrib. L. & Prac. § 16:6 (2023) (survey on farm equipment distribution statutes does not include any statutes from the USVI); Legal Aspects of Selling & Buying, App'x O, State Petroleum Dealer Laws (3d ed. 2021) (survey of petroleum distribution laws does not include any statutes from the USVI).
8. 15 U.S.C. § 1222.
9. Northview Motors, Inc. v. Chrysler Motors Corp., 227 F.3d 78, 92 (3d Cir. 2000).

failed to act in good faith, injuring the plaintiff dealer.[10] A lack of good faith cannot be established by merely demonstrating that the manufacturer acted arbitrarily, unreasonably, or unfairly.[11] Rather, the dealer must establish that the manufacturer's conduct constituted coercion, intimidation, or threats of coercion or intimidation directed at the dealer.[12]

Termination—even without cause—alone is not enough to invoke the Dealer's Act.[13] Rather, to make a claim, manufacturer must have used the danger of termination as a threat in an attempt to force the dealer to do certain things.[14] The Dealer's Act is a limited remedy for dealers compared to the VIFBA, which creates a cause of action for any termination without good cause.[15] However, if a manufacturer acts in bad faith and ultimately terminates the franchisee without good cause, a plaintiff may pursue both Dealer's Act and VFIBA claims.[16]

2. Annotations

In *Gassett v. Nissan*, the plaintiff franchisee alleged that Nissan had terminated its franchise agreement in bad faith, which violated the Dealer's Act, *and* failed to give 120 days' notice of termination and lacked good cause, as required by the VIFBA.[17] The court analyzed both claims and ultimately granted Nissan's motion for summary judgment, concluding that the lack of a written contract precluded recovery under the Dealer's Act.[18] While the lack of a written contract was not an impediment to a claim pursuant to the VIFBA, the expiration of the Act's two-year statute of limitations barred recovery under the VIFBA.[19]

C. Termination

1. What Constitutes Termination or Cancellation

a. Commentary

Written notice of termination, cancellation, or intention not to renew a franchise for any reason must be given at least 120 days in advance of any termination, cancellation, or failure to renew.[20]

b. Annotations

Under Virgin Islands law, it is unlawful for a franchisor to terminate, cancel, or fail to renew a franchise for any reason whatsoever without having first given

---

10. Gen. Motors Corp. v. New A.C. Chevrolet, Inc., 263 F.3d 296, 326 (3d Cir. 2001).
11. *Id.*
12. *Id.* (citing 15 U.S.C. § 1221(e)).
13. Buono Sales, Inc. v. Chrysler Motors Corp., 449 F.2d 715, 724 (3d Cir. 1971).
14. *New A.C. Chevrolet, Inc.*, 263 F.3d at 326.
15. V.I. CODE ANN. tit. 12A, § 132.
16. *See* Gassett v. Nissan N.A., Inc., 877 F. Supp. 974, 986 (D.V.I. 1994).
17. *Id.* at 975.
18. *Id.* at 981.
19. *Id.* at 982.
20. V.I. CODE ANN. tit. 12A, § 131.

written notice of such termination, cancellation, or intent not to renew the franchisee at least 120 days in advance of such termination.[21]

2. Restrictions on Termination or Cancellation

a. Commentary

Under the VIFBA, the franchisor must have good cause for terminating or failing to renew the franchise agreement.[22] Pursuant to the VIFBA, "good cause" shall be (1) failure by the franchisee to substantially comply with the requirements of the franchise agreement, so long as those requirements are both essential and reasonable, or (2) bad faith of the franchisee in carrying out the terms of franchise.[23]

b. Annotations

The author found no cases related to termination restrictions under the VIFBA.

3. Notice Requirement

a. Commentary

Under Virgin Islands law, it is unlawful for a franchisor to terminate, cancel, or fail to renew a franchise for any reason whatsoever without having first given written notice of such termination, cancellation, or intent not to renew the franchisee at least 120 days in advance of such termination.[24]

b. Annotations

The author found no cases related to termination notice requirements under the VIFBA.

4. Grounds for Termination

a. Commentary

Failure by the franchisee to substantially comply with the requirements of the franchise agreement, so long as those requirements are both essential and reasonable, or bad faith of the franchisee in carrying out the terms of franchise.[25]

b. Annotations

The author found no case law addressing grounds for termination under the VIFBA.

5. Required Cure Period

a. Commentary

Not applicable.

---

21. Fleming v. Orange Crush of P.R., Inc., 30 V.I. 268, 270–71 (D.V.I. July 11, 1994).
22. V.I. CODE ANN. tit. 12A, § 132.
23. *Id.*
24. *Id.* § 131.
25. *Id.* § 132.

b. Annotations
Not applicable.

6. Repurchase Obligations
a. Commentary
Not applicable.

b. Annotations
Not applicable.

D. Restrictions on Nonrenewal
1. What Constitutes Nonrenewal
a. Commentary
Written notice of termination, cancellation, or intention not to renew a franchise for any reason must be given at least 120 days in advance of any termination, cancellation, or failure to renew.[26]

b. Annotations
Under Virgin Islands law, it is unlawful for a franchisor to terminate, cancel, or fail to renew a franchise for any reason whatsoever without having first given written notice of such termination, cancellation, or intent not to renew the franchisee at least 120 days in advance of such termination.[27] The author has not found any case law related to constructive termination claims under the VIFBA.

2. Notice Requirement
a. Commentary
Before a franchisor may choose to terminate, cancel, or not to renew a franchise agreement, it must first give the franchisee written notice 120 days before terminating the agreement.[28]

b. Annotations
Under Virgin Islands law, it is unlawful for a franchisor to terminate, cancel, or fail to renew a franchise for any reason whatsoever without having first given written notice of such termination, cancellation, or intent not to renew the franchisee at least 120 days in advance of such termination. The author found no case law addressing notice requirements for termination under the VIFBA.

---

26. *Id.* § 131.
27. Fleming v. Orange Crush of P.R., Inc., 30 V.I. 268, 270–71 (D.V.I. July 11, 1994).
28. V.I. CODE ANN. tit. 12A, § 131.

3. Grounds for Nonrenewal

a. Commentary

Under Virgin Islands law, there are two grounds for nonrenewal of a franchise: failure by the franchisee to substantially comply with the requirements of the franchise agreement, so long as those requirements are both essential and reasonable, or bad faith of the franchisee in carrying out the terms of franchise.[29]

b. Annotations

The author found no case law addressing grounds for nonrenewal under the VIFBA.

4. Required Cure Period

a. Commentary
Not applicable.

b. Annotations
Not applicable.

5. Limitations on Franchisors' Right to Impose Conditions for Renewal

a. Commentary
Not applicable.

b. Annotations
Not applicable.

6. Repurchase Obligations

a. Commentary
Not applicable.

b. Annotations
Not applicable.

E. Transfers and Succession

1. Commentary
Not applicable.

2. Annotations
Not applicable.

---

29. *Id.* § 132.

F. Other Regulation of the Franchise Relationship

1. Commentary

It is a violation of the VIFBA for any franchisor, directly or through any officer, agent, or employee to engage directly or through any officer, agent, or employee to engage directly or indirectly in methods of competition with any franchisee that constitute unfair methods of competition within the meaning of the FTC Act.[30]

The VIFBA does not invalidate other laws and is intended to be read in conjunction with all other laws of the United States Virgin Islands unless there is a direct conflict.[31]

2. Annotations

The author found no case law addressing unfair competition from the franchisor under the VIFBA or how a direct conflict between the VIFBA and other laws are to be resolved.

G. Remedies and Administrative Action

1. Restrictive Covenants

a. Commentary
Not applicable.

b. Annotations
Not applicable.

2. Damages

a. Commentary
A franchisee may bring an action against a franchisor for violation of the VIFBA in the District Court of the Virgin Islands and shall recover the damages by him sustained by reason of the franchisor's failure to comply with the VIFBA, together with the costs of the action, including reasonable attorneys' fees.[32]

b. Annotations
The author found no case law addressing damages under the VIFBA.

3. Rescission

a. Commentary
Not applicable.

b. Annotations
Not applicable.

---

30. *Id.* § 134.
31. *Id.* § 138.
32. *Id.* § 135.

4. Injunctive Relief

a. Commentary
Not applicable.

b. Annotations
Not applicable.

5. Control Person Liability

a. Commentary
It is a violation of the VIFBA for any officer, agent, or employee of a franchisor to engage directly or indirectly in methods of competition with any franchisee that constitute unfair methods of competition within the meaning of the FTC Act.[33] Damages are available.[34]

b. Annotations
The author found no case law addressing control person liability under the VIFBA.

6. Attorneys' Fees

a. Commentary
A franchisee that is successful in bringing an action against a franchisor for violation of the VIFBA is entitled to an award of reasonable attorneys' fees.[35]

b. Annotations
The author found no case law addressing an award of attorneys' fees under the VIFBA.

7. Limitations on Damage Waivers

a. Commentary
While binding arbitration before the American Arbitration Association or "other similar rules" is permitted where such a provision is included in a written franchise agreement, any damages awarded for a violation of the VIFBA "shall be no less than" those permitted by the VIFBA.[36]

b. Annotations
The author found no case law addressing limitations on damage waivers under the VIFBA.

---

33. *Id.* § 134.
34. *Id.* § 135.
35. *Id.*
36. *Id.* §§ 133, 135.

8. Administrative Action

a. Commentary

The Department of Licensing and Consumer Affairs of the Virgin Islands (DLCA) is responsible for the administration and enforcement of the VIFBA.[37] A written complaint may be filed with the DLCA.[38]

b. Annotations

The author found no case law addressing the administration and enforcement of the VIFBA by the DLCA.

H. Dispute Resolution

1. Limitations on Franchisors' Ability to Restrict Venue

a. Commentary

As noted earlier, binding arbitration of franchise disputes is permitted where the arbitration provision appears in a written franchise agreement so long as the arbitration is conducted in accordance with the rules of the American Arbitration Association or "other similar rules"; the criteria applied by the arbitrator(s) when determining whether a "good cause" termination, cancellation, or refusal to renew of the franchise occurred are the same as those contained in the VIFBA; and the damages available are the full measure of damages available pursuant to the damages provisions of the VIFBA.[39]

b. Annotations

In *Spenceley Office Equipment v. Ricoh Latin America, Inc.*, the District Court of the Virgin Islands enforced an arbitration clause in an office products distributorship agreement in part based on the arbitration provisions of the VIFBA.[40]

2. Limitations Period

a. Commentary

Any action brought pursuant to the VIFBA must be commenced within two years after the cause of action shall have accrued.[41]

b. Annotations

In *Gassett v. Nissan N.A., Inc.*, a franchisee asserted in part a VIFBA claim that the franchisor had acted in bad faith and violated the VIFBA by failing to give 120 days' notice of termination prior to termination and by competing directly

---

37. *Id.* § 139.
38. Government of the U.S. Virgin Islands, Department of Licensing and Consumer Affairs (DLCA), https://secure.dlca.vi.gov/license/Asps/complaint/AddComplaint.aspx?Busseq/ (last visited Mar. 30, 2025).
39. V.I. CODE ANN. tit. 12A, § 133.
40. 48 V.I. 848 (D.V.I. Feb. 28, 2007).
41. V.I. CODE ANN. tit. 12A, § 136.

with the franchisee.[42] The court granted summary judgment respecting the VIFBA claims because it determined that the franchisee had filed its VIFBA claim "more than two years after the claim accrued."[43] Specifically, in May 1991, the owner of the franchisee had informed the franchisor of his belief that any termination was improper but the legal action had not been filed until June 1993.[44]

---

42. 877 F. Supp. 974, 975 (D.V.I. 1994).
43. *Id.* at 982.
44. *Id.*

Virginia

John Edson and Ben Reed

I. Introduction to Statute

The Virginia Retail Franchising Act (the Act) seeks to remedy the perceived inequities underlying the franchisor-franchisee relationship by establishing mechanisms that create a fairer balance of power between the parties.[1] The Act primarily regulates franchise offerings through registration and disclosure obligations on franchisors.[2] However, the Act also includes a provision that regulates the relationship between a franchisor and franchisee with respect to the cancellation of a franchise relationship.

II. Commentary and Annotations

A. Definition of a Franchise

The Act applies a three-element test to determine whether a business relationship qualifies as a "franchise" and, in turn, is subject to the provisions of the Act governing the relationship between the parties.[3] Specifically, section 13.1-559(A) of the Act states that a "franchise" means a written contract or agreement between two or more persons, by which:

- A franchisee is granted the right to engage in the business of offering, selling, or distributing goods or services at retail under a marketing plan or system prescribed in substantial part by a franchisor;
- The operation of the franchisee's business pursuant to such plan or system is substantially associated with the franchisor's trademark, service mark, trade name, logotype, advertising, or other commercial symbol designating the franchisor or its affiliate; and
- The franchisee is required to pay, directly or indirectly, a franchise fee of $500 or more.[4]

---

1. *See* VA. CODE ANN. § 13.1-558; Ansaripour v. Air Transit, Inc., No. 9956, 1989 WL 646218, at *3 (Va. Cir. Ct. Mar. 15, 1989); Crone v. Richmond Newspapers, Inc., 238 Va. 248, 254 (1989).
2. *See generally* VA. CODE ANN. §§ 13.1-557 to 13.1-574.
3. VA. CODE ANN. § 13.1-559(A) to (B).
4. *Id.* § 13.1-559(A).

1. Written Agreement

a. Commentary

In order for the Act to apply to a relationship, the terms of the "franchise" must be contained in a written agreement. For example, where there was no written agreement, the arrangement between a manufacturer and distributor was not considered a "franchise" under the Act.[5] Indeed, even when there was previously a written agreement between a purported franchisee and purported franchisor, if that agreement has expired, the relationship post-expiration will not be deemed a franchise under the Act because there is no written agreement governing the relationship.[6]

b. Annotations

The Act did not apply to an arrangement between an automobile distributor and manufacturer because the written agreement with the manufacturer's predecessor expired, such that there was no written agreement between the manufacturer and the distributor sufficient to create a "franchise" at the time the distributor sued the manufacturer. *Turner v. Subaru of Am., Inc.*, 566 F. Supp. 143, 147–50 (W.D. Va. 1983).

2. Trademark Element

a. Commentary

In order to satisfy the "trademark" element of a "franchise," the Act requires that "the operation of the franchisee's business pursuant to [a franchisor's] plan or system" be "substantially associated with the franchisor's trademark[.]"[7] The Virginia Administrative Code defines a "trademark" as "include[ing] trademarks, service marks, names, logos, and other commercial symbols."[8] However, simply using another party's logo standing alone may not be sufficient to satisfy the "trademark" element of a franchise.[9] The critical issue is whether the services provided by the purported franchisee are "substantially associated with the purported franchisor's mark.[10] Instead, "there must be something special and distinct with not only the plan or system but also with the logo,"[11] such that display of the purported franchisor's mark would call to the mind of customers a substantial association with the plan or system, comparable to how McDonald's "golden arches signify to a hungry person a hamburger prepared a certain way."[12]

---

5. *In re* JGB Indus., Inc., 223 B.R. 901, 908 (Bankr. E.D. Va. 1997).
6. Turner v. Subaru of Am., Inc., 566 F. Supp. 143, 147–50 (W.D. Va. 1983).
7. VA. CODE ANN. § 13.1-559(A).
8. VA. ADMIN. CODE § 5-110-10.
9. *See* Ansaripour v. Air Transit, Inc., No. 9956, 1989 WL 646218, at *3 (Va. Cir. Ct. Mar. 15, 1989); Dulles Mut. Ben. Ass'n v. Air Transit, Inc., 15 Va. Cir. 140, 1988 WL 619368, at *7–8 (Va. Cir. Ct. Oct. 21, 1988).
10. *Id.*
11. *Id.*
12. *Id.*

b. Annotations

An arrangement between a manufacturer and distributor was not considered a "franchise" under the Act because, in addition to the lack of a written agreement, the distributor presented no evidence that it paid the manufacturer a franchise fee or that the distributor's business was substantially associated with manufacturer's trademark. *In re JGB Indus., Inc.*, 223 B.R. 901, 908 (Bankr. E.D. Va. 1997).

Use by taxi drivers of the airport transit authority's logo on taxicabs servicing customers at Dulles Airport did not satisfy the trademark element of the Act because the service of providing taxicab services at the airport was not "substantially associated" with the logo. The importance of the owner-operator agreement between the parties was not the logo on the side of the taxis but the right to operate taxis at the airport. *Ansaripour v. Air Transit, Inc.*, No. 9956, 1989 WL 646218, at *3 (Va. Cir. Ct. Mar. 15, 1989); *Dulles Mut. Bens. Ass'n v. Air Transit, Inc.*, 15 Va. Cir. 140, 1988 WL 619368, at *7–8 (Va. Cir. Ct. Oct. 21, 1988).

3. Franchise Fee Element

a. Commentary

A "franchise fee" is broadly defined under the Act to include any "fee or charge for the right to enter into or maintain a business under a franchise, including a payment or deposit for goods, services, rights, or training."[13] However, the Act does make some exceptions. Payments of a bona fide wholesale price for starting and continuing inventory of goods for resale or the payment at fair market value for the purchase or lease of real property, fixtures, equipment, or supplies necessary to enter into or maintain the business are not considered a "franchise fee."[14] De minimis payments under $500 are also not considered "franchise fees."[15]

b. Annotations

An arrangement between a manufacturer and distributor was not considered a "franchise" under the Act because, in addition to the lack of a written agreement, the distributor presented no evidence that it paid the manufacturer a franchise fee or that the distributor's business was substantially associated with manufacturer's trademark. *In re JGB Industries, Inc.*, 223 B.R. 901, 908 (Bankr. E.D. Va. 1997).

An arrangement between a manufacturer and a dealer was not considered a franchise because the underlying contract did not require the dealer to pay a franchise fee. The dealer argued that it paid a "fee" because it was required to purchase training videos, programs, tools, parts, and other goods and/or services from the manufacturer and also had to make payments for the use of cooperative advertising. But the court found that the language in the dealer agreement stating that the dealer had "not paid any fee for this agreement" was

---

13. VA. CODE ANN. § 13.1-559(A).
14. *Id.*
15. *Id.*

conclusive as to whether the dealer paid a "franchise fee." *Ward's Equipment, Inc. v. New Holland North America, Inc.*, 254 Va. 379, 493 S.E.2d 516 (1997).

4. Community of Interest; Significant Degree of Control; Joint Marketing Plan

a. Commentary

The Act does not provide a statutory definition for what constitutes a "marketing plan or system prescribed in substantial part by a franchisor," and there are limited Virginia cases that interpret the language of the statue.[16] One court has indicated that the level of detail a company sets forth in a plan or system is a determining factor in whether that plan or system has been prescribed in substantial part by the company.[17] The Virginia State Corporation Commission (the Commission) has also offered insight into what may constitute a "marketing plan or system" and when such a system has been prescribed in "substantial part." Specifically, the Commission has concluded that a company prescribed a "marketing plan or system" when it (1) provided a third party with exclusive territories; (2) allowed the third party to use the company's sign and name; (3) supplied the third party with billing statements prepared by the company; (4) retained copies of new member contracts entered into by the third party; and (5) provided training for the third party's sales people and brochures to help enroll new members.[18] The Commission also clarified that a marketing plan or system is only "prescribed in substantial part by a franchisor" when participation in the marketing plan or system is required by a company, as opposed to merely suggested.[19] In addition, the marketing plan must relate to goods or services that are sold at retail.[20]

b. Annotations

Owner-operator agreements between taxi drivers and the airport transit authority "provide a very detailed plan or system under which the owner-operators must provide taxicab services at Dulles Airport" sufficient to satisfy the marketing plan element of the Act. *Ansaripour v. Air Transit, Inc.*, No. 9956, 1989 WL 646218, at *3 (Va. Cir. Ct. Mar. 15, 1989). However, the court found that the services offered under the marketing plan were not substantially associated with the transit authority's marks. *See also Dulles Mut. Ben. Ass'n v. Air Transit, Inc.*, 15 Va. Cir. 140, 1988 WL 619368, at *7–8 (Va. Cir. Ct. Oct. 21, 1988) (same).

A title insurance service business was not a franchise because the services were performed for professional mortgage lenders and attorneys, not the ultimate consumers of a retail sale (i.e., the purchasers of the property for which the title services were provided). *Erdmann v. Preferred Rsch., Inc. of Georgia*, 852 F.2d 788, 791 (4th Cir. 1988).

---

16. *See id.*
17. *See* Ansaripour v. Air Transit, Inc., No. 9956, 1989 WL 646218, at *3 (Va. Cir. Ct. Mar. 15, 1989).
18. Commonwealth of Virginia *ex rel.* Y&G Co. v. Am. Trade Exch., No. SEC870114, Bus. Franchise Guide (CCH) § 9,267 (Va. State Corp. Comm'n June 27, 1988).
19. *Id.*
20. *See* Erdmann v. Preferred Rsch., Inc. of Georgia, 852 F.2d 788, 791 (4th Cir. 1988).

B. Scope and Jurisdiction

1. Commentary

This Act only applies to franchises that operate or maintain a place of business within the Commonwealth of Virginia.[21] The Act does not apply to out-of-state franchises offered by Virginia franchisors.[22] This is the case even where the franchisor's franchise agreement designates Virginia law as governing all claims between the parties.[23] However, the Virginia Supreme Court has clarified that the requirement of a place of business located in Virginia does not necessarily mean that the purported franchisee must operate a retail establishment. Rather, it is sufficient that "the business transacted under the franchise agreement . . . have a nexus to the Commonwealth."[24]

2. Annotations

The Act did apply to the relationship between newspaper publisher and distributors of newspapers who agreed to distribute newspapers to vending machines located in Richmond, Virginia, because the agreement obligated the distributors to conduct business in Virginia, even if the distributors did not operate a business from any physical place of business. *Crone v. Richmond Newspapers, Inc.*, 238 Va. 248, 254, 384 S.E.2d 77, 80–81 (1989).

The Act did not apply to a relationship where the agreement granted the franchisee the right to operate anywhere in the United States because that fact did not establish a sufficient nexus with the Commonwealth of Virginia nor any obligation to transact business in Virginia. *Keurig Green Mountain, Inc. v. Global Baristas U.S., LLC*, No. 18-CV-0095 (LAK), 2018 WL 4926446, at *3 (S.D.N.Y. Oct. 10, 2018).

The Act did not apply to a franchisee operating a business in Arkansas because the franchisee never operated a business in Virginia. *Britelink, Inc. v. TeleCorp PCS, Inc.*, No. 3:03-CV-00207 GTE, 2004 WL 5509416, at *7 (E.D. Ark. May 6, 2004).

C. Termination

1. What Constitutes Termination or Cancellation

a. Commentary

The Act does not specifically address what constitutes termination or cancellation of a franchisee.

b. Annotations

Not applicable.

---

21. VA. CODE ANN. § 13.1-559 (B).
22. Silver v. JTH Tax, Inc., No. CIV.A. 2:05CV126, 2005 WL 1668060, at *4 (E.D. Va. June 21, 2005).
23. JTH Tax, Inc. v. Hines, Civ. No. 2:15cv558, 2017 WL 9772103, at *2–3 (E.D. Va. Dec. 15, 2017).
24. Crone v. Richmond Newspapers, Inc., 238 Va. 248, 254, 384 S.E.2d 77, 80–81 (1989).

2. Restrictions on Termination or Cancellation

a. Commentary

The Act states that it is unlawful for a franchisor to cancel a franchise without reasonable cause.[25] "Cancellation" means that the franchisor ends an existing franchise relationship prior to the end of the term of the franchise agreement.[26] While the Act itself does not define what constitutes "reasonable cause," the issue has been addressed in several Virginia cases.[27] First, the Virginia State Corporation Commission has made clear that notifying a franchisee of an at-will termination prior to the expiration of the term of the franchise agreement is not reasonable cause.[28] However, it is not clear that termination for defaults specified under the franchise agreement will suffice to meet the "reasonable cause" standard. For example, the U.S Court of Appeals for the Fourth Circuit, in an unpublished decision, upheld a jury finding that franchisee's failure to pay fees due under a contract was not reasonable cause for a franchisor to terminate the franchise because the franchisee disputed the amount purportedly unpaid.[29] And no other cases elaborate on when a breach of the franchise agreement is sufficient to constitute reasonable cause to terminate the agreement.[30] In contrast, it is clear that a franchisor has reasonable cause to terminate a franchise when a franchisee informs the franchisor that it intends to abandon the franchise or cease operating its business.[31]

b. Annotations

While failure to pay disputed fees might be a cause for termination, the court refused to overturn a jury's conclusion that a termination for failure to pay disputed amounts was not "reasonable cause" under the Act. *G.M. Garrett Realty, Inc. v. Century 21 Real Estate Corp.*, 2001, 17 F. App'x 169, 172 (4th Cir. 2001).

A franchisee could claim that the franchisor terminated its franchise without reasonable cause after franchisee notified the franchisor that it was ceasing operation of the franchised business, even if the franchisee alleged that the franchisor "retaliated" for the franchisee ceasing operation by terminating the franchise agreement. *Bans Pasta, LLC v. Mirko Franchising*, LLC, No. 7:13-CV-00360 JCT, 2014 WL 637762 (W.D. Va. Feb. 12. 2014).

A hotel franchisee that alleged that the franchisor cancelled its franchise without reasonable cause by requiring the franchisee to change the brand and segment of its hotel to a less desirable brand and segment adequately alleged

---

25. VA. CODE ANN. § 13.1-554.
26. *See* Grandstaff v. Mobil Oil Corp., No. 78-512-A, 1978 WL 1458, at *16 (E.D. Va. Dec. 7, 1978).
27. *See* G.M. Garrett Realty, Inc. v. Century 21 Real Estate Corp., 2001, 17 F. App'x 169 (4th Cir. 2001); Bans Pasta, LLC v. Mirko Franchising, LLC, No. 7:13-CV-00360-JCT, 2014 WL 637762 (W.D. Va. Feb. 12. 2014).
28. *See* Final Order & Opinion, Petition of Betsy-Len Motor Hotel Corp., Case No. SEC880073, 1988 WL 385823, at *4 (Va. State Corp. Comm'n Dec. 29, 1988).
29. *See G.M. Garrett Realty*, 17 F. App'x at 172.
30. *Id.*
31. *See Bans Pasta*, 2014 WL 637762, at *7.

cancellation without reasonable cause sufficient to survive a motion to dismiss, even though the franchisor pointed out that the hotel franchisee continued to operate the hotel under the less desirable brand. *LTD Mgmt. Co., LLC v. Holiday Hosp. Franchising, Inc.*, No. CIV.A. 2:07CV530, 2008 WL 7281926, at *9 (E.D. Va. Mar. 11, 2008).

3. Notice Requirement

a. Commentary
Not applicable.

b. Annotations
Not applicable.

4. Grounds for Termination

a. Commentary
Not applicable.

b. Annotations
Not applicable.

5. Required Cure Period

a. Commentary
Not applicable.

b. Annotations
Not applicable.

6. Repurchase Obligations

a. Commentary
Not applicable.

b. Annotations
Not applicable.

D. Restrictions on Nonrenewal

1. What Constitutes Nonrenewal

a. Commentary
The Act does not explicitly impose restrictions on the nonrenewal of a franchise, although it does require a franchisor to have reasonable cause to "cancel" a franchise. As already discussed, Virginia courts have interpreted this obligation to prohibit the termination of a franchise agreement during the term of the agreement. But in so doing, the Virginia Supreme Court has held that "the Act does not proscribe the parties to a franchise from, as here, agreeing that it shall be in force for a limited duration and that it shall extend for an identifiable

period of time."[32] Thus, the Act "does not ... require renewal or extension of a franchise after it lawfully terminates according to its terms."[33] However, no case has considered whether a franchisor must have "reasonable cause" to elect not to renew a franchise where the franchise agreement expressly provides for the possibility of renewal or whether the refusal to renew without reasonable cause when the agreement provides for renewal would violate section 13.1-564.

b. Annotations

The Act does not prohibit a franchisor from electing not to renew a franchise agreement that expires on its own terms and does not impost "a continuing duty of renewal in the absence of reasonable cause for nonrenewal." *Grandstaff v. Mobil Oil Corp.*, No. 78-512-A, 1978 WL 1458, at *16 (E.D. Va. Dec. 7, 1978).

2. Notice Requirement

a. Commentary
Not applicable.

b. Annotations
Not applicable.

3. Grounds for Nonrenewal

a. Commentary
Not applicable.

b. Annotations
Not applicable.

4. Required Cure Period

a. Commentary
Not applicable.

b. Annotations
Not applicable.

5. Limitations on Franchisors' Right to Impose Conditions for Renewal

a. Commentary
Not applicable.

b. Annotations
Not applicable.

---

32. *See* Betsy-Len Motor Hotel Corp. v. Holiday Inns, Inc., 238 Va. 489, 492, 385 S.E.2d 559, 560 (1989).
33. *Id.* 489 Va. at 492, 385 S.E.2d at 560–61.

6. Repurchase Obligations

a. Commentary
Not applicable.

b. Annotations
Not applicable.

E. Transfers and Succession

1. Commentary
Not applicable.

2. Annotations
Not applicable.

F. Other Regulation of the Franchise Relationship

1. Use of Undue Influence to Induce Surrender of Contractual Rights

a. Commentary
In addition to the restriction on cancelling a franchise, the Act prohibits a franchisor from using "undue influence to induce a franchisee to surrender any right given to him by any provision contained in the franchise."[34] Franchisees claiming that a franchisor used undue influence to induce the surrender of a right must clearly define the surrendered right and how the franchisor influenced the franchisee to surrender it.[35] Further, when a franchisor takes an action that is expressly allowed under an agreement, the franchisee cannot claim that it was unduly influenced to surrender a right under that agreement.[36] For example, a court dismissed a franchisee's claim that the franchisor used undue influence to induce the franchisee to surrender its claimed right to assign the franchise agreement because the franchisee did not have a unilateral right to assign its rights under the franchise agreement.[37] The court rejected the franchisee's argument that the franchise agreement did afford it the right to assign the agreement, but the court pointed out that the provision actually provided that the franchisee could not assign the agreement without the prior written consent of the franchisor.[38] According to the court, the franchisor could not induce the franchisee to surrender a right that it did not actually possess.[39]

---

34. VA. CODE ANN. § 13.1-564.
35. *See* Sherman v . Ben & Jerry's Franchising, Inc., No. 1:08-CV-207, 2009 WL 2462539, at *9 (D. Vt. Aug. 10, 2009).
36. *See Betsy-Len Motor Hotel*, 238 Va. at 492, 385 S.E.2d at 561.
37. *See* McDonald's Corp. v. Turner-James, No. CIV.A. 05-804, 2005 WL 7873649, at *2 (E.D. Va. Nov. 29, 2005).
38. *Id.*
39. *Id.*

b. Annotations

Summary judgment was appropriate on a hotel franchisee's claim under section 13.1-564 that the franchisor had used "undue influence" to coerce the franchisee to surrender its rights under the franchise agreement by allegedly requiring the franchisee to choose between (1) exiting the system and paying a termination fee; (2) converting to another of the franchisor's hotel brands; or (3) continuing to operate under its existing brand, which the franchisor had to cease developing. There was no evidence that the hotel franchisee surrendered any right, however, because the franchisor committed to continuing to maintain support for the brand through the expiration of the franchise agreement and offered to pay for the cost of changing the signage for franchisees that converted to another brand, which comported with the Act's requirement (in section 13.1-558) that "franchisors . . . deal fairly with their franchisees." *Lake Wright Hosp., LLC v. Holiday Hosp. Franchising, Inc.*, No. CIV.A 2:07CV530, 2009 WL 2606254, at *41–42 (E.D. Va. Aug. 20, 2009).

2. Choice of Law

a. Commentary

The Act provides that "[a]ny condition, stipulation or provision binding any person to waive compliance with any provision of [the Act] shall be void."[40] Based on this language, a choice of law provision choosing a state law other than Virginia will not be enforced to the extent it would prevent a Virginia franchisee from asserting a claim under the Act.[41]

b. Annotations

A franchise agreement choice of law provision was not enforced because the anti-waiver provision of the Act "prevent[s] franchisees from waiving protection under the statute, even by signing a choice-of-law agreement," and that the law of the state chosen in the franchise agreement did not afford the same level of protection to franchisees as that afforded by the Act. *Cottman Transmission Sys., LLC v. Kershner*, 536 F. Supp. 2d 543, 551 (E.D. Pa. 2008).

G. Remedies and Administration Action

1. Restrictive Covenants

a. Commentary
Not applicable.

b. Annotations
Not applicable.

---

40. VA. CODE ANN. § 13.1-571(c).
41. *See Cottman Transmission Sys., LLC v. Kershner*, 536 F. Supp. 2d 543, 551 (E.D. Pa. 2008).

2. Damages

a. Commentary

If a franchisor is found to have cancelled a franchise without reasonable cause or used undue influence to induce a franchisee to surrender any right given to it by any provision contained in the franchise, the franchisee may bring an action against its franchisor to recover the damages, including costs and reasonable attorneys' fees.[42] Although no court has opined on how damages under the Act should be calculated, one court has made clear that the claimed damage must have been caused by the violation of the Act.[43] In that case, the franchisee operated a retail cellular phone sales franchise as part of its larger electronics business. The court found that the franchisee's calculation of alleged lost profits failed to "segregate damages based on the cellular portion of its business from those stemming from the electronics business."[44] The court also concluded that the franchisee failed to demonstrate how the franchisor's actions "caused the electronics business to suffer lost profits" or to "provide records from which the profitability of the cellular business could reasonably be determined" and instead simply estimated the value of the whole business.[45] That was insufficient to establish with reasonable certainty the amount of damages purportedly attributable to the franchisor's conduct. The fact that the franchisee failed to quantify the damages allegedly caused by the franchisor's undue influence or eliminate other possible causes of the business failure was also problematic for the court with respect to causation.[46]

b. Annotations

An appellate court vacated and remanded a jury award of damages to a franchisee because the amount of the checks the franchisee tendered to the franchisor after termination, as calculated by the franchisee's expert, was not supported by evidence at trial that that amount corresponded to damages incurred by the franchisee. Instead, the appellate court concluded that the amount of $50,000, which the franchise testified was his estimated damages, less a $39,000 offset for amounts the jury found that the franchisee owed to the franchisor, was the proper measure of damages. *G.M. Garrett Realty, Inc. v. Century 21 Real Estate Corp.*, 2001, 17 F. App'x 169, 174 (4th Cir. 2001)

3. Rescission

a. Commentary

Not applicable.

b. Annotations

Not applicable.

---

42. VA. CODE ANN. § 13.1-571(a).
43. *See* Hampton Audio Elecs., Inc. v. Contel Cellular, Inc., 23 F.3d 401, 1994 WL 200729, at *1 (4th Cir. 1994) (unpublished).
44. *Id.* at *2.
45. *Id.*
46. *Id.*

4. Injunctive Relief

a. Commentary

The Act allows a franchisee to pursue any remedies that may exist at law or in equity against a franchisor who has violated relationship provisions of the Act.[47] Section 13.1-568 of the Act also authorized the State Corporation Commission to issue temporary or permanent injunctions to prevent violations of the Act. However, that power has only been exercised in connection with the Act's presale registration and disclosure obligations.

b. Annotations

No cases address this issue.

5. Control Person Liability

a. Commentary

Not applicable.

b. Annotations

Not applicable.

6. Attorneys' Fees

a. Commentary

Under section 13.1-571(a) of the Act, a franchisee who successfully brings a claim for any violation of section 13.1-564 is entitled to the costs of the action, including reasonable attorneys' fees.[48]

b. Annotations

No cases address this issue.

7. Limitations on Damage Waivers

a. Commentary

Not applicable.

b. Annotations

Not applicable.

8. Administrative Action

a. Commentary

The Act does provide for the State Corporation Commission to take action to prevent violations of the Act. Under section 13.1-567, the Commission can initiate an investigation to determine whether a person has violated the act,

---

47. Va. Code Ann. § 13.1-571(d).
48. *Id.* § 13.1-571(a).

including the issuance of subpoenas for testimony or documents.[49] Depending on its findings in the investigation, the Commission can initiate a formal hearing by providing 30 days' prior notice to a party accused of violating any provision of the Act.[50] If the Commission proves that the accused party violated the Act, the Commission may impose a civil penalty not exceeding $25,000 for each violation.[51] The Commission may also request, but not require, that a franchisor found to have violated the Act offer the franchisee rescission.[52]

b. Annotations

No cases address this issue.

H. Dispute Resolution

1. Limitations on Franchisors' Ability to Restrict Venue

a. Commentary

Not applicable.

b. Annotations

Not applicable.

2. Limitations Period

a. Commentary

Suits must be brought within four years after the date that cause of action upon which it is based occurred.[53]

b. Annotations

No cases address this issue.

---

49. *Id.* § 13.1-567.
50. *Id.* § 13.1-570.
51. *Id.*
52. *Id.*
53. *Id.* § 13.1-571(a).

Washington

Vanessa Wheeler

I. Introduction to Statute

When Washington enacted the Franchise Investment Protection Act (FIPA) in 1972, it became the second state in the nation with comprehensive franchising legislation,[1] and the first to adopt a comprehensive relationship statute that extended to relationship issues beyond merely termination and nonrenewal.[2] The state legislature enacted FIPA in response to both the growth in popularity of the franchising model[3] and public perceptions that the model was rife with abusive business practices.[4] Washington enacted FIPA shortly after California, the forerunner in such state legislation, enacted its franchise statute.

FIPA was later amended in 1991[5] and again in 2012.[6] FIPA contains extensive provisions related to registration and disclosure of the franchise offerings as well as the franchise relationship itself. The sections of the statute regulating the performance of the franchising relationship are often referred to as the Franchisee Bill of Rights and they prohibit certain acts and practices in the franchisee relationship.[7]

---

1. Howard E. Bundy & Daniel J. Oates, *in* THE FRANCHISE DESK BOOK (Garner ed., 3d ed. 2017).
2. Donald S. Chisum, *State Regulation of Franchising: The Washington Experience*, 48 WASH. L. REV. 291, 335 (1973) (noting that FIPA's broad relationship statute was based on a proposed bill from the state of Massachusetts that failed to obtain sufficient support to pass into law) (citing Fair Dealing in Franchising Act, H. 2279 (Mass. 1970), *reproduced in Report of the Senate Select Comm. on Small Business on the Impact of Franchising on Small Business, Based on Hearing Before the Subcomm. on Urban and Rural Economic Development*, 91st Cong., 2d. Sess., at 1 (1970)).
3. Douglas C. Berry, David M. Byers & Daniel J. Oates, *State Regulation of Franchising: The Washington Experience Revisited*, 38 SEATTLE U.L. REV. 811, 812–14 (2009).
4. David Gurnick & Steve Vieux, *Case History of the American Business Franchise*, 24 OKLA. CITY U.L. REV. 37, 47 (1999). A particular spark for greater regulation of franchising in Washington resulted from public outrage over a 1968 incident in which a foreign company persuaded Washington resident to purchase vending machine franchises, took payment, and never provided the machines. *See* Berry, Byers & Oates, *supra* note 3, at 817. The precipitating event would not constitute a franchise under today's standards. *Id.* at 817 n.42.
5. An Act Relating to Franchise Investment Protection, ch. 226, 1991 Wash. Sess. Laws 1123.
6. An Act Relating to Franchise Investment Protection, ch. 336, 2012 Wash. Sess. Laws 5045.
7. WASH. REV. CODE § 19.100.180; *see also* East Wind Express, Inc. v. Airborne Freight Corp., 95 Wash. App. 98, 102, 974 P.2d 369 (1999) (describing the relationship protections of Wash. Rev. Code § 19.100.180 as the "Franchisee Bill of Rights").

II. Commentary and Annotations

A. Definition of Franchise

Pursuant to Washington Revised Code (RCW) section 19.100.010, a franchise exists where there is an oral or written agreement, express or implied, that requires a person (1) directly or indirectly pay a fee to the owner of a trademark[8] in exchange for operating a business that (2) is substantially associated with that trademark, (3) for the offering, sale, or distribution of goods or services under a marketing plan controlled by that trademark owner. RCW section 19.100.010(a)(i)–(iii). Provided all three requirements are met, a franchise exists whether the parties intended to create such a relationship or even knew that they were doing so.[9] For this reason, to determine whether the relationship provisions of the statute apply to regulate the parties' ongoing activities, it is important for both potential franchisors and franchisees to understand the elements of a franchise and how they can be met in Washington.

1. Trademark Element

a. Commentary

No franchise relationship exists unless the franchisee is given the right to operate a business that is "substantially associated" with a trademark (or other trade name or service mark) by the franchisor or its affiliate.[10] This definition was adopted in 1991 amendments to the statute.[11] Unlike in some jurisdictions, where a franchisee need only show authorization to use the mark, in Washington, there must be actual proof of use and association.[12]

b. Annotations

In *Atchley v. Pepperidge Farm, Inc.*, plaintiff, a distributor of defendant's products, argued that its distributor agreements were franchise agreements governed by FIPA.[13] The court determined that a distributor is associated with a company's products rather than the company's trademarks, and to prevail on an argument on the "substantial association" element, a plaintiff must show that it's business is substantially associated with a franchisor's trademarks beyond merely

---

8. The term "trademark" is being use broadly here to cover trademarks, trade names, service marks, advertising, and other commercial symbols designating affiliation with a particular source or brand, the use of any of which in this context is sufficient to meet this element. *See* WASH. REV. CODE § 19.100.010(4)(a)(2).

9. *See* Jon K. Morrison, Inc. v. Avis Rent-A-Car Sys., Inc., Bus. Franchise Guide (CCH) ¶ 12,701 (W.D. Wash. Nov. 1, 2003).

10. WASH. REV. CODE § 19.100.010(a)(ii).

11. *See* Bundy & Oates, *supra* note 1 ("The trademark element of the definition of a franchise was significantly modified by the 1991 amendments to FIPA. The legislature added the requirement—that "the operation of the business is substantially associated with" the franchisor's trademark or other commercial symbol.") (citing WASH. REV. CODE § 19.100.010(6)(a)(ii)).

12. Daniel J. Oates, Shannon L. McCarthy & Douglas C. Berry, *Substantial Association with a Trademark: A Trap for the Unwary*, 32 FRANCHISE L.J. 130, 134–35 (2013).

13. Atchley v. Pepperidge Farm, Inc., 2012 WL 6057130 (E.D. Wash. Dec. 6, 2012).

distributing product.[14] De minimus use of defendant's trademark, such as on business cards, forms, even delivery trucks and some apparel, was insufficient.[15]

2. Franchise Fee Element

a. Commentary

The definition of a franchise fee for the purposes of FIPA has remained unchanged since its enactment in 1972. A franchise fee is:

> any fee or charge that a franchisee or subfranchisor is required to pay or agrees to pay for the right to enter into a business or to continue a business under a franchise agreement, including but not limited to, the payment either in lump sum or by installments of an initial capital investment fee, any fee or charges based upon a percentage of gross or net sales whether or not referred to as royalty fees, any payment for the mandatory purchase of goods or services or any payment for goods or services available only from the franchisor, or any training fees or training school fees or charges.[16]

However, FIPA excludes from the definition, among other things, bona fide loans from franchisors, the purchase of goods at a bona fide wholesale price, a bona fide loan from a franchisor, goods purchased on consignment and bona fide wholesale prices, leasing of real estate, supplies, or fixtures for the business at fair market value, and various provisions relating to trading stamps.[17]

The parties do not need to intend for a fee to constitute a franchise fee to satisfy the statute.[18] There are many cases, however, concluding that hidden franchise fees are present in the form of percentage lease agreements (that result in potentially above-market leasing rates),[19] and unlawful tying arrangements.[20] Generally, however, courts analyze a franchise fee in terms of whether it is an unrecoverable capital investment by the franchisee in the franchisor,[21] whether

---

14. *Id.* at *8.
15. *Id.* at *9; *but see* Huebner v. Sales Promotion, Inc., 38 Wash. App. 66, 69, 684 P.2d 752 (1984), *cert. denied*, 474 U.S. 818 (1985) (applying pre-1991 amendment version of the statute requiring only authorization to use the trademark); Lobdell v. Sugar N' Spice, Inc., 33 Wash. App. 881, 890, 658 P.2d 1267 (1983) (same pre-1991 amendment conclusion).
16. Bundy & Oates, *supra* note 1, at n.23.
17. WASH. REV. CODE § 19.100.010(8).
18. *See* Jon K. Morrison, Inc. v. Avis Rent-A-Car Sys., Inc., Bus. Franchise Guide (CCH) ¶ 12,701 (W.D. Wash. Nov. 1, 2003).
19. Corp v. Atlantic Richfield Co., 45 Wash. App. 563, 726 P.2d 66 (1986).
20. Blanton v. Mobil Oil Corp., 721 F.2d 1207, 1220 (9th Cir. 1983) *cert denied*, 471 U.S. 1007 (1985) ("It is irrelevant that a forced overcharge is not specifically denominated as a franchise fee [because] FIPA is intended to reach 'franchisors who might attempt to extract a hidden franchise fee in the form of overcharges for property sold to the franchisee.'") (citing Chisum, *supra* note 2, at 343).
21. Corporate Res., Inc. v. Eagle Hardware & Garden, Inc., 115 Wash. App. 343, 350, 62 P.3d 544 (2003); *Jon K. Morrison, Inc.*, Bus. Franchise Guide (CCH) ¶ 12,701; Atchley v. Pepperidge Farm, Inc., 2005 WL 1213959 (E.D. Wash. May 20, 2005).

it is paid to the franchisor directly,[22] and whether the fee is for the right to conduct the business.[23] Generally, ordinary business expenses and optional program fees are not hidden franchise fees.[24]

b. Annotations

In *Atchley v. Pepperidge Farm, Inc.*, the supplier's charge of a pallet fee to plaintiff pursuant to a distribution agreement was not a franchise fee under FIPA because it was merely a deduction to the commission plaintiffs received from the sale of corresponding products, not an unrecoverable investment.[25] The court further found that the "bona fide wholesale price" exception applied to the pallet fee, because the fee was a reasonable charge for the expense incurred by the defendant in packaging and delivering the product.[26] The *Atchley* court's focus on the requirement that there be some form of unrecoverable investment by the franchisee in the franchisor is in line with the legislative intent behind the statute: to protect franchisees from the monetary loss of a franchise investment.[27]

3. Community of Interest; Significant Degree of Control; Joint Marketing Plan

a. Commentary

For a franchise to exist, the franchisee must be offered the right to offer, sell, or distribute goods or services "under a marketing plan prescribed or suggested in substantial part by the grantor or an affiliate."[28] Marketing plan is defined under FIPA as "a plan or system concerning an aspect of conducting business," and may include price specifications, systems or discount plans, sales or display equipment or merchandising devices; sales techniques, materials for promotions or advertising; training regarding advertising, operation, or management of a business; or guidance or assistance on the operational, managerial, technical, or financial aspects of a business.[29] Although there is little case law assessing the existence of a marketing plan, the key question is generally whether, overall, there is a certain level of control of the franchisee's operation by the franchisor.[30]

---

22. *See* Bryant Corp. v. Outboard Marine Corp., Bus. Franchise Guide (CCH) ¶ 10,604 (W.D. Wash. Sept. 29, 1994); *aff'd*, 77 F.3d. 488 (9th Cir. 1996); *Atchley*, 2005 WL 1213959.

23. *Bryant Corp.*, Bus. Franchise Guide (CCH) ¶ 10,604; *Jon K. Morrison, Inc.*, Bus. Franchise Guide (CCH) ¶ 12,701; Atchley v. Pepperidge Farm, Inc., 2006 WL 696317 (W.D. Wash. Mar. 20, 2006), *reconsideration denied*, 2006 WL 2585028 (E.D. Wash. Sept. 7, 2006).

24. *Id.*; *see also* Atchley v. Pepperidge Farm, Inc., 2012 WL 6057130, at *9 (E.D. Wash. Dec. 6, 2012) ("Ordinary business expenses are not franchise fees because they are paid during the regular course of business, not as a right to do business."). Conversely, mandatory product purchases of excess inventory likely satisfy the requirement of an indirect franchise fee. Atchley v. Pepperidge Farm, Inc., 2010 WL 1936275 (9th Cir. 2010) (citing Blanton v. Mobil Oil Corp., 721 F.2d 1207, 1220 (9th Cir. 1983)).

25. *Atchley*, 2012 WL 6057130, at *10.

26. *Id.*

27. *Jon K. Morrison, Inc.*, 2003 WL 2319903; Bus. Franchise Guide (CCH) ¶ 12,701; *see also* Lobdell v. Sugar 'N Spice, Inc., 33 Wash. App. 881, 658 P.2d 1267 (1983) (holding that FIPA was intended to protect franchisees from losing investments in the franchised business).

28. Wash. Rev. Code § 19.100.010(a)(i)–(iii).

29. *Id.*

30. *Atchley*, 2012 WL 6057130, at *8 (citing Berry, Byers & Oates, *supra* note 3, at 838).

b. Annotations

In *Atchley v. Pepperidge Farm, Inc.*, the court assessed the degree of control a franchisor exerts over a franchisee by looking to nine factors: (1) times of operation; (2) advertising and marketing; (3) business environment; (4) staff uniforms; (5) pricing; (6) trading stamps; (7) hiring; (8) sales quotas; and (9) training of management employees.[31] Plaintiffs showed that the supplier had control over product pricing for products sold directly by the supplier, and pricing schedules used to calculate commissions.[32] The court held that this was insufficient to show that the supplier exercised control over prices.[33] The court also rejected plaintiff's argument that the supplier provided anything more than financial support,[34] and that it had failed to show any of the nine factors, much less a majority of factors.[35] As such, plaintiff had failed to establish the existence of a marketing plan.[36]

B. Scope and Jurisdiction

1. Commentary

Courts have arrived at different conclusions regarding the geographical reach of the FIPA statute depending on the provision in question.[37] The application of FIPA's registration and presale disclosure provisions only apply "in this state," that is, Washington, based on a strictly defined set of situations.[38] Conversely, the post-sale relationship provision contained in the franchisee bill of rights has been found to have no such explicit jurisdictional limit.[39] In addition, however,

---

31. *Atchley*, 2012 WL 6057130, at *8.
32. *Id.*
33. *Id.*
34. The court had previously noted that a marketing plan "may" include financial assistance. *Id.* at *7 (quoting WASH. REV. CODE § 19.100.010(11)). By implication, the fact that the supplier provided financial assistance (in the form of guaranteeing a loan) was insufficient, standing alone, to show the existence of a marketing plan. *Id.* at *8.
35. *Id.* at *8.
36. *Id.*
37. *Compare* Taylor v. 1–800–Got–Junk?, LLC, 632 F. Supp. 2d 1048 (W.D. Wash. 2009), *aff'd*, 387 Fed. App'x 727 (9th Cir. 2010) *with* Red Lion Hotels Franchising, Inc. v. MAK, LLC, 663 F.3d 1080 (9th Cir. 2011).
38. *Taylor*, 632 F. Supp. 2d at 1052 ("FIPA's legislative history confirms that its language defining conduct 'in this state' was intended to provide a territorial limitation on the scope of the Act."); *see also id.* (citing WASH. REV. CODE § 19.100.020, which defines four discrete situations where conduct occurs "in this state" such that it subjects the parties to the jurisdictional reach of the statute). The court's decision in *Taylor* is in accord with the legislative history of the statute, as noted by commentator Donald S. Chisum, who critiqued the original version of the statute for failing to define the phrase "in this state." *Taylor*, 632 F. Supp. 2d at 1052 (citing Chisum, *supra* note 2, at 337–38 and noting that "When FIPA was amended in 1991, the legislature apparently responded to this critique and inserted a specific definition for what constitutes conduct 'in this state.'" That now-codified definition is substantially similar to the provision of California's law. This amendment demonstrates a clear intent to limit the territorial coverage of the act to specific conduct that can be said to occur "in this state.") (internal citations omitted).
39. *Red Lion*, 663 F.3d at 1087 ("FIPA's bill of rights does not contain—indeed, has never contained—language limiting its application to the relation between a franchisor and franchisee 'in this state.'").

claims under the franchisee bill of rights have no express private right of action, and as such, the mechanism for dealing with alleged violations of the franchisee bill of rights provisions is to bring a claim under Washington's Consumer Protection Act, which contains its own separate territorial limit.[40] No court has determined whether the CPA's territorial limit applies, only that a claim for violation of the franchisee bills of rights provisions is not precluded by the jurisdictional restrictions of FIPA's registration and disclosure provisions.[41]

2. Annotations

In *Red Lion Franchising, Inc. v. Mak, LLC*, the franchisor terminated the franchisee for failing to implement required upgrades at the franchised business.[42] The franchisee counterclaimed, alleging that the termination was wrongful under FIPA's franchisee bill of rights because the franchisor had failed to provide adequate notice and opportunity to cure the breach, as required by the statute.[43] On summary judgment, the district court ruled in favor of the franchisor, noting that based on earlier case law limiting the jurisdictional reach of the FIPA statute to claims "in this state," the statute did not apply to the franchisor's termination of a franchise located in California.[44] The franchisee appealed the summary judgment ruling to the Ninth Circuit.[45] Contrary to recent Ninth Circuit case law limiting the jurisdictional reach of the FIPA statute, the court reversed, distinguishing the prior cases based on its conclusion that the franchisee bill of rights contained no similar limiting language applying the statute to claims "in this state."[46] The franchisor's principal place of business was located within the state of Washington, and, as such, the court held that the statute applied, noting that the Washington legislature "might have wanted to apply FIPA's bill of rights to all franchises and franchisees of Washington franchisors."[47] The Ninth Circuit therefore remanded to consider the merits of the counterclaim.[48]

---

40. Daniel J. Oates, Vanessa L. Wheeler & Katie M. Loberstein, *A State's Reach Cannot Exceed Its Grasp: Territorial Limitations on State Franchise Statutes*, 37 FRANCHISE L.J. 187, 198–99 (2017).
41. *Id.*
42. Red Lion Hotels Franchising, Inc. v. MAK, LLC, 707 F. Supp. 2d 1110, 1114 (E.D. Wash. 2010).
43. *Id.*
44. *Id.*
45. *Red Lion*, 663 F.3d 1080.
46. *Id.* at 1090.
47. *Id.* at 1090. The Ninth Circuit's ruling is curious, given that the actual legislative history from the 1991 amendments made no mention of this hypothetical intention by the legislature. To the contrary, the legislature at the time was seeking to implement changes recommended by Dr. Chisum in his article, and to bring consistency of Washington's statute in line with proposed uniform statutes that were under consideration at the same time. *See, e.g.*, Berry, Byers & Oates, *supra* note 3, at nn.117–21. The *Red Lion* decision rests on dubious legal reasoning. The more appropriate analysis is likely to assess the jurisdictional scope of Washington's Consumer Protection Act in litigating bill of rights claims, as it represents the sole mechanism for pursuing relief.
48. *Red Lion*, 663 F.2d at 1091.

C. Termination

1. What Constitutes Termination

a. Commentary

FIPA does not explicitly define "termination" for the purposes of the statute, but suggests that it is a franchisor's decision to end a franchise agreement at any time "prior to the expiration of its term."[49] Washington courts that have addressed the issue identify termination as specifically ending a franchisee trademark license prior to the conclusion of the term.[50] Courts have distinguished this from termination of the franchisee's business, which does not constitute "termination" of the franchise.[51] As a result, Washington law does not recognize a claim of constructive termination, and "termination" requires actual termination of the right to use the trademarks.[52]

b. Annotations

In *Coast to Coast Stores, Inc. v. Gruschus*, plaintiff argued that franchisor terminated its franchise by repossessing franchisee's inventory, subject to a valid security agreement, resulting in the suspension of franchisee's business.[53] The court held that the "franchise" that must be terminated for the purposes of the statute is the franchise agreement, not the franchisee's business, and thus forcing the closure of franchisee's business, is not sufficient to constitute termination.[54] A franchise is only terminated "when the agreement between the franchisee and franchisor is brought to an end, terminating the franchisee's right to use the franchisor's trade name, service mark, or the like."[55]

2. Restrictions on Termination

a. Commentary

Under FIPA, franchisors may not terminate any franchise prior to the expiration of its term except for "good cause."[56] The statute doesn't expressly state what constitutes "good cause," but FIPA does state that it includes the franchisee's breach of a material provision of the franchise agreement or other agreement with the franchisor, and the failure to cure such breach after reasonable notice.[57] Reasonable notice is not required to be more than 30 days, unless the default is one that by its nature cannot be cured in 30 days, in which case franchisee

---

49. WASH. REV. CODE § 19.100.180(2)(j).
50. Coast to Coast Stores, Inc. v. Gruschus, 100 Wash. 2d 147, 667 P.2d 619 (1983).
51. *Id.* at 152 (holding that a franchisor did not terminate a franchise merely by refusing to provide the franchisee with additional inventory, which ultimately caused the franchisee to cease doing business).
52. Carlock v. Pillsbury Co., 719 F. Supp. 791, 852 (D. Minn. 1989) ("Constructive termination of a franchise is not actionable under Wash. Rev. Code Ann. § 19.100.180(2)(j).").
53. *Coast to Coast Stores, Inc.*, 100 Wash. 2d at 148–49.
54. *Id.* at 152.
55. *Id.*
56. WASH. REV. CODE § 19.100.180(2)(j).
57. *Id.*

must at least initiate material and ongoing action toward cure within a 30-day period.[58] However, a franchisor may terminate for a willful and material breach, without providing notice or opportunity to cure, if the franchisee has already engaged in three willful, material breaches in the 12 months prior and been given notice and opportunity to cure in each case.[59] The statute further enumerates a number of specific situations in which termination without notice is permissible.[60]

b. Annotations

Franchisees sued for unspecified violations of FIPA's relationship provision, arguing that the franchisor had so completely failed to provide promised support and commitment to franchisees that the franchisees had in many cases been forced to shut down operations.[61] The franchisor moved to dismiss any claim arising under FIPA's termination provision, arguing that it had not terminated the franchisees' trademark licenses, nor the parties' agreements, and that FIPA does not provide a cause of action for constructive termination.[62] The court agreed, and granted the franchisor's motion.[63]

A franchisor offered renewal to the franchisee on new terms.[64] The franchisee rejected updated renewal terms of the franchise agreement and demanded renewal on prior terms.[65] The franchisor's refusal to renew on prior terms did not constitute "termination" under FIPA's relationship provision, even if the franchisee did not like or approve of the new terms.[66]

3. Notice Requirement

a. Commentary

Although notice of termination is not explicitly required under FIPA, franchisors may not terminate any franchise early except for "good cause," which is defined to "include" a franchisee's breach of a material provision of the franchise agreement or other agreement with the franchisor and failure to cure after reasonable notice.[67] Reasonable notice is not required to be more than 30 days, unless the default is one that by its nature cannot be cured in 30 days, in which case franchisee must at least initiate material and ongoing action toward cure within a 30-day period.[68] The statute is not clear on its face as to whether a

---

58. *Id.*
59. *Id.*
60. *Id.*
61. Carlock v. Pillsbury Co., 719 F. Supp. 791, 800 (D. Minn. 1989).
62. *Id.* at 852.
63. *Id.*
64. Thompson v. Atlantic Richfield Co., Bus. Franchise Guide (CCH) ¶ 9080 (W.D. Wash. June 17, 1987).
65. *Id.*
66. *Id.*; *see also* Corp v. Atlantic Richfield Co., 122 Wash. 2d 574, 585, 860 P.2d 1015 (1993) ("[A] franchisee's dissatisfaction with new terms does not equal a refusal to renew or a termination by the franchisor.").
67. *Id.*
68. *Id.*

franchisor can terminate without providing prior notice, except in five discrete circumstances that are specifically called out. Specifically, a franchisor may terminate without providing notice or opportunity to cure if (1) the franchisee has already engaged in three willful, material breaches in the 12 months prior and been given notice and opportunity to cure in each case; (2) the franchisee is adjudicated bankrupt or insolvent; (3) the franchisee makes an assignment for the benefit of creditors; (4) the franchisee voluntarily abandons the business; or (5) the franchisee is convicted of or pleads guilty to a charge of violating any law relating to the franchise business.[69] While the statute does not explicitly state that these five scenarios are the exclusive means for terminating without notice, at least one court has held that list to be exclusive.[70]

b. Annotations

In *Beutlich v. ARCO Products Co.*,[71] the franchisee falsely reported sales to the franchisor to obtain promotional allowance rebates. The franchisor terminated based on fraudulent conduct.[72] Although the franchisee operated a convenience store, covered by FIPA, he also operated a gasoline station, governed by the federal Petroleum Marketing Practices Act (PMPA).[73] Ignoring the FIPA issues, the court found that the PMPA preempted any claims, and that the termination was proper under the PMPA.[74]

The same judge that ruled in *Beutlich* reached the opposite conclusion in *Malek v. Southland Corp.*[75] In that case, after the franchisee was caught misappropriating money orders, the franchisor terminated without providing notice and opportunity to cure.[76] Without the effect of the PMPA's the federal preemption, the court concluded that termination without notice was improper because the theft of the money orders didn't fall into the specific exceptions to notice enumerated in the act.[77]

4. Grounds for Termination

a. Commentary

A franchisor may terminate without providing notice or opportunity to cure if (1) the franchisee has already engaged in three willful, material breaches in the 12 months prior and been given notice and opportunity to cure in each case; (2) the franchisee is adjudicated bankrupt or insolvent; (3) the franchisee makes an assignment for the benefit of creditors; (4) the franchisee voluntarily abandons the business; or (5) the franchisee is convicted of or pleads guilty to a

---

69. *Id.*
70. *See* Malek v. The Southland Corp., Bus. Franchise Guide (CCH) ¶ 11,386 (W.D. Wash. 1998).
71. Bus. Franchise Guide (CCH) ¶ 11,657 (W.D. Wash. Mar. 13, 1998), *aff'd*, 182 F.3d 924 (9th Cir. 1999).
72. *Id.*
73. *Id.*
74. *Id.*
75. Bus. Franchise Guide (CCH) ¶ 11,386 (W.D. Wash. 1998).
76. *Id.*
77. *Id.*

charge of violating any law relating to the franchise business.[78] Alternatively, a franchisor may terminate for a material breach of the franchise agreement, provided the franchisee is given notice of the breach and a reasonable opportunity to cure.

b. Annotations

There are no cases that affirm proper grounds for termination of the franchise agreement outside those enumerated in FIPA.

5. Required Cure Period

a. Commentary

FIPA requires only a "reasonable" opportunity to cure, which need not be more than 30 days.[79] A longer cure period is only required if it would take longer than 30 days to effectuate a cure, in which case the franchisee need only have commenced efforts to cure within 30 days.[80]

b. Annotations

There are no cases that address the reasonableness of a cure period under FIPA.

6. Repurchase Obligations

a. Commentary

In any situation where the franchisor terminates for good cause, the franchisor is then required to pay the franchisee fair market value for the "franchisee's inventory and supplies, exclusive of (i) personalized materials which have no value to the franchisor; (ii) inventory and supplies not reasonably required in the conduct of the franchise business; and (iii), if the franchisee is to retain control of the premises of the franchise business, any inventory and supplies not purchased from the franchisor or on his or her express requirement."[81] However, the franchisor is allowed to offset against this payment obligation, any amounts owed by the franchisee.[82]

b. Annotations

There are no cases that address repurchase obligations under FIPA.

D. Restrictions on Nonrenewal

1. What Constitutes Nonrenewal

a. Commentary

FIPA does not expressly define nonrenewal, but its language suggests that nonrenewal includes any decision by the franchisor not to continue the franchise

---

78. WASH. REV. CODE § 19.100.180(2)(j).
79. Id.
80. Id.
81. Id.
82. Id.

relationship following the expiration of then-current franchise term.[83] Based on Washington case law, nonrenewal does not include situations in which a franchisor offers different terms for renewal than the franchisee operates under during the prior term, particularly where the franchise agreement does not include a right to renew on the same terms.[84]

A franchisor did not include a right of renewal in original agreement and stated that any subsequent agreement would contain whatever terms were then being offered new licensees. Thus, the franchisor may include new terms in subsequent franchise offers.[85] Such modifications will generally not constitute a nonrenewal of the franchise agreement.[86] Furthermore, a franchisee's decision not to renew based on new terms does not entitle the franchisee to any compensation from franchisor under this provision.[87]

b. Annotations

There is no case law addressing this issue.

2. Restrictions on Nonrenewal

a. Commentary

In its current form, FIPA places no restriction on a franchisor's decision not to renew,[88] but does require that a franchisor fairly compensate a franchise at the time the franchise agreement expires.[89] Specifically, a franchisor must compensate a nonrenewed franchisee for fair market value of the franchisee's "inventory, supplies, equipment, and furnishings purchased from the franchisor, and good will, exclusive of personalized materials which have no value to the franchisor, and inventory, supplies, equipment, and furnishings not reasonably required in the conduct of the franchise business."[90] However, if the franchisor gives the franchisee at least one years' notice of nonrenewal and agrees in writing not to enforce any noncompete agreement against the franchisee, the franchisor will not have to pay for good will.[91] Additionally, a franchisor is entitled to offset any required compensation by any amounts franchisee owes to franchisor.[92]

---

83. WASH. REV. CODE § 19.100.180(2)(i).

84. Corp v. Atlantic Richfield Co., 122 Wash. 2d 574, 589, 860 P.2d 1015 (1993) ("FIPA contains no explicit prohibition against a franchisor making substantial change without good cause and it is difficult to read the act's nonrenewal and termination provisions as providing an implied prohibition.").

85. Id.

86. Id.

87. Id.

88. FIPA originally required renewal of franchise relationships, but the statute was amended to its current form before it took effect. Compare Franchise Investment Protection Act, ch. 252, § 18(2)(i), 1971 Wash. Sess. Laws, 1st Ex. Sess. with An Act Relating to Franchises, ch. 116, 1972 Wash. Sess. Laws 2d Ex. Sess.

89. Corp v. Atlantic Richfield Co., 122 Wash. 2d 574, 860 P.2d 1015 (1993).

90. Id.

91. Id.

92. Id.

b. Annotations

FIPA places no restriction on a franchisor's decision not to renew; a franchisor can decline to renew a franchise agreement for any reason or for no reason at all.[93] Absent other contractual rights, a franchisor may choose not to renew a franchise agreement at will so long as that franchisor pays the required compensation.[94]

A franchisor did not include an automatic right of renewal in original agreement, but rather stated that any subsequent agreement would contain whatever terms were the being offered new licensees.

The franchisor may include new terms in subsequent franchise offers.[95] Such modifications will generally not constitute a nonrenewal of the franchise agreement.[96] Furthermore, a franchisee's decision not to renew based on new terms does not entitle the franchisee to any compensation from the franchisor under this provision.[97]

3. Notice Requirement

a. Commentary

As described earlier, there are no notice requirements for nonrenewal outside of the terms of the franchise agreement itself. However, a franchisor can avoid paying compensation for the goodwill of a franchise business if it provides at least one years' notice of nonrenewal (and agrees not to enforce any post-expiration noncompete).

b. Annotations

Franchisor that provided one year's notice of nonrenewal in the context of a franchise agreement that allowed either party to terminate on 30 days' notice satisfied FIPA's notice requirements and the franchisor was not obligated to pay for the goodwill value of the franchisee's business.[98]

4. Grounds for Nonrenewal

a. Commentary

Not applicable.

b. Annotations

Not applicable.

5. Required Cure Period

a. Commentary

Not applicable.

---

93. Thompson v. Atlantic Richfield Co., 663 F. Supp. 206 (W.D. Wash. 1986).
94. Id.
95. Corp v. Atlantic Richfield Co., 122 Wash. 2d 574, 585, 860 P.2d 1015 (1993).
96. Id.
97. Id.
98. Dr Pepper/Seven Up, Inc. v. A&W Bottling, Inc., No. C03-3659Z (W.D. Wash. Nov. 23, 2004).

b. Annotations
Not applicable.

6. Limitations on Franchisor's Rights to Impose Conditions for Renewal
a. Commentary
Not applicable.

b. Annotations
Not applicable.

7. Repurchase Obligations
a. Commentary
A franchisor is obligated in all cases of nonrenewal by the franchisor to pay the franchisee fair market value for (1) inventory, supplies, equipment, and furnishings that are either purchased from the franchisor or "not reasonably required in the conduct of the franchise business," with the exception of personalized items that have no value to the franchisor; and (2) good will.[99] In cases where the franchisor has provided at least one years' notice of nonrenewal and agrees not to enforce any covenant not to compete against the franchisee, the franchisor need not pay for the value of goodwill.[100]

b. Annotations
There are no cases that address repurchase obligations under FIPA.

E. Transfers and Succession
1. Commentary
FIPA does not address transfers of succession beyond its provisions around termination. As originally drafted, FIPA would have prohibited the franchisor from putting unnecessary restrictions on a franchisee's right to transfer the franchised business, but that language was first replaced with language that prohibited such restrictions without just cause,[101] and eventually all language related to transfer was removed in its entirety before FIPA's effective date.[102]

2. Annotations
Not applicable.

---

99. WASH. REV. CODE § 19.100.180(2)(i).
100. *Id.*
101. James Fletcher, Franchise Investment Protection Act, June 1971 (unpublished thesis available for the University of Washington Law School Library); 135 Wash. Sess. Laws, 1st Exec. Sess., ch. 252 § 18(2)(j) (1971).
102. WASH. REV. CODE § 19.100.180(1).

F. Other Regulations on the Franchise Relationship

1. Restrictions on Sources of Supply

a. Commentary

FIPA prohibits a franchisor from requiring a franchisee to buy any goods or services, except initial inventory, from an approved vendor, unless the franchisor can prove that there is a justifiable business reason for the restriction and that the restriction does not materially affect competition.[103] This provision was drafted with antitrust laws in mind[104] and specifically requires courts to consider decisions made by federal courts in antitrust cases when interpreting its application.[105]

b. Annotations

Plaintiff failed to prove that requiring a franchise to use specific computer software would violate antitrust laws.[106] Furthermore, federal courts have generally found that a franchisor may require a franchisee to use its proprietary computer systems without issue.[107]

A plaintiff alleging a violation of FIPA's anti-tying provision will only be successful if they can prove that (1) the franchisor tied together the sale of two distinct products or services; (2) the franchisor possesses enough economic power in the tying product market to coerce the franchisee into purchasing the tied product; and (3) the tying arrangement affects a "not insubstantial volume of commerce" in the tied product market.[108] The franchisee failed to plead the relevant market, or the franchisor's coercive power, and therefore its complaint was dismissed.[109]

2. Prohibition Against Discrimination

a. Commentary

FIPA prohibits a franchisor from discriminating between franchisees "in the charges offered or made for royalties, goods, services, equipment, rentals, advertising service, or in any other business dealing unless the franchisor shows

---

103. WASH. REV. CODE § 19.100.180(2)(b).

104. Chisum, *supra* note 2, at 372 ("[S]ince the legislative intent is to avoid creation of differing state and federal standards on the legality of franchise tying agreements, section 18(2)(b) will have little impact on supply restrictions."). Accordingly, the intent of these provisions appears to be to preclude illegal tying arrangements under the Sherman Act or the Clayton Act. *See* Berry, Byers & Oates, *supra* note 3, at 877 n.406 (citing 15 U.S.C. §§ 1, 17).

105. WASH. REV. CODE § 19.100.180(2)(b) ("In determining whether a requirement to purchase or lease goods or services constitutes an unfair or deceptive act or practice or an unfair method of competition the courts shall be guided by the decisions of the courts of the United States interpreting and applying the anti-trust laws of the United States.").

106. JDS Grp. Ltd. v. Metal Supermarkets Franchising Am., Inc., 2017 WL 2643667, at *3 (W.D.N.Y. June 20, 2017).

107. *Id.*

108. BP W. Coast Prods. LLC v. Shalabi, 2012 WL 2277843, at *9 (W.D. Wash. June 14, 2012) (citing Rick-Mik Enters., Inc. v. Equilon Enters., LLC, 532 F.3d 963, 971 (9th Cir. 2008)).

109. *Id.*

that such discrimination is (1) reasonable; (2) based on franchise as granted at materially different times; (3) reasonably related to such differences in times or based on other proper justifiable distinctions considering the purposes of FIPA; and (4) not arbitrary."[110] However, a franchisor may negotiate the terms of a franchise without violating the antidiscrimination provision, if the franchisee initiates the negotiation.[111]

b. Annotations

To succeed on a claim for violation of FIPA's antidiscrimination provision, a plaintiff must prove that franchisor treated similarly situated franchisees differently.[112] Unlike federal antitrust laws, such as the Robinson-Patman Act, the franchisee need not be in direct competition with similarly situated franchisees to obtain the benefit of the antidiscrimination provision.[113]

Where a franchisor has more than one franchise system, it does not contravene FIPA by treating franchisees in each system differently.[114]

A plaintiff franchisee alleged that its franchisor violated FIPA's antidiscrimination provision by suing the plaintiff for breach of a noncompetition agreement but not suing other former franchisees for the same conduct.[115] The court determined that franchisor made a "rational business decision" not to pursue the others based on the litigation compared to the likely recovery, and therefore did not violate the antidiscrimination provision.[116]

Franchisor did not violate the antidiscrimination provision in selectively enforcing a covenant not to compete where the covenant was reasonable, and where different covenants were signed by franchisees at different times.[117]

3. Reasonable Pricing Restrictions

a. Commentary

The franchisee bill of rights prohibits franchisors from selling any product or service to a franchisee for "more than a fair and reasonable price."[118] Courts have applied the plain meaning of this provision to conclude that a price is fair and reasonable when it accords with a price acceptable to a prudent person in similar

---

110. WASH. REV. CODE § 19.100.180(2)(c).
111. *Id.* § 19.100.184.
112. *Shalabi*, 2012 WL 2277843, at *9 ("To survive a motion to dismiss, it is sufficient under FIPA to allege that two franchises from the same franchisor are subject to different sets of standards.").
113. *Id.*
114. BP W. Coast Prods. LLC, v. SKR, Inc., 145 989 F. Supp. 2d 1109 (W.D. Wash. 2013); *see also* Madison House, Ltd. v. Sotheby's Int'l Realty Aff., Inc., 2007 WL 564151, at *2–3 (W.D. Wash. Feb. 20, 2007).
115. Precision Enters., Inc. v. Precision Tune, Inc., Bus. Franchise Guide (CCH) ¶ 10,472 (W.D. Wash. 1993).
116. *Id.*
117. Armstrong v. Taco Time Int'l, Inc., 30 Wash. App. 538, 635 P.2d 1114 (1981); *see also* Chico's Pizza Franchises, Inc. v. Sisemore, 544 F. Supp. 248 (E.D. Wash. 1981), *aff'd*, 685 F.2d 440 (9th Cir. 1982) (discrimination permissible so long as franchisor "demonstrate[s] that disparate treatment is rationally and justifiably based on sound business practices.").
118. WASH. REV. CODE § 19.100.180(2)(d).

circumstances.[119] A claim under this section of the statute therefore necessarily raises a fact question as to whether the price charged is a reasonable price.[120]

b. Annotations

A franchisee challenged the franchisor's practice of selling printed advertisements to the franchisee at more than double the franchisor's cost.[121] The franchisee obtained a summary judgment on the claim, with the district court concluding that the franchisor's cost was a reasonable price, and that twice that amount was unreasonable as a matter of law.[122] The case was certified to the Washington Supreme Court, which concluded that the franchisor's cost was not the standard for whether or not the price was reasonable.[123] Rather, that was a fact question for the fact finder.[124] Similarly, charging twice the cost of the product was not a per se unreasonable price; rather that, too, was a fact question for the jury's determination.[125] The court listed a nonexclusive list of factors to consider when assessing the reasonableness of the price, including (1) the franchisor's price; (2) the prices of competitors; (3) the franchisor's profit margin; (4) the franchisor's charges to other franchisees for the same or similar products or services; (5) business and industry practices; (6) the price at which the franchisee could obtain the same or equivalent products or services on the market; and (7) the value that the franchisor adds to the product or service, if any.[126]

In another case, however, the court held that a pure markup of a product, bought by the franchisor at a bona fide wholesale price, with no value added by the franchisor, constituted a per se unreasonable price.[127]

4. Supplier Rebates and Kickbacks

FIPA prohibits franchisors from obtaining money, goods, services, or anything of value from a third party who does business with a franchisee on account of such business unless the benefit is disclosed to the franchisee in advance.[128]

a. Commentary

FIPA's original draft precluded supplier rebates.[129] Amended before it officially took effect, the provision, also known as the "anti-kickback" provision, now only requires disclosure of rebates and discounts that the franchisor receives

---

119. Money Mailer, LLC v. Brewer, 194 Wash. 2d 111, 119, 449 P.3d 258 (2019).
120. Id.
121. Money Mailer, LLC v. Brewer, 2018 WL 3156901, at *2–4 (W.D. Wash. June 28, 2019).
122. Id.
123. *Money Mailer, LLC*, 194 Wash. 2d at 115–16.
124. Id. at 118.
125. Id.
126. Id. at 121–22.
127. Nelson v. Nat'l Fund Raising Consultants, Inc., 120 Wash. 2d 382, 385, 842 P.2d 473 (1992). In *Money Mailer*, the Washington Supreme Court subsequently walked back this ruling, noting that it was unclear from the record in *Nelson* whether there were other reasons why the court upheld the prior ruling. *Money Mailer, LLC*, 194 Wash. 2d at 126 n.6. As such, *Nelson* likely no longer stands for a per se prohibition.
128. WASH. REV. CODE § 19.100.180(2)(e).
129. Franchise Investment Protection Act, ch. 252, 1971 § 18(2)(e) Wash. Sess. Laws, 1st Ex. Sess.

from third party vendors who do business with franchisees.¹³⁰ Unlike FIPA's other relationship provisions, which apply to post-sale conduct, the anti-kickback statute requires presale disclosures of amounts a franchisor receives from designated or required suppliers.¹³¹

b. Annotations

A franchisee sued its franchisor, arguing that a markup on products purchased from a third party was not disclosed prior to the purchase of the franchise.¹³² After the franchisee prevailed in the lower courts, the Washington Supreme Court affirmed, noting that the evidence showed that the franchisee did not know about the markup until it received its first invoice from the franchisor, long after signing the franchise agreement.¹³³ This constituted an impermissible undisclosed kickback in violation of the statute.¹³⁴

A franchisee failed to show a violation of the anti-kickback prohibitions in FIPA by merely alleging that high prices implied the existence of otherwise unknown or undisclosed kickbacks.¹³⁵

A franchisee's claim that its franchisor's affiliated entity was receiving benefits did not rise to a claim under FIPA's anti-kickback provisions because the affiliate was related to the franchisor and the entities effectively acted as a single unit.¹³⁶ The anti-kickback provision does not prohibit franchisors from benefiting from their own fee collection practices, only if it benefits from a third party's relationship with the franchisee.¹³⁷

5. Exclusive Territories

a. Commentary

If a franchisee is granted an exclusive geographical territory in its franchise agreement, FIPA prohibits a franchisor from granting competing franchises in that same territory or competing directly with the franchisee in the territory.¹³⁸

b. Annotations

There are no cases discussing the exclusive territory provision under FIPA.

6. Standards of Conduct

a. Commentary

Under FIPA, a franchisor must prove that any "standard of conduct" it imposes on any franchisee through "contract, rule, or regulation" is reasonable and necessary.¹³⁹

---

130. WASH. REV. CODE § 19.100.180(2)(e).
131. *Nelson*, 120 Wash. 2d at 390–92.
132. *Id.* at 385–86.
133. *Id.* at 386.
134. *Id.* at 390–91.
135. BP W. Coast Prods., LLC v. Shalabi, 2012 WL 2277843, at *10 (W.D. Wash. June 14, 2012).
136. Money Mailer, LLC v. Brewer, 2018 WL 3156901, at *2 n.3 (W.D. Wash. June 28, 2018).
137. *Id.*
138. WASH. REV. CODE § 19.100.180(2)(f).
139. *Id.* § 19.100.180(2)(h).

b. Annotations

The only court to have addressed this provision of the statute noted as a preliminary matter that franchise systems rely on uniformity and limiting franchisee discretion to deviate from the business system.[140] As such, the reasonable conduct provision should not be used "to undercut a franchisor's business judgment in establishing standards for its franchise system."[141] Accordingly, the court refused plaintiff's invitation to a take a "supervisory role over the franchisor" and felt such a role would be inconsistent with statute's legislative intent.[142] As such, claims under this relationship provision turn on proof by the franchisor that it exercised reasonable business judgment in implementing, adopting, or enforcing the business standard in question.

G. Remedies and Administration Action

1. Restrictive Covenants

a. Commentary

FIPA does not directly address the issue of noncompetition covenants, nor has any case addressed the issue head on. The only cases addressing noncompetes in the franchising context have held such agreements to similar standards as those in the employment context.[143]

Washington has recently banned noncompetition agreements in most contexts, but limited the definition of "noncompetition covenant" to agreements affecting "an employee or independent contractor," and explicitly excluded from the definition of "noncompetition covenant" any "covenant entered into by a franchisee when the franchise sale complied with RCW 19.100.020."[144] Furthermore, RCW section 49.62.010 specifically excluded from the definition of "noncompetition covenants," inter alia, "a covenant entered into by a person purchasing or selling the goodwill of a business or otherwise acquiring or disposing of an ownership interest[.]"[145] That definition was updated, effective June 6, 2024, to clarify that such exclusion applies to situations in which "the person signing the covenant purchases, sells, acquires, or disposes of an interest representing one percent or more of the business."[146]

In addition, Washington does explicitly prohibit franchisors from restricting, restraining, or prohibiting a franchisee from "soliciting or hiring any employee of" (1) another franchisee in that franchise system or (2) a franchisor.[147]

---

140. JDS Grp. Ltd. v. Metal Supermarkets Franchising Am., Inc., 2017 WL 2643667 (W.D.N.Y. June 20, 2017).
141. *Id.* at *4.
142. *Id.*
143. Armstrong v. Taco Time Int'l, Inc. 30 Wash. App. 538, 635 P.2d 1114 (1981).
144. Wash. Rev. Code § 49.62.010.
145. *Id.*
146. An Act Relating to Noncompetition Covenants, ch. 36, 2024 Wash. Sess. Laws 5935.
147. Wash. Rev. Code § 49.62.060.

b. Annotations

A court enforced a noncompetition covenant contained in a franchise agreement, concluding the restrictions (as modified) were reasonable in geographic and temporal scope.[148] The court expressly rejected the argument that FIPA prohibits noncompetition agreements.[149]

2. Damages

a. Commentary

FIPA does not provide for any specific damages, or other remedy, for a violation of the relationship provisions. Rather, FIPA makes clear that any such violation may be an "unfair act or practice" under the Washington Consumer Protection Act (CPA), as long as the plaintiff can prove all required elements.[150] Pursuant to the CPA, successful plaintiffs are entitled an award of actual damages, as well as treble damages, capped at $25,000, at the court's discretion.[151]

b. Annotations

Not applicable.

3. Rescission

a. Commentary

Not applicable.

b. Annotations

Not applicable.

4. Injunctive Relief

a. Commentary

A franchisee may seek injunctive relief for a violation of FIPA's relationship provisions. Such franchisee would need to both (1) file a claim under Washington's CPA, requesting injunctive relief, and (2) serve a copy of that complaint, or other initial pleading, on the Washington attorney general.[152]

b. Annotations

There are no cases discussing the injunctive relief for violations of FIPA's relationship provisions.

---

148. *Armstrong*, 30 Wash. App. at 548.
149. *Id.* ("Armstrong contends the enforcement of the covenant is prohibited by the Washington Franchise Investment Protection Act, RCW 19.100. We disagree."). This conclusion is consistent with the nonrenewal section of the bill of rights, which express limits the obligation to pay the franchisee the value of the goodwill of its business if enough advance notice is given, and the franchisor agrees to waive the noncompete in the franchise agreement. WASH. REV. CODE § 19.100.180(2)(i). This section specifically contemplates the use of noncompetes in franchise relationships.
150. WASH. REV. CODE §§ 19.86 *et seq.*
151. *Id.* § 19.86.090.
152. *Id.* § 19.86.095.

5. Control Person Liability

a. Commentary

FIPA's relationship provision makes it an unfair or deceptive act or practice in violation of the state's consumer protection act for any "person" to engage in any of the prohibited acts enumerated in the statute.[153] The statute broadly defines "person" as "a natural person . . . as well as the individual officers, directors, and other persons in act of control of the activities of [the franchisor or its ownership]."[154] As such, directors and officers that are "in act of control" of the activities of the franchisor, and which are directly involved in any of the prohibited actions that violate the relationship protections under the statute, are subject to possible liability.

b. Annotations

There are no cases discussing director and officer liability for violations of FIPA's relationship provisions.

6. Attorneys' Fees

a. Commentary

Pursuant to the CPA, which is the statute through which franchisees can seek a remedy for a violation of the franchisee bill of rights provisions, a successful plaintiff will be entitled to attorneys' fees.

b. Annotations

There are no cases discussing attorneys' fee awards for violations of FIPA's relationship provisions.

7. Limitation on Damage Waivers

a. Commentary

FIPA contains an anti-waiver provision that prohibits any waiver that would relieve a person of liability imposed by FIPA.[155] This waiver extends beyond damage waivers and includes the waiver of any right granted by the statute's relationship protections, and prohibits choice-of-law provisions that would result in waiving FIPA's protections.[156] The anti-waiver provision does not apply if it is part of a negotiated settlement in connection with a bona fide dispute between a franchisee and a franchisor, arising after their franchise agreement has taken effect, provided that the franchisee is represented by independent

---

153. *Id.* § 19.100.180(2).
154. *Id.* § 19.100.010(13).
155. *Id.* § 19.100.180(2)(g).
156. *Id.* § 19.100.220(2) ("Any agreement, condition, stipulation, *including a choice of law provision* purporting to bind any person to waive compliance with *any provision* of this chapter or any rule hereunder is void.").

legal counsel.[157] The statute also does not prohibit negotiated changes implemented at the initiative of the franchisee.[158]

b. Annotations

A franchisee entered into a settlement agreement with a franchisor to resolve a claim of presale fraud and misrepresentation.[159] While the franchisee was generally represented by counsel in most matters, it elected not to retain counsel for purposes of negotiating the settlement agreement.[160] Thereafter, the franchisee sued the franchisor on the same fraud and misrepresentation claims that were the subject of the prior settlement and release.[161] The franchisee argued that the negotiated settlement was an improper waiver in violation of FIPA's anti-waiver prohibitions.[162] The franchisor argued that the franchisee had the opportunity to retain independent legal counsel to represent it in connection with the settlement agreement, and that it elected not to do so.[163] The trial court agreed with the franchisee, concluding that the statute requires actual representation and review by legal counsel for a waiver to be effective.[164]

8. Administrative Action

a. Commentary

FIPA provides a suite of administrative remedies. The Washington attorney general can enter into an assurance of discontinuance with franchisors to resolve violations.[165] The department of financial institutions, a separate Washington state agency, can also investigate potential violations.[166] The director of financial institutions can also issue a stop order, preventing the sale or registration of franchises in the state.[167] If it appears that the franchisor has violated the statute, the department of financial institutions can issue cease and desist orders.[168]

b. Annotations

There are no cases assessing the scope of administrative remedies available to the state for violations of the FIPA's relationship provisions.

---

157. *Id.*
158. *Id.* § 19.100.184.
159. Taylor v. 1-800-Got-Junk?, LLC, 632 F. Supp. 2d 1048, 1051 (W.D. Wash. 2009), *aff'd*, 387 Fed. Appx. 727 (9th Cir. 2010).
160. *Id.*
161. *Id.*
162. *Id.*
163. *Id.*
164. *Id.* ("The dispositive issue in this case therefore turns on whether FIPA's anti-waiver provision applies. If it does, then the settlement and release would be invalid since the Taylors were not represented by counsel at the time of the agreement."). The holding is arguably dicta, however, as the court ultimately concluded that FIPA did not apply at all to the dispute because the claim was beyond the jurisdictional scope of the statute. *Id.* at 1054.
165. WASH. REV. CODE § 19.100.210(5).
166. *Id.* § 19.100.245.
167. *Id.* § 19.100.120(2).
168. *Id.* § 19.100.248.

H. Dispute Resolution

1. Limitations on Franchisor's Ability to Restrict Venue

a. Commentary

The Washington Department of Financial Institutions has adopted an interpretive statement that limits a franchisor's ability to require arbitration outside the state of Washington.[169] Under the auspices of the relationship prohibitions on the unreasonable standards of conduct provision, the interpretive statement "finds that it is not in good faith, reasonable, or a fair act or practice for a franchisor to set the site of arbitration, mediation, and/or litigation in a state other than Washington."[170]

b. Annotations

There are no cases assessing the franchisor's ability to restrict venue under FIPA.

2. Limitations Period

a. Commentary

Although FIPA itself does not have a process through which franchisees may seek remedy for violations of the statute's relationship provisions, franchisees bring claims under the CPA.[171] The CPA itself contains a four-year statute of limitations.[172]

b. Annotations

There are no cases discussing the statute of limitations for violations of FIPA's relationship provisions.

---

169. 4 Franchise Act Interpretive Statement, Sec. Div., Wash. Dep't of Fin. Insts. (1991).
170. *Id.*
171. WASH. REV. CODE § 19.100.180(2); *id.* § 19.100.190(1).
172. *Id.* § 19.86.120.

Wisconsin

Andy Beilfuss and Mark Leitner

I. Introduction to Statute

Like many state laws that regulate the franchisor-franchisee relationship during the relationship's term, the Wisconsin Fair Dealership Law (WFDL) prohibits in-term termination or cancellation unless based on "good cause." Unlike most of those relationship laws, the WFDL imposes additional regulations that go well beyond a prohibition against good-cause termination:

- The WFDL protects "dealers," not merely "franchisees."[1] Protected "dealer" status extends to a wide range of distributors of goods and services well beyond traditional franchisees, in some cases to businesses that derive less than 10 percent of their revenues or profits from a grantor's products or services. (The WFDL's term for the supplier or franchisor side party is "grantor.")[2]
- The WFDL prohibits not only in-term "termination" and "cancellation" but also forbids a grantor from failing to renew a dealership without good cause.[3]
- The WFDL forbids a grantor from "substantially chang[ing] the competitive circumstances" of a dealership without good cause.[4]
- The WFDL contains a "deemer" clause providing that "any violation of this chapter by the grantor is deemed an irreparable injury to the dealer for determining if a temporary injunction should be issued," giving a significant advantage to a dealer that is able to prove under preliminary injunction standards that a grantor arguably violated the WFDL.[5]

Even experienced franchise counsel should tread carefully in their first forays into litigation under the WFDL. Fortunately, there are hundreds of cases that, taken together, address almost every issue that could be disputed under the law. This chapter provides a guide to the most important WFDL issues.

---

1. WIS. STAT. § 135.02(2), (3).
2. *Id.* § 135.02(5).
3. *Id.* § 135.03.
4. *Id.*
5. WIS. STAT. § 135.065.

II. Commentary and Annotations

A. Definition of Franchise/Dealership

Under the WFDL, the existence of a protected "dealership" requires three elements: "(1) the existence of a contract or agreement between two or more persons; (2) by which a person is granted one of the rights specified; and (3) in which there is the requisite 'community of interest.'"[6] The "rights specified" are either a right to sell or distribute goods or services, or the right to use a trade name, trademark, logotype, or other commercial symbol.[7] Unlike franchise relationship laws in other states, the WFDL does not require a franchise fee, or the existence of a marketing system or plan prescribed by a franchisor. Instead, the Wisconsin statute is intended to protect a range of commercial relationships beyond "the telltale trappings of the traditional franchise."[8] "In most cases, there is rarely an obvious answer to the question of whether a business is a dealership[.]"[9]

B. Annotations

The existence of a protected statutory dealership requires (1) the existence of a contract or agreement between two or more persons; (2) by which a person is granted the right to sell or distribute goods or services, or the right to use or display a trademark, trade name, logotype, or other commercial symbol; (3) in which there is the requisite "community of interest." *Benson v. City of Madison*, 2017 WI 65, ¶ 35, 376 Wis. 2d 635, 651, 897 N.W.2d 16.

The definition of "dealership" under the WFDL is broad, because the statute is intended to protect a wide range of commercial relationships extending beyond "the telltale trappings of the traditional franchise." *Bush v. National School Studios, Inc.*, 139 Wis. 2d 635, 651, 407 N.W.2d 883 (1987).

Many types of entities can be dealers under the Wisconsin Fair Dealership Law if the statutory elements are met. For example, in *Builder's World, Inc. v. Marvin Lumber & Cedar, Inc.*, 482 F. Supp. 2d 1065, 1072–73 (E.D. Wis. 2007), *modified sub nom. Builders World, Inc. v. Marvin Lumber & Cedar, Inc.*, No. 06C0555 (E.D. Wis. July 23, 2007), the district court held that a co-op organized under Wisconsin Statutes section 185.02 could qualify as a "dealer" that was party to a "dealership." In *Girl Scouts of Manitou Council, Inc. v. Girl Scouts of the United States of America, Inc.*, 549 F.3d 1079, 1090–94 (7th Cir. 2008), the Seventh Circuit held that a nonprofit, local Girl Scouts council qualified as a WFDL "dealer." And in *Benson v. City of Madison*, 2017 WI 65, ¶¶ 23–33, 376 Wis. 2d 635, 897 N.W.2d 16, the Wisconsin Supreme Court held that a municipality could be a "grantor" under the WFDL, suggesting that any entity that contracts with a municipality and that can meet the statutory requirements could be a party to a protected "dealership."

---

6. Benson v. City of Madison, 376 Wis. 2d 35, 897 N.W.2d 16 (2017).
7. WIS. STAT. § 135.02(3)(a).
8. Bush v. Nat'l Sch. Studios, Inc., 139 Wis. 2d 635, 651, 407 N.W. 883 (1987).
9. *Bush*, 139 Wis. 2d at 647.

1. Right to Sell or Trademark Element

a. Commentary

A putative dealer can satisfy the trademark requirement in either of two ways: first, by demonstrating it has the "right to sell" the grantor's product or service;[10] or second, by showing that it has not only been granted the right to use the grantor's commercial marks but has actually made substantial use of those commercial symbols.[11]

The Wisconsin Supreme Court defines the "right to sell or distribute" goods or services as "the 'unqualified authorization to transfer the product at the point and moment of the agreement to sell' or the 'authority to commit the grantor to a sale.'"[12] Under this general rule, the "single most important factor" is the dealer's "ability to transfer the product itself (or title to the product) or commit the grantor to a transaction at the moment of the agreement to sell."[13] The "hallmarks of control" over the sales process "include transfer of title to customers, maintenance of inventory, approval of sales terms, and collecting payment."[14] According to the Wisconsin Supreme Court, the "most important[]" of these factors is the receipt of the customer's payment by the dealer, which is then remitted in whole or in part to the grantor.[15]

Alternatively, this element can be satisfied through compliance with the commercial-symbols prong of the statutory definition. Despite the literal wording of the statute, which requires merely the existence of the "right to use" commercial symbols, courts unanimously hold that more is required.[16] Specifically, a protected dealership "must either put those symbols 'to such use that the public associates the dealer with the trademark,'"[17] or "prominently display the logo as a[n] implicit guarantee of quality."[18] "Sufficiently substantial use of a grantor's corporate symbol typically requires a purported dealer to 'make a substantial investment in the trademark.'"[19] Mere "de minim[i]s investment in a trademark"[20] will not suffice. For example, a few thousand dollars' worth of expenditures on advertising and including the putative grantor's marks on the dealer's website is not enough.[21]

---

10. John Maye Co. v. Nordson Corp., 959 F.2d 1402, 1406 (7th Cir. 1992).
11. Moodie v. Sch. Book Fairs, Inc., 889 F.2d 739, 743 (7th Cir. 1989).
12. *Benson*, 376 Wis. 2d at 61 quoting Foerster, Inc. v. Atlas Metal Parts Co., 105 Wis. 2d 17, 313 N.W.2d 60, 64 (1981).
13. *John Maye*, 959 F.2d at 1406.
14. PMT Machinery Sales, Inc. v. Yama Seiki USA, Inc., 941 F.3d 325, 329 (7th Cir. 2019).
15. *Benson*, 376 Wis. 2d at 61.
16. *John Maye*, 959 F.2d at 1410.
17. *PMT Machinery Sales*, 941 F.3d at 330.
18. Moodie v. Sch. Book Fairs, Inc., 889 F.2d 739, 743 (7th Cir. 1989).
19. *PMT Machinery Sales*, 941 F.3d at 330 (quoting Van Groll v. Land O'Lakes, Inc., 310 F.3d 566, 570 (7th Cir. 2002)).
20. *Moodie*, 889 F.2d at 743.
21. *PMT Machinery Sales*, 941 F.3d at 330.

b. Annotations

The Wisconsin Supreme Court defines the "right to sell or distribute" goods or services as "the 'unqualified authorization to transfer the product at the point and moment of the agreement to sell' or the 'authority to commit the grantor to a sale.'" *Benson v. City of Madison*, 2017 WI 65, ¶ 41, 376 Wis. 2d 635, 897 N.W.2d 16, quoting *Foerster, Inc. v. Atlas Metal Parts Co.*, 105 Wis. 2d 17, 313 N.W.2d 60, 64 (1981). The "single most important factor" in addressing this issue is the dealer's "ability to transfer the product itself (or title to the product) or commit the grantor to a transaction at the moment of the agreement to sell." *John Maye Co. v. Nordson Corp.*, 959 F.2d 1402, 1406 (7th Cir. 1992).

A sales representative that has no authority to commit the grantor to any contract, represents other companies, and paid no franchise fee likely will not qualify as a dealer under the Wisconsin Fair Dealership Law. *Kornacki v. Norton Performance Plastics, Inc.*, 956 F.2d at 129; *Northland Sales, Inc. v. Maax Corp.*, 556 F. Supp. 2d 928 (E.D. Wis. 2008).

A few thousand dollars' worth of expenditures on advertising, coupled with including the putative grantor's marks on the dealer's website, is mere de minimis use of those marks that is insufficient to satisfy the WFDL. *PMT Machinery Sales, Inc. v. Yama Seiki USA, Inc.*, 941 F.3d 325, 330 (7th Cir. 2019). Instead, "[s]ufficiently substantial use of a grantor's corporate symbol typically requires a purported dealer to 'make a substantial investment in the trademark.'" *PMT Machinery Sales*, 941 F.3d at 330, quoting *Van Groll v. Land O'Lakes, Inc.*, 310 F.3d 566, 570 (7th Cir. 2002).

A protected dealership makes a substantial investment in the grantor's commercial symbols by putting them to such use that the public associates the dealer with the trademark, or by prominently displaying the logo as an implicit guarantee of quality. *Moodie v. School Book Fairs, Inc.*, 889 F.2d 739, 743 (7th Cir. 1989).

2. "Contract or Agreement" Element

a. Commentary

The WFDL expressly extends to "a contract or agreement, either express or implied, whether oral or written[.]"[22] When the evidence fails to establish the existence of a contract, then no dealership exists.[23] Nevertheless, the express inclusion of coverage for both implied and oral contracts leaves ample but not unlimited room for argument. For example, where the putative dealer failed to support its argument for an oral agreement with evidence of the parties' supposed course of dealing, the court rejected the plaintiff's WFDL claim.[24]

---

22. WIS. STAT. § 135.02(3)(a).
23. Century Hardware Corp. v. Acme United Corp., 467 F. Supp. 350 (E.D. Wis. 1979); Bong v. Cerny, 158 Wis. 2d 474, 463 N.W.2d 359 (Wis. Ct. App. 1990).
24. Lakeshore Distrib. Co. v. H. Schmitt Sohne, Inc., 606 F. Supp. 1, 2 (E.D. Wis. 1984).

b. Annotations

When the evidence fails to establish the existence of a contract, no dealership exists. *Century Hardware Corp. v. Acme United Corp.*, 467 F. Supp. 350 (E.D. Wis. 1979); *Bong v. Cerny*, 158 Wis. 2d 474, 463 N.W.2d 359 (Ct. App. 1990).

The WFDL specifies that the "contract or agreement" necessary for a "dealership" may be "express or implied." "Implied" means a contract implied in fact. *Bong v. Cerny*, 158 Wis. 2d 474, 481, 463 N.W.2d 359 (Ct. App. 1990).

When a putative dealer claiming an oral dealership contract fails to supply evidence of the parties' course of dealing, the plaintiff has no claim under the WFDL. *Lakeshore Distributing Co. v. H. Schmitt Sohne, Inc.*, 606 F. Supp. 1, 2 (E.D. Wis. 1984).

When there are multiple agreements between an alleged dealer and its grantor, the court should evaluate the following factors to determine whether one or more of the agreements may qualify for WFDL protection: (1) the language and history of the agreement; (2) the distinct nature of the activities in each agreement; (3) the extent to which the activities are treated distinctly by the grantor in the operation of the dealer's business; and (4) whether there are third parties performing the activities separately. *Team Electronics of Janesville, Inc. v. Apple Computer, Inc.*, 773 F. Supp. 153, 155 (W.D. Wis. 1991).

An operating division or business unit of a corporation claiming to be a "dealer" cannot itself have an "agreement" with a grantor that is separate and apart from the agreement between the plaintiff corporation and the alleged grantor. *Kayser Ford, Inc. v. Northern Rebuilders, Inc.*, 760 F. Supp. 749, 753, Bus. Franchise Guide (CCH) ¶ 9815 (W.D. Wis. 1991).

3. Community of Interest Element; Significant Degree of Control; Joint Marketing Plan

a. Commentary

The "community of interest" requirement is the most frequently litigated element of a WFDL claim. It is this element, according to the courts, that "most distinguishes [protected] dealerships from other forms of business agreements" left unprotected by the WFDL.[25] The statute itself is vague: it specifies only that a community of interest is defined as "a continuing financial interest between the grantor and grantee in either the operation of the dealership business or the marketing of such goods or services."[26]

In an important 1987 decision, the Wisconsin Supreme Court sought to clarify the "community of interest" requirement. Rejecting a fixed percentage-of-business test as inconsistent with the flexibility that the legislature had built into the WFDL,[27] the court identified two "guideposts" in the broad statutory definition. The first of these guideposts, "continuing financial interest," "contemplates a shared financial interest in the operation of the dealership or the

---

25. Ziegler Co. v. Rexnord, Inc., 139 Wis. 2d 593, 600, 407 N.W.2d 873 (1987).
26. WIS. STAT. § 135.02(1).
27. *Ziegler Co.*, 139 Wis. 2d at 602.

marketing of a good or service."[28] The second guidepost, which the court called "interdependence," helped distinguish a dealership from "an ordinary vendor-vendee relationship" by focusing on "the degree to which the dealer and grantor cooperate, coordinate their activities and share common goals in their business relationship."[29] These two guideposts "appear to require a person to demonstrate a stake in the relationship large enough to make the grantor's power to terminate, cancel, or not renew a threat to the economic health of the person (thus giving the grantor inherently superior bargaining power)."[30] A dealer's "economic health is threatened where a termination, cancellation, failure to renew, etc., a business relationship would have a significant economic impact on the alleged dealer."[31]

After explaining the "guideposts," the Supreme Court went on to identify what have become known over the ensuing decades as the "*Ziegler* factors," ten facets of a business relationship for courts to examine in order to guide their inquiry into the two "guideposts":

- How long the parties have dealt with each other;
- The extent and nature of the obligations imposed on the parties in the contract between them;
- What percentage of time or revenue the alleged dealer devotes to the alleged grantor's products or services;
- What percentage of the gross proceeds or profits of the alleged dealer derives from the alleged grantor's products or services;
- The extent and nature of the alleged grantor's grant of territory to the alleged dealer;
- The extent and nature of the alleged dealer's uses of the alleged grantor's proprietary marks (such as trademarks or logos);
- The extent and nature of the alleged dealer's financial investment in inventory, facilities, and good will of the alleged dealership;
- The personnel which the alleged dealer devotes to the alleged dealership;
- How much the alleged dealer spends on advertising or promotional expenditures for the alleged grantor's products or services; and
- The extent and nature of any supplementary services provided by the alleged dealer to consumers of the alleged grantor's products or services.[32]

The Supreme Court concluded its list by declaring that "[e]ach of the facets may relate to one or both of the guideposts and we do not intend this list to be all inclusive."[33] Unsurprisingly, these fact-intensive inquiries led to extensive litigation over the community of interest issue.

---

28. *Id.* at 603.
29. *Id.* at 605.
30. *Id.*
31. *Id.*
32. *Id.* at 606.
33. *Id.*

Seventeen years after *Ziegler*, the Wisconsin Supreme Court revisited its approach to the existence of a community of interest but did not break any new ground in defining or applying the two "guideposts" or the ten "facets" initially established in *Ziegler*. Instead, the court in *Central Corp. v. Research Products Corp.*[34] appeared to be most interested in reemphasizing that no specific aspect of either guidepost and no one factor was to be considered dispositive in evaluating the factual record at the summary judgment stage: "Where there are genuine issues of material fact or reasonable alternative inferences to be drawn from undisputed material facts, the determination of whether there is a community of interest is one which will be made by the trier of fact, based on an examination of all of the facets of the business relationship."[35] The *Central Corp.* court also reiterated *Ziegler*'s rejection of a hard-and-fast percentage test to resolve the existence of a community of interest: "While we recognize that the sale of Research's products does not comprise a large percentage of Central's gross revenues or profits, this fact alone is not dispositive, but is a matter to be weighed by the trier of fact."[36]

In 2017, the Wisconsin Supreme Court addressed the community of interest requirement for a third time.[37] The decision in *Benson v. City of Madison* is important for a number of reasons, most significantly because it holds that a municipality can be a "grantor" of a dealership protected by the WFDL.[38] For purposes of this chapter, however, *Benson* is significant mainly because it makes clear for the first time that use of the *Ziegler* factors is not mandatory in judicial evaluation of community of interest disputes: "Although we have said that these extra statutory items 'should' be considered by courts . . . it is more accurate to say that some or all 'may' be considered; the factors are meant to be a helpful aid in addressing the overriding community of interest question, not an unwieldy burden."[39] This left lower courts with even less guidance on how they should resolve disputes over the existence of a community of interest.

In contrast to the multifactor evaluation adopted by the Wisconsin Supreme Court, the Seventh Circuit holds that the *Ziegler* factors "may be distilled into two highly important questions in establishing a community of interest: (1) the percentages of revenues and profits the alleged dealer derives from the grantor; and (2) the amount of time and money the alleged dealer has sunk into the relationship. Neither of these is sufficient alone, but strong facts in one area can make up for weaker facts in another area."[40] The Seventh Circuit has further elaborated on the latter "sunk costs" standard: it concerns the situation "when the alleged dealer has made sizable investments (in, for example, fixed assets, inventory, advertising, training) specialized in some way to the grantor's

---

34. 272 Wis. 2d 561, 681 N.W.2d 178 (2004).
35. *Id.* at 585.
36. *Id.* at 584.
37. Benson v. City of Madison, 376 Wis. 2d 35, 897 N.W.2d 16 (2017).
38. *Id.* at 50–57.
39. *Id.* at 64 n.15.
40. Home Protective Servs., Inc. v. ADT Sec. Servs., Inc., 438 F.3d 716, 720 (7th Cir. 2006).

goods or services, and hence not fully recoverable upon termination."[41] When a putative dealer can easily turn its assets to selling the products of a different manufacturer,[42] or can sell off its inventory at a profit, courts are less willing to find the kind of sunk costs that will support a community of interest.

No discussion of the WFDL's community of interest requirement is complete without considering the beliefs of the dealership bar in Wisconsin that the state courts' application of the *Ziegler* factors tend to favor dealers, while the federal courts' approach to the community of interest requirement weighs in favor of grantors.[43] The Seventh Circuit itself has sought to deny that there is a difference, reasoning that the federal and state courts have merely developed "two ways of saying the same thing. A grantor can exploit a dealer's fear of termination (our words) only if termination will have severe economic consequences (their words). Severe economic consequences will attend termination (theirs) because the dealer will be unable to recover its sunk costs (ours). The ten *Ziegler* factors structure any inquiry into these matters."[44] Notwithstanding the Seventh Circuit's attempt to smooth the waters, one need only consider the frequency with which grantors' counsel seek to remove to federal court WFDL lawsuits commenced by dealers' counsel in state courts to question its accuracy.

b. Annotations

The "community of interest" element most clearly distinguishes protected "dealerships" from other types of business relationships left unprotected by the WFDL. *Ziegler Co. v. Rexnord, Inc.*, 139 Wis. 2d 593, 600, 407 N.W.2d 873 (1987).

Courts may not use a fixed percentage-of-business calculation as the exclusive test for the presence of a community of interest, because it is inconsistent with the flexibility the legislature built into the WFDL. *Ziegler Co. v. Rexnord, Inc.*, 139 Wis. 2d 593, 602, 407 N.W.2d 873 (1987).

The Wisconsin Supreme Court has identified two "guideposts" to aid courts in resolving the community of interest issue. The first guidepost is "continuing financial interest," which "contemplates a shared financial interest in the operation of the dealership or the marketing of a good or service." The second guidepost is "interdependence," which helps distinguish a dealership from "an ordinary vendor-vendee relationship" by focusing on "the degree to which the dealer and grantor cooperate, coordinate their activities and share common goals in their business relationship." *Ziegler Co. v. Rexnord, Inc.*, 139 Wis. 2d 593, 603–05, 407 N.W.2d 873 (1987).

When a community of interest exists, the putative dealer will be able to "demonstrate a stake in the relationship large enough to make the grantor's power to terminate, cancel, or not renew a threat to the economic health of the person (thus giving the grantor inherently superior bargaining power)." A

---

41. *Frieburg Farm Equip., Inc. v. Van Dale, Inc.*, 978 F.2d 395, 399 (7th Cir. 1992).

42. *Home Protective Servs.*, 438 F.3d at 720.

43. *See, e.g.*, Brian Butler & Jeffrey A. Mandell, The Wisconsin Fair Dealership Law § 4.7 (5th ed. 2022).

44. *Freiburg Farm Equip. Inc.*, 978 F.2d at 399.

putative dealer's economic health is threatened when "a termination, cancellation, failure to renew, etc., a business relationship would have a significant economic impact on the alleged dealer." *Ziegler Co. v. Rexnord, Inc.*, 139 Wis. 2d 593, 605, 407 N.W.2d 873 (1987).

Factors that may be relevant to assessing one or both of the "guideposts" include the length of the parties' relationship; the nature of the obligations of the parties contained in the agreement; the percentage of time or revenue devoted by the dealer to the grantor's products or services; the percentage of the gross proceeds that the dealer derives from the grantor's products or services; the extent and nature of the grant of territory to the alleged dealer; the extent and nature of the alleged dealer's use of the grantor's proprietary symbols, marks, or logos; the extent and nature of the alleged grantor's investment in inventory, facilities, and goodwill; the personnel devoted to the alleged dealership; the alleged dealer's spending on advertising and promotion for the grantor's products or services; and the extent and nature of supplementary services provided by the alleged dealer. *Ziegler Co. v. Rexnord, Inc.*, 139 Wis. 2d 593, 606, 407 N.W.2d 873 (1987).

No specific aspect of either the "continuing financial interest" or the "interdependence" guideposts, and no one of the ten "*Ziegler* factors," should ever be considered dispositive at the summary judgment stage. Instead, "where there are genuine issues of material fact or reasonable alternative inferences to be drawn from undisputed material facts, the determination of whether there is a community of interest is one which will be made by the trier of fact, based on an examination of all of the facets of the business relationship." *Central Corp. v. Research Products Corp.*, 2004 WI 76, ¶ 37, 272 Wis. 2d 561, 681 N.W.2d 178.

The requirement that an alleged grantor's threatened termination must pose a threat to the economic health of the dealer is "intended to weed out the typical vendor-vendee relationship." *Central Corp. v. Research Products Corp.*, 2004 WI 76, ¶ 32, 272 Wis. 2d 561, 681 N.W.2d 178.

Courts are not required to use the *Ziegler* factors in deciding whether a "community of interest" is part of the "contract or agreement" between an alleged dealer and an alleged grantor. "Although we have said that these extrastatutory items 'should' be considered by courts . . . it is more accurate to say that some or all 'may' be considered; the factors are meant to be a helpful aid in addressing the overriding community of interest question, not an unwieldy burden." *Benson v. City of Madison*, 2017 WI 65, ¶ 49 n.15, 376 Wis. 2d 35, 897 N.W.2d 16.

When the facts are undisputed and do not give rise to reasonable competing inferences, a court may conclude that a business relationship does not exhibit sufficient interdependence and continuing financial interest and grant summary judgment for the alleged grantor, especially when the alleged dealer does not prominently display the alleged dealer's products, and when the alleged grantor's products amount to between 1 percent and 5 percent of the alleged dealer's revenues over several years' time. *Moe v. Benelli USA Corp.*, 2007 WI App. 254, ¶¶ 21–23, 743 N.W.2d 691.

In contrast to the Wisconsin Supreme Court's approach to "community of interest" questions, the U.S. Court of Appeals for the Seventh Circuit has held that the *Ziegler* factors "may be distilled into two highly important questions in establishing a community of interest: (1) the percentages of revenues and profits the alleged dealer derives from the grantor; and (2) the amount of time and money the alleged dealer has sunk into the relationship. Neither of these is sufficient alone, but strong facts in one area can make up for weaker facts in another area." *Home Protective Services, Inc. v. ADT Security Services, Inc.*, 438 F.3d 716, 720 (7th Cir. 2006).

C. Scope and Jurisdiction

1. Commentary

After several decisions from courts outside Wisconsin in the first few years after enactment of the WFDL determined—based on Wisconsin choice-of-law provisions—that the WFDL governed relationships with dealers who did no business whatsoever in Wisconsin,[45] in 1977 the Wisconsin Legislature amended the statute to limit its geographic scope, providing that it would apply only to dealerships "situated in this state."[46]

The Wisconsin Supreme Court has interpreted "situated in this state" to focus on "the substance of the dealership, not the location of the dealer."[47] To determine whether a dealership has sufficient connection to Wisconsin, courts have adapted the multifactor "community of interest" test in *Ziegler* to the following factors: (1) percent of total sales in Wisconsin (and/or percent of total revenue or profits derived from Wisconsin); (2) how long the parties have dealt with each other in Wisconsin; (3) the extent and nature of the obligations imposed on the dealer regarding operations in Wisconsin; (4) the extent and nature of the grant of territory in this state; (5) the extent and nature of the use of the grantor's proprietary marks in this state; (6) the extent and nature of the dealer's financial investment in inventory, facilities, and good will of the dealership in this state; (7) the personnel devoted to the Wisconsin market; (8) the level of advertising and/or promotional expenditures in Wisconsin; and (9) the extent and nature of any supplementary services provided in Wisconsin.[48] These factors are not exhaustive, and the focus of the inquiry is "on the nature and extent of the dealership's development of, investment in and reliance upon the Wisconsin market."[49]

The Seventh Circuit has held that a dealer with multistate operations whose Wisconsin business is protected by the WFDL cannot recover damages for "any amounts attributable to the termination of [its] right to serve states other than Wisconsin."[50] Similarly, a multistate dealer whose Wisconsin operations are

---

45. C.A. May Marine Sup. Co. v. Brunswick Corp., 557 F.2d 1163 (5th Cir. 1977); Boatland, Inc. v. Brunswick Corp., 558 F.2d 818 (6th Cir. 1977).
46. WIS. STAT. § 135.02(2).
47. Baldewein Co. v. Tri-Clover, Inc., 233 Wis. 2d 57, 70, 606 N.W.2d 145, 150 (2000), *opinion after certified question answered*, 221 F.3d 1338 (7th Cir. 2000).
48. *Baldewein*, 606 N.W.2d at 152.
49. *Id.*
50. Morley-Murphy Co. v. Zenith Elecs. Corp., 142 F.3d 373, 381 (7th Cir. 1998).

protected against termination by the WFDL (and who obtains an injunction to that effect) is not entitled to injunctive relief against termination of its relationship in other states[51] unless it can show that it is entitled to protection under statutes of other states that afford protections against termination.[52]

2. Annotations

Several decisions in the late 1970s applied the WFDL to relationships with dealers who did no business in Wisconsin. *C.A. May Marine Supply Co. v. Brunswick Corp.*, 557 F.2d 1163 (5th Cir. 1977); *Boatland, Inc. v. Brunswick Corp.*, 558 F.2d 818 (6th Cir. 1977). In response to these decisions, the Wisconsin Legislature amended the WFDL in 1977 to limit its application to only those dealerships "situated in this state." Wisconsin Statutes section 135.02(2).

The "situated in this state" requirement reflects the legislature's intent to make the WFDL apply exclusively to dealerships that do business exclusively within the geographic confines of the state of Wisconsin. *Swan Sales Corp. v. Jos. Schlitz Brewing Co.*, 126 Wis. 2d 16, 22, 374 N.W.2d 640, 644 (Ct. App. 1985).

The "situated in this state" requirement addresses the substance of the dealership relationship, not the geographic location of the dealer. *Baldewein Co. v. Tri-Clover, Inc.*, 2000 WI 20, ¶ 22, 233 Wis. 2d 57, 70, 606 N.W.2d 145, 150, *opinion after certified question answered*, 221 F.3d 1338 (7th Cir. 2000).

A court deciding whether the substance of a dealership is "situated in" Wisconsin applies a variant of the "*Ziegler* factors" to the following issues: (1) percent of total sales in Wisconsin (and/or percent of total revenue or profits derived from Wisconsin); (2) how long the parties have dealt with each other in Wisconsin; (3) the extent and nature of the obligations imposed on the dealer regarding operations in Wisconsin; (4) the extent and nature of the grant of territory in this state; (5) the extent and nature of the use of the grantor's proprietary marks in this state; (6) the extent and nature of the dealer's financial investment in inventory, facilities, and good will of the dealership in this state; (7) the personnel devoted to the Wisconsin market; (8) the level of advertising and/or promotional expenditures in Wisconsin; and (9) the extent and nature of any supplementary services provided in Wisconsin. *Baldewein Co. v. Tri-Clover, Inc.*, 2000 WI 20, ¶ 30, 233 Wis. 2d 57, 75, 606 N.W.2d 145, 152, *opinion after certified question answered*, 221 F.3d 1338 (7th Cir. 2000).

These factors are not exhaustive or exclusive, and the focus of judicial inquiry should be on the nature and extent of the dealership's development of, investment in, and reliance on the Wisconsin market. *Baldewein Co. v. Tri-Clover, Inc.*, 2000 WI 20, ¶ 30, 233 Wis. 2d 57, 75, 606 N.W.2d 145, 152, *opinion after certified question answered*, 221 F.3d 1338 (7th Cir. 2000).

An agreement for the manufacture of machines that the seller was forbidden by contract to sell in Wisconsin was not a dealership "situated in this state." *Generac Corp. v. Caterpillar Inc.*, 172 F.3d 971, 976 (7th Cir. 1999).

---

51. Brava Salon Specialists, LLC v. Swedish Haircare, Inc., 2023 WL 1795512, at *4 (W.D. Wis. Feb. 7, 2023).
52. Keen Edge Co. v. Wright Mfg., Inc., 2020 WL 4926664, at *7 (E.D. Wis. Aug. 21, 2020).

A dealer with multistate operations whose Wisconsin business is protected by the WFDL cannot recover damages for "any amounts attributable to the termination of [its] right to serve states other than Wisconsin." *Morley-Murphy Co. v. Zenith Electronics Corp.*, 142 F.3d 373, 381 (7th Cir. 1998).

A multistate dealer whose Wisconsin operations are protected against termination by the WFDL is not entitled to injunctive relief against termination of its relationship in other states, *Brava Salon Specialists, LLC v. Swedish Haircare, Inc.*, Case No. 22-cv-695-wmc, 2023 WL 1795512, at *4 (W.D. Wis. Feb. 7, 2023), unless it demonstrates that it is entitled to protection against termination by the laws of other states where it does business. *Keen Edge Co. v. Wright Manufacturing, Inc.*, Case No. 19-CV-1673-JPS, 2020 WL 4926664, at *7 (E.D. Wis. Aug. 21, 2020).

The effective date of the WFDL is April 5, 1974. Applying the WFDL to govern a relationship that predates the statute's effective date would violate the Contract Clause of the U.S. Constitution. *Wipperfurth v. U-Haul Co.*, 101 Wis. 2d 586, 588, 304 N.W.2d 767 (1981).

After November 24, 1977, a renewal or amendment of an agreement is sufficient to bring the renewed or amended agreement within the scope of the WFDL, even though the initial agreement would not have been subject to the statute because of the federal Contracts Clause. *Swan Sales Corp. v. Jos. Schlitz Brewing Co.*, 126 Wis. 2d 16, 23, 374 N.W.2d 640, 644 (Ct. App. 1985).

Modifications to an existing dealer agreement that predates the effective date of the WFDL qualify as "amendments" or "renewals" of the agreement when they are both substantial changes to the agreement and were not anticipated by the parties when they made their original agreement. *Builder's World, Inc. v. Marvin Lumber & Cedar, Inc.*, 482 F. Supp. 2d 1065, 1072–73 (E.D. Wis. 2007), *modified sub nom. Builders World, Inc. v. Marvin Lumber & Cedar, Inc.*, No. 06C0555 (E.D. Wis. July 23, 2007).

D. Termination

1. What Constitutes Termination or Cancellation

a. Commentary

A grantor may not take any of the following actions vis-à-vis a dealership without good cause: (1) termination, (2) cancellation, (3) nonrenewal, or (4) substantially changing the competitive circumstances of a dealership agreement.[53] While termination, cancellation, and failing to renew are mutually distinct concepts, they are all actions taken by the grantor to end the relationship between the parties.[54]

The WFDL does not define a "substantial [] change [of] the competitive circumstances of a dealership agreement," so courts are left to determine its meaning. For example, courts have held that a dealer with a nonexclusive geographic territory may not assert a substantial change in competitive circumstances of a

---

53. Wis. Stat. § 135.03.
54. Meyer v. Kero-Sun, Inc., 570 F. Supp. 402, 406 (W.D. Wis. 1983).

dealership agreement where the grantor appoints a second dealer in its distribution territory.[55] On the other hand, a court found that a grantor substantially changed a dealership agreement's competitive circumstances when it began selling directly to customers in the dealer's territory.[56]

Under certain circumstances, "[f]ranchisors may make system-wide nondiscriminatory changes in order to adapt market conditions" that do not amount to a substantial change in competitive circumstances, even if those nondiscriminatory changes adversely affected a dealer on an individual basis.[57] Permitting such changes "serves the interest of the franchisees as a whole."[58] Thus, a franchisor who implements a policy with respect to all of its dealers in a system-wide fashion does not substantially change the competitive circumstances of a dealership agreement.[59] However, discriminatory actions that target a particular dealer (or class of Wisconsin dealers) are prohibited.[60]

Courts also recognize "constructive termination" in WFDL disputes which "occur when the grantor takes actions that amount to an effective end to the commercially meaningful aspects of the dealership relationship, regardless of whether the formal contractual relationship between the parties continues in force."[61] Thus a grantor may not be able to alter a dealer's geographic territory that functionally terminates the dealership, absent good cause.[62] Grantors may also be liable for constructive termination under a theory of "economic duress."[63]

b. Annotations

As implied earlier, whether a grantor's proposed change to a dealership agreement amounts to a substantial change in competitive circumstances presents one of the most challenging questions in WFDL disputes. In *Brava Specialists, LLC*, a cosmetic manufacturer permitted an authorized Florida distributor to sell its products online through Amazon.com. *Brava Salon Specialists, LLC v. Label.M*

---

55. The Wis. Compressed Air Corp. v. Gardner Denver, Inc., 571 F. Supp. 2d 992, 1001 (W.D. Wis. 2008) (collecting cases).

56. Builder's World, Inc. v. Marvin Lumber & Cedar, Inc., 482 F. Supp. 2d 1065, 1074 (E.D. Wis. 2007).

57. Re/Max N. Cent., Inc. v. Cook, 272 F.3d 424, 431 (7th Cir. 2001); Conrad's Sentry, Inc. v. Supervalu, Inc., 357 F. Supp. 2d 1086, 1099 (W.D. Wis. 2005) ("Despite the impact of the ban on plaintiff, the court held that because it was a system-wide ban, it was non-discriminatory and therefore, not a change in competitive circumstances.").

58. E. Bay Running Store, Inc. v. NIKE, Inc., 890 F.2d 996, 1000 (7th Cir. 1989).

59. *Id.*

60. Remus v. Amoco Oil Co., 794 F.2d 1238, 1240 (7th Cir. 1986); Conrad's Sentry, Inc. v. Supervalu, Inc., 357 F. Supp. 2d 1086, 1099, (W.D. Wis. 2005) (holding that a grantor may not substantially change the competitive circumstances in a way "that had a discriminatory effect on [dealers]" or were "intended to eliminate" a grantor's Wisconsin dealers).

61. Girl Scouts of Manitou Council Inc. v. Girl Scouts of U.S. of Am. Inc., 700 F. Supp. 2d 1055, 1079 (E.D. Wis. 2010), *aff'd in part, rev'd in part on other grounds*, 646 F.3d 983 (7th Cir. 2011) (internal sources omitted).

62. Girl Scouts of Manitou Council, Inc. v. Girl Scouts of U.S. of Am., Inc., 646 F.3d 983, 989 (7th Cir. 2011).

63. JPM, Inc. v. John Deere Indus. Equip. Co., 94 F.3d 270, 272 (7th Cir. 1996).

USA, Inc., No. 15-CV-631-BBC, 2016 WL 632649, at *2 (W.D. Wis. Feb. 17, 2016). Thereafter, the manufacturer confirmed to its Wisconsin-based distributor that it permitted the Florida distributor to sell its products online because of "the number of unauthorized resellers of [the manufacturer's] products already online, as well as a changing sales environment." *Id.* The Florida distributor was even permitted to sell products to customers in the Wisconsin-based distributor's exclusive territory. *Id.*

In considering the Wisconsin-based distributor's motion for preliminary injunction, the court found that the manufacturer's decision to move sales of its products online likely resulted in a substantial change in the competitive circumstances of the distributor's dealership. *Id.* The court specifically noted that the manufacturer would violate the WFDL if it made that change "without providing 90 days notice *and* resulted in intrabrand competition by other authorized distributors or dealers within [the Wisconsin-based distributor's] protected territory." *Id.* at *5. The court also noted that the manufacturer failed to prove at the preliminary injunction stage that its decision to move sales online was "essential, reasonable and nondiscriminatory." *Id.* at n.3.

2. Restrictions on Termination or Cancellation

a. Commentary

Absent "good cause," the WFDL prohibits a grantor from terminating, cancelling, failing to renew, or substantially changing the competitive circumstances of a dealership agreement.[64]

b. Annotations

As one of the key protections afforded to dealers under the WFDL, whether a grantor has "good cause" to terminate a dealership agreement is an oft-litigated question. Given that "good cause" is also a highly context-specific inquiry, courts continually address the subject, which is replete with decisional law.

Often, an aggrieved party asserting a wrongful termination WFDL claim will also promptly seek preliminary injunctive relief. *Homesteader's Store, Inc. v. Kubota Tractor Corp.*, No. 24-CV- 23-JDP, 2024 WL 2015687 (W.D. Wis. May 7, 2024). In *Homesteader's Store, Inc.*, an equipment manufacturer attempted to terminate a distributor based upon a failure to meet sales goals, failure to meet the facility standard for appearance of its stores, and a failure to comply with the manufacturers advertising requirements. *Id.* The distributor filed an action, asserting that the manufacturer wrongfully terminated its dealership agreement based upon three theories.[65] First, the distributor argued that the manufacturer made it impossible for the distributor to meet its sales goals because the manufacturer did to provide adequate inventory to the distributor.[66] Second, the manufacturer purportedly applied its market share metrics in a discriminatory manner because it sent a notice of termination to only the plaintiff distributor

---

64. WIS. STAT. § 135.03.
65. *Homesteader's Store, Inc.*, 2024 WL 2015687 at *3.
66. *Id.*

and did not send termination notices to other underperforming distributors. *Id.* Third, the distributor asserted that the manufacturer's performance metric is not an essential and reasonable requirement of the distributor agreement. *Id.*

The court dispensed with the distributor's first and second theories for termination because the distributor failed to carry its burden to demonstrate likelihood of success on the merits. *Id.* However, the court agreed with the distributor that the manufacturer's market share performance metric was not an essential and reasonable requirement of the distributor agreement. *Id.* While sales quotas can be "reasonable and necessary requirement[s]," the manufacturer's particular metric was based upon market data defined by counties, rather than by the distributor's "real-world market." *Id.* So although "[n]orthern Green County is much closer" to the distributor's store "than any part of Columbia County," the manufacturer did not attribute sales from Green County customers to the distributor because Green County was not considered a part of the distributor's local market area. *Id.* The court granted the distributor's motion for preliminary injunction. *Id.* Presently, the parties are briefing the manufacturer's appeal of the preliminary injunction. *Homesteader's Store, Inc. v. Kubota Tractor Corp.*, No. 24-CV-23-JDP (W.D. Wis.), Dkt. 68. Accordingly, counsel should endeavor to review the current case law when assessing the relative strengths and weaknesses of a wrongful termination WFDL claim.

3. Notice Requirement

a. Commentary

A grantor must generally provide the dealer with 90 days' prior written notice before termination, cancellation, nonrenewal, or effecting a substantial change in competitive circumstances,[67] regardless of whether the parties' agreement provides for shorter notice periods.[68] The notice must state all the reasons for the termination of, or change in, the dealership relationship. If the basis for the termination or change is a deficiency (i.e., "a dealer's failure to live up to the grantor's expectations of it"[69]), then the notice must also generally provide that a dealer has 60 days by which to cure the deficiency.[70] No notice is required if the reason for the termination or change is insolvency, an assignment for the benefit of creditors or bankruptcy.[71] However, this exception to the notice requirement can only be invoked where insolvency, assignment, or bankruptcy is the "motivating factor" leading to the final decision to terminate.[72]

Note that courts construe Wisconsin Statute section 135.04's use of "substantial change in competitive circumstances" more broadly than Wisconsin Statute section 135.03's use of "substantial [] change [in] the competitive circumstances *of a dealership agreement*" (emphasis added). Courts interpret the former

---

67. WIS. STAT. § 135.04.
68. Paul Reilly Co. v. Dynaforce Corp., 449 F. Supp. 1033, 1036 (E.D. Wis. 1978).
69. The Wis. Compressed Air Corp. v. Gardner Denver, Inc., 571 F. Supp. 2d 992, 1003 (W.D. Wis. 2008).
70. WIS. STAT. § 135.04.
71. *Id.*
72. Bruno Wine & Spirits, Inc. v. Guimarra Vineyards, 573 F. Supp. 337, 340 (E.D. Wis. 1983).

to encompass *any* substantial change in competitive circumstances. For example, a grantor substantially changes the competitive circumstances of a dealer by "allowing or engaging in any intrabrand competition likely to have a serious effect on a dealer's ability to continue to compete in that market," even if such change is permitted under the dealership agreement.[73] Thus, if a substantial change in competitive circumstances does not tie to a dealership agreement (and therefore trigger Wisconsin Statute section 135.03's good cause requirements), a grantor must *nevertheless* provide written notice consistent with Wisconsin Statute section 135.04.[74]

b. Annotations
Not applicable.

4. Grounds for Termination

a. Commentary

The WFDL's "explicit purpose" is "to protect dealers against unfair treatment by grantors, who inherently have superior economic power and superior bargaining power in the negotiation of dealerships."[75] Therefore, a grantor can only terminate a dealer for "good cause," which is limited to the following grounds: (1) failure by a dealer to comply substantially with essential and reasonable requirements imposed upon the dealer by the grantor or sought to be imposed by the grantor, which requirements are not discriminatory as compared with requirements imposed on other similarly situated dealers either by their terms or in the manner of their enforcement or (2) dealer bad faith.[76]

Grantors may also terminate for good cause based upon their own economic circumstances.[77] However, this type of termination is limited; the grantor must show (1) an objectively ascertainable need for change, (2) a proportionate response to that need, and (3) a nondiscriminatory action.[78] That said, a grantor need not show "financial ruin" in order to establish good cause for economic reasons.[79] Discontinuation of an unprofitable product line is sufficient to meet the good cause standard.[80] Note that the grantor may still need to comply with applicable notice provisions.[81]

A grantor's basis for termination must be "essential and reasonable," considering the facts and circumstances of the parties' relationship.[82] Courts have

---

73. *The Wis. Compressed Air Corp.*, 571 F. Supp. 2d at 1002 (citing Jungbluth v. Hometown, Inc., 201 Wis. 2d. 320, 336, 548 N.W.2d 519 (1996)).
74. *See generally The Wis. Compressed Air Corp.*, 571 F. Supp. 2d at 992.
75. *Jungbluth*, 201 Wis. 2d 320, 330 (internal sources omitted).
76. Wis. Stat. § 135.02(4).
77. Morley-Murphy Co. v. Zenith Elecs. Corp., 142 F.3d 373, 377 (7th Cir. 1998).
78. *Id.*; *see also* Ziegler Co. v. Rexnord, Inc., 147 Wis. 2d 308, 314, 433 N.W.2d 8, 11 (1988).
79. Lee Beverage Co. v. I.S.C. Wines of Cal., Inc., 623 F. Supp. 867, 869 (E.D. Wis. 1985).
80. *Id.*
81. Jungbluth v. Hometown, Inc., 201 Wis. 2d 320, 334, 548 N.W.2d 519 (1996).
82. Deutchland Enters., Ltd. v. Burger King Corp., 957 F.2d 449, 453 (7th Cir. 1992) (upholding franchisor's termination of franchisee for failure to comply with contractual provision that prohibited franchisee from operating competitor restaurants).

rejected a grantor's ability to issue blanket terminations based upon an "inadequate rate of return" from dealers.[83] Whether contract terms are "essential and reasonable" is often a "close case."[84] Courts and juries are often put in the unenviable position of "sit[ting] as economic commissars intermediating disputes between business entities or opining on the wisdom of various corporate structures" for which they "have little training in assessing whether business activities are 'reasonable' or 'essential.'"[85]

The burden of proving good cause rests with the grantor and is generally a question of fact for the jury.[86] However, the good cause requirement is not implicated unless there is an initial finding that the grantor terminated, cancelled, failed to renew, or substantially changed the competitive circumstances of the dealership agreement.[87]

b. Annotations

The Western District of Wisconsin recently reaffirmed that grantors may make changes to a dealership agreement—even if it amounts to a "substantial change"—"as long as the requirement for new dealers is 'essential, reasonable and non-discriminatory.'" *Queen v. Wineinger*, No. 21- CV-378-WMC, 2022 WL 3027004, at *7 (W.D. Wis. Aug. 1, 2022), *appeal dismissed sub nom. American Dairy Queen Corp. v. Wineinger*, No. 22-2533, 2023 WL 5624068 (7th Cir. Mar. 14, 2023).

5. Required Cure Period

a. Commentary

A notice of termination or change in a dealership (i.e., termination, cancellation, nonrenewal, or a substantial change in competitive circumstances) must notify the dealer that it has 60 days in which to rectify any asserted deficiency.[88] If the deficiency is cured within the 60-day cure period, the notice is void.

While the WFDL does not expressly require that proposed steps to cure be reasonable, courts construe the WFDL broadly to require that "the steps that a grantor requires a dealer to take in order to rectify a deficiency must be reasonable."[89]

b. Annotations

There are several important exceptions to the cure requirement. First, if the reason for the termination or change in the dealership is nonpayment of sums

---

83. Kealey Pharmacy & Home Care Servs., Inc. v. Walgreen Co., 761 F.2d 345, 350 (7th Cir. 1985).
84. Kaeser Compressors, Inc. v. Compressor & Pump Repair Servs., Inc., 781 F. Supp. 2d 819, 824 (E.D. Wis. 2011).
85. *Id.* at 827.
86. WIS. STAT. § 135.03; Frieburg Farm Equip., Inc. v. Van Dale, Inc., 978 F.2d 395, 401 (7th Cir. 1992).
87. Re/Max N. Central, Inc. v. Cook, 272 F.3d 431 (7th Cir. 1989) (internal sources omitted).
88. WIS. STAT. § 135.04.
89. Al Bishop Agency, Inc. v. Lithonia-Div. of Nat. Serv. Indus., Inc., 474 F. Supp. 828, 835 (E.D. Wis. 1979).

due, then the grantor need only provide a 90-day[90] written notice with a ten-day cure period.[91] Second, if the basis for the substantial change in competitive circumstances is *not* because of dealer deficiency, the notice need not provide the 60-day cure period.[92]

6. Repurchase Obligations

a. Commentary

At the option of the dealer, upon termination (with or without cause), the grantor must repurchase all inventories sold by the grantor to the dealer at "fair wholesale market value."[93] This obligation only applies to inventory that is marked with a name, trademark, label, or other mark that identifies the grantor. "Fair wholesale market value" is an undefined term, but at least one Wisconsin court has interpreted it to mean "wholesale price."[94]

b. Annotations

Not applicable.

E. Restrictions on Nonrenewal

In addition to prohibiting termination or cancellation of a dealership during its term, the WFDL also prohibits a grantor from refusing to renew a dealership when it expires under the terms of the parties' agreement.

1. What Constitutes Nonrenewal

a. Commentary

The Wisconsin Supreme Court has held that the WFDL's prohibition against nonrenewal does "force by law the renewal of a contract which was entered into for a limited term[.]"[95] This decision makes clear that a grantor desiring to end its relationship with a dealer solely in reliance on the expiration of a specified contract term cannot do so. Thus, "[t]he statute's main purpose is to give dealers a kind of tenure—like federal judges, or teachers, or workers in establishments covered by collective bargaining contracts."[96]

---

90. White Hen Pantry v. Buttke, 100 Wis. 2d 169, 177, 301 N.W.2d 216, 220 (1981) (holding that "if the reason for termination, cancellation, nonrenewal or substantial change in competitive circumstances is nonpayment of sums due under the dealership, the grantor must provide the dealer with at least 90 days' prior written notice").

91. WIS. STAT. § 135.04.

92. The Wis. Compressed Air Corp. v. Gardner Denver, Inc., 571 F. Supp. 2d 992 (W.D. Wis. 2008) (citing Designs in Med., Inc. v. Xomed, Inc., 522 F. Supp. 1054, 1060 (E.D. Wis. 1981)).

93. WIS. STAT. § 135.045.

94. Roedel-Hanson & Assocs., Inc. v. Environamics Corp., 242 F. Supp. 2d 582, 584 (E.D. Wis. 2003).

95. Martino v. McDonald's Corp., 101 Wis. 2d 612, 615, 304 N.W.2d 780 (1981).

96. Remus v. Amoco Oil Co., 794 F.2d 1238, 1240 (7th Cir. 1986).

b. Annotations

The WFDL's prohibition against nonrenewal of a dealership forces by law the renewal of a contract that was entered into for a limited term. *Martino v. McDonald's Corp.*, 101 Wis. 2d 612, 615, 304 N.W.2d 780 (1981).

2. Restrictions on Nonrenewal

a. Commentary

Like termination, cancellation, and changing the competitive circumstances of a dealership, a grantor may implement nonrenewal only with both good cause[97] and proper notice.[98]

b. Annotations

Not applicable.

3. Notice Requirement

a. Commentary

The same 90-day notice requirement that governs termination, cancellation, and changes in competitive circumstances also applies to nonrenewals.[99] Every WFDL notice must contain all of the reasons that the grantor wishes to rely on as a basis for ending or changing the dealership relationship;[100] a grantor may not rely on a reason that is not expressly stated in the notice,[101] meaning that the grantor is under a "use it or lose it" rule governing reasons for nonrenewal.

b. Annotations

Not applicable.

4. Grounds for Nonrenewal

a. Commentary

The same definition of good cause that governs grantor efforts to terminate, cancel, or change the competitive circumstances of a dealership also applies to nonrenewal.[102]

b. Annotations

Not applicable.

---

97. WIS. STAT. § 135.03.
98. WIS. STAT. § 135.04.
99. *Id.*
100. *Bruno Wine & Spirits, Inc. v. Guimarra Vineyards*, 573 F. Supp. 337, 339 (E.D. Wis. 1983).
101. *Id.*
102. WIS. STAT. § 135.03.

5. Required Cure Period

a. Commentary

The required cure periods—ten days for "nonpayment of sums due under the dealership," and 90 days for all other stated reasons for nonrenewal—govern nonrenewal as well.[103]

b. Annotations

Not applicable.

6. Limitations on Franchisors' Right to Impose Conditions for Renewal

a. Commentary

The WFDL's definition of "good cause" includes "failure to comply substantially" with "essential and reasonable" requirements not only actually imposed but also those "sought to be imposed by the grantor."[104] Applying to grantor actions that will have their effect in the future, this component of the statute can be implicated when a grantor seeks to impose new contract terms upon renewal. The general governing principle is that courts "hesitate to conclude that the Wisconsin legislature meant . . . to prevent franchisors from instituting non-discriminatory, system-wide changes without the unanimous consent of the franchisees."[105]

Courts will find that changed terms in a new agreement are "essential and reasonable" when they are directly responsive to a genuine business issue confronted by the grantor. For example, in *Wisconsin Music Network v. Muzak Limited Partnership*, the Court of Appeals for the Seventh Circuit found that the implementation of a new program to deal with national accounts "met a competitive need to offer national accounts national treatment," and the dealer failed to undermine that conclusion.[106] The Court of Appeals also ruled that the grantor complied with the WFDL's nondiscrimination requirement by seeking to impose the new program only when its contracts with local franchisees were up for renewal.[107] Similarly, when a dealer refused to sign a new standard-form agreement upon renewal, and the dealer failed to show facts demonstrating that the terms imposed by the new agreement would alter the competitive circumstances of its dealership, the district court concluded that the grantor had not proposed a substantial change in the dealer's competitive circumstances and thus had not failed to renew the agreement.[108]

---

103. WIS. STAT. § 135.04.
104. WIS. STAT. § 135.02(4).
105. Wis. Music Network, Inc. v. Muzak Ltd. P'ship, 5 F.3d 218, 224 (7th Cir. 1993), (quoting Remus v. Amoco Oil Co., 794 F.2d 1238, 1241 (7th Cir. 1986)).
106. *Wis. Music Network*, 5 F.3d at 224.
107. *Id.* at 224.
108. Bresler's 33 Flavors Franchising Corp. v. Wokosin, 591 F. Supp. 1533, 1537–38 (E.D. Wis. 1984). Notably, the district court's placement of the burden of proof on the dealer on the "substantial change in competitive circumstances" issue is inconsistent with the WFDL's directive that "the burden of proving good cause is on the grantor." WIS. STAT. § 135.03.

However, courts do not blindly accept every economic justification that grantors offer for changes to a standard dealership agreement. A grantor's asserted need for uniformity in its dealer contracts was deemed insufficient to support summary judgment when unsupported by economic data, especially when the desired change—the elimination of dealers' exclusive rights to sell within their territories—was contrary to the parties' long-established practice.[109]

b. Annotations

The WFDL's definition of "good cause" covers not only failure to comply with essential and reasonable requirements that have already been imposed by a grantor but also extends to such requirements "sought to be imposed." Thus, the WFDL comes into play when a grantor seeks to impose new contract terms, including at time for contract renewal. The Seventh Circuit holds that courts should "hesitate to conclude that the Wisconsin legislature meant . . . to prevent franchisors from instituting non-discriminatory, system-wide changes without the unanimous consent of the franchisees." *Wisconsin Music Network, Inc. v. Muzak Limited Partnership*, 5 F.3d 218, 224 (7th Cir. 1993), quoting *Remus v. Amoco Oil Co.*, 794 F.2d 1238, 1241 (7th Cir. 1986).

Courts are likely to find that terms "sought to be imposed" by a grantor in a renewal agreement if they are directly responsive to a legitimate business need faced by the grantor and they are imposed uniformly across the grantor's system. A new program for dealing with national accounts met a competitive need to offer national accounts uniform national treatment, and the dealer could not claim that it was being singled out because the grantor rolled out the new agreement terms as its old agreements expired across the country. *Wisconsin Music Network, Inc. v. Muzak Limited Partnership*, 5 F.3d 218, 224 (7th Cir. 1993).

When a dealer refused to sign a new standard-form agreement even though it could not show that the new terms would adversely change its competitive circumstances, the grantor was allowed to refuse to renew the dealer's agreement. *Bresler's 33 Flavors Franchising Corp. v. Wokosin*, 591 F. Supp. 1533, 1537–38 (E.D. Wis. 1984).

A grantor's purported desire for national uniformity in its revised renewal dealer agreements was not sufficient when the grantor failed to support the change with economic data demonstrating a need for the change, especially when the change was contrary to the parties' long-established course of dealing. *Kaeser Compressors, Inc. v. Compressor & Pump Repair Services, Inc.*, 781 F. Supp. 2d 819, 826–27 (E.D. Wis. 2011).

7. Repurchase Obligations

a. Commentary

The WFDL's repurchase requirement is contained in Wisconsin Statute section 135.045, which provides that "[i]f a dealership is *terminated* by the grantor," the

---

109. Kaeser Compressors, Inc. v. Compressor & Pump Repair Servs., Inc., 781 F. Supp. 2d 819, 826–27 (E.D. Wis. 2011).

grantor must repurchase certain inventory.[110] This is true whether termination is for good cause or without cause. On its face, the inventory repurchase obligation does not extend to cancellations or nonrenewal, although there is no good reason why the obligation would extend to one form of ending the relationship but not the other two regulated by the statute. A grantor seeking to avoid the repurchase obligation in the wake of a nonrenewal should therefore tread carefully.

b. Annotations

The authors were unable to locate any case law addressing repurchase obligations.

F. Transfers and Succession

1. Commentary

Not applicable.

2. Annotations

Not applicable.

G. Other Regulation of the Franchise Relationship

1. Commentary

a. Special Protection for Dealers of Intoxicating Liquor

In 1999, the WFDL was amended to provide a new category of protection, extending to wholesalers of intoxicating liquor, who may qualify as "dealerships" without having to show the existence of a "community of interest."[111] A partial veto of the amendment by the governor eliminated statutory protection for wine dealers, and nearly 20 years after the amendment went into effect, the Wisconsin Supreme Court upheld an interpretation of the statutory language that confirmed wine dealers did not qualify for the new protected status.[112] Several Wisconsin circuit courts, however, have ruled that wine dealers can still obtain WFDL protection if they can meet the pre-amendment requirements, including the community of interest.[113]

Not all wholesalers of intoxicating liquor are protected under the new statutory provisions, however. The definition of "dealership" contains a carve-out excluding two categories from protection: (1) when the grantor's total annual production of spirits is below 200,000 gallons, and (2) when the dealer derives less than 5 percent of its annual net revenues from intoxicating liquor from the

---

110. WIS. STAT. § 135.045.
111. *Id.* § 135.066.
112. Winebow, Inc. v. Capitol-Husting Co., 381 Wis. 2d 732, 914 N.W.2d 631.
113. L'Eft Bank Wine Co. v. Bogle Vineyards, Inc., Case No. 2020CV001563 (Wis. Cir. Ct. Dane, Apr. 26, 2021); Gen. Beverage Sales Co. v. Duckhorn Portfolio, Inc., Case No. 2021CV001180 (Wis. Cir. Ct. Dane Cnty. May 21, 2021). Beer distributors can also attempt to qualify for standard community-of-interest protection under the WFDL, and if they fail in that effort, their interests are granted some protection by WIS. STAT. § 125.33(10), a statutory scheme for compensating a beer distributor that loses distribution rights. The details of that statute are beyond the scope of this chapter.

grantor's products.[114] If neither of these statutory exceptions applies, then an intoxicating liquor dealer is protected against termination, cancellation, non-renewal, or substantial change in its competitive circumstances without having to contend with the sometimes vexatious community of interest requirement.

2. Annotations

The governor's partial veto power was properly exercised to eliminate special statutory protection for wine dealers under the legislature's 1999 amendments to the WFDL. *Winebow, Inc. v. Capitol-Husting Co.*, 2018 WI 60, 381 Wis. 2d 732, 914 N.W.2d 631.

Even though wine dealers do not qualify for protection under the new statutory provisions protecting intoxicating liquor dealers, wine dealers may be protected by the WFDL's general provisions, including the community of interest requirement. *L'Eft Bank Wine Co. v. Bogle Vineyards, Inc.*, Case No. 2020CV001563 (Wis. Cir. Ct. Dane Cnty. Apr. 26, 2021); *General Beverage Sales Co. v. Duckhorn Portfolio, Inc.*, Case No. 2021CV001180 (Wis. Cir. Ct. Dane Cnty. May 21, 2021).

H. Remedies and Administrative Action

1. Restrictive Covenants

a. Commentary

A provision of a dealership agreement that prohibits the dealer from operating a "same or similar" business during the term of the parties' agreement is enforceable under the WFDL as an "essential and reasonable" requirement. *Deutchland Enterprises*, 957 F.2d at 452–53. The WFDL contains no provision affecting a grantor's ability to impose restrictions on competition after the termination of a dealership.

b. Annotations

In *Deuthchland Enterprises, Ltd. v. Burger King Corp.*, the U.S. Court of Appeals for the Seventh Circuit concluded, among other things, that because Burger King franchisees "have advance notice of the franchisor's marketing strategies, and access to its operating methods and polices" it was reasonable to enforce an in-term covenant not to compete, restricting a franchisee's ability to own and operate a competing brand in order to "protect its information, marketing strategies, and operating policies from appropriation." *Deutchland Enterprises, Ltd. v. Burger King Corp.*, 957 F.2d 449, 453–54 (7th Cir. 1992).

2. Damages

a. Commentary

The WFDL allows a wrongfully terminated dealer to elect preliminary injunctive relief, damages, or both.[115] One federal court has held that a terminated dealer must elect before trial whether it will pursue damages or permanent injunctive

---

114. Wis. Stat. § 135.02(3)(b); *id.* § 135.066(5)(a), (b).
115. *Id.* § 135.06.

relief, because allowing the dealer to pursue both theories at trial would place the grantor in the untenable position of arguing both that the dealer had an adequate remedy at law and that it had not offered sufficient evidence of its damages.[116]

A dealer may seek two basic types of damages: past and future lost profits, and lost business value.[117] However, it cannot pursue both lost profits and lost business value, because they are duplicative.[118] Generally, the lost profits approach results in a higher damages claim than the loss in business value.[119]

The standard Wisconsin rules governing the recovery of lost profits control in damages claims under the WFDL: they must be proved to a reasonable certainty, but mathematical precision is not required.[120] Costs avoided as a result of the grantor's WFDL violation must be subtracted from revenue when calculating an award of lost profits, and no offset is allowed for fixed costs.[121] As noted in the preceding section on the geographic scope of WFDL protection, damages for losses arising from territory outside Wisconsin cannot be awarded in a WFDL case,[122] however, a recent decision by the U.S. Supreme Court[123] has some commenters believing that the Seventh Circuit Court of Appeals may reconsider the Commerce Clause's application to extraterritorial lost profits damages under the WFDL.

b. Annotations

Punitive damages are not available in WFDL claims. *White Hen Pantry, Division Jewel Cos. v. Johnson*, 599 F. Supp. 718, 719 (E.D. Wis. 1984).

In *Track, Inc. v. ASH North American, Inc.*, the question of whether extraterritorial sales "arising from sales by the Wisconsin dealership to customers in other Midwest states" was presented for consideration. *Track, Inc. v. ASH North American, Inc.*, No. 21-CV-786-JDP, 2023 WL 2733679, at *5 (W.D. Wis. Mar. 31, 2023) (denying motion to dismiss WFDL claims). While the court declined to answer the question at the motion to dismiss stage, it hinted at the possibility that sales made to buyers located both within and outside Wisconsin by a dealer located in and operating exclusively from Wisconsin could be appropriate damages under the WFDL. *Id.*

Damages may also be awarded for wrongful nonrenewal or substantial change in competitive circumstances and for improper notice, confirming that damages are not merely limited to terminations of a dealer agreement. *Lindevig v. Dairy Equipment Co.*, 150 Wis. 2d 731, 737–38, 442 N.W.2d 504, 507, Bus. Franchise Guide (CCH) ¶ 9431 (Ct. App. 1989).

---

116. Lakefield Telephone Co. v. Northern Telecom, Inc., 679 F. Supp. 881, 883–84 (E.D. Wis. 1988).
117. Bush v. Nat'l School Studios, 131 Wis. 2d 435, 444, 389 N.W.2d 49 (Wis. Ct. App. 1986), *aff'd*, 139 Wis. 2d 635, 407 N.W.2d 883 (1987).
118. *Bush*, 131 Wis. 2d at 444.
119. Moodie v. Sch. Book Fairs, Inc., 889 F.2d 739, 745 (7th Cir. 1989).
120. Esch v. Yazoo Mfg. Co., 510 F. Supp. 53, 56 (E.D. Wis. 1981).
121. Morley-Murphy Co. v. Zenith Elecs. Corp., 142 F.3d 373, 382 (7th Cir. 1998).
122. *Id.* at 381.
123. *See* Nat'l Pork Producers Council v. Ross, 143 S. Ct. 1142 (2023).

Although a terminated dealer may allege in its complaint claims for damages and for permanent injunctive relief, at trial the dealer must elect between the two. *Lakefield Telephone Co. v. Northern Telecom, Inc.*, 679 F. Supp. 881, 883–84 (E.D. Wis. 1988).

A dealer may seek two general types of damages: past and future lost profits, or lost business value, but it may not pursue both in the same action, because the theories are duplicative. *Bush v. National School Studios*, 131 Wis. 2d 435, 444, 389 N.W.2d 49 (Ct. App. 1986), *aff'd*, 139 Wis. 2d 635, 407 N.W.2d 883 (1987). A lost profits analysis will ordinarily yield higher damages than a lost business value calculation. *Moodie v. School Book Fairs, Inc.*, 889 F.2d 739, 745 (7th Cir. 1989).

Lost profits claims under the WFDL follow the general rules for recovery of lost profits: they must be proved with reasonable certainty, but mathematical precision is not required. *Esch v. Yazoo Manufacturing Co.*, 510 F. Supp. 53, 56 (E.D. Wis. 1981).

A terminated dealer's costs avoided as a result of a grantor's termination in violation of the WFDL must be subtracted from revenue when calculating lost profits, and no offset is allowed for fixed costs. *Morley-Murphy Co. v. Zenith Electronics Corp.*, 142 F.3d 373, 382 (7th Cir. 1998).

3. Rescission

a. Commentary
Not applicable.

b. Annotations
Not applicable.

4. Injunctive Relief

a. Commentary
The WFDL expressly provides for injunctive relief as one of the remedies available to an aggrieved dealer. More specifically, section 135.06 reads that a dealer "may be granted injunctive relief against unlawful termination, cancellation, nonrenewal or substantial change of competitive circumstances."[124] Section 135.065 partially relieves a dealer of the burden to show the traditional elements of injunctive relief, where a dealer can establish a reasonable likelihood of a violation of the WFDL by the grantor; such a violation "is deemed an irreparable injury to the dealer for determining if a temporary injunction should be issued."[125] This represents a substantial assist to the dealer, as irreparable harm is typically a very high bar to surpass. Notably, however, the presumption is simply a "rebuttable" presumption. The effect of the WFDL is to transfer from the dealer to the grantor "the burden of going forward with evidence on the question of irreparable injury."[126]

---

124. WIS. STAT. § 135.06.
125. *Id.* § 135.065.
126. S & S Sales Corp. v. Marvin Lumber & Cedar Co., 435 F. Supp. 2d 879, 885 (E.D. Wis. 2006).

b. Annotations

In *S & S Sales Corp. v. Marvin Lumber & Cedar Co.*, the U.S. District Court for the Eastern District of Wisconsin determined that where evidence rebutting the existence of irreparable harm was presented, "the presumption falls out of the case," thus requiring the moving party to establish that it "(1) is likely to become insolvent or lose its business; (2) will be unable to finance the litigation; (3) will incur losses that are difficult to calculate; or (4) that defendant is likely to become insolvent," a burden the party was unable to meet. *S & S Sales Corp. v. Marvin Lumber & Cedar Co.*, 435 F. Supp. 2d 879, 886, 2006 WL 1707260 (E.D. Wis. 2006) (denying request for temporary injunction for failure to establish irreparable harm, an essential element of a request for injunctive relief).

In *Rustic Retreats Log Homes, Inc. v. Pioneer Log Homes of Brit. Columbia Inc.*, Rustic Retreats Log Homes, Inc. ("Rustic") moved for a preliminary injunction to prevent the termination of its dealership agreement with Pioneer Log Homes of British Columbia, Ltd. ("Pioneer") prior to trial. *Rustic Retreats Log Homes, Inc. v. Pioneer Log Homes of British Columbia Inc.*, No. 19- CV-1614, 2020 WL 3415645 (E.D. Wis. June 22, 2020). As the party seeking a preliminary injunction against a grantor, Rustic was entitled to a presumption of irreparable harm under the WFDL. Pioneer attempted to rebut the presumption, arguing that Rustic failed to present evidence beyond lost sales and that, therefore, a money judgment would sufficiently compensate Rustic for any damages. The court disagreed and concluded that Rustic sufficiently alleged "not just lost sales but the potential destruction of its business" and thus was still entitled to a presumption of irreparable harm, paving the way to successfully seeking a preliminary injunction preventing the termination of the dealership agreement during the pendency of the litigation. *Id.*

5. Control Person Liability

a. Commentary

The WFDL's prohibition on the cancellation and alteration of dealerships, absent good cause, expressly provides that it is applicable not only to grantors but also to those grantors acting "directly or through an officer, agent or employee."[127] The text might be interpreted to suggest then, that the individual directors and officers of a grantor in the corporate form, as well as the members of a grantor in the form of a limited liability company, could be subject to personal liability for a violation of the WFDL. Or perhaps the same individuals might be called upon to defend against claims of tortious interference involving the dealership agreement between the grantor (as a business entity) and the dealer. There is no current judicial authority reading section 135.03 to suggest this is a correct conclusion. It is much more likely that any individual liability would require further proof by the dealer, of the kind necessary to pierce the corporate veil.

b. Annotations

Not applicable.

---

127. WIS. STAT. § 135.03.

6. Attorneys' Fees

a. Commentary

A dealer successfully proving a WFDL claim is entitled to recover its "reasonable actual attorney fees" as provided in section 135.06.[128] In calculating the amount to be charged against the grantor, "the starting point . . . is the calculation of the 'lodestar.'"[129] The "lodestar" is a two-step process. First, the court is required to determine "the number of hours reasonably expended on the litigation multiplied by a reasonable hourly rate."[130] Once this is accomplished, a court may "make appropriate adjustments to increase or decrease the award in light of a number of considerations that include 'the amount involved and the results obtained.'"[131] Importantly, the WFDL does not permit attorney fees to be measured by the applicable percentage where a case is taken by the dealer's counsel on a contingent fee basis. Fees are permitted, however, where they are incurred upon the prosecution of a successful appeal. Fee awards are limited solely to the dealer's claims, or portions of claims, that are met with success.

b. Annotations

In *Lindevig v. Dairy Equipment Co.*, the dealer was not awarded its fees and costs to the extent they were incurred in its failure to favorably litigate the merits of its WFDL claim. Nonetheless, because the dealer's counsel had earlier procured a temporary injunction, the dealer was eligible to recover its fees related to that initial phase of the litigation. *Lindevig v. Dairy Equipment Co.*, 150 Wis. 2d 731, 442 N.W.2d 504, Bus. Franchise Guide (CCH) ¶ 9431 (Ct. App. 1989).

7. Limitations on Damage Waivers

a. Commentary

Section 135.025(3) reads that "the effect of this chapter may not be varied by contract or agreement."[132] It continues: "[a]ny contract or agreement purporting to do so is void and unenforceable to that extent only."[133] While this provision is championed by dealers most often in disputes involving the enforceability of choice-of-law and forum selection clauses, it is very likely that a dealer could successfully invoke section 135.025 to invalidate any contract terms purporting to waive or limit the damages (or other WFDL remedies) available to that dealer under section 135.06.

b. Annotations

Not applicable.

---

128. *Id.* § 135.06.
129. Wis. Compressed Air Corp. v. Gardner Denver, Inc., 2008 WL 4379227, at *2 (W.D. Wis. Sept. 22, 2008).
130. *Id.*
131. *Id.*
132. Wis. Stat. § 135.025(3).
133. *Id.*

8. Administrative Action

a. Commentary
Not applicable.

b. Annotations
Not applicable.

I. Dispute Resolution

1. Limitations on Franchisors' Ability to Restrict Venue

a. Commentary
Wisconsin courts generally recognize that contracting parties may expressly agree that the law of a particular jurisdiction shall control their relationship. However, this principle of party autonomy is limited, particularly where an important public policy would be violated by enforcement of a choice-of-law clause. The WFDL's purpose is "[t]o protect dealers against unfair treatment by grantors, who inherently have superior economic power and superior bargaining power in the negotiation of dealership" and "[t]o provide dealers with rights and remedies in addition to those existing by contract or common law."[134] Consistent with these policies, the WFDL expressly prohibits dealership agreements that attempt to vary its effect; such contracts are "void and unenforceable to that extent only." Courts have interpreted these provisions to void choice-of-law clauses in dealership agreements.[135] The Seventh Circuit has concluded that traditional choice-of-law principles are not applicable to WFDL claims; whether the purported dealer is entitled to WFDL protection depends on whether it meets the definitions of "dealer" and "dealership."[136]

Courts have reached a different conclusion with respect to forum selection clauses in dealership agreements. While the WFDL provides that a dealer has a right to bring suit "in any court of competent jurisdiction,"[137] forum selection clauses are not expressly proscribed.[138] Early case law invalidated forum selection clauses in dealership agreements.[139] However, recent jurisprudence aligns with the strong public policy favoring enforcement of forum selection clauses.[140] Thus, "absent extraordinary circumstances," courts enforce forum selection clauses in dealership agreements.[141]

---

134. *Id.*
135. Bush v. Nat'l Sch. Studios, Inc., 139 Wis. 2d 635, 641–45, 407 N.W.2d 883, 886–88 (1987).
136. Generac Corp. v. Caterpillar, Inc., 172 F.3d 971, 975–76 (7th Cir.1999); *but see* Crazy Lenny's E.Bikes, LLC v. Alta Cycling Grp., LLC, 2022 WL 1537029, at *3 (C.D. Cal. May 12, 2022) (enforcing a California choice-of-law clause to dismiss a WFDL claim because "[p]laintiff's invocation of the WFDL assumes its conclusion, which is that Wisconsin law applies in the first place").
137. WIS. STAT. § 135.06.
138. Rolfe v. Network Funding LP, 2014 WL 2006756, at *2 (W.D. Wis. May 16, 2014).
139. Cutter v. Scott & Fetzer Co., 510 F. Supp. 905, 909 (E.D. Wis. 1981).
140. Brava Salon Specialists, LLC v. Label.M USA, Inc., 2016 WL 632649, at *2 (W.D. Wis. Feb. 17, 2016).
141. Watch & Accessory Co. v. Garmin Int'l, Inc., 2021 WL 6197892, at *2 (E.D. Wis. Dec. 30, 2021).

Note that the Wisconsin Legislature designed the WFDL to afford protections to "dealership[s] situated in this state."[142] The Wisconsin Supreme Court has interpreted this phrase to focus on "the substance of the dealership, not the location of the dealer."[143] To determine whether a dealership focuses on Wisconsin, courts have adapted the multifactor "community of interest" test in *Ziegler* to the following factors: (1) percent of total sales in Wisconsin (and/or percent of total revenue or profits derived from Wisconsin); (2) how long the parties have dealt with each other in Wisconsin; (3) the extent and nature of the obligations imposed on the dealer regarding operations in Wisconsin; (4) the extent and nature of the grant of territory in this state; (5) the extent and nature of the use of the grantor's proprietary marks in this state; (6) the extent and nature of the dealer's financial investment in inventory, facilities, and good will of the dealership in this state; (7) the personnel devoted to the Wisconsin market; (8) the level of advertising and/or promotional expenditures in Wisconsin; and (9) the extent and nature of any supplementary services provided in Wisconsin.[144]

These factors are not exhaustive, and the focus of the inquiry is "on the nature and extent of the dealership's development of, investment in and reliance upon the Wisconsin market."[145]

b. Annotations

The WFDL does not expressly prohibit litigation in a non-Wisconsin forum. The WFDL does, however, incorporate Wisconsin's strong public policy of protecting franchisees and dealers from unfair treatment by franchisors and grantors and states that a dealer can bring suit "in any court of competent jurisdiction." Wisconsin Statute section 135.06. Nevertheless, "absent extraordinary circumstances," a court will enforce a forum selection clause in a dealership agreement. *Brava Salon Specialists, LLC v. Label.M USA, Inc.*, No. 15-CV-631-BBC, 2016 WL 632649, at *2 (W.D. Wis. Feb. 17, 2016).

2. Limitations Period

a. Commentary

Claims under the WFDL must be "commenced with one year."[146] The limitations period begins to accrue "where there exists a claim capable of present enforcement, a suable party against whom it may be enforced and a party who has a present right to enforce it."[147] Thus, where a grantor sends a notice of termination to a dealer that does not comply with the WFDL's notice and cure provisions or provide the reasons for termination, the cause of action begins to

---

142. WIS. STAT. § 135.02(2).
143. Baldewein Co. v. Tri-Clover, Inc., 233 Wis. 2d 57, 70, 606 N.W.2d 145, 150 (2000).
144. *Id.* at 152.
145. *Id.*
146. WIS. STAT. § 893.93(3)(b); *see also* DeTemple v. Leica Geosystems, Inc., 2009 WL 1871710, at *2 (E.D. Wis. June 24, 2009), *vacated in part on other grounds* DeTemple v. Leica GeoSystemes, Inc., 2009 WL 3617616 (E.D. Wis. Oct. 29, 2009).
147. Les Moise, Inc. v. Rossignol Ski Co., 122 Wis. 2d 51, 57, 361 N.W.2d 653, 656 (1985).

accrue from the date of receipt of the written notice—not the date of termination pursuant to that notice.[148]

b. Annotations

The WFDL has a one-year limitations period. Wisconsin Statute section 893.93(3)(b).

The WFDL's limitations period begins to run the date that written notice of termination is received by the dealer. *Les Moise, Inc. v. Rossignol Ski Co.*, 122 Wis. 2d 51, 53, 361 N.W.2d 653, 654, Bus. Franchise Guide (CCH) ¶ 8293 (1985); but see *Chili Implement Co. v. CNH America, LLC*, No. 2014AP1496, 2015 WL 193450 (Wis. Ct. App. Apl. 30, 2015) (unpublished) (finding that certain violations of the WFDL may start to run after the dealer receives a termination notice).

For suits under the WFDL against a governmental entity, Wisconsin Statute section 893.80 (the notice of claim statute) increases the WFDL's limitations period by 120 days. *Benson v. City of Madison*, 376 Wis.2d 35, 897 N.W.2d 16 (2017).

---

148. *Id.* at 656.

About the Editors

Julianne Lusthaus has been practicing franchise law for more than 24 years, representing both franchisors and franchisees. Services for franchisors include assisting with the development of franchise programs, corporate structuring, preparation and registration of FDDs, onboarding franchisees, compliance with franchise sales and relationship laws, and ongoing operational issues.

Julie also represents single unit, multiunit and multibrand franchisees as well as master franchisees, guiding them through franchise acquisitions and renewals, the purchase and sale of existing franchise businesses, and real estate matters. She has extensive experience assisting sophisticated operators navigating the risks associated with multiunit and multibrand development.

Julie is a past member of the Governing Committee of the ABA Forum on Franchising and a past director of the LADR Division of the ABA Forum on Franchising. She was program co-chair for the 2018 ABA Franchise Forum. Julie has published extensively on franchise law issues and is the co-author of the chapter on "Representing Franchisees" in *Fundamentals of Franchising*, 4th edition, and the co-author of the chapter on "FDD Review and Franchise Agreement Negotiation" in *Representing Franchisees*. Julie is also a frequent speaker on franchise issues at events hosted by various organizations including the ABA, Strafford Webinars, the IFA, NYS Bar Association, and WCBA.

Elliot Ginsburg has been a practicing attorney for more than 14 years. Elliot's primary focus is on representing franchisees, franchisee associations, and distributors in both transactional matters and disputes with franchisors and suppliers. Elliot has been an editor for the *Franchise Law Journal* and is recognized as a knowledgeable authority in franchising and distribution. He has written numerous articles and co-authored the *Annual Franchise and Distribution Law Developments* in 2018. He frequently speaks on franchise topics at ABA-hosted events.

In addition to his work representing franchisees, Elliot represents businesses of all types, handling a diverse array of matters, including corporate formation, business transactions, contract drafting and negotiations, trademark issues, regulatory matters, employment questions, capital raises, and litigation.

Index

A

abandonment, termination for, in Missouri, 357–358
administrative action
  in Arkansas, 28–35
  in California, 72–83
  in Connecticut, 119–123
  in Delaware, 139–141
  in Hawaii, 162–165
  in Illinois, 192–197
  in Indiana, 216–218
  in Iowa, 235–237
  in Michigan, 265–270
  in Minnesota, 303–322
  in Mississippi, 342–344
  in Missouri, 363–367
  in Nebraska, 384–388
  in New Jersey, 411–417
  in Puerto Rico, 444–450
  in Rhode Island, 470–472
  in Virginia, 494–497
  in Washington, 516–517
  in Wisconsin, 543–548
agreement
  in Arkansas, 6–7
  in Wisconsin, 524–525
alcohol, special considerations with, in Wisconsin, 542–543
arbitrary standards, in Hawaii, 162
arbitration
  in California, 86–89
  in Puerto Rico, 453–454
Arkansas
  administrative action in, 28–35
  agreement in, 6–7
  ancillary documents in, 26
  attorneys' fees in, 33–34
  community of interest in, 11
  conduct standards in, 24–26
  control in, 11
  damages in, 30–31
  discrimination between franchisees in, 26–27
  dispute resolution in, 35–38
  distribution right in, 9–10
  franchise defined in, 4–10
  franchise fee in, 11
  franchisor provision of information in, liability with, 26
  franchisor venue restriction in, 35–37
  injunctive relief in, 32–33
  joint marketing plan in, 11
  jurisdiction in, 12–13
  limitations period in, 37–38
  location requirement in, 7–9
  nonrenewal in, 18–21
  offer right in, 9–10
  oral agreement in, 6–7
  remedies in, 28–35
  rescission in, 32
  restrictive covenants in, 28–30
  right of free association in, 26
  sale right in, 9–10
  scope in, 12–13
  succession in, 22–24
  termination in, 13–19
  territory requirement in, 9
  trademark element in, 10–11
  transfers in, 22–24
  waiver limitations in, 34
  written agreement in, 6–7
associational rights. *See also* free association, right of
  in California, 64
  in Illinois, 190
  in Minnesota, 295–296

attorneys' fees
- in Arkansas, 33–34
- in California, 81–82
- in Connecticut, 122
- in Delaware, 140–141
- in Hawaii, 164
- in Illinois, 195–196
- in Iowa, 236
- in Michigan, 269
- in Minnesota, 319–320
- in Mississippi, 344
- in Missouri, 366
- in Nebraska, 388
- in New Jersey, 417
- in Puerto Rico, 449
- in Rhode Island, 471–472
- in U.S. Virgin Islands, 482
- in Virginia, 496
- in Washington, 518
- in Wisconsin, 547

B

bankruptcy, termination for, in Missouri, 358

C

California
- administrative action in, 72–83
- arbitration in, 86–89
- attorneys' fees in, 81–82
- choice of law in, 90–92
- community of interest in, 47–49
- control in, 47–49
- control person liability in, 80–81
- damage waivers in, limitations on, 82
- damages in, 75–79
- discrimination between franchisees in, 69–70
- dispute resolution in, 83–92
- emergencies in, state or federal, 82
- encroachment in, 65
- franchise defined in, 40–49
- franchise fee element in, 43–47
- franchisor venue restriction ability in, 83–85
- injunctive relief in, 80
- joint marketing plan in, 47–49
- jurisdiction in, 49–50
- jury trial waiver in, 89
- limitations period in, 85–86
- liquidated damages in, 78
- material modifications in, 65–67
- no waiver clauses in, 67–68
- nonrenewal in, 56–61, 75–76
- policy rationale in, 40
- price control in, 71–72
- protected classification in, 69–70
- remedies in, 72–83
- rescission in, 79
- restrictive covenants in, 72–75
- royalties in, damages for lost, 77–78
- scope in, 49–50
- succession in, 61–63
- supply sources in, 70–71
- termination in, 50–56
- trademark element in, 41–43
- transfers in, 61–63
- unfair competition law in, 68–69

cancellation. *See* termination

choice of law
- in California, 90–92
- in Puerto Rico, 454–455
- in Virginia, 494

community of interest
- in Arkansas, 11
- in California, 47–49
- in Connecticut, 102–106
- in Delaware, 131
- in Hawaii, 149–151
- in Illinois, 176–178
- in Iowa, 222
- in Michigan, 250 254
- in Minnesota, 278–279
- in Mississippi, 333
- in Missouri, 351–353
- in Nebraska, 373–374
- in New Jersey, 394–396
- in Rhode Island, 460–461
- in Virginia, 488
- in Washington, 502–503
- in Wisconsin, 525–530

competition law, in California, 68–69

complete defense, in New Jersey, 411

conduct standards
- in Arkansas, 24–26
- in Indiana, 216

Index   **555**

in Minnesota, 297–298
in Washington, 515–516
Connecticut
  administrative action in, 119–123
  community of interest in, 102–106
  control in, 102–106
  control person liability in, 122
  damage waivers in, limitations
      on, 122
  damages in, 119–121
  dispute resolution in, 123–125
  franchise defined in, 93–97
  franchisor right to impose conditions
      for renewal in, 118
  franchisor venue restriction in,
      123–124
  injunctive relief in, 121–122
  joint marketing plan in, 102–106
  jurisdiction in, 106–109
  limitations period in, 124–125
  nonrenewal in, 115–118
  remedies in, 119–123
  rescission in, 121
  scope in, 106–109
  termination in, 109–115
  trademark element in, 97–102
Connecticut Business Opportunity
     Investment Act, 93
Connecticut Franchise Act, 93
contract element, in Wisconsin, 524–525
control
  in Arkansas, 11
  in California, 47–49
  in Connecticut, 102–106
  in Delaware, 131
  in Hawaii, 149–151
  in Illinois, 176–178
  in Iowa, 222
  in Michigan, 250–254
  in Minnesota, 278–279
  in Mississippi, 333
  in Missouri, 351–353
  in Nebraska, 373–374
  in New Jersey, 394–396
  in Rhode Island, 460–461
  in Virginia, 488
  in Washington, 502–503
  in Wisconsin, 525–530

control person liability
  in Arkansas, 32–33
  in California, 80–81
  in Connecticut, 122
  in Delaware, 140
  in Hawaii, 164
  in Illinois, 195
  in Indiana, 217
  in Iowa, 236
  in Michigan, 267–268
  in Minnesota, 316–319
  in Mississippi, 343–344
  in Missouri, 366
  in Nebraska, 387
  in Rhode Island, 471
  in U.S. Virgin Islands, 482
  in Virginia, 496
  in Washington, 518
  in Wisconsin, 546
criminal liability, in Hawaii, 165–166
criminal misconduct, termination for, in
     Missouri, 357
cure period
  with nonrenewal
    in Arkansas, 21
    in Connecticut, 117
    in Delaware, 137
    in Illinois, 187
    in Indiana, 212
    in Minnesota, 293
    in Mississippi, 340
    in Missouri, 360
    in Nebraska, 380
    in New Jersey, 408
    in Rhode Island, 467
    in Washington, 510
    in Wisconsin, 540
  with termination
    in Arkansas, 18
    in California, 54–55
    in Connecticut, 114
    in Delaware, 135
    in Hawaii, 154
    in Illinois, 183–185
    in Indiana, 211
    in Michigan, 260
    in Minnesota, 289–290
    in Mississippi, 338

cure period,
   with termination, *continued*
      in Missouri, 359
      in Nebraska, 378
      in New Jersey, 405
      in Rhode Island, 465–466
      in Washington, 508
      in Wisconsin, 537–538

D

damages
   in Arkansas, 30–31
   in California, 75–79
   in Connecticut, 119–121
   in Delaware, 139
   in Hawaii, 163
   in Illinois, 192–194
   in Indiana, 217
   in Iowa, 236–237
   limitations on, in Minnesota, 320–321
   liquidated, in California, 78
   for lost royalties, in California, 77–78
   in Michigan, 266–267
   in Minnesota, 307–310, 320–321
   in Mississippi, 342
   in Missouri, 363–365
   in Nebraska, 386–387
   in New Jersey, 413–414
   for nonrenewal, in California, 75–76
   in Puerto Rico, 445–447
   in Rhode Island, 470
   for termination, in California, 75–76
   in U.S. Virgin Islands, 481
   in Virginia, 495
   waivers, limitations on
      in California, 82
      in Connecticut, 122
      in Hawaii, 165
      in Illinois, 196
      in Puerto Rico, 450
      in Rhode Island, 472
      in U.S. Virgin Islands, 482
      in Virginia, 496
      in Washington, 518–519
      in Wisconsin, 547
   in Washington, 517
   in Wisconsin, 543–545
dealer, in Puerto Rico, 425–428
dealer contract, in Puerto Rico, 428–429
dealership, defined, in Wisconsin, 522–530
Delaware
   administrative action in, 139–141
   attorneys' fees in, 140–141
   community of interest in, 131
   control in, 131
   control person liability in, 140
   damages in, 139
   dispute resolution in, 141–142
   franchise defined in, 127–131
   franchise fee element in, 129–131
   franchisor ability to restrict venue in, 141–142
   franchisor right to impose conditions for renewal in, 138
   joint marketing plan in, 131
   jurisdiction in, 132
   limitations period in, 142
   nonrenewal in, 135–138
   remedies in, 139–141
   rescission in, 140
   restrictive covenants in, 139
   scope in, 132
   succession in, 138
   termination in, 132–135
   trademark element in, 128–129
   transfers in, 138
discrimination, between franchisees
   in Arkansas, 26–27
   in California, 69–70
   in Hawaii, 159–160
   in Illinois, 189
   in Indiana, 213–214
   in Minnesota, 294–295
   in Missouri, 368
   in Puerto Rico, 441
   in Washington, 512–513
dispute resolution
   arbitration in
      in California, 86–89
      in Puerto Rico, 453–454
   in Arkansas, 35–38
   in California, 83–92
   in Connecticut, 123–125
   in Delaware, 141–142
   in Hawaii, 166–167

in Illinois, 197–201
in Indiana, 217–218
in Iowa, 237–238
in Michigan, 270–271
in Minnesota, 322–328
in Mississippi, 345
in Missouri, 367–368
in Nebraska, 388
in New Jersey, 418–420
in Puerto Rico, 450–455
in Rhode Island, 472–473
in U.S. Virgin Islands, 483–484
in Virginia, 497
in Washington, 520
in Wisconsin, 548–550
distribution right, in Arkansas, 9–10
documents, ancillary, in Arkansas, 26

E

emergency, state or federal, in California, 82
encroachment
   in California, 65
   in Hawaii, 160–161
   in Indiana, 214
   in Iowa, 231–233
   in Minnesota, 296–297
exclusive territory
   in Indiana, 214
   in Minnesota, 296–297
   in Washington, 515
exclusivity impairment, in Puerto Rico, 442–443

F

fee, franchise. *See also* attorneys' fees
   in Arkansas, 11
   in California, 43–47
   in Connecticut, 102
   in Delaware, 129–131
   in Hawaii, 145–149
   in Illinois, 172–176
   in Indiana, 206–208
   in Iowa, 221–222
   in Michigan, 242–250
   in Minnesota, 276–278
   in Mississippi, 332–333
   in Missouri, 351
   in Nebraska, 372–373
   in New Jersey, 394
   in Rhode Island, 460
   in Virginia, 487–488
   in Washington, 501–502
franchise
   definition of
      in Arkansas, 4–10
      in California, 40–49
      in Connecticut, 93–97
      in Delaware, 127–131
      in Hawaii, 144–151
      in Illinois, 169–178
      in Indiana, 204–208
      in Iowa, 220–222
      in Michigan, 240–254
      in Minnesota, 275–279
      in Mississippi, 330–333
      in Missouri, 348–353
      in Nebraska, 370–374
      in New Jersey, 390–396
      in Rhode Island, 459–461
      in U.S. Virgin Islands, 475–476
      in Virginia, 485–488
      in Washington, 500–503
      in Wisconsin, 522–530
   fee element in
      in Arkansas, 11
      in California, 43–47
      in Connecticut, 102
      in Delaware, 129–131
      in Hawaii, 145–149
      in Illinois, 172–176
      in Indiana, 206–208
      in Iowa, 221–222
      in Michigan, 242–250
      in Minnesota, 276–278
      in Mississippi, 332–333
      in Missouri, 351
      in Nebraska, 372–373
      in New Jersey, 394
      in Rhode Island, 460
      in Virginia, 487–488
      in Washington, 501–502
   joint marketing plan in
      in Arkansas, 11
      in California, 47–49
      in Connecticut, 102–106

franchise,
  joint marketing plan in, *continued*
    in Delaware, 131
    in Hawaii, 149–151
    in Illinois, 176–178
    in Indiana, 205–206
    in Iowa, 222
    in Michigan, 250–254
    in Minnesota, 278–279
    in Mississippi, 333
    in Missouri, 351–353
    in Nebraska, 373–374
    in New Jersey, 394–396
    in Rhode Island, 460–461
    in Virginia, 488
    in Washington, 502–503
    in Wisconsin, 525–530
  trademark element in
    in Arkansas, 10–11
    in California, 41–43
    in Connecticut, 97–102
    in Delaware, 128–129
    in Hawaii, 144–145
    in Illinois, 170–171
    in Indiana, 204–205
    in Iowa, 221
    in Michigan, 241–242
    in Minnesota, 275–276
    in Mississippi, 330–332
    in Missouri, 349–351
    in Nebraska, 370–371
    in New Jersey, 392–393
    in Rhode Island, 459–460
    in Virginia, 486–487
    in Washington, 500–501
    in Wisconsin, 523–524
  written agreement
    in Arkansas, 6–7
    in Virginia, 486
franchisor
  liability with provision of information by, in Arkansas, 26
  right to impose renewal conditions
    in Connecticut, 118
    in Delaware, 138
    in Hawaii, 157
    in Illinois, 187–188
    in Indiana, 213
    in Michigan, 263
    in Minnesota, 293
    in Mississippi, 341
    in Missouri, 360–361
    in Nebraska, 380
    in New Jersey, 408
    in Puerto Rico, 438–439
    in Rhode Island, 467
    in Wisconsin, 540–541
  venue restriction ability of
    in Arkansas, 35–37
    in California, 83–85
    in Connecticut, 123–124
    in Delaware, 141–142
    in Hawaii, 166
    in Illinois, 197–199
    in Indiana, 217
    in Iowa, 237–238
    in Michigan, 270–271
    in Minnesota, 322–327
    in Missouri, 367
    in Nebraska, 388
    in New Jersey, 418–420
    in Puerto Rico, 450–452
    in U.S. Virgin Islands, 483
    in Wisconsin, 548–549
fraud, termination for, in Missouri, 357
free association, right of. *See also* associational rights
  in Arkansas, 26
  in Hawaii, 158
  in Iowa, 231

G

good faith, in Iowa, 234

H

Hawaii
  administrative action in, 162–165
  anti-waiver provision in, 161–162
  arbitrary standards in, 162
  attorneys' fees in, 164
  community of interest in, 149–151
  control in, 149–151
  control person liability in, 164
  criminal liability in, 165–166
  damage waivers in, 165
  damages in, 163

discrimination between franchises in, 159–160
dispute resolution in, 166–167
franchise defined in, 144–151
franchise fee element in, 145–149
franchisor right to impose renewal conditions in, 157
franchisor venue restriction ability in, 166
freedom of association in, 158
injunctive relief in, 163–164
jurisdiction in, 151–152
limitations period in, 166–167
nonrenewal in, 154–157
remedies in, 162–165
rescission in, 163
restrictive covenants in, 163
scope in, 151–152
secret rebates in, 160
succession in, 158
supply sources in, 159
termination in, 152–154
trademark element in, 144–145
transfers in, 158
unreasonable standards in, 162

I

Illinois
administrative action in, 192–197
association rights in, 190
attorneys' fees in, 195–196
community of interest in, 176–178
control in, 176–178
control person liability in, 195
damage waivers in, 196
damages in, 192–194
discrimination between franchisees in, 189
dispute resolution in, 197–201
franchise defined in, 169–178
franchise fee in, 172–176
franchisor right to impose renewal conditions in, 187–188
franchisor venue restriction ability in, 197–199
injunctive relief in, 194–195
jurisdiction in, 178–180
limitations period in, 199–201
nonrenewal in, 185–188
remedies in, 192–197
rescission in, 194
restrictive covenants in, 192
scope in, 178–180
succession in, 188
termination in, 180–185
trademark element in, 170–171
transfers in, 188
waiver restrictions in, 190–191
Illinois Franchise Disclosure Act, 169
impairment, in Puerto Rico, 440–441
Indiana
administrative action in, 216–218
conduct standards in, 216
control person liability in, 217
damages in, 217
discrimination between franchises in, 213–214
dispute resolution in, 217–218
encroachment in, 214
franchise defined in, 204–208
franchise fee in, 206–208
franchisor right to impose renewal conditions in, 213
franchisor venue restriction ability in, 217
injunctive relief in, 217
jurisdiction in, 208–209
limitations period in, 218
marketing plan in, 205–206
nonrenewal in, 211–213
release restrictions in, 215–216
remedies in, 216–218
rescission in, 217
restrictive covenants in, 216
scope in, 208–209
succession in, 213
supply restrictions in, 214–215
system element in, 205–206
termination in, 209–211
trademark element in, 204–205
transfers in, 213
waiver restrictions in, 215–216

injunctive relief
    in Arkansas, 32
    in California, 80
    in Connecticut, 121–122
    in Hawaii, 163–164
    in Illinois, 194–195
    in Indiana, 217
    in Iowa, 236
    in Minnesota, 311–316
    in Mississippi, 343
    in Missouri, 365–366
    in Nebraska, 387
    in New Jersey, 415–416
    in Puerto Rico, 447–448
    in Rhode Island, 471
    in Virginia, 496
    in Washington, 517
    in Wisconsin, 545–546
insolvency, termination for, in Missouri, 358
Iowa
    administrative action in, 235–237
    attorneys' fees in, 236
    community of interest in, 222
    control in, 222
    control person liability in, 236
    damages in, 236–237
    dispute resolution in, 237–238
    encroachment in, 231–233
    franchise defined in, 220–222
    franchise fee in, 221–222
    franchisor venue restriction ability in, 237–238
    free association in, 231
    good faith in, 234
    injunctive relief in, 236
    joint marketing plan in, 222
    jurisdiction in, 222–223
    limitations period in, 238
    nonrenewal in, 226–228
    no-waiver clauses in, 234
    releases in, 234
    remedies in, 235–237
    rescission in, 236
    restrictive covenants in, 235–236
    scope in, 222–223
    succession on, 228–230
    supply restrictions in, 233–234
    termination in, 224–226
    territory exclusivity in, 231–233
    trademark element in, 221
    transfers in, 228–230

J

jurisdiction
    in Arkansas, 12–13
    in California, 49–50
    in Connecticut, 106–109
    in Delaware, 132
    in Hawaii, 151–152
    in Illinois, 178–180
    in Indiana, 208–209
    in Iowa, 222–223
    in Michigan, 254–255
    in Mississippi, 334–335
    in Missouri, 353–354
    in Nebraska, 374–376
    in New Jersey, 396–400
    in Puerto Rico, 429–430
    in Rhode Island, 461–462
    in U.S. Virgin Islands, 476–477
    in Virginia, 489
    in Washington, 503–504
    in Wisconsin, 530–532
jury trial waiver, in California, 89

K

kickbacks, supplier, in Washington, 514–515

L

liability
    control person
        in Arkansas, 32–33
        in California, 80–81
        in Connecticut, 122
        in Delaware, 140
        in Hawaii, 164
        in Illinois, 195
        in Indiana, 217
        in Iowa, 236
        in Michigan, 267–268
        in Minnesota, 316–319
        in Mississippi, 343–344
        in Missouri, 366
        in Nebraska, 387

in Rhode Island, 471
in U.S. Virgin Islands, 482
in Virginia, 496
in Washington, 518
in Wisconsin, 546
criminal, in Hawaii, 165–166
with franchisor information provision, in Arkansas, 26
limitations period
in Arkansas, 37–38
in California, 85–86
in Connecticut, 124–125
in Delaware, 142
in Hawaii, 166–167
in Illinois, 199–201
in Indiana, 218
in Iowa, 238
in Michigan, 271
in Minnesota, 327–328
in Mississippi, 345
in Missouri, 367
in Nebraska, 388
in New Jersey, 420
in Puerto Rico, 452–453
in Rhode Island, 473
in U.S. Virgin Islands, 483–484
in Virginia, 497
in Washington, 520
in Wisconsin, 549–550
liquor, special considerations with, in Wisconsin, 542–543
location requirement, in Arkansas, 7–9

M

marketing plan, joint
in Arkansas, 11
in California, 47–49
in Connecticut, 102–106
in Delaware, 131
in Hawaii, 149–151
in Illinois, 176–178
in Indiana, 205–206
in Iowa, 222
in Michigan, 250–254
in Minnesota, 278–279
in Mississippi, 333
in Missouri, 351–353
in Nebraska, 373–374

in New Jersey, 394–396
in Rhode Island, 460–461
in Virginia, 488
in Washington, 502–503
in Wisconsin, 525–530
material modifications, in California, 65–67
Michigan
administrative action in, 265–270
attorneys' fees in, 269
community of interest in, 250–254
control person liability in, 267–268
damages in, 266–267
dispute resolution in, 270–271
franchise defined in, 240–254
franchise fee in, 242–250
franchisor venue restriction ability in, 270–271
joint marketing plan in, 250–254
jurisdiction in, 254–255
limitations period in, 271
nonrenewal in, 260–263
remedies in, 265–270
rescission in, 267
restrictive covenants in, 265–266
scope in, 254–255
successions in, 263–264
termination in, 255–260
trademark element in, 241–242
transfers in, 263–264
Minnesota
administrative action in, 303–322
association rights in, 295–296
attorneys' fees in, 319–320
community of interest in, 278–279
control in, 278–279
control person liability in, 316–319
damages in, 307–310, 320–321
discrimination between franchisees in, 294–295
dispute resolution in, 322–328
encroachment in, 296–297
exclusive territory in, 296–297
franchise defined in, 275–279
franchise fee in, 276–278
franchisor right to impose renewal conditions in, 293

Minnesota, *continued*
   franchisor venue restriction ability in, 322–327
   injunctive relief in, 311–316
   jurisdiction in, 279–286
   limitations period in, 327–328
   nonrenewal in, 290–293
   releases in, 297–303
   remedies in, 303–322
   rescission in, 310–311
   residents *vs.* nonresidents in, 280–283
   restrictive covenants in, 303–307
   scope in, 279–286
   standards of conduct in, 297–298
   statutory scope in, 279–280
   succession in, 294
   termination in, 286–290
   trademark element in, 275–276
   transfers in, 294
   waivers in, 297–303
Mississippi
   administrative action in, 342–344
   attorneys' fees in, 344
   community of interest in, 333
   control in, 333
   control person liability in, 343–344
   damages in, 342
   discrimination between franchisees in, 368
   dispute resolution in, 345
   franchise defined in, 330–333
   franchise fee in, 332–333
   franchisor right to impose renewal conditions in, 341
   injunctive relief in, 343
   joint marketing plan in, 333
   jurisdiction in, 334–335
   limitations period in, 345
   nonrenewal in, 339–341
   remedies in, 342–344
   rescission in, 342
   restrictive covenants in, 342
   scope in, 334–335
   succession in, 341
   termination in, 335–339
   trademark element in, 330–332
   transfers in, 341

Missouri
   administrative action in, 363–367
   attorneys' fees in, 366
   community of interest in, 351–353
   control in, 351–353
   control person liability in, 366
   damages in, 363–365
   dispute resolution in, 367–368
   franchise defined in, 348–353
   franchise fee in, 351
   franchisor right to impose renewal conditions in, 360–361
   franchisor venue restriction ability in, 367
   injunctive relief in, 365–366
   joint marketing plan in, 351–353
   jurisdiction in, 353–354
   limitations period in, 367
   nonrenewal in, 359–361
   preemption in, 368
   remedies in, 363–367
   rescission in, 365
   restrictive covenants in, 363
   scope in, 353–354
   succession in, 361
   termination in, 355–359
   trademark element in, 349–351
   transfers in, 361
monetary threshold, in New Jersey, 398–400

N

Nebraska
   administrative action in, 384–388
   attorneys' fees in, 388
   community of interest in, 373–374
   control in, 373–374
   control person liability in, 387
   damages in, 386–387
   dispute resolution in, 388
   franchise defined in, 370–374
   franchise fee in, 372–373
   franchisor right to impose renewal conditions in, 380
   franchisor venue restriction ability in, 388
   gross sales during year prior in, with jurisdiction, 376
   injunctive relief in, 387

joint marketing plan in, 373–374
jurisdiction in, 374–376
limitations period in, 388
nonrenewal in, 379–381
place of business in, 374–376
remedies in, 384–388
rescission in, 387
restrictive covenants in, 384–386
scope in, 374–376
succession in, 381–382
termination in, 377–379
trademark element in, 370–371
transfers in, 381–382
New Jersey
  administrative action in, 411–417
  attorneys' fees in, 417
  community of interest in, 394–396
  complete defense in, 411
  control in, 394–396
  damages in, 413–414
  dispute resolution in, 418–420
  franchise defined in, 390–396
  franchise fee in, 394
  franchisor right to impose renewal conditions in, 408
  franchisor venue restriction ability in, 418–420
  injunctive relief in, 415–416
  joint marketing plan in, 394–396
  jurisdiction in, 396–400
  limitations period in, 420
  monetary threshold in, 398–400
  nonrenewal in, 406–408
  place of business in, with jurisdiction, 396–397
  prohibited practices in, 410–411
  remedies in, 411–417
  rescission in, 414–415
  restrictive covenants in, 411–413
  scope in, 396–400
  succession in, 409
  termination in, 400–405
  trademark element in, 392–393
  transfers in, 409
  unreasonable standards in, 410
no waiver clauses
  in California, 67–68
  in Iowa, 234

nonrenewal
  in Arkansas, 18–21
  in California, 56–61
  in Connecticut, 115–118
  cure period with
    in Arkansas, 21
    in Hawaii, 157
    in Illinois, 187
    in Indiana, 212
    in Minnesota, 293
    in Mississippi, 340
    in Missouri, 360
    in Nebraska, 380
    in New Jersey, 408
    in Rhode Island, 467
    in Washington, 510
    in Wisconsin, 540
  damages for, in California, 75–76
  defined
    in Arkansas, 18
    in California, 56–57
    in Connecticut, 116
    in Delaware, 135–136
    in Hawaii, 155
    in Illinois, 185–186
    in Indiana, 211
    in Michigan, 260
    in Minnesota, 290–291
    in Mississippi, 339
    in Missouri, 359–360
    in Nebraska, 379
    in New Jersey, 406
    in Puerto Rico, 437
    in Rhode Island, 466
    in Washington, 508–509
    in Wisconsin, 538–539
  in Delaware, 135–138
  grounds for
    in Arkansas, 20
    in California, 59–60
    in Connecticut, 117
    in Delaware, 137
    in Hawaii, 156–157
    in Illinois, 187
    in Indiana, 212
    in Iowa, 227
    in Michigan, 261–262
    in Minnesota, 292–293
    in Mississippi, 340

nonrenewal,
    grounds for, *continued*
        in Missouri, 360
        in New Jersey, 407–408
        in Puerto Rico, 438
        in Rhode Island, 467
        in U.S. Virgin Islands, 479
        in Wisconsin, 539
    in Hawaii, 154–157
    in Illinois, 185–188
    in Indiana, 211–213
    in Iowa, 226–228
    in Michigan, 260–263
    in Minnesota, 290–293
    in Mississippi, 339–341
    in Missouri, 359–361
    in Nebraska, 379–381
    in New Jersey, 406–408
    notice requirement with
        in Arkansas, 20
        in California, 58–59
        in Connecticut, 116–117
        in Delaware, 137
        in Hawaii, 156
        in Illinois, 186–187
        in Iowa, 226–227
        in Michigan, 261
        in Minnesota, 291–292
        in Mississippi, 340
        in Missouri, 360
        in Nebraska, 380
        in New Jersey, 407
        in Rhode Island, 467
        in U.S. Virgin Islands, 479
        in Washington, 510
        in Wisconsin, 539
    in Puerto Rico, 437–439
    repurchase obligations with
        in Arkansas, 21
        in California, 60–61
        in Connecticut, 118
        in Hawaii, 157
        in Illinois, 188
        in Iowa, 227–228
        in Mississippi, 340
        in Nebraska, 380–381
        in New Jersey, 408
        in Rhode Island, 467–468
        in Washington, 511
        in Wisconsin, 541–542
    restrictions on
        in Arkansas, 19–20
        in California, 57–58
        in Connecticut, 116
        in Delaware, 136
        in Hawaii, 155
        in Illinois, 186
        in Indiana, 211
        in Michigan, 260–261
        in Minnesota, 291
        in Mississippi, 339
        in Nebraska, 379
        in New Jersey, 406–407
        in Puerto Rico, 438
        in Rhode Island, 466–467
        in Virginia, 491–492
        in Washington, 509–510
        in Wisconsin, 539
    in Rhode Island, 466–468
    in U.S. Virgin Islands, 479–480
    in Virginia, 491–493
    in Washington, 508–511
    in Wisconsin, 538–542
nonresidents, in Minnesota, 280–283
notice requirement
    with nonrenewal
        in Arkansas, 20
        in California, 58–59
        in Delaware, 137
        in Hawaii, 156
        in Illinois, 186–187
        in Iowa, 226–227
        in Michigan, 261
        in Minnesota, 291–292
        in Mississippi, 340
        in Missouri, 360
        in Nebraska, 380
        in Rhode Island, 467
        in U.S. Virgin Islands, 479
        in Washington, 510
        in Wisconsin, 539
    with termination
        in Arkansas, 15–16
        in California, 52–53
        in Connecticut, 111–112
        in Delaware, 134
        in Hawaii, 153
        in Illinois, 180–181
        in Indiana, 210
        in Iowa, 224–225

in Michigan, 257–258
in Minnesota, 287
in Mississippi, 337–338
in Missouri, 355–356
in Nebraska, 377–378
in New Jersey, 404–405
in Puerto Rico, 431–432
in U.S. Virgin Islands, 478
in Washington, 506–507
in Wisconsin, 535–536

O

offer right, in Arkansas, 9–10
oral agreement, in Arkansas, 6–7

P

payment terms, in Puerto Rico, 442
place of business
   in Nebraska, 374–376
   in New Jersey, 396–397
preemption, in Missouri, 368
price control, in California, 71–72
pricing, reasonable, in Washington, 513–514
protected classification, in California, 69–70
Puerto Rico
   administrative action in, 444–450
   arbitration in, 453–454
   attorneys' fees in, 449
   choice of law in, 454–455
   damage waivers limitations in, 450
   damages in, 445–447
   dealer contract in, 428–429
   dealer defined in, 425–428
   discrimination in, 441
   dispute resolution in, 450–455
   exclusivity impairment in, 442–443
   franchisor right to impose renewal conditions in, 438–439
   impairment in, 440–441
   injunctive relief in, 447–448
   jurisdiction in, 429–430
   limitations period in, 452–453
   nonrenewal in, 437–439
   payment terms in, 442
   remedies in, 444–447
   rescission in, 447
   restrictive covenants in, 444–445
   scope in, 429–430
   shipment delays in, 442
   shipping terms in, 442
   succession in, 439–440
   termination in, 430–437
   transfers in, 439–440
   venue restriction ability of franchisor in, 450–452

R

rebates
   secret, in Hawaii, 160
   supplier, in Washington, 514–515
releases
   in Iowa, 234
   restrictions on
      in Indiana, 215–216
      in Minnesota, 297–303
remedies
   in Arkansas, 28–35
   in California, 72–83
   in Connecticut, 119–123
   in Delaware, 139–141
   in Hawaii, 162–165
   in Illinois, 192–197
   in Indiana, 216–218
   in Iowa, 235–237
   in Michigan, 265–270
   in Minnesota, 303–322
   in Mississippi, 342–344
   in Missouri, 363–367
   in Nebraska, 384–388
   in New Jersey, 411–417
   in Puerto Rico, 445–447
   in Rhode Island, 470–472
   in Virginia, 494–497
   in Washington, 516–517
   in Wisconsin, 543–548
repurchase obligations
   with nonrenewal
      in Arkansas, 21
      in California, 60–61
      in Connecticut, 118
      in Hawaii, 157
      in Illinois, 188
      in Iowa, 227–228
      in Mississippi, 340
      in Nebraska, 380–381
      in New Jersey, 408
      in Rhode Island, 467–468
      in Washington, 511

repurchase obligations,
  with nonrenewal, *continued*
    in Wisconsin, 541–542
  with termination
    in Arkansas, 18–19
    in California, 55–56
    in Connecticut, 115
    in Hawaii, 154
    in Illinois, 185
    in Michigan, 260
    in Mississippi, 338–339
    in Missouri, 359
    in Nebraska, 379
    in New Jersey, 405
    in Puerto Rico, 437
    in Rhode Island, 466
    in Washington, 508
    in Wisconsin, 538
rescission
  in Arkansas, 32
  in California, 79
  in Connecticut, 121
  in Delaware, 140
  in Hawaii, 163
  in Illinois, 194
  in Indiana, 217
  in Iowa, 236
  in Michigan, 267
  in Minnesota, 310–311
  in Mississippi, 342
  in Missouri, 365
  in Nebraska, 387
  in New Jersey, 414–415
  in Puerto Rico, 447
  in Rhode Island, 471
  in Virginia, 495
  in Wisconsin, 545
restrictive covenants
  in Arkansas, 28–30
  in California, 72–75
  in Delaware, 139
  in Hawaii, 163
  in Illinois, 192
  in Indiana, 216
  in Iowa, 235–236
  in Michigan, 265–266
  in Minnesota, 303–307
  in Mississippi, 342
  in Missouri, 363
  in Nebraska, 384–386
  in New Jersey, 411–413
  in Puerto Rico, 444–445
  in Rhode Island, 470
  in Virginia, 494
  in Washington, 516–517
Rhode Island
  administrative action in, 470–472
  attorneys' fees in, 471–472
  community of interest in, 460–461
  control in, 460–461
  control person liability in, 471
  damage waivers limitations in, 472
  damages in, 470
  dispute resolution in, 472–473
  franchise defined in, 459–461
  franchise fee in, 460
  franchisor right to impose renewal
      conditions in, 467
  franchisor venue restriction ability in,
      472–473
  injunctive relief in, 471
  joint marketing plan in, 460–461
  jurisdiction in, 461–462
  limitations period in, 473
  nonrenewal in, 466–468
  remedies in, 470–472
  rescission in, 471
  restrictive covenants in, 470
  scope in, 461–462
  succession in, 468
  termination in, 462–466
  trademark element in, 459–460
  transfers in, 468
royalties, damages for lost future, in
    California, 77–78

S

sale right
  in Arkansas, 9–10
  in Wisconsin, 523–524
sales, gross, in Nebraska, with
    jurisdiction, 376
scope
  in Arkansas, 12–13
  in California, 49–50
  in Connecticut, 106–109
  in Delaware, 132
  in Hawaii, 151–152

in Illinois, 178–180
in Indiana, 208–209
in Iowa, 222–223
in Michigan, 254–255
in Minnesota, 279–286
in Mississippi, 334–335
in Missouri, 353–354
in Nebraska, 374–376
in New Jersey, 396–400
in Puerto Rico, 429–430
in Rhode Island, 461–462
in U.S. Virgin Islands, 476–477
in Virginia, 489
in Washington, 503–504
in Wisconsin, 530–532
shipment delays, in Puerto Rico, 442
shipping terms, in Puerto Rico, 442
succession
   in Arkansas, 22–24
   in California, 61–63
   in Delaware, 138
   in Hawaii, 158
   in Illinois, 188
   in Iowa, 228–230
   in Michigan, 263–264
   in Minnesota, 294
   in Mississippi, 341
   in Missouri, 361
   in Nebraska, 381–382
   in New Jersey, 409
   in Puerto Rico, 439–440
   in Rhode Island, 468
   in Virginia, 493
   in Washington, 511
   in Wisconsin, 542
supplier rebates, in Washington, 514–515
supply restrictions
   in Indiana, 214–215
   in Iowa, 233–234
   in Washington, 512
supply sources
   in California, 70–71
   in Hawaii, 159
system element, in Indiana, 205–206

T

termination
   for abandonment, in Missouri, 357–358
   in Arkansas, 13–19
   for bankruptcy, in Missouri, 358
   in California, 50–56
   in Connecticut, 109–115
   for criminal misconduct, in Missouri, 357
   cure period with
      in Arkansas, 18
      in California, 54–55
      in Hawaii, 154
      in Illinois, 183–185
      in Indiana, 211
      in Michigan, 260
      in Minnesota, 289–290
      in Missouri, 359
      in Nebraska, 378
      in New Jersey, 405
      in Rhode Island, 465–466
      in Washington, 508
      in Wisconsin, 537–538
   damages for, in California, 75–76
   defined
      in Arkansas, 13–14
      in California, 50–51
      in Connecticut, 110–111
      in Delaware, 132–134
      in Hawaii, 152
      in Illinois, 180
      in Indiana, 209
      in Iowa, 224
      in Michigan, 255–256
      in Minnesota, 286
      in Mississippi, 335–336
      in Missouri, 355
      in Nebraska, 377
      in New Jersey, 400–401
      in Puerto Rico, 430
      in Rhode Island, 462
      in U.S. Virgin Islands, 477–478
      in Virginia, 489
      in Washington, 505
      in Wisconsin, 532–534
   in Delaware, 132–135
   for fraud, in Missouri, 357
   grounds for
      in California, 53–54
      in Connecticut, 112–114
      in Delaware, 134–135
      in Hawaii, 153–154

termination,
  grounds for, *continued*
    in Illinois, 181–183
    in Iowa, 225–226
    in Michigan, 259
    in Minnesota, 287–288
    in Mississippi, 338
    in Missouri, 356–358
    in Nebraska, 378
    in New Jersey, 405
    in Puerto Rico, 432–437
    in Rhode Island, 464–465
    in U.S. Virgin Islands, 478
    in Washington, 507–508
    in Wisconsin, 536–537
  in Hawaii, 152–154
  in Illinois, 180–185
  in Indiana, 209–211
  for insolvency, in Missouri, 358
  in Iowa, 224–226
  in Michigan, 255–260
  in Minnesota, 286–290
  in Mississippi, 335–339
  in Missouri, 355–359
  in Nebraska, 377–379
  in New Jersey, 400–405
  notice requirement with
    in Arkansas, 15–16
    in California, 52–53
    in Connecticut, 111–112
    in Delaware, 134
    in Hawaii, 153
    in Illinois, 180–181
    in Indiana, 210
    in Iowa, 224–225
    in Michigan, 257–258
    in Minnesota, 287
    in Mississippi, 337–338
    in Missouri, 355–356
    in Nebraska, 377–378
    in New Jersey, 404–405
    in Puerto Rico, 431–432
    in Rhode Island, 463–464
    in U.S. Virgin Islands, 478
    in Washington, 506–507
    in Wisconsin, 535–536
  in Puerto Rico, 430–437
  repurchase obligations with
    in Arkansas, 18–19
    in Connecticut, 115
    in Hawaii, 154
    in Michigan, 260
    in Mississippi, 338–339
    in Missouri, 359
    in Nebraska, 379
    in New Jersey, 405
    in Rhode Island, 466
    in Washington, 508
    in Wisconsin, 538
  restrictions on
    in Arkansas, 14–15
    in California, 51–52
    in Connecticut, 111
    in Delaware, 134
    in Hawaii, 152–153
    in Illinois, 180
    in Indiana, 209–210
    in Iowa, 224
    in Michigan, 256–257
    in Minnesota, 287
    in New Jersey, 401–404
    in Puerto Rico, 430–431
    in Rhode Island, 462–463
    in U.S. Virgin Islands, 478
    in Virginia, 490–491
    in Washington, 505–506
    in Wisconsin, 534–535
  in Rhode Island, 462–466
  in U.S. Virgin Islands, 477–479
  in Virginia, 489–491
  in Washington, 505–508
  in Wisconsin, 532–538
territory requirement. *See also* exclusive territory
  in Arkansas, 9
  in Indiana, 214
  in Iowa, 231–233
trademark element
  in Arkansas, 10–11
  in California, 41–43
  in Connecticut, 97–102
  in Delaware, 128–129
  in Hawaii, 144–145
  in Illinois, 170–171
  in Indiana, 204–205
  in Iowa, 221
  in Michigan, 241–242
  in Minnesota, 275–276
  in Mississippi, 330–332
  in Missouri, 349–351

in Nebraska, 370–371
in New Jersey, 392–393
in Rhode Island, 459–460
in Virginia, 486–487
in Washington, 500–501
in Wisconsin, 523–524
transfers
in Arkansas, 22–24
in California, 61–63
in Delaware, 138
in Hawaii, 158
in Illinois, 188
in Indiana, 213
in Iowa, 228–230
in Michigan, 263–264
in Minnesota, 294
in Mississippi, 341
in Missouri, 361
in Nebraska, 381–382
in New Jersey, 409
in Puerto Rico, 439–440
in Rhode Island, 468
in Virginia, 493
in Washington, 511
in Wisconsin, 542

U

undue influence, to induce surrender of contractual rights, in Virginia, 493–494
unfair competition law, in California, 68–69
unreasonable standards
in Hawaii, 162
in New Jersey, 410
U.S. Virgin Islands
attorneys' fees in, 482
control person liability in, 482
damage waivers in, 482
damages in, 481
dispute resolution in, 483–484
franchise defined in, 475–476
franchisor venue restriction ability in, 483
jurisdiction in, 476–477
limitations period in, 483–484
nonrenewal in, 479–480
scope in, 476–477
termination in, 477–479

V

venue restriction, limitations on franchisor ability with
in Arkansas, 35–37
in California, 83–85
in Connecticut, 123–124
in Delaware, 141–142
in Hawaii, 166
in Illinois, 197–199
in Indiana, 217
in Iowa, 237–238
in Michigan, 270–271
in Minnesota, 322–327
in Missouri, 367
in Nebraska, 388
in New Jersey, 418–420
in Puerto Rico, 450–452
in Rhode Island, 472–473
in U.S. Virgin Islands, 483
in Wisconsin, 548–549
Virgin Islands. *See* U.S. Virgin Islands
Virginia
administrative action in, 494–497
attorneys' fees in, 496
choice of law in, 494
community of interest in, 488
control in, 488
control person liability in, 496
damage waivers limitations in, 496
damages in, 495
dispute resolution in, 497
franchise defined in, 485–488
franchise fee in, 487–488
injunctive relief in, 496
joint marketing plan in, 488
limitations period in, 497
nonrenewal in, 491–493
remedies in, 494–497
rescission in, 495
restrictive covenants in, 494
scope in, 489
termination in, 489–491
trademark element in, 486–487
transfers in, 493
undue influence to induce surrender of contractual rights in, 493–494
written agreement in, 486

W

waivers
- anti-waiver provision, in Hawaii, 161–162
- damages, limitations on
  - in California, 82
  - in Connecticut, 122
  - in Hawaii, 165
  - in Illinois, 196
  - in Puerto Rico, 450
  - in Rhode Island, 472
  - in U.S. Virgin Islands, 482
  - in Virginia, 496
  - in Washington, 518–519
  - in Wisconsin, 547
- in Illinois, 190–191
- of jury trial, in California, 89
- limitations, in Arkansas, 34
- no waiver clauses, in California, 67–68
- restrictions on
  - in Indiana, 215–216
  - in Minnesota, 297–303

Washington
- attorneys' fees in, 518
- community of interest in, 502–503
- conduct standards in, 515–516
- control in, 502–503
- control person liability in, 518
- damage waivers limitations in, 518–519
- damages in, 517
- discrimination in, 512–513
- dispute resolution in, 520
- exclusive territory in, 515
- franchise defined in, 500–503
- injunctive relief in, 517
- joint marketing plan in, 502–503
- jurisdiction in, 503–504
- limitations period in, 520
- nonrenewal in, 508–511
- pricing restrictions in, 513–514
- remedies in, 516–517
- restrictive covenants in, 516–517
- scope in, 503–504
- succession in, 511
- supplier kickbacks in, 514–515
- supplier rebates in, 514–515
- supply restrictions in, 512
- termination in, 505–508
- trademark element in, 500–501
- transfers in, 511

Wisconsin
- administrative action in, 543–548
- agreement element in, 524–525
- alcohol in, 542–543
- attorneys' fees in, 547
- community of interest in, 525–530
- contract element in, 524–525
- control in, 525–530
- control person liability in, 546
- damage waivers in, 547
- damages in, 543–545
- dispute resolution in, 548–550
- franchise defined in, 522–530
- franchisor right to impose renewal conditions in, 540–541
- franchisor venue restriction ability in, 548–549
- injunctive relief in, 545–546
- joint marketing plan in, 525–530
- jurisdiction in, 530–532
- limitations period in, 549–550
- liquor in, 542–543
- nonrenewal in, 538–542
- remedies in, 543–548
- rescission in, 545
- sale right in, 523–524
- scope in, 530–532
- succession in, 542
- termination in, 532–538
- trademark element in, 523–524
- transfers in, 542

written agreement
- in Arkansas, 6–7
- in Virginia, 486